"This book is a remarkable achievement. It is f[...] its interrelation of pedagogical theory, philos[...] sentation, ecclesial locatedness, pastoral aware[...] reflection, and historical contextualizing. The book is a 'must' for theological educators and education."

— **Tom Greggs**
University of Aberdeen

"Through this important textbook, Edie and Lamport invite us into an amazing conversation about nurturing faith. It is at once fresh and comprehensive, culturally aware and theologically faithful. Through sidebars, a foreword, and six stimulating responses, they invite others to join us in the dialogue. How to nurture Christian disciples who make a difference serving God's realm of hope and justice is the conversation they host. Indeed, I recommend you join with them in the dialogue."

— **Jack L. Seymour**
Garrett-Evangelical Theological Seminary

"This detailed overview of the field of Christian education, viewed from a broadly Protestant perspective, is grounded in biblical theology and Christian doctrine while maintaining a clear focus on the contemporary cultural influences that affect Christian learners in a variety of contexts and at different life stages. The authors' light and engaging style, and their concern for both the practice of Christian formation and the importance of critical reflection within it, makes for an easy and illuminating read, despite the extent and depth of their reading and the weightiness of the topic."

— **Jeff Astley**
Durham University

"This is a highly synthetic work, novel and unique in how it integrates so many different strands of issues and thought. It is irenic and inclusive, reflective of a lifetime (indeed, lifetimes—and not just as a coauthored piece since there are many more voices here in a kind of symphonic unity) of lived experience and practical wisdom."

— **Bryan T. Froehle**
Palm Beach Atlantic University

"Edie and Lamport engage Christian education as a comprehensive process of human formation that nurtures faith through embodied, communal, contextual practices. Combining principles and proposals, the authors model their conviction that dialogue and discernment will help teachers of Christian faith cooperate with

God's grace in shaping people's capacity to accept Christian beliefs and, most importantly, also to enflesh Christian behaviors as developing disciples. Current and aspiring teachers and faith leaders will find hope for the church's future in these pages."

— **Anne McGowan**
Catholic Theological Union

"In this time of crisis for the Christian church in America, *Nurturing Faith* provides a deeply biblical, faithful witness to the practices and thinking that can transform Christian discipleship and enliven the Christian community for a world that, more than ever, needs a faithful witness, deliberate discipleship, and faithful service to all in need. Get this book; it can and will transform your church."

— **James K. Wellman Jr.**
University of Washington

"The education minister on a given church staff has become a relic of history, but so too has the church priority of educating believers. Lamport and Edie's book cries loudly and unashamedly, in a wilderness of weak-kneed faith, for the church to do something about its theologically uneducated members. I highly recommend this exciting book!"

— **Earl Waggoner**
Colorado Christian University

"With 'generous humility,' Edie and Lamport skillfully navigate the contemporary terrain of multiculturalism, postmodernism, and Christian nominalism while guiding us toward a robust, embodied framework for learning, teaching, and 'nurturing' others of all ages in the faith. This is no ordinary textbook—it is thoroughly engaging, wrestling boldly with the interdependency of faith and practice for the global church."

— **Ronald T. Michener**
Evangelische Theologische Faculteit, Belgium

"What are ways to nurture faith in the twenty-first century? Fred Edie and Mark Lamport take on the task of identifying problematic cultural and theological dynamics in the nurturing of faith and propose a wide range of theological and educational perspectives to address these challenges. The result is an original and accessible textbook with a rich diversity of angles from which to approach the task of forming disciples."

— **A. L. van Ommen**
University of Aberdeen

NURTURING FAITH

A Practical Theology for Educating Christians

Fred P. Edie and Mark A. Lamport

WILLIAM B. EERDMANS PUBLISHING COMPANY
GRAND RAPIDS, MICHIGAN

Wm. B. Eerdmans Publishing Co.
4035 Park East Court SE, Grand Rapids, Michigan 49546
www.eerdmans.com

27 26 25 24 23 22 21   1 2 3 4 5 6 7

ISBN 978-0-8028-7556-3

Library of Congress Cataloging-in-Publication Data

Names: Edie, Fred P., 1960– author. | Lamport, Mark A., author.
Title: Nurturing faith : a practical theology for educating Christians / Fred P.
    Edie and Mark A. Lamport.
Description: Grand Rapids, Michigan : William B. Eerdmans Publishing Com-
    pany, [2021] | Includes bibliographical references and index. | Summary:
    "A comprehensive guide to Christian educational ministries geared toward
    the nurturing of faith in a variety of contexts"—Provided by publisher.
Identifiers: LCCN 2021007976 | ISBN 9780802875563
Subjects: LCSH: Christian education. | Education (Christian theology)
Classification: LCC BV1471.3 .E35 2021 | DDC 268—dc23
LC record available at https://lccn.loc.gov/2021007976

To Helen, my first teacher of Christian education; to Chuck, mentor, friend, and hero; and to Alison, who embodies grace.

—Fred

To Tresi—simply the best person I know and an incisive instrument in the nurturance of my own evolving (sometimes wander-prone, sketchily irresolute, itchy-footed) journey of faith.

—Mark

CONTENTS

List of Sidebars   xiii

List of Tables   xv

List of Figures   xvi

Foreword *by Charles R. Foster*   xvii

Introduction   1
Introduction   2
Teaching Conceptions of Jesus   5
Questions in Christian Educational Theory   6
The Purpose of the Book   8
Defining Our Terms   9
The Authors   14
Organization of the Book   16
Interactive Dialogue   19
For Further Reading   19

PART ONE: CULTURAL DYNAMICS OF NURTURING FAITH   21

1. Leaving the Faith: Eulogies of Disenchantment,
    Lethargy, and Irrelevance   27
    Introduction   28
    Challenges to Nurturing Faith   30
    Learning from Other Faith Traditions   35
    Here's the Problem . . .   46
    Conclusion   49
    Interactive Dialogue   49
    For Further Reading   50

2. Stories We Tell Ourselves: How Concepts of Modernism and
    Postmodernism Inform and Inhibit Nurturing Faith   51
    Introduction   52
    The Story of Faith   53

How We Got Here: Stages of Modern Thought   57
The Call to Faith   60
The Story of Modernism/Postmodernism   62
Conclusion   73
Interactive Dialogue   73
For Further Reading   73

3.   Fusing Belief and Practice: How Religious Nominalism Informs
     and Inhibits Nurturing Faith   75
     The Assent of Nominalism   76
     Contributors to and Manifestations of Christian Nominalism   79
     The Dance of Belief and Practice   83
     Conclusion   95
     Interactive Dialogue   95
     For Further Reading   96

4.   Keeping the Faith: Sketching a Practical Theology
     for Nurturing Faith   97
     Challenges of and Opportunities for Nurturing Faith   98
     Distinctives of and Gifts for Nurturing Faith   115
     Conclusion   119
     Interactive Dialogue   120
     For Further Reading   120

PART TWO: CRITERIA FOR NURTURING FAITH   121

5.   Revelation, Experience, and the Hope of
     Profound Transformation   127
     Introduction   128
     Coming to Terms with Revelation   129
     Mediating Sources of Revelation   133
     Revelation in the Modern and Postmodern Worlds   138
     Implications for Revelation and Nurturing Faith   141
     Conclusion   146
     Interactive Dialogue   147
     For Further Reading   147

6.   Humanity, Embodiment, and the Trust of Interdependent Kinship   148
     Introduction   149
     Coming to Terms with Human Being   150
     Human Portraiture   150
     Steps toward a Theological Anthropology   159
     Implications for Faith Formation   162
     Conclusion   166

	Interactive Dialogue	167
	For Further Reading	167
7.	**Jesus, Sin, and the Grace of Cruciform Resurrection**	168
	Introduction	168
	Story	174
	Theological Musings on Paschal Mystery for Faith Formation	180
	Implications for Nurturing Faith	184
	Conclusion	185
	Interactive Dialogue	186
	For Further Reading	186
8.	**Church, Reconciliation, and the Faith of a Countercultural Community**	187
	Introduction	188
	Coming to Terms with the Church	189
	"We Believe in the Church":	
	Faith as Participation in Alternative Community	191
	(Two of) the Church's Failures	195
	Implications for Nurturing Faith	198
	Conclusion	202
	Interactive Dialogue	202
	For Further Reading	202
9.	**Virtue, Character, and Joy in Kingdom Practices**	203
	Introduction	204
	Theories of Practice from Aristotle through Aquinas to MacIntyre	205
	Christian Practices	206
	Theologizing Practice: Practicing the Kingdom	209
	Practicing God's Realm, Receiving Divine Joy	212
	How Do Practices Work?	213
	Practices in Practice	214
	Implications for Faith Formation: Practicing God's Realm Today	215
	Conclusion	217
	Interactive Dialogue	217
	For Further Reading	218
10.	**Prophecy, Reflection, and the Freedom of Discerning Community**	219
	Introduction	220
	Coming to Terms with Critical Reflection in Education	221
	Critical Reflection for Personal Transformation	222
	Critical Reflection for Social Transformation	225
	Theological Themes in Critical Reflection	229
	Implications for Nurturing Faith	231
	Conclusion	236
	Interactive Dialogue	236
	For Further Reading	237

PART THREE: COLLEAGUES IN NURTURING FAITH — 239

11.	**Nurturing Atmospheric Faith in Children**	245
	Introduction	246
	The Mandate for Nurturing Faith with Children	247
	Foundational Insights on Educating Children in Faith	248
	A Traditional Strategy for Nurturing Faith with Children: Schooling as Miscalculated Model of Learning	251
	Cultural Incursion: Protection, Innocence, and Premature Exposure	254
	A Proposed Strategy for Nurturing Faith with Children: Atmospheric Faith	256
	Propositions for Nurturing Faith with Children	263
	Conclusion	264
	Interactive Dialogue	265
	For Further Reading	265
12.	**Nurturing Passionate Faith in Adolescents**	266
	Introduction	267
	What Is Adolescence?	268
	Nurturing Passionate Faith in Young People	275
	Conclusion	282
	Interactive Dialogue	283
	For Further Reading	283
13.	**Nurturing Vocational Faith in Adults**	285
	Introduction	286
	Dynamic Adulthood	287
	Faith-Forming Implications of Dynamic Adulthood	295
	Conclusion	301
	Interactive Dialogue	302
	For Further Reading	302

PART FOUR: CONTEXTS FOR NURTURING FAITH — 303

14.	**Nurturing Intergenerational Faith through Congregations**	311
	Introduction	312
	Challenges to Faith Communities	313
	Congregations as Communities That Nurture Faith	314
	Congregations as Intergenerational Communities That Nurture Faith	316
	Intergenerational Community Faith Formation in Action	319
	Conclusion	328
	Interactive Dialogue	328
	For Further Reading	328

15. Nurturing Integrative Faith through Christian Schools   330
    Introduction   331
    Theological, Social, and Cultural Impacts upon Christian Schooling   332
    Theological and Educational Considerations for Christian Schooling   336
    A Case Study in Deliberative Vision and Practice in
       Christian Schooling   342
    Church in the Education of the Public   345
    Whither Christians? Private, Public, or Home Schooling?   346
    Conclusion   349
    Interactive Dialogue   350
    For Further Reading   350

16. Nurturing Intentional Faith through Theological Education   351
    Introduction   352
    Conceiving the Craft of Professor in Theological Education   352
    Best Practices for Teaching in Higher Education   353
    Prevailing Misperceptions of Educational Philosophy, Psychology, and
       Practice in Theological Education   355
    Conclusion   367
    Interactive Dialogue   368
    For Further Reading   368
    Additional Resources   370

PART FIVE: CONVERSATIONS IN NURTURING FAITH   373

17. A Teaching Agenda for the Global Church in
    a Postmodern World   379
    The Uniqueness of Christian Teaching and Faith   380
    Translating John Dewey into Our Faith-Nurturing Agenda   381
    Noneducation, Miseducation, and Education   383
    Wisdom and Our Modest Proposal for a Teaching Agenda   389
    Interactive Dialogue   393
    For Further Reading   393

18. A Conversation among Practical Theologians   394
    Response 1: Reflections on the Nature of Revelation and
       Religious Experience by Martyn Percy   396
    Response 2: Kinship and Difference: Relationships Aren't Easy
       by Almeda M. Wright   401
    Response 3: Participation in the Means of Grace by Craig Dykstra   405
    Response 4: Redeeming Hope: An Alternate Kingdom
       Informing Culture by Kirsten Sonkyo Oh   409

Response 5: Lived Faith in Communities of Charitable Critique
  by Elizabeth DeGaynor   414
Response 6: Knowing for Living Faith by Thomas Groome   418

Rejoinder and Epilogue   423
The Law of Unintended Consequences   423
Galvanizing Issues of Convergence   424
Faith in, Obedience to, and Praise for God   428
Parting Plea—Compromise Elsewhere   430
Interactive Dialogue   431

Acknowledgments   433

List of Contributors   435

Notes   439

Index of Names and Subjects   499

Index of Scripture References   510

The diversity of the writers of the sidebars is an effort toward inclusion of various perspectives not always found in the same volume. They may express views that are different from our own, and we are very comfortable with that. Our thanks for their contributions!

The sidebars are adapted from George Thomas Kurian and Mark A. Lamport, eds., *Encyclopedia of Christian Education*, 3 vols. (Lanham, MD: Rowman & Littlefield, 2015), and used with permission.

Chapter	Sidebar	Author	Page
Introduction	Learning	Alison Le Cornu	7
	Knowledge	Robert W. Pazmiño	12
1	Doubt	Kevin P. Emmert	32
	Ritual	Timothy D. Son	39
2	Postmodernism	Ronald T. Michener	56
	Cultural Influences	Oliver V. Brennan	63
3	Nominal Christian	Daniel Bennett	77
	Experiential Learning	Leona M. English	93
4	Socialization	James P. Bowers	103
	Critical Thinking	Patrick Bruner Reyes	116
5	Experience	HiRho Y. Park	136
	Mystery	Tom Schwanda	142
6	Reason	HiRho Y. Park	155
	Reflective Engagement	Doug Blomberg	159
	Anne E. Streaty Wimberly	Fred P. Edie	163
7	Imagination	Fred P. Edie	172
	Sacraments	Fred P. Edie	178

8	Images of God	Finola Cunnane	192
9	Spiritual Learning	Jeff Astley	208
10	Freedom	Jeff Astley	227
	Thomas H. Groome	James P. Bowers	231
11	Prayer and Children	R. Kevin Johnson	257
	Horace Bushnell	James P. Bowers	260
12	Adolescent Religious Identity	David M. Bell	272
	Mentoring Adolescent Boys	Derek Jones	275
	Mentoring Adolescent Girls	Emily A. Peck-McClain	280
13	James W. Fowler III	James P. Bowers	289
	Generational Issues	Ivy Beckwith	292
	Life Span Development	Alison Le Cornu	296
14	John H. Westerhoff III	James P. Bowers	315
	Godly Play	Jerome Berryman	321
15	Influence of Public Education	Laura Barwegen	334
	Home Schooling	Ron J. Bigalke	347
16	Behaviorism	Laura Barwegen	357
	Cone of Learning	Larry H. Lindquist	359
	Constructivism	Bernard Bull	363
17	Curriculum	Robert W. Pazmiño	382
	Jane Vella and Curriculum Planning	Leona M. English	387

TABLES

1   Projected Cumulative Change Due to Religious Switching,
2010–2050   29

2   The Potential Educational Value of One Aspect of Mormon
Religious Education   37

3   The Potential Educational Value of One Aspect of Jewish
Religious Education   40

4   The Potential Educational Value of One Aspect of Muslim
Religious Education   43

5   Comparing the Three Alternate Faith Traditions and Relevant
Educational Practices   45

6   Fundamental Obstacles to Educating in Faith, Observable
Symptoms, and Misconstrued Results   47

7   Meanings of Faith   54

8   Outworking of Humanistic Traits in Postmodern Thinking and
Nurturing Faith   66

9   Results of Postmodernism in the Human Experience   70

10   Countries That Will No Longer Have a Christian Majority in 2050   78

11   Religious Composition of the United States, 2010–2050   79

12   Juxtapositions of Religious Belief and Practice   85

13   Contextual Circumstances in Educating Christians   99

14   Prevalent Challenges and Corresponding Practices for
Educating in Faith   101

15   Differing Theological Orientations   336

16   Differing Educational Orientations   337

17   Proposed Stance for Theological Education Correlated with
Best Practices   361

FIGURES

1   America: A Christian Nation?   81
2   The Flow of the Teaching Experience—Colossians 1:9–12   242
3   The Divine-Human Communication Process   242
4   Learning as Past-Present-Future   243
5   Age Distribution of Religious Groups, 2010   248
6   Foundational Elements of Developing Intentional Educational Design   356
7   Cone of Learning   360
8   Grenz and Olson's Five Types of Theology   365

FOREWORD

Charles R. Foster

Nurturing Faith is among the most comprehensive and provocative introductions to Christian education available to students and church and academic leaders in the field. Although written as a textbook, it goes beyond describing the field to envisioning its future shape and responsibilities. It is reader friendly. Edie and Lamport introduce each chapter in *Nurturing Faith* with a "road map" to guide readers through its content. It does more. When gathered together, these road maps create an expansive map of the field of Christian education. It is a useful metaphor. It prompted me to recall road maps other Protestant Christian educators developed to introduce the field to their readers. Lewis Sherrill's *The Rise of Christian Education* (1950), Mary Boys's *Educating for Faith* (1989), Karen Tye's *Basics of Christian Education* (2000), and Robert Pazmiño's *Foundational Issues in Christian Education* immediately came to mind (1988).[1] Two other road maps influenced my own engagement with the field.

The first mapped continuities and changes in American Protestant Christian education from the early nineteenth century into the late 1960s. I was introduced to this historical map shortly after joining the faculty of the Methodist Theological School in 1968. My senior colleague Robert Browning had graciously invited me to teach with him the introductory course. Together we engaged students in mapping the movements of American Protestant Christian education they might encounter in the congregations they would be serving as pastors. We hoped, by the end of the semester, they would be able to recognize that expectations in their congregations for biblical literacy could be traced back into the Sunday school movement in the nineteenth century; attention to a critical understanding of the origins and meaning of biblical texts had been emphasized in the religious education movement in the early twentieth century; and commitments to age-appropriate theological reflection in the new curriculum resources in many denominations in the 1960s had been influenced by writings of neo-orthodox theologians from the 1930s. Along the way, we highlighted religious educators whose road maps of the field not only directed readers into the assumptions and practices of these movements but also significantly influenced their purposes and practices: Frederick Packard's *Teacher Taught* (1839) and *Teacher Teaching* (1861) in the early Sunday school movement; Horace Bushnell's *Christian Nurture* (1888) in the religious education movement that George Albert Coe's *A Social Theory of Religious Education* (1917) helped define; and H. Shelton Smith's *Faith and Nurture* (1941), inspiring at the time the transformation of the field's theological assumptions.[2]

Nearly twenty years later, I participated in a project initiated and directed by Jack Seymour and Donald Miller (1982) to distinguish among various approaches Protestant Christian educators were taking to reenvision the assumptions and practices of Christian education after the collapse of what Robert W. Lynn and Elliott Wright (1971) had called the partnership of public and Sunday schools and the loss of institutional support for the field in the wake of denominational restructuring.[3] To create a map of these approaches to Christian education in its changing cultural and religious environment, Seymour and Miller invited representatives of each approach to write essays to guide readers through the distinctive ways they envisioned the relationship of faith and tradition, biblical authority and personal experience, and teaching and learning in their view of the field. The compilation of these essays in *Contemporary Approaches to Christian Education* created a disciplinary map of the shared yet often disparate strands of the discourse in and about the field in the 1980s.[4]

These thoughts about mapping the field drew my attention to a number of books and events that refocused, expanded, and sometimes transformed the discourse and practice of the field, including those by Bushnell, Coe, and Smith. More recently, I thought of C. Ellis Nelson's focus on the congregation as educator (1967), Maria Harris's work on religious imagination and teaching (1987), Thomas Groome's emphasis on praxis (1980), Lawrence Richards's evangelical theological framework (1975), and Anne Wimberly's expansion of our vision of the field through the story-forming faith traditions in African American churches (1994).[5] To these, we may well be adding Edie and Lamport's *Nurturing Faith* for reconfiguring in Christian education the relationship of belief and practice in nurturing faith. I come to this conclusion for several reasons.

The first is its theological, educational, and contextual comprehensiveness. The authors introduce readers to a map of the contexts of Christian education, reclaiming for Protestant Christian educators and reminding Catholic and Orthodox Christian educators of the range of their responsibilities in drawing on their theological traditions to envision, shape, and practice faith nurturing in a postmodern world with both a local and a global consciousness in a wide variety of social, cultural, and religious institutional contexts. They map, in other words, the responsibilities of nurturing faith in children, adolescents, and adults as well as the intergenerational nurture of faith in congregations and the nurture of faith in Christian schools and theological seminaries—with a reminder that nurturing faith across the life span builds up Christian communities of faith, conscious of the challenges of being faithful as a global church in a postmodern world.

They also map a fresh approach to the discourse about Christian education as a field of study and practice among its many stakeholders. It includes several features. The first occurred in the decision Edie and Lamport made to collaborate on this project, knowing that in doing so they would be negotiating sometimes differences in approach and perspective associated with their personal faith journeys, educational backgrounds, professional experience, and theological commitments. In an era when partisan politics permeate the discourse in both church and governmental agencies, they chose to create a map of the field rooted in their struggles to draw on differences they brought to the project as resources to their shared commitments about Christian education and the nurture of faith in Christian community. Their collaborative effort alters our experience of the text and, by inference, expands our sense of the breadth of their vision of the field. It encourages us, in other words, to reach across our theological and epistemological differences to engage critical questions together about its shape and future.

A second feature distinguishing the text occurs in the ways Edie and Lamport expand the conversation about Christian education. They explore sources for certain emphases in Christian education in biblical, theological, and historical texts. They draw on the insights for nurturing faith from the practices of Mormon, Jewish, and Muslim religious education. They rely on the experience and wisdom of a wide range of conversation partners in the field. They incorporate definitions of key terms and concepts and include commentaries by scholars from other disciplines and colleagues in the field on some question or issue in accompanying sidebars. And then they invited six Christian educators—colleagues from across the field—to reflect critically upon a chapter given to them from the text. They model in their map of the field, in other words, fresh ways to explore and reflect on the field itself.

The epistemological map they create is, to my mind, their most important contribution to our reflections about the purposes and practices of a Christian education. For Edie and Lamport, this map is unapologetically theological, both in the articulation of its purposes in nurturing our relationship to God in Jesus Christ and in the practices of encountering and living into belief in Jesus Christ. They describe this theological epistemological map this way: the "objectives for education for nurturing faith seem relatively simple: the Christian way is to be enmeshed in all aspects of a person's being and in Christ's corporate body, leading to radical transformation and resulting in the continued mission of God through individuals and the faith community to participate in God's redemption of the world. In the process, God's gracious character may become embodied in humans, and human nature may reach its fullest development as it exemplifies divine character: peace, joy, love" (pp. 8–9 below). That statement becomes the impetus to the development of a systematic theological epistemology giving purpose and form to a Christian education nurturing faith. Its dialogical character becomes evident in chapter titles, as in the chapter on the doctrine of God: "Revelation, Experience, and the Hope of Profound Transformation," or the chapter on the theological grounding of their understanding of practice: "Virtue, Character, and the Joy of Kingdom Practices." The intent in these explicitly theological chapters and those focused on the doctrines of humanity, Christology, church, and wisdom is to develop what they describe as balance between "cogent theology" and "action-oriented practice" (p. 84 below).

Edie and Lamport, however, have done more in *Nurturing Faith* than creating a comprehensive map of the field. The book is a serious challenge to local church leaders satisfied with what the authors call "curricu-tainment" or what I have described as "random moments of religious enrichment"; to denominational leaders and curriculum producers preoccupied with the supervision of educational "programs" and the marketing of curriculum resources; and to professors and teachers in colleges and seminaries often more focused on specific problems or issues in Christian education than on nurturing faith in building up communities of faith as the body of Christ engaged in Christ's reconciling ministry in a postmodern and religiously pluralistic world. They remind us that the future of a faith community relies on the interdependence of its educational contexts in the consistency of nurturing the faith of children with that of adolescents, adults, and the students who will become, as religious leaders, the agents of the nurture of faith in their congregations. *Nurturing Faith* then is more than an overview of the field; it is an invitation to participate in a lively conversation across the field about its future.

That conversation is built into the structure of the book. Road maps guide readers through the terrain they are exploring. They do not include all that can be seen or examined. If used appropriately, they become resources to new discoveries and new possibilities. Edie and Lamport embraced these features of a map, in their request to colleagues from across the field to reflect critically on one of the chapters in *Nurturing Faith*, in the responses included in the final section of the book. The development of the map they created continues, in other words, in the constructive responses of those who read those chapters and then enriched them from the vantage point of their own perspectives. Thomas Groome, for example, encourages readers to continue exploring distinctions in how experiential and praxis ways of knowing are relevant to our expectations of a Christian education in nurturing faith. Almeda Wright wonders about the extent to which Edie and Lamport's vision of Christian education accounts adequately for the challenge of nurturing faith across the lines of difference. Her attention was especially attuned to differences associated with the personal and social consequences of oppression, marginalization, suppression, or abuse typically rooted in cultural practices of racism, sexism, homophobia, and classism. In her essay, Kirsten Sonkyo Oh offers Edie and Lamport one response to Wright's question by suggesting that, rather than viewing "nurturing faith" in congregations as a countercultural practice, we might begin to think about the church as representing an "alternative culture of the kingdom of God" in nurturing faith. Wright's and Oh's comments encourage Christian educators to be more self-conscious about nurturing justice, compassion, and hope in public life when nurturing faith in communities of faith.

While reading the manuscript, I often found myself wanting to enter directly into their conversation with each other, sometimes to affirm, sometimes to question, and other times to expand the topic under consideration. *Nurturing Faith* conveys a robust vision and is a compelling guide for pastors and lay leaders, Christian education faculty and students, curriculum producers, and denominational staff engaged in the nurture of a faith deeply rooted in Christian tradition, with the constructive capacity to address challenges of living faithfully in our postmodern world. At a point in time when young adults are not just leaving but often fleeing our various religious communities, Edie and Lamport offer a fresh and powerful alternative way of living into the practices of Christian education in nurturing faith in Jesus Christ.

The end of learning is to repair the ruins of our first parents by regaining to know God aright, and out of that knowledge to love him, to imitate him, to be like him, as we may the nearest by possessing our souls of true virtue, which being united to the heavenly grace of faith, makes up the highest perfection.

—JOHN MILTON

I was made merely in the image of God, but not otherwise resembling him enough to be mistaken for him by anybody but a very near-sighted person.

—MARK TWAIN

ROAD MAP

Note to reader: Road maps in this book guide and orient readers to the themes in a given chapter.

Faith is not a natural instinct for Mark (coauthor of the book); hard facts, sequential logic, predictable safety, and empirical evidence are modes of knowing with which he is much more comfortable. Living by faith has been a learned activity, and that with unevenness and a pronounced lack of symmetry—inclusive of some wrestling and handwringing, retreating and advancing. One night in a small group Bible study, Mark was struck with empathy for the disciples' consternation with Jesus's style as they said to him: "Now you are speaking clearly and without figures of speech" (John 16:29), implying metaphorical language was more typical and not readily grasped by them. So Mark asked the group why Jesus—in a time near the end of his life, when his message and mission needed to be shored up by those disciples who were soon to carry the torch of Jesus into a hostile climate of disbelief—would use analogical, less-than-concrete clarity about the nature of God, Jesus, and the coming of the Spirit. Mark's friend, Bill, an astute design engineer, offered an explanation to his puzzlement with an insight that struck him: Jesus used this analogical language ("Though I have been speaking figuratively, a time is coming when I will no longer use this kind of language . . ." [John 16:25]) as an intentional device so those who truly followed in the Jesus way would not believe based on clarity and logic and easy-to-grasp instructions. Jesus purposefully tested those who would seek him based on an inherently compelling trust based on faith. The Spirit confirmed that rendering, and it has helped Mark understand more about navigating a life of faith in God—with plenty of room for augmentation pending.

So yes, blessed are they who have not seen—as Jesus points out in the case of the apostle Thomas's doubt—and yet believe (John 20:29). In other words, our father Abraham would say to us "go, without knowing"; likewise, nineteenth-century Danish philosopher Søren Kierkegaard would tell us "leap, and find." Blessed are those who take God at his word without requiring any evidence or proof to validate what they believe. The task to which Christians are called is belief by faith and not sight (2 Cor. 5:7), and *this single, complex concept pivots as the center of this book: faith, and how it is nurtured.*

Introduction

Nurturing faith anticipates and responds to Christ's baptismal gift. Baptism incorporates persons into Jesus's death and resurrection life (Rom. 6). Through Christ, we are born anew by water and the Spirit (John 3). In Christ, we become "new creations" (2 Cor. 5), cleansed from the power of sin that otherwise enslaves us (1 John 1:7). We are made brothers and sisters of Jesus (Col. 1:2) and heirs to his kingdom (James 2:5). All this is God's free gift, and a gift only God can give: While we were still sinners, Christ died for us (Rom. 5:8).

And yet, while the triune God alone remains the creator, sustainer, and redeemer of all life, the nature of a gift requires that it be received. This is even truer when that gift is the offer of God's unqualified, unmerited love. Love, by definition, may not be coerced or forced upon us, for then it ceases to be love. Instead the quality of love is to invite relationship. God's salvation consists of the invitation to participate intimately in God's own life. This is the meaning of *grace*.[1]

Baptism beckons disciples of Jesus not only to unwrap this gift of relational love but also to delight in it, to explore the depth of its mysteries, and then to put it to use by returning love to God and lavishing it upon others. This project is at once the most beautiful ever undertaken, and the riskiest. Ask Jesus. That is why baptismal waters also gush Spirit empowerment to link Christians together in mutuality and dependence in one body, the church. Put differently, we are joined together for the purpose of learning to be what Christ makes us, the new creation. We are yoked for nurturing faith.

Theological ethicist Stanley Hauerwas frames this journey of becoming as learning to live within the story of God. Learning that story and living that story may by grace characterize those who locate themselves within it: "The Church is but God's gesture on behalf of the world to create a space and time in which we might have a foretaste of the Kingdom. It is through gestures that we learn the nature of the story that is the very content and constitution of that Kingdom. The way we learn a story, after all, is not just by hearing it. It must be acted out."[2] Nurturing faith, then, is the training in those stories and gestures through which we learn to participate in God's story and to glimpse the kingdom.

Perhaps a more familiar name for this characterizing activity is discipleship. If nurturing faith requires gathering in a baptismal community, it is also a sending. Not only are disciples called by Jesus and blessed by Jesus, they are sent out to minister in Jesus's name. They become "God-bearers," to use the traditional language; they embody the "abundant life" (John 10:10) Jesus promises. This calling to follow in Jesus's way—itself a sending for the sake of mission—is the flip side of the baptismal gift. It is the means through which the Spirit continues the work of transformation in us and, ultimately, all of creation. In a movement of graced circularity, faith may be nurtured by doing the things Christians do: worshiping God, loving neighbors, especially the unloved, earning daily bread justly, living simply, unencumbered by pursuit of empire, and stewarding all that God has given. In turn, lived faith constitutes the church's principal witness to the truth, beauty, and goodness of its story.

We insist, however, even here in the preliminaries, that an essential component of nurturing faith is learning to confess and repent of the church's and our own repeated failures to live into Christ's baptismal gift of new creation. Instead, as Paul warned the Romans, we have allowed ourselves to be controlled by the power of sin (7:21–23). Not only have we failed to be an obedient church, but historically Christians have actively distorted faith, using it as an excuse for colonial conquest, for the creation of the category of race and racialized hierarchies, for the oppression of marginalized persons (who might be Jesus's *best* friends), for the desecration of the created world, and for grabbing at the power of empire. Yes, the gospel is *good* news. In Christ, by the power of the Spirit, we may become new creations. However, without acknowledging our history of failure, we who seek to nurture faith (especially those who, like the authors and perhaps many of our readers, enjoy great privilege relative to the majority of our brothers and sisters in Christ) risk nurturing nothing more than pious platitudes, or, worse, we twist truth into a terrible lie.

While God's revelation is without flaw, our words about this revelation (i.e., theology) may be blemished, and so we tread lightly, trying not to speak for God where the divine does not speak. In the effort to avoid this fate, we seek to pay attention to Jesus.[3] To quote Tom Wright, "Christian faith isn't a general religious awareness. Nor is it the ability to believe several unlikely propositions. It is certainly not a kind of gullibility which would put us out of touch with any genuine reality. It is the faith which hears the story of Jesus, including the announcement that he is the world's true Lord, and responds from the heart with a surge of grateful love."[4]

What does Jesus want us to seek and accomplish? Simply put, *transformation*. Jim Samra teases out the illustrative image of spiritual newness embedded in the doctrine of creation. Paul, in his second epistle to the Corinthians (4:6, quoting Gen. 1:3: "Let light shine out of darkness . . ."), explicates that just as God spoke the world into existence and took existing material to bring life and order it, so the Creator takes an existing human life and brings life and order to it—transformation. This theme is repeated in 2 Corinthians 5:17 ("The new creation has come: The old has gone, the new is here!") and "places the anthropological transformation of humans within the larger scope of the cosmological transformation/renewal/recreation of all things."[5]

Individual believers and communities of faith are to be changed in thinking, feeling, and doing. First, those who grow in faith will increasingly *love and obey God* rather than focusing their worship and devotion on other things. Second, maturing disciples will *love their neighbors* as themselves. Compassion, forgiveness, and submission will be the rule rather than selfishness, bitterness, and pride. Third, they will seek to *honor God* in all they do, including their jobs and the way they spend their time. Last, they will feel the need and develop the ability to *share their faith* with those around them in an honorable way—in a way that would reflect the teaching intentions of Jesus. This "full life" is the innate human quest to find fulfillment; it is the higher life that searchers and nontheists seek but cannot acquire. Or, as Diana Butler Bass would proclaim, the Christian way is a mechanism for searchers to find rest from their spiritual longings and "offers pathways of life-giving spiritual experience, connection, meaning, vocation, and doing justice in the world."[6]

Teaching Conceptions of Jesus

The enterprise of Christian education for the purpose of nurturing faith, as it exists in churches and parachurch organizations, has traditionally been long on teaching tips and innovations and rather limited on thinking with intention about its goals, theories, and philosophies of educating in Christian-specific ways. The educational mission of the church is to be accomplished with redoubtable effect in all geographical locations, in all sociopolitical environments, through all the Christian centuries, with all developmental life stages, and across the spectrum of abilities. While Jesus emphatically commanded the church to baptize in his name and teach all the things he did (Matt. 28:19–20), he was not particularly specific about how this was to be accomplished.

Yet Jesus is known even by those of non-Christian religions as a "master teacher," no doubt because his influence has continued uninterrupted through twenty centuries and that one-third of the world population claim Christianity as their faith. In his day, he was called *rabbi* both by those who sympathized and opposed. So, what may be gleaned from the teaching ministry of Jesus about the content and methods that inform Christian education in our twenty-first-century postmodern context?

Certainly, there are clues from Jesus's own content and methods. He spoke much of the kingdom of God and introduced distinctive ethics in the Sermon on the Mount. And Jesus used a variety of teaching methods, most often through stories, visual demonstrations, and mentoring. Madeleine L'Engle quips that Jesus was God who told stories. More often than not, these stories came in the form of parables. Parables are common images used in uncommon ways in order to goad learners into new ways of seeing and being in the world—to reveal then conceal. They work on a strategic pattern of orientation, disorientation, and reorientation.[7] Jesus also taught by *aphorism*—a subversive saying wearing the disguise of a proverb that attempts to challenge, even undermine, the hearer's perspective (e.g., Mark 8:35; 10:25; Luke 14:11).[8] He utilized metaphor ("I am the bread of life" [John 6:35]), paradox (give life to have life [Matt. 10:39]), and other poetic means of speech. Jesus also taught through his manner of life. He ate with outcasts, healed even on the Sabbath, and turned temple business-as-usual upside down. And this is to say nothing of the considerable teaching impact of the events of his passion and resurrection.[9]

Remarkably, the Bible Jesus knew—the Old Testament—had stories, but Jesus did not tell those stories exactly. Nevertheless, the Gospels clearly imply that Jesus's teaching through precept and practice can only make sense through the memory of God's saving work in and through the stories of Israel. Jesus is variously styled as the "New Adam," or the "New Moses." Indeed, without Israel's memory of God's creative and redeeming work, Jesus would be unintelligible to us. His stories relied upon Israel's stories but spoke something new. They often left hearers (and later, readers) uncertain about their meaning. In addition, Jesus had no materials, no meeting space, and no schedule. His curriculum, therefore, seemed rather haphazard and spontaneous, without discernible scope and sequence. However, Jesus's teaching was relational and reality oriented, authoritative and effective, loving and affirming, imaginative and engaging, prophetic and practical. In this book, we intend to cull from Jesus's pedagogical practices (his ways of educating for nurturing faith) to inform appropriate translations for contemporary Christian educational efforts.[10]

Questions in Christian Educational Theory

How does one move from "Jesus the Master Teacher" to theorizing for nurturing faith in our Christian communities? Or, in different terms, to what extent ought churches and parachurch organizations have a plan that details the faithful educational ends they seek—plus the curricular content and the pedagogical means to reach those ends? D. Campbell Wyckoff appropriately asserts: "The ultimate test of any program of Christian education is this: Is it a true and appropriate way for the church of Jesus Christ to carry on its educational work?"[11] Further, he adds, as a crucible for a properly located launching point: "the most promising clue to orienting Christian education theory so that it will be both worthy and communicable is to be found in recognizing and using the gospel of God's redeeming activity in Jesus Christ as its guiding principle."[12] Wyckoff also sets out this educational vision in practical terms by posing an important set of questions:[13]

1. What purposes is it intended to achieve?
2. Who is necessarily involved in the educational transaction?
3. With what knowledge and experiences is it concerned?
4. By what essential processes is it to seek to achieve its ends?
5. What are its duration, it sequences, and its rhythms likely to be?
6. What is its characteristic timbre—its sound and feel?
7. In what setting or settings may it best take place?
8. What institutional forms are necessary?

These are questions of curriculum (*what* we teach), pedagogy (*how* we teach), teaching/learning (*who* is teaching/taught), the nature of the educational environment (*where* we teach), and educational ends (*why* we teach). Answers to these queries constitute one important dimension of Christian educational theory. These are also *theological* questions, at least implicitly. Wyckoff argues that Jesus is to be the barometer for *what* we teach, *who* teaches and *who* is taught, *how* we teach, and *where* we teach, and *why* we teach. While there is only one Jesus, the good news he offers and embodies will be interpreted differently by different communities. Answers will vary depending upon communal contexts and a community's specific theological commitments. Some communities will focus upon full inclusion and belonging of marginalized persons, for example, others upon Christ's lordship over against the caesars of this world. These theological particularities affect how faith is nurtured and what kind of faith is taught. Questions like these must be addressed if faith communities wish to bring relevant resources from Scripture and tradition to bear upon their processes of nurturing faith. Lacking a vision for educational ends, any means will get you there! All too often congregations mistake means for ends and then profess dismay that their members fail to live as disciples. These questions in both their educational and theological garb will inform our work throughout as we attempt to distill the most effective, transcultural, faith-enhancing efforts for educating Christians in the global church.[14] (They will be developed in chapter 2 and fleshed out further in chapters 5 through 10.)

LEARNING

Implicit in any understanding of learning is the notion of change, although the nature of that change varies. A familiar emphasis is on the acquisition of knowledge, but this quantitative focus is gradually giving way to an appreciation of more qualitative aspects that are concerned with the processes of learning and the corresponding growth and development experienced by individuals. Outside a specifically Christian context, the study of learning has been approached from a number of perspectives, including *theoretical* (behaviorist, cognitivist, interactionist, and experiential learning theories); *epistemological* (which emphasizes learners as knowers); *situational* (especially the place where learning is occurring, such as the workplace); and *promotional* (strategies for promoting and fostering learning).

Learning, of course, occurs throughout life, which has encouraged a more extensive investigation beyond how children learn. One such theory—experiential learning—represents an attempt to bring together the whole person (both body and mind) and the social situations encountered, which results in the transformation of experience and the continually changing person. The person is, therefore, more at the center of thinking about learning than has been the case thus far.

Christian understandings of learning have tended to follow secular trends, especially in the emphasis on how children learn and how they might be disciples within a church setting or appropriately informed within a secular school context.

Each of these issues raises questions about whether Christian learning has specifically different characteristics from other subject disciplines. Distinctions are to be
made between learning *about* Christianity and learning Christianity; nevertheless,
all Christians, at whatever age, have to receive information about their faith, its
traditions, and practices. A crucial dimension of nurturing faith is one's ability to
critically reflect on the Christian tradition and people's personal faith—a practice
(and skill) often weakly exercised among many adult Christians. While faith development may well be the central goal of Christian learning, this is something
that incorporates many dimensions, both in terms of learning and of faith. In a
contemporary climate that prizes the articulation of learning outcomes that can
be assessed both formatively and summatively, the development of a distinctly
Christian character often eludes identification, through a range of activities that
contribute to sacred learning, such as active reading, meditative prayer and reminiscence, and the fostering of a biblical imagination.

ALISON LE CORNU

The Purpose of the Book

The story of God is a narrative of unrelenting compassion for all creation and
especially for human beings. In fact, God loves people so much, the depiction
in Scripture is of one who risks everything to find them and to invite them to
join in the saving kingdom work. The mission of the church is to represent
this God to the world in which we live, to invite lost people to become found,
to proclaim the gospel by word and deed, and to glorify God to and with all
the people groups on earth. In this way, the church also witnesses to God's
redeeming love.

And while speaking God's truth to the world is vital, evangelism has been
seen, in some quarters, as the most important function of the church. It is
not. For evangelism is only the first part of discipleship. Yes, these two concepts—evangelism and discipleship—should not be separated either in the
theologies or practices of our mission. Certainly, the goal of the church is not
simply to produce those who would acknowledge Christianity as truth; the
more desirable outcome is that these "believers" would advance to "followers."
So, an underlying value of this book is to recognize the synergetic notion that
evangelism leads to discipleship, and discipleship leads to mission, including
evangelism, and that neither is complete until the other is embraced. In these
pages, we will explore the theological implications and essential practices of
discipleship for the purpose of discerning biblical principles for relevant application in various contexts.

In light of this story, the objectives for education for nurturing faith seem
relatively simple: the Christian way is to be enmeshed in all aspects of a per-

son's being and in Christ's corporate body, leading to radical transformation and resulting in the continued mission of God through individuals and the faith community to participate in God's redemption of the world. In the process, God's gracious character may become embodied in humans, and human nature may reach its fullest development as it exemplifies divine character: peace, joy, love, truth, and the image of God (Gal. 5:13–25).[15]

Even if the educational task is at once God-given and grace-driven and seemingly straightforward, human beings display an amazing knack for messing things up. Hence, we seek to learn from the past by inviting readers to explore educational theory and theology and then to see how it unfolds in actual educational practices. We take seriously the rapid cultural changes (globalism, postmodernism, political movements for liberation or repression, the urgency of environmental crisis) and attempt to assess how these present both challenge *and opportunity* for nurturing faith in the present and future. As practical theologians, we believe that reflection on the practices of educational ministry is critical to nurturing faith even as it does not guarantee success. The book is an invitation to imagine faithful educational practice and to reflect upon the ingredients and dynamics that make it so. Join us!

Defining Our Terms

Terminology within the field of practical theology can be confusing. For example, writers and practitioners use *Christian education, religious education,* or *educational ministry* as umbrella terms for all efforts toward nurturing faith. Others prefer *discipleship, sanctification, catechesis, faith,* or *spiritual formation.* We are not purists in this regard, though the title of the book suggests what we are after, *nurturing faith,* even as it is named differently in different settings.

As implied above, we understand "nurturing faith" to be a *practical theology* task in the following ways.[16] First, it involves a ministry *practice* of the church—its call to make disciples. At risk of pinning the obvious to the mat, we mean by *practice* that faith communities *do things* in order to nurture faith in their members. They teach, mentor, and seek to love and serve others as God loves. After all, as Rebecca Konyndyk DeYoung reminds, "discipleship . . . is the work of straightening what is bent, retraining and strengthening our capacities, and working loose the bonds that constrain us."[17]

Second, in addition to practice itself, practical theology in our understanding includes considered *reflection,* self-conscious examination, of the church's practices of educational ministry. Educational leaders are called not only to do things but also to think about their doings. Practice gives rise to theological implication, and theology likewise informs practice; it is a symbiotic, reciprocal, and natural process. Though human beings never exist above or beyond the particular contexts they inhabit, to a certain extent, we may stand back from the educational practices of ministry we are engaged in, holding them at arm's length, so to speak, to ask questions about what we are doing, how we are doing it, and assessing whether we are practicing as we intend or achieving the results (nurtured faith) we seek.

Third, educational leaders rely upon more than their intuitions when reflecting upon their ministry practice. They will need to be informed by a number of fields, principally *theology*. Theology may be conceived as an informed, extended conversation over time about the nature of God's loving and saving intent for all creation. The conversation began with the people of Israel but for Christians continues and is centered in God's self-revelation in and through Jesus Christ as narrated in the Scriptures. We call theology a "conversation" because even though the events of Israel and Jesus occurred in the past, God is still acting toward the kingdom in the present through the power of the Spirit. Discerning what God is up to requires discernment on the part of educational leaders. Returning to the importance of theology in the task of education for nurturing faith, educational leaders will look to Scripture and tradition as "norms" for evaluating not only the content of their formational efforts but also the processes and dynamics of providing that content, as well as the ends they seek.

At the same time, Christian educational leaders may be informed by the fields of education, philosophy, and the social sciences to help them understand better what awakens love of learning in persons, how learning is related to forming identity, the relation between knowing and doing, and so on. With James Loder we affirm that the adequacy of nontheological knowledge should be evaluated in light of the theological, but we welcome this conversation. For example, because of our theological convictions, we would be somewhat wary of educational curricula that seek merely to cultivate "self-affirmation." While avowing that God's intent for human beings is to become (again) authentically, fully human, our theological convictions also cause us to reject the possibility of human beings affirming themselves apart from God's saving affirmation.

On the other hand, social science has provided a lens for critically evaluating formational practices once broadly approved by the church. For example, does corporal punishment teach children respect for authority by breaking devilish little wills already depraved by sin, or does it teach them to be violent? Regardless of the answer, if our only source on the subject were a cursory reading of Proverbs 13:24 ("Whoever spares the rod hates their children, but the one who loves their children is careful to discipline them"), the question could not even arise. As Arthur Holmes is oft quoted—and we affirm as well—all truth is God's truth, wherever it may be found.[18] In short, we find the careful research of scholars of many disciplines useful in our work. In being faithful to our task, we are charged with the responsibility of being exegetes of Scripture and tradition, culture, and human development.

Finally, *context* matters to practical theology. In this case, educational ministry must meet people in the language and on the cultural footings familiar to them. Put differently, educational ministry is not "one size fits all." Congregations on some street corners will look to Jesus to liberate them from economic injustice. Congregations on other street corners will want to practice Jesus's simple life unencumbered by too much stuff.

Mission is still another term that appears frequently in these pages. With contemporary missiologists, we affirm that "God is a missionary" whose quest is to restore all creation to loving communion with the Holy Trinity. God has a mission, and that mission has a church. An important corollary of this missional retrieval is that educational ministry can no longer be content with disseminating faith content to church members. Instead, this missional emphasis rightly focuses the educational task on a life lived. Education for nurturing faith must seek to form disciples for active participation in God's mission of reconciliation and restoration.

Which leads, finally, to a consideration of our term *nurturing faith*—that faith that is the crux of this entire book. We are indebted to the sixteenth-century reformers for heightened distinctions in its meaning. Martin Luther was careful to speak of a "vital faith" or "living faith" as that which was properly associated with "saving faith" or "true faith." Vital faith is to be contrasted with comatose faith, which is clarified by James's commentary: "faith without works is dead" (2:14-26). No, faith produces fruit. Luther's contemporary Philip Melanchthon drew important interrelated gradations of the various usages of the concept of faith:[19]

> *Nōtitia*—the *content* of faith, or those things to be believed; that is, to believe
>   in God one must know things about him (cognitive component).
> *Assensus*—one's *assent* of the intellect to truth; the conviction *nōtitia* is true;
>   for example, one can know about the Christian faith but not trust it;
>   this concept implies a convictional certainty (affective component).
> *Fiducia*—a personally appropriated *trust* or reliance; even demons have
>   *nōtitia* and *assensus* (James 2:19), but *fiducia* combines cognition with
>   affect to act in ways that demonstrate faithful living (behavorial com-
>   ponent). Implicitly, *fiducia* points to faith as *embodied*, embedded deep
>   in our marrow, an important truth sometimes lost on our forebears.

Conveniently, Paul expresses the shades of meaning for all three concepts in 1 Thessalonians 2:13: "And we also thank God continually because, when you received the word of God [*nōtitia*], which you heard from us, you accepted it not as a human word [*assensus*], but as it actually is, the word of God, which is indeed at work in you who believe [*fiducia*]." And the tangible result of this faith, as spelled out in the next verse, is "For you, brothers and sisters, became *imitators* of God's churches in Judea, which are in Christ Jesus" (2:14, emphasis added)—a knowledge-based, conviction-established, action-oriented trust. Obviously all of these have significance for the meaning of faith; however, as we speak throughout this book about "nurturing faith," it is *fiducia* that we seek to nurture.

Though there will be much more about faith in the pages to come, we also note briefly two additional dimensions of it crucial to this project. First, faith is always faith *together*. Faith brings us into relation together with the triune God and together with the faithful. There is no such thing as solitary faith. Second, faith consists of more than internal dispositions toward conviction and trust. Faith is also performed. Fred's professor, James Fowler, described this as "*faithing*." In addition to overcoming the dichotomy of faith and works, faithing, including, for example, participation in worship and mission, makes space for inclusion of children, adolescents, and differently abled persons among the faithful.

KNOWLEDGE

Knowledge in the Bible refers to a whole life response to God and creation that embraces revelation as the essential source for both truth and wisdom. Knowledge in general as a cognitive apprehension of reality (Hebrew *yada*) is distinguished from wisdom (*khakmah*) that issues in life. In the Old Testament, the reverence of God (Prov. 1:7; 9:10) is the beginning of wisdom: "for the Lord gives wisdom; from his mouth come knowledge and understanding" (Prov. 2:6). In the New Testament, the claim is that in Jesus Christ "are hidden all the treasures of wisdom (Greek *sophia*) and knowledge (*gnōsis*)" (Col. 2:3). Therefore, a biblical view of knowledge is one that is holistic in the sense of involving knowledge in the cognitive sense along with feeling and action.

The Bible regards knowledge as something that arises from personal encounter, and knowledge of God is related to the revelation of God in the historic past and the promised future. Yet God is also revealed in the present earthly sphere in which God's creatures have their being and live out their history. The knowledge of God is inseparably bound up with God's revelation in time and space and in historical contexts. In the Bible, knowledge implies the awareness of the specific relationship in which the individual person and corporate community stand with the person or object known. Just as the individual is considered as a totality rather than a being composed of body and mind, knowledge is an activity in which the whole individual is engaged.

Knowledge is also recognized as a social and cultural construction related to the sources drawn upon to gain understanding of the world, ourselves, and the meaning of life. Knowledge is discerned through nature and science that studies the natural world, through rationality, experience, tradition, history, intuition, and even imagination. Parker Palmer suggests that knowledge as understood in our societal context must be related to human interests and passions—namely, the three human interests or passions of control, curiosity, and compassion. The knowledge gained through applied empirical and analytical study generally seeks to gain control over a body of information. The knowledge that liberates is described in 1 Corinthians 8:1-3: "We know that we all possess knowledge. Knowledge puffs up, but love builds up. The man who thinks he knows something does not yet know as he ought to know. But the man who loves God is known by God." This knowledge is one that is associated with the interest of compassion or love and recognizes the web of relationships in which knowledge is embraced. The New Testament maintains that knowledge or truth must be related to love (Eph. 4:15; 2 John 1) and that all truth is God's truth. The problem posed for the Christian is how to maintain in creative tension those truths discerned through study in various disciplines with the truths revealed in Scripture, while at the same time being guided by love for God, others, and the creation. It is Jesus's prayer that his disciples be sanctified by God's truth, recognizing that God's word is truth (John 17:17). Christ declares that he incarnates truth (John 14:6).

Christians recognize the limits of human knowledge and the place of no-knowledge or what mystics describe as the "cloud of unknowing." This recognition honors the place of mystery and reverence in relation to knowledge and all of life. Christians can recognize the place of paradox and always be open to new light and truth from God's word—written, created, and incarnate.

The highest knowledge is of God and is conditioned by faith and obedience. As the Holy Spirit encounters human spirits, life and growth are possible as God is known in new ways. Again, the words of the apostle Paul directed to the issue of food sacrificed to idols in Corinth serve to warn Christians regarding our knowledge and its potential idolatry: "We know that we all possess knowledge. Knowledge puffs up, but love builds up. The man who thinks he knows something does not yet know as he ought to know. But the man who loves God is known by God" (1 Cor. 8:1b-3). Human knowledge is transcended by being known by God and encountering God's love. Paul's warning does not negate the quest for knowledge but sets that quest in a wider context of biblical faith and commitment.

ROBERT W. PAZMIÑO

Nurture is also an important term most often associated in the modern era with Horace Bushnell.[20] Like Bushnell, while we fully affirm that faith is a graced gift of God, we do not believe it drops out of heaven and knocks folks on the head fully formed. Even Peter had Cornelius, and John Wesley had the Moravians to encourage, mentor, and assist in their faith formation. As Wesley, borrowing from Augustine, famously observed, "Without God we cannot, without us God will not."[21] Truthfully, taking up educational ministry makes no sense absent this conviction. We are convinced that faith communities (including those depicted in the Scriptures), families, friends, and mentors all play crucial roles in nurturing faith. We also believe that faith, like Bushnell's "hot house plant" (as we attempted to emblemize in the image on the front cover), may grow and bear ever more fruit when carefully cultivated in communities devoted to nurturing it.

The Authors

We are products of our experiences: Fred is a southerner by heritage and a divinity school professor; Mark is a midwestern graduate school professor and for thirty years has taught regularly in Europe.[22] Fred took his baccalaureate degree from Furman University, a master of divinity from Vanderbilt Divinity School, a PhD from Emory University, and has gained considerable ministry experience on both US coasts before his current appointment as a professor of practical theology at Duke Divinity School/Duke University. Mark has a PhD in curriculum and instruction, with graduate theological degrees in practical theology, church history, and biblical and theological studies, which he applies in his teaching in practical theology—assisting students to consider how to educate Christians in various cultures. Fred was raised Methodist and is an ordained elder in that denomination; Mark is Wesleyan-ish—though prefers not to be pigeonholed by derivatives—but favors, due to his inclusive transdenominational ministries in various national and global settings, simply to be labeled "Christian."

Fred only half facetiously claims that teenaged girls in the community church youth group functioned as instruments of God's "prevenient grace" in his youthful conversion to Christ. His faith was nurtured by adult leaders who loved and accepted him and in a congregation that cultivated and celebrated his gifts. The journey continued as the same congregation invited him, out of the blue, to become their summer youth worker while in college, and then entrusted him with real responsibility in that task.

Equally surprising, a youth ministry stint out west in the 1980s immersed him in worship that attended to Christian timekeeping and to sacrament as well as word. He found liturgical spirituality to be at once down-to-earth, employing the basic material things of life—water, food, community, the rhythms of creation—yet devoting these ordinary things to invoking the grace of holy mystery. Faith grounded in practices of worship has helped him name care for God's creation, overcoming racialized and gender oppression, and learning to see God's saving work in the midst of the ordinary, material everydayness of life as crucial tasks for educational ministry and for his own discipleship.

Still another gift to Fred's vocational becoming was his apprenticeship under Helen Rogers in the 1990s, who showed him how to envision and lead an effective congregational educational ministry. Before Fred enrolled in graduate school to study Christian educational theory, Helen had already formed Fred in the praxis of educational leadership. That rich experience, coupled with Helen's encouragement to continue to refine his gifts for teaching, completes the grounded experience Fred continues to work out of at present.

Mark was raised in a Christian home and spent much of his childhood and adolescence participating (and joyfully, at that!) in Sunday school, Christian camps and retreats, a Christian version of Boy Scouts, and church and parachurch youth groups. After attending a Christian liberal arts university, then three graduate theological schools, he began a three-decade-long career teaching in Christian liberal arts colleges, universities, and seminaries. Christian parents and grandparents, other Christian adult role models and institutions, and the sustaining friendship of peers around the globe have significantly fortified his faith experience and journey in the Christian faith.[23]

Mark's academic sojourn—and resultant major emphases in his operating assumptions of how Christians are most effectively educated—has been influenced by the classroom presentations and publications of several of his graduate school professors, and for that he is grateful. Lawrence O. Richards (at Wheaton College) demonstrated in the classroom a teaching style that evoked thinking and observation, and his writing highlighted the social science theories that were most applicable to teaching and learning faith. D. Campbell Wyckoff and James Loder (both at Princeton) expanded his understanding of how cultural and human development factors may be brought to bear on the educational mission of the church. Finally, Ted W. Ward (at Michigan State) reinforced the role of critical thinking and research for leadership in designing curriculum and facilitating learning experiences for students.

We devote writing space to describing ourselves not because we imagine we are *that interesting* but because readers deserve to know the contexts out of which we think and write. We are blessed with considerable pastoral experience and academic training. At the same time, we, undoubtedly, by dint of sin or accidents of history, remain unaware of certain implications of the gospel for educational ministries and for ourselves. We may even be blinded at times to the insights of those our world has judged to be "other." At the same time, we—perhaps like you, the reader—continue to seek maturity in faith.[24] We hope this book represents growing awareness of the God willing to leave the ninety-nine sheep in order to bring the one more into the sheepfold.

Perhaps a word about "blending voices" is appropriate here. While Fred and Mark are passionate about the themes and contents of the material, we sometimes have slightly different takes on issues—for example, Scripture, culture, experience. That is not surprising, even a welcome reality, and it is one of the reasons we think that makes us compatible teammates. So while we have taken primary responsibility for discrete chapters, we have also read and contributed vigorously to one another's work. Even so, not everything voiced by one partner is necessarily the settled posture of the coauthor.[25] We hope that is not a distracting feature for the reader. Nevertheless, we are comfortable with these few dissonances and have practiced a generous humility with each other.

Organization of the Book

The book is designed as a textbook and is best studied in dialogue among colearners and over the course of some weeks during a concentrated period. Of course, individuals who provide leadership to local congregations, small groups, mission organizations, parachurch ministries, and theological schools will find guidance applicable to those settings, yet interactive dialogue may yield more comprehensive and creative results. The task of this book, we submit, is relevant to the breadth and length of the Christian tradition—Anglican, Orthodox, Protestant, and Roman Catholic—and nonsectarian venues. Constructed for application of instructional design in the global church, this book therefore attempts to expound principles that are transcultural and in need of specific programmatic application to various contexts. And while the text is in English and released by a fine publisher in the United States, we intend it to be considered by theological institutions, denominational and missiological training centers, and local church implementation in all of the English-speaking world, including, but not limited to, North America, the United Kingdom and Ireland, Australia, and segments of Europe, the Middle East, Africa, and Asia.

Part 1 seeks to provide a full and honest assessment of nurturing faith in the Western church at present. We seek to tell it like it is, at least as we see it from our vantage point. *Chapter 1* includes both an examination of faith communities for whom the predominant narrative is one of decline, as well as a frank conversation about the culpability of educational ministries in this decline. Yet that is not the only story. We continue to believe that educational ministries, thoughtfully conceived, still hold the potential for contribution to a more faithful and effective future for nurturing faith.

The next two chapters examine broader cultural trends and their impacts upon faith communities seeking to nurture faith. Given the rapidity of cultural and social change, we do not consider our examination either exhaustive or as current as your favorite blog. We do believe that our chosen themes hold important implications for educational ministry primarily because they may function to disrupt "the ways we have always done it." Yet we do not consider disruption to be synonymous with decline. The dynamics we name describe change, but they also imply opportunity. *Chapter 2* details the mysterious beckoning of postmodernism. We discuss the nature of belief and how Christian allegiance must result in concomitant behaviors, attitudes, and dispositions. In *chapter 3*, the focus is how staid nominalism stunts meaningful experience of encountering the Christian faith, and it emphasizes the necessary leadership behaviors that stem from intentionality and design to keep these two together in meaningful partnership. *Chapter 4* presents our potential remedies for "keeping the faith" and sets up a practical theology for nurturing faith in the global church.

Part 2 is the heart of the book. As we suggested at the outset, the very possibility of nurturing faith is premised upon the revelatory agency of God, whose love, by definition, seeks expression through relationship with creation. God's nature and mission are revealed in the person and work of Jesus Christ. Only through Jesus do we know the extent of God's love and receive anew the possibility of loving relationality with God, one another, and all of creation. Finally, only through the Spirit's sustaining power may we live into this new creation. To put this plainly, the triune God nurtures faith. Faith at its root comes as divine gift. At the same time, as we have noted, since God's desire is loving response to God's initiative, the door is left open to human participation in nurturing the faith God offers. With this in mind, theologian Randy Maddox describes grace (God's offer of relational love) as "responsible" (meaning response-able).[26] Maddox is attempting to emphasize the (secondary) role humans play in working out their salvation. Hence, education for nurturing faith is one dimension of the church's "response-ability," something it can and must do for its members.

In these six chapters, therefore, we flesh out the theological convictions undergirding the strategic means by which Christians are most enduringly, most profoundly, and most engagingly educated in faith. *Chapter 5* expounds the role of revelation through the Bible and traditioned church practice or conversely how we (mis)handle mediators of revelation and lose our orientation to transformation. *Chapter 6* highlights theological anthropology—that is, views of humanness—and the nature of learning through relationships in the faith community in contrast to our culture's preference for individualistic self-seeking. *Chapter 7* describes the possibility of Jesus and the gospel as humble yet true in a world suspicious of Christians as players of power games. *Chapter 8* addresses the critical issues of the church—its necessity for shaping Christian identity while discerning its legitimate exercise of authority and leadership, including how respect for Christian diversity is key to that legitimacy. *Chapter 9* explores how an array of practices for nurturing embodiment promotes faith's stability in a climate of fragmentation. Finally, *chapter 10* promotes a culture of critical thinking and reflection toward transformation as we consider faith and church or fall prey to ideologies that subvert it.

Part 3 attempts to envision our theology in action through the life cycle. *Chapter 11* highlights the formative nature of "atmosphere" for the Christian education of children. *Chapter 12* advances the distinct role that "passion" plays in the Christian education of adolescents. Finally, *chapter 13* addresses the critical importance of "vocation" in the Christian education of adults.

Part 4 demonstrates the practical theological importance of considering context in nurturing faith. *Chapter 14* directly hits on how those who give leadership to congregational education should plan for faith-affirming activities. *Chapter 15* considers the task of schooling and home schooling and how it interacts with spiritual formation. A reconceptualization of how the church equips its leadership through theological education is the focus of *chapter 16.*

Finally, in **part 5** we attempt an experiment—to engage in a scholarly and pragmatic dialogue with practical theologians to test whether our ideas about culture and church and nurturing within these confines hold up under scrutiny. In *chapter 17*, we suggest an agenda for the heightened effectiveness of nurturing faith for the global church. Then, in *chapter 18*, we invite six leading thinkers in practical theology to critique our six chief tenets for nurturing faith—fleshed out in chapters 5 through 10—and our specific proposal for the global church. These six outstanding practical theologians—Elizabeth De-Gaynor (Episcopal), Craig Dykstra (Presbyterian), Thomas Groome (Roman Catholic), Kirsten Sonkyo Oh (United Methodist), Martyn Percy (Anglican), and Almeda Wright (American Baptist)—engage our main themes in chapter 18 with meaty "responses." (See their biographies at the back of the book.) Finally, we offer a *rejoinder and epilogue* that responds to the contributors and poses a final appeal.

We have included several *special features* in the book. Emory University/ Candler School of Theology practical theologian Chuck Foster (United Methodist) has written an exceptional foreword that nobly introduces the task set before us. He has expressed great insight into how the mission of nurturing faith can be faithfully intertwined with other aspects of the work of the global church as it exists in a postmodern world.

Additionally, two *interactive elements* are included: (1) each chapter concludes with "interactive dialogue," that is, *questions* intended to tease further probing into the embedded themes (professors and students and church and parachurch leaders alike may choose to engage in discussion upon them); and (2) *sidebars*—which aim to elucidate and enrich a number of points we make—have been scattered through the contents of the book. (The sidebars are adapted from George Thomas Kurian and Mark A. Lamport's *Encyclopedia of Christian Education* and are included with gracious permission of the publisher.)[27]

Interactive Dialogue

1. How do you define "faith," and how does culture view this concept? What is the correlation of your description of faith with 2 Corinthians 5:7 (cited above)? How do you demonstrate Christian faith with regard to your life practices?
2. How do you prioritize the church's comprehensive mission of worship, service, evangelism, and discipleship? Why have various churches ranked one over the other through the Christian centuries?
3. What are your preliminary theories—before reading the author's ideas still to come in the book—about how the Christian faith is best nurtured? Recount one or more stories about how your faith has been enhanced in significant ways.

For Further Reading

Browning, Don. *Fundamental Practical Theology: Descriptive and Strategic Proposals*. Minneapolis: Fortress, 1995.

Carroll, Jackson W., and Wade Clark Roof. *Bridging Divided Worlds: Generational Cultures in Congregations*. San Francisco: Jossey-Bass, 2002.

Dykstra, Craig. *Growing in the Life of Faith: Education and Christian Practices*. Louisville: Geneva, 1999.

Foster, Charles R. *Educating Congregations: The Future of Christian Education*. Nashville: Abingdon, 1994.

Maddox, Randy. *Responsible Grace: John Wesley's Practical Theology*. Nashville: Kingswood, 1994.

Nelson, C. Ellis. *Where Faith Begins*. Louisville: John Knox, 1967.

Osmer, Richard R. *Practical Theology: An Introduction*. Grand Rapids: Eerdmans, 2008.

Veling, Terry A. *Practical Theology: "On Earth as It Is in Heaven."* Maryknoll, NY: Orbis, 2005.

Wolfe, Alan. *The Transformation of American Religion: How We Actually Live Our Faith*. Chicago: University of Chicago Press, 2005.

Part One
Cultural Dynamics of Nurturing Faith

Mark grew up in Peoria, Illinois, a blue-collar, middle-class city splashed with midwestern values in the bread basket of the United States, where folks were hospitable and most people—at least as it seemed to him as a child in the 1960s—went to church and believed in the same God he did. In his comfortable suburban setting, the neighbors on one side were Methodist; on the other side, Roman Catholic; and across the street, some brand of Baptist. At public school, he prayed and pledged allegiance "under God." In the family living room, there were Bibles, *Halley's Bible Handbook*, and a 1940s Warner Sallman's mass-produced painting: "Christ at Heart's Door."[1] It is possible at his tender age that he didn't know very many who were not—or at least did not appear to be—related to some church or variety of Christianity. The world of Mark's formative years was small and sheltered and happy and simple, and he is grateful for his narrow childhood socialization.[2]

For centuries, and across much of the Western world, many could have recounted roughly similar homogeneous stories of *their* childhoods. In fact, as late as 1900, over 80 percent of the world Christian population was Caucasian, and over 70 percent resided in Europe.[3] But while the *World Christian Encyclopedia* assesses the percentage of Christians worldwide to have been 33 to 34 percent for the last several generations, and projects the same proportion in the coming half-century,[4] the European-Caucasian majority is definitely *not the case* at the start of the twenty-first century. Nevertheless, it is possible that half of all the Christians who have ever lived are living now—perhaps two billion. This is a remarkable, unprecedented opportunity for nurturing faith. With a (self-reported) Christian population of over 250 million, there are more Christians in the United States than in any other country in the history of the world.[5] But what can be said about the world condition in which these Anglican, Protestant, Orthodox, and Roman Catholic adherents are being educated in faith?

As is quite clear, *this* is not twentieth-century religious-leaning Peoria anymore, and instead broad socializing undercurrents dominate the twenty-first-century global village. "Enchanted world" is a phrase used by social philosopher Charles Taylor in *A Secular Age* to describe these conditions of culture that favored religious belief.[6]

Three macrofactors have a role to play in nurturing faith on the world Christian scene today:

First, the teaching of the church is related to the social condition of the people it serves. Certainly, the heuristic circumstances of a given culture and the experiences of Christians within it are bound to interact with the content of what is taught in faith communities—acting as a sort of countermeasure in dealing with hostile or dangerous or distracting or theologically charged life situations. For example, the apostle John had a vision behind the scenes of world history and into the supernatural realm, as recorded in the apocalyptic book of Revelation. The message of persistence in the face of long odds to those who were in the minority and experiencing unjust persecution was of great encouragement to those believers.

One can imagine that the most urgent and most culturally pressing teachings in the parts of Asia where the church today exists in a rather hostile and repressive environment may be markedly different from churches, say, in England where Christianity still claims a comfortable share of the historical voice from its Church of England heritage and is not subjected to harsh persecution or despotic governmental forces. In sum, the most salient themes of Christian teaching are likely to be influenced by the social circumstances of the people.

Second, the relationship of church and state affects Christian education. While it may seem obvious, the governmental authorities of a given country may have varying relational degrees ranging from congenial to totalitarian. Detrimental conditions for Christianity exist in some countries—for example, North African countries are overwhelmingly Islamic; in contrast, some countries have adopted religious postures that, at least on the surface, are decidedly convivial and virtually inseparable from their political philosophies—for example, several nations in southern Europe possess deep Roman Catholic ties.[7]

One of the debilitating consequences with unusually close associations between state and Christianity can be witnessed in some Scandinavian countries, where some 90 percent claim Lutheranism yet a minimal number actually practice the Christian faith. In any situation, the government plays a role in how faith communities exist, practice, and teach Christianity.

Third, when a society experiences rapid change, its teaching of faith is also likely to be adapting. The pace of Western cultural change is frenetic and driven largely by media—including movies, music, social media, and popular culture—and unlikely to reduce its velocity any time soon. With such change, society is confronted with an array of new, often avant-garde topics, and the teachings of the church must respond by assisting believers in the task of theological reflection upon this rapid change, rather than naively capitulating to cultural drift.

What are those social conditions in the current time that are prevalent and in need of explicit understanding from a faith perspective? Numerous points could be listed. In our Western culture, Christians need to continually and critically engage in cultural assessment, especially as Christians face ethical issues about economic and justice issues, medical and technological advances, political and media influences, and sexual and educational agendas. Societal change understandably affects the topics and even the means of Christian education.

Perhaps we lack proper historical perspective, but this first-third of the twenty-first century may be the most challenging time in the history of the Christian centuries to nurture faith. What rationale supports such a bold claim? Well, in the Western world, culture looks askance at old-time, faith-based metanarratives; and globally, the fight continues to be inflamed by fierce battles between Christianity and other worldviews. Such political oppression and cultural allurements are powerful and detrimental. But *nurturing faith is the educational mission of the global church, its destiny and calling.* The gates of hell will not prevail against it (Matt. 16:18) and increasing faith is what God intends for followers (2 Cor. 3:18; Gal. 4:19; 5:22–23; Col. 1:9–14).

Part	Theme
1	Cultural Dynamics for Nurturing Faith
	› Leaving the Faith (chapter 1)
	› Modernism/Postmodernism (chapter 2)
	› Religious Nominalism (chapter 3)
	› Keeping the Faith (chapter 4)
2	Criteria for Nurturing Faith
3	Colleagues in Nurturing Faith
4	Contexts for Nurturing Faith
5	Conversations in Nurturing Faith

So, what holds part 1 together? These four chapters provide "the lay of the land" and name key contextual realities (for good and for ill) that must be taken into account when considering the task of nurturing faith. Part 1 chronicles various "cultural dynamics in nurturing faith"—contrasting the factors and tendencies of how and why Christians leave and keep their faith. Individual, cultural, educational, and religious factors play roles in each case. Some themes under consideration include the shift from premodern to modern to postmodern social imaginaries; the church's interaction with increasingly hostile or indifferent cultures (pressure from the outside) plus the church's own internal failings and struggles (pressure from the inside); and finally, we will turn to specifically Christian educational considerations, including the need to push beyond the paradigm of the school and to develop a more holistic anthropology/epistemology.

Specifically, *chapter 1* explores the challenges faith communities confront in educating believers and seeks insight from other faith traditions to learn how better to nurture our own. *Chapter 2* tells two stories—one of modernism/postmodernism and the other of faith. We will voice the message each contributes to the mission of God. *Chapter 3* speaks of time-worn religious traditionalism and addresses the scourge of nominalism and nationalism and their place in the (mis)education of Christians. Finally, *chapter 4* advances our main theses, propelled by practical theology and social science research, for fostering the life-sustaining educative experiences in the Christian way and for sustaining vital growth in faith.

CHAPTER ONE

Leaving the Faith: Eulogies of Disenchantment, Lethargy, and Irrelevance

O to grace how great a debtor, Daily I'm constrained to be!
Let Thy goodness, like a fetter, Bind my wandering heart to Thee.
Prone to wander, Lord, I feel it, Prone to leave the God I love;
Here's my heart, O take and seal it, Seal it for Thy courts above.

—ROBERT ROBINSON

Why was it virtually impossible not to believe in God in, say 1500, in our Western society, while in 2000 many of us find this not only easy but even inescapable?

—CHARLES TAYLOR

ROAD MAP

We suppose this chapter could just as easily been called "Confessions of a Humbled Church." In *chapter 1* we somberly rehearse the church's failure to nurture faith effectively and divest itself of counterproductive educational strategies. While we ought not to hide the church's failures, we also need to take the words above of Charles Taylor (in the epigraph) seriously—for cultural forces have indeed conspired against even the possibility of transcendence. Therefore, here we explore the dismal statistics and mounting social and cultural obstacles that tell a narrative of decline within the Christian fold. While we face the growing embrace of other narratives beyond the Christian story, we confess a million ways the church has been either feckless or evil and failed to prioritize or execute faith formation. For this, on behalf of the church, we repent, seek forgiveness, and ask for wisdom to reverse what has so gravely injured Christians and non-Christians alike. But do not be dismayed: in these beginning pages, we concede there may be a good bit of hand-wringing and even shouting in the name of righteous indignation. Our strategy is a balancing act in being honest in our lament over what seems like Christian decline in the West while yet holding on to love, hope, and *faith*.

Introduction

Roughly half of those who grow up in Christian families (regardless of denomination) leave the faith, at least at some point in their lives.[1] Up to 10 percent (more than thirty million) of all Americans are *former* Catholics.[2] The same trend is well-documented in Europe, where belief in God has decreased in Britain, the Netherlands, Germany, and France.[3] Many crestfallen parents and aggrieved faith communities are then left to wonder why attempts to pass along their faith have been ineffectual—a condition that would not have surprised Danish philosopher Søren Kierkegaard, who thought Christian education was *the main obstacle* to Christian belief.[4] So, spurred along with the goal of growing more successful in transmitting the Christian religion, the church must make more concerted efforts at better teaching practices.

This chapter is about the concern for *loss* in far too many who have called Christianity their home base—loss of faith and loss of communion with the community of faith. The upshot of this loss is manifest in disenchantment, lethargy, and irrelevance: *disenchantment*, in that a faith once embraced now tastes bitter; *lethargic*, in that a faith once vibrant now drifts to a listless and ineffectual shadow of itself; and *irrelevant*, in that a faith meant to invoke hope for the day slides to an extraneous façade.[5] These eulogies signify that the ache driving this chapter is for the lamentable state of affairs in which Christians lose faith.[6] But what are the reasons people lose faith, and what can be done to enhance teaching ministries in the church to diminish such loss?

John Westerhoff somewhat counterintuitively warns: "Teaching religion is not very important"; at best, it only produces "educated atheists."[7] Consider the unfortunate experience of Sergei Bulgakov. He was born into a family of Russian Orthodox priests and went to seminary to train for the same profession, and *this* is where he experienced a loss of faith. He later returned to the church and reminisced: "How did I come to lose my faith? . . . It occurred when the poetry of my childhood was squeezed out of my life by the prose of seminary education. I realized that I could not be satisfied with the apologetics of the textbooks. Instead of helping me, they further undermined my faith."[8] What Bulgakov describes is tragic and obviously represents exactly the *opposite* effect of what any educational efforts in faith would seek. Why is the church so ineffective at transmitting its faith to succeeding generations? And what are the challenges that undermine such attempts at fostering faith?

As of 2020, Christianity is the dominant world religion with roughly 2.2 billion adherents. This is good news: for over twenty centuries, the teachings of Jesus have spread from a trifling patch of land on the Mediterranean Sea, and the faithful have grown exponentially. Islam is the second largest religion, with about 1.6 billion adherents. However, according to the Pew Research Study on "The Future of World Religions,"[9] if current demographic trends continue, Islam is expected to catch up with Christianity midway through the twenty-first century. Why? Several factors are at work, but most relevant to our discussion, Christians are expected to see the largest net losses from *religious switching*—leaving the faith of one's childhood and deciding to opt for another or none at all (see table 1).[10] Is it reasonable to ascribe at least partial blame for religious switching on faltering Christian educational efforts?

Table 1. *Projected Cumulative Change Due to Religious Switching, 2010–2050*

	Switching in	Switching out	Net Change
Unaffiliated	97,080,000	35,590,000	+61,490,000
Muslims	12,620,000	9,400,000	+3,220,000
Folk Religions	5,460,000	2,850,000	+2,610,000
Other Religions	3,040,000	1,160,000	+1,880,000
Hindus	260,000	250,000	+10,000
Jews	320,000	630,000	-310,000
Buddhists	3,370,000	6,210,000	-2,850,000
Christians	40,060,000	106,110,000	-66,050,000

Source: The Future of World Religions: Population Growth Projections, 2010–2050. Pew Research Center.

The religiously unaffiliated (atheists, agnostics, nonaffiliated) are expected to see the largest net gains from switching, adding more than 61 million to their number.[11] And, as suggested by the Pew Research Center study, many of those being added to the ranks of the "religious unaffiliated" are evacuees from the Christian faith (66 million).[12] This is most decidedly not good news: those who have previously been affiliated with Christianity for various reasons are *leaving the faith*.[13] If we are to be honest, it is frustrating. We are disappointed by certain cultures that scoff, belittle, and excoriate those who embrace non-empirical faith; discouraged by the ineffective teaching strategies communities of faith inflict on followers that result in a faith that appears to be irrelevant; and disheartened by individuals who are caught up in the pursuit of self and lack the character, obedience, and sacrifice to stay the course. Of course, all this is the result of spiritual battles (Eph. 6:10–18), but the result certainly stirs passions within us to ameliorate these conditions.

The Pew Research Center projections attempt to incorporate patterns in religious switching in 70 countries, where surveys provide information on the number of people who say they no longer belong to the religious group in which they were raised. Some social theorists have suggested that as countries develop economically, more of their inhabitants will move away from religious affiliation.[14] While that has been the general experience in some parts of the world, notably Europe, it is not yet clear whether it is a universal pattern. Philip Jenkins considers this very point in *The Next Christendom*,[15] in which he compellingly articulates one of the reasons global Christianity is decisively shifting its movement from north and west to south and east: as societies gain wealth, the practice of Christianity diminishes. As Christians are seduced by the promise of economic safety propelled by wealth and self-reliance, a faith-based life is more easily sidelined. Switching from Christianity to other belief systems plays directly into the hand of imagined self-sufficiency and corresponding lack of faithful dependence.

So, in sum, over the coming decades, Christianity is expected to experience the largest net losses from "switching," which often amounts to just "quitting." One wonders, what is defective in the experience of some who taste Christianity but decide not to partake? Globally, about 40 million people are projected to relocate into Christianity, while 106 million are projected for an *en masse* exodus, with most joining the ranks of the religiously unaffiliated.[16] Some of this, we propose, can be accounted for by *postmodern dynamics* (to be addressed in chapter 2); other factors no doubt derive from off-putting *religious nominalism*, manifested as authoritarianism, arrogance, exclusion and perceptions of patriarchy, and racism (to be addressed in chapter 3 and elsewhere).[17]

Challenges to Nurturing Faith

These "big picture" themes impact Christian strategies for faith formation. Any obstacle that diminishes or thwarts the salvation of God from finding a home in the minds, hearts, and lives of Christians and the church is a challenge to the objectives of Christian education. As noted, some of these challenges are provoked from *outside* the church (e.g., secularism, pluralism, consumerism); while others are fueled from *inside* the church (e.g., nominalism, misguided faith-forming content and methods, plus unhealthy internal dynamics within faith communities). Still other challenges, seemingly promulgated by individual Christians (e.g., defiant attitudes, glaring hypocrisy, unrelenting sin, nominal commitment), also point to the power of cultural individualism in the global north. This part examines how these inner and outer dynamics along with the church's too frequent failure to critically evaluate and renew its teaching strategies are impacting its efforts toward nurturing faith.

The Explicit Teaching/Learning Process as Starting Point

At present, Christian faith communities give little attention to educational theory or practice in their efforts to nurture faith. They seldom pause to ask what sort of learning they wish to promote or even what *Christian* learning consists in. The typical educational default is to learn for cognitive competence (knowing *about* subject matter) promoted by pedagogies that presume knowledge is passively absorbed by students. Much of this default mode is simply "wrong" by even secular educational standards. In addition, Christian educational leaders ought to question whether it suits Christian educational ends.

The basic axiom of learning in any explicitly educational setting is based on the students' motivation and capability. This is "educational psychology 101": a student may be willing but not able; a student may be able but not willing; and of course, a student may be neither willing nor able. If any of these three conditions exist, learning will be muted.

Questions about motivation and capability for being educated in the Christian faith are not often considered with clarity. Whereas rewards through high grades or awards may drive a student in formal school settings to learn, no such formal evaluation is part of most church-based informal growth in faith.[18] Whereas cognitive wherewithal is the primary operating vehicle for formal school education, Christian education is primarily about nurturing faith and spiritual virtues.[19]

In his fine chapter "Pedagogy for the Unimpressed" in *Awakening Discipleship*, David White squarely blames the consumerist culture for diminishing attention spans. In his perceptive *Virtually You: The Dangerous Powers of the E-Personality*,[20] Elias Aboujaoude looks more broadly at how technology use restructures our perception and construction of identities and relationships, all of which directly impact how learning works. Likewise, Chuck Foster's chapter "Why Can't They Remember?" in *From Generation to Generation* recounts the same idea: cultural preoccupations and social institutions actively prevent learning focus and perceptual awareness. How then are people motivated or unmotivated to learn?[21]

An understanding of salient principles of intentional human learning can only increase students' motivation and nurture their abilities: (1) students cannot recall and apply knowledge unless they practice retrieval and use; (2) better learning results when teachers vary the conditions of learning; (3) when learners integrate knowledge from both verbal and visual representations, they can recall it and apply it with greater ease; (4) prior knowledge or belief impacts what students will learn; (5) what instructors and learners believe about knowledge acquisition (epistemology) influences what will be learned; (6) experience is a poor teacher absent self-reflection upon it; (7) lectures may fail to promote understanding if students are not engaged by them in an interpretive process; (8) remembering is a creative process that influences what learners will and will not be able to recall and apply; (9) trying to cover large amounts of material and information reduces understanding and recall; and (10) what learners do will determine what they will learn, how well they can recall it, and the conditions under which they can use it.[22] These basic principles emphasize the critical nature of student engagement in learning. No input without output. No impression without expression. Not teaching, but learning. What these principles should convey for Christian educators is that passivity must be replaced by student engagement in thought and practice.

DOUBT

Religious doubt takes on many different forms. Some people doubt God because they want to believe but do not dare to or do not find it easy to believe. Others doubt God because they believe but do not want to. Others doubt because they wrestle with philosophies and ideas contrary to their faith, or because they encounter certain experiences that contradict their beliefs. Doubt is not primarily an obscure philosophical or theological concept, nor simply a state of spiritual or psychological anguish; it is a matter of truth—knowing who God really is and whether we can trust him. Doubt involves questions like, Is God real? How can I be sure? Does God love me? Is Jesus Christ the only way to salvation?

Doubt is a universal experience, regardless of religious belief or stage of life. Doubt will be included in faith, even mature faith, as a structural feature of it. This means Christians are not immune to doubt. John Calvin explained that faith is neither untouched by doubt nor assailed by no worry. Rather, Christians battle a lack of confidence because of the imperfection of our faith. The existence of doubt does not imply the absence of faith but is rather a continual reminder of our sinful nature, which hinders us from knowing God perfectly. This is why Augustine asserts that Christians love God by faith now but will love God by sight in the new creation. In the eschaton, sin will no longer create a barrier between us and God, for we will see God for who God truly is.

Christians should, therefore, not be surprised when they or their loved ones encounter seasons of doubt. We are broken and sinful people who live in a broken and sinful world. Christians, therefore, should aim to understand doubt and how to rightly address it. As Os Guinness explains, doubt can act as a "sparring partner both to truth and error." While doubt may hinder us from embracing the truth, it can also aid us in deflecting lies and therefore grow in our faith. This means there is a positive element of doubt, for the Christian. By wrestling with and through doubt, Christians can become more assured of the truth and who God is. Scripture explains that the "testing of [our] faith produces perseverance," and that perseverance renders us "mature and complete" (James 1:2–4).

Doubt, therefore, can be instrumental in the perfection of our faith and should be battled courageously. Creel explains that self-conscious faith "is an act of courage, a daring affirmation of one's deepest desires." This does not mean, however, that one simply believes whatever one hopes to be true. Rather, true faith wrestles to affirm what the biblical faith holds to be true, despite one's spiritual and psychological anguish.

The Christian cannot do this alone. Rather, doubt is best addressed in the context of Christian community. As Dietrich Bonhoeffer explained, the Christian "needs his brother solely because of Jesus Christ. The Christ in his own heart is weaker than the Christ in the word of his brother; his own heart is uncertain; his brother's is sure." The goal of Christian education is to nurture and strengthen faith. Christian education is, therefore, a fundamental tool in instilling and restoring a believer's confidence in God.

KEVIN P. EMMERT

Educational Factors Inside the Church

James Smart's classic analysis, in *The Teaching Ministry of the Church: An Examination of the Basic Principles of Christian Education*, of the rigor of educating in faith continues to illuminate the present situation.[23] He warned that challenges to Christian education arise, first, from *the rigidity of tradition* (in which tired and ineffective means continue to sway theory and practice, including the reinforcement of assumptions that learning is a passive "top-down" process); second, from *the prevalence* of *moralism* (when Bible stories are employed to enforce weak moralisms instead of imaginative conviction for transformation); third, from *the imbalance of the burden* (in which forces in the lives of the students compete with focus on Christian education); fourth, from *the inadequacy of time* (a disproportionately small amount devoted to faith formation); fifth, from *the subordination of priorities* (implied by the degree to which churches fail to emphasize meaningful learning for their students); sixth, from *the poor quality of programs* (exhibited by the inferior training of the teachers and haphazard investment in educational resources); seventh, from *the timidity of curriculum* (in which culturally inoffensive postures are taken on urgent ethical issues); eighth, from *the fragmentation of revelation* (demonstrated by the lack of awareness Christians exhibit for the overarching story and mission of God and their inability to perceive God's activity in the present); and ninth, from *the confusion of purpose* (indicated by the lack of cohesion or demonstrable goals in program design and lack of measurable results from Christian education initiatives).

Educational Factors outside the Church

As Charles Taylor has made clear, secularism, the presumption that there is no frame of existence other than the "immanent" one, appears to challenge Christian faith at its core.[24] Secularism denies the very possibility of *transcendence*, let alone the existence of a God who is revealed in the person of Jesus Christ by the power of the Spirit. In its destructive wake, secularism also appears to swamp truth. Absent God, truth loses its ground and credibility, causing skeptics to characterize it as mere power discourse, a form of ideology intended to maintain the power of one group over others. Critics of the church claim that in its pretense of mediating the revealed truth of God, it has instead maintained the dominance of White European men over women and people of color and even children. They have a point.

Secularism has impacted the possibility of faith and the task of nurturing it in indirect ways as well. Sundays no longer exhibit a Sabbath-like character; they look much like every other day of the week in North America and Europe. Individual people are far more likely to "trust their guts" when it comes to discerning the proper course of their lives than to look to authorities claiming to speak for God. Even practicing Christians who profess to value Scripture as God's word are nevertheless more likely to read it to see what's in it for them than to ask what God is up to and how they may join up.

In sum, secularism has become a powerful, even dominant dimension of culture in the global north. Human creators of culture seldom notice how it is forming their imaginations and desires. Faith-forming leaders will require eyes wide open in order to understand and appreciate how it presents a challenge to the fundamental possibility of faith as well as the task of nurturing it. On the other hand, by casting the sins of Christendom in stark relief and forcing Christianity to the margins of society, secular critics may have done the church a service. Now more than ever it is becoming clear to Christians that truth must serve *love*. As more than one pastor has noted, Christians expended much effort in recent centuries, arguing with others that they were *right*. Perhaps now it is time to try being good. With John Wesley, therefore, we affirm that God's mercy is God's justice. And as the old KJV puts it, "mercy and truth are met together" (Ps. 85:10) in God's providence.

In short, reliable data indicate Christians leave the faith decidedly, often, and for a variety of reasons. While secularizing influences eschew the faith as primitive and old-fashioned, just as often the church shoots itself in the foot through poor educational strategies. A rather unorthodox line of inquiry perhaps might be entertained here: How do other faith traditions transmit their faith with notable success? In light of their present failures, can Christian efforts toward nurturing faith gain insight from others?

Learning from Other Faith Traditions

Rethinking Practices for Faith-Forming Christian Education

Granted, Christianity is susceptible to fallout, but other faith traditions seem to do better in retaining their adherents. Jews, despite suffering unparalleled devastation over the centuries, maintain their collective identity. Mormons are justifiably admired for passing on the faith of their forebearers. Muslims, too, effectively form and retain their members. So, faced with the prospects of losing Christians in disquieting numbers, what clues can be discerned from observing how other faith traditions transmit faith across generations?[25]

We propose that Christian educators, in the spirit of humility, could learn from other religious traditions with respect to their most distinctive means for nurturing faith.[26] The search here is pedagogical rather than theological.[27] Admittedly, as McDermott observes, "Rarely, if ever, has evangelicalism (or European Christianity in general) regarded non-Christian religion as something from which it can learn."[28] Perhaps this historic arrogance—Christians assuming they possess all the answers—partly accounts for our own present struggle. With McDermott again, we are convinced that "Most learning is a matter not of seeing entirely new things but of seeing old things in a new way."[29] Hence our aim is to see with sufficient appreciation different dynamics of faith formation in other traditions that, in turn, may assist Christians in discovering or recovering helpful analogues in their own. Consider this.

In the graduate-level course Mark teaches called "The Educational Mission of the Church," he invites articulate lay and professional spokespersons from various traditions to talk on a panel about their faith. Presenters may be Mormon, Jewish, Buddhist, Muslim, Jehovah's Witness, or Christian Scientist. Students in the course listen to these religious educators reflect on how their particular faith is inculcated, nurtured, and otherwise taught to their children, youth, and adults, and then ask an array of questions—often focusing on what drew the panelists to embrace their faith, what means they use to transmit their faith effectively to their members, and to what extent the general nature of secularization and loss of religiosity in society impacts their faith.

From our reflection on the comments from several dozen panelists over the years, three main themes have emerged as we have listened to other faith traditions share their practices of transmission:[30]

1. **People** are more influential than doctrine in drawing others to a faith and sustaining it. A faith lived out by exemplars is a powerful apologetic for faith.

2. The **ritual(s)** of a faith community serve as a binding force for embrac-

ing and owning a faith. Action fosters, cements, and sometimes embodies belief and intensifies the practice and experience of a group.

3. Sacrificial **commitment** and radical **discipline** are expected of individuals and modeled by the faith community, which means that there is a strong emphasis on the centrality of community. Where much is expected, much support is extended.

As a result of these observations, it becomes apparent that some of our currently employed educational perspectives and practices may even be frustrating the spiritual growth of our constituents. Our overemphasis upon classroom learning to the exclusion of more active approaches, for example, or the growing popularity of "edu-tainment" curricula for children and youth—letting consumerist cultural values override the gospel, or persistently characterizing faith itself as a purely interior disposition of the soul with no integration into life—are three cases in point.

In light of these preliminary insights, we explore in further detail Mormon witness, Jewish ritualizing, and Muslim daily prayer. Nevertheless, we do so while remaining aware of the tension between the desire to learn from Mormon, Jewish, and Muslim ways of propagating faith and the claim to some level of uniqueness to Christian educational practice, given the particularity of our revelation. Again, the point of this exercise is to invigorate our own faith-forming imagination, perhaps to reawaken dormant memories of our past faith-forming efforts and to innovate in light of them. Therefore, the following is (1) an attempt to describe a laudable faith practice, (2) an effort to contrast this exemplary practice with an alternate approach, and (3) suggestions of what Christian educators might learn from this practice.

Mormon Religious Education: Pragmatizing Apologetics and Ownership

That Mormonism is growing around the world at phenomenal rates is not in question.[31] And it is also evident that the Mormon religion is being absorbed and its tenets sustained by its members.[32] Certainly, a number of factors can account for such remarkable fidelity, but one particular practice, mission, as attested to by those who have experienced it, is also a significant educational and concretizing ingredient in the faith formation of Mormons.

Describing an Alternate Faith-Forming Practice

One of Mormonism's most distinctive, albeit indirect, educative strategies is to enlist young men and young women, normally in their upper teens and early twenties, to become "missionaries." Most North Americans, although fewer Europeans in recent days, have encountered these earnest evangelists on our doorsteps. What then is the ingenuity of this form of education? (See table 2.) In the process, these young adults leave home and are displaced to geographical locations around the world where through listening to others, they are forced to become intimately conversant with the doctrine and practices of their faith. Their preparation begins years prior with explicit training in Bible, theology, doctrine, apologetics, and rhetoric. It is mostly through their numerous door-to-door encounters (often with skeptics), however, that Mormon missionaries become adept at defending and owning their faith.

Table 2. *The Potential Educational Value of One Aspect of Mormon Religious Education*

Faith Tradition	Religious Practice	Potential Value of Adapted Practice	Recovered Practice from Christian History	Educational Learning Theory
Mormon	Missional service	Increased action-oriented grasp of a too often verbally dominant faith	Pursuing dynamic, urgent, lay-oriented leadership, and faith-enhancing religious passion	Conceptual disequilibrium

Experiencing faith in this manner comes at a critical point in a believer's lifecycle. At a time when many leave the church—young adulthood—Mormons intentionally engage their adherents in a faith-forming educational experience that cements their place in the church. This form of hands-on educational activity increases an action-oriented grasp of a religious faith that can otherwise become a more stagnant verbally dominant dogma, even though their practice is primarily linguistic (to speak to others) and conceptual (to articulate the tenets of the faith). Because no practice is beyond corruption, it is possible that some Mormon missionaries grow more skilled at winning arguments than at living faithfully. Yet we are reminded of the words of Peter Bohler, Moravian friend to a spiritually anxious John Wesley: "Preach faith until you have it; then, because you have it, you will preach faith."[33] There is something about the public performance of faith that makes it stick to its bearers.

Contrasting Faith Tradition Practices

Compare the Mormon practice of calling young adults to intentional mission with the far more common practice of congregations sending post–high school young people into their futures with the vague injunction to "find a church." In this instance, it appears that Christian faith communities have acceded to the cultural script portraying young adulthood as the season for *finding* or *making* something of one's *self*. By contrast, Mormons tell their young, in effect, by following God, *God* will make something of you.

Considering an Alternate Faith-Forming Practice

To be sure, those Mormon young adults have come to know their faith by the end of the two-year mission. They have experienced a life-transforming event that will likely ingrain their identities and future commitments in the Mormon Church. They will be uniquely prepared to draw upon their faith resources to provide leadership and service to their families and local churches for the rest of their adult lives. (This includes the capacity to interpret the Scriptures and other sacred texts.) Check this theory by talking to those who have experienced it. We have encountered some of these young adults after having returned from mission service. They demonstrate confidence in faith and themselves and know what it means to be Mormon.

For Christians to more effectively nurture faith, there is an urgent need to conceive of and promote sustained faith-forming efforts where young adult Christians in particular have skin in the game. These could include participation in mission, featuring regular encounters with people who believe differently for purposes of real-world dialogue about the truth claims of the Christian faith. With the support of communities of reflection, these emerging disciples will be grafted into the Christian faith through the proven benefit of *conceptual disequilibrium*—the intentional practice of challenging our assumptions through doubt, reality testing, and intense analysis of a particular system of beliefs.[34] Certainly, one may argue that the Christian mission is not theologically and practically identical to Mormon mission, again, given the uniqueness of Christianity vis-à-vis Mormonism. However, such "missionary activities" (as described above) certainly are unusual and risky proposals to introduce to communities of faith, and Christian parents, and they have little precedent within Christianity, but the results could yield nothing less than groups of prepared and committed young people for sustaining an intentional Christian life.

Finally, it seems likely that calling young Christians into mission will promote long-term dynamic, urgent, lay-oriented leadership, and faith-enhancing religious passion. In this regard, we certainly have something to learn from Mormon practices of mission.

Jewish Religious Education: Ritualizing Action and Socialization

One of Mark's favorite books is Chaim Potok's *Wanderings: A History of the Jews*—a well-woven story touching upon the historical markers and watershed events of the remarkable faith-journey of one of the world's most persecuted peoples.[35] The resiliency of the Jewish people is unparalleled in religious history. Therefore, a better grasp of how they have educated their members in the faith can suggest helpful possibilities for the Christian effort.[36]

Describing an Alternate Faith-Forming Practice

Christian education practice has something to learn from Jewish religious education. Lauren Winner, a Jewish convert to Christianity, provides a unique perspective for those in her new religion:

> Christian practices . . . would be enriched, that is, they would be thicker and more vibrant, if we took a few lessons from Judaism. . . . Jews do these things with more attention and wisdom not because they are more righteous nor because God likes them better, but rather because doing, because action, sits at the center of Judaism. *Practice is to Judaism what belief is to Christianity.* That is not to say that Judaism does not have dogma or doctrine. It is rather to say that for Jews, the essence of the thing is a doing, an action.[37]

It is just the opposite for much of Western Christianity—a statement-of-faith-oriented, somewhat less behavior-measured, creed. In fact, an emerging "practices movement" may just be reshaping Christianity.

This form of religious practice inculcates in its students a renewed sense of located placement in the story of God by practicing the community's story in expressions of binding social ritual. (See table 3.) Keeping weekly Sabbath, for example, proclaims the identity of God as creator, liberator, and sustainer while "performing" Jews into grateful dependence upon that God.

RITUAL

Participating in ritual may provide participants with a rich array of learning experiences. Ritual performed in a congregation communicates the central aspects of a congregation's core beliefs, vision, and identity to participants. Contrary to the common misunderstanding that ritual is thoughtless action or bodily movement devoid of intrinsic logic and grammars, ritual practice discloses a significant body of information and knowledge about the collective nature of a congregation. The most critical core values and convictional beliefs held dearly within a congregation are disclosed through ritual practice. In this sense, ritual is an indispensable aspect in the religious socialization process, incorporating new adherents into the corporate life and culture of a congregation.

Ritual is a religious or solemn ceremony of some kind that consists of a series of actions performed according to a prescribed order, or a rite of passage during one's lifecycle, such as a *bar mitzvah*, wedding, funeral and the like, usually performed in accordance with social custom or normal protocol. Some of the distinctive and constitutive elements involved in ritual practice are a group of people enacting some forms of patterned movements, a ritual space, and time apart from the mundane schedule of everyday life. And ritual often incorporates internal desires and intention when the participants perform rituals.

The educational potencies of ritual practice have critical influence in the formative process of a community. These effects of ritual practice are best seen when they are located within the two educational dynamics of congregational ministry—socialization and transformation. Ritual often stands at the critical intersection of a congregational life, where both socialization and transformation interact with each other and push and pull from each other, and yet remain fully complementary to each other. From the above examples of ritual functions and roles, we can see how the critical roles that ritual plays in a congregation allow for an educational condition where this dialectic between seeking to maintain social stability and continuity and searching for transformation is embraced and honored, even when clear foresight is nowhere to be seen. The formative impact of rituals when performed in a congregation collectively and intentionally can only be imagined, as both its pedagogical and generative functions are seriously acknowledged in the learning process.

TIMOTHY D. SON

Table 3. *The Potential Educational Value of One Aspect of Jewish Religious Education*

Faith Tradition	Religious Practice	Potential Value of Adapted Practice	Recovered Practice from Christian History	Educational Learning Theory
Judaism	Socializing ritual	Renewed sense of located placement in grander metanarrative of story of God	Reinvigorating rituals that enable participants to experience their place in God's story	Experiential ownership

Contrasting Faith Tradition Practices

Contrast Jewish identity-shaping rituals, especially their integration into the daily life of the household, with much of Western Christianity, where gaping inconsistencies exist between stated belief and living it out. It is just this tendency—an oddball tenet of a *nominal faith* that Christian belief need not find any expression in one's behavior (particularly visible among some Christians)—that needs this corrective stance from Judaism.[38] William Hutchison, former church historian at Harvard, says in many Western societies there is a gap between profession of belief and committed Christian practice, but it is most striking in the United States and the West in particular.[39] The pagan religions of the ancient world usually separated belief and conduct in a fashion unknown to first-century Christianity. The priests and priestesses of the ancient idols did not insist on a change of behavior. Rather, devotees of some pagan religions could live much as they pleased so long as they worshiped the deities in deference to public expectation.[40] At present, this phenomenon of "undisciplined disciples" contributes to nations becoming post-Christian even as many of their citizens nonetheless believe they *are* Christian.[41] This undesirable state extends across the spectrum of the Christian family—conservative, evangelical, mainline; Protestant, Roman Catholic, Orthodox, Anglican.[42]

Considering an Alternate Faith-Forming Practice

Judaism, especially through its utilization of communal ritual, demonstrates the power and importance, not only of intentional instruction but of religious socialization. Michael Warren poetically expresses this truth: "Faith can be elaborated, explained, and systematized in books, but it shouts, it dances, it lives and takes flesh in people."[43] In this similar vein, Jewish theologian Abraham Joshua Heschel has keenly observed: "What we need more than anything else is not textbooks but text-people."[44] Learning faith is as much about engendering intimacy in human relationships nurtured by faith as about articulated parsing or indoctrinating systems of belief. Ask honestly what Christian educators wish there were more of—Bible study groups or faith-practicing communities led by exemplars?—and the answer is clear.

Through worship and study, community governance and catechesis, spiritual direction and household prayer, Jews and some Christians over time have been educated and formed (socialized) within a web of practices transmitted and transformed by the communities that live out such practices in daily life. Engaging in these practices—whether highly ritualized or thoroughly quotidian—individuals and communities come to know themselves, others, and God in specific ways. In them, multiple layers of enculturation, resistance, and negotiation—orientations within the world—are both expressed and absorbed.[45]

Christian educators need to conceive of and promote their own practices of socialization, including rituals that personalize and humanize the convictions and ethos of a community. Through this process, these believers will be more readily grafted into the Christian faith through the proven benefit of *experiential ownership*—being assimilated into a value system that assigns significant human meaning through the intentional practice of communal rites and symbolic life-affirming commitment.

The most correlational applications of experiential ownership, as distilled from the social learning theories of Albert Bandura, are these: first, the highest level of observational learning is achieved by first organizing and rehearsing the modeled behavior symbolically and then enacting it overtly; second, coding modeled behavior into words, labels, or images results in better retention than simply observing; third, individuals are more likely to adopt a modeled behavior if it results in outcomes they value; and finally, individuals are more likely to adopt a modeled behavior if the model is similar to that of the observer and has admired status and functional value.[46] Each of these important social science principles has tremendous relevance for modeling, experiencing, and nurturing faith in children, adolescents, and adults.[47]

Christian educators have something to learn from this socializing dimension of Jewish education.[48]

Muslim Religious Education: Radicalizing Kinesthetic and Symbolic Commitment

What comes to mind when the average Westerner contemplates followers of Islam? Possibly, the first notion that takes shape is a mental image of Muslims' demonstrative practice of prone public prayer. What does this practice mean, and how may Christians learn from it?

Describing an Alternate Faith-Forming Practice

Lamin Sanneh grew up as the son of a Muslim tribal chief in Senegal, West Africa. He was until his recent passing a Christian missiologist and a professor at Yale Divinity School in the United States.[49] Sanneh attests to the powerful influence of prayer in Islamic religious faith practice. Muslims, individually or in a group, punctuate their daily routines with prayer. Facing Mecca, they pray five times a day—early morning, noon, midafternoon, sunset, and evening. And a good Muslim washes forearms, feet, mouth, and nostrils three times and recites a memorized prayer of faith, praise, and gratitude.[50] Sanneh emphasizes two primary reasons that make Muslim prayer so powerful: first, the physicality involved, where both kinesthetic and symbolic action may invoke conscious thought; and second, the radical, countercultural commitment, often public, demonstrated by such unabashed behavior.

In the Christian faith, kneeling, standing, singing, praying, communion, baptism, all involve physical action that can be educational and formative. They are intended to shape attitudes and make theological statements but are underutilized and underappreciated and lack the zealous, countercultural intentions of the corresponding Muslim practice.[51] Evangelical Christians in particular are likely to view kinesthetic practices as external representations of faith instead of embodiments of it. (See table 4, below.)

Contrasting Faith Tradition Practices

Contrast this, once again, with another of the most prominent flaws of Western Christianity, namely, that historians have commented on the shallowness of personal commitment that accompanies much of the post–World War II religious resurgence in the United States. Church membership can mean little more than culturally prescribed respectability and belief in the modern way of life.

The middle-class subculture has existed in such a close relationship with some versions of American Christianity, it sometimes is difficult to distinguish what is consumerist from what is Christian. Added to that, the self-styled messiah of national religiosity is now crowned prince of a new civil religion. The result? Sociologist Peter Berger speaks what church-people know is true but are afraid to admit: "The spirit has gone out of religious institutions to shape and they rather have been shaped by society's agenda."[52] Friedrich Nietzsche lambastes those who relabel the divine in comfortable button-down, middle-class tones: "You have caged Jesus, tamed him, domesticated him. . . . The roaring bull has become a listless ox. You have gelded God!"[53]

Table 4. *The Potential Educational Value of One Aspect of Muslim Religious Education*

Faith Tradition	Religious Practice	Potential Value of Adapted Practice	Recovered Practice from Christian History	Educational Learning Theory
Islam	Transforming prayer	Reinvigorated valuation of symbolic prostration to shape interaction with God	Practicing a more tangible presence with an invisible yet time-and-space inhabiting God	Kinesthetic symbolism

The gospel, as represented in the teachings of Jesus, is characterized in the New Testament as an "offense," but some of today's abridged versions seem anything but offensive. The cross frequently is adopted as a popular symbol, a fashion statement. Theologian Carl Henry warned: "Western evangelicalism is being spiritually thwarted by its affluence. No group of Christians has . . . more to learn about sacrifice. Our lifestyles are clearly non-Christian . . . marked by greed, extravagance, self-gratification, and lack of compassion for the needy."[54] The striking words of Jesus are blunted. Perhaps these are a primary motivation for the entire emerging church or fresh expressions movements.[55]

Considering an Alternate Faith-Forming Practice

Although there is some overlap here with the previous consideration of Jewish practices of ritualized socialization, in this instance, we are especially interested in the dynamics of shaping personal moral and spiritual character in relation to communion with transcendence. In *The American Religion: The Emergence of the Post-Christian Nation*, literary critic Harold Bloom identifies the quintessential Western religion as that devoted to self-affirmation and human freedom and asserts that evangelical Christianity is the most representative example of this religion. He claims: "This is faith more in self than Christ, concerned more with individual expression than care for community and seeking more freedom *for* the self than freedom *from* sin."[56] What Christian educators should perceive, then, is that Muslim prayer actions are tangible, powerful, visible practices of dependence transcending the self and an uncompromising commitment to faith.

Debra Dean Murphy explains how formative the *actions* of worship (specifically prayer) can be:

> Even our bodies are implicated in the formation and transformation that prayer effects. Kneeling in worship is an act of the production of Christian bodies. Kneeling, bowing, genuflecting, closing the eyes, and clasping the hands do not so much express or communicate certain subjective inner states as much as they produce particular kinds of people. Kneeling and other liturgical bodily postures are not mere *displays* of ritualized behavior. Rather, the act of kneeling itself "generates a body identified with subordination." This is not the subordination of forced enslavement or quiescent obedience—despite the lamentable abuses and misunderstandings in the church's past—but is the willing surrender, inscribed on one's very body, to the will of God.[57]

Christian educators need to conceive of faith-forming efforts that promote a reinvigorated valuation of symbolic prostration to shape interaction with holy mystery. In the process, these believers will be more handily absorbed into a Christian faith through the practice of *kinesthetic symbolism*—a literal, physical action meant to enact a religiously symbolic gesture of dependence, obedience, and other-worldly devotion.[58] We are not arguing here specifically for prostration, but rather for a greater awareness and inculcation of physical expressions in practicing our faith, from prostration in prayer, to raising hands in praise, and so on. Through this practice, a more tangible and affective presence with a transcendent yet time-and-space inhabiting God is more easily envisaged.

In addition to specific insights, what is to be learned from this brief exploration of other religious traditions? Dorothy Bass teaches: "Educating people of faith did not in the past (and cannot today) take place only or even primarily in places recognizable as 'school.' Rather, *this process takes place through and with practices*—some of them deliberately and intentionally educational, but most pursuing other goods, such as communion with God or love of neighbor."[59]

In summary, we suggest that appreciation for certain formational dynamics resident within the faith-forming, faith-renewing practices of other religious traditions can awaken us to the need to discover or recover similar dynamics within our own. These include sufficient practice with sharing, teaching, and translating faith to others as a means to faith ownership; attention to ritualization, including domestic rituals as a means to Christian socialization and enculturation; and, finally, the need to reclaim prayerful postures of praise and obedience to God in order to connect personally with God and learn to depend upon divine grace. (See table 5.)

Table 5. *Comparing the Three Alternate Faith Traditions and Relevant Educational Practices*

Faith Tradition	Religious Practice	Potential Value of Adapted Practice	Recovered Practice from Christian History	Educational Learning Theory
Mormon	Missional service	Increased action-oriented grasp of a too often verbally dominant faith	Pursuing dynamic, urgent, lay-oriented leadership, and faith-enhancing religious passion	Conceptual disequilibrium
Judaism	Socializing ritual	Renewed sense of located placement in grander metanarrative of story of God	Reinvigorating rituals that enable participants to experience their place in God's story	Experiential ownership
Islam	Transforming prayer	Reinvigorated valuation of symbolic prostration to shape interaction with God	Practicing a more tangible presence with an invisible yet time-and-space inhabiting God	Kinesthetic symbolism

Christian educators may learn from other faiths, but that alone will not solve all their problems. There are deep-seated societal and institutional facets that must be addressed head-on. To this we now turn our attention.

Here's the Problem . . .

Based on the phenomenon of "religious switching," challenges to nurturing faith from individuals and practices within and outside the church, and observations from other faith traditions, the following six obstacles impact and in some cases actively thwart efforts to fulfill the Christian educational mission. While we will more fully flesh them out in chapter 4, as well as propose remedial action, we briefly introduce them here.

First, *there is disconnectedness between the Christian tradition and the lives of believers.* Forgetfulness plagues Christianity when its sources and traditions are underappreciated. People in the global north are formed to devalue tradition and think the future is all that matters. In the digital age, our future orientation and our utilitarian/economic orientation are primary causes of this disconnect. The digital age makes the boundaries between various traditions and their communities fuzzy, fluid. A future orientation causes us to look at tradition as more often a hindrance rather than a help in facing what is ahead. Christians need grounding. *Without rootedness, Christian education is mere drifting.*

Second, *there is an assumption that the Christian life is a solitary journey filled with personal decisions to be individually negotiated with a corresponding diminution of the community of faith.* Our utilitarian orientation predisposes us to view tradition only pragmatically, as merely a depository or chest of old ideas that can be used or discarded at will. This, of course, is done very individualistically. Americans are more likely to identify with *their* faith, which they consider personal to them, than with the institutions, including denominations and congregations that have historically represented their faith to them.[60] In the context of religious community, education is our attempt to help one another understand this mystery (the Body of Christ) in its breadth and depth and to reflect on its implications for ourselves and for the world. *Without community, Christian education is mere speculation.*

Third, *in an age where Truth is increasingly decided by the loudest voice, and authority, including religious authority, is suspect, Christian education is vulnerable to the whims of entrepreneurs, harbingers of self-improvement, and self-styled biblical interpretation.* The most telling thing about contemporary Christians, claims philosopher Dallas Willard in *The Divine Conspiracy*, is they have no compelling sense that Jesus's teachings are of vital importance to their lives. Granted, one reason so many no longer trust authority purporting to speak truth is that it has so often shown itself to be interested in little more than retaining its own power and privilege. (Consider the revelations of child sexual abuse in Roman Catholic as well as some Protestant denominations and the longstanding coverups to protect offenders.) We acknowledge that questioning authority is often legitimate (e.g., biblical prophets) and address this further in our chapters on revelation and church for offering insights into discerning where and how truth can be discerned, and authority rendered trustworthy. *Nevertheless, without a commitment to truth and authority in the local faith community, Christian education is limited to teaching subjectivist experience.*

Table 6. *Fundamental Obstacles to Educating in Faith, Observable Symptoms, and Misconstrued Results*

Obstacle to Educating in Faith	Observable Symptoms	Result
Disorienting amnesia	Disconnectedness between Christian tradition and present purpose	Lack of memory; mere drift
Autonomous determinism	Prevalence of solitary journey and diminution of the community of faith	Lack of community; mere speculation
Interpretive pluriformity	Increasing prevalence of pragmatic and self-help experientialism	Lack of truth; mere utilitarianism
Cultural constructionism	Cultural entrenchment that relativizes values and truth as historical and cultural	Lack of authority; mere relativism
Fragmented faith	Absence of substantive change in the practice of life and faith	Lack of faith practice; mere nominalism
Conceptual bricolage	Deficiency of theological reflection and honest searching for God's ways	Lack of reflection; mere activism

Fourth, *at their own peril, many Christians passively acquiesce to the environmental ambiance without the discernment to critically assess how the dominant culture is certainly, albeit imperceptibly, changing them.* As cultural beings, Westerners become secularized simply by the contexts in which they grow up and live. Of course, secularism is not only outside the church but inside as well. Christians passively absorb varieties of cultural contexts they inhabit. People do not suddenly lose their secularism when they enter the church. Andy Crouch's insightful observations in *Culture Making: Recovering Our Creative Calling* detail how despite its ardent mission to change the dominant culture, the church has largely been remade by the culture it eschews.[61] A fish, as the saying goes, does not know it is wet; likewise, people are rarely as aware of their own masked cultural postures as they think. Teaching for cultural awareness is essential. Yet, awareness alone is not sufficient. Cultural awareness by itself may cause persons to conclude that since formation through varieties of cultures is inevitable, all are equally valuable. The issue for Christian nurture is that the ethics of the kingdom of heaven often are at odds with societal ideologies. Christians, therefore, sometimes must practice cultural resistance in addition to embrace. On the other hand, because the gospel is always mediated through cultures, there is also the need for engaging with cultures that seem, even on the face of things, threatening to Christian purposes. On the whole, however, the church and Christians would rather not, it seems, consider cultural engagement. As the twists and turns of this paragraph demonstrate, it is hard work. *Without reflective cultural awareness, Christian education is mere capitulation to cultural constructionism.*

Fifth, *there is a flawed presumption that those who hear biblical truth will ipso facto make the leap to living it out and revise their thoughts, attitudes, and actions toward virtuous ends.* A. W. Tozer, the noted author and pastor, warned: "A notable heresy has come into being throughout . . . [the] Christian circle: the widely accepted concept that we humans can choose to accept Christ only because we need Him as Savior, and that we have the right to postpone our obedience to Him as long as we want to!"[62] Salvation apart from discipleship is unknown in Scripture, which unambiguously teaches that true obedience is one of the toughest requirements in the Christian life. When Christians are unwittingly wooed into a view that discipleship is not difficult and can be accommodated to embrace the comfortable life of prevailing social aspiration, a flawed orientation is promulgated. Creativity and innovation will mark effective teaching in the Christian realm, which engages the student in learning and stretches faith by interacting with lived reality. Where passivity dominates Christian education, words are the primary motif. *Without faith practice in action, Christian education is mere verbalism.*

Sixth, *there is a lack of theological reflection and honest searching for God's ways in the world.* In addition to disregard for the past, what drives amnesia is a lack of reflection. When church education does not introduce laypeople to methods of theological reflection on biblical and theological texts, they are confined to their own opinions and interpretations. This strategy of piecing fragmented beliefs together lacks coherence. Theological naivete is due to a lack of critical thinking rooted in and modeled by the educational practices of the church. *Without reflection, Christian education is mere activism.*[63]

Conclusion

An untenable line of thinking goes like this: Traditional ways are outdated and lack vitality for contemporary life (#1 obstacle above). As a result, we must make up our own minds about what to believe, but this presupposes hyperindividuality and defaults to our own wants and needs, fitting primarily with our own self-composed biography (#2). There is little room for authority in this scheme (#4), and truth defaults to what works (#3). It is no wonder we live out faith incoherently, piecemeal, so to speak, without a sense of unified, corporate faith practice (#5). It is no wonder we lack wise mentors to guide us; because it is not valued, we seldom nurture faith wisdom (#6). For these reasons, countervailing strategies introduced briefly above for nurturing authentic faith will be developed in detail in subsequent chapters and then put into play in parts 3 and 4.

Let us be reminded of the ground covered in chapter 1: We acknowledge that to the extent the Christian faith has been unintentionally or even intentionally disenchanting, lethargic or irrelevant, the church has regrettably nurtured the *loss of faith* through its teaching mission. Yet, despite such discouragements, we have hope. We remain confident that these inadequacies may be corrected and that Christian faith may again resound deeply within human lives. While the first epigraph laments the predisposition of some who are "prone to wander," the preeminent task of Christian educators is to assist persons with (re)establishing their relationship to divine love, to connect biblical truth to life, to participate intimately in a community of faith, to examine their cultural surroundings in light of kingdom values, to embrace the call to obedience and sacrifice, and to critically reflect about God in the world, and in doing so, in the words of another old hymn, to discover blessing in "the tie that binds" to God, neighbor, and creation.

Interactive Dialogue

1. Does it surprise you that 10 percent of *all* Americans have left the Roman Catholic Church? Why or why not? What do you make of table 1 (p. 29) with regard to "religious switching"?
2. As stated on page 30: "Any obstacle that diminishes or thwarts the salvation of God from finding a home in the minds, hearts, and lives of Christians and the church is a challenge to the objectives of Christian education." What challenges do the authors suggest from outside or inside the church hinder the truth of God from being more effectively

integrated in the lives of Christians? Do you agree with their analysis? Are there other challenges you would include?

3. Besides elements of Mormon, Jewish, and Muslim religious education, what other faith traditions might Christian educators learn from? Explain specific formational dynamics that seem valuable and why. What are the risks of looking for formational insights beyond Christian communities?

4. Which obstacle to educating in faith, that is, disorienting amnesia, autonomous determinism, social constructionism, interpretive pluriformity, fragmented faith, or conceptual bricolage, is most threatening to your faith community? (See table 6 on p. 47.) Why?

For Further Reading

Bisset, Tom. *Why Christian Kids Leave the Faith*. Grand Rapids: Discover House/ RBC Ministries, 1992.

Chaput, Charles J. *Strangers in a Strange Land: Living the Catholic Faith in a Post-Christian World*. New York: Henry Holt, 2017.

Foster, Charles R. *From Generation to Generation: The Adaptive Challenge of Mainline Protestant Education in Forming Faith*. Eugene, OR: Wipf & Stock, 2012.

Kinnaman, David. *You Lost Me: Why Young Christians Are Leaving the Church . . . and Rethinking Faith*. Grand Rapids: Baker, 2011.

Volf, Miroslav, and Dorothy C. Bass, eds. *Practicing Theology: Beliefs and Practices in Christian Life*. Grand Rapids: Eerdmans, 2002.

Stories We Tell Ourselves: How Concepts of Modernism and Postmodernism Inform and Inhibit Nurturing Faith

Error never shows itself in its naked reality, in order not to be discovered. On the contrary, it dresses elegantly, so that the unwary may be led to believe that it is more truthful than truth itself.

—IRENAEUS OF LYONS

We are not content with life, with the limits that the present and the possible press upon us, but we strive and strain for something or other, we know not what.

—JOHN D. CAPUTO

ROAD MAP

This chapter is about two stories—modernism/postmodernism and faith. As such, this is an exercise in epistemology—that is, how we know what we know—and the task is to critique the stories we encounter in order to understand how each contributes to and detracts from nurturing faith. Yes, postmodernism can be nihilistic, but it has its uses. Therefore, we regard postmodernism warily but also with sufficient charity to glean from its critiques of modernism, rejecting a wholesale skepticism about or demolition of any and every claim to truth, but taking on board the value of critically analyzing the claims we encounter instead of thoughtlessly accepting them. We navigate between two stories—each with its own narrative and path for meaning-making.

Introduction

Chapter 1 laments the loss of Christian faith due, in part, to factors inside and outside the church. The next two chapters attempt to describe the most influential cultural dynamics that challenge the nurturing of faith, namely, modernism and postmodernism (in chapter 2) and nominalism (in chapter 3).

The 2010 Sophia Coppola–directed movie *Somewhere* pursues many of the issues of the twenty-first-century postmodern experience. Johnny Marco (Stephen Dorff) is a Hollywood actor who, even with his recent rise to fame, does not feel much meaning in his daily life. Despite drinking and socializing occasionally with a childhood friend, Marco spends much time alone, driving his Ferrari, drinking beer, taking pills, and indulging in polyamorous relationships. When he receives an unexpected visit from his eleven-year-old daughter, Cleo (Elle Fanning), they spend time together in his hotel suite, and Johnny brings her with him on his daily routine and on a publicity trip to Milan. Gradually, Johnny's fatherly emotions emerge and force him to reassess his otherwise "successful" life. After Cleo leaves for camp, Johnny calls his ex-wife and tearfully breaks down, admitting his unhappiness at his empty life. His ex-wife is indifferent to his pain and declines his request to come see him. At the end, Johnny checks out of the hotel, promising not to return, and drives his Ferrari into the countryside. He randomly stops and gets out, leaving the keys in the ignition, and then walks down the highway smiling. This highly symbolic act—eschewing all the worldly pleasures that ultimately bring no joy—exchanges faith in one way of life for faith in another, even though there is uncertainty about the journey to come. In sum, the storyline of the protagonist is a haunting reminder of the themes of Ecclesiastes (i.e., meaninglessness, empty lives despite numerous experiments to find pleasure), which are apt correlations to the dissatisfaction with life that many postmoderns experience.[1] In what, then, should we place our faith? What constitutes an authentic source for happiness and meaning?

Postmodernism rejects many philosophical stances that have traditionally been used to talk meaningfully about reality, and, as Stephen Hicks points out, postmodernism leans more heavily on social-linguistic constructs of reality.[2] Although there are what may be called varieties of postmodernism, with different agendas, it is not unreasonable to derive implications for how it affects our intention to nurture faith in the people of God.[3] Some Christians need to rally against a singularly sinister agent for causing (in their view) the ruination of culture. For some, the creeping, pervasive, and increasingly powerful pandemic of postmodernism would fit that bill nicely. Nevertheless, our view also sees redeeming qualities through interaction with postmodernism. As such, the task here is to measure those forces wrought by postmodernism that inhibit and those that may even inform nurturing faith.

The concept of "story" is an approved postmodern tool for expressing one's truth. At the same time, postmoderns may accuse stories (described as meta-narratives below) of underwriting social perversion. This chapter is ultimately about stories, and each story has lessons from which the wise will learn. In the end, it boils down to two countervailing, diametrically opposing stories and the choices created based on each. For as the ancient poet-philosopher Virgil contends: "Fortunate is the one who understands the cause of things." So true, but which story?

The Story of Faith

Jesus hauntingly asks: "When the Son of Man comes, will he find faith on the earth?" (Luke 18:8). Apparently, the possibility there may be a lack of faith is of some concern to Jesus. Faith is of extreme importance to God, and faith must reside within humans in their quest for right living. Clearly, faith was something the apostles recognized as important as they begged Jesus to "increase our faith!" (Luke 17:5). *Faith* is such a familiar religious word, but it might be the case that its overuse has made us inattentive to its significance. What is meant by the faith spoken of throughout Scripture and in religious dialogue? Common usage of *faith* in the Christian world normally surfaces in two essential contexts. (See table 7, below.) In the first case, over the centuries, councils and denominations have codified "statements of faith" that express, to the best of their well-intended but finite abilities, the essence of Christianity. This is a theological enterprise—faithfully attempting to make sense of divine revelation—and a vital one. Such belief statements are designed not as walls for exclusion (although such exclusion can materialize if statements become tests of orthodoxy) but rather as common affirmations to which faith communities pledge allegiance. Faith in this sense is a series of convictions to which we, as members of a believing community, give mental assent. Faith is also a profession of loyalty.

In the second case, faith is conceived as a way of life (albeit certainly intertwined with theological convictions), yet is less categorical, more adventurous, often messy, certainly emotional, and keenly experiential, all because it is a life lived in dependence upon God and others. Christian philosopher Nicholas Wolterstorff likens faith to a footbridge that you do not know will hold over the chasm until you are forced to walk out onto it.[4] This faith is like a pilgrimage, and like a pilgrimage, it is ongoing. The end of lived faith is a Christian's mission to enter into and participate in the kingdom of God, which is here but not yet completely. And because the ways of living out faith through our unique personalities and in our disparate locations is different, the faithful life of Christian adventure will also vary from person to person and community to community. The pilgrim's journey then is not as predictable or as uniform in the second meaning of the term as in the first, which is largely governed by words and cognitive content. So, when Paul says, "One Lord, one faith" (Eph. 4:5), to which "faith" is he referring?

Table 7. *Meanings of Faith*

Faith as knowing	Faith as living
A statement of beliefs, as in "the Christian faith"	A predisposed way of living life, as an adventure
A series of propositions to which we may agree	An emotional, messier sense of how we deal with God
Internal; residual	External; active
Increasing tendency toward rationalization	The experience of a faithful pilgrim, a sojourner

Even Paul's attempt to define faith is rather elusive, lacking the concrete specificity one might expect for such a critical theological notion. The oft-quoted aphorism from the author of Hebrews describes (rather than defines) faith as "the substance of things hoped for and the conviction of things not seen" (Heb. 12:1). For the Christian, this elusive and allusive lack of vision symbolizes faith; for scientific-minded secularists, faith seems a fairytale based on misguided foolishness.[5] Where is the proof, they taunt? For nonbelievers, the idea of faith conveys a nonempirical, somewhat abstract concept not easily grasped. Thomas Aquinas offers the following illustrative sentiments: Augustine says faith is a virtue whereby we believe what we do not see, and John Damascene says faith is an assent without research. Aquinas claims "faith is a habit of the mind, whereby eternal life is begun in us, making the intellect assent to what is non-apparent."[6] In this way, faith, though related to thinking, is distinguished from many capacities pertaining to the intellect.

One may observe those who live by faith. It is evident by the attitudes, values, language, and behaviors exhibited as they navigate with dependence upon God for clues to life. Of course, for the believer (who, in its best sense, is defined as one who trusts), faith is something beyond one's immediate grasp and demonstrates the affective dimension of walking not by sight or evidence but in a childlike dependence upon a supernatural being. From the outside, faith may appear to be nothing more than a psychological condition based on optimistic positive thought. From the inside, for those who grasp the nature of the life Jesus introduces, a pilgrimage in faith—both personal and corporate—is a well-placed expression of utter dependence in an invisible yet immanent reality. Martin Luther considered faith as a free surrender and joyous wager on the unseen, unknown goodness of God.

Perhaps more than any other character in the Bible, Abraham seems to crystalize what the life of faith is intended to look like. Not only is he singled out by God due to his prominence as progenitor of God's elect, but as a result of his spiritual journey, he is revered thousands of years later, as the author of Hebrews includes him as the paragon of faith—as one who believes in God and who acts with no assurance of certainty other than that he has decided to trust God. Not only does Abraham abandon his homeland, he goes obediently "even though he did not know where he was going" (Heb. 11:8). Further, he moved ahead faithfully despite his bewilderment with God's instruction to sacrifice his son—the long-anticipated link to the promised people (11:17–19). These examples, offered for the nourishment of future generations of God's followers, are meant to be indelibly imprinted on the consciousness of those who will live by faith in the presence of God. We are not permanent citizens of the country named in our passports—one day we will die and leave—but we can be permanent dwellers in the kingdom of God. We will be tested on our commitments to him, and based on how we respond to his invitations, we will join in his mission in this world. The Christian's life is not guided by sight or logic or certainty, but by faith in God alone. This is the concept that nontheists cannot grasp, as for them a life abandoned to the will of God appears foolish. Seeing the world in the way God sees it is another task of theology. The moral of our stories begins to emerge. But the bottom line is this: *Without faith it is impossible to please God* (11:6).

Simply put, the task of the Christian educator is to *nurture this Abrahamic-like gift of faith* in those God loves. Paul identifies "faith" as such a signature quality of the Christian teaching and places it alongside "hope" and "love" as ultimate expressions (1 Cor. 13:13). Paul also emphasizes his fatherly desire in a rather graphic way about the enablement of faith in his beloved brothers and sisters: "My dear children, for whom I am again in pains of childbirth until Christ is formed in you" (Gal. 4:19). In faith, the apostle Peter jumped out of the boat sailing on the Sea of Galilee because he believed, yes, but he also *acted* on his beliefs. This is the reckless, risky, even dangerous life God calls his would-be followers to—dependence on God and not their own instincts. These clues to the meaning of faith further divulge how to properly order the relationship in cognitive-contented knowledge, affective-valued longings, and behavioral-oriented faith. All these have a place in the Christian life, but what the biblical authors desire for us is a life marked by faith—an utter dependence upon God for our sustenance, worth, mission, and identity. The byproduct of a faithful life results in human freedom. "You will know the truth, and the truth will set you free" (John 8:31–36). Not a freedom *from*, but a freedom *to*—to realize service to others, obedience to God, and joy for ourselves.

POSTMODERNISM

One of the most ambiguous, controversial words of the past several decades is *postmodernism*. In Christian circles, the notion has had mixed reviews. Unfortunately, it has sometimes been used as a scapegoat term for all evils of contemporary society and culture. In this regard, the *post* in *postmodernism* implies a radical continuation of modernist relativism and secularism. Some of this sentiment stems from Friedrich Nietzsche's full-scale assault on the notion of "truth" as both arbitrary and illusory. This type of nihilistic leaning has fostered the idea that anything postmodern must include a denial of truth and, hence, the truth of God.

Others, however, see the religious potential in postmodernism by viewing it as a critique of extreme modern biases toward empiricism and rationalism. Here, postmodernism is seen as the attempt to move beyond the hubris and pretension of human reasoning as the primary or sole means to discover truth. This type of radical suspicion of modernism can be readily observed in the writings of French philosophers Jean-François Lyotard, Jacques Derrida, Michel Foucault, and Emmanuel Levinas, along with American philosopher Richard Rorty, among others. A critical appropriation of these strains of postmodernism provides an instructive critique to those who have wittingly or unwittingly embraced a paradigm of knowledge that is too restrictive to allow space for Christian truth. This version of postmodernism questions the modernist optimism of human ability, knowledge, and progress. It brings to the forefront both the finiteness and basic corruption of humankind. But in so doing, it opens the door to the possibility of the religious and, in turn, Christianity.

The postmodern critique of modernism provides rich opportunities for Christian multivalent learning that would extend beyond the limitations of the propositional, rational, or empirical means of learning. Postmodernism is not about denying reality; it is rather affirming that reality is broader than the epistemological confines of modernism. Further, it radically questions the confident optimism of individual knowledge and its presumed objectivity, and it provides a call to contextually based community learning that would not only include human reasoning abilities but also comprise the imagination and emotions. It suggests that reality cannot be reduced to rational, objective discourse; it is always contextually situated and embedded. Hence, a Christian appropriation of this understanding allows for a priority of the Holy Spirit's work through Scripture in community and practice, without exclusive emphasis on cognitive-based learning through logical propositions.

RONALD T. MICHENER

How We Got Here: Stages of Modern Thought

The life of faith does not emerge naturally. Jesus commends childlike faith, but the evolution of contemporary thought excoriates such immature allegiance. How did we get here? August Comte, arguably the father of modern sociology, offers a rudimentary three-stage evolution of the modern mind.[7] Following are Comte's progressive stages of secular thought that have ushered Western thinking from modernity into the postmodern mindset:

1. **Theological stage.** God is the center of the universe, the source of all. Society employed theology to explain all elements of reality and to legitimate all its social institutions. All knowledge was deduced from religious assumptions. This stage in time gave way to the . . .

2. **Scientific stage.** Gone are the days of mystery and unknowing; enter the age of rationality. The religio-magical constructions of reality are doomed to extinction in most societies, as, little by little, observations and discoveries lead people to realize that there are also scientific explanations for things. Sociologist Max Weber explains this process as the "increasing tendency toward rationalization." Social construction of reality is based on the laws of nature. Empirical evidence is the hallmark of truth. This stage in time gave way to the . . .

3. **Humanistic stage.** Humans make free choices guided by their own values and needs. The source of moral authority is neither divine (as in the theological stage) nor data-driven (as in the scientific stage), but personal or societal. The major doctrines of the Christian faith are reexamined in light of new thinking with the intent of debunking the fatal flaws of "old-time religion."

Each previous stage does not disappear but is slowly marginalized—pushed to the background as the more *avant-garde* way of thinking emerges. In other words, theistic belief is obviously still part of Western thinking, as evidenced by the persistence of Christian doctrine and practice, yet its influence is diminished. And certainly, the scientific age remains one of the primary means of pacifying contemporary curiosities about the world, among other notions, but even more preeminent is the advancement of the self as center of the universe. Those ideas held prior to the latest stage are now held in low regard. The radical idea to be grasped is "everything we once knew and accepted as fact was wrong." Not that previous epistemologies cease to exist, but they in fact persist. New ways of thinking are added as concentric circles—the old remains but is largely assigned a less influential role. The past is old-fashioned, irrelevant, and maybe even offensive to our postmodern sensibilities. And, for some, this even includes truth mediated through sacred words of God.[8]

In sum, the shift in the evolution of modern to postmodern thinking has moved from the Creator's commandments to the creatures' whims. Postmodernism flourishes, and Romans 1:20–22 describes this brand of collective thinking: "For since the creation of the world God's invisible qualities—his eternal power and divine nature—have been clearly seen, being understood from what has been made, so that men are without excuse. For although they knew God, they neither glorified him as God nor gave thanks to him, but their thinking became futile and their foolish hearts were darkened. Although they claimed to be wise, they became fools." These two stories—of biblical faith and secular humanism (as manifested in modernism/postmodernism)—and these two versions of reality resist coalescing.

Let's unpack this third stage of preoccupying thought that dominates popular culture. Comte's third stage, the humanistic stage, is more fully illustrated by Langdon Gilkey.[9] He describes four traits that form the basis of the postmodern mindset:

- **Contingency.** Everything that is was caused by some natural phenomenon that preceded it. Through a process of evolution and natural selection, *homo sapiens* emerged, and humans took their place in this universe. (The concept of contingency makes God irrelevant.)
- **Autonomy.** Because God is not in the picture—symptomatic of the collapse of authority—humans are free to determine their own destiny and meaning. Life is an uncharted adventure into the future, and the ends and purposes it may have are none other than the ones humans create for it. (This is exactly the terror-filled *angst* that Søren Kierkegaard has described so well—left on our own with too many choices and nowhere to turn for certain guidance.)
- **Relativity.** Since we each make our own meaning, those in each society bring into being a system of thought and values that has meaning to those who create and live in it. While not necessarily determined arbitrarily, there are therefore no absolutes, only relative truths. (Dosto-

yevsky poignantly pens in *The Brothers Karamazov*: "If there is no immortality then everything is permissible."[10])

- **Temporality.** Life on this planet is all there is. Existence is limited by time. Death is the end of everything, and everything must die. (No life after death.)

These worrisome traits frame the thoughts, actions, policies, and rhetoric of many in our communities. And just as such beliefs underlie the worldview of many twenty-first-century citizens of the world as they develop their view of reality, they also reshape traditionally held views on spiritual meaning, authority, destiny, and faith. The doctrine of toleration is ingrained in our culture. "Everything is right somewhere, and nothing is right everywhere," Taylor says, "thus relativism absolutizes pluralism . . . truth is merely opinion, goodness only what the majority says it is. . . . Relativism is the spirit of our age. The intolerant person is the one thing that can't be tolerated, the one person who must be shamed or silenced."[11] To be narrow-minded is offensive. And, yes, in some instances for the Christian, our narrow-mindedness can be a result of arrogance. Perhaps there is too easy a separation of goodness and love from truth.

Now, we also believe for one to live in the world without God takes an immense amount of faith as well, maybe *more* than theistic faith. Everyone, whether they acknowledge it or not, lives based on faith in something—faith in love, faith in education, faith in wealth, faith in the common good, faith in doing one's best, faith in government, faith in technology, faith in societal advancement, and so on. And it is not hard to spot a culture's gods—they are what people swear by, embedded in stories that need no explanation.

While we normally put little stock in what "celebrities" say, these theological statements strike us as representative of what many believe in our world. Reporter Mick Brown of the *London Telegraph*, talking to Meryl Streep about the movie *Doubt* (2008), in which she plays a nun, asked her where she found consolation in the face of aging and death. Streep, raised Presbyterian, postulated: "Consolation? I'm not sure I have it. I have a belief, I guess, in the power of the aggregate human attempt. In love and hope and optimism—you know, the magic things that seem inexplicable." Confidence in humans, love, hope, and optimism. We wish we had such faith in the human character in our world; alas, we do not. Watch the news; observe culture, media, and popular music. Is an overt pessimism a fair grasp of the current situation?

Consider cultural incivility, racial injustice, and the list of worsening societal woes. Can a postmodern ethic turn this tide? Is it the case in a culture where it is possible, even likely, not to believe in God that these dark nights of the soul represent the triumph of modernity or the possibility of confession of God's apparent absence even for some people of faith? Nevertheless, we wonder how postmoderns might respond to these questions about their brand of faith and how it may contribute to positive morality in the Western world:

- What gives comfort in faith in humanity or the world given the proclivity of hatred, violence, war, greed, bitterness, and narcissism as performed nightly on the evening news?
- What manifestations of convincing (non)belief in nontheistic faith might provide encouragement in humanity as individuals experience sadness, absence of meaning, disassociation and alienation from others, and the void of something of substance beyond this facile existence in life?
- What stories do we in the global north tell that give hope, purpose, and confidence in living an existence of meaning, significance, and betterment?
- To what extent are these stories illustrated in societal virtue and individual character?
- Where are the overt communities that radiate happiness based on such stories?
- What segments of the world community serve others who have less rather than serving themselves?
- Why are the most vocal expressions in our collective consciousness laced with overwhelming anger, frustration, loneliness, and distrust?
- What wisdom informs our technologically superior world?

A loss of faith in each other and in our place in the cosmos runs parallel with the abandonment of God. New York University sociologist Eric Klinenberg claims American society is amid a fundamental social and demographic shift, the "greatest social change of the last 60 years."[12] What is this radical change—the increasing prominence represented by *postmodernism*?

The Call to Faith

The call of God is a summons to embark upon a journey of faith whose destiny is not always apparent, smooth, or easy. Mark has appreciated the writings of Dartmouth College professor Randall Balmer, who wrote a rather personal tale recounting his spiritual past and present called *Growing Pains: Learning to Love My Father's Faith*. As he read Balmer's reminiscence it seemed as though he was reading his own journey of childhood, adolescence, and a period of wrestling with the call of God. Mark learned their fathers had even died the same year and at the same age. As Balmer writes about his own pilgrimage of faith:

> The path of faith is not tidy. For many, belief in itself is an affront to intelligence and even to sanity, especially when you can explain the spiritual quest in psychological or sociological or physiological terms. For me, the path to faith has been rocky and my steps uneven. I am plagued by doubts and fears and anxieties. I feel desolate, at times, and my cries to God meet with silence. I have been locked in a lovers' quarrel with my father, the preacher, for the better part of three decades, a quarrel over faith and belief and theology that has not so much abated as it has taken a different form since his sudden passing a few months ago. Like Abraham, I'm not always certain where I'm going on this pilgrimage, and my progress is slowed, I'm sure, whenever I pause to wrestle with God—or someone—lurking there in the darkness. My trajectory is rarely straight and not always upward. It resembles at times the woven, brown cord of a toaster trailing off the table.
>
> And yet what sustains me is a sense, or at least the hope, of divine presence, that I am not alone on this pilgrimage, but I am in the company of friends who will pick me up from time to time, dust me off, and point me in the right direction.
>
> I believe because of the epiphanies, small and large, that have intersected my path—small, discrete moments of grace when I have sensed a kind of superintending presence outside of myself. I believe because these moments—a kind word, an insight, an anthem on Easter morning, a chill in the spine—are too precious to discard, and I choose not to trivialize them by reducing them to rational explanation. I believe because, for me, the alternative to belief is far too daunting. I believe because, in the waning decades of the twentieth century, belief itself is an act of defiance in a society still enthralled by the blandishments of Enlightenment rationalism.[13]

We resonate with these words, and in some ways, they illustrate a postmodern sensibility for faith—openness to transcendence, loving mystery, an unwillingness to concede all knowledge to empiricism or rationalism. Sometimes Mark prays, "Oh, Lord, I come to you, because there is no other place to go. I have tried appealing places and found them to be empty and ultimately wrongly directed." Although God knows us intimately and wishes us to be in intimate relations together, there is far more that we do not know about God than we do know of him. Augustine expressed this concept: "God is greater in our thoughts than in our words and greater in reality than in our thoughts." While some may be unsettled by this notion, yet there is a transcendent and mysterious element to this mover of the universe. God is not something to be "figured out," as this too would diminish the amount of faith required to continue in the way. We acknowledge he is trustworthy and deserving of faith. Yet we revel in what we do know and pledge our trust even with uncertainty all around.

The Story of Modernism/Postmodernism

Postmodernism is an ambiguous overarching term for skeptical interpretations of culture, literature, art, philosophy, economics, architecture, fiction, and literary criticism. It is often associated with deconstructionism, an approach that upends our notions of "meaning." Many people in the modern era had a belief in the triumph of science and technology and the decline in religion.[14] This is something that has not happened. Interest in religion has not declined, and reports, such as in Philip Jenkins's writings, show fervor in these days, which is more pronounced in the global south. There was also a strong or naive view in metanarratives in the modern era, such as continual progress for humanity, which does not exist in a postmodern era. Part of the decline in such a view is the two massive world wars.

Sociologist Rodney Stark in *The Victory of Reason* provocatively contends that Europe and North America thrived because Christianity made possible political and economic freedoms, modern science, and resulting advancement. However, once Americans developed "an extraordinary faith in reason,"[15] Christian belief shifted to become a religion that was called upon to serve the practical interests of the people (civil religion), and then the interests of the self (therapeutic religion). It moved from pragmatism to existentialism and, consequently, to relativism, the conduit for postmodernism.

The postmodern aversion to truth is well expressed by Allan Bloom in *The Closing of the American Mind*:

> The danger . . . is not error but intolerance. Relativism is necessary to openness; and this is the virtue, the only virtue, which all primary education for more than fifty years has dedicated itself to [teaching]. Openness—and the relativism that makes it the only plausible stance in the face of various claims to truth and the various ways of life and kinds of human beings—is the great insight of our times. The true believer is the real danger. The study of history and of culture teaches that all the world was mad in the past; men always thought they were right, and that led to wars, persecutions, slavery, xenophobia, racism and chauvinism. The point is not to correct the mistakes and really be right; rather it is not to think that you are right at all.[16]

Gianni Vattimo takes postmodern thought to its logical conclusion, and his message taps into the postmodern mentality of many contemporary Europeans and Americans.[17] He defines postmodernity as "the time of contamination, everything is contaminated, nothing has value, nothing has meaning."[18] There is obviously a pronounced pessimism conveyed. Postmodernism, Vattimo contends, embraces tension, confusion, contradiction, and ambiguity as an inevitable product of the multiple levels of systems of knowledge and narratives circulating at one time.[19] And where little ambiguity or confusion exists, the postmodernist is generally very suspicious, since we have to suspect that there are powerful forces at work creating coherence that is making everything and everyone conform. And so, whereas a modernist often would have seen confusion as a sign of faulty knowledge or a lack of knowledge, contradiction as a problem yet to be worked out, and finally ambiguity as simply a lack of clarity or perhaps an unfortunate misunderstanding, postmodernists generally look for these elements as the inevitable product of living within systems of meaning.[20] Indeed, these aspects can be extremely creative, since they can cause new systems of meaning to be generated and can sometimes allow us to free ourselves (at least in some ways) from the webs of discourse and meaning that demarcate our particular circumstances, by giving us a range of meanings to choose from.

CULTURAL INFLUENCES

The importance of understanding cultural influence in educating Christians should never be underestimated. The better one understands contemporary culture, the more effective one will be as a Christian educator. At the heart of any culture lies meanings, values, and a particular pattern of thinking and behaving. Contemporary culture shapes the meaning systems and values of people. Thus, when cultural change occurs, people's meanings, values, and ways of behaving change. This is especially true in the case of the younger generation, and it offers a significant challenge to those involved in the ministry of Christian education, not only for the young but for all age groups.

Economic change always leads to social change, and this, in turn, brings about cultural change. Economic and social changes occur at the level of observable data, whereas cultural change occurs in a covert manner, beneath the surface of what can be easily measured. *Cultural* change concerns meaning and values, and it is this type of paradigm shift that affects religious belief and practice, presenting a new challenge to one's inherited understanding and approach to Christian education.

Since culture constitutes a total context that shapes each person, how then can the culture of the present time—postmodernism—be best described? While there is a rejection of absolutes and, at best, an indifference toward institutionalized religion, especially among the rising generation, there is, on the other hand, a new openness to interactive community and to the spiritual as a reaction to the rationality and individualism of modernity.

This renewed openness to the spiritual dimension of life, in whatever form it takes, provides an opportunity for Christian religious educators to build on an existing foundation. The search for wholeness and for meaningful spirituality offers the possibility of dialogue with the Christian story in its institutionalized, symbolic, and liturgical expression.

One feature of the philosophy of postmodernity that argues well for a community-based religious faith is the nonindividualistic attitude that is replacing the individualism of modernity. This renewed sense of the importance of community does not deny the significance of the individual; rather, the conception is that the individual cannot be understood apart from his or her place in the community. From the postmodern perspective, Christian communities that are open to diversity will be more attractive to the postmodern sensibility, whereas communities that strive to be homogeneous will close themselves off from the diversity that is inherent in postmodern thought and way of life.

Commentators on Christian faith and culture point to the importance of enabling people to engage in cultural discernment, critique, and analysis by providing them with skills whereby they can reflect on and critically examine the culture in which they are immersed. Furthermore, there is need for explicit gospel-rooted discernment of culture in religious education classes and in parish or congregational youth groups. If Christian education is to be relevant to the lives of today's adolescents, it must take seriously the issue of gospel-rooted cultural discernment.

The manner in which people experience reality is culture bound and any Christian educational endeavor that does not take account of the contemporary cultural milieu in which all age groups are immersed is destined to be less than adequate. The relationship between religious nurture and religious education needs to be reconsidered, and the two aims of religious education should be taken into account—namely, formation in the faith (religious nurture) and the academic understanding of religion (religious studies).

OLIVER V. BRENNAN

The Faith of Postmodernism

Whatever postmodern is, it is not the next big thing. In other words, this is not "stage four" to come after the humanistic stage *à la* Comte (above). As A. J. Conyers compellingly explains, first, *every culture attempts to speak universally*.[21] This is true of most societies: to see the world through their own lenses and wish for others to emulate their ideas. Some cultures even attempt to force their cultural mores on others. This phenomenon has been seen of course in our checkered Christian history. Richard Bauckham, in *The Bible in Mission: Christian Mission in the Postmodern World*, suggests the movement in Scripture is always from the particular to the universal, without ever leaving the particular behind.[22] Second, *no culture succeeds in speaking universally*. Some, however, have succeeded to an astonishing degree. Conyers claims: "more than all, Christianity, that swept together the disparate strains of Hebrew prophetism, Greek philosophy, drawing upon streams of traditions from Asia, Europe, and Africa, presented the first—and perhaps the only truly—catholic version of the world."[23] This is an amazing and very interesting contention and one that Christians have worked hard to foster. The spread of the gospel, per Jesus's departing command, was to teach all he had taught. Over the centuries in which Christianity has had a hearing, however, a triumphalism and even counter productivity has emerged. For example, Yale theologian Willie Jennings argues rather convincingly for the church's culpability in the conquest and subjugation of the global south.[24] Yes, Christianity has been successful, but the preferred status of Christianity in the world landscape has changed. Third, as Conyers continues, cultures also suffer fatigue. As a result, *postmodernism is not a culture but the fatigue of culture*. It is a sign of the end of modernity, and for that reason its critique of modernity is telling. But it is not a new age, nor the sign of a new kind of culture. It despairs of culture. It cannot become a vessel for gospel, asserts Conyers, for it is fundamentally antigospel. Culture depends upon life, not decay, and it is there—not in the decadent features of a modern West, but perhaps in the revivals of Africa and Asia—that we shall truly find the gospel at work. However, we think postmodernism has played an important iconoclastic function, namely, freeing us from the false certainties of modernism, including modernist efforts at justifying faith in modernist terms. Postmodernism has opened us to the possibilities of reclaiming the union of truth and goodness.

We will return to the issue of the role of the Christian message in the postmodern world, but for now we offer four implications of living in a world imbued by contingency, autonomy, relativity, and temporality. These powerful forces containing their own postmodern "doctrines" require critique.

Postmodern Doctrine 1: Certainties Have Been Replaced by Alternatives

Postmodernism repudiates large-scale narratives and challenges authority. "I define postmodern as incredulity toward metanarratives," says Jean-François Lyotard.[25] As a result, new, hybrid disciplines develop without connection to old epistemic traditions, especially philosophy, and this means science only plays its own game and cannot legitimate others, by giving moral prescriptions.[26] The loss of a continuous metanarrative therefore breaks the subject into heterogeneous moments of subjectivity that do not cohere into an identity. But as Lyotard points out, while the combinations we experience are not necessarily stable or communicable, we learn to move with a certain nimbleness among them. In other words, while the story of God, once believable and worthy of faith, was a guiding force for interpreting the meaning of existence, humans have become adept at piecing together and even creating their own ideas about what the purpose of life might be.

As Lyotard notes, "Lamenting the 'loss of meaning' in postmodernity boils down to mourning the fact that knowledge is no longer principally narrative." The postmodern sensibility does not lament the loss of narrative coherence any more than the loss of being. Inventing new codes and reshaping information is a large part of the production of knowledge, and the metaprescriptives of new story lines and their rules are themselves objects of invention and experimentation for the sake of producing new statements. The life-giving message of Christianity then becomes obsolete in the postmodern mentality. No moral imperatives should properly rise to trump and inform other moral imperatives. Parity means nonexclusivity. Jesus is *a* way, not *the* way. Christianity is *one* of the ways, among an array of world religions, to reach a god-figure.[27]

When the table legs are kicked from under the metanarrative of the Bible (i.e., certainty), the search for meaning in our closed and natural world scrambles to provide its own answers (i.e., alternatives). The seeds of doubt then handcuff our attempts to nurture faith in a skeptical world.

Table 8. Outworking of Humanistic Traits in Postmodern Thinking and Nurturing Faith

Traits of Humanism	Implications for Postmodern Thinking	Postmodern Doctrines
Contingency	Certainties have been replaced by alternatives	Meaning is created
Autonomy	Divine authority has been replaced by self-authority	Sovereignty is mine
Relativity	Thinking has been replaced by experience	Feelings trump all
Temporality	Permanence has been replaced by unceasing change	Reality is determined

Postmodern Doctrine 2: Divine Authority Has Been Replaced by Self-Authority

With the rejection of ultimate sources of meaning and truth (postmodern doctrine 1), humans must step in to take back control of their lives and moral direction. All authority is suspect—schools, governments, communities, and so forth; in fact, any force that may impose a certain way of seeing that reduces the prominence of our instinctive sensibilities is deemed a problem. Thus, as many Westerners have come to assume, we must rely on ourselves as a personal source of authority.[28]

The metanarratives, or the "big stories" such as Christianity's story of sin and redemption, allow us to make ultimate sense of the world. But the problem with metanarratives is that they are so important to us that we tend to try to make other narratives and the people who hold them fit into them—whether they like it or not. Postmoderns are careful to point out that Christianity can be used to justify systems of domination and control. The authority of God, then, is stifling to human freedom and so is something from which many would prefer to be distanced. Postmodernists point out that metanarratives are illusory and furthermore tend to be used for the purpose of oppression. And so many postmodernists have tried to debunk these metanarratives, including Christianity, as fictitious.

The premise here is that multiple viewpoints and multiple interests enlarge our comprehension of the finally incomprehensible universe, whereas a singular and definitive perspective denies this irreducible multiplicity of viewpoints. This posture witnesses both high sensitivity toward toleration and respect of all views of life and the world—with the exception of any who disagrees with this chief virtue of toleration—and high reactionary pushbacks toward those who defensively champion their strongly held story.

With the authority of God displaced from our community consciousness, people are promoted to and supported in personal sovereignty. An entitled status for humanity supplants the divine. Overconfidence in ourselves reduces our ability to nurture faith.

Postmodern Doctrine 3: Thinking Has Been Replaced by Experience

Left to ourselves (no certainty and self-authority, doctrines 1 and 2), we prefer the most readily accessible instrument as guide—our senses and experiences. "If objectivist reason gone mad is the perfect description of modernity, the subjectivist denial of reason is the dementia of postmodernity," Ralph Wood colorfully explains.[29] Emotions, feelings, intuition, reflection, magic, myth, and mystical experience are now center stage. "I know" has been replaced by "I feel." Feelings are harder to refute than knowledge; in fact, they cannot be.

Postmoderns do raise valid points for consideration. As with rationalist modernism, so with irrationalist postmodernism: there is truth in it. As Wood points out, it is true all our seeing is indeed subjective and culture-bound. Humans default in seeing the world through their own lenses. Truth is filtered, and understanding is rooted in time and place. There is no view from nowhere, no godlike perch from which we can view the world neutrally—as if it were God's own view. But from the valid premise that there is no such thing as naked knowledge, postmodern relativists reach invalid conclusions. They hold that we can make no comparative moral judgments, engage in no time-transcending religious arguments, allow no privileging of certain cultures—even cultures that dignify women over cultures that demean them, or even governments that enhance democratic freedoms over those that destroy them.

With the elevation of personal experience as advancing truth and authority, how one feels, chooses, and desires gains a foothold for governing how we live and act. To nurture a faith grounded in historic events and supernatural revelation, we must compete with those who would rather believe what they wish and not confer obedience to any source outside themselves.[30]

Postmodern Doctrine 4: Permanence Has Been Replaced by Unceasing Change

With these three postmodern doctrines entrenched in the Western psyche, every human thought and endeavor seems tentative, malleable, and subject to alteration. Two French words are illustrative here. *Bricolage* is used to describe "do-it-yourself projects" and is the construction or creation of a work from a diverse range of things that happen to be available, or a work created by such a process. *Pastiche* is related, combining or pasting together multiple elements. With a lack of certainty, absence of authority, and socially negotiated truth, humans are left to cobble together the various fabrics of life and meaning and truth as best they can, like a patchwork quilt. The only cohesive element in postmodernism is lack of cohesive elements. While this may seem freeing, the result is a world in chaos. (See table 9, below.)

The outcome of these postmodern doctrines brings a culture marked by palpable sadness. First, enlightened humans who are weary from searching for truth and meaning do not find it. What people ultimately desire is rest and peace. This concept of "rest" is one of the most central concepts running throughout the Old and New Testaments. The people of Israel are offered rest in the promised land, that is, freedom from wandering, if they depend on the sovereign God instead of themselves (Josh. 1). Jesus invites lost and burdened people to come to him, and he will give rest, peace, hope, truth (Matt. 11:28). Second, the result of tasting a season of self-authority is the inevitable realization of our limits. Like children who wish to be in charge, they ultimately realize they have parents for a reason. Third, the experiential attempts to discover meaning in life is dashed by futility (e.g., like "a chasing after the wind," as in Eccles. 1:14; 2:11). Humans, perhaps more than anything else in the postmodern world, seek meaning. Life without meaning is an endless circuit of futility. Jesus promises profound life that is worthy of living (John 10:10). Fourth, consigned to our own devices, humans are preoccupied with busyness in experience that may satisfy our longing for validity. And if this cannot be realized, at least we can stay busy and maybe not notice the void. The reality is, many would trade everything they have for happiness and a deep-seated countenance of joy and fulfillment (Rom. 15:13). All told, the human experience driven by self-styled meaning-making and the illusive quest for truth has produced an intense, sarcastic bitterness with life and a deep disappointment with the world, other people, and ourselves.

The most fundamental axiom in the wisdom literature of the Old Testament is that the fear of the Lord is the beginning of wisdom. Whereas, Solomon, as exampled in Proverbs and Ecclesiastes, learned these lessons through difficult life experiences, it is preferred that humans learn these same lessons through didactic means. Learning through other peoples' experiences (rather than our own) is less titillating, less satisfactory, but far wiser and safer. The postmodern culture, however, cries out for experiences and lambastes learning from anything except one's own heuristic taste buds and craving sensations. This can be related to the decline of and disinterest in historical perspective. In other words, a wise person will read these words, heed these lessons, and avoid some life pain. The less wise person will have to undergo a series of experiments, ultimately unfulfilling, learning the same exact lesson Solomon has already offered (Prov. 3:5–18). The postmodern resolve is to see how far a person can go with no such basis for wisdom. To believe in nothing is much easier than to believe in something. Menachem Mendel, a rabbi in the nineteenth century, put it this way: "For the believer there are no questions, and for the unbeliever there are no answers."[31] What humans want, but cannot admit out loud so as not to betray their postmodern indoctrination, is the assurance of a truthful story, which teaches that life is about serving God by serving others. Humans are sadly mistaken in the adolescent waywardness fueling these postmodern doctrines and need to be found. We are the prodigal sons and daughters, and the waiting, loving father is only too happy to welcome us, provide rest, reveal true meaning, and help us discover peace.

Table 9. Results of Postmodernism in the Human Experience

Traits of Humanism	Implications for Postmodern Thinking	Results for the Human Experience	Desired Outcome
Contingency	Certainties have been replaced by alternatives	Weariness from searching	Rest
Autonomy	Divine authority has been replaced by self-authority	Resignation to human limitation	Meaning
Relativity	Thinking has been re-placed by experience	Preoccupation with sensate activity	Happiness
Temporality	Permanence has been replaced by unceasing change	Bitterness from disappointment	Assurance

The Story We Locate Ourselves In

While our position here has tended toward critique of modernism and post-modernism, might there not be ways in which these worldviews could inform the nurturing of faith? Perhaps this question comes late to the party, but suitable awareness of our cultural mood and how we have arrived at this societal location is warranted. Ronald Michener is not as despairing as Conyers (above) regarding the inevitable triumph of postmodern thought.[32] He sees opportunities for nurturing faith in this climate as well. So do we. For example, some associate postmodernism with a full-scale assault on the notion of truth. Granted, postmodernism questions the modernist optimism of human ability, knowledge, and progress—it brings to the forefront both the finiteness and basic corruption of humankind. And with denial of truth, some conclude, comes also the denial of God's truth. But, as Michener posits, a postmodern critique of modernism provides rich opportunities for Christian multivalent learning that would extend beyond the limitations of propositional, rational, or empirical truth that has dominated since the Enlightenment. Postmodernism is not about denying reality; it is rather affirming that reality is broader than the epistemological confines that modernists claim.[33] It fittingly questions the confident optimism of individual knowledge and its presumed objectivity, and it provides a call to contextually based community learning that would not only include human reasoning abilities but also comprise the imagination and emotions. Postmodernism suggests that reality cannot be reduced to rational, objective discourse and that it is always contextually situated and embedded.

Based on this critique, we contend that postmodernism may inform how we nurture faith in four ways:

First, a renewed priority for nurturing faith will consider *the role of the Holy Spirit's work* through Scripture in community and practice, without exclusive emphasis on cognitive-based learning through logical propositions. Harvey Cox in his *The Future of Faith* describes three "ages" of the Christian religion: the Age of Faith (faith *in* Jesus, which lasted about 300 years), the Age of Belief (belief *about* Jesus, roughly 1500 years), and the Age of the Spirit (*experience* of Jesus, 200 years, including now).[34] A modernist-based Christian education errs toward information-based models of instruction, emphasizing cognitive input and logical, rational analysis. Postmodern perspectives accent humans as affective, emotional, imaginative learners in combination with cognitive aspects of humanity. Nurturing faith in our time must account for these tendencies. Our experiential interaction with the Spirit of God is a necessary component of faith formation.

Second, Christian education should *engage the imagination* to a greater degree. Rather than a tendency in modernistic approaches toward acceptance, agreement, and acquiescence, provoking creative thought about faith and its interaction with life has the potential of evoking change. As J. Marian Snapper claims: "Imagination is that human function closest to the heart, qualifying and shaping the intellect, emotion and will as they come to expression in life. Imagination is central to the learning process by which we are changed (transformed)."[35] Insofar as human beings are made in the image of God, it follows that they should imitate either God or the Creator's prime image. Right-brained activity is needed as a balancing and supplementary expression of the Christian faith. One example of a call for this approach is found in James K. A. Smith's *Desiring the Kingdom*. He wishes to reframe Christian education as more formative rather than informative.[36] Nurturing faith must rightly order its teaching priorities in being less cognitive and more affective— that is, shaping people who love, hope, desire, then think and translate these into virtuous affections.

Third, many would assume that knowing leads to doing. However, this cause-and-effect relationship can be turned on its head as we acknowledge the powerful teacher of *doing that informs knowing*. The postmodern sensibility embraced here is that our experiences are rich instructors in understanding our faith. Effective pedagogical strategies will consider ways in which faithful actions and service can be practiced in community, then debriefed to distill discoveries. Educators, as seen throughout the works of American pragmatist John Dewey, have long known that students' ability to own and experience and make discoveries for themselves has a more profound effect than when students are passive recipients of information about a given topic.

Fourth, a postmodern Christian education would presuppose the need for both knowledge of Scripture and the nurturing of *Christian practices in community* for the ongoing development of our beliefs. To alleviate the alienation that many feel in the postmodern climate, intimate interaction with the community of faith provides a tremendously motivating impetus in growing faith. Positive peer examples and "lived faith" punctuates kingdom values through action.[37] And the consistent application of Christian practices actually takes a major priority in the development of our faith. When the practices become habits, they become automatic and central to our identity formation and Christian character. Nurturing faith in postmodern times, Michener contends, might best look to a recurring integrative relationship between philosophy of education and pedagogical practice. Further, postmodern Christian education will also emphasize learning by practicing with others in community more than learning merely by explaining to others. Teachers will be more inclined to model the importance of relationality, community, and participation in a climate of postmodernity.

Christians have had varying rates of success in faithfully navigating culture.[38] As Andy Crouch estimates, the story of Christian engagement with culture is primarily unidirectional—greater and greater accommodation paradoxically accompanied by smaller and smaller influence. He challenges:

> The gospel constantly challenges every human culture with the possibility that we live within misplaced horizons. The gospel, precisely because it so powerfully confronts all the human ways we try to supplant God, from the tower of Babel to the cross, is always mysterious and even dangerous to cultures that want to maintain their uneasy bargains with sin—whether those bargains take the form of tribalism or individualism, collectivism or consumerism. No human society—not even Israel, as the prophets lamented and insisted—can fully "enculturate" the gospel. Christendom is always purchased at the price of a reduced gospel that all too often reduces the cross to a piece of jewelry.[39]

Crouch offers insightful commentary on these two competing stories we have been discussing. He says the eager conformers to the allure of postmodernism, propelled by an economic dream, will buy the biggest house they can afford, send their children to the best schools they can find, and take the highest-paying job they can get (to pay for their children's college education, of course). It all will make perfect sense, because it all will fit in the only story most postmoderns have left, the only religion in which our culture still believes: "the story of us," as witnessed by cult devotion to self-improvement, self-reliance, self-validating, self-referencing, and, well, "selfies."[40]

There is another story though—the story of faith. In this story, wisdom looks like foolishness (and vice versa), infants have an edge on the educated, and the earth belongs to the meek, not the loudest. The one who was last in the class becomes both salutatorian and valedictorian, the one who welcomes us into the feast and the one who bids farewell to the world we thought we knew. Jesus's alternate version of reality expounds a story of a strange banquet whose unexpected guests "get in" through no fault or merit of their own. Jesus's story stands conventional metanarratives on their heads. Full of upset expectations and undeserved gifts, it squares no more easily with the postmodern dreams than a camel squeezing through the eye of a needle.[41]

Conclusion

Having considered the prevailing influence of modernism and postmodernism as influential players in Western thought and action for their interaction with nurturing faith, we turn in *chapter 3* to another force with strong presence in Christian education—the strident dynamic of religious nominalism.

Interactive Dialogue

1. What is your story of faith, including episodes of advance and retreat? How do you juxtapose your faith with that of Abraham? Is his exemplary level of faith possible to achieve in our lives?

2. Postmodernism, which may seem to replace divine authority with self-authority, influences the way Christians interpret Scripture. As a result, some Christians come to the Bible with postmodern, individualistic assumptions and can shape the text into meaning what they may wish. How do you see the role of the Holy Spirit in this matter?

3. One constructive aspect of postmodernism is its hunger for community. How do you view it as an opportunity to nurture Christian faith through Christian practices in your local congregation?

For Further Reading

Beiner, Ronald. *Civil Religion: A Dialogue in the History of Political Philosophy.* Cambridge: Cambridge University Press, 2010.

Downing, Crystal. *How Postmodernism Serves (My) Faith: Questioning Truth in Language, Philosophy and Art.* Downers Grove, IL: IVP Academic, 2006.

Grenz, Stanley J. *A Primer on Postmodernism*. Grand Rapids: Eerdmans, 1996.
Juergensmeyer, Mark. *Religion in Global Civil Society*. Oxford: Oxford University Press, 2005.
Michener, Ronald T. *Engaging Deconstructive Theology*. Aldershot: Ashgate, 2007.
Oliver, Anita. "Postmodern Thought and Christian Education." *Journal of Research on Christian Education* 10 (2001): 5–22.
Smith, James K. A. *Desiring the Kingdom: Worship, Worldview, and Cultural Formation*. Grand Rapids: Baker Academic, 2009.
———. *Who's Afraid of Postmodernism: Taking Derrida, Lyotard, and Foucault to Church*. Grand Rapids: Baker Academic, 2006.
Smith, David I., and James K. A. Smith, eds. *Teaching and Christian Practices: Reshaping Faith and Learning*. Grand Rapids: Eerdmans, 2011.

Fusing Belief and Practice: How Religious Nominalism Informs and Inhibits Nurturing Faith

The Christian churches and Christianity have nothing in common save in name: they are utterly hostile opposites. The churches are arrogance, violence, usurpation, rigidity, death; Christianity is humility, penitence, submissiveness, progress, life.

—LEO TOLSTOY

Does our life together in the church, including our ways of talking, behaving, organizing ourselves, and relating to one another . . . refer to anything other than ourselves? . . . Or, is it all something that has no grounding beyond our own thinking and doing?

—CRAIG DYKSTRA

ROAD MAP

The previous chapter documents global epistemological challenges (distrust of all truth claims, the rise of secularism) confronting those who would nurture faith. This chapter is about Christian nominalism as a byproduct of its love affair with nationalistic tendencies and cultural symbolisms. When cultural and political appendages glom on to the Christian message, perverse results are the outcome. Nominalism is a condition where Christian belief and practice have little purchase on the lives of persons who profess to be Christian. In addition to defining nominalism, the chapter describes varieties of contributors to and manifestations of this ailment, including exceptionalism, nationalism, and traditionalism. Contending that nominalism arises in part out of either improper Christian belief, practice, or erroneous configurations of the relationship between belief and practice, the chapter analyzes three ways this relationship becomes distorted, providing a grid of sorts to assist educational leaders with the task of analyzing their own contexts. It also seeks to point toward the promise of belief and practice properly interrelated.

The Assent of Nominalism

Mark spent a six-month sabbatical teaching graduate students at a fine theological school just outside Nairobi, Kenya. There, in the course "Teaching and Learning the Christian Faith,"[1] Mark and the students (who represented some two dozen African countries and had been largely handpicked to attend the seminary for advanced education and training) brooded over the greatest obstacles they faced educating Christians in faith, and what they had to say was particularly revealing and instructive for him as a newcomer to the African continent. One by one, students recounted the Christian legacy of fruitful missionary movements in their respective countries. But, as the stories piled up, the atmosphere in the room turned somber. The students acknowledged gratefulness for their Christian heritage, yet it had in some instances garnered unanticipated consequences.[2]

Like almost any movement that is ideological or social—which Christianity is, to the extent that it is affected by human contextualization—naturally occurring patterns emerge: first, there is evidence of dynamic personal and societal change; then, after a period of gradual accommodation to culture, a stabilization period appears as a normalizing albeit taming feature.[3] However—according to what the students had to say—what ultimately can transpire is retrenchment, which then fades to lethargy. In other words, to the extent that Christianity makes permeating inroads in the psyche and fabric of a society, there tends to be an eventual backlash—a rather subliminal diminution of faith and a hapless routinization emerges to replace the initial liveliness. The result, as we hashed through the grim implications of this theory, was perhaps one of the most dreaded enemies of Christian education: *nominalism*—being Christian . . . in name only.[4]

Nominal claims to Christian identity often coexist alongside other features of human identities; their ancestral, ethnic, or familial associations, for example. Nominal Christians are Christian because of their background, which likely means that they (or their parents) were raised in Christianity as children; they *inherited* a Christian identity.

NOMINAL CHRISTIAN

A nominal Christian is one who professes belief in the teachings of Jesus in form only, though lacking substance or authenticity. The size and scope of nominality can exist in any culture or context where the church is more than one generation old. In addition, the term is difficult to quantify based on inferences, statistics, or other descriptors. The following are types of nominality in the individual's relationship to the local church: one who attends church regularly and worships devoutly but who has no vital personal relationship with Jesus as Savior and Lord; one who attends church regularly but for cultural reasons only; one who attends church only for major church festivals (Christmas, Easter, etc.) and ceremonies (weddings, baptisms, funerals); one who hardly ever attends church but maintains a church relationship for reasons of security, emotional or family ties, or tradition; and one who has no relationship to any specific church and who never attends but considers himself a believer in God (in a Protestant traditional sense).

DANIEL BENNETT

The students' vivid experiences supported this hypothesis and added traction by their remarkably similar reports coming from a number of countries in the Christian-oriented regions of sub-Saharan Africa.[5] It seemed that in some countries/cultures where there is or has been a prominent or historically influential relationship with Christianity, the residual effect observed is often a significant percentage of people, who by virtue of nothing more than custom, believe they are Christian. This faith-by-association status is a tremendous detriment to nurturing faith and is *ironically* the result of the church's failure to nurture faith! Christian nominalism presents itself as either an uncritical syncretism of Christian identity with other sorts of identities or prescribes an equally uncritical coexistence of the differing identities wherein the Christian dimension exhibits no creative or disciplinary influence over the others. Each form tacitly denies that Jesus is Lord. While dimensions of identity can and do overlap, nurturing faith requires forming identities consistent with God's saving and missional work. Christianity is not simply an assemblage of beliefs and practices; it intends a coherent way of life along with a promised end—the fullness of God's realm—that makes real the need for proper interrelation between beliefs and practices.[6] Religions, including Christianity, which come to be defined by nominalism, are more likely to neglect such intentionality and lack coherence.[7]

As the class continued in this line of thinking, we observed similar trends that had marked Christianity in Europe over the centuries. Students commented on how active faith diminished as Christian nominalism grew, and also how it spread through all wings of the church—in Protestantism (as in much of sub-Saharan Africa, most of Scandinavia, and more recently in South Korea), in Roman Catholicism (as in large swaths of southern Europe and South America), and in the Orthodox Church (as in significant regions of central and eastern Europe). As noted, the data suggest continuing diminishment of faith in "Christian countries."[8]

Table 10. *Countries That Will No Longer Have a Christian Majority in 2050*

	Majority Religion 2010	% of Population 2010	Majority/Largest Religion 2050	% of Population 2050
Australia	Christians	67.3	Christians	47.0
United Kingdom	Christians	64.3	Christians	45.4
Benin	Christians	53.0	Christians	48.5
France	Christians	63.0	Unaffiliated	44.1
Republic of Macedonia	Christians	59.3	Muslims	56.2
New Zealand	Christians	57.0	Unaffiliated	45.1
Bosnia-Herzegovina	Christians	52.3	Muslims	49.4
Netherlands	Christians	50.6	Unaffiliated	49.1

Source: The Future of World Religions: Population Growth Projections, 2010–2050. Pew Research Center.

At one point, having delayed inquiry into the largest geographic Christian population, perhaps out of deference to their professor, our working "socio-religious nominalism hypothesis" turned to the United States—a very reasonable line of inquiry indeed. (See table 11, below.) And so, it seems right that we now examine as a case study the issue of *nominalism* as a detriment to nurturing faith with respect to the historic and present situation of Christianity in the United States. While this book is not intended to narrowly focus on the US, we wish to amply illustrate our point from the most-researched group of Christians in the world. By doing so, what we find may also be relevant for dozens of other countries, where their Christian population acquires nominalist tendencies.

As we have learned so far, the Christian faith is affected by the environment in which it exists, often an adaptation to cultural factors. Much as Christians wish to change their wider culture, Christianity is more often refashioned by dominant cultures.[9] In addition, the informal sociological analysis above suggests a tendency toward decline in religious fervor over succeeding generations. Whether the preferred explanation is cultural or sociological, the result is nominalism. For Christians, this means declining importance of faith for persons and communities and, critical to what follows below, a growing risk for distortion or cooptation of Christian faith by social/cultural forces antithetical to it.

Contributors to and Manifestations of Christian Nominalism

We turn now to specific species of the *genus nominalus*. A variety of factors contribute to Christian nominalism, including but not limited to exceptionalism, nationalism, and traditionalism. Each of these displays naivete with respect to authentic Christian faith and life. These factors not only contribute to nominalism, however; they become expressions of it.

Table 11. Religious Composition of the United States, 2010–2050

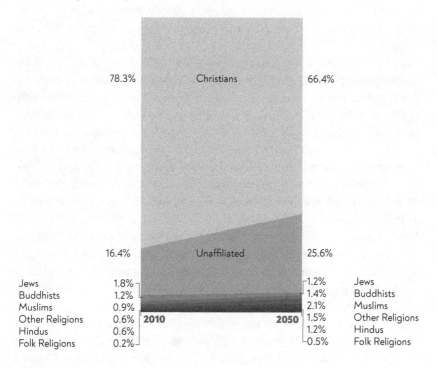

Source: The Future of World Religions: Population Growth Projections, 2010–2050.
Pew Research Center.

Nominalism and American Exceptionalism

To various classes or groups, Mark sometimes poses the question whether the United States is a "Christian country" and then sits back and watches the action. Many, of course, claim a sort of divine mysticism in the nation's creation—that America was an especially elect nation and that the founders acted as they did due to God's providential guiding hand. The nation's past and founding documents, according to this view, assume an almost sacred quality. As can be appreciated, due to the variety of potential understandings and fluidity between perspectives, it can be difficult to decipher what one means when speaking of America's Christian heritage or of it being a "Christian nation." Steven K. Green characterizes the resiliency of a belief in America's religious origins, particularly of its "chosen" status, as perplexing, especially in that American religious exceptionalism has not been taught in the nation's public schools for two generations. Nevertheless, the narrative persists, much of it from a religio-patriotic rhetoric, actively fueled by popular literature and media and channeled by pastors, politicians, and commentators.[10]

A 2015 Public Religion Research Institute (PRRI) survey finds that nearly two in three Americans (62 percent) say God has granted America "an exceptional role in human history." (See figure 4, below.) "American exceptionalism is a deep and abiding belief that's fundamental to the American DNA," said Daniel Cox, PRRI research director.[11] Of course, the promises of God for the nation of Israel so clearly presented in the Old Testament declared their "chosen" status among the nations, but the self-identifying "exceptional" sense some Christians in the US embrace seems to occur without peer in the world church today. This as a form of supersessionism—the "Christian" United States as the new Israel—and it certainly fits with Western modernity's view of its own preeminence. What then can be said of an historical, national ethos that reflects such a sentiment? And how does this special (shall we say *entitled*) status play out in its commitment to living faith in the postmodern world?

A central question in Mark Noll's *The New Shape of World Christianity: How American Experience Reflects Global Faith* considers what Christianity in the United States means for the worldwide Christian community. One view is that US Christians *control* events; a second view is one of *influence* (not manipulation); and a third view describes the relationship of American and world Christianity as merely *shared historical experience*.

Which of these views is most accurate in the case of the influence of the United States on global Christian education? It is hard to know. To what extent is Christian education in the United States (or, Christianity, for that matter) qualitatively different than world Christianity? Here some argue that it is aggressive and therefore abusive. Rather baldly, Noll opines: "No body of Christians has been as capable at exercising power as American believers, though few have been more reluctant to address questions of power face-on."[12]

Noll's operating thesis is that Christianity in its United States form is important for the world, but not primarily because of direct influence. Instead, money and prestigious educational institutions exert disproportionate influence upon the world Christian scene. And while the majority of Christians reside elsewhere, the United States minority has a loud presence. In his diplomatic way, Noll calls the phenomenon "adolescent exuberance."[13] Some find US Christianity off-putting, to say the least. Of course, while US Christians tend to see their contributions as nothing other than offering help in extending the faith, others view this with more suspicion, seeing it as intrusive. With global mission advancement and evangelistic zeal comes the presumption that the US knows best when it comes to everything from mission to education in faith, and often with missionary church-planting come US cultural values, practices, and systems.

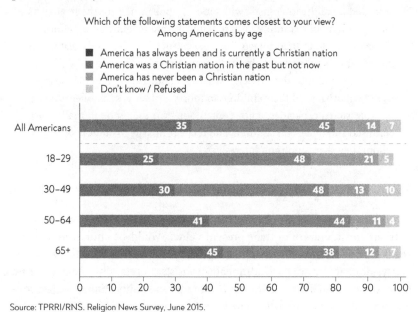

Source: TPRRI/RNS. Religion News Survey, June 2015.

Figure 1. *America: A Christian Nation?*

Nominalism and Christian Nationalism

Religious and social forces have also birthed a spirit of Christianity that is confused with *nationalism* in some regions where the church exists. This unnatural mingling of religion and citizenship is another form of *nominalism*—a faith born loosely of accommodation to wider culture or affiliation with non-Christian ideologies—and such a faith no doubt exacerbates the initial mingling. The inevitable result of nationalism is a pronounced naivete that confuses the nature of Christian discipleship and prevents radical commitment to the countercultural teachings of Jesus. Christian nationalism presumes alliance between the realization of God's realm and the means and ends of the nation-state.[14] In the US, Christian nationalism often has uncritically sanctioned the exercise of military power as commensurate with God's will. Similarly, it has presumed that God will not rest until every last person on the planet learns to shop like Christians in the US. On the equivocation of Christianity with cultural and civil religion, Alan Wolfe offers this spot-on pronouncement:

> Believers in America are neither an exotic nor an endangered species. They ought not to be treated as holding fast to ways of life that, if not faithfully recorded by anthropologists, will soon disappear, nor are they cabalists hiding from public scrutiny until the time is right to launch their efforts to shape the world in their image. They believe in a supernatural creator, but there is little supernatural about the ways in which they do so. Religious believers blend into the modern American landscape. They increasingly live in suburbs, send their children to four-year liberal arts colleges, work in professional capacities, enjoy contemporary music, shop in malls, raise confused and uncertain children, and relate primarily to other people with whom they share common interests.[15]

Nominalism and Christian Traditionalism

Traditionalism, for our purposes, means retaining past belief and practice without consideration of their present value. Would-be church innovators regularly find themselves brought up short by the traditionalist chorus: "We've always done it that way!" Traditionalism insists on retaining the past for no other reason than it is past. The effect is to squash vitality, innovation, or conviction that God is still working new creation in the world. Its further effect is to foist a kind of inertia upon believers.

Nominalist traditionalism is not a new threat. It has existed at least as long as Christians have invoked a *tradition*. John Wesley's efforts toward renewal in the eighteenth-century Church of England are a case in point. Wesley criticized the church's status-quo satisfaction with the outer form of religion unaccompanied by its lively, transforming spirit. The church of Wesley's day required little more of members than minimal religious duties—baptism of children plus annual communion. Unsurprisingly, British Christians, in turn, had little use for Christianity. Wesleyanism (later institutionalized as Methodism) overcame traditionalism and injected new life into British and ultimately world Christianity. As we have seen, however, religious renewal and vitality are seldom sustained long-term, and these days Methodism in the global north struggles with its own nominalist traditionalism.

Traditionalism is proof that tradition can become an idol. Traditionalism implies a fixation with the past and a desire to maintain the status quo. Historian Jaroslav Pelikan perhaps put it the best: "Tradition is the living faith of the dead; traditionalism is the dead faith of the living," and "it is traditionalism that gives faith such a bad name."[16] Mary Boys aptly points out that the historic Christian faith is a continuing dance between tradition and transformation.[17] Charles Foster claims being entrapped by traditionalism is chiefly responsible for the "cultural captivity" of church education.[18] The issue at hand is, what is worth handing on (tradition), and how should it be appropriated given the learners' life situation (transformation)? Our beliefs and expressions of faith connote something weighty (tradition) and are not to be downgraded to meagerly voiced platitudes or lifeless noises (Matt. 6:7–8). These convictions are to be distilled into vigorous, evident, faith-forming practices (transformation). Christians ought then to embark upon the theological task of interpreting the world—a faithful negotiation of past and present, tradition and transformation. And by engaging in the activity of life-hermeneutics, we must be quite certain that our presumptions of how to engage are sound and not merely loaded with cultural accretions that distort the meaning of the gospel.

The Dance of Belief and Practice

Nominalism, whether it takes the form of exceptionalism, nationalism, traditionalism or others, squashes, blurs, or misdirects faith. The only acceptable endgame for Christianity springs from orthodox belief, faithfully executed practice, and apt interplay between the two. Our word "belief" can be inadequate or even misleading. What the early Christians meant by "belief," says Tom Wright, included both believing *that* God had done certain things and believing *in* the God who had done them. This is not belief that God merely exists, but loving, grateful trust.[19] For the gospel to seep into any society, Christianity must cultivate this form of belief and live the story of Jesus. Where Christianity overemphasizes belief without enough concern for practice, it becomes a verbally oriented dogma (verbalism), which focuses lopsidedly on cognitive understanding to the exclusion of its ethical dimension. It then sadly lacks the moral example to salt society. Correspondingly, where Christianity overemphasizes action-oriented practice without due concern for cogent theology, it becomes too experientially based and risks losing its dependence upon God's grace (activism). The Christian message then appears devoid of the requisite truth and moral authority necessary to guide persons and communities.

While this regard for balance has long been a concern for the church, *it is our contention that nominalism, as manifested in exceptionalism, nationalism, traditionalism, and other forms of religious naivete, is at once cause and effect of Christian educational efforts that fail to pursue the proper juxtaposition between belief and practice.* Is this pronouncement fair? Well, theologian Ronald Sider observes that scandalous behavior from *within* is rapidly destroying Christianity. He charges: "By their daily activity, most Christians regularly commit treason."[20] Author Michael Horton laments that in survey after survey, there is evidence that Christians are as likely to embrace lifestyles every bit as hedonistic, materialistic, self-centered, and sexually immoral as the non-Christian world in general.[21] Additionally, scholar Alan Wolfe claims today's evangelicalism (in particular) exhibits so strong a desire to copy the culture of hotel chains and popular music that it loses what religious distinctiveness it once had. The truth is there is increasingly little difference between an essentially secular enterprise, such as the popular entertainment industry, and the "bring 'em-in" at any cost efforts of some megachurches.[22]

Belief and practice must go hand in hand, but often the way the two interact with each other can be problematic. There are at least three different combinations of belief and practice that need addressing (see table 12, below).[23] *First*, Christians may display right belief but wrong practice, which betrays the intent of the gospel. *Second*, Christians may believe wrongly and act wrongly, which mocks both the intent and meaning of the gospel. *Third*, we may hold wrong beliefs yet surprisingly exhibit right practice, which confuses the true meaning of the gospel as God's initiative for the world. And *fourth*, we may hold right beliefs backed up by right practice. This is the interrelationship to which the Christian educational ministries aspire. Simply put, the educational mission of the church is to nurture faith in its adherents such that their minds and wills embrace right beliefs, while their lives are marked by right attitudes and practices. The judicious exhibition of right belief interplaying with right practice powerfully illustrates the truest meaning of the gospel. Three unintended results appear when belief and practice are wrongly related. These include unintended outcomes, curious inventions, and misshapen creatures, but most alarmingly, a distortion of the Christian witness to the surrounding culture. Admittedly, Christians will try (and fail) to get this combination right until Christ returns. Yet try we must. Fortunately, God can transform even our imperfections to accomplish God's purposes.

Table 12. *Juxtapositions of Religious Belief and Practice*

Common Tendencies	Characteristic Inferences	Corresponding Results
Right belief/ wrong practice	Betrays true intent of gospel	Unintended outcomes
Wrong belief/ wrong practice	Mocks intent and meaning of gospel	Curious inventions
Wrong belief/ right practice	Confuses true meaning of gospel	Misshapen creatures
Right belief/ right practice	Exposes true meaning of gospel	Faithful disciples

Right Belief/Wrong Practice—Jonah: Theological Orthodoxy Meets Practical Apostasy

There is a temptation to turn to exemplary cases when talking about the relationship between religious beliefs and practices, but as Pauw reminds us, there is also something to be said for looking at efforts by less than exemplary believers to bridge the troublesome gaps that keep appearing in the disparity of stated belief and lived behavior.[24] In doing so, we see the struggles of slippage and compromise. Less exemplary believers point us away from notions of heroism and mastery in religious practice. They draw our gaze instead toward the gracious God who works in and through them.

Obviously, it is coherence of belief and practice that is sought. The ordinary struggles of Christian people lay bare the ligaments that hold beliefs and practice together. Their discords reveal how easily these connections become strained and broken when admirable belief fails to nurture admirable practice, or conversely when vibrant practice fails to stimulate vibrant belief.[25] For practices shape religious beliefs, but religious beliefs also shape practices. It is a tensive relationship, which means beliefs influence, but are not reducible to, certain actions, attitudes, and interests.

As the case of the prophet Jonah demonstrates, belief in divine mercy frequently coexists in religious life with the failure of resolve to be merciful. Jonah seems to believe in an unhelpful version of Israel's exceptionalism that turns into arrogance. The history of Christian thought is littered with examples of self-justifying appeals to religious beliefs. Yet in their role of helping us make sense of the world, beliefs may temper resistance to our current desires and practices and may at times interrogate or even temporarily disband them.[26]

Jonah holds admirable beliefs but struggles mightily with how to live them out. Jonah's inclusion in the books of the prophets, specifically for his less than exemplary record, has served as an ongoing source of encouragement to generations of believers who know the same struggles in integrating belief and practice. The book of Jonah is filled with miraculous events: a man who was swallowed by a fish and remained entombed for three days, the sudden growth of a gourd, and the repentance of the Ninevites. Another miracle, however, is that in spite of wrong behavior (on the part of the begrudging messenger), God brings salvation. Ultimately, the prophetic book, and specifically Jonah chapter 4, is about the revelation of God's character, and more than that— Jonah's character. We suppose this story invites us to laugh at ourselves—our hypocrisy, our mixed motives.

Wrong practice is observed in Jonah but not wrong belief. Jonah's orthodox religious beliefs are evident throughout the story. Jonah pronounces: "I am a Hebrew and I worship the Lord, the God of heaven, who made the sea and the land" (1:9) and "Salvation comes from the Lord" (2:9). Further, he correctly offers: "You are a gracious and compassionate God, slow to anger and abounding in love, a God who relents from sending calamity" (4:2). Yet Jonah's beliefs fail in part to shape his practice. God summons Jonah to the practice of testimony, yet his practice lacks integrity.

Regardless, the whole city repents, even the livestock! But true beliefs and good results are not sufficient conditions for excellent practice. How many wrong practices have been justified in the name of good results? A religious community's best insight into the possibilities and deformities of its beliefs and practices often comes from the outside. Critical theological reflection is required to unmask perennial human tendencies toward triumphalism and self-deception, and those within the circle of communal self-understanding may not be sufficiently alert to these tendencies in their midst.

Excellence in belief involves the critical self-knowledge that we are often antagonistic toward the good and prone to self-deception. Excellence in practice involves confessing our inability to practice our faith in a consistent way. When belief shapes practice in an excellent way, we celebrate God's grace, not human effort. For us as a people of faith who want to love God, the communal settings of proclamation, sacraments, and confession frame our hopes for closing the gap between beliefs and practice. In those settings, we can reaffirm the truth about our dependence on the richness of God's grace and pray for greater integrity between our beliefs and our practices.[27] Engagement in these practices, with other people, over time, can give rise to new knowledge and new capacities for perception that are not accessible otherwise, especially as individuals are left to their own devices.

The problem is not that Jonah fails to believe the right things; he fails to *desire* the right things. As the Augustinian tradition insists, the link between belief and practice is forged by human longing and attitude. The most accessible indication of my spiritual state is not in my words but in my thoughts and emotions. These can be the most accessible—and terrifyingly so—moral thermometer of our character. And our character is an accurate barometer of the state of our faithfulness to the Spirit-led life in God.

The byproduct of right beliefs but wrong practices in nurturing faith is *unintended outcomes*. The intended outcome of our best efforts at nurturing faith will be hospitable welcome of persons into belief in the triune God and the holistic formation of disciples who follow Jesus in practice. Unintended outcomes betray Christian hypocrisy and arrogance, and these have soured (even wounded) those who search for God.

Wrong Belief/Wrong Practice—The End of Religion?!

The intent of Christian faith formation is to become fully alive in Christ as human beings with potential for moral integrity, even Christ-likeness. Sometimes we fail in this effort through the combination of erroneous belief *and* bad practice. The woefully misconfigured and curious inventions that result from wrong beliefs and wrong practices detract and alienate people from participation in the vision for reconciliation with God and each other as well as the journey toward holiness.

One case in point has been Christianity's tangled interactions with colonialism. This "wrong belief" has historically confused Christian faith with a vision of supersessionist superiority, a misappropriated presumption of God's favor of European Christianity, and an ensuing confusion of European expansionist ambitions and economic treasure-hunting with gospel. As if this ideology were not sufficiently problematic all by itself, it was accompanied by "wrong practice" in the newly "discovered" world that featured enslavement or extermination of whole peoples; environmental exploitation and destruction; stealing wealth; destroying indigenous cultures; creating separate and unequal Christianity for native converts; and failure to live into inclusive community in the one body of Christ. Obviously, as in this case, wrong belief/wrong practice on the part of the church has sometimes proven disastrous, effectively sanctioning evil in the name of God.

Perhaps as a result, there are movements afoot at present seeking to characterize *religion itself* (including especially Christianity) as, *ipso facto*, a form of wrong belief/wrong practice that must be eradicated.[28] According to this argument only the complete extermination of religious faith altogether will permit enlightenment in the world. Even as we here acknowledge that the existence of the gospel does not guarantee the good life God intends, we view its eradication as far more problematic than its presence. We shudder to imagine living without Jesus's witness to even the possibility of reconciliation, peace, justice, holiness, joy, and faith.

An Excursus on the Relationship of Secularism to Nominalism

Nineteenth- and twentieth-century pundits confidently predicted *the death of religion* as the natural consequence of secularization. As Stark and Bainbridge note with irony: "Most Western intellectuals have anticipated the death of religion as eagerly as ancient Israel awaited the messiah."[29] They maintain that religion, and most notably Christianity, simply cannot survive in a rationalist, science-dominated society. Indubitably, the neurosis of superstitious faith will be outgrown.[30] Indeed, students of religion regularly encounter new accounts of a decisive death blow for those "dinosaurs" who believe they still live under Peter Berger's "sacred canopy." The bleak vision of religion's demise led Max Weber to gloomily paint it as a "polar night of icy darkness and hardness."[31] And in this vein, Berger foresaw a "world without windows" to describe the resultant effect of the increasing prominence of rational calculation, typical of science and technology, thus shutting out the light of life-sustaining wisdom. Those who hold a strong belief in secularization see it as an irresistible force, moving steadily forward wherever modernity has a foothold, and having more or less the same effects in all contexts.

Yet, reports of the death of religion seem greatly exaggerated. As loudly as the adamant and vocal nonreligious minority blasts the silliness or danger of nonempirical faith throughout academia, media, popular culture, and other societal venues, faith in the Christian way remains. Indeed, *outbursts of Christianity* across the globe are definitively robust, unexpectedly diverse, and surprisingly innovative.[32] The hallowed secularization doctrine has predicted a vanishing not in evidence. Marx, Freud, and Nietzsche would be stunned by the persistence of Christianity were they alive today. The *World Christian Encyclopedia* assesses the percentage of Christians worldwide to have been 33 to 34 percent for the last several generations and projects the same proportion in the coming half-century.[33] Admittedly, the attenuation of religion in some quarters is disconcerting, yet sustained Christian vitality, which has evaded rationalization or the encroachments of the secular state, appears to be more than an odd mutation blocking the road to human progress. In fact, theories of postmodernity generally, and of contemporary religion more specifically, are predicated on the belief that Western societies have moved *beyond* secularism. Ironically, according to postmodernist writers, a new liveliness of religion results from the uncertainty of meaning produced by a too certain secularism. And as a result of this liveliness spurred by secularization, two countervailing processes have occurred: revival and religious innovation.

Yet, while secularization studies cannot ignore resilience of common religion, which has outlived the moribund atrophy of the church's public impact, secularization is a valuable tool for assessing the state of Christianity. Secularization *opens our eyes to the marginalization of nominalist Christianity*. Permit the following use of the contemporary church in England, which retains some representative elements of the formerly Christianized Western culture, as an extensive case study for this point. Some, including its own leaders, have described the English Church as a punctured balloon, a deflated remnant of a grand idea. The ostentatious cathedrals are tourist Meccas for the curious, but anathema for the young—historically interesting, existentially irrelevant. Peter Ball, co-National Youth Officer of the Church of England, resonates with this gloomy depiction, and he wonders aloud whether the imposing and historic buildings, hierarchical ecclesiastical structures, and seeming inflexible practices of worship have alienated youth. He may be right. Regardless, the church in England is languishing, and youth are fleeing. Estimates of up to one thousand young people leave the church every week. And England offers a model case study of dechristianization and flailing attempts to reintroduce the Christian religion afresh to its alienated postmodern citizens; it should be a thunderous caution to other countries that share such rich Christian heritages. Former Archbishop of Canterbury George Carey says England has developed something of an allergy to religion. David Lyon grieves the lessening shadow of the land's church steeples: "Once a respected and central pillar of society, the Church has been demoted from prominence, and relegated to the social fringes."[34] In this case, secularist forces from without and traditionalist responses within have contributed to British Christian nominalism, thereby relegating the church to the fringes of British society. (Later we will consider whether "fringe locations" may in fact be good places for Christians to inhabit.)

Martin E. Marty in *The Modern Schism: Three Paths to the Secular* further explains British nominalism:

> England knew a few minor god-killers and now and then provided a home
> for continental ideas or advocates of ideas about the deaths of God, Church,

and Christian culture. But twentieth-century heirs of the legacy of those ideas do not have to deal seriously with the thought about the death of God in England. Rather, they have to reckon with people who began to ignore Christian claims, to become impervious to them; people who found that God, Church, and Christian teaching were superfluous to their thought and action.[35]

In contrast with the French version of secularizing, he characterizes the English experience as drab and bland. Marty concludes that secularization did not mean the disappearance of Christianity so much as its relocation. This observation—made a generation ago—still persists, yet with a postmodern twist.[36]

Return to Wrong Belief/Wrong Practice: The End of Religion?!

Within the church, the outcome of wrong belief/wrong practice leads to curious or even grotesque inventions. At minimum, this combination looks like the indifferent British nominalism (a form that effectively characterizes not only England but much of Christianity across the global north). At worst, Christian forms of wrong belief/wrong practice have unleashed enormous evil upon the world and brought upon Christians justified scorn and condemnation. Once criticized for its failure to practice what it preached, Christian faith is now cast by secularism in more radical terms as a flawed premise *en toto*. In other words, for secularism, the presumption that religious faith could *ever* lead to flourishing life is itself and at its root wrong belief/wrong practice. Christianity itself and not just its deformed manifestations in belief and practice are now cast as a curious invention.

Wrong Belief/Right Practice—Where Is the Grace?

Being *practical* theologians, we are tempted to settle for right practice even if accompanied by wrong belief. As the song goes, Christians aspire to be known by their love more than what they have to say about it. In fact, love is what wins in the end, not perfect belief systems. But poor theology or, more often, inadequate theology remains less than ideal. Without it, laudable practice goes wanting for lack of proper vision or motivation. This category also points to the paucity of faithful imagination, without which, persons and communities often cannot recognize how their good practices become grafted into God's cosmic mission.

Fred once studied a congregation (it happened to be the one he grew up in) that displayed a remarkable knack for calling young people into ministry (he was one of them).[37] Conversations with dozens of people, including a number of current pastors and church workers also nurtured by that congregation, revealed key factors contributing to this congregation's success. These included a number of excellent practices: first, a vibrant faith community where young people were integrated into every facet of community life, including its central practices of worship and mission; second, adult mentors, all exemplary Christians, modeled to youth lives of joyful abundance; third, a very high percentage of the congregation, including adults, participated in classes and studies with the intent of growing in faith; fourth, as young persons' gifts for leadership became evident, they were given real ministry responsibilities while continuing to receive training and support.

Those called by God through this congregation expressed profound gratitude for its impact upon them. Their stories varied in the details, but all coalesced around the sense of being welcomed into a joyous community with a shared identity and purpose. They simply could not imagine a more compelling way to spend the rest of their lives.

Yet for all the commendable practices of this community, there was one surprising lacuna. More than one interviewee commented that language of "calling" and "vocation" were absent from the congregation's dictionary. To be clear, it was not as if there was no dictionary whatsoever. Folks knew they were gathered around the triune God, and, oh, how they loved Jesus best of all. But a calling to ministry? That was left to the mysterious workings of the Spirit upon the private meditations of individual hearts. Said one present-day pastor who grew up in the church, "I wish we had talked about [calling to ministry vocations] more, it would have saved me a lot of confusion." To be sure, there was plenty of biblical teaching on the love of Jesus transforming sinful lives into good ones, especially where adolescent virtue was perceived to be lacking. No one interviewed could recollect, however, appreciative tellings of biblical call stories, no overheard testimonies of calls received, no sermons describing how persons who served the common good might do so in response to a call from God. Fred didn't learn the language of calling and vocation, much less connect it to baptism, until seminary.

Admittedly, leveling a complaint about poor or inadequate belief in relation to the otherwise sterling practices of nurturing faith in future church workers can seem more than a little snippy. Yet a lack of theological clarity on the belief in vocation holds implications for the entire community, not just a few would-be religious professionals. Absent belief in calling, congregations will have difficulty imagining themselves as a pilgrim people whose purpose transcends their own comfort. Further, individual Christians may never learn to value their (paid or volunteer) work toward reconciliation, health, or justice as forms of vocation participating in God's mission. The lack of vocational language can also abet clericalism, where everyone assumes that the pastor alone is capable of thinking spiritual thoughts.

Considering in broader terms the strange juxtaposition of right practice with wrong or inadequate belief, often the result is failure to perceive or receive God's grace. (Allow "grace" here to mean God's promise of abiding relational love.) Pastors and church workers observe that some in their communities are driven either by pride or its inverse, shame and guilt, each fostered by inadequate belief. The prideful "take charge" in faith communities. They are the first to volunteer to chair the fundraising campaign, to write the *big* check, and to exhort the congregation to charity as great as their own. Apparently unaware of Jesus's injunctions against too much public piety or perhaps imagining themselves to be indispensable to God's success, they manifest belief in what amounts to a self-assured works righteousness, convinced that living well is what puts them at God's right hand. Others quietly volunteer for multiple committees, plus teaching Sunday school and singing in the choir, too, all in desperate hope that God may one day find them acceptable. This, too, is belief in works righteousness—this time not for the proud but for the anxious.

As readers easily grasp, whatever form it takes, the conviction that we find God's favor by doing good things is a wrong (if widely subscribed) belief. Obviously, the missing piece here is Christian belief in the primacy of grace, that God's good favor finds *us*. Indeed, we profess that the world turns on God's relational love as revealed in Jesus Christ. It is in and through *Christ*, not our own devices, that we may do all things. God's grace assures the anxious and humbles the haughty. Practice hinges upon grace. Practice is at once the gift of grace, a response to grace, a means of grace, and a sharing in grace. Believing in grace, therefore, is absolutely key to grasping gospel. Without imaginations formed into the biblical stories of God's mighty *grace-filled* acts, practice falls short of incorporating Christians into awareness of the cosmic significance of their lives. Further, practice without proper cognizance of grace attenuates the wonder of Christian life. And where there is too little wonder, there is too little joy.

An inescapable correlation, to be sure, must be endorsed in Christian education for the seamless interaction of belief and action. But the tendency has been to observe the lockstep sequence of a belief leading to an action—in other words, to know something must be in place prior to being and doing. While this may be legitimate, it is not definitive. In fact, human experience teaches that *to do* is also a powerful instructor in *being and knowing*. An entire academic domain called *"experiential education"* explores the value and interplay of these concepts and is particularly relevant for nurturing Christians.

EXPERIENTIAL LEARNING

Experiential learning refers broadly to a collection of practices and perspectives on learning and teaching that involve active and engaged education. Christian educators who work with children will be familiar with the importance of learning by doing, but this may be less apparent to those working with adults. Experiential approaches can be traced to the seminal work of John Dewey in the early 1900s when he promoted the role of experience and activity in learning.

Experiential learning helps us to understand that what children, youth, and adults bring to a learning environment is not incidental. It matters in that learners need to be able to connect what they are learning to previous experiences and to use this experience as a basis for further learning. The educator's task within experiential learning is not to impart knowledge and to dispense information on topics such as ritual, sacred texts, or religious teaching but to help learners understand how these topics might connect to their previous knowledge, and to have them actively engage in learning new insights. When experiential learning is honored in an educational setting such as a theological seminary, learners are honored as decision makers, as people who bring a lifetime of experience to the classroom, and as those who have a need to learn in various ways, which may include lectures but are not limited to them.

Experiential learning can be misunderstood. A close look at Dewey's scholarship shows that his basic idea of learning by doing, and centering on what the person wanted to learn, was more complicated than having activity in a Christian education class or asking learners what they needed to learn. Though these are laudable, Dewey had a notion that activity must be accompanied by reflection and analysis, and it had to be about more than meeting the learners' needs. In his classic work, *Experience and Education* (1938), he outlined his understanding of the role of experience in learning, and he presented it as a complex and intricate system of working from experience to reflection to analysis and to action. To plan and organize such an educational opportunity is a challenging exercise. Yet it allows for all the dimensions of the person—physical, emotional, spiritual, intellectual—to be engaged in learning.

One of the least recognized ways that experiential learning is practiced in religious settings is through informal learning or learning that occurs apart from a teacher or an organized learning event such as a Bible study class. Informal learning might take place when one gains insight about liturgical reform while participating in and observing a liturgical event. Informal learning might also take place while reading a spiritual text, making a pilgrimage to a holy site, or participating in events and meetings sponsored by a Christian group.

One of the key roles of the teacher in experiential education is as a support or facilitator of reflection in this learning. In the case of informal learning, the educator might be the one who debriefs with a travel or service-learning group. In this case, the Christian educator may provide opportunities for journal writing and group discussion, drama or role play, or art activities. Such reflection may have ethical implications, such as when uncomfortable feelings are acknowledged by learners or when there is a conflict of positions with the organizing religion. In engaging in experiential education, the educators can and must be aware of the possible outcomes and be prepared to negotiate them.

LEONA M. ENGLISH

One might rightly ask which is more important in the spiritual life of an adherent: belief or practice. G. K. Chesterton is famously noted as having quipped that Christianity has not so much been tried and found wanting, as it has been found difficult and left untried. Certainly, University of Southern California philosopher Dallas Willard agrees: "For at least several decades, the churches of the Western world have not made discipleship a condition of being a Christian. One is not required to be . . . a disciple in order to become a Christian, and one may remain a Christian without any signs of progress toward or in discipleship. . . . Discipleship is clearly optional."[38]

The requirement for being a Christian has become that one believes the proper things about Jesus—merely a mental assent to orthodoxy. Christians have heard, especially from Dietrich Bonhoeffer, about the cost of discipleship, but consider the cost of nondiscipleship. Besides thwarting the teaching of Jesus, nondiscipleship costs the loss of abiding peace, a life penetrated throughout by love, faith that sees everything in the light of God's overriding good, hopefulness that stands firm in the most trying circumstances, and power to do what is right. It then appears lamentably devoid of the requisite absolute truth and moral authority to influence society.[39]

The byproduct of wrong beliefs but right practices in nurturing faith produces *misshapen creatures*. Followers who are properly shaped display zeal for embarking on the long and uneven road to discipleship. Yet right practices of Christian-like endeavors—such as attending to the rituals of the faith community and identifying with the people of God, when teamed with the wrong practices, or lack of effort, in becoming a viable disciple of Jesus—are nowhere to be found in Scripture. Misshapen creatures are those who appear to have the form of a follower but lack the determined will to become who they are meant to be in God.

Blaise Pascal forcefully asks (and answers): "Why is it so hard to believe? Because it is so hard to obey." It is just this sentiment that steers us to the fourth category of belief and practice, after having considered three misguided correlations in this chapter—right belief *and* right practice. The result is "faithful disciples," which we shall discuss more fully in part 2 (chapters 5 through 10).

Conclusion

As Mark and the African graduate students concluded the discussion about forming faith in Christians responsive to the temptations of nominalism (begun in the first paragraphs of this chapter), we renewed our commitment to model and mentor habits through Christian belief and practice that could be affirmed in balanced and life-affirming ways. We were reminded of the dangers of nationalism that consorts with Christianity in a way that conflates the two and imposes a nationalistic vision on the radical teachings of Jesus. It was a sobering dialogue and reminiscent of Philip Jenkins's assessment: "Religions die, but they leave ghosts. . . . Ghosts haunt the new religions that succeed the old."[40] Nationalistic ghosts. And finally, in this chapter, we have challenged ourselves, given the limitations of our leadership opportunities, to shed light upon any educational practice in the church that might unintentionally or—worse—neglectfully promote naivete about the obligations of those who choose to follow Jesus, thereby ensuring that discipleship is seen as an optional endeavor instead of something that must be taken up by anyone who will claim association with the mission of God.

To review, *chapter 2* outlined several ways in which the slippery and varied concepts of postmodernism inhibit and inform faith. Here in *chapter 3*, we acknowledge how nominalism is an unwelcome conspirator in our attempts to nurture faith. Finally, as we move to *chapter 4*, we will suggest solutions to these insipient problems and propose six critical means by which education in faith may best to be nurtured.

Interactive Dialogue

1. What do you make of the authors' contention that Christianity can become nationalistic? And how do you respond to the quotation from Wolfe on page 82 in this context? How, if it all, do you view yourself and your faith community in this tension?

2. The authors wonder why so many call themselves Christian and yet do not have a Christian religious identity. What do you think? And what can faith communities do to reduce "cultural Christianity" and other forms of nominalism?

3. To what extent do you agree with the notion (from p. 92) that "*to do* is also a powerful instructor in *being and knowing*"? How do you "know"? And how has this been applicable in your faith journey? In your local congregation?

4. Why do you think religion (in general) and Christianity (in partic-

ular) will not just "go away," as the secularists predicted? How does secularization open our eyes to the cultural isolation of Christianity? (See p. 89.)

For Further Reading

Allen, Diogenes. *Christian Belief in a Postmodern World: The Full Wealth of Conviction.* Louisville: Westminster John Knox, 1989.

Grenz, Stanley J. *A Primer on Postmodernism.* Grand Rapids: Eerdmans, 1996.

Hauerwas, Stanley. "The Gesture of a Truthful Story." *Theology Today* 42 (July 1985): 181–89.

Kinnaman, David. *You Lost Me: Why Young Christians Are Leaving Church . . . and Rethinking Faith.* Grand Rapids: Baker, 2011.

Lamport, Mark A., and Darrell Yoder. "Faithful Gestures: Rebooting the Educational Mission of the Church." *Christian Education Journal* 3 (Spring 2006): 53–73.

Plantinga, Alvin. *Warranted Christian Belief.* New York: Oxford University Press, 2000.

Sider, Ron. "The Evangelical Scandal." *Christianity Today* 49 (April 2005): 70–73.

CHAPTER FOUR

Keeping the Faith: Sketching a Practical Theology for Nurturing Faith

We will not hide them from their children; we will tell the next generation the praiseworthy deeds of the Lord, which He commanded our forefathers to teach their children, so that the next generation would know them, even the children yet to be born, and they in turn would tell their children. Then they would put their trust in God and would not forget His deeds but would keep His commands.

—PSALM 78:4-7

I am not trying, O Lord, to penetrate thy loftiness, for I cannot begin to match my understanding with it, but I desire in some measure to understand thy truth, which my heart believes and loves. For I do not seek to understand in order to believe, but I believe in order to understand. For this too I believe, that unless I believe, I shall not understand.

—ANSELM

ROAD MAP

Think of *chapter 4* as an appetizer for the main course to follow; a springboard into *part 2*. This chapter is an introduction to Christian education/formation as practical theology and also an exploration of how theology informs educational practice. It is a vision for all that follows. We have arrived at the sobering realization that Christians—due to disenchantment, lethargy, and irrelevance—have too often left the faith (*chapter 1*); we have found ourselves awash in the powerful effects of both modernism and postmodern sympathies that have transmuted but also clarified the faith (*chapter 2*); and we have chided religious systems for too easily allowing the vital, dynamic Christian faith to shrivel into a nominal status (*chapter 3*). But now, we unfold our emerging theses on nurturing faith for the global church. Six themes—commemoration, disclosure, humility, citizenship, gestures, reflection—constitute our strategy for provoking renewal in faith nurture.

Challenges of and Opportunities for Nurturing Faith

In *chapter 1*, we rehearsed and lamented six fundamental obstacles to nurturing faith—disorienting amnesia, autonomous determinism, interpretive pluriformity, cultural constructionism, fragmented faith, and conceptual bricolage. In this chapter (summarized in tables 13 and 14 below), we propose rectifying *countermeasures*—six practices that we contend are ultimately vital to effective Christian education and nurturing faith:

Number One: Disorienting Amnesia and Meaningful Commemorations

The First Encroaching Challenge: Disorienting Amnesia

Some observe a discontinuity between the historical traditions of the faith and the current lived experience of Christianity. When the biblical and historical roots of the Christian belief system become estranged, serious consequences emerge. Stephen Prothero, citing E. D. Hirsch's classic *Cultural Literacy*, chides our current state of affairs as "a gradual disintegration of cultural memory,"[1] which has led to an inability to communicate in an articulate way. This applies not only to societies in general but also the religious components of them. Granted, this condition may be more of a Western phenomenon. French sociologist Danièle Hervieu-Léger describes Europe's loss of faith as amnesia, not so much rooted in doubt, but forgetting. Certainly, much of the same can be observed in American Christianity in the United States and in many quadrants of the global church. The "chain of memory" has been broken.[2]

In a similar vein, Pulitzer Prize–winning historian Carl Schorske notes the modern mind has grown indifferent to history because history has become useless to it.[3] The present experience trumps all else: the future is intriguing but not something that can be accessed in the immediate, and history seems to be simply the accumulation of all that we are trying to recover from—such as uncivilized ways, antiquated beliefs, and undesirable styles of being. In other words, when history is deemed as irrelevant by segments of a culture or even entire cultures, this leads only further to the diminution of the insights previously appreciated from its history. Moderns know everything about the last twenty-four hours but little about the last twenty centuries or last fifty years. Media is biased toward supplying images and fragments but bereft of historical perspective. Remembering requires a contextual basis—a theory, a vision, a metaphor—something within which facts can be organized.[4]

It is not just Protestants who bemoan this loss of religious understanding in modern culture; Catholics and Jews observe the same basic ignorance of their traditions and sacred articles.[5] But some, primarily Protestants, still seethe about banned school prayer and Bible reading in the United States from the early 1960s—*Engel v. Vitale* (1962) and *Abington v. Schempp* (1963)—and correlate illiteracy problems and wayward civility to those Supreme Court decisions, as contributors to this lack of memory.[6] Perhaps—who can know for sure?

Table 13. Contextual Circumstances in Educating Christians

Encroaching Challenges to Christian Education	Engaging Resources for Christian Education
Disorienting amnesia	Meaningful commemorations
Autonomous determinism	Mutual disclosure
Interpretive pluriformity	Generous humility
Cultural constructionism	Intentional citizenship
Fragmented faith	Faithful gestures
Conceptual bricolage	Probing reflection

The First Engaging Resource: Meaningful Commemorations

The main cause of this disconnect between faith and life (and consequently, a loss of memory) may be an improperly constructed process of merely acquiring information or skills. The church must make conspicuous campaigns that rejoice in "remembering" the heritage and truth given it. To be sure, it is not the revelation of God as witnessed in Scripture that is forgettable or wearisome, but the inability of those teaching to coax relevant connections with those studying. As Craig Dykstra reminds us, education in faith must be at once an *investigative* process that guides people in the exploration of our experience with God; a *critical* process that liberates us from the patterns of thinking, feeling, valuing, and behaving that make it difficult for us to participate in this experience; and a *caring* process through which we graciously invite one another to enter freely and ever more deeply into this experience.[7] To be memorable, Christian education moves beyond mere history and engages fervidly at the intersection of faith and life.

Insight from Practical Theology: Worship Incubates Faith

Worship is certainly a most accessible form of Christian commemoration. In corporate worship, the lives of Christians are formed and transformed, and Christian identity is conferred and nurtured. Encounters with God in worship reveal simultaneously the profundity of our waywardness and the magnificence of God's being. Conscious intentions along with embodied habits that emerge from such a worshipful encounter are part of our Christian formation. They include the recognition of the need to receive and give love; the desire for personal reform; and rehearsal of faithful actions.[8] In worship, "people are characterized, given their life and their fundamental location and orientation in the world."[9] As the church worships, faith is incubated, and the believer's place in the cosmos is most clearly understood. Murphy distills: "In corporate worship the lives of Christians are formed and transformed, Christian identity is conferred and nurtured."[10]

By worship, we mean corporate worship including preaching, singing, baptism, the Lord's Supper, as well as personal worship. It is in this context that a sinful person comes into the Lord's presence in the midst of the redeemed community to praise, honor, and petition the Creator. Although some have placed importance on worship *services*, they have sometimes failed to see corporate worship as being vitally connected to education in Christ. The reasoning has been the following: we worship in church, but we get education in schools. Because of this, our education has little to do with our worship, and our worship has little to do with our education.

The main cause of this disconnect is that we have improperly seen education as little more than the process of acquiring information or skills. However, as we have argued, education for Christians is something much broader and richer, because it deals with transforming an entire person from a sinner characterized by self-love/self-loathing to a pristine image of Christ characterized by love for God and neighbor.

Where do we begin making these changes? It starts with repositioning worship at the center of Christian education and personal transformation. It declares one's faith and one's fear of the Lord as the "beginning of knowledge" (Prov. 1:7).

Through worship, Christians grasp their *place* in the cosmos—loved by their Creator.

Table 14. Prevalent Challenges and Corresponding Practices for Educating in Faith

Challenges to Educating in Faith	Misconstrued Result	Practical Theology for Lived Faith	Transcendent Vision
Disorienting amnesia: disconnectedness between Christian tradition and lived reality	Lack of meaning; mere history	Worship incubates faith	Place
Autonomous determinism: prevalence of solitary journey and diminution of the community of faith	Lack of community; mere speculation	Community makes faith operational	Position
Interpretive pluriformity: increasing prevalence of self-help hermeneutic based on experientialism	Lack of truth; mere experience	Divine guidance properly locates faith	Power
Cultural constructionism: cultural entrenchment that relativizes values and truth as historical and cultural	Lack of authority; mere capitulation	Kingdom values demand a culturally aware faith	Perception
Fragmented faith: absence of discipleship in life and faith	Lack of faith practice; mere verbalism	Engagement makes faith alive	Passion
Conceptual bricolage: deficiency of theological reflection for God's story of redemption in the world	Lack of reflection; mere activism	Reflection on Scripture makes faith meaningful	Perspective

Number Two: Autonomous Determinism and Mutual Disclosure

The Second Encroaching Challenge: Autonomous Determinism

Simply put, this condition comes from stories that we global northerners laud in culture—of self-made conquerors who are brave and triumph in spite of long odds against them, buoyed only by persistent resolution and personal conquest. Endemic in the American spirit, for example, is the stubborn and rugged individualist mentality. Just as the self-made person is a distortion, so is the "mind-made self" (the false assumption that humans know and act based upon only their rational thoughts), which we will more fully explore in chapter 6. Movies, media, and other sources of inspiration tout what humans can accomplish if only they put their minds and spirits to meet all the challenges that stand in their way (e.g., losing weight, getting a degree, starting a business, and experiencing spirituality). Sadly, the go-it-alone mindset is revealed to be an ultimately sad and lonely path. Yet, Robert Putnam's best seller *Bowling Alone: The Collapse and Revival of American Community* recounts how people have become increasingly detached from family, friends, neighbors, and community structures.[11]

Mark was fortunate to live for two years in beautiful Northern Ireland.[12] What he discovered was the most gracious, welcoming, convivial people anywhere he has travelled in the world. Perhaps some have a first impression of the "troubles" (as they call it) associated with violence, which have sharply diminished, though tensions persist. Despite such a past, illustrations of the kindnesses extended to him are far too numerous to recall let alone include here, but the impact of these acts has not been lost on him and has encouraged him all the more to invoke such kindness on others. Over time Mark developed a couple of (unproven) hypotheses about why their consideration was extended: first, the prevalence of the Anglican and Presbyterian Churches, which compose a substantial segment of Northern Irish population, has infiltrated society with its beautiful manifestation of kingdom hospitality;[13] and second, the area is relatively small geographically (about half the size of Indiana) and in population (less than two million). With the smaller contexts, an enhanced sense of interdependence and civility tends to characterize the social relationships; in contrast, with large populations and geographical size, the sense of close community is not commonly well developed or practiced. This phenomenon of impersonal communities can be readily observed in chat rooms and opinion-centers on the internet. When dialogues regarding news stories or ethical issues ensue, the absurdity, hostility, and ugliness of human depravity is often on full display. People, not physically present or personally known, are free to hide behind their obscurity to brandish hate and promote discordance because they are dislocated and anonymous.

Yet, the Christian faith is not meant to be experienced alone as an individually negotiated relationship with God. The nature of the Christian ethic, its doctrine, and the nature of the people of God is communal. A regrettable phenomenon of aloneness can even exist when individuals self-select megachurches and do so to remain anonymous. While it is difficult to be invisible in small churches, one can easily become intentionally disassociated from interpersonal contact and merely experience a corporate existence without personal interaction. For many, their greatest fear is exclusion, and their greatest desire is inclusion. We are fickle: how would we expect to find community while we intentionally withdraw from it?[14]

The Second Engaging Resource: Mutual Disclosure

As attested to by Putnam's most sobering observations introduced earlier, there is a tremendous desire by people who are frenetically preoccupied yet desperately lonely for authentic community that allows for self-disclosure, honesty, transparency, and trusting relationships.[15] Human beings are not meant to be alone.

However, there is one huge obstacle to mutual disclosure: people do not trust each other, and wariness has drastically increased over recent decades. A 1972 Associated Press–GfK and General Social Study found that two-thirds of US residents said that most people could be trusted, whereas in 2013, only one-third of people thought so.[16] Americans are a suspicious people. And when trust is low, the way we react and behave with each other becomes less civil. Some studies suggest it is too late for most Americans to become more trusting. That research claims the basis for a person's lifetime trust levels is set by his or her midtwenties and is unlikely to change, other than in some unifying crucible such as a world war. Some may become a little more trusting as they age, but beginning with the baby boomers, each generation has started off adulthood less trusting than those who came before them, say the AP-GfK/GSS results. There is no single explanation for Americans' loss of trust, but this is obviously a major barrier for developing relational faith.

The recent "small group movement" is now a staple within congregations with varying degrees of effectiveness. Nevertheless, Christians lament their inability to connect with people and groups that satisfy a deep longing for intimacy and genuine association where faith and life can be experienced in consort. Hear the eloquent writing from Dietrich Bonhoeffer in *Life Together: The Classic Exploration of Faith in Community* as he describes various expectations of community: "Let him who cannot be alone beware of community. . . . Let him who is not in community beware of being alone. . . . Each by itself has profound perils and pitfalls. One who wants fellowship without solitude plunges into the void of words and feelings, and the one who seeks solitude without fellowship perishes in the abyss of vanity, self-infatuation and despair."[17]

SOCIALIZATION

Socialization refers to the process of interaction between persons and their social environment that shapes self-identity, values, and worldview. While the concept has become quite common in the disciplines of anthropology, sociology, and psychology, the reality also has deep historical roots and has gained much contemporary attention in Christian education. Generally speaking, socialization is understood to involve three major interrelated and simultaneous processes.

Externalization refers to persons revealing needs, desires, capacities, and possibilities in a social environment. *Objectification* is the reification of our externalizing activity into objective social reality in the form of traditions, laws, political structures, social expectations, roles, and economic systems. *Internalization* is the personal internalizing of the social, cultural, religious, economic, and political possibilities and parameters created by externalizing and objectification and shapes self-identity, self-image, and self-consciousness. John H. Westerhoff III provided the most comprehensive definition of socialization as the lifelong formal and informal ways one generation seeks to sustain and transmit its understanding and way of life; seeks to induct its young into and reinforce for its adults a particular set of values and responsible adult roles; and seeks to help persons develop self-identity through participation in the life of a people with their more or less distinctive ways of thinking, feeling, and acting. Westerhoff also specifically defines religious socialization as a process consisting of lifelong formal and informal mechanisms, through which persons sustain and transmit their faith (worldview, value system) and lifestyle.

Socialization as an intentional strategy of formation can be traced to early Christian practice—at least to the catechetical work of the early church. Those initiated into the Christian faith were enrolled in a process of discipleship involving an extended period of sponsorship by other believers, limited participation in congregational life, and demonstration of conversion by lifestyle change. Horace Bushnell understands Christian formation of children through the organic nature of family, church, society, and state, represented by an anticipation of the modern attention given to socialization in the social sciences and in Christian education.

Subsequently, Christian educators from all theological persuasions and traditions have acknowledged the importance of socialization and developed theories and theologies of Christian formation grounded in the idea. George Albert Coe, C. Ellis Nelson, John Westerhoff III, Bernard Marthaler, Lawrence O. Richards, Thomas H. Groome, and, most recently, James K. A. Smith, among others, have all built their understandings of Christian education on some form of socialization theory. Indeed, one can hardly talk about the work of Christian education in any context or culture without taking account of the role played by socialization.

JAMES P. BOWERS

Mark and his wife are invested in a small group of trusted friends from their local church where they study the Bible and grapple with its implications for the societal, familial, and personal issues encountered.[18] His wife's innate tendency is to expose the innermost states of her anxieties and ask for input from the others in the group; Mark envies that. Regrettably, his first instinct and default tendency as a first-born child—marked with an unassailable independent streak—is to withhold expressions of his difficulties, fearing it will give him away as weak and lacking in proper self-sufficiency. He is learning to trust others more because he needs to . . . and wants to. The result of his vulnerability with others in the community of faith is always rewarded by their wisdom, affirmation, challenge, and clarity to engage life choices with greater insight than any one person has on his or her own.

Insight from Practical Theology: Participation in Christ's Body Makes Faith Operational

Involvement in a faith community describes believers' positions as colearners in a mutual quest. Community symbiotically binds us to others. Perhaps we should ask ourselves whether we really want to be bound to others, even in the name of religion. Westerners are ferociously independent and disinclined to submit to cramping restrictiveness of "others." Yet there is no other way to join Jesus than to enter his Body. Through mutual disclosure, we enter into this sustaining presence that offers interdependent kinship.

Fueled by a society that preaches we are the captains of our own destinies, some are too stubborn to acquiesce to others. And so, for the sake of nurturing faith in community, we must ask ourselves these questions: Does a democratic spirit of independence reduce the possibility of community life? Do we want to submit ourselves to community rituals?

C. Ellis Nelson describes it this way:

> Why this insistence on the communal nature of the church? Because it is by this process that faith can be incubated and nurtured. Faith is a concomitant of human association. This is why the church must be a gathering of Christians which is permanent enough to allow individuals to know each other in various facets of their life and regular enough in its meetings to be able to develop a sense of solidarity in Christ and in their mission to the world. The human interaction is the most powerful process we know for creating and sustaining values, and for shaping a distinctive style of life.[19]

Of course, some have been horribly "burned"—maltreated, even abused—by experiences in Christian community.[20] This is heartrending: a significant disruption to one's spiritual nurture furthers an already tenuous reputation held by those about the goodness of the church. Again, Bonhoeffer sheds light:

> Those who love their dream of a Christian community more than they love the Christian community itself become destroyers of that Christian community even though their personal intentions may be ever so honest, earnest and sacrificial. God hates this wishful dreaming because it makes the dreamer proud and pretentious. Those who dream of this idolized com-

munity demand that it be fulfilled by God, by others and by themselves. They enter the community of Christians with their demands set up by their own law, and judge one another and God accordingly. It is not we who build. Christ builds the church.[21]

Christian faith is nurtured in community marked by a supernatural, somewhat risky, *inspired trust*.

Through mutual disclosure, Christians grasp their *position* in the cosmos— relationally embedded in community.

Number Three: Interpretative Pluriformity and Generous Humility

The Third Encroaching Challenge: Divisive Interpretation

The fundamental themes of Luther's reforms locate the Bible as the ultimate foundation of all Christian belief and practice. But the problem that emerged (and continues still) is "How can one speak of the Bible as having any authority when it is so clearly at the mercy of its interpreters?"[22] The fundamental problem of Protestant theological identity, as Alister McGrath extrapolates, as other branches within Christianity perceived, was primarily about a certain way of doing theology that could lead to an uncontrollable diversity of outcomes. And who would have the definitive prerogative to decide what is orthodox and what is heretical? This was "a dangerous idea," McGrath argues, that opened the floodgates to "a torrent of distortion, misunderstanding, and confusion."[23]

A current example, which dominates the church where it is growing with the most global gusto, is Pentecostalism's resonance with postmodernism. Pentecostals, while affirming the traditional Protestant notion of the accessibility of the Bible and the right of every believer to interpret the text, stress the multiple dimensions of the meaning that arise—not because of the indeterminate nature of the text, but on account of the "leading of the Spirit" into the true meaning of the text, which that same Spirit originally inspired.[24] Of course, the underlying issue is the source of authority for interpreting the text and practicing the faith.

The Third Engaging Resource: Generous Humility

While divergent ways of interpreting Scripture manifest themselves within faith traditions, the church rejoices in the pluriform unity of God's revelation.

One of the primary descriptors of Christian education is its emphasis on studying the Bible. And there may be no other time where the church needs to display trust in the Holy Spirit's guidance as individual Christians and as faith communities interpret the Scriptures. Certainly, children are taught Bible verses and stories at a very young age, which has instilled in many a deep respect for God's word. However, at the same time, it seems many of these very people struggle as adults to have meaningful conversations about the most basic of biblical concepts. Interpretive skills are often forfeited to facts about the Bible and acceptance of others' interpretations. Adults may know snippets of biblical content but lack the ability to deal with the overarching themes, which restricts their ability to intelligently critique the culture around them and develop their faith. And, as a result, the ability to deal gently and faithfully with other Christians who may hold variant understandings is not a well-developed gift. Then in the face of alternate interpretations, a *de facto* ungraciousness emerges to squelch possible false teachings.

We contend, then, it is just as important *that* believers learn the Bible and theology and hermeneutical skills as it is *how* they learn it. Educators need to teach the Bible and theology not merely as additional subjects but as the *central and pervasive focus of all education* and with a nod to a gracious understanding of the breadth and value in various ways of seeing the truth of Scripture from sister faith communities. What needs converting is not just our minds but also our whole imagination, our heart's desires for God and greater trust in how the Spirit is speaking across cultures and perspectives. Such an integrated approach will provide a much-needed depth of meaning and significance to the learning experience. However, the overarching posture must model a gracious, generous humility as the church moves to faithful ways of encountering both the word and the world.

Insights from Practical Theology: Divine Guidance Properly Locates Faith

The Holy Spirit is the teacher and enables Christians with insight to see how the truth of Scripture is to be rightly interpreted and acted upon. Yet other competing interpretations creep in. How else would one explain scriptural justifications for war, slavery, church splits, bigamy, racism, bombing abortion clinics, and a virtually never-ending multitude of cultural, political, and ethical conflicts? It is no wonder theologian Stanley Hauerwas resorts to hyperbole: "No task is more important than for the Church to take the Bible out of the hands of individual Christians in North America. North American Christians are trained to believe that they are capable of reading the Bible without spiritual and moral transformation. They read the Bible not as Christians, not as a people set apart, but as democratic citizens who think their common sense is sufficient for the understanding of scripture."[25] The Bible is not simply a repository of true information about God, Jesus, and the hope of the world. It is, as Tom Wright posits, part of *the means by which,* in the power of the Spirit, the living God rescues people and the world and takes them forward on the journey toward God's new creation, making them agents of that new creation even as they travel.[26] However, as Harvard Divinity School professor Harvey Cox warns,[27] the cultural influence of the Bible today fosters a wary suspicion of current scholarship, and it makes readers fall back on a literalistic understanding of its contents.

But Scripture is authoritative: it has the power to change lives and cultures and deserves to be proclaimed with confidence. In *Scripture and the Authority of God: How to Read the Bible Today,* Wright reminds us that living with the authority of Scripture means living in that story that Scripture tells. It means soaking ourselves in that story, as a community and as individuals. It means Christian leaders and teachers must themselves become part of the process, part of the way in which God is at work not only *in* the Bible-reading community but also *through* that community in and for the wider world. The revelation of God through Scripture is the wellspring from which faith is nurtured.[28] Spirit-given wisdom is required, however, to discern the intention of Scripture and sound hermeneutical practices, and to identify duplicitous agendas proffered by those who wish to manipulate theological truth to serve narrowly held positions.

Our conviction is that the Bible has both authority and relevance, and that the secret to both is Jesus Christ. Scripture ought to be read (rightly interpreted) through the "key" of Jesus's ministry, life, death, and resurrection. Proper readings of Scripture cannot be opposed to God's self-revelation in Jesus. Secondarily, Christians look to the witness of persons and communities, past and present, who offer exemplary performances of Scripture as keys to faithful interpretations of it.

The Bible is not a weapon but an instrument of healing and reconciliation, a divine instrument that sits above cultures and religions and individuals for evaluation of them and not the reverse. A pronounced and cautious humility should be observed when attempting to speak for God. Because our love remains frail and partial—subject to our own hopes and fears—our hearing of God's voice as we read Scripture always needs testing by reference to other fellow Christians, past as well as present, and indeed other Scripture passages themselves. Listening to God's voice in Scripture does not put us in the position of having infallible opinions.

Through supernatural direction, Christians grasp their source of *power* in the cosmos—a unity of faith.

Number Four: Cultural Constructionism and Intentional Citizenship

The Fourth Encroaching Challenge: Redoubtable Postmodernism

Granted, contemporary society with its waning forgetfulness has diminished the impact of Christian education. Have social secularization and religious pluralism severely diminished the Christian consciousness and education in faith? Or, can these cultural developments open new possibilities for faithfulness and faith formation? Postmodernism is not a culture, but the fatigue of culture. It is a sign of the end of modernity, and for that reason its critique of modernity is telling. But it is not a new age, nor the sign of a new kind of culture.[29] Does this spell doom or is it an opening to a new kind of culture as the teaching of the church considers its version of truth, life, and virtue?

Sociologist Peter Berger, reflecting on a generation of theorizing about the correlation of modernity and secularization, admits he and his colleagues were wrong: *Most of the world today is not secular, but very religious.*[30] A 1997 Gallup World Poll among 160 nations (representing 97 percent of the world population, though China was excluded from the religion questions) reveals that 53 percent had attended a religious place of worship within the last seven days, and 76 percent confirmed religion was an important part of their lives.[31]

In fact, vigorous religiosity *arises along with* pluralism, Rodney Stark asserts.[32] Upsurges of Christianity coexist with—and are even due to—postmodernity. But what are the consequences of such identifications and divergent values? Despite these flashes of global spiritual arousal, unintended outcomes, curious inventions, and misshapen creatures have sometimes been produced by socially compromising attempts in faith shaping.[33]

The Christian relationship with culture has been (and continues to be) an uneasy dance.[34] Culture, for good or for ill, is the collection of practices, beliefs, and stories that carve out a sense of personal and communal identity. But the people who most carefully study culture tend to stress how much they are *transformed by it*. So, we ask with Andy Crouch, what does it mean to be more than cultural consumers but instead to be culture-makers? What does it mean to be not just culturally aware but culturally responsible? What is our calling in this or any culture? How might congregations shape cultures resistant to or resilient in response to the excesses of mass culture? If we are to be culture makers, where in the world do we begin? And how does this affect how we effectively educate Christians?[35]

The Fourth Engaging Resource: Intentional Citizenship

In spite of some humans who revel in self-sufficiency, the church could opt to rejoice and rest in the cruciform sovereignty of God in this world. The countercultural nature of the Christian kingdom, manifested without geo-political borders, has its own ethic (in the Sermon on the Mount), its own language (loving-kindness), its own epistemology (theistic revelation), and its own agenda (worship of God by service to the world). The Jewish theologian Abraham Heschel claimed that when God's creatures come together, a holy space is created between them. It is in this realm that they can always find the Creator still at work.

As postmodernism cannot ultimately satisfy the quests of the humans who search for happiness, the uncompromising beauty of the Christian life could attract previously exhausted and unfulfilled devotees to a newfound peace. And so, the church ought not shrink from engagement with the world but treat such interactions as occasions to enliven faith and commitment befitting citizenship in God's kingdom. To be properly oriented amid a wayward post-modern culture, Christian education emphasizes the true-north guidance of the Holy Spirit to negotiate our place in the world.

Insights from Practical Theology: Kingdom Values of Faith Communities Inform Cultural Awareness

Because we are embodied beings, we are also beckoned by the allure of ma-terial and sensate culture. But our membership in the heavenly realm gives Christians the ability to discriminate between their (good) materiality and material*ism*. When the apostle John sees the apocalyptic revelation from God behind the scenes of world history, his purview, enhanced by the interpretive grid from God, sees with clarity instead of "through a glass darkly" (1 Cor. 13:12). Yes, although we see only "in part" now, we are nevertheless able to interpret the ideologies of this day with greater insight than those who do not yet dwell in faithful communities. While that presumption may sound arrogant, the promise of cultural insight is enabled by the knowledge and promises of God. The Spirit guides the church to confident reliance upon the gospel, which is at the same time permeated through and through by loving humility. Much of faith formation depends, therefore, on the church learning to live (again) as the church.

Through kingdom values lived out in shared community, Christians find proper *perception* of the cosmos and clarity of vision and purpose.

Number Five: Fragmented Faith and Faithful Gestures

The Fifth Encroaching Challenge: Muddled Approaches

While Christianity has been affected by memory problems and experienced mixed influences from postmodernism, a pronounced misunderstanding persists with respect to how the church best educates Christians.[36] What, in its most basic form, is Christian education, and how is the effective nurturing of faith to occur?

One pattern that emerges from the development of Protestantism, especially as it may be influenced by Western individualism, is a seemingly endless cycle of birth, maturing, aging, and death, leading to renewal and reformulation.[37] The relentless energy and creativity of one generation gives rise to a new movement; a later generation, anxious because the original dynamism and energy of the movement appears to be dissipating, tries to preserve it by petrification—that is, by freezing the original vision in the hope that its energy will thus be preserved. Yet all too often, petrification leads to the conservation of only a structure, not the life-giving vision itself. These trends have affected the structures, strategies, and methods of Christian education to a tremendous degree.

Faith education has been subject to fluid understandings and has through the Christian centuries eventuated in less than ideal results. Once again, Dallas Willard in *The Great Omission*, lambasting the church, goes straight to the heart of the issue: "For at least several decades the churches of the Western world have not made discipleship a condition of being Christian."[38] Religious literacy is not just the accumulation of facts or memorizing and regurgitating dogma. To what extent does its meaning from previous generations relate to what would be relevant in the twenty-first century? What is the proper balance between an intellectual and experiential knowledge of faith?

Christian education, we contend, is the cultivation of wisdom and virtue by nourishing the soul on truth, goodness, and beauty, so that, in Christ, the learner is enabled to better know, glorify, and enjoy God. As Irenaeus declares, "The glory of God is the one fully alive." The central concepts to grasp regarding our Christian expressions are irreducible: *faith* that requires obedience in submission to God and in mission to the world; *hope* that sees a transcendent story of this life and the next; and *love* that binds us into a nurturing community and extends to despairing humanity (1 Cor. 13:13).

The Fifth Engaging Resource: Faithful Gestures

Despite some bungled schemes to educate Christians, the church rejoices in the faithful expression of celebrating the gifts of God. To be clear, what it means to be Christian is that we are a people who affirm locating our lives within the story of God. Hauerwas summarizes, "The Church is but God's gesture on behalf of the world to create a space and time in which we might have a foretaste of the Kingdom. It is through gestures that we learn the nature of the story that is the very content and constitution of that Kingdom. The way we learn a story, after all, is not just by hearing it. It must be acted out."[39] Simply put, Christian education is the training in those gestures through which we learn the story of God and God's will for our lives. The primary task of being educated Christianly is not the achievement of better understanding, but faithfulness. Indeed, we can come to understand only through faithfulness, as the story asks for nothing less than our lives.[40]

Insight from Practical Theology: Engagement Makes Faith Come Alive

Interaction outside the church has the potential to test, strengthen, correct, and even substantiate faith. Through this interface with other cultures, philosophies, and faith traditions, Christians find opportunities to explain the faith and often identify weaknesses in thinking, such as the perennial human tendencies toward triumphalism and self-deception. It is just this necessary form of engagement that supplies us with passion to join with God in mission.

Our faith comes alive as we confront issues, develop answers to difficult questions, witness the plethora of human need, and humbly demonstrate the life of one surrendered to Jesus. In contrast, it seems that an isolated faith is often a weak faith because it is untested and too often unused.

One significant way to facilitate faith-stretching experiences is to encourage learners to participate in cross-cultural immersions (a more intentionally educational version of mission trips). Under the guidance of good leadership, students can benefit from such endeavors. While in another country, the time should be spent engaging the culture, learning from its history, and discussing its theological assumptions. All of these will serve to broaden the students' perspective, ability to relate to others, and confidence when presented with a chance to explain the faith.

This principle should also be applied to adult congregations within Christian circles. Some adults (especially from more traditional backgrounds) struggle to appreciate or even acknowledge the genuine faith of other Christian denominations or Christian expressions in other cultures than their own.

Rather than understanding the difficult questions within the Christian faith that stimulated denominations, many well-intentioned believers find it hard to avoid judgmental attitudes (motivated often by ignorance). A widened perspective will inevitably diminish needless dogmatism and judgmentalism when discussing difficult questions.

By moving beyond the familiar, Christians grasp *passion* in the cosmos and can become partners in the mission of God.

Number Six: Conceptual Bricolage and Probing Reflection

The Sixth Encroaching Challenge: Suppressed Thinking

In sectors of the Christian family, some educational practices frustrate spiritual growth—whether intentionally or unintentionally—by devaluing, even belittling, the role of reason and critical reflection.[41] In provocative interview-based research, Ruth Tucker deduces two traits of a typical "walk away" from Christian faith: one's association with a fundamentalist or highly conservative religious background, and one's inability to grapple with philosophical, theological, or scientific challenges to Scripture's reliability.[42] What does truth, we ask, have to fear from engagement with any topic in the world? Whether out of fear or control or poor educational modeling or ignorance, some assume for the sake of unity (or uniformity?) that Christians should merely accept (in a mentally passive way) the teaching they hear in church and not question the authority of those who teach. Critical engagement with other Christians and Christian faith itself can only enhance our understanding of faith and practice. A conception of educating that plays upon acquiescence and uncritical reasoning is a standard practice of cults and other mind-control initiatives. So, why is "thinking" to be eschewed in churches, small groups, missions, parachurch ministries, and, even in some cases, theological schools?[43]

Perhaps there is a fundamental misunderstanding of the role of "knowledge" in educating Christians. In our view, one's ability to think, to analyze, to critique, and then adapt to contextual Christian practice is critical and ultimately a great deal more important than merely knowing faith facts and other trivial minutiae, even of the Bible.

Consider, for example, Jesus's educational intentions in the so-called Sermon on the Mount as a template for guiding how Christians should live as faithful sojourners.[44] Notice that Jesus taught theological principles and ethical guidelines and not primarily knowledge-oriented information. He had in mind that subsequent generations would be able to apply these values across cultures and eras. Therefore, it is perhaps more consequential today to learn the art of Christian imagination that can be enacted in changing societal conditions—that is, learning to think critically, to think theologically, to think constructively. The lasting teaching from the Sermon on the Mount comes to us in information about the kingdom of God; provides a framework to develop life skills for living in the kingdom; challenges us to pursue motivating interests in the kingdom; and commits to an alternate society based on these kingdom values. While the most desired educational result might be a changed society, the most effective means to achieve this is fostered by a Christian educational philosophy that nurtures theological thinking and application.[45]

The Sixth Engaging Resource: Probing Reflection

Christian theology means reflecting on and articulating beliefs about God and the world that Christians share as followers of Jesus. By "reflecting," Stanley Grenz and Roger Olson claim, "We use our minds to organize our thoughts and beliefs, bring them into coherence with one another by attempting to identify and expunge blatant contradictions, and make sure that there are good reasons for interpreting Christian faith in the way we do. Reflection, then, involves a certain amount of critical thinking—questioning the ways we think and why we believe and behave the way we do."[46]

Christian education should promote learning cultures where people confront intriguing sociocultural issues. The routine quest for Christian education, we advance, is to explore authentic tasks that challenge students to grapple with ideas, rethink their assumptions, and examine their mental models of reality. While teaching methods vary, these conditions are best fostered to the degree that learners feel a sense of control over their learning; work collaboratively with others; believe their contributions will be considered fairly and honestly; and receive substantial feedback.

Insight from Practical Theology: Reflection Makes Faith Meaningful

Whereas worship incubates faith and community makes faith operational, the second tent-post for Christian education is *theological reflection*, which makes faith meaningful. It is this exercise that gives Christians perspective on the meaning of Scripture and the world's issues. With the ability to reflect theologically on the questions and issues of life, a believer's faith in and relationship with God will be most meaningful. Pauw claims: "Engagement in these practices, with other people, over time, can give rise to new knowledge and new capacities for perception that are not accessible otherwise."[47]

In addition to biblical instruction and current theological understandings, it is vital for believers to learn historical theology. Past believers dealt with so many of the questions and issues that come up today, and when we ignore their insights, we rob ourselves of a wealth of knowledge and wisdom. Churches and parents could help connect a student's public education with his or her faith by teaching the church's history alongside what the student learns in class (i.e., by asking "What was the church doing at this time?"). This would also provide opportunities to correct the secularizing assumptions that undergird many modern history textbooks.

Further, regarding historical theology, Christian educators need to teach philosophy and logic not merely as parts of information but rather to *map out the development of thought throughout the history of humanity*. Humans have always had questions, and today's students (even as young as middle schoolers) are asking those same questions. As educators, we respect students more when we address their questions directly than when we ignore or patronize them with thoughtless, textbook answers. However, to faithfully follow the assumption that Scripture is our ultimate authority, the philosophy of the Bible and Christianity should be taught as the filter through which all other philosophies are critiqued. We echo Murphy: "Christians . . . must be trained to see what is going on—to become critical readers of culture."[48] With this approach, students will see why philosophers developed their ideas, what the consequences of their beliefs were, and what needs to be retained, fixed, or thrown out.

Through theological reflection, Christians grasp God's *perspective* in the cosmos—a way of wisdom for the journey.

In sum, the *content* of Christian education is the story of God that the church is called to live out, and the *task* of Christian education is to create conditions in which this story can do its transformative work. Cannon projects this call to action in this way: "Engagement in spiritual practices leads to Christ-centered action through works of justice such as service, discipleship and reconciliation. At the same time, justice-oriented action also leads back to reflection through spiritual practices such as silence, prayer and study. The correlation between reflection and increased social action is not linear. . . . The spiritual practices are recursive disciplines that simultaneously draw people closer to the heart of God through reflection and action."[49]

Distinctives of and Gifts for Nurturing Faith

Education is the creation, acquisition, transmission, and preservation of knowledge. The Christian education that nurtures faith is concerned not with the simple exchange of facts and information but with their epistemological dimensions. It is different from secular knowledge, because it is also concerned with transcendent purposes of human life. For a Christian, education is not an otiose exercise of mental faculties as in learning for learning's sake. It is purpose-driven by the urge to find meaning in existence. But unlike Buddhism and Gnosticism, knowledge itself has no salvific value in Christianity. Knowledge and education in and of themselves are not pathways to spiritual wisdom, nor do they provide the students with a moral compass or sense of existential direction.

Christian education may not necessarily be different from secular education in its pedagogy or methodology, but its origins and ends are deeper. Education is multifunctional. First, education in schools develops professional skills and talents, provides book learning from manuals, transfers ideas from teachers to students, and adapts the mind to be receptive to new experiences. In the case of Christian education, it goes one stage further and transforms the mind or, as Paul says, endows the students with a new mind—the mind of Christ. Thus, the goal of Christian education is *metanoia* or transformation or transmutation. It is said that all of us stand on the shoulders of giants. But in the case of Christian education, there is an additional factor, and that is revelation or revealed knowledge that comes through meditation, prayer, and direct communication with the divine. Without revealed knowledge, human experience remains one-dimensional. Revealed knowledge is not merely a state of knowing but also a state of being.

CRITICAL THINKING

Critical thinking in Christian education is the reflective thought and interrogation of one's beliefs, faith commitments, assumptions, traditions, and actions. The act of critical thinking involves logic: the use of sound inductive or deductive reasoning to assess the validity and value of beliefs, assumptions, claims, and actions.

Critical thinking can be traced to the Socratic method originating in ancient Greece. This dialectical method is a discourse in which individuals ask and answer questions to evaluate concepts, beliefs, and truth claims. Later, Scholasticism (1100–1500) marked a period of critical thinking that used this dialectical method to investigate and defend the dogma and teaching of the church. In contrast, during the Enlightenment (1650–1800), critical thinking emerged as the systematic challenging of traditions and assumptions using reason and scientific skepticism. Because much of this inquiry and examination was directed at the church's teaching, critical thinking during this period was seen at odds with Christian education.

In the twentieth century, following the work of Jean Piaget and John Dewey, critical thinking became an integral part of Christian pedagogy. Dewey asserted that critical thinking is suspended judgment; and the essence of this suspense is inquiry to determine the nature of the problem before proceeding to attempts at its solution. Following this theme of inquiry, critical thinking in Christian education was further enhanced by the insights of critical theorists, notably the Frankfurt School, and later educational theorists such as Paulo Freire, among others. These theorists came to identify critical thinking as both integral to the process of education and a crucial outcome of critical pedagogy. No pedagogue's work has had more of an impact on critical thinking in Christian pedagogy than Paulo Freire. Most notably his works *Education for Critical Consciousness* (1974) and *Pedagogy of the Oppressed* (1970) laid the foundation for pedagogical concepts in Christian education such as problem-posing education, conscientization, and dialogical education.

Given this history, critical thinking in Christian pedagogy is regarded in three distinct ways: (1) critical thinking is a skill to be learned, (2) which involves examining the lived experience of the learner, (3) and is a dialectical experience among a community of learners that can lead to the transformation of the particular historical situation, similar to notions of critical reflection.

Today, critical thinking in Christian education reflects Henry Giroux's definition of critical pedagogy that it is about more than a struggle over assigned meanings, official knowledge, and established modes of authority. It is also about encouraging students to take risks, act on their sense of social responsibility, and engage the world as an object of both critical analysis and hopeful transformation. Following this reasoning, critical thinking in Christian pedagogy is a dialectical method with the purpose of social and ecclesial transformation. In order to engender critical thinking and advance Christian education, this definition invites critical inquiry and investigation of its epistemological foundations, definitive claims, and tacit assumptions.

PATRICK BRUNER REYES

Education thus has profound theological significance, and even the early apostolic fathers realized it. Justin Martyr founded the first Christian school in the first century. For him, as well as the great Christian educators who followed him, education was the principal conduit for the transmission of knowledge and the most powerful instrument for Christian growth and maturity. Faith and knowledge are intimately connected. The metaphor most used in the Scriptures to represent knowledge is light, because light illuminates the world and dispels darkness. In Proverbs, the fear of the Lord is the beginning of knowledge, and Samuel uses the term "a God of knowledge" (1 Sam. 2:3). Hosea laments that people are perishing for lack of knowledge. In the New Testament, Christ calls himself "the light of the world" (John 8:12).

Thus, Christian education, ultimately, is unlike any other educational venture in the cosmos. No other curricular enterprise has equivalent content (revelation, including through Scripture), goals (Christocentric transformation), and dynamic (power of the Holy Spirit). It is distinct in what it attempts, and it dispatches extraordinary gifts to accomplish the task. (See the chart below.)

The Christian faith is outrageously astonishing in that the God of the universe wants to know us and be known by us. The task of Christian education, then, is nothing less than seizing a most inconceivable, even implausible idea: humans become intimate with divinity . . . and *vice versa*!

Encroaching Challenges to Nurturing Faith	Engaging Resources for Nurturing Faith	Exclusive Uniquenesses of Nurturing Faith	Extraordinary Gifts for Nurturing Faith	Expounded in Chapter Number
Disorienting amnesia	Meaningful commemorations	Penetrating Scripture	Transformative hope	5
Autonomous determinism	Mutual disclosure	Interdependent kinship	Inspired trust	6
Interpretive pluriformity	Generous humility	Resurrected image	Restorative grace	7
Cultural constructionism	Intentional citizenship	Supernatural guidance	Countercultural faith	8
Fragmented faith	Faithful gestures	Focused proclamation	Fortifying love	9
Conceptual bricolage	Probing reflection	Discerning community	Principled freedom	10

Here is how J. I. Packer spins it:

> Why has God spoken? . . . The truly staggering answer which the Bible gives to this question is that God's purpose in revelation is to *make friends* with us. It was to this end that He created us rational beings, bearing His image, able to think and hear and speak and love; He wanted there to be genuine personal affection and friendship, two-sided, between Himself and us . . . He speaks to us simply to fulfill the purpose for which we were made; that is, to bring into being a relationship in which He is a friend to us, and we to Him, He finding His joy in giving us gifts and we finding ours in giving Him thanks.[50]

In this chapter, we have chronicled encroaching factors that impede the divine-human "friendship" from flourishing as intended. However, the Christian education enterprise offers supernatural Spirit-given resources to accomplish the reality of Psalm 78:4–7, quoted at the beginning of this chapter—hope, trust, grace, faith, love, and freedom:

- While loss of Christian memory diminishes effectiveness in the educational task, Jesus remains the source of revealed truth for living. This alone, and the story it tells, provides a *transforming hope* that casts out fear and extends eternity to earth. (See chapter 5.)
- While collaboration and insight from intimate associations in the community of faith take effort and submission, the nature of faith is best lived with inspired trust placed in *interdependent kinship*—the gift of others. (See chapter 6).
- While some branches of the Christian education over- or underemphasize various interpretations of Scripture and, in some cases, bow to postmodern patterns of subjectivism, the church is being transformed into the image of Jesus, which nevertheless may have a spectrum of perspectives. We are comforted by God's resurrection miracle of *restorative grace* in our lives. (See chapter 7.)
- While modern cultural settings steer persons away from God, Christian education relies upon the supernatural guidance of the Spirit of holiness to keep the church grounded. This posture takes a *countercultural faith* that lives both within and beyond human understanding. (See chapter 8.)
- While practices of Christian education sometimes falter in a focused integration of the story of God, the infusion of the practice of relentless, gracious, *fortifying love* is the most powerful educator in faithful compassion to each other and the world. (See chapter 9.)
- While critical thinking seems undervalued in educating Christians, the nature of the church is collectively a discerning community who together reason with godliness. The result is a *principled freedom* to experience reality as God intended humans to abide. (See chapter 10.)

Conclusion

In our quest to nurture faith, we celebrate *people*: people who embark upon the opportunity for teaching and learning the historical and vibrant faith. Christian education is as much about engendering intimacy in human relationships nurtured by faith as it is about articulated parsing or indoctrinating systems of belief. Although the inspired truth of the gospel is persuasive, the beckoning love, unremitting concern, and personal involvement in the lives of people are also extremely forceful.

Whereas postmodern culture and other factors may impact the spiritual dimensions of the mission of the church, we seek wisdom to apply human development research, theological scholarship, and educational theory and practice for the creative and faithful application of biblical truth to permeate the values of children, adolescents, and adults, as well as families, faith communities, institutions, voluntary associations, and societal structures, recognizing dimensions of our communal and corporate lives in the deeply meaningful, life-affirming, radicalizing Christian way.

Interactive Dialogue

1. Why are Westerners so intent on being individualistic in life and faith when the hope of authentic community is one of humans' deepest longings? Why is it so difficult for Christians to develop intimate spiritual relationships? Share a personal story of community-found or community-lost.

2. The authors suggest that a generous humility must be displayed in how Christians interpret Scripture and practice faithful living. How can that practically be achieved in a way that maintains a high view of Scripture and truth, given our postmodern context?

3. Which of the six practices suggested to counteract the six challenges to nurturing faith is most necessary for your faith community to improve the quality of Christian formation? How might that be accomplished?

For Further Reading

Groome, Thomas H. *Will There Be Faith? A New Vision for Educating and Growing Disciples*. San Francisco: HarperOne, 2011.

Murphy, Debra Dean. *Teaching That Transforms: Worship as the Heart of Christian Education*. Grand Rapids: Brazos, 2004.

Pauw, Amy Plantinga. "Attending to the Gaps between Beliefs and Practices." In *Practicing Theology: Beliefs and Practices in Christian Life*. Edited by Miroslav Volf and Dorothy C. Bass. Grand Rapids: Eerdmans, 2002.

Roberts, Carlos C. *Christian Education Teaching Methods—From Modern to Postmodern: Teaching the Faith to Post-Moderns*. Bloomington, IN: AuthorHouse, 2009.

Saliers, Don E. "Liturgy and Ethics: Some New Beginnings." In *Liturgy and the Moral Self: Humanity at Full Stretch Before God*. Edited by Bryon Anderson and Bruce Morrill. Collegeville, MN: Liturgical, 1998.

Wilson, Douglas, ed. *Repairing the Ruins: The Classical and Christian Challenge to Modern Education*. Moscow, ID: Canon, 1996.

Part Two

Criteria for Nurturing Faith

A recent scientific paper—by Edward Dutton, of the Ulster Institute for Social Research in the United Kingdom, and Dimitri Van der Linden, of Rotterdam University in the Netherlands—suggests that atheists are more intelligent than people who believe in God. Not because one belief system is more correct but because atheists can overcome the *instinct* of religion.[1]

These authors propose that if religion can rightly be considered "an instinct," then intelligent people have the ability to overcome mere impulse, sensate intuition, innate urges; in other words, in this case, they can resist placing unqualified belief in symbolic divine beings or gods.[2] Being intelligent by embracing atheism—tending toward reason and logic, seeking empirical proof, not yielding to sentimentality—helps people rise above their lesser yearnings. For Dutton and Van der Linden, then, to embrace faith in God is an instinct to be sublimated, and those who cannot do this are simply less intelligent. What does that say about the brainpower of Jesus and, well, you, and all those who live by faith? Admittedly, living by faith may appear not to be reasonable, and defy logic, but intelligence is neither a spiritual gift nor one of the keys to the kingdom.[3] Without apology, Christianity demands *resilient trust, childlike innocence,* and *audacious faith*—a foolhardy concept to those who want assurances rested in proof.

For example, in AD 203 in Roman Carthage, a twenty-two-year-old woman, still breastfeeding her infant child, was brought before the local administrator. Her name was Vibia Perpetua, and her crime was belonging to the emerging cult of Christianity.[4]

Perpetua squared off against the Roman procurator—a midlevel government bureaucrat, playing the role of Christian-hunting inquisitor—and a small assembly of gawkers. She was given every opportunity to recant her faith. But she would not. When asked point-blank whether she was a Christian, Vibia Perpetua signed her own death sentence, asserting, *Christiana sum* (Latin for "I'm a Christian").

Her prosecutor was seemingly confounded by her decision to die for her faith, desperately urging her to recant. The procurator pleaded, "Have pity on your father's grey head; have pity on your infant son. Offer the sacrifice for the welfare of the emperors." She didn't and was martyred by the sword.

A modern reader may share this bafflement. Like, "Do it! Just cross your fingers and repudiate Christ! You have a kid! It's not worth it! Apostatize! C'mon!" Maintaining a vital, unapologetic faith in a world that treats it as infantile is difficult. One is tempted to capitulate and slide into a skeptical mode—to substitute rational thought for faith.

Faith was patently the current, the content, of Jesus's curriculum—not knowledge, not rationalized discourse, and not kowtowing to what appeared reckless by others. An overarching theme of the master teaching endeavor of Jesus was his intentional engagement with willing and unwilling learners: to test their confidence in what was hoped for and to demonstrate assurance about what was not seen (Heb. 11:1). This was Jesus's strategy for nurturing faith— *growing in faith by becoming faithful*. Not only did his life and decisions model the nature of faith in his Father, but also the dialogue and circumstances most often recorded in the Gospels evidence the centrality of having unreserved, seemingly rash, faith in spite of the circumstances—for example, seekers were healed because of it, followers were raised from the dead as a consequence of it, and apostles walked on water as a demonstration of it. All due to faith.

How can a person of faith not be moved by these testimonies of faith— convictional belief translated into gritty action—exhorting perseverance in spite of our life struggles, which are negligible in comparison to those of these heroes:

> And what more shall I say? I do not have time to tell about Gideon, Barak, Samson and Jephthah, about David and Samuel and the prophets, who *through faith* conquered kingdoms, administered justice, and gained what was promised; who shut the mouths of lions, quenched the fury of the flames, and escaped the edge of the sword; whose weakness was turned to strength; and who became powerful in battle and routed foreign armies. Women received back their dead, raised to life again. There were others who were tortured, refusing to be released so that they might gain an even better resurrection. Some faced jeers and flogging, and even chains and imprisonment. They were put to death by stoning; they were sawed in two; they were killed by the sword. They went about in sheepskins and goatskins, destitute, persecuted and mistreated—the world was not worthy of them. They wandered in deserts and mountains, living in caves and in holes in the ground. (Heb. 11:32–38)

If the reader has achieved such a mentality, you probably do not need to finish this book; if the reader has some ground to gain, then, by all means, follow with us the rest of the way. Thomas Groome, one of our "response" contributors, identifies three modes of engaging religion (in general) and the Christian faith (in particular): learning *about* it, learning *from* it, and *becoming* it.[5] These complement our three meanings of faith discussed earlier in this book's introduction (see pp. 11–12). To settle for the first two seems like a lost opportunity.[6] Faith is to be enfleshed, incarnated—as Jesus has shown us.

To nurture faith that evokes the unshakeable life force expected by Jesus and demonstrated by the heroes above, a sound understanding of how theology drives our practices is vital. Part 2 explores major categories of Christian doctrine, with an eye to translating this grounded belief into practical means for believers to morph into intentional followers, obedient disciples, and faithful pilgrims in a world that tells a radically alternate story of life, meaning, and purpose.

Part	Theme
1	Cultural Dynamics for Nurturing Faith
2	**Criteria for Nurturing Faith** › **Revelation and Hope (chapter 5)** › **Humanity and Trust (chapter 6)** › **Jesus and Grace (chapter 7)** › **Community and Faith (chapter 8)** › **Virtue and Love (chapter 9)** › **Reflection and Freedom (chapter 10)**
3	Colleagues in Nurturing Faith
4	Contexts for Nurturing Faith
5	Conversations in Nurturing Faith

The fact is, each culture creates, sustains, and defends its own tales—self-justifying stories that drive its moral, social, and even religious climate. Some stories are so embedded in our collective consciousness that we may not even be fully aware of how greatly we have been conditioned to unquestionably serve them. The reality is that Christians have another story—a greater story, a transcendent story—that trumps stories of nationalism and ethnic exclusion. A story so incredible, so beyond what seems sensible that it takes supernatural faith to believe it and practice it. Christians are new citizens, who speak a new language and embody a new set of militant values that challenge other human stories. Regrettably, yet undeniably, many Christians consider themselves first as geographical citizens of a human country rather than citizens of the kingdom of God.

The main tenets of the Christian way, set out in chapters 5 through 10, explain why hope from divine revelation, trust from human kinship, grace through Jesus's cruciform resurrection, faith through supernatural reconciliation, love through virtuous joy, and freedom through reflective wisdom are the most compelling reasons to experience the mission of God and fight against disorienting amnesia, autonomous determinism, interpretive pluriformity, social constructionism, fragmented faith, and conceptual bricolage.

CHAPTER FIVE

Revelation, Experience, and the Hope
of Profound Transformation

To infinity and beyond!

—(THEOLOGIAN!?) BUZZ LIGHTYEAR IN *TOY STORY*

For God so loved the world that he gave his one and only Son, that who-ever believes in him shall not perish but have eternal life.

—JOHN 3:16

ROAD MAP

This chapter explores the nature of God, revelation, and human experience in light of the present challenge of "disorienting amnesia." Nurturing faith in Christian communities presumes the existence of a divine being who is up to something good. We name this being-in-action "God." God is creator, we declare, and is above us and beyond us, yet in relation to us. But how do we know? Imagining ourselves to be rational beings, we may attempt to reason as much, positing a "first cause," an "unmoved mover," a big bang of a God who creatively kick-starts the universe. Yet reasoning to or from a first cause can take us only so far. For example, what about the relationship part? Reason appears to require a God who is exclusively other than creation, distant from creation, one who completely transcends the creation in order to cause this cosmic effect. How can such a remote God be said to be in relation with creation? For that matter, how would we even notice a God who utterly transcends the limits of our experience? Do amoebas know what an elephant is?

Introduction

The crucial theological term Christians use to address questions posed above is *revelation*. We claim that God bridges the gap between divine transcendence and creaturely finitude through God's initiative, God's self-revealing, a "how do you do" of cosmic proportions. Enter Jesus Christ. Speaking theologically, Jesus is at once the content of Christian revelation, the means of Christian revelation, and the key to interpreting multiple revelatory modes. Christ as revelation of God enables creatures not only to know God as fully as God intends but also to discover themselves to be among God's beloved, a cure for disorienting amnesia. Hence, revelation offers the hope of personal and social transformation.

This chapter explores shades of meanings and implications of the doctrine of revelation (the classics as well as emerging insights) for the purpose of discerning the doctrine's relation to the ministry of nurturing faith. (See the chart below.) It considers the content and means of revelation and offers a preliminary account of faithful responsiveness to revelation. Along the way, we seek to reclaim revelation as a legitimate epistemological category (a way of knowing truth), one whose mediating sources include Scripture, tradition, and the lived experience of the church.

To that end, we first invite faith-formational leaders into the ongoing theological conversation about revelation. We judge it better for leaders to reflect upon nuanced and sometimes competing claims for revelation than to operate out of unreflective assumptions. Second, the chapter presumes a relationship, imaginative not mechanical, between the content and means of God's self-revealing and the ministries of nurturing faith in a revealing God. Finally, the chapter considers the "reveal-ees." How does revelation involve creatures, especially human ones? How can it transform them? What role, if any, do humans play in receiving or responding to revelation? How may revelatory truth be distinguished from falsehood? The chapter concludes with three specific implications of revelation for the ministry of nurturing faith.

Encroaching Challenges to Nurturing Faith	Engaging Resources for Nurturing Faith	Exclusive Uniquenesses of Nurturing Faith	Extraordinary Gifts for Nurturing Faith
▸ Disorienting amnesia	Meaningful commemorations	Penetrating Scripture	Transformative hope
Autonomous determinism	Mutual disclosure	Interdependent kinship	Inspired trust

Encroaching Challenges to Nurturing Faith	Engaging Resources for Nurturing Faith	Exclusive Uniquenesses of Nurturing Faith	Extraordinary Gifts for Nurturing Faith
Interpretive pluriformity	Generous humility	Resurrected image	Restorative grace
Social constructionism	Irresistible citizenship	Supernatural guidance	Countercultural faith
Fragmented faith	Faithful gestures	Focused proclamation	Fortifying love
Conceptual bricolage	Probing reflection	Discerning community	Principled freedom

Coming to Terms with Revelation

Scripture and the theological tradition offer rich and varied characterizations of revelation. Sometimes described in terms of "God's mighty acts in history," "sacramental presence," or as "saving knowledge," each portrayal signals nuanced imagining about the meaning of revelation, the God who reveals, and how the creation participates in it. This brief "coming to terms" with revelation sets the stage for the more explicit theologizing to follow.

Terms such as *disclosure* and *unveiling* signal revelation's origins beyond the limits of human knowledge.[1] God is the ultimate mystery, and only God can make Godself known. These terms also at least imply the blessed character of revelation; shared from beyond, it bears the nature of *gift*.[2] As we shall see, the gift of revelation offers an apprehension of reality that would otherwise escape us. Revelation offers transformational imaginative possibilities.

The word *encounter* provides additional insight.[3] It suggests that God's revelation, in addition to being a gift from God, consists of the gift of God's relational *presence*. God shows up to the world. God, who transcends material, social, and historic reality, nevertheless participates in it.

Confrontation, a term favored by twentieth-century Reformed theologian Karl Barth, further qualifies the nature of this revelatory encounter.[4] The active force of his language makes plain that God is not present as an impartial observer. Confrontation connotes judgment upon creation. Principally, however, Barth believed confrontation to consist of an intervention in and through Jesus Christ, resulting in the transformation of the world. Whereas human beings have made a mess of their own history (hence their desire to escape or forget the past), Jesus Christ reveals God's initiative to redeem history and to inaugurate God's realm. Contemporary theologians describe God's confrontation in light of God's *mission* (*missio Dei*).[5] Through revelation, we discover God to be an agent, an actor, one who is working toward the culmination of God's good intent and whose work we humans may join.

Evident in this survey of terms, Christians perceive God's revelatory engagement as more than a cosmic public service announcement; instead of "I EXIST," revelation intends *relationship*, "I AM WITH YOU!" "First cause" and "unmoved mover" fail at this point. Focused on logical necessities, they transact their business in the economy of limitless power and transcendence of being. In contrast, Christian revelation suggests that the God who exists enters into *communion* with creation. To be sure, God is more than personal, but God is never only a limitless force, the impossible possibility, the cosmological constant, or whatever abstraction reason can conjure. God does not allow humanity to remain lost in its forgetfulness.

Collectively, these terms also depict revelation as *loving* through and through. God comes from beyond the world to save the world. God seeks creation's prospering. In contemporary terms, God's self-revelation pursues the *flourishing* of creation.[6] This revelation is transformational. It makes clear the difference between the present and God's promised future. It grounds Christian hope.

Christ as Content *of Revelation*

The Scriptures, especially the four canonical Gospels and the writings of Paul, witness to Jesus as the revelation of God. Similar to visual artists, the biblical writers shape literary "portraits" of Jesus, each with its own unique emphasis. The author of Mark, for example, depicts a young man in a hurry to announce God's coming realm—notice how many times the adverb *immediately* appears in the text—but whose identity remains mostly a mystery to his followers. Their best reckoning suggests he is like the prophets of Israel's past condemning injustice, warning of God's judgment, bringing good news of inclusion to God's beloved—widows, orphans, and sojourners—plus healing the sick and freeing the imprisoned. Only at the very end comes the emerging awareness, "Truly this man was the Son of God" (Mark 15:39). Mark's Gospel makes us privy to the first-century church's dawning (and mind-bending) revelatory insight: The one who announces God's kingdom actually *embodies* this kingdom. Jesus the proclaimer of good news becomes Christ proclaimed as good news. If you want to know God, then take up your cross and join yourself to Jesus.

By adding fulsome accounts of Jesus's advent and resurrection, Matthew and Luke deepen the church's insight into the Son's divine origins and identity.

They also demonstrate how the revelation of Jesus's divine sonship is filtered through social and cultural lenses. Scholars agree that Matthew was writing for a largely Jewish community, hence his development of the "Jesus as new Moses" motif. Luke, whose community was mostly gentile, and who himself was a physician, portrays Jesus as the "great physician."

The Gospel of John clarifies Jesus's divine status. To John, he is the preexistent Word, God's creative power become flesh. John also hints at the manner of Jesus's resurrected presence to the faith community through sacramental means, the bread that satisfies all hungers, the wine that exudes divine presence, and the living water that quenches all thirst.

Paul concentrates on Jesus's saving work. He portrays Jesus as the one who battles the powers of sin and death, ultimately defeating them through his own death and resurrection. Baptismal incorporation into Christ's body transforms persons into the "new creation" and joins them together in a new form of sociality, the church, where they strive to live faithful to Christ until he returns.

Much more could be said about biblical portraits of Jesus's identity. The writer of Hebrews, for example, portrays Jesus as the great high priest, interceding on behalf of humankind before the Father (Heb. 4:14–16). We need not be exhaustive in our descriptions to draw the conclusion that, so far as the Scriptures are concerned, Jesus reveals God because, mysteriously, Jesus *is* God. The content of revelation is a person, Christ crucified and risen.

Christ as Means of Revelation

The doctrines of incarnation and Trinity are critical to discerning how Christ is also the means of God's revelation. Although the New Testament canon crystallized by the fourth century, the church continued to ponder the mystery of God revealed in and through the life, death, and resurrection of Jesus. Jesus's full divinity and full humanity were affirmed in the doctrine of the incarnation, his triunity with Father and Spirit hammered out in church councils of the fourth and fifth centuries. These formal descriptions not only reveal God as related to creation but also explain how the Godhead is fundamentally a being-in-relation.

The doctrine of the Trinity reveals God as three persons so deeply in love with one another as to constitute a unity. John of Damascus (eighth century) describes this quality of relationship as a dance of ecstasy.[7] Imagine each partner leaping with joy in perfectly choreographed step with the other two. Their dance of love reveals the harmony of each person freely giving themselves and freely receiving the others as gift. That the Godhead is a relationship constituted by a superabundance of love means that its nature is to seek relationships with other beings, including human ones. Christ is the exemplar of divine relationality.

Equally important is the incarnation. In an act of loving condescension, God takes on flesh in the person of Jesus of Nazareth. God becomes relatable in terms that we creatures ourselves may naturally comprehend. In Jesus, God assumes human form. Jesus shares human flesh and blood.

In the 1997 movie *Contact* (perhaps the longest film ever produced without an intermission), Jodi Foster plays a scientist listening through radio telescopy for evidence of extraterrestrial intelligent life.[8] It arrives in the form of computerized code for building a space travel device, one that will take a human being to meet these intergalactic neighbors. After endless squabbling, construction delays, and very little film editing, Ms. Foster herself finally sets sail. The moment of contact comes in an ethereal scene without much gravity around. The ET appears to Ms. Foster in the form of her beloved father. "We thought it would be easier for you this way," the ET explains. Here Hollywood emulates incarnation.

The ideas embedded in the doctrines of the incarnation and Trinity are also suggestive of the nature of this divine personal relationship with creation. Jewish philosopher Martin Buber helps at this point by contrasting relations of two kinds: "I-Thou" with "I-It."[9] In the "I-It," knowing subjects (ourselves, for example) establish relationship with some other by distancing ourselves from it. Figuratively speaking, we hold the other up for inspection at arm's length and then spin it on our fingers like a basketball. In this way, we turn this other into an object of our scrutiny, which may then be reduced to our description of it. This form of relationship projects the "I's" mastery over the "it." For example, objectifying relations turn a human patient fighting for life in a hospital intensive care unit into "the pancreatic cancer in 3-A."[10] With respect to revelation, this "I-it" way of relating is a problem, as it tempts humans to think of relationships in abstract terms that can be distilled to a set of principles or propositions. When humans objectify God, however, God easily becomes the object of human preferences and manipulations. That moves theologian Douglas John Hall to rejoin, "the Emmanuel who will be 'with us' will not be possessed by us."[11]

Buber insists, therefore, that God and humans share an "I-thou" relationship. This is the case in part because even as God is revealed, God remains hidden. God may never be mastered or reduced to an object. Instead, God is the "eternal thou" who relates to human creatures subject to subject. As theologian Noel Leo Erskine puts it, revelation ultimately "is not the sharing of information but the communication of one mind to another."[12] This communication implies mutuality, reciprocity, and love in the revelation of divine-human relationship. It insists upon the irreducible integrity of the relating parties. Just as God comes to us in love and not coercion, human beings dare not invoke God for their self-serving ends.

In summary, revelation is God's gift in the person and work of Jesus Christ. Revelation includes content (it is good *news* after all!), but, finally, the news is of a relational God doing what God does—seeking relationship in love. Revelation is God's loving self-offering of communion with creation in and through Jesus, who teaches his disciples to pray to "Abba" (Father) by the power of the Holy Spirit. It reveals human beings as woven into God's story of creation, redemption, and fulfillment of history. It locates us in the cosmos (creatures not creators); it provides us an identity (God's beloved, little sisters and brothers of Jesus).

Mediating Sources of Revelation

Historically, Christians have utilized a variety of sources and patterns of experiencing to open themselves to meeting the divine. These include corporate worship and other Christian practices, such as contemplation, engagement with the Scriptures, ecstatic union with the Spirit, imitating Christ and the saints who exemplify Christly virtue, and discerning the Spirit's promptings to the human heart to "do justice, love kindness, and walk humbly" with the Lord (Mic. 6:8). Christians often describe their apprehensions of revelation in sensory and experiential terms: "hearing God's voice," "seeing the vision," "following in Christ's way," or "feeling the Spirit's promptings" in their minds or hearts. The mediating sources of revelation most often named usually include some combination of the following: Scripture, tradition, reason, and experience. Together these sources respond to the crisis of disorienting amnesia by inviting persons to locate themselves within communities who see in them a blessed past and the promise of a hope-filled future.

Scripture

Christians look to the Bible, their holy Scriptures, as a primary source of revelation. The Scriptures disclose the paradigmatic story of God: God's creation, God's covenant relationship with Israel, the grafting of gentiles into Israel's promise through the life, death, and resurrection of Jesus, and the Spirit-born church making pilgrimage toward God's reign. Proponents of scriptural revelation also claim a relational character to this revelatory content—the living word of God *addresses* hearers through the words of Scripture.

The church has always upheld the entire Bible, including the Old and New Testaments as revelational. Even as Jesus becomes the church's interpretive "key" for receiving biblical revelation, the church rightly acknowledges the necessity of the record of the faith of Israel for making any sense of Jesus.

Christian students of Scripture who believe the Old Testament to be irrelevant to their study misread the New Testament and diminish the revelatory potential of the Bible.

Whereas Scripture is critical to any account of revelation, a little historical context is in order. Protestant Christians tend to forget that the church was born and prospered for roughly three centuries without a formal New Testament. Undoubtedly, many first- and second-century communities read and interpreted letters of Paul and what became canonical Gospels in their worship, but it would be historically inaccurate to say that the Bible in its present form has always been considered the exclusive source of revelation. Second, as noted, the Bible was read in the context of the liturgy. Believers did not possess Bible apps—not to mention the fact that most couldn't read. The Bible originally offered its revelatory power in worship in concert with other liturgical means, including the sacraments.

Tradition

Tradition is the name given to the practices and teachings of the Christian church. Some Christian communities separate the Bible from tradition, and others include the Bible within tradition. Consistent with their devaluation of the past, moderns typically associate tradition with moldy books gathering dust in a dark library basement. Contemporary Protestants are also at least dimly aware that they are not supposed to like tradition either, though for theological more than asthmatic reasons. With prompting, they recall Martin Luther's declaration for *sola scriptura*, "Scripture alone," Scripture over and against tradition, as the sole trustworthy source of revelation.[13]

Luther's criticisms of corrupted traditions of the church's life in his day were undeniably just, but they served to diminish other more constructive contributions of tradition. Luther imagined discontinuity between the churches of the New Testament and those that followed them. Yet the records of these slightly later (but still ancient) churches of antiquity show that they understood themselves to be in continuity with the faith of their forebears. It was self-evident to the church of antiquity that God's revelation was active in community worship, inclusive of word and sacrament, in its evangelical success, in the continuing discernment and written doctrinal statements of God's triune identity and upon Jesus as incarnate of God, and in the courage of church leaders who persisted in faith by resisting the Roman Empire on one side and heretics on the other. Ignatius (first century) and Justin (second century), for example, not only led churches through difficult times but also contributed (inspired?) theological treatises on the nature and practice of Christian faith. Modern Christians read their Scriptures through the interpretive lenses of these and other church fathers and mothers even as their historical amnesia blinds them to this reality. To drill down on the continuity issue, just as in the case of the biblical apostles, many of the greatest church leaders of antiquity sealed their witness in martyrdom.

None of this negates Luther's critique or the primary importance of Scripture. If anything, the Bible's witness to the original and transformative revelation of Jesus grows in proportion to the ever-widening historical gap between then and now. Even so, where Luther's rallying cry *sola scriptura* helped launch a Reformation, what he actually bequeathed to the church was more than a return to Scripture unvarnished by the accretion of tradition; he also beckoned a return to an already traditioned reading of Scripture to which he himself contributed! Contemporary Protestants take for granted that they are "justified by faith," for example, because of Luther's own "traditioned" and "traditioning" readings of Scripture.[14]

"Dead" tradition turns turn out to be alive after all. Emphasizing its dynamism, moral philosopher Alasdair MacIntyre paints tradition as an "argument extended through time" about the goods of the tradition.[15] In MacIntyre's view, tradition is not made from granite; instead the tradition is the church's continuing conversation about what constitutes the tradition.

Because tradition is dynamic, it invites prophetic (re)interpretation of God's story. Following Walter Brueggemann, we are convinced that when this story is entrusted exclusively to the courtiers of the king, to the powerful and privileged in other words, it becomes ossified and distorted.[16] Presuming God's favor, the rich and powerful of the Global North declare without a trace of irony, "the state of the union is strong!" And we hear this while the poor lose access to education, jobs, and health care, our earth home is treated like an apple for the picking, and (in our own country at least) the implicit power of whiteness operates to determine all that is true, good, and beautiful in the world. Beginning with the prophets of Israel and continuing through Saint Francis to Martin Luther to MLK to Maya Angelou, the tradition of the prophets repeatedly reclaims the truth of the paradigmatic scriptural stories for God's redemption of those who cry out of their suffering. Discerning God's continuing revelation will require learning to listen to these traditioning voices.

Reason

As Christianity spread westward into Greco-Roman culture, a revived Neoplatonism attempted a synthesis between the logic of Athens and the passions of Jerusalem for early Christianity. Reason came to be regarded as pointing beyond an abstract metaphysics to the holy Trinity. Reason also provided the nuanced language critical to fighting heresy.

Further, reason can extend the implications of God's revelation into settings that trusted sources do not address. Reason was employed to determine the status of baptized Christians who lapsed under Roman persecution or, more recently, in the effort to explain the moral limits of warfare.

But reason can lead to cleverness more than to wisdom. Hence Christians need also learn how to attend to reasons of the heart where reason is bent to the service of love. The apostle Paul exercises reason in service of love when he determines not to flaunt his freedom from the law. Though Paul reasons that he is free to eat meat sacrificed to idols, he abstains in order to spare less mature brothers and sisters moral confusion (1 Cor. 8).

As noted in the introduction, however, a God conjured by reason alone tends to wind up being characterized by speech that struggles to express ideas that go beyond our earthly sense of limits: infinity, immutability, and eternity. The most reason can say about God by itself is "God is not like us." Historically, this has led to a devaluation of all things material and human. Infinity beats rock, paper, and scissors every time. When, due to the excesses of philosophical reason, transcendence swallows immanence, eternity holds time captive, and the spiritual realm escapes the material, the consequences have been detrimental to finite, temporal, material creatures.

Experience

To this growing list (Scripture, tradition, reason) John Wesley—who in the eighteenth century founded the movement called "Methodism"—added experience.[17] In contrast to what he characterized as the empty "shell of religion" in the English state church, Wesley encouraged believers to seek God's loving presence through spiritual experience.

Wesley, therefore, advocated participation in "means of grace" for perceiving God's relational love. Wesley believed that persons could experience the grace of God's loving relational presence through sacramental worship, Bible study, accountability groups, service with the poor, even through singing wild and crazy *hymns*! As Henry Knight explains, these means were not only sources of God's loving presence for Wesley, but they also revealed God's triune identity and missional purposes.[18]

EXPERIENCE

Aristotle (384–322 BC) postulated an intellectual meaning to both human experience and cognitive development. John Locke's epistemological theory and John Stuart Mill's utilitarianism, which emphasizes individual freedom to pursue the experience of happiness, set the foundation for the experiential learning theory in the eighteenth and the nineteenth centuries. The premise of experiential learning theory is that knowledge is formed and executed subject to individual experience.

John Dewey argued that personal experience should be considered within the framework of learning, in his book *Experience and Education* (1938). More recently, two major theories provoked a paradigm shift to a traditional discourse of learning: *Multiple Intelligence Theory* by Howard Gardner and *Experiential Learning Theory* by David Kolb. The premise of these two theories is that the fusion of knowledge (cognition) and experience (behavior) form intellectual development. The traditional view of intelligence includes only logic and cognition. Robert Stemberg also argued that individual experience and cultural context differentiate individual learning style and its outcome. As a social entity, a person carries social practice and experiences into learning and the formation of intelligence; navigation of environmental context, personal choices, family and cultural experiences, and religious practices influence the blend of complex human intelligence.

In a similar way, Scripture does not offer either-or choices but includes human experience, reason, and tradition. Experience is a critical source for both Christian education and theology. The revelation of God through Scripture should be interpreted according to the signs of the time, including human experiences, which can be explained with reason and expressed through traditions. This does not mean that we deny the primacy of canonical heritage as the normative source of Christian education. Incorporation of human experience in the pedagogy of Christian education enables educators and learners to avoid a dichotomy between theological assumptions and the practice of faith. Empirical pedagogy allows Christian education to be a living theology, which provokes action along with faith development through education. John Wesley, founder of Methodism, considered human experience essential for keeping theology a practical discipline. Practical theology is based on a new pedagogy that starts with human experience, reflects on a theory, and then suggests a strategic way to incorporate the learning in our daily life—versus applying human experience to a theoretical theme. Albert C. Outler integrated empiricism for contemporary use of interpretation in faith-accentuating practice. Human experience shapes Christian practice, and Christian practice forms tradition.

The current generation demands visual and image-driven experiential learning because of technological development and the expansion of online learning. The implication of experience for Christian education would be that learning based on Christian faith should connect cognitive and experiential learning to provoke the embodiment of knowledge, encouraging and inspiring students to participate in the creation of communities of justice and diversity.

HIRHO Y. PARK

Wesley does not encourage religious experience for its own sake. He rightly perceives that believers who focus too heavily upon experience can mistake feeling good for feeling God. Yet Wesley is equally convinced that well-intended efforts to protect God from human domestication—by insisting upon God's transcendence and sovereignty, God's *dis*continuity with the created world—foreclose upon the relational nature of revelation. In order to mediate between these poles, Wesley (or perhaps those who interpret Wesley) describes God's initiative as response-able.[19]

Revelation in the Modern and Postmodern Worlds

Wesley sought to prevent revelation from being discarded as a way to engage God in the modern world. He asserted revelation's origins in God but also stressed its relational, responsive nature. He sought to demonstrate how the divine-human relationship employed interdependent mediating sources (Scripture, tradition, reason, experience) for apprehending revelation. However, such a position was already being challenged. Calvinists emphasized the sole authority of Scripture, while Catholics retrenched themselves in tradition. Christian pietists looked to religious experience as the true mediator of faith. The Enlightenment's growing advocacy for science or reason as exclusive arbiters of knowledge threatened to eclipse all the others.

Modern intellectuals found it increasingly difficult to retain revelation as an epistemological category, as a legitimate way of knowing. Reason and experience, once considered servants of revelation, commenced to hang out their own shingles and go into business for themselves. In other words, Western scholars became persuaded that everything worth knowing derived from human empirical investigation of or reasoned reflection upon the material world. God was no longer required as revealer of truth or even as first cause. As sociologist Max Weber observed, for the first time in history, it became possible to imagine a "disenchanted" world.[20] This epistemological stance led to the rise of the "secular age" (described in part 1) in communities in Europe and North America.[21]

Where in premodern times the existence and activity of God was presumed, that presumption now required defense. Where premodernity accepted God's sovereignty and unlimited power over all creation, modernity focused on the power of human beings to "conquer nature." Where premodernity took for granted God's mysterious presence-in-absence, modernity either wrote God out of the equation altogether or argued that "God" was merely a name for deep human experience.

Returning to Jodi Foster in *Contact* for a moment, our star, ecstatic over her meeting with the extraterrestrials (no doubt because she believes it to have justified the first two hours of the movie), returns home joyfully, only to be plunged into another half hour of public squabbling. Subpoenaed to testify before Congress about cost overruns and the small matter of her space pod, suspended between an enormous Ferris wheel–sized mixer attachment containing electromagnets pulsing gigawatts of power, *appearing never to have left the launch site,* she defends the veracity of her account. All that electricity somehow opened up a hole in the space-time continuum, she testifies, through which she connected to reality beyond herself. Against her assertion, an expert witness argues instead that the electromagnetism scrambled Ms. Foster's brain to the point of inducing a vivid hallucination, one that acquainted her not with extraterrestrials but with her own deepest psychic projections. Welcome to modernity!

In the early twentieth century, religious education, especially in the United States, came to imagine itself as the catalyst of a progressive social movement. Educating people in faith meant teaching them to engineer the "Democracy of God," thought George Albert Coe, founder of the Religious Education Association.[22] By being forward-looking and embracing constructive experience as their teacher, Christians would complete God's project all on their own. In this scenario, God is no longer a mystery but becomes a cipher for American progressivism. Faith means (at least for White Americans) activism for just working conditions, access to schooling for children, and women's suffrage.

In response to a world war in which tens of millions died and to the emerging threat posed by Hitler, Reformed theologian Karl Barth roared his prophetic "No!" against human progressivism and the natural theology underwriting it.[23] He believed the church had abetted this slaughter. Instead of appealing to the revelation of God in Jesus Christ by the power of the Spirit, it had, Barth declared, settled for a theology that featured humanity "speaking of [itself] in a loud voice."[24] Barth reiterated the hiddenness of God, the sovereignty of God, the incommensurability of divine revelation with human experience or knowledge. He pointed to the Nazis as the horrid outcome of presuming an easy alliance between God and human ambition. Only God's saving action in Jesus Christ mattered for human redemption. Humanity's best hope was to point to God's revelation, to repent, and to witness.

In response to Barth, the practices of nurturing faith pivoted once again. Where progressive religious educators taught faith commensurate with the experience of a progressive political agenda, Barthian religious education, born out of mistrust of that same experience, reemphasized God's otherness and therefore the necessity of focusing upon the exclusive revelation of Jesus Christ. For Barthian Christian educators, encounter with Jesus as Word of God alone saves humanity. Educators, therefore, doubled down on teaching Scripture and theological reflection upon it. They did not waste time inviting students to name their "experiences" of God in life, because they believed God to be radically other than humanity.

Even as Barth partly succeeded in chastening the church, his theology could not hold back the rising tides of secularism or the growing influence of experience. The twenty-first century finds the church of the Global North relegated to its margins. By contrast, scientism and rationalism, their ascendency seemingly complete, have fostered a world in which revelation no longer seems necessary or credible.

But no sooner had reason and science built their own epistemological fortress than cracks began to appear in its walls. Postmodern critical thinkers argue convincingly that these presumably unimpeachable foundations of knowledge are, in fact, rooted in their own "faithful" presuppositions.[25] In other words, science and reason cannot by their own rules establish their truth claims as "self-evident." They, too, require "belief" in their explanatory power, for any ideology, any mode of knowing, rests on certain fundamental premises that cannot be proved and so must simply be believed. William James foresaw this epistemological crisis when he observed how scientists, too, "dogmatize like infallible popes."[26]

We return briefly to *Contact*, that cinematic trove of theological wisdom. Hollywood hunk Matthew McConaughey plays opposite Jodi Foster as, rather unbelievably, a *public theologian*. Part-time antagonist, always the love interest, McConaughey stirs up the story by asserting the value of faith amidst all these scientific proceedings. When Jodi Foster can summon no evidence of her encounter with ETs, she declares her experience to be true nonetheless. She is forced to make the postmodern turn in other words, one that McConaughey names "faith."

Postmodernity tears down the walls of modern epistemic certainty, leaving science and reason in its wake. This can be good news for the church, however, because these new epistemological circumstances can open the door again for rehabilitating revelation as a valid means of knowing. If it turns out that *all* epistemological systems, science and reason included, require faith in their premises, then a system claiming to know by way of a special revelation from God cannot on the face of things be dismissed from the epistemological table. This does not mean, however, that Christians can return to the good old days when everyone presumed divine enchantment. Once out of the bag, secularism or the exclusive authority of personal experience will not automatically submit themselves to revelation. Christians will need to contend for their special revelation amidst all kinds of other believers, including rationalists, scientists, and secularists of many stripes. Yet Christians have an advantage. Social philosopher Charles Taylor maintains that the secular West will continue to experience "haunting" by a ghost in the machine, as it were, an anxiety born of the possibility that there is something more than just the earthly "immanent frame," even as secularists live as if there were not.[27] Christians call this ghost "Holy."

Present-day ministries of faith formation inherit all the tensions described above. Where Wesley attempted to hold multiple mediating sources of revelation in a constructive relationship, nineteenth- and twentieth-century faith traditions once again tended to gravitate toward one or the other of the sources. Some communities continued to focus exclusively upon God's revelatory initiative and therefore upon teaching the content of Scripture or tradition that purports to contain it. When faced with difficult questions, however, concerning the authority or proper interpretation of these sources, they sometimes simply insist upon Scripture's self-interpretive power, or their God-given authority for interpretation. More recently, fundamentalists have sought to defend the authority of Scripture on rationalist and evidentiary terms. How positively modern of them! Other communities focus upon the experiential (human) dimensions of revelation and the possibilities of transformation through it. These communities that focus upon human transformation risk the "inadequate belief, right-practice" conundrum described in part 1, namely, forgetting the identity and mission of the God who authorizes it.

Implications for Revelation and Nurturing Faith

This part returns to the problematic of "disorienting amnesia" described in part 1. It suggests specific Christian forms of meaningful commemoration, participation in transcendence for the purpose of transformation, and missional encounters with difference as key to apprehending Christian revelation.

Consider Worship

Modernity taught the church how to separate the whole into many parts. Symptomatic of this fragmentation, Christians now speak of faith formation and worship as if these are separate endeavors. This was not always the case, however, and nor should it be in the future.

The catechumenate, the ancient church's process of forming persons for participation in its rites of initiation, offers a case in point. The church required candidates for membership ("catechumens") to participate in an interdependent ecology of teachings, disciplined practices of daily life, and series of worshiping rites. Completion of the process could require as many as three years. Commenting on the rigor of the catechumenate, theologian Will Willimon observes that the church determined that "one must be a whole Christian or one must be no Christian at all."[28]

From the perspective of the catechumenate, the "awesome" mystery of God's revealed identity, presence, and transforming power were experienced most consequentially through the thin spaces of sacramental liturgies.[29] To cite historian Thomas Finn once again, faith in the early church was the result of "symbols deeply lived."[30] The church believed that ritual symbols did more than point to God, however; they mysteriously invited relational participation in the revelation of God's triune life. In turn, worship was regarded as the source and means of converts' transformation into Christ's new creation. During the triduum—the three days beginning with worship on Holy Thursday evening, and inclusive of Good Friday and Holy Saturday and the great Vigil for Easter—catechumens participated ritually in the revelation of Christ's death, burial, and resurrection. They embodied the biblical story in other words. They were "incorporated into Christ's Body" (mystically, historically, sociologically) by way of baptismal new birth and eucharistic communion with his living flesh and blood. Faith, in this case, manifests itself as corporate doxological performance—participation in shared, God-focused liturgical practices—where God is at once actor and audience.

MYSTERY

Pedagogically, mystery communicates that the learning process is more than rational and analytical thought, and more than the accumulation of information and facts. Education must also be attentive to the knowledge that comes through love and contemplation. Biblically, mystery can refer to paradox, as when Paul speaks of the nature of the cross (1 Cor. 2:1–5). Neither Jews nor Greeks could logically grasp the unfathomable nature of God's saving act through Jesus Christ. Mystery can also express the secrets of that which is hidden. For Paul, the great mystery is that "Christ [is] in you, the hope of glory" (Col. 1:27). The apostle employs the same term in relation to the allegory between the marriage of husband and wife and the relationship between Christ and the church (Eph. 5:32). *Mystērion*, the Greek word for mystery, was later translated into Latin as *sacramentum* or sacrament. When C. S. Lewis seeks to explain communion, he declares that Jesus's "command, after all, was Take, eat: not Take, understand." Many people are fearful of mystery, and while there have been aberrant expressions that have led some astray, the above Scripture demonstrates that there is also a biblical manifestation of mystery. Educators should, therefore, follow Paul's example of seeking to be "servants of Christ and stewards of God's mysteries" (1 Cor. 4:1).

Historically, the best models of education see no contradiction between doctrine and biblical teaching, and mystery and contemplation. Examples as diverse as Bernard of Clairvaux in the twelfth century, the Puritans, the Dutch and German Pietists in the seventeenth century, and early Evangelicals of the eighteenth century all confirm this emphasis. Significantly, believers from the Christian East (i.e., the Orthodox Church) have never separated doctrinal teaching from contemplative experience. All of these divergent traditions acknowledge that there are limits to human reason and that it is more important to experience God than to be able to explain something about God.

Richard Osmer contrasts the distinction between "teaching about mystery" and "teaching for mystery." Christianity and theology both recognize the necessity of mystery. No one can adequately explain the doctrines of the Trinity, incarnation, atonement, or a person's communion with God through prayer and worship. God is ineffable and beyond human knowledge, yet God graciously reveals the most significant aspects necessary for us to know, love, and serve him.

While there is an important place for this "teaching about mystery" within the educational life of the church, the "teaching for mystery" provides a more helpful foundation upon which to begin. "Teaching for mystery" affirms that this is the natural state of young children. The innate wonder, imagination, and curiosity of a child are naturally attracted to mystery. One of the keys to guide adults into appro-priating mystery comes as young children are observed at play and worship. Osmer employs paradox and parables in his model of "teaching for mystery." Through "reframing" of what the students already know and by presenting the "contraries of insight" (i.e., employing paradox as two different perspectives are communi-cated concurrently), he challenges learners to see the subject through different eyes. Jesus, as rabbi or "teacher" (Matt. 19:16; Mark 4:38; Luke 10:25), illustrates "teaching for mystery" more specifically through his use of parables (e.g., Matt. 13; Mark 4; Luke 15–16). Parables have an allegorical or symbolic nature that requires greater reflection and wonder. One of the best-known examples of allegory has been John Bunyan's epic *Pilgrim's Progress*. Jesus also frequently employed the use of questions (e.g., Matt. 16:15; Mark 10:51; Luke 6:46; 9:25; John 1:38) and silence (e.g., Matt. 21:23–27; 27:12–14).

Educators seeking to cultivate a greater appreciation for mystery can encour-age their students as well as themselves to grow in the attitude of humility and childlike wonder and play. This prerequisite reminds all learners of the limitations of the human achievement and comprehension, the importance of ambiguity, and a proper reverence and awe before God. Teachers can also create opportunities for silence, contemplation of God, and more meditative and prayerful methods of reading Scripture that, instead of offering explanation, create greater opportuni-ties for experience.

TOM SCHWANDA

Once Christianity became the officially sanctioned religion of the Roman Empire and its members were no longer subject to religious persecution, the pressure to form persons capable of cruciform faithfulness lapsed. Instead of resisting Rome all the way to martyrdom, the church went to battle against heretics. Over time, orthodoxy, which literally means "right [worshipful] praise" (and aptly characterizes the meaning of faith in this early period), was reduced to a requirement for affirming revealed "right belief" as a condition of membership. Hence the catechumenate—a fully orbed process of holistic formation for body, mind, and spirit preparing for entry into relational life in Christ—gradually shrinks to "catechism," memorization of responses to questions about the content of Christian faith. Put differently, it becomes possible to separate faithful beliefs from faithful life (for faith to become disembodied, in other words) and thus to acquire and practice such beliefs outside the context of worship. Worship becomes a space where a faith that resides within *ideas* is interpreted through preaching or playacted through ritual.

It was no longer sufficient, in other words, to allude to revelation by pointing to worship and exclaiming "Look there!" The same was true of revelation's classical sources. Once, elements of a worshiping ecology, inclusive of Scripture, sacrament, and spiritual experience, all joined together in a graced complementarity. But things fell apart. As a result, these sources increasingly were made to stand on their own, even pitted against one another. Protestants especially, as we have seen, learned to distrust or ignore sacraments and tradition and, in some forms, experience. Catholics forgot about Scripture.

Times are changing. Christians today live in a smaller and more diverse world. Lutherans rub shoulders with Pentecostals who regularly bump into Catholics. Unsurprisingly, Roman Catholics are now poring over the Scriptures, Protestants are overcoming their fear of sacraments, Pentecostals are reminding everyone of the revelatory power of experience, and the Orthodox are chanting, "Hey sisters and brothers, we never gave up on the original ecology!" Faith formational leaders, therefore, will increasingly look to worship that is inclusive of multiple revelational sources as critical to the ministry of nurturing faith.

You Can Run (from Experience), but You Can't Hide

Prophets, biblical and ecclesial, repeatedly warn the human community not to confuse its own experience with God's revelation. The danger cannot be overstated. Throughout history, human beings have authored unspeakable evil in the name of God, an agenda God reviles. Yet while prophets rightly condemn this idolatry, they, too, speak for God out of their own experiences, particularly of suffering and injustice. Postmodernism has elevated this observation to the level of truism. Try as we may, we cannot fully disentangle revelation from human lived experience. Our contexts deeply impact what and how we know, including what we name as revealed truth from God. Even when revelatory sources are deemed God-given, free from any human imprint (a claim likely to sink in a bog), human communities receive, interpret, and respond to revelation in light of their particular burdens and hopes.

So how does the church assure its experience participates in revelation or is at least in service to revelation, especially in light of the explosive growth of experiential faith in the Global South? John Wesley hinted that practices of loving God and neighbor assured the presence of the one toward whom they pointed. Scholars have turned to the pivotal role of "welcoming the stranger" for ensuring continuity between Christian experience and revelation. "Stranger" in this case means persons or entire communities whom the church defines as outside or other than itself. Strangers can be complete outsiders, members of other faith traditions, for example, or insiders whom the church has marginalized or kicked to the curb—a list that has included at various times in history, women, LGBTQ persons, and persons whose ancestry is not European.

In *Reading in Communion*, theologians Stephen Fowl and L. Gregory Jones search for norms to promote truthful interpretation of scriptural revelation.[31] They contend that accurate reading must first be communal so that individualized, self-serving readings are checked. Further, they insist that communities reading together also be characterized by the experience of welcome and inclusion of strangers into the task of biblical interpretation. The authors point to the Bible itself to justify this norm. The Old and New Testaments repeatedly witness to encounters with supposed strangers who turn out to bear (or be) God. The authors also testify to the appalling consequences where this norm is not upheld. They highlight the failure of the Dutch South African Church to denounce apartheid as the result of its having lost the capacity to read the Bible in community with Black African Christians.[32] Fowl and Jones do not contend that the experience of reading the Bible in community with persons different from oneself automatically yields revelation, only that not doing so almost always falls short of it.

The Church Becomes Revelation as It Participates in God's Mission

In his article on revelation and Christian education, Daniel Schipani suggests that the church's task, more than receiving or stewarding revelation, is to "become revelation," thereby providing "grace-filled glimpses" of God's promised abundant life.[33] This claim connects with current renewed emphasis on the church's participation in God's mission as a primary strategy for nurturing faith. Michael Warren puts this plainly:

Even if you have trouble believing in the traditional teachings, you can still see the gospel being lived. It is observable, discernable, and visible. You might not want to be part of it, or you might judge it to be insane or stupid, but the "it" cannot be denied. That was the way Jesus himself spoke to the disciples of the Baptist when they asked him if he were the promised one. "The blind recover their sight, cripples walk, lepers are cured, the deaf hear, dead people are raised to life, and the poor have the good news preached to them" (Matt 11:5; Luke 7:22).[34]

This renewed vision for a missional church as revelatory—one that we wonder, frankly, what happened to in the first place—suggests that revelation may be encountered and faith nurtured as persons participate in this communal way of life. Revelation becomes trustworthy as persons live into its promises together.

Conclusion

Christian faith is the gift of a revealing God. It is a gift of relationship, a gift of love, and a gift of hope. As such, revelation is a cure for disorienting amnesia. It frees human beings and human communities from the impossible burden of shaping the good life on their own. Educational leaders will employ a variety of tried and true, as well as innovative, means for nurturing it. For large segments of the Global North, this will require (re)awakening persons to the possibility of belief in transcendence in the wake of modernity. For them, gestures toward re-enchantment likely will win the day over angry apologetics. Worship is one such setting where creative use of symbol, ritual, music, and other forms invite reawakening to holy mystery. In addition, educators will employ the entire ecology of Scripture, tradition, reason, and experience (especially the experience of others who challenge our assumptions) as trusted means for receiving God's word in Christ. Worship and mission are especially appropriate contexts for engaging these means and the God who communicates through them.

Even so, the crisis of confidence confronting Christianity today stems less from the incredibility of its revelation and more from the "un-credibility" of Christian witness. Put plainly, persons standing outside of Christianity must see Christians *living* as if their revelation were true. Educational leaders will, therefore, involve Christians in soul-searching discernment, lamentation, repentance for sin, faithful missional practices, and sustained relationships with persons different from themselves (where they mostly listen). They will strive to become once again known by their love. Living into this hope, they may shine as beacons of hope.

This task is not an impossible one. As we shall see in the next chapter, human beings are fashioned by God out of love for lives of loving. To practice loving relationality is to practice who we are!

Interactive Dialogue

1. What does it mean to claim "Jesus Christ is the revelation of God"?
2. Rank by order of importance the four mediating sources of revelation (Scripture, tradition, reason, experience) for your own faith community. Explain why this is the case. Consider whether the account of these sources in the chapter has caused you to reevaluate your rankings.
3. How may persons and communities of faith ensure the truthfulness of their received revelation?
4. Does revelation continue in the present?

For Further Reading

Finn, Thomas M. *Early Christian Baptism and the Catechumenate: West and East Syria*. Collegeville, MN: Liturgical, 1992.

Fowl, Stephen E., and L. Gregory Jones. *Reading in Communion: Scripture and Ethics in Common Life*. Eugene, OR: Wipf & Stock, 1998.

Outler, Albert C., ed. *John Wesley*. Oxford: Oxford University Press, 1964.

Smith, James K. A. *Who's Afraid of Postmodernism: Taking Derrida, Lyotard, and Foucault to Church*. Grand Rapids: Baker Academic, 2006.

Taylor, Charles. *A Secular Age*. Cambridge, MA: Harvard University Press, 2007.

CHAPTER SIX

Humanity, Embodiment, and the Trust of Interdependent Kinship

The Glory of God is the human being made fully alive.

—IRENAEUS OF LYON

My humanity is caught up, inextricably bound up, in yours. I am, because you are. To live this reality is to live the truth.

—DESMOND TUTU

ROAD MAP

The focus of this chapter is on how faith coheres with the "stuff" of humanity. Simply put, we wonder, "What makes human beings tick?" How do they learn? What motivates them? How are they susceptible to the transformative work of the Spirit? As we've suggested previously, every educational leader has answered these questions at least intuitively. No doubt by this point, readers will also remember our refrain: We judge it better for formational leaders to make their intuitions explicit and to challenge or deepen them, if necessary, in order to practice well the ministry of nurturing faith. In a postmodern era, this means rethinking outdated if deeply entrenched assumptions that have grown out of cultures of individualism, the certainty of rationality, and the free and autonomous construction of the personhood (the so-called self-made "man"). We seek to replace these with convictions we deem closer to God's creative intent: fully embodied beings who are constitutively relational; beings motivated as much or more by their "hearts" as by reason; and as story-bearing "imaginers," working out of the past while oriented to the future.

Introduction

In Pat Conroy's novel *The Great Santini*, the author provides a thinly veiled account of his own upbringing under the iron fist of his father, a Marine fighter pilot.[1] Santini is the personification of the modern American warrior: fearless, bombastic, ruthlessly competitive, tyrannical, and supremely confident in his own abilities. As the story unfolds, readers also discover that dear old dad is a racist, misogynist bully who runs his household like boot camp. Under the pretext of discipline, he regularly beats his wife and children. The very same man, however, experiences no greater joy than worshiping with his family, especially at Christmas Eve Mass. The tyrant who rules through intimidation and violence also loves God and, in a strange way, loves his family too.

Conroy's complex portrait of his complicated father, a man in turn capable of beastliness and beatitude, sets the stage for our consideration of "theological anthropology." This subcategory of theology explores the nature of human being and the possibility of human transformation through God's initiative of grace in Jesus Christ.[2] It demands, therefore, that we attend to the "What makes people tick?" question. As we shall see, when portraits of human being depart from primary Christian assumptions, then efforts to nurture persons in Christian faith turn out to be shallow or misdirected. The good news is that faith as gift from God coheres with the "stuff" of our humanity, *all* of it. This chapter seeks to uncover all that stuff.

The chapter proceeds, after defining a few key terms, by presenting three historically influential portraits of human being. Next, and in light of these portraits, it provides a set of theological anthropological convictions. Finally, we highlight promising insights from the field for nurturing real faith, not pretend piety, matching God's redemptive work with our own best judgment about human motivation, aspiration, and destiny—all tied to the power of imagination.

Encroaching Challenges to Nurturing Faith	Engaging Resources for Nurturing Faith	Exclusive Uniquenesses of Nurturing Faith	Extraordinary Gifts for Nurturing Faith
Disorienting amnesia	Meaningful commemorations	Penetrating Scripture	Transformative hope
▸ Autonomous determinism	Mutual disclosure	Interdependent kinship	Inspired trust
Interpretive pluriformity	Generous humility	Resurrected image	Restorative grace

Encroaching Challenges to Nurturing Faith	Engaging Resources for Nurturing Faith	Exclusive Uniquenesses of Nurturing Faith	Extraordinary Gifts for Nurturing Faith
Cultural constructionism	Intentional citizenship	Supernatural guidance	Countercultural faith
Fragmented faith	Faithful gestures	Focused proclamation	Fortifying love
Conceptual bricolage	Probing reflection	Discerning community	Principled freedom

Coming to Terms with Human Being

The word *human* shares the same root as "humus," the organic component of soil and, interestingly, "humble." To be human is to be born out of the stuff of the earth. Christians remind themselves of their humble origins (and destiny) annually when receiving the cross-shaped imprint of ashes on their foreheads, accompanied by these words: "From dust you have come and to dust you shall return" (Gen. 3:19).

At the same time, humans appear to transcend the mere facts of biological existence. Put succinctly (if ungrammatically) we humans *be*, or, better, we have *be-ing*.[3] We can become present to our experience and to ourselves in ways we suspect clams cannot. The source of this being is the subject of endless speculation. Greek philosophy attributed it to the indwelling of the immaterial soul. The Bible points to divine in-spiriting of the body. Current science equates human being-ness with synaptic networks in the brain amounting to a powerful background feeling that we *are*.

Our scientific classification, *homo sapiens*, is also pertinent. *Homo* means human while *sapiens* connotes wisdom. Implied here is the sense that humans display intellective capacities beyond those of other species. *Sapiens* also implies that thinking is at the center of being.

The purpose of our being is also the subject of speculation. Is it to love God and neighbor? To successfully transmit our genes to the next generation? To fulfill every desire? To win at the game of life?

Human Portraiture

Below we offer three "portraits" of human being. These three portraits have been so influential that readers' own assumptions about what makes humans tick are likely shaped by them at least in part. Equally true, the church's theology in the Global North has also been influenced by these portraits for better or for worse. In what follows, we try to show which dimensions of these portraits may be congenial to Christian convictions and which have proven destructive.

The Solitary Thinker

Readers may know the sculpture, actually the bronze casting. It's the naked male sitting pensively, chin resting on the knuckles of his forehand. The nineteenth-century artist Rodin cast a number of these larger than life figures, most of which remain on public display in Europe and North America. Some art historians suggest that Rodin's inspiration was the poet Dante contemplating the harrowing description of hell he had penned in the *Inferno*. In the present cultural imagination, however, The Thinker all by himself—minus the backstory—has become a prominent symbol for human being. It implies we exist in order to think, or maybe, we think in order to exist. Thinking is our exclusive *modus operandi*.

Internet tourist photos typically depict one or two or twenty-two actual living humans posed pensively at the feet of The Thinker, their chins resting upon their own knuckles. The photos suggest we assume this thinking position quite naturally, so the portrait must be accurate, yes? Perhaps we are even better at mime.

The origins of The Thinker as a portrait of human being extend at least as far back as the ancient Greeks. Plato and others believed rational thought to be a function of the immaterial soul. Its highest use was contemplation of eternal transcendent ideals, though it was also handy for problem solving. In addition, the Greeks believed in reason's capacity to escape bodily baggage to focus upon transcendence. For the ancients, this unique capacity served to elevate humans above mere animals in the hierarchy of being.

Later, in the seventeenth century, the philosopher René Descartes argued *Cogito, ergo sum* ("I think, therefore I am") and more deeply entrenched in the West the portrait of humans as primarily thinkers. It is important to attend to Descartes because he and other enlightenment scholars represent a watershed in human self-understanding. Looking for a place to stand in a world increasingly up for epistemological grabs, Descartes believed thinking, at least, to be secure, especially as Copernicus and Galileo had made it impossible to trust the senses in traditional ways. Equally important for his work, Europe was then awash in passionate nationalisms, and these often boiled over into violent continental warfare. Descartes was searching for the means to ascend to high moral ground in order to lay claim to the truth. He concluded that, although all else was suspect, he could not doubt finally his own capacity to doubt. Rationality, as Descartes constructs it, is the last and only place to stand. The exercise of reason, therefore, is what makes human beings human. It also holds the key to saving the world.

One corollary of Descartes's dictum is of particular relevance for this discussion. Descartes says, "From that I knew I was a substance, the whole essence or nature of which is to think, and that for its existence there is no need of any place, nor does it depend on any material thing; so that this 'me,' that is to say, the soul by which I am what I am, is entirely distinct from body, and is even more easy to know than is the latter; and even if body were not, the soul would not cease to be what it is."[4]

However well intended, Descartes's rationalist portrait had profound and harmful long-term consequences. For example, he convinced us (and we remain widely convinced) that mind and body are separate entities, the former an essential one, the latter not so. Further, we are also persuaded that the rational mind is destined for constant struggle for control over the impassioned body. Such a conclusion is understandable when we witness so much violence, abuse, and lack of self-control in the world. The image of the so-called civilized and virtuous human requires that we be cut off from our body and its messy emotions, feelings, and passions. The mind alone becomes the location for reason, for discerning truth and therefore for moral judgment, even for experiences of suffering or joy. Ultimately, our essence is judged to be separate from our organism.

It would be a mistake to assert that Descartes introduced the world to dualism. Indeed, the Greeks made their own distinctions between mind and body, but these distinctions were neither as rigid nor as at odds with one another nor as strongly hierarchical as they became for Descartes. Not coincidentally, this portrait also expresses a politics—one where the knowing that promotes caring for children, for example, or the creative handwork of the craftsperson, or the artist working with physical media are devalued, while the so-called pure reasoning of a select educated elite is privileged exclusively. Taken to extremes, such dualism functioned to exclude women (deemed too bodily, too emotional) and people of color (same general reasons) from the human species altogether, and also justified the mistreatment of children, persons with disabilities, the elderly, and the infirm.

Descartes's model, beyond denigrating the body and dividing the self against itself, also holds implications for human relationships. Simply put, it serves to isolate us from our neighbors. Since, as the logic goes, human beings are most often responsible for the stirring of one another's desires, and desire is automatically antithetical to reason, the best strategy for virtue is to minimize human contact. The logical outcome of this thinking is *Emile*, Rousseau's theoretical child raised in "natural" social isolation and away from the corrupting influence of others until he has first mastered his passions. The adult Emile is not a hermit; he is socially engaged, but the relationships he establishes with others are purely contractual and utilitarian.[5] Kant, too, speaks of being besieged by desire when in the company of others. He makes no distinction between good and bad company or, for that matter, good and bad desires. Instead, human beings are to be cut off from their bodies and cut off from one another if they wish to be fully human. The Enlightenment introduces the world to the fully autonomous, self-constructing, disembodied, isolated, rational individual—a portrait that resembled the ideals and assumptions of its creators.

A Bunch of Animals

Try as we may, human beings never seem to fully escape the portrait that we are "a bunch of animals." As if history and the news media alone were not sufficient evidence for its veracity, the "human as beast" literary trope is available for instant purchase on iTunes, or in print for old timers like the authors. These are the stories where somebody grows horns or claws or a tail and then perpetrates some serious scariness on a mostly expendable cast of characters (plus the audience). We scream out of fear *and* because we find this portrait of ourselves as animals *believable*, at least a little bit. However friendly the human façade, we suspect the beast simmers just below the surface, ready to do violence. Portraying humans as animals has also served to justify and reinforce racist tropes and to dehumanize wartime enemies.

Beginning in the late nineteenth century, Sigmund Freud attempted to dress up this way of viewing humans in the garb of modern European respectability. His theory of personality hypothesized deep recesses of the human subconscious, a realm oozing with instincts and erotic bodily drives (for example, the desire to possess one's parents, or to kill them, or both) itching to get out.[6] Whether in their expression or suppression, he believed these drives consistently confounded their bearers. Freud credits civilization with damming the psychic waters of destruction, as it were, but suspected that restraint comes at high personal cost.[7] In response, Freud offers "psychoanalysis" to help patients peer into their subconscious and, if not to fix it, at least to come to terms with it.

Regardless of readers' personal opinions about Freud's theory, just as with The Thinker, the belief that humans are beasts now permeates many of the cultures of the Global North. We take the subconscious for granted, we blame

Freud for sexually suggestive "slips," we complain about our inability to get out from under our "superego," or to rein in our "id," we describe ourselves and others in terms of "neuroses" ("compulsion," "passive aggression," etc.), all without a second thought. Many residents of the Global North are more fluent in psychoanalytic language than biblical language. For example, we are more likely to describe ourselves and others as "neurotic" than "sinful."

Recently, a slightly different version of this view of humans has attained scientific respectability. Scientists of all stripes—evolutionary biologists, psychologists, primate ethologists, and neuroscientists, to name a few—are painting a new picture of the human as animal. Instead of a mythology of instinctual drives, however, the characterizing agent in this portrait is natural selection.[8] According to Charles Darwin, "natural selection" describes the main process of evolution "whereby organisms better adapted to their environment tend to survive and produce more offspring."[9] Most controversial, Darwin believed that human history, too, was subject to the same process of natural selection as other species. Life is all about species advancing their genes to the next generation. Also emphasizing the continuity of human animals with other animals, scientists note the overlap between human evolutionary processes and those of similar species, including primates. From the other direction, animal behaviorists report observing signs of intelligence once exclusively attributed to humans. Dogs empathize, crows use tools, chimpanzees solve problems and learn language, elephants are moved to altruism. So much for the hierarchy of being!

The field of neuroscience builds upon Darwin's legacy. Specifically, neuroscience posits shared neural architecture between human forebears and present-day humans. Located near the base of the skull in what may be described euphemistically as "the downstairs," evolutionarily ancient brain regions manage basic homeostatic functions—respiration, heart rate, skin conductance, hunger or satiation—and are mostly or entirely automated. Older brain regions also tend to basic emotional responses—fear and desire, for example. Without putting too fine a point on it, neuroscience portrays human ancestors as desiring, emoting beings long before they developed capacities for language or reflective thought. Layered on top, the more recently evolved neocortex, the brain's "upstairs," contains neural networks for language, for spatial mapping, for reasoned decision-making—all those functions typically associated with cognition, reason or intelligence. What brain science suggests, however, is that natural selection has not only added new "floors" to the human brain over time; it has also wired old and new together. Something like a nineteenth-century British manor house, the evolutionary "upstairs," even as it imagines its own superiority (it can *speak* after all), remains dependent upon, if not always aware of, the powerful influence of the evolutionary downstairs. In the case of "high-level" reasoning, for example, basic biological desire for homeostasis is always influencing reason's object and direction, even to the point of suggesting what is reasonable when reason itself can't decide! Nor does every brain response occur in top-down fashion. Following William James's famous illustration, we do not see a bear on the trail, ponder awhile whether it represents a threat to our existence by performing a cost-benefit analysis on the encounter, then decide whether to respond with fear. No, we see the bear and are immediately afraid without pausing to think about it.[10] Readers can see the evolutionary logic at work here. It makes sense in this case to run first and think second. Reversing this order can make one lunch. Even as reasoned reflection constantly seeks pride of place in human beings' musings upon the nature of their being, minding the body is always first on the brain's to-do list.

REASON

Discussion about the interactive relationship between faith and reason in philosophy and theology has produced various approaches: mutual exclusivity, synthesis, and integration. Aristotelian philosophy opened the question of the relationship between faith and reason focused on an empirical world. Plato (428–348 BC) and Aristotle (384–322) suggested new possibilities for the systematic ordering of all knowledge, how faith is formulated by rational reflection on concrete reality. Saint Augustine of Hippo (354–430) advocated compatibility of faith and reason. Augustine believed that intellectual inquiry is an act of faith seeking understanding (*fides quaerens intellectum*). Therefore, natural sciences and logic enhance understanding of Christian faith. Influenced by Augustine, Saint Anselm (1033–1109) sought intelligible truth (*intellectus fidei*), not to understand in order to believe but to believe in order to understand Christian faith.

Thomas Aquinas (1225–1274) believed that both affirmed faith and reason formed the foundation for the theological reasoning required to obtain the knowledge of God. God is the foundation of all things, and the revelation of God is known through faith (supernatural revelation) and through reason (natural revelation). Aquinas constructed his theology on the balance between faith and reason; knowledge could be obtained using "both-and" methodology. Whereas the Bible is a good source of knowledge derived from faith, scientific skepticism challenges ideas grounded in tradition and faith.

In the Middle Ages, faith and reason became separate entities. For example, the Protestant reformer Martin Luther (1483–1546) rejected the power of human reason to illuminate faith. Luther asserted that salvation is possible only by faith through the grace of God, without reason. Scholars of rationalism, such as René

Descartes (1596–1650) and Baruch Spinoza (1632–1677), tried to answer epistemological and metaphysical problems by reason alone, against empiricism, and they believed that anything appealing to the intellect must be true.

Immanuel Kant (1724–1804) synthesized that both reason and experience are necessary for obtaining knowledge. Faith is distinct from knowledge but has a rational basis. Influenced by the Enlightenment in the seventeenth and the eighteenth centuries, John Wesley (1703–1791), the founder of Methodism, constructed a new way of theological reflection that understood the living core of the Christian faith to be revealed in Scripture, illumined by tradition, vivified in personal experience, and confirmed by reason.

Reason is used to interpret human experiences and to seek to understand God's action and God's will in individuals and within communities. By reason, we test the congruence of the Christian witness to human knowledge, experience, and service. The mutually critical conversations among reason, experience, and Scripture enable the emergence of an ethical voice, which is crucial to Christian education. The dialectical relationships between faith and works, love and reason, individual and society, small group and community solidarity, praxis and theory are ways of balancing the totality of Christian faith and its practice in Christian education. Christian education seeks holistic understanding of the revelation of God and its relationship to explicit (social and cultural) and implicit (individual and spiritual) Christian experiences. Faith and reason are compatible sources for Christian education; theological claims are refined or supplemented by reason. The uniqueness of Christian education lies in the integration of Christian faith and reason that creates a paradigm of learning about the truth, which contains practical wisdom of life.

HIRHO Y. PARK

On the plus side of the ledger, this portrait highlights the significance of the human *body* for human *being*. Contra Descartes, it suggests that humans are not motivated by reason alone, nor are they ever capable of pure, objective, reason. Human being is constitutively embodied being. This focus on embodiment over "pure mind" also supports a crucial theological inclusion of all sorts of people historically sidelined from the species. Dualistic thinking also illustrates the human tendency to befuddle ourselves. Frequently, we simply don't know what motivates our actions or thoughts because the body's desires regularly escape conscious attention. Indeed, humans seem to possess a near endless capacity to deceive ourselves over our motivations. However, understanding that we are embodied creatures, subject to needs and desires, highlights the human predilection to descend into destructive behaviors, even violence. To its credit, neuroscience has helped explain the interplay between genetic inheritance and environments of formation for faulty wiring in the brain. Further, if environments of formation matter to the brain's health, it therefore grounds hope for the therapeutic value not only of medications but also of healthy communities for forming healthy people. Neuroscience may also support theological contentions for redemptive desires. Embodied beings may be moved to love as well as hate. We will have more to say about this below.

Negatively, if we focus on our material and animal being, this often encourages capitulation to fatalism about human life, which Christians cannot abide. We too easily presume that once we really come to know another, we will discover the violent sociopath within, not the very good creature of God. Nor does the overused confession "I'm only human" excuse the basest of my human tendencies. Sin still applies even in a therapeutic age.

Lovers

Depicting persons as guided by their hearts is an ancient theme presently being recovered in earnest. The heart symbolizes the human center of value, motivation, empathy, and desire. It may carry an erotic connotation. The heart may also stand for character or virtue. God chooses David for his heart, his strength of character, and not his physical appearance (1 Sam. 16:7). Mary is so heartbroken over Lazarus's death, she accuses Jesus of dereliction of duty (John 11:32).

For the early church, the heart and its loves were a prominent feature of its Neoplatonic "psychology." This psychology is often illustrated through the image of the charioteer driving a chariot powered by two horses. The horses represent the two oppositional life forces within all living beings that help shape the interaction between those beings and their world. The "appetitive" force, sometimes called "desire," draws things into beings, including human beings. The "spirited" force, sometimes called "anger," pushes beings (again including human beings) against other things in the environment.[11] These horses are part of God-given human nature. The tension they create between attraction and resistance animates all life.

For humans, the charioteer controlling these push-me pull-you ponies is reason. Reason is a uniquely human capacity enabling a quality of considered interaction with the world not driven exclusively by the appetitive or the spirited. In other words, reason helps guide the horses through the course of life. Sometimes reason applies the brakes or reins in the horses or even occasionally shows them the whip. At other times, the running is smooth, and only a light touch is required. According to theological historian Roberta Bondi, Christians of antiquity who presumed this psychology believed that reason provided the capacity "to see and know God, to see as God sees, and to love God and other people. Acts of compassion and forgiveness, worship, insight into others all stem from reason which is fueled by desire and anger."[12] In other words, unlike Enlightenment thinkers, ancient Christians believed that reason worked in concert with bodily desires, habits, and emotions toward the cultivation of deep affections. Love is the primary example. Thus, the role of reason is not merely constraining or inhibitory in relation to bodily desire and anger; rather it is to direct those natural life forces toward their proper loving ends. After all, a charioteer without horses is going nowhere, except maybe into a Monty Python skit. Bondi continues, "Reason serves love," and "love draws reason to the good, to God."[13]

Saint Augustine—who himself knew the strength of the body's desires—famously prays in the *Confessions*, "my heart is restless until it rests in thee, O Lord."[14] Similarly, Pascal observes, "there is a God-shaped hole in the human heart."[15] Each suggests that desire is at the center of the human relationship with God and the world. According to Augustine, human beings are created for loving relationship with God; however, human love often desires improper ends—things, status, power—or confuses lesser goods with ultimate ones. The love intended for God fastens upon idols instead.

Philosopher James K. A. Smith has reasserted the importance of the heart for human flourishing in the present day. Building upon Augustine while skewering Descartes, he paints human beings as "lovers" more than thinkers.[16] Utilizing philosophies of embodiment, he constructs an account of desire as the spark of human being. Next, he demonstrates how desires (loves) become habituated within persons through practices (see chapter 9), causing them to seek after certain ends often without consciously attending to them.[17] Indeed, according to Smith, desired ends may contradict the ones humans articulate by way of reason. Katherine Turpin, author of *Branded: Converting Adolescents from Consumer Faith*, illustrates Smith's point with an ironic chapter title placed on the tongues of young people (though she could be quoting any of us): "Consumerism Is Bad, Let's Go Shopping!"[18] Smith challenges the Enlightenment view of human being as a quintessentially rational being. Pascal, too, would have agreed with Smith. "The heart has reasons," Pascal sagely perceives, "of which reason knows not."[19]

Lovers are made for relationships. As we've noted, love is relational by definition. Moderns, however, typically assume that loving relationships begin when two autonomous and self-constructed individuals choose to enter into one. Once again, science and philosophy are challenging this enlightenment perspective. Studies of parental interactions with infants suggest that infants, rather than bringing a fully constructed self with them each morning to the changing table, acquire a sense of themselves through repeated daily interactions with their caregivers. The "dance" on the changing table, for example, with mom or dad gently (but quickly!) removing a soiled diaper from baby and then strapping on a fresh one features adult and child mirroring each other's expressions and sounds. In turn, these gestures provide the means for baby and caregiver to construct not only a loving relationship but also, more fundamentally, a sense of their own identities as beings-in-relation.

Steps toward a *Theological* Anthropology

New Testament scholar Susan Eastman focuses upon the faith-formational significance of Paul's injunction "to imitate me as I imitate Christ" (1 Cor. 11:1) by underlining neuroscientific claims for "mirror neurons."[20] These neural networks are hypothesized as being associated with a person's internal imitation of the body states of others.[21] They may explain in part why emotional distress can be contagious or viewing a dance performance can be so invigorating. Emotion systems in brain and body resonate with the emotions of others, and the brains of audience members join in as dancers leap. For Eastman, as for others, the endgame is this: Human beings are created for and through relationships. We are irreducibly and consistently interdependent with others for our own being and identity. We are not born merely with the capacity for relationships; we are constitutively relational. Indeed, without a "we," there could be no "me." Further, if Eastman (and Smith too) is correct, imitation of others especially through Christian practices not only forms our identities but also orients our desires to certain ends. If we are beings-in-relation, then we need to be in good relationships, participants in Christ even, if we hope to be good.

Theological ethicist Richard Bondi makes important additions to this emerging portrait. Describing four "elements of character," he names first the "capacity for intentional action."[22] Similar to Descartes, Bondi here highlights the possibility of acting based on reasoned decision-making. Importantly, however, he also speaks of human involvement with "affections" and "passions" (the emotional analogues of virtue and vice).[23] Unlike Descartes but similar to Smith and Eastman, Bondi acknowledges the essential role, for better or for worse, of desire in virtuous living. Passions may overwhelm the capacity for intentional action, while affections may promote it.

REFLECTIVE ENGAGEMENT

The concept of reflective engagement owes its immediate provenance to Donald Schön, though its roots lie with John Dewey. It may be seen as a species of experiential learning, but there are links also with problem-based learning and action research.

Dewey defines education as that reconstruction or reorganization of experience that adds to the meaning of experience. What one should ask about any situation or experience proposed to induce learning is what quality of problem it involves, because thinking starts with a problematic situation; ideas are only authentic when they are tools in a reflective examination that tends to solve a problem.

In contrasting the "high, hard ground" of academic theorizing and the "swampy lowland" of (professional) practice, Schön encapsulates the challenge he sees in the notion of reflective practice to the paradigm of technical rationality, according to which professional activity consists in instrumental problem solving made rigorous by the application of scientific theory and technique. The practitioner is not confronted immediately with problems to be solved but problematic situations characterized by uncertainty, disorder, and indeterminacy; thus, first of all, the problem must be framed by defining appropriate ends and acceptable means, rather than rushing to a putative technical solution. Whereas most of our knowing is tacit, embedded in action, we are often surprised by something we experience, and we try to make sense of it by reflecting on implicit understandings that have been disrupted in some way. This is reflection-in-action; reflection-on-action occurs after practical engagement.

Paulo Freire contributed to critical pedagogy generally and to Christian education specifically. A notable impact has been that on Thomas Groome, who outlines a shared Christian praxis approach, which he describes as bringing life to faith and faith to life. Groome identifies two significant influences in the development of this approach. One is Jesus's encounter on the road to Emmaus; the other is a statement from Vatican Council II, asserting that the "split between the faith which many profess and their daily lives deserves to be counted among the more serious errors of our age." Groome does not offer a methodology to be slavishly applied but a number of movements to be employed flexibly according to context. It begins with consideration of present engagement with the cultural milieu, leading to critical reflection on what would most often be taken for granted. This internal dialogue that should then be externalized, for this is a communal process, is ultimately shared with the living tradition of which one is part, the story that constitutes the overarching narrative within which personal stories are (to be) lived.

James Fowler's research into faith development suggests that during late adolescence or adulthood, as people begin to take personal responsibility for their commitments and lifestyle, they may embrace the "capacity for critical reflection on identity (self) and outlook (ideology)." However, he also points to what might be termed the tragic flaw of this Stage 4, when critical thought is overly trusted and the reflective self subsumes reality and the perspectives of others into its own worldview. Faith can then ossify into "clear distinctions and abstract concepts" incapable of comprehending life's complexities, so that a person is pushed toward an orientation that is more dialectical and multileveled. This, Stage 5, is dialogical in character: The knowable is invited to disclose itself, and knowers seek to accommodate their cognitive structures to it, rather than vice versa. A person could then be said to have adapted to the uncertainty and problematic character of life, discerning the powerful residues of meaning that escape our strategies of reductive interpretation and thus being capable of genuine reflective engagement.

DOUG BLOMBERG

The third element Bondi proposes is what he calls the human "subjection to the accidents of history."[24] These accidents describe elements of ourselves that we did not choose to receive but are part of us nevertheless. Such accidents include gender, place in the birth order, family of origin or its absence, social location, access to education or other cultural resources, and in the Global North, at least, racialized identity. These accidents speak to the particularity of formation in context. Each human being is unique and ought not be generalized or stereotyped. Bondi also suggests that these accidents are so important to the formation of human character that they may seem to exert controlling influence over the entire course of human life. To offer one tragic example, statistically speaking, persons raised in poverty are likely to remain in poverty as adults and to raise their own children in poverty, thus perpetuating the cycle of intergenerational poverty.

Fourth, and consistent with other contributors to this portrait, Bondi envisions the "capacity of the heart," one consisting of a matrix of memory, imagination, and hope. Building upon Augustine's "restless heart" motif while appropriating the language of narrative ethics, Bondi argues that it is the capacity of the heart that causes human beings to desire union with the good (as in the case of the gospel story of God's mission to establish a kingdom of loving inclusion) and to "reach out" toward those stories.[25] In turn, the capacity of the heart is also the means through which humans perceive *being embraced* by truthful stories themselves. (Bondi is proposing a narrative means of envisioning the divine-human relationship prompted and undergirded by divine grace, hence being embraced by a truthful story.) Equally important, as potential remedy to misdirected reason, distorted passions, and destructive accidents of history, the capacity of the heart as a means to mediate grace provides proper reasons for action and helps to expunge sinful passions and to cultivate loving affections, while offering persons the means to reinterpret their subjection to the accidents of history. With respect to this last element of character, union with the truthful story of God's new creation in Christ enables persons to discover they are not fated to poverty, to second class citizenship, to self-loathing, to forces of dehumanization, or to repeated patterns of violence and abuse.

We find much to commend here. This emerging portrait corrects the hyperrationality and individualism handed down by the Enlightenment. With respect to theology, it reclaims the significance of the human body. It preserves an element of mystery for human being and cautions against facile presumptions about their motivations. It provides space for the insights of contemporary science. It insists on the essential relationality of persons with one another and their wider environment. It acknowledges and protects human particularity. It places embodied loving desire at the center of the human moral project and allows for the possibility of forming those desires to the good. Finally, by way of the "capacity of the heart," Bondi opens the door to a form of Christian imagining, a kind of perception that is as much intuited or received as it is thoughtfully constructed. Is this the portal to the Spirit's promptings? Is it the "mind of Christ"?

A growing number of scholars are linking this embodied relational and desiring existence with mostly nonconscious, nonlinguistic ways of perceiving. This elevates the "listen to your heart" argument we've been making to a different plane. In a scholarly revisitation of the differing roles of left and right brain hemispheres, Iain McGilchrist makes a powerful case for the primacy of the aesthetically inclined right hemisphere over the more linguistic and logical left.[26] He suggests that the right hemisphere is where the "big picture" (our term) gets processed even as the left hemisphere manipulates and reduces all this data to manageable bits for the sake of efficient action. At the same time, McGilchrist suggests that the Global North has created a culture where the left hemisphere rules. It provides little incentive (or opportunity) for self-transcending wonder, awe, or contemplation of reality beyond the pragmatic "what you see is what you get" bent toward efficient action. Instead of receiving the gift of immersion in life, human beings furiously work to make their mark on it.

If McGilchrist is correct, then faith-formational leaders will also seek to cultivate these global, if mostly allusive and illusive, right hemisphere imaginative sensibilities, for they awaken us to transcendence—to the other side of the wardrobe, as it were. McGilchrist suggests that participation in the aesthetic and artistic dimensions of culture offers the best prospect for forming this powerful, if subtly influential, dimension of human selves.

Implications for Faith Formation

By hammering shut the coffin of individual self-construction, this chapter seeks to respond to the problem of "autonomous determinism" and its correlative individualism described in part 1. From the very beginning, God saw that it was not good for the human to be alone (Gen. 2:18)—that Adam and Eve, more than opting for partnership, *completed* one another. We would extend this fundamental human relationality to our connection with the entire creation. Persons are created for (and through) communion with God and *all* that God has created. In addition to this focus on relationality, the chapter sought to re-emphasize the significance of human embodiment for relational communion. In the effort to move past captivity to the Cartesian anthropological portrait, we have highlighted the role of bodily desire, habit, and imagination in human life. Human beings are far too wonderfully made to be limited to mere thinking.

Below we offer a few insights from the field of Christian education as it grows in its own awareness of what makes persons tick. The continuing emergence of "imagination" as a locus of faith formation is driving the field at present.[27] The standard account of imagination describes it as the human capacity to call to mind what does not exist in the senses. Much more has been added to this definition that is relevant to faith formation, so we summarize important themes below.

Imagination as Story-Linking

Christian educator Anne Wimberly advocates a process of "story-linking" for African American Christian education whereby biblical stories are imaginatively connected with the life stories of African American persons and communities with the hope that contemporary African American Christians will imagine and appropriate redemptive possibilities for the unfolding stories of their own lives.[28] Stories are among those aesthetic forms capable of speaking both to conscious awareness and to the underground imagination of embodied desires. They fill human minds with powerful images, and they tug on human hearts.[29]

Wimberly allows that she is not so much developing an educational method as making plain how African Americans have always engaged the Scriptures. Wimberly points out that African American Christians, once enslaved and still oppressed people, imaginatively identify with the story of God's deliverance of Israel out of Egypt to the promised land. They look to Jesus with hope that he (aka the "new Moses") will deliver them into his promised reign of justice, inclusion, and dignity. Put simply, they link biblical stories of God's redeeming action to their own stories.

ANNE E. STREATY WIMBERLY

Anne E. Streaty Wimberly (b. 1936), professor emerita of Christian education at Interdenominational Theological Center (ITC) in Atlanta, GA, is the foremost scholar of African American Christian education in the United States. She earned a bachelor's degree in music and education from Ohio State University in 1957 and a master's in music education from Boston University in 1965.

Early in her teaching career, Wimberly mentored girls of color at a Methodist-supported school and later served in public school systems in Detroit and the

Boston area. Her teaching coincided with the integration of public schools in the US. Wimberly found herself mocked and derided by white students and teachers. Fortunately, these experiences deepened her trust in God and reinforced her sense of belovedness by God. Her purpose grew, and she earned a PhD in curriculum and instruction from Georgia State University in 1981.

Dr. Wimberly sensed a call to ministry in the 1980s. She returned to school at Garrett-Evangelical Theological Seminary and began a project that later became the contemporary classic *Soul Stories: African American Christian Education*. *Soul Stories* revealed Dr. Wimberly's genius for incorporating stories into Christian educational curricular method. Recognizing the value of stories in African American culture, Wimberly's "story-linking" approach juxtaposes everyday African Americans' stories of oppression and hope with scriptural stories and also with stories of exemplary African American Christians.

Aware of the dehumanizing forces to which African Americans are subject, she views Christian education as offering the means to resist them and, further, to help persons take up vocations that will support their own dignity while offering uplift to the black community. Her commitment to hope-building is evident in multiple books on adolescents, including *Youth Ministry in the Black Church: Centered in Hope* with Sandra Barnes and Karma Johnson (2013); *Empowering Black Youth of Promise: Education and Socialization in the Village-Minded Black Church* with Sandra Barnes (2016); and *Raising Hope: Four Paths to Courageous Living for Black Youth* with Sarah Farmer (2017).

Recently, Dr. Wimberly, along with Nathaniel West and Annie Lockhart-Gilroy, edited *From Lament to Advocacy: Black Religious Education and Public Ministry* (2020). Undertaken as a response to repeated police killings of black people in the US, the book exhorts black Christian educators to redouble their efforts to shape their ministries toward the development of critical consciousness and liberative imagination in pursuit of social justice. They point to mother-daughter relationships, spiritual retreats sponsored by urban parishes for marginalized youth, and the need for Christian education to disrupt the school-to-prison pipeline. The book links Dr. Wimberly's commitment to hope-building vocations to the struggle against racialized violence and other injustice.

FRED P. EDIE

Following this pattern, womanist theologian Delores Williams more recently has linked the biblical story of Hagar with the experience of contemporary African American women. Noting that Hagar was enslaved as well as the object of class, gender, and sexual exploitation, Williams imaginatively describes how this single mother resists her oppressors and secures existence for herself and her son, Ishmael, in the wilderness.[30] As a fighter and a survivor, Williams depicts Hagar's story as offering hope for many contemporary Black women.

For her part, Anne Wimberly promotes still another layer of story-linking as part of her educational strategy. Not only does she invite connections between learners and the biblical story, she further invites learners' imaginative connections to the stories of African American Christian exemplars. She draws upon exemplars like Harriet Tubman and Howard Thurman as embodiments of dimensions of the biblical story. When it comes to employing the Bible for African American faith formation, therefore, Wimberly is far more interested in imagination as a means to transformation than mere precept or application.

Affectivity, Diverse Communities, and Transformed Imagination

A new generation of Christian educators continues to innovate with respect to imagination. Educator and biblical scholar Amanda Jo Pittman traces the significance of imagination in the book of Acts.[31] In one of three case studies, she describes and analyzes Peter's decision to go to the house of Cornelius, a gentile centurion, and to eat with him and his family. Pittman reminds readers that centurions struck terror in the hearts of Jews. They symbolized the unchecked power of empire, and their unpredictable violent actions inflamed a climate of fear in occupied communities. She also points out how Peter's vision, full of "unclean" foods, conjured in him palpable disgust at the prospect of following God's call. Peter has all kinds of reasons to beg off this invitation. Through this attention to the context of the story, however, Pittman enables readers to appreciate how Peter's change of heart requires more than a change of mind. The transformed imagination that enables Peter to envision Cornelius and family as God's beloved and then to enter intimately into (bodily) relation with them by sitting down at their table also involves the transformation of Peter's bodily passions. Through his vision (a gift of the Spirit mediated by the aesthetic dimensions of his humanity), God offers Peter new reasons of the heart, new ends for his love. Yet the vision becomes reality only as Peter and his hosts enter into this surprising and diverse communion with one another. It is in the act of eating together that disgust turns to delight and where they discover their common ties before God. Once again, we see the crucial importance of encountering different kinds of people for nurturing faith.

Imagination and (Serious) Play

On another tack, Christian educator Courtney Goto also traces the possibility of forming the imagination of Christians by aesthetic means, this time through practices of play.[32] Play is not a new theme in educational circles; it has been creatively appropriated for children's educational ministries by a number of scholars.[33] Goto envisions play as more than child's play, however, and as encompassing more than conventional assumptions about its frivolity and fun. In one of her own case studies, Goto demonstrates how adults at play were critical to the transformation of her congregation. She first describes a garden created by her Japanese American Christian elders on the church grounds during the congregation's early years. It became an oasis of peace in a busy urban area. It symbolized the church's identity. It seemed to Goto a perfectly fitting expression of Japanese American Christian spirituality. Over time, however, the garden (and the congregation) fell into disrepair. Teenaged Goto, assisted by now elderly gardeners, set out to restore it. Goto movingly chronicles learning the culturally choreographed dance of gestures required for Japanese gardening—the right way to trim hedges, to realign rock features and to reinscribe pathways. Inspired by this restoration, Goto's mother, the church's educator, re-created the garden out of papier-mâché and fabric *inside the church sanctuary*. Over a season, the congregation played ritually in this pretend garden during its worship. Congregants experimented with moving things around, adding new plantings, and undertaking a range of worshipful practices in relation to different garden features. Goto suggests that over time this liturgical playing enabled the community to remember the distinctiveness of its founding identity as well as provided the freedom to imagine what God's future might offer them. Long simmering conflicts arose but were playfully reinterpreted in this imaginative garden.

We do not think Goto would immediately counsel readers to drop this book, go plant a garden, then re-create it in their church sanctuary. This brilliant endeavor in ministry is also a highly contextualized one. We do hope, however, that readers will give these experiments by Wimberly, Pittman, Goto, and others due consideration. Aesthetic appeals to the human imagination—an imagination lodged in the mind, heart, belly, and bones of its bearers as well as in the collective ethos of communities—awaken our loves and hold the potential to direct them to their proper ends. Faith is another name for that direction. Faith is the deepest imaginings of the human heart finding repose in divine embrace.

Conclusion

This chapter began with the claim that faith, while a gift, also coheres with the stuff of humanity. Estimations of the content of this "stuff" have varied over time. Consistent with biblical wisdom and contemporary sensibilities, we have chosen to highlight human being's essential embodiment, desire, and relationality. The project of nurturing faith in light of these emphases is presently coalescing around "imagination," a term that embraces complexity over the too simplistic (and ultimately destructive) Enlightenment views of persons as rational agents or irrational beasts. We've attempted to describe not only what makes persons tick but also what makes them open to receiving God's presence and grace.

Imagination requires an object, a telos, however. Jesus Christ can provide it. In the next chapter, we turn to how Jesus empowers human beings to imagine themselves rightly and therefore to become transformed as God intends.

Interactive Dialogue

1. With which of the portraits of human being—solitary thinker, beast, or lover—do you most identify? Is there another portrait that captures you better?
2. According to the authors, what is wrong with rationalism?
3. What do you make of the claim that human beings are more "lovers" than "thinkers"? How do the authors suggest it will impact the ministry of nurturing faith? What other impacts can you imagine?
4. What is at stake in the effort to reimagine human beings as embodied and relational? As imaginative?
5. The authors contend that cultivating Christian imagination requires sustained relations with different kinds of Christians. Why? Defend, modify, or rebut this claim.

For Further Reading

Bondi, Roberta C. *To Love as God Loves: Conversations with the Early Church*. Philadelphia: Fortress, 1987.

Damasio, Antonio. *Descartes' Error: Emotion, Reason, and the Human Brain*. New York: G. P. Putnam's Sons, 1994.

Eastman, Susan Grove. *Paul and the Person: Reframing Paul's Anthropology*. Grand Rapids: Eerdmans, 2017.

Edie, Fred P. *Book, Bath, Table, and Time: Christian Worship as Source and Resource for Youth Ministry*. Cleveland: Pilgrim, 2007.

Goto, Courtney T. *The Grace of Playing: Pedagogies for Leaning into God's New Creation*. Eugene, OR: Pickwick, 2016.

McGilchrist, Iain. *The Master and His Emissary: The Divided Brain and the Making of the Western World*. New Haven: Yale University Press, 2009.

Smith, James K. A. *Desiring the Kingdom*. Grand Rapids: Baker Academic, 2009.

Wimberly, Anne E. Streaty. *Soul Stories: African American Christian Education*. Rev. ed. Nashville: Abingdon, 2005.

CHAPTER SEVEN

Jesus, Sin, and the Grace of Cruciform Resurrection

We acknowledge and bewail our manifold sins and wickedness.

—"PRAYER OF CONFESSION,"
BOOK OF COMMON PRAYER

Just as this [bread and wine] turns into you when you eat and drink it, so you for your part turn into the body of Christ.

—AUGUSTINE OF HIPPO

ROAD MAP

Jesus is the reason for Christian faith. He is the beginning and the end of all things. He is faith's subject and object—at once its medium and message. For leaders in faith formation, Jesus is the "curriculum," the "pedagogy," and the primary "instructor." In one way or another, every chapter in this book is about Jesus. He is a master teacher, and he calls his pupils to practice an embodied, communal way of life. Limited by space considerations, this chapter does double duty. It focuses upon *two* crucial dimensions of what is called "Christology": first, the person of Jesus as incarnation of God; and second, the saving nature of his "paschal mystery." By way of Scripture, tradition, and the church's lived experience, it spells out how these convictions shape the task of nurturing faith.

Introduction

Back in the twentieth century, Fred arrived home from work to the spectacle of crayoned crosses Scotch-taped side by side around an entire family room—to walls, chairs, cabinets, even a potted plant, all at the eye level of a two-year-old. The artist pointed to his creation and said with emphasis: "Having a Jesus *Crisis!*" Though he may have meant to say "Christ" instead of "crisis," no one could dispute his point. Jesus's death on the cross forces us to confront the crisis of sin. Acknowledging the human condition while gazing into a mirror is no easy task. Yet Jesus also presents us with a crisis of opportunity. He has promised us re-creation. Shall we receive it?

To place this introduction in a more prosaic key, Jesus is *Who* we nurture faith in. Jesus is God's self-revelation, the second person of the Trinity, incarnate Son of the Father. Jesus reveals God's identity and mission while drawing us into the joy of divine triune existence. Incarnation is a critical theme here, for it suggests particular approaches to nurturing faith, which we shall explore in some detail. Second, Jesus is also *Why* the church nurtures faith. Through the mystery of his life and ministry, death and resurrection, Jesus delivers human beings and all creation from captivity to sin to the freedom of new creation. Trusting faith in his graced work is redemptive, restorative, and liberative. As we shall see, at one level, the question is why Jesus elicits trust and gratitude as the only adequate faith responses to his self-giving. At another level, Christ also invites faithful participation in himself, in his living body, as members of the new creation. With respect to the problem of interpretive pluriformity described in part 1, this chapter insists upon Jesus as Christianity's hermeneutical key. At the same time, it illustrates how the meanings and significance of Jesus himself are pluriform, therefore making humility an essential ingredient of participation in him.

Encroaching Challenges to Nurturing Faith	Engaging Resources for Nurturing Faith	Exclusive Uniquenesses of Nurturing Faith	Extraordinary Gifts for Nurturing Faith
Disorienting amnesia	Meaningful commemorations	Penetrating Scripture	Transformative hope
Autonomous determinism	Mutual disclosure	Interdependent kinship	Inspired trust
▸ Interpretive pluriformity	Generous humility	Resurrected image	Restorative grace
Social constructionism	Intentional citizenship	Supernatural guidance	Countercultural faith
Fragmented faith	Faithful gestures	Focused proclamation	Fortifying love
Conceptual bricolage	Probing reflection	Discerning community	Principled freedom

Coming to Terms with Incarnation

From the outset of his ministry Jesus taught "as one who had authority." People were "amazed" by his teachings and healings (Mark 1:22). They speculated that he was a *prophet* of God. Slowly, however, it dawned upon Jesus's followers that he was more than a godly human; he was humanly God. Oddly, the Gospels suggest that outsiders and demons were the first to recognize Jesus's divine *identity*. Only after his crucifixion and resurrection did the inside crowd figure things out. As noted in chapter 5, Jesus is said to "reveal" God. Jesus discloses God's nature, which would otherwise transcend human comprehension. (Recall the splendid *Contact* analogy.) In Jesus, we know God's loving creativity and relationality. Jesus also reveals God's *mission*. God seeks restoration of all creation from sin and full establishment of God's realm. In Jesus, we learn that God's identity and mission are fully consistent with one another. Who God is and what God does are the same.[1]

Over time, the church came to speak of Jesus as *incarnation*, God in the flesh (*carnus* means meat or flesh). It affirmed that Jesus is at one and the same time truly God and truly human, two natures in one person. This doctrine was refined over several centuries at church councils in the effort to refute competing claims. On one side were those who asserted that Jesus's divinity must certainly trump his humanity. In effect, they held that Jesus only pretended to be human or to suffer and die. In response, Gregory of Nazianzus (fourth century) asserted "that which he [Jesus] has not assumed he has not healed."[2] A second position contended for the opposite of the first. It asserted that Jesus was not divine but was only, exclusively, human. True, he was an unusual man, perhaps even uniquely intimate with God but, in the end, just a mere human, not a savior. A third position held that Jesus was a divine-human hybrid. Like a holy piñata, he was one thing on the outside (flesh) and something wonderful within (divine).

Each flawed position is understandable, given the limits of human comprehension. Nor did conciliar clarifications squelch them for all time. These heresies persist into the present. With respect to nurturing faith, they appear, on the one hand, in the form of spiritualized faith unconcerned with bodies or communal life or social cultural realities and, on the other hand, as moral activism without faithful attunement to transcendence.

The church continues to insist upon Jesus as fully human and fully divine, however. In the language of creeds and councils, Jesus is of "one being with the Father," he is "begotten not made," and he assumed humanity by being born of Mary. According to Cyril of Alexandria, Jesus's divine and human natures coexist in *hypostatic union*, two natures dwelling together in one single concrete existence.[3]

Origen (185–254) speaks of God's *condescension* to human beings in Jesus.[4] In other words, because God meets us on our terms by sharing our humanity, God crosses the gulf between divine transcendence and creaturely finitude. This insight serves as still another reminder that faith is first a gift from God. Had God not assumed creaturely existence, human beings would remain ignorant of God's loving intent.

Coming to Terms with the Paschal Mystery

The *paschal mystery* refers to God's saving and restorative work in and through Christ. Christians profess that the life, death, and resurrection of Jesus redeem the world from its captivity to sin and reorient it to the flourishing God intends. A variety of theories of *atonement* purport to explain how Christ accomplishes this work. For example, the Scriptures sometimes gesture to Jesus's death as paying the legal *penalty* for God's judgment against human sin. Elsewhere Jesus is imagined as offering himself as a *ransom* to free captive humanity. Another oft-used term is *sacrifice*, as in the case of Paul's description of Jesus as the "paschal lamb" (1 Cor. 5:7). No single atonement theory can account for the depth of Christ's saving work, so none of them is elevated to the level of doctrine. Each points in its own way toward the breadth and depth of holy mystery—the infinitely fathomable significance of God's love.

Since only God in Christ can save, there would seem little more to say about it, let alone do about it, in relation to nurturing faith. Yet as we will suggest below, faith goes hand in hand with learning to understand ourselves as sinners trapped in a web of sin. We receive Christ's gift of freedom from sin in part through growing acknowledgment of the extent of its hold on ourselves and the world. Christian freedom consists of more than freedom *from* sin, however. It means freedom *for* relational interdependence, including love of God and neighbor, and freedom for life as a member of Christ's postascension body on earth, the church. Paul considers *baptism* to be the means of entry into Christ's body, because for him it washes persons into Jesus's death on the cross and the hope of sharing in his resurrection life (Rom. 6). Juxtaposing the imagery of John 3 and Romans 6, baptism serves as both *tomb* wherein persons die to sin and *womb* where they are born again to new life in Christ.[5]

Theological Musings on Incarnation for Faith Formation

Stepping beyond doctrine, we offer a theology of imagination in relation to incarnation. Whereas the previous chapter considered aspects of human imagination, we propose to consider Jesus Christ as the *Imagination of God*.

Revealed in the incarnation is all of God's past, present, and future saving intent. Jesus's imaginative sayings combined with Jesus's imaginative doings disclose creation's destiny. We do not mean to imply by this claim that Jesus is a figment of God's imagination. Rather, as Robert Jenson suggests, Jesus "is the person in whom the Father hears and sees himself and so determines who and what God is."[6] In the person of the Son, divine imagination condescends to meet human imagination.

IMAGINATION

Imagination, as Maria Harris observes, is "far too complex a reality to be reduced to mere definition. It is imagination's nature *not* to pin down." Hence when tempted to settle for just the standard definition—the capacity to see in the mind what does not exist in the senses—we quickly grant her point. At times, for example, imagination attends not to fantasy but to what *exists* with the purpose of rendering the familiar strange again. Imagination is frequently associated with art and aesthetic ways of knowing that stir the heart. While powerful, aesthetic insights resist logical or empirical agendas of specificity and certainty. Further still, imagination is integral to the capacity for self-transcendence, a decidedly mixed blessing (as Adam and Eve discovered). Given this ambiguity, it is inevitable that imagination be implicated in both doxology and devilry within Christian tradition.

The Bible's assessment of imagination holds theological themes in tension. On the one hand, imagination finds itself indicted for its propensity to incline humans to idolatry. The Bible repeatedly warns against "imaging" God out of concern for domesticating God for human purposes. Imagination also may prompt a kind of creativity on the part of humans inappropriate to their creaturely status. The capacity for transcendence may (wrongly) tempt human beings to usurp God's unique creative role, even to fancy themselves as God.

On the other hand, the writer of Colossians imaginatively portrays Jesus as the "image" (*eikōn*) of God (Col. 1:15). Gazing upon Jesus, Christians are provided a window into holy mystery. More than that, Jesus as "image" not only functions to point toward God, but also Jesus fully participates in the divinity he images. Here the door is opened to the faithful use of imagination within the Christian tradition. If flesh and blood may faithfully image the invisible God, then, by analogy, humans may make imaginative use of material things for their own iconographic purposes. Water, bread, and wine become ingredients of sacraments. Music, drama, storytelling, stained-glass windows, and other visual arts proliferate for doxological purposes.

Of what does the Christian imagination consist, and what is its purpose? Minimally, it would seem to require a rich trove of images—symbols, stories, practices, and more—that display God's history of covenant association with Israel, self-revelation through the life, death, and resurrection of Jesus Christ, and intent to build a realm consistent with God's creating and redeeming nature. Imaginative knowing is associative and expansive, not specifying and reductive; therefore, the larger the image trove, the greater possibility for faithful imagining. In addition, Christian imagination includes awareness that Christian images themselves always bear a surplus of meaning. When Christians use even a single symbol, story, ritual, or metaphor, they speak and enact limitless possible associations. "Bread," for example, implies companionship, thanksgiving, abundance, feasting, trust, value, community, life, and also (broken) body. This plurality is entirely appropriate when the imagination's ultimate referent is a God who transcends human capacities for description.

As Dykstra observes, Christian imagination "sees what is 'not yet' and works to create it." It interpretively correlates the images from its trove with the present fears, hopes, joys, and sufferings of human beings and communities. Where persons are yearning for or claiming identity as God's beloved children in Christ, seeking and finding healing from personal and social ills, or where hope-filled transformative action toward justice is "rolling down like the waters," the Christian imagination sees the Spirit at work. More than creatively linking God's saving past with the present, then, it also seeks to equip persons to participate in God's saving work. Christian imagination *acts* in anticipation of the future it imagines with hope.

FRED P. EDIE

Nor do we wish to imply, as have various heretical streams of modalism over the history of Christianity, that God made up Jesus a little later in the creative process in order to solve unanticipated problems in creation, bugs in the system that required patching with new code. As we have seen, Jesus is the creative (imagining) Word, present from the very beginning, now made flesh. He is not a savior-come-lately.

The apostle Paul helps clarify what we intend for Jesus as the Imagination of God, in his letter to the Colossians. He describes Jesus as the "image" (*eikōn*) of God (Col. 1:15). "Image," of course, is also the root of "imagination." Further, in Jesus, the *eikōn*, "all the fullness of God was pleased to dwell" (1:19). In this passage, Paul is painting the first brush strokes in what will eventually become the formal doctrine of incarnation. Jesus as *eikōn* is anything but an abstract fanciful solution to a problem of metaphysical logic. Instead, and this is crucial for nurturing faith in Jesus, his materiality is assumed to be the essential channel through which the revelation of God (and human redemption) is offered.

To reiterate, Jesus Christ, the Imagination of God, is at one and the same time (1) utterly grounded in the ordinary earthly materiality of human life (he is fully flesh and blood); (2) the bearer of the fullness of God (fully divine). This is decidedly good news! In Jesus, both God and human beings may imagine themselves rightly. Hence a fundamental task of Christian education for faith formation is pointing to Jesus as God's imaginative intent for all creation. Endemic to faithful response to Jesus Christ as God's Imagination is a properly trained human imagination.

In addition, God's "enfleshment" in Christ affirms human embodiment as the means to perceive him as God. As noted in chapter 6, human imagination encompasses the desires of human hearts, the habitual dispositions of human bodies, emotions, feelings, and thoughts, plus human core relationality. God in Christ utilizes all of these human capacities to make God's self known. Jesus's embrace of embodiment vouchsafes human bodies (corporate and personal) as loci for receiving divine revelation.

Further still, God's embrace and redemption of earthly existence in Jesus assures the church that materiality in general, the "stuff" of creation that is, may mediate Jesus's presence and grace by the power of the Spirit. Jesus not only inhabited a body, he dwelt within a human culture too. He learned to speak and read language, probably Aramaic. He embraced the religion of Judaism through participation in its language, stories, rituals, symbols, and practices.[7] He taught by way of culturally accessible means.

Even as Jesus reveals God, incarnation remains mysterious. It cannot be contained by simplistic platitudes or reductive systems. Flattening incarnation becomes just another form of idolatry. Therefore, the task of nurturing faith is found in knowing that Jesus is one who simultaneously reveals and conceals a God who comes as near as human flesh while continuing to transcend human experience and knowledge. Fortunately, Scripture and tradition are full of cultural tools for awakening this kind of faith, tools continuously updated as cultures change over time. We turn now to exploring some of these central cultural tools.

Story

Prior chapters have pointed to story as a primary means for stirring faithful imagination. This part explains in more detail why this is so. Matthew, Mark, Luke, and John offer their Gospels for the purpose of nurturing faith. Notably, their invitation to faith comes in story form. For each of them, Jesus is a "storied" revelation. Inviting others into life in Christ requires telling his story. To suggest that the Gospels assume storied or "narrative" shape means that each follows certain literary conventions. There is a central protagonist (Jesus), certain supporting characters, and a few antagonists. The Gospels also develop a plot—Jesus comes on the scene, he creates dramatic tension by stirring up the status quo, the plot thickens, then the story climaxes with his passion and resurrection.

The storied nature of the Gospels has not always been appreciated even by the church. Especially from the period of the Enlightenment to the middle of the twentieth century, esteem for stories suffered at the hands of rationalism and empiricism. In these epistemological systems, truth came to consist of facts that could be established through observation and reason. Stories, including biblical stories, were demoted to the realm of fantasy or child's play. Influenced by the Enlightenment, theologians and biblical scholars of that time became embarrassed by the church's own dependence upon stories. Their responses took at least two forms. Bible scholars sought to dig beneath the "fantastic" stories of Scripture, the Gospels in particular, in order to establish "the facts" about Jesus verifiable through intertextual investigation, historical research, or reason. As a result, fully orbed gospel narratives were reduced to a few bullet points on the "historical Jesus":

- Jesus was a Jewish teacher, probably affiliated with one or another Jewish sect.
- He likely received baptism from John the Baptist, *not* because this was an important public epiphany of Jesus as God's Son empowered for ministry by the Spirit but because it sent mixed messages over the identity of the Messiah. Put in different terms, that the Gospels are at such pains to reiterate John's subordination to Jesus implies that Jesus receiving baptism from John had been an issue of confusion and conflict for the early church, hence the baptism *must* have taken place.
- He was executed by the Roman authorities for stirring up social unrest. Independent confirmation of Jesus's crucifixion exists outside the Gospels.

The search for the historical Jesus leaves only a shell of a man, hardly worthy of the church's faith.

A second response was to search for meaning behind or above the story of Jesus. Friedrich Schleiermacher (1768-1834) sought to lift Christianity out of all its messy particularity (for example, that its founder was a poor Jew) and to portray it instead as one means to open persons to a universally available God-consciousness, a "feeling of absolute dependence" that persons discover within themselves. In this case, Jesus functions as a symbol of what fully realized God-consciousness consists in.[8]

Inspired by theological ethicist Stanley Hauerwas and others in the later decades of the twentieth century, the storied nature of Christian faith was recovered.[9] Hauerwas's simple yet profound observation is this: speaking of Jesus (or in our case, nurturing faith in him) isn't possible apart from telling his story. Discussing the meaning of Jesus or his impact depends first upon the stories about him. Gospel stories, therefore, are more than window dressing for abstract moral points or universally available God-consciousness; they *are* the point. The gospel is essentially, irreducibly narrative.

God also uses story to communicate gospel to beings who are themselves fundamentally "storied." Humans, created by a storied God, also make meaning in and through stories they tell and hear. For humankind, it is stories "all the way down."

There is more. The story of Jesus speaks to the aesthetically tuned dimensions of the human quest for meaning. It induces participants to wonder and delight. It disarms defensiveness and distanced speculation. It suspends disbelief and builds bridges to transcendent experience. We identify bodily—somatically— with a story. That is why readers and hearers become so involved with characters in stories, be they Harry Potter, Frodo, or Jesus. As beings relational at their core, humans assimilate empathically stories of others into their own.

The ministry of nurturing faith will, therefore, face down temptations to reduce the gospel to abstract principles or "four spiritual laws" and wean itself from Bibles that purport in their margins to explain the meaning *behind* stories. In their place, leaders in faith formation will substitute more occasions and contexts for telling the gospel story as *story*. It will invite learners to tell the stories of their own lives and to invite their transformation by reimagining themselves in light of Jesus's story. In addition to Scripture, it will welcome and utilize the extensive Christian literature featuring Christ-figures as protagonists. From *The Chronicles of Narnia* to *Babette's Feast*, to the southern novel *Walking across Egypt*,[10] this literature stimulates faithful imagining by inserting Christlike characters into circumstances beyond the (too?) well-traveled paths of Palestine. Portraying Jesus as lion (*Narnia*), chef (*Feast*), or an old woman (*Egypt*) invites readers of stories to be incorporated through their embodied imaginations into the relational reality of the incarnational imaginal presence.

Metaphor and Other Linguistic Devices

Nurturing incarnational faith also requires cultivating capacity to "play" with language through the use of a variety of poetic conventions, including but not limited to metaphor, meter, parallelism, paradoxical juxtaposition, and so on. Figurative language covers the pages of the Bible and fills the hymns, homilies, teachings, and poems of the early church. Ephrem, the fourth-century deacon of the Syrian church, offers both a theology and pedagogy for nurturing faith through poetic imagination. Though relatively unknown in the present day, he has been called "the greatest poet of the patristic age and, perhaps, the only theologian-poet to rank beside Dante."[11] Notably he also arranged many of his poems to be sung by choirs.

Poetically, of course, Ephrem proposes a theology of figurative speech. First, he declares it impossible to exhaust the mystery of God. Nevertheless, he allows that God "puts on names," that is "metaphors," out of loving condescension to human "weakness."[12]

> We should realize that,
> had He not put on the names
> of such things,
> it would not have been possible for Him
> to speak with us humans.
> By means of what belongs to us did He draw
> close to us:
> He clothes Himself in language,
> So that He might clothe us
> In His mode of life. (*On Faith* 31.2)[13]

Ephrem is clear that this naming is possible only through God's loving initiative.

Motivated by love, God assumes a great many names (Lord, Judge, Rock, Lamb) in order to appeal to the human imagination. At the same time, Ephrem is equally certain that God may put on and "strip off" these names. In other words, while metaphor remains an important means of imagining incarnation, Ephrem insists upon the metaphoric character of the language in order to preserve God's otherness. To literalize a metaphor is to miss its function to simultaneously reveal and conceal.

Ephrem is also expert in paradox. His poems contain juxtapositions of opposites:

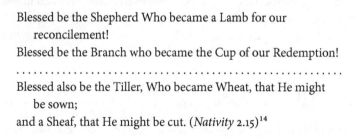

> Blessed be the Shepherd Who became a Lamb for our
>   reconcilement!
> Blessed be the Branch who became the Cup of our Redemption!
> . . . .
> Blessed also be the Tiller, Who became Wheat, that He might
>   be sown;
> and a Sheaf, that He might be cut. (*Nativity* 2.15)[14]

As illustrated by the juxtaposition of "Shepherd" to "Lamb," Ephrem's practice is to break metaphors upon one another to foster allusive, playful imagination in those who participate in his poetry or sing his hymns. One cannot be shepherd and lamb at the same time, and, yet, this both/and is somehow true for Jesus. This wordplay elicits in participants wonder, joy, and delight, which leads to praise. The effect is to create a "thin space" where the material and the spiritual intermingle. In other words, poetics connects persons to the relational presence and mystery of Christ in such a way as to dispose them to worship. It is no accident, therefore, that so much of Scripture engages in figurative and poetic speech. Its invitation is for persons to know Christ and to sense themselves participating in his living, if enigmatic, presence.

Symbol and Ritual

As referenced in chapter five, Thomas Finn's explorations of baptismal rites of initiation from the first through the fifth centuries in communities around the Mediterranean basin reveal a range of Christian ritual symbolic practices we might consider exotic today: anointings, exorcisms, fasting, vigil keeping, kissing, full submersion in baptismal waters often while naked, followed by a first partaking in the Eucharist. Finn's descriptions starkly contradict any view of faith as a private internal disposition of the disembodied soul. He points instead to faith-making that is publicly ritualized, necessarily communal, fully embodied and therefore imaginatively evocative.

The early church obviously privileged *experiential* faith. To a certain extent, candidates for baptism were kept in the dark about the baptismal rites awaiting them. Ambrose (c. 340-397) explained the need for candidates to receive faith through participation in the sacraments of baptism and communion before they discussed this gift. He implies that the experience of the rites "speaks" more than anything we can say about them.[15] We are suggesting here that graced meaning and transforming power of incarnation may be proffered through these and other ritual symbols themselves. They provide appropriately incarnational means for imaginative participation in the mystery of incarnation. As Paul explains to the Christians in Rome, through baptism new Christians share in Christ's death and in the hope of his resurrection (Rom. 6). The newly baptized are sacramentally made over *into* Christ as members of Christ's body. More on this below.

SACRAMENTS

Three relationships typically describe approaches to sacraments and responses of faith.

1. Sacramental Participation *Is* Education—Historian Thomas Finn artfully suggests that the "theology of the church of antiquity was the result of symbols deeply lived." This claim is supported through awareness of *anamnēsis* and prolepsis in relation to liturgical action. *Anamnēsis* is usually translated "remembrance" in English—as in Jesus's eucharistic bidding: "Do this in remembrance of me" (1 Cor. 11:24). To do Jesus's *anamnēsis* summons all his past saving actions into the present sacramental moment and seeks to bind worshippers into them. Similarly, characterizing sacraments as proleptic is to acquire through them a "foretaste" of God's realm, the future shalom made present. To participate in the sacraments is educative, therefore, because it incorporates worshippers into all of God's storied past, present, and future salvation. Hence sacramental participation gains credibility as education for inviting Christians to *perform* their identities by way of embodied language uniquely available through liturgical action, for enacting worshippers into God's *story* of salvation, or for the ways liturgy engages human affectivity and imagination to shape the *heart* in virtue.

2. Sacramental Participation *Prompts* Education—The emphasis here is upon sacraments as objects of study in relation to the life of the believer. Assisting persons in reflecting upon the implications of sacramentally enacted stories and theologies described above is one common educational means toward faithful discipleship. To that end, catechetical instruction often utilizes action/reflection pedagogies to prepare persons for sacramental participation and then to invite their reflections upon their experiences. Beyond linking Scripture and theology to sacraments and faith, educators may also facilitate learners' linkage of sacramental practice with justice-seeking practices of everyday life. Hence hunger sated at the Eucharist table propels believers outward to meet and fill the many hungers of the world.

3. Sacramental Participation *Shapes* Education—Here, assumptions about epistemic and theological dimensions of sacramentality shape educators' curricular, pedagogic, and teaching practices whether these practices are expressly oriented to the sacraments or not. Sacramentally related concerns for eliciting or cultivating persons in aesthetic capacities for surprise, wonder, creativity, playfulness, and dwelling in the mystery of paradox are primary in this approach. In addition, sacramentally shaped education invites learners imaginatively to tap into the surplus of meaning resounding within metaphorical and ritualistic symbols such as water, bread, and wine. This form of education taps into human creativity to support engagement with a God who is at once immanent and transcendent.

Obviously, Christian education shaped by sacramentality is not merely aesthetic, nor is that its end. Consistent with the sacraments themselves, it is fundamentally christological. Its aesthetic bent, however, along with its openness to linking the spiritual with the material, and because it fosters associative and expansive modes of knowing, inclines it to see Christ's saving work broadly within the historical, material, and social practices of the world.

FRED P. EDIE

The question is, were the churches of the New Testament and antiquity more "primitive" than ours (thus the need for all these rites and symbols), or did they possess more wisdom about how God is revealed and faith nurtured than the contemporary church (especially its Protestant variations)? We favor the lost-wisdom theory. And, consistent with this and other chapters in this part, we view Christian ritual symbols, including engagement with the Scriptures (the church's "Book"), its baptismal waters ("Bath"), its holy meal ("Table"), and its temporal patterning of Christ's life ("Time"), as being both "culturally" and "theologically" "efficacious."[16] They too open thin spaces where divine grace meets material humanity. They speak to and through our embodiment, and they offer and invite participation in incarnational mystery. Further, we view congregational participation in these "holy things" as examples of Fowler's "faithing." Corporate praise of God *is* faith, at least one dimension of it.

These reflections on story, poetics, and ritual symbols also hold true for the practices of dance, music and song, visual arts, and drama. In the lyrical words of Emily Dickinson, all of these bear potential to tell "the truth but tell it slant."[17] They invite encounter with God while refusing the temptation to make God subject to our own prejudices.

Theological Musings on Paschal Mystery for Faith Formation

Jesus is not only the incarnate means to nurturing faith; he is also faith's subject and object. Through Jesus's life, death, and resurrection, humanity and all of creation are freed from enslavement to sin and death. If Christian teenagers in the US know anything about their faith (and this is not a given), they know this formula: "Jesus died for my sins." True enough, but not nearly adequate to grasping the depth and breadth of sin or the surpassing love of God's redemptive work in Christ. For help explaining these fundamental Christian convictions, we turn to Paul the apostle, as interpreted by New Testament scholar Susan Eastman.

Eastman suggests that Paul offers multiple overlapping accounts of sin. Paul first describes it as "what all human beings do."[18] Sin consists of evil actions persons commit. This story of sin, familiar to Euro-American Christians, is a valuable one. It holds humans accountable for their sins by insisting upon their "complicity in interlocking systems of lies and violence."[19] It also explains why they fall under judgment and deserve the wrath of God. For Paul, these human sins are idolatrous at their core (Rom. 1:21; see also vv. 22–27). They amount to the failure to honor God as God.

That human beings are idolatrous beings is beyond doubt. Yet this account by itself suits a climate of cultural individualism perhaps a little too well. It assumes humans are radically free and autonomous agents who choose to sin all by themselves and therefore have no one to blame either for their sin or its consequences but themselves. Eastman notes how Paul resists oversimplifying. Even in this first story, he suggests that human sin results in a "debased mind," implying a distortion of perspective that renders human beings less than fully able to acknowledge or obey God (Rom. 1:28).

According to Eastman, Paul builds upon his first account by offering additional ones in which he characterizes sin as an actor on a cosmic stage, an agent weaving itself into death-dealing relationships with humans. We turn to those in a moment, but first a brief summary of Paul's assumptions about how human beings are formed as persons—in other words, what makes them tick.

Similar to many postmoderns, the very *pre*modern Paul holds a thoroughgoing relational view of human beings. (See again chapter 6.) In brief, because the Enlightenment had not yet invented its individualistic and rationalistic portrait, Paul does not imagine that human beings independently choose to become who they are. Rather, for Paul, the individual person emerges throughout the course of life in and through relationships with other persons, those persons also emerging in and through their web of personal relationships. In other words, "I" am a product of "we." I am a relational being to the core. (Indeed, for Paul, human relational connection to Adam and Eve is what makes them sinners.) Similar to what we noted previously, for Paul, human beings are "constitutively relational." Paul could not conceive of humans any other way. He had no vision of radical individual freedom or individual autonomy that Christians of the Global North (mistakenly) presume. This is important to keep in mind as we move to Paul's second story of sin.

In this second account, Paul's grammar for sin switches from the verb form (something humans do) to the noun form (a personified agent warring against God in a drama of cosmic proportions). Eastman describes sin here as an "external" and "oppressive power": a force acting upon humans in opposition to God and God's good mission. Distinct from the first story's emphasis on humans as sinners, Eastman explains that Paul's second account treats "sin itself [as] the surpassing 'sinner.'"[20] Paul describes human beings falling "under the power of sin" (Rom. 3:9) and becoming sin's "slaves" (6:20). Indeed, sin's power catches up everyone and everything in its web of destruction, deceit, and violence.

This is a crucial addition to Paul's first account for at least three reasons. First, it insists that all creation—including the natural world, as well as human social and cultural systems, and not just individual sinners of their own initiative—falls under sin's power. Second, it refutes the temptation to identify other humans entirely with their sin, to call them "evil." This restraint is crucial, for when I judge others to be "evil sinners," I may believe myself justified in doing violence to them in the name of wiping out evil. This thinking, we might call it "other-izing," is the root of demonization of people groups, slavery, war, and even genocide. It also contradicts Jesus's nonviolent witness. Perpetrating violence in the name of truth or righteousness only reveals sin's continuing sway over everything, "sinner" and "saved" alike. Third, sin as alien power best explains how children, persons with disabilities, or persons with dementia may also be described as being "under sin" even while lacking full agency. Although they cannot be said to freely "choose" sin in any conventional sense, their personhood is compromised to the extent that they too become bound up in sin's web. They are denied relations of mutuality and love in a world corrupted by sin and instead are subjected to sin's relations, characterized by objectification, fear, or resentment of their inability to contribute to Pharaoh's economy.

In the third story of sin, Paul links relational personhood to sin's agency. He confesses his own inability to do the good he wants to do, instead doing "the very thing I hate" (Rom. 7:15). Yet he adds this crucial insight: In fact it is no longer I who do it, but sin that dwells within me (7:17). Recall the assertion above that human beings are always being constituted and reconstituted as persons in relationship with others ("others" in this case can include all kinds of beings or agents). Human interaction with sin is no different. Sin preys upon then co-opts human relationality. Paul describes this as the battle between the "I" and "not I." Eastman calls this phenomenon "conflicted dyadic agency." Through relationship with sin, humans assimilate its perspective within themselves, only to find they have fallen into its grasp. Moreover, persons who have internalized sin's power discover their own agency diminished through this relationship. Like drug users enslaved to their drugs, humans become slaves to sin. Eastman summarizes: "The Self here is described as occupied territory, its subjectivity colonized by an oppressive foreign power, its members mobilized for actions contrary to its deepest wants, but yet it remains cognizant of its loss of freedom. It experiences this combination of cognizance and crippled capacity as inner division, which is the internalization of sin's lethal embrace."[21]

This diminished agency manifests itself as lost capacity for healthy relations with others. Since "no one is good, not even one" (Rom. 3:9–11), instead of entering into healthy relational participation in mutual embrace and submission, sin's dominion over human beings enlists them in relations of domination and exploitation. Persons created in love by God to be formed in and through loving relationships promoting mutual flourishing find themselves deformed by them instead.

In summary, Paul offers several descriptions of sin. In the first, human beings are "sinners" who commit sins. For this idolatrous failure to trust God, they fall under God's wrath. In the second, sin is characterized as an alien cosmic force acting upon humans. Third, sin preys upon persons' relational constitutions, enslaving them by taking over their relational agency.

This discussion of sin is an essential preamble for rightly perceiving the redeeming work of God in Jesus Christ through the power of the Spirit. For humans are at once guilty of committing sin and have become slaves to its power. They are both sin's perpetrators and its victims. With regard to our guilt, it makes sense to claim that Jesus died *for* our sin. Something or some-One was required to save human beings from God's wrath. But if sin is a cosmic force contending not only against creation but also against God, an enslaving power that turns even the best impulses of creation to its own deceitful purposes, then we may say more fundamentally that Jesus died on the cross for *sin itself*. He was "made to be sin" (2 Cor. 5:21), put to death by the most violent of means, in order to put to death sin's power. In the process, humanity and creation are forgiven, redeemed, and delivered from God's wrath. A "new creation" in Christ begins.

At present this new creation continues to battle against sin's power. Because of the resurrection, we are assured that the future belongs to Christ, but the present is no picnic. Even as the paschal mystery defeats sin, sin's influence lingers. Paul urges Roman Christians to act in a manner consistent with the freedom Christ has won for them by refusing to fight evil with evil and instead to "overcome evil . . . in a communal life that replicates Christ's grace toward all."[22] This stance is honest yet hopeful. It explains why even Christians continue to struggle with sin and evil while affirming their power to resist it through participation in Christ's body, the church.

Having described bondage to sin in relational terms, "not I but sin within me," Paul chooses the parallel form, "no longer I . . . , but Christ who lives in me," to describe the new creation.[23] Baptism into Christ becomes the way human beings die *to* sin by incorporation into Christ's death *for* sin. At the same time, baptism incorporates persons into the future promise for sharing Christ's resurrection life (Rom. 6). Eastman points out that just as was the case for life in sin, relational participation characterizes life in Christ. In addition, unlike the old life under sin, this new life expands the human capacity for loving and creative agency. Human participation in Christ enables the "flourishing of human actors" through relationships characterized by mutual encouragement and self-giving.

Implications for Nurturing Faith

Faith as Relational Participation in Christ

Faith, like sin and redemption, is relational and participatory. Christian faith is not merely "faith about"; it is "faith in" and "faith with" the crucified and risen Christ. Though God carries out saving work on a cosmic scale, Christians experience it through relational *participation* in Christ's body. They begin by being incorporated into Christ's life, death, and resurrection through baptism into the church, Christ's body on earth (Rom. 6). They continue to participate in Christ through regular encounters with his living word in Scripture, his saving love in the sacraments, or by imitating him, as with walking the stages of the cross. Persons receive Christ through graced practices beyond the sanctuary, as well as, for example, through their efforts toward healing the sick, serving the poor, and seeking the justice of God's realm for all God's people. To paraphrase Eastman, by imitating Christ, we discover how Christ is already imitating us, God taking on human flesh and blood for the sake of creation. In turn, Christ's imitation is what makes human imitation of and participation in Christ possible. Participation in the church provides the means to partake in Christ's relationality by assimilating his perspective to our own at the same time as Christ further assimilates us into the divine life.[24]

"You Can Run, but You Can't Hide" Again, This Time from Sin

Nurturing faith occurs at the nexus of hope and humility. Even as Christians stake the future on Christ's sacrificial death for sin and resurrection to new life, they do so aware that the unwavering light of Christ continues to expose sin's grip on them. This is why we call for generous humility for interpreting Scripture. And this is why Christian faith will always consist of prayers of repentance over calls for vengeance. Those who lead educational ministry may never lead from the stance of spiritual superiority. Claims to unblemished virtue only mean that sin has educational leaders right where it wants them.

Nurturing faith will therefore require an unending struggle for clear-sightedness. Sin's capacity to deform human minds, to trap them in a web of deceit, to take over human agency, and to pose as righteousness points to the need for ongoing confession, lamentation, and repentance as part of faith. Christians will be beseeching God to extract them from sin's matrix, at least until Christ's return. Christian colossal failures of the past—anti-Semitism, endorsement of human slavery, collusion with empires—provide evidence of the persistence of sin but also of Christ's surpassing power to expose and overturn it. Participation in Christ means relations of domination may be seen for what they are and then transformed for mutual flourishing and joy.

Battling Sin

Finally, and perhaps surprisingly for an account of faith formation stressing the need for humility, we suggest that nurturing faith will require *fighting* to the very end. Paul describes the battle as requiring "the whole armor of God" (Eph. 6:10). Christian educator Emily Peck-McClain urges this different kind of battling in a book evocatively titled *Arm in Arm with Adolescent Girls.*[25] In it she teaches Paul's rendition of sin and redemption (recounted in this chapter) in order to offer teenaged girls crucial gospel insights. First, she reads Paul so girls will know that they and their bodies are not coincident with sin but are subject to distortion by the power of sin. In this, Peck-McClain stands with Paul's words to the Ephesians: "Our fight is not with flesh and blood but principalities and powers" (6:12). As with all human beings, adolescent girls find themselves trapped in a web of sin not of their own creation. The relational matrix of sin, not the choices of individual girls by themselves, is what constructs the sexual objectification of their bodies that girls eventually internalize. Second, Peck-McClain equips girls to fight back against the powers arm in arm with mentoring sisters and mothers in Christ's body. She utilizes many of the weapons we have described: participation in Christ through deep attention to the Scriptures, to the baptismal covenant, plus cultivating clear-sightedness, vigilance, and sharing community bent toward relations of mutual flourishing.

Conclusion

The incarnation of Christ means that faith may be nurtured through participation in human relationships, material human symbols, language, and other cultural patterns and products. Faith is not procured by way of otherworldly spiritual gnosis. At the same time, while incarnation reveals God's loving condescension to meet humans where they are, it will not allow God to be captured by them or their cultures. Even as it reveals, incarnation remains a mystery, open to new interpretations of its significance. The death and resurrection of Christ rescue humanity from sin, including their temptations to demystify God. More, the paschal mystery invites relational participation "in Christ" where new creation may be at least partially realized. Yet this mystery, too, remains infinitely fathomable. While properly centering their faith-forming efforts upon the person and work of Jesus, therefore, those who seek to nurture faith will retain (and also teach) a generous humility with respect to multiple, novel, and sometimes competing interpretations of his significance.

Participation in Christ means participation in his body, the church. The church is on exactly nobody's list of top ten most popular institutions just now, but faith comes in and through it. We turn now to the church, warts and all, in the effort to discover how it is integral to nurturing faith.

Interactive Dialogue

1. According to the chapter, Jesus is a storied Savior. What does that mean, and how does it matter for the ministry of nurturing faith?
2. In addition to telling scriptural stories, the chapter proposes participation in ritual symbols and learning to speak and imagine poetically. Why?
3. In your own life, where have you understood yourself as sinner? As sin's victim?
4. What is relational participation in Christ? How and why is it critical to warding off sin's power?

For Further Reading

Brock, Sebastian. *The Luminous Eye: The Spiritual World Vision of Saint Ephrem the Syrian*. Kalamazoo, MI: Cistercian, 1985.

Hauerwas, Stanley, and L. Gregory Jones. *Why Narrative? Readings in Narrative Theology*. Eugene, OR: Wipf & Stock, 1997.

Peck-McClain, Emily A. *Arm in Arm with Adolescent Girls*. Horizons in Religious Education Book Series. Eugene, OR: Pickwick, 2018.

CHAPTER EIGHT

Church, Reconciliation, and the Faith
of a Countercultural Community

The church does not have a social ethic; the church is a social ethic.

—STANLEY HAUERWAS

It is not the church which 'undertakes' mission, it is the mission of God which constitutes the church.

—DAVID BOSCH

ROAD MAP

Once, the church was the humblest of institutions, a loose alliance of communities gathering to worship the crucified and risen Jesus and determined to submit to his lordship. Later the Christian church became one of the most powerful institutions on earth. Emperors sought alliances with it, peasants and crafts people devoted decades to erecting massive artifices in its honor, and its earthly treasure grew to rival all the crown jewels of the planet. Ordinary Christians revered and feared the church because they believed it held the keys to their eternal fate. At present the church is more often the object of scorn or indifference. Centuries of arrogance, unjust power moves, confusing citizenship in God's reign with that of the nation-state, and what can only be described as complicity with evil have scared off many of the faithful, plus many others who may once have looked to the church in order to meet God. In light of its abysmal track record of late, what help could the church be to the process of nurturing faith? Surprisingly, this chapter, while conceding the enormity of the church's sin and declaring the need for its repentance, considers church as an essential expression of faith and even a gift to faith. In turn, it calls for the church to reimagine its life and mission in faithfulness to the triune God.

Introduction

On Easter Sunday in 2017, Ross Douthat, an editorial writer for the *New York Times*, half facetiously challenged his largely secular readership to return to the churches of their upbringing.[1] Asking "what could it hurt?," he even suggested that going to church might alleviate liberal guilt. Readers responded ferociously. Some, victimized by sex crimes and other forms of ecclesial mistreatment, had washed their hands of the thing for all time. Others simply could not conceive of choosing church (even mainline Protestantism, which Douthat describes as only minimally burdened by spiritual baggage) as anything but a wishful-thinking waste of time for suckers. Still others cited a litany of readings from "The Book of Stupid and Egregious Things Christians Have Done": protesting "fags" at funerals; burning Korans; reducing Jesus's gospel to feel-good consumerism, and these are just the latest chapters in a very long book. David Kinnaman, evangelical pollster and author of *You Lost Me*, confirms that these opinions are often shared not just by *Times* readers but also by young adult evangelical Christians. Frustrated by the church's perceived hypocrisies—dogmatism without love, certainty untempered by humility—they too are leaving it behind and striking out on their own.[2] African American pastor Joy K. Challenger notes that while African American churches are not yet experiencing outward migration of young adults, movements for justice historically housed in the Black church have begun to operate independent of it.[3] For Christians and non-Christians alike, the church, rather than birthing and bolstering faith, is ever more perceived as a barrier to it.

Into this climate of popular loathing for the church, we advance the unpopular thesis that Christian faith is not possible without it. Borrowing from Cyprian of Carthage, we insist that "no one can have God for his Father, who does not have the Church for his mother."[4] With Cyprian, we affirm the church as a special locus of revelation and redemption. Unlike Cyprian, however, our claim stems less from convictions for the church as God's gatekeeper and more from the nature of faith, which we contend is irreducibly relational and therefore essentially social and communally embodied.

In other words, faith is coextensive with church. That said, we do not go easy here on the church. In this chapter, we focus our own critique on two related issues—one being the church's failure to enact its unity in Christ, and the second, its failure to resist sinful principalities and powers Christ unveiled.

Encroaching Challenges to Nurturing Faith	Engaging Resources for Nurturing Faith	Exclusive Uniquenesses of Nurturing Faith	Extraordinary Gifts for Nurturing Faith
Disorienting amnesia	Meaningful commemorations	Penetrating Scripture	Transformative hope
Autonomous determinism	Mutual disclosure	Interdependent kinship	Inspired trust
Interpretive pluriformity	Generous humility	Resurrected image	Restorative grace
➤ Social constructionism	Intentional citizenship	Supernatural guidance	Countercultural faith
Fragmented faith	Faithful gestures	Focused proclamation	Fortifying love
Conceptual bricolage	Probing reflection	Discerning community	Principled freedom

Coming to Terms with the Church

As part of its inheritance from Israel, the church understood itself as *God's People*, the flock living under the protection of the "Good Shepherd" (John 10). Elsewhere, the New Testament describes newly baptized Christians as "built into a *spiritual house*, to be *a holy priesthood*, to offer spiritual sacrifices acceptable to God through Jesus Christ" (1 Pet. 2:5). This imagery evokes the church's primary vocation for worship. Similarly, the writer of Ephesians describes Christians as "members of the *household of God* . . . with Christ Jesus himself as the cornerstone," in whom this household becomes a "*dwelling place for God*" (Eph. 2:19–22). Implied here is a degree of correlation between the community of Christians and the living presence of God's own self.

Paul strengthens this connection through the image of church as the *body of Christ*. In the Pauline Epistles, this imagery also describes the church's unity (Eph. 4:4), as well as the essential interdependence of its members (1 Cor. 12; Rom. 12). Eyes, feet, and hands require one another for the health of the body. Hence the unified body also is necessarily a *diverse* one. Paul speaks of differently distributed *gifts of the Spirit* shared for the common good. Some members of the body teach, some serve, some discern the Spirit. Perhaps because these gifts involve agency—*doing* something—we are less inclined to imagine *receiving* teaching or *receiving* service as emblematic of giftedness. Yet children, by receiving the gifts of others, also witness to the interdependence of the body. This is not to suggest that children or for that matter persons with disabilities or demented persons do not have active gifts to contribute; it is only to expand our notion of what constitutes giftedness. The gift of vulnerability, the grace for receiving, seems essential to the sharing of other gifts.

As the church grew and as it came to terms with a delayed eschaton, concerns for its identity, institutional form, and for the orthodoxy of its beliefs increased. Faced by challenges from within and without, it became necessary to stipulate what the church was and was not. The councils at Nicaea (325) and at Constantinople (381) defined the church as "one, holy, catholic, and apostolic" entity.[5] While space does not allow detailed exposition of these terms, they are rooted in the Scriptures and the church's lived experience. If, for example, the church is Christ's body, it must therefore be *one*. That it somehow embodies Christ in the world and its founding is attributed to the Spirit at Pentecost means that it must be *holy*. *Catholic* simply means that all Christians were members of the same universal church, while *apostolic* signaled that the church preserved the original revelation of God in Christ by the power of the Spirit as passed down by the apostles along with their mission to share the gospel across the world.

Unfortunately, these positive descriptors were often deployed to exclude or punish persons or movements deemed heretical. More than joyous witness to God's continuing mission, the descriptors "one, holy, catholic, and apostolic" were made to stand guard against perceived threats to the church's authority. Augustine (354–430) recognized the difficulty in discerning this one holy church. He therefore proposed the existence of an invisible church, known only to God, mixed in with the visible one.

While not abandoning the language of Nicaea, the leaders of the Reformation focused upon more practical *marks* of the church—the *word faithfully proclaimed* and the *sacraments rightly celebrated*.[6] Of course, they spent several centuries feuding over the meaning of "faithfully" and "rightly."

Which brings us to the modern era. After centuries of ecclesial infighting that contributed to unprecedented warfare and carnage across Europe, theological gymnastics explaining how, despite all appearances to the contrary, the church is in fact "one, holy, catholic, and apostolic" proved ever less convincing. As theologians Peter Hodgson and Robert King put it, "the Christian church is not only united but also divided; not only catholic . . . but also partisan, particular, heterodox, and in continual need of renewal; not only holy but also profane and sinful; not only in possession of apostolic authority but also under constraint to serve the world and enhance human freedom."[7]

Equally grounded in present reality, Hans Kung, a Roman Catholic theologian, suggests that these descriptors signify gifts of grace to the church but also "tasks" set before the church.[8] The church has work to do if it is to become what it is.

"We Believe in the Church":
Faith as Participation in Alternative Community

We asserted in chapter 6 that human beings are constitutively relational beings. Put simply, we hold that "I" could not emerge were there not already a "we" surrounding us. This conviction makes the authors communitarians, at least in one sense: we hold that the church precedes the possibility of personal faith. There is far more to say about the church than its role in constituting Christian identity, however.

The biblical and theological descriptions of the church (unity, Christ's body constituted by interdependent members) would seem to make evident its necessity for faith. Yet by the turn of the twentieth century, liberal European theologians were convinced otherwise. Adolf von Harnack offers this widely representative view: "The kingdom of God comes by coming to *individuals*, making entrance into their *souls*, and being grasped by them. The kingdom of God is indeed God's *rule*—but it is the rule of a holy God in individual hearts."[9]

Influenced by the widespread climate of cultural individualism, Harnack and others sought to strip Christian faith of what they imagined to be its external encumbrances in order to reveal its essence—a private interior disposition of the soul. Likewise, with faith reduced to internal piety, the church becomes at most a voluntary association of like-minded individuals. Christians begin to imagine they may take it or leave it.

This diminishment of community also contributes to the church becoming nearly indistinguishable from the wider culture. Recently, Fred read about a nearby congregation hosting Father's Day (yes, the greeting-card holiday) by extending a special invitation for men to wear hunting camouflage, to check out a professional race car displayed in the sanctuary narthex, to light up cigars, and then to smoke venison, along with their stogies, in the parking lot. This was uncommon hospitality (and we are not entirely without a sense of humor), yet we wonder whether this Sunday communal assembly sanctified anything more than a stereotypical version of North American masculinity. In the midst of all that smoke, church nearly disappears into the wider culture.

Since the late twentieth century, however, cultural individualism has come under scrutiny from many camps. For philosophers and political scientists, the question is this: If individualism rules the day, what is the basis for social cohesion? For theologians and biblical scholars, the issue is more pointed: Did Jesus intend for his followers to form a distinctive community? If so, what should it look like? To the second question, the answer across the spectrum from Catholics to Mennonites is a resounding "yes" to community. The answer to the first is more complex. As we will seek to show, renewed explorations of the church not only advocate for communalism to counter unbridled individualism; they also contend that the *shape* of the church's life (its "politics") needs to be distinctively cruciform. Allegiance to a crucified Messiah means the church can no longer align itself with the violence of nation-states or cater to oligarchs. Instead, the gospel calls it to offer a counterwitness. Below we attempt to support these claims.

New Testament scholar Gerhard Lohfink describes Jesus's mission as fundamentally communal. He contends that careful reading of the New Testament reveals Jesus's intention to gather and restore Israel, reconstituting it once again as a holy people in order it to fulfill its purpose as light to the nations.[10] In other words, Jesus's mission was directed to a particular community for the sake of establishing a universal community into which even those considered beyond the pale of membership would be welcomed. Toward this mission, Jesus and the twelve disciples (symbolic of Israel) preach the kingdom, heal the sick, and share table fellowship with sinners. Those who were lost become found. For Lohfink, the new community is being constituted through these practices of community building. And as with the prodigal son, sinners' joy is the gift of more than filled bellies; it is a homecoming, a restoration to community.

If Jesus's mission is for the sake of establishing a new community, it also implies a distinctive configuration of relations, a politics, what Lohfink calls a "contrast-society."[11] Already we have seen the pervasiveness of practices of welcome, forgiveness, and restoration for persons once regarded as outsiders. Additional practices follow from these. Jesus commands his disciples to love their enemies because God, too, is kind to the ungrateful and the wicked (Luke 6:32–36). (For a further consideration of how people may view God, see the "Images of God" sidebar.) Likewise, Christians are to turn the other cheek, give the clothes off their back, and go the extra mile. Lohfink reminds his readers that these examples are not metaphors, and nor are they depictions of an inner spiritual attitude; they are "concrete social practices," because "for the people of God to exist . . . , its social order has to be put into practice."[12]

IMAGES OF GOD

Coming from the Latin word *imago*, an image may be described as a visual representation, a mental picture, idea, or conception of someone or something. It also includes the perception of someone or something held by a group. Images are not abstract thoughts but, rather, paint pictures that are laden with perceptions and feelings. In this way, they differ from ideas.

Image of God refers to one's operative and perceptive insight concerning that which is supreme in our lives. An individual may hold several images of God that may change and develop throughout the life cycle. Common images of God include an old man with a beard, an absent God, a remote God, a judging God, an unforgiving God, a serious God, a God who loves conditionally or unconditionally, a challenging God, a loving, caring, forgiving God, and so many more. Evolving through stages of psychological development, the negotiation of life experiences and social factors, one's images of God influence the manner in which one relates to God, self, and the world. Images of God differ from ideas about God and may be at variance with the doctrinal professions one makes about God.

Whatever one's image or images of God, it is important that they are authentically grounded in theology. Although Scripture offers a plethora of images of God, no image fully captures who God is. The variety of images offered in Scripture include God as a father full of mercy and compassion, a mother who gives life and nurtures, a generous creator, a judge, and ultimately Jesus Christ, the image of the unseen God. These words and images used to describe God in both the Old and New Testaments are free to paint mental pictures (images) in the human mind and to challenge any false or stale images that may be held.

The God presented in the Hebrew Scriptures is an adult, male God whose name is YHWH as was revealed in Exodus. This is a God who is a generous creator, who blesses all of creation and who enters into a covenant with his people. The Old Testament reveals many images of God—a God who, in the cool of the evening, walks through the garden of Eden; a God who invites Abram to become the father of a great nation and who blesses Abraham and Sarah, in their old age, with a son; a God who later puts Abraham to the test, telling him to sacrifice his only son, Isaac, yet stopping him before the deed was done; a God who turned Lot's wife into a pillar of salt, who led the Israelites through the desert and brought them back to their homeland, who spoke to Moses from the burning bush and to Elijah in the gentle breeze, who loved Israel more than a mother with the child at the breast, and who longed to communicate divine wisdom to all who valued it.

The God of the New Testament is revealed in the person of Jesus Christ, the image of the invisible God. He is the good shepherd, the bread of life, the living water, the prodigal father, the one who invites to "come, follow me," to "do this in memory of me," the one who challenges his followers to be like the good Samaritan, the tax collector at the back of the temple, or the poor widow who put all she had into the box.

In sum, the authors of the Old and New Testaments used illustrations from the created world in terms of man and woman, cloud, dove, eagle, fire, light, rock, wind, water; from roles in life, such as mother, father, host, visitor, and wrestler; and from such occupations as gardener, potter, judge, king, landowner, and shepherd to provide images of God. It is important to note that no image teaches everything about God. Rather, these are the images that God has chosen to reveal to God's people.

FINOLA CUNNANE

Ironically, Christian communal nonviolence is born out of Jesus's violent death on the cross. Jesus's crucifixion was a political punishment. Jesus and his followers threatened equally the limited power of Jewish officials over Jews and an entire empire based upon *pax Romana*. Each of these entities maintained themselves through violence or threats of violence. By refusing to meet violence with violence, however, Jesus reveals violent power as incapable of determining the course of history. He is the first to observe that the emperor has no clothes.

Some protest that this vision of church as communal witness to peace is unrealistic. Admittedly, the church has been party to more outbreaks of violence than we care to count. Yet when it has found itself outside the halls of power, it has become better aligned with Jesus's peace. According to Lohfink, whether this peaceable social ethic can be fulfilled depends upon "groups of people which consciously place themselves under the gospel of the reign of God and wish to be real communities of brothers and sisters—communities which form a living arena for faith, in which everyone draws strength from each other."[13]

The Pauline Epistles offer similar evidence for salvation as communal and for church as the nonviolent community of those being saved. In addition to the body imagery described above, Paul depicts a new form of sociality in Galatians. "In Christ" (a baptismal inference), social boundaries that once divided persons are surmounted or relativized; there is no longer Jew or Greek, male or female, slave or free (Gal. 3:28–29). Instead, the church is one community swimming together in shared baptismal waters. Here again we see (though this time from Paul) that a central intent of Jesus's saving work is the restoration of community. Indeed, if Paul had conceived of salvation as merely saving individual souls, why would he repeatedly tackle problems of disunity in the churches he served? Ephesians 2 best captures Paul's sense of Christ's mission: "[Christ] has abolished the law with its commandments and ordinances, so that he might create in himself one new humanity in place of the two, thus making peace, and might reconcile both groups to God in one body through the cross, thus putting to death that hostility through it" (Eph. 2:15–16). Sin divided once unified humanity—in Paul's case, Jews from gentiles. Christ joined humanity back together in his body. Faith requires receiving Christ's gift of reconciling community.

Paul's advocacy for the church as countercommunity also hinges on his account of "principalities and powers" (Eph. 6:12). For Paul, these are structures, forces, and systems, both cosmic and earthly, that order life. They exist in the realm of God's providence, yet they, too, are distorted by sin. Examples include government, public opinion, the workings of the natural order, and social imaginaries. Engaging with principalities and powers includes our present awkward reliance upon fossil fuels. We can't live without them, yet we can't really live with them either. Paul contends, however, that Jesus unveils the hidden distortions of these powers. In the end, he refuses to save himself from them, and for this act of defiance, the powers kill him. Yet Jesus's faithfulness to the point of death (and subsequent resurrection) defeats the powers by exposing their perversions and false claims to absolute power (Col. 2:13–15).

For Paul, Jesus's life and ministry, along with the social life it enacts, consist in the struggle to live free from distorted powers. In contrast to the politics of violence practiced by Rome (pitting people groups against one another while exploiting them all), Jesus reveals the illusory nature of Roman power, the futility of its violence, and therefore its inability to prevent God's rejoining of humanity into one beloved community. Paul sees the birth of Christian churches as evidence of God's saving work coming to pass.

What is the point in a book about faith of traveling alongside of church? We think the two are inextricably connected. As noted, many Christians default to the assumption that faith consists of a sense of interior communion with God. For some Christians, a warmed heart is the total saving significance of Jesus's life, death, and resurrection. For us this version of Christianity is not altogether false but is woefully insufficient. Instead we contend that any account of "new creation" in Christ must include participation in the community striving to be Christ's communal body. Unlike interior faith, this faith is expressed in a politics of face-to-face relational inclusion marked by repeated reconciliation, forgiveness, justice, and a social witness whose peaceableness often places it in conflict with principalities and powers. Faith requires and consists of participation in church. Only through this form of social participation may faith avoid the traps of sentimental piety or unwitting endorsement of the politics of violence.

(Two of) the Church's Failures

The description of church as a "contrast society" prompts educational leaders to ask whether it is living at present as Jesus intends. In at least two cases, the answer is this: "Warning: Major System Failure!" The cases we consider below include Christian communities' unwillingness to address and overcome their racism (a failure of unity) and (therefore) their failure to witness fully to a way of life that counters the politics of empire.

In 1960, Martin Luther King Jr. observed that "eleven o'clock on Sunday morning is one of the most segregated hours . . . in Christian America."[14] How have things changed more than half a century later? Our answer is "not so much." Admittedly, the ecumenical movement captured the imagination of Christians around the world in the twentieth century. At present individual Christians and a small number of American congregations have devoted themselves to reconciling racialized divisions in the church. Some Christian denominations have also promoted reconciliation by diversifying pastoral appointments. All in all, these efforts have not moved the dial much. In the US at least, the church remains nearly as racially segregated as it has always been.[15] This in a cultural climate where racialized division, antagonism, fearmongering, and violence are on the upswing.

Remember, for Jesus, redemption consisted of a new community of inclusion. Authentic faith looks like a unified church. In Paul's view, gentile and Jewish Christians were not merely to share the same zip code; together as one body, they were to become a new social reality, a polis whose existence serves as witness to God's reconciling and redeeming work. However difficult the task of overcoming preexisting culture differences, food preferences, status hierarchies, worshiping customs, and so on, Paul insists upon it because this is what salvation in Christ consists of! This unity is the gift and task of the church. Hence American Christians (especially White ones) who shelter themselves in segregated congregations persist in disobedience. They remain under the power of sin even as Christ has freed them from it. Remember also that imagining this segregated way of life to be Christian is attributable, in part, to imagining faith as consisting exclusively of inward spiritual devotion.

In *The Christian Imagination*, theologian Willie James Jennings seeks to uncover the root causes of racism and racialized segregation in the church. The book proceeds with Jennings sharing a number of firsthand accounts from church officials during the era of European colonization of the "new world," including the Americas and Africa. These accounts mostly are authored by highly educated theologians/pastors/missionaries who purport to describe indigenous peoples, lands, and resources along with the shape of their missionary enterprises to them. One particularly horrifying account is authored by Zurara, official chronicler for Prince Henry of Portugal.[16] Zurara is present as Henry presides over a slave auction in African Guinea in 1444. According to his report, when auctioneers begin to divide purchased slaves into lots, African family members wailed in protest, mothers and fathers were beaten back again and again from desperate efforts to retrieve children and spouses taken from them. Finally, the slaves are led out to different slave galleys, never to see one another again.

According to Jennings, these missioners also justified the colonizers' practices of conquest, displacement of peoples from their lands, and the extraction of their wealth. He demonstrates how these same chroniclers of colonial expansion, in an effort to make sense of it all to the European church, repeatedly contrast their own world of "civilization" and "intelligence" with black bodies. Over time a hierarchical scale developed. It "naturally" located white skin at the top of the hierarchy, shades of yellow, red, and brown in the middle, and very black ("burnt" or "harmed") skin at the bottom.[17] The scale also was employed to predict the salvific probability of indigenous peoples. Once again dark-skinned bodies ranked the lowest.

In addition, after native peoples were stripped of their former markers of identity—lands, kinship links, cultural inheritances—a new transportable and universal marker was required. "Race" became the "transcendental" that fit the bill.[18] In place of farmer, spouse, father of three, whose ancestors farmed this valley in central Africa from the beginning of time and whose village had always stood in the shade of this ancient stand of trees, one became merely *Black*, an individual, a commodity, and barely, if at all, human. The reports of Zurara and others witness to the church's complicity in this distorted yet highly theological imagining.

Jennings contends that the pre-Reformation European church could have imagined its role differently.[19] Faced with making sense of heretofore unknown peoples living in exotic places, it could have *wondered* (as in offering praise, delight, gratitude, awe, glory, and joy) at God's unparalleled creativity. It could have realized again through this revelatory encounter with new peoples and new lands its mission to become an inclusive communion. Alternately, faced with growing evidence of the suffering, dislocation, and mass death of native peoples, the church might have sensed resonance between their pathos and that of the crucified Christ and taken up its cross in solidarity with them. Instead, clouded by its own untested assumptions of superiority, it justified enslavement, genocide, and conquest as God's providential intent.

Not only did the European church create the categories of race and racialized hierarchies, however; Jennings shows how this "racial calculus" also led to a disunited church body.[20] Native peoples did become Christian, but baptism, for example, "as performed in the slaveholding Christian West, . . . enacted no fundamental change in the material conditions of Christian existence."[21] This includes no change to patterns of human social belonging, no loving interdependence between Europeans and indigenes. The church's mission was reduced to, as Jennings says, a "presentation of salvation without communion."[22] Once again, the theological imagination of the church foundered upon colonizing hubris. The church's mission could have moved "forward as the Son came forward and wishes to go forward in *intimate joining*."[23] Instead the church reimagines itself based upon racialized divisions that the church itself created, divisions that for centuries Christians assumed were normal and good, divisions that continue to exact suffering upon Christian brothers and sisters of color and make a mockery of the one body.

Implications for Nurturing Faith

Faith Requires Community with Others

In light of the enormity of the church's sin, Jennings is "not ready to make nice," at least with the theological tradition of Europe.[24] Perhaps this is understandable given the exculpatory nature of his work. Practical theologian Christena Cleveland, while no more conciliatory regarding racialized injustice, is of a more pragmatic bent. In her book *Disunity in Christ*, she writes from the perspective of social psychology, venturing both explanations and solutions to racialized segregation in congregations.[25] Cleveland premises her account upon basic human tendencies to categorize differences, to associate with those like themselves, and to value self over others in order to boost personal esteem and social status.

According to Cleveland, this human tendency to imagine and categorize differences enables persons to navigate complex social/cultural environments by simplifying them. Instead of learning everything about every human being we encounter every single day (introverts are already hiding!), it is more efficient to describe them as "that basketball player" or "those hospital volunteers." Simplicity comes at a cost, however. Cleveland demonstrates how differentiation risks stereotyping, which readily slides down the slope toward disdain. All hospital volunteers everywhere become "mean ladies in pink" (even the men!), should one of them have the gall to look sidewise at dear old granddad drooling while he sleeps off his hip replacement surgery. Nor do we typically notice these biases at work in ourselves. We presume to monopolize Goodness, Truth, and Beauty, while those *others* (even other Christians) are at best Bad, Lying, Uglies. As Cleveland wryly observes, we never really escape our adolescence.[26]

If this is a problem for human communities on a crowded planet, it is a deal breaker for the church. Echoing Jennings, Cleveland likens the divided church to a body with an "auto-immune" disease, its members consuming one another out of enmity instead of flourishing together in shared health.[27] On a different tack, she rightly emphasizes the "cross cultural" nature of discipleship.[28] She points out how discipleship requires Christians to find companionship with all kinds of Christians in order to encounter more deeply the limitless mystery of God's love.

Dorotheus of Gaza, a sixth-century monk, illustrates Cleveland's point. He imagines himself standing in a circle together with his fellow monks. All have fixed their gaze upon God at the center of the circle. He next imagines the group taking one step closer to God. Obviously, the circle tightens up, and the brothers draw closer to one another at the same time. Dorotheus concludes that deepened encounter with God goes hand in hand with deepened relationships with his brothers in community. He notes (with joy no less) how brothers he finds especially difficult to love will teach him greater humility, which in turn leads to increased receptivity to God's love.[29] Just as in a human family, we don't get to pick our brothers and sisters in Christ. Put simply, the faith we seek to nurture requires us to step with humility and hope into relations with others not like us.

Cleveland counsels a number of practices to this end, some preventive of division, others prescriptive for reconciliation. First, she recommends regularly subjecting our insider/outsider distinctions to critical analysis. We should ask, "Do the differences we imagine between them and us exist in fact?" Most often the answer is "no." In the early 1980s' climate of cold war, the artist Sting sang plaintively, "I hope the Russians love their children too."[30] The song was a stinging rebuke to ginned-up political and cultural division between and demonization of peoples that we might assume actually share a common hope and destiny. Similarly, suggests Cleveland, we should also scrutinize assumptions for "our" virtues in relation to "their" vices. Jesus diagnosed this illness as the log-eye syndrome, the tendency to see only our own goodness in relation to others' sin (Matt. 7:3).

In addition to critical analysis, Cleveland counsels a number of practices for reconciling disunity and creating churches hospitable to previously excluded brothers and sisters in Christ. She urges groups alienated from one another, first, to focus on language that emphasizes wider commonalities and, second, to work together to achieve shared goals. Neighboring congregations segregated by race could intentionally employ "body of Christ" language, in reference to each other, for example. Further, Cleveland suggests that churches sharing responsibility for a joint task—say, painting a mural on a vacant building in their neighborhood—are more likely to imagine themselves as "we" or "us" than churches that merely talk the talk of unity.

Yet, this too is complicated. Cleveland also addresses inequities of power between people groups. She points out how historically privileged Christians and congregations may not notice how they habitually tend to take charge of even "shared" projects. (It's what the powerful have always done!) Returning to the mural for a moment, imagine the misunderstandings and hurt feelings when Jesus begins to appear on the wall sporting blond hair and blue eyes. (Apparently, no one from the differently hued congregation was in on the planning.) Cleveland points out how difficult it is especially for White congregations to learn truly to share the power they historically have monopolized.

Doing so requires not only inviting different kinds of people to the table but also tasting the food they offer. It may even mean becoming guests at *their* tables. It requires repentance on the part of the powerful, plus humility, a commitment to restored justice and power sharing, and the determination to speak less and listen more. On the other hand, for Christians historically oppressed by other Christians, the challenge is forgiveness, and the list of sins is long. For both groups the undertaking is immense. It requires wading way out of comfort zones into deeply troubled waters. Moreover, the way ahead is mined with inevitable misunderstandings tempting travelers back to the safety of Pharaoh's shore: "At least we knew what to expect in Egypt!" we wail.

According to Cleveland, this is the *best-case* scenario for reconciliation leading to Christian unity: misunderstanding, unintentional offense, and embarrassment. The politics of Christian life are costly! Yet we are convinced that there is no other way forward for the church. Repeat: there is no other option. The cultivation of personal faith requires and presumes interdependence and social intimacy with other members of Christ's body, including especially those whose experience of the body is very different from our own.

Faith Is Devoted to the Mission of God

Not only has the church sought to get its own house in order, so has it recast its mission to the world. Once, the churches of the Global North imagined that mission looked like traveling overseas for the purpose of turning peoples native to those lands into Christians. As Jennings demonstrates, these missionary efforts often underwrote cultural, economic, and political domination. In search of a better way, theologians have recovered an ancient phrase, *missio Dei*, meaning "mission of God." In place of imagining mission as an initiative of the church for the purpose of church expansion and cultural conquest (learning to love crown and commonwealth along with Jesus), they have sought to discern and articulate what *God* is doing in the world and how the church may best serve *God's* mission. They wonder what it means to imagine God as the preeminent missionary. According to the oft-repeated phrase in missional theology, they insist that the church does not have a mission; God has a mission, and that mission has a church. Mission begins with God. The church is its servant.

Hence mission is less an operation the church undertakes and more what it is at its core if it takes seriously its identity as Christ's body. The church exists to serve its neighbors wherever it finds them. We Christians are not here for ourselves. Our mission is less about saving souls and more about inviting neighbors to help us discover the beloved community Christ envisions. Again, the shape of this mission is cruciform. The church pours out its life for the poor and marginalized in imitation of Christ who poured out his. In this way of mission, the church witnesses to Christ's coming reign. Freed from contending for truth in the ideological marketplace ("my gospel is truer than your atheism"), the missional church may instead offer anyone it encounters hospitality, and the intimacy of mutual joining—all of this characterized by the humility to learn from the relationship.

If the church is a leaky vessel easily drifting off course, it nevertheless sails by the wind of the Spirit in the current of living baptismal waters toward the land of God's promise. It bears the life-giving story of God. No one would learn this story if communities of faithful Christians did not tell it. The church also shares the sacramental presence of graced mystery (God's relentless loving embrace) and occasionally even reflects the holiness of its calling. A congregation in Bermuda, one of the oldest on the west side of the Atlantic, has gathered to proclaim the word and receive the Eucharist every Sunday for four hundred years. Perhaps not always, but presently worshippers and liturgical leaders of many hues rub shoulders easily. Together they receive with open arms many vacationing guests. In another setting, Ash Wednesday finds ministers and laypersons of a New York parish standing on their busy Manhattan sidewalk in front of their church, offering imposition of ashes and prayer to passersby. Surprised and grateful, many accept. A church on the Florida gulf features differently abled children and youth as leaders of congregational worship. United Methodist churches in North Carolina have begun to reimagine themselves as community hubs consistent with the *missio Dei*. Their formerly underused kitchens hum all summer with food preparation for community children and the aged. They also support rural chefs and food entrepreneurs. In this effort, congregations not only sponsor persons' vocations for feeding the world, they also help assure the availability of nutritious local food to their communities. Recently, numerous churches in North America have stood publicly with refugees and against the basest of human racialized hatred, lately emboldened to crawl out from under the rocks where it usually hides. Anywhere in the world where the church is present, so are hospitals, clinics, schools, shelters, community-development projects, homes for displaced persons, Bible translators, and adoption agencies. In the United States, the Federal Emergency Management Agency factors the compassionate participation of tens of thousands of Christians into its disaster relief efforts. Christian churches and relief organizations also stay to rebuild communities long after floods and hurricanes have passed.

In each of these examples, the church reveals its true unity and its faithfulness to God's mission through countercommunal practices of social interdependence. Not always, but far more often than scoffers admit, the church gives grace away. Living in community with others who seek that good end, even if imperfectly, is key to faith.

Conclusion

Nurturing faith is the gift and cause of the church's constitution of its own faithful politics. Christian educational leaders within the church will therefore strive to accomplish two critical tasks. First, they will teach disciples to reflect critically upon themselves and their world in order to sniff out their sin, including their corporate sin as members of churches. Second, it will invite them to practice Jesus's way together as a contrast society, so that Christians may again be known by their love. We take up those tasks in the final chapters of this part.

Interactive Dialogue

1. When have you been frustrated with the church? Why?
2. The authors insist upon the church as essential to faith. Why? Do you agree?
3. Gerhard Lohfink declares that Jesus intended to establish a "contrast society." What does he mean? Do you agree with his proposal?
4. Summarize the main points of the account of the colonizing churches' creation of the category of "race." Do you agree or disagree with it? How does this account affect the church's authority to speak for God?
5. Where do you see the church either captive to or overcoming its fear of "otherness"? What solutions do you envision?

For Further Reading

Cleveland, Christena. *Disunity in Christ*. Downers Grove, IL: IVP, 2013.

Jennings, Willie James. *The Christian Imagination*. New Haven: Yale University Press, 2010.

Kinnaman, David. *You Lost Me: Why Young Christians Are Leaving the Church . . . and Rethinking Faith*. Grand Rapids: Baker, 2011.

Lohfink, Gerhard. *Jesus in Community*. Philadelphia: Fortress, 1984.

CHAPTER NINE

Virtue, Character, and Joy in Kingdom Practices

Now everybody hopes to be saved by a superficial faith, without the fruits of faith, without the baptism of trial and tribulation, without love or hope, and without truly Christian practice.

—CONRAD GREBEL

Love takes practice.

—PARAPHRASE OF 1 JOHN 4:7 (*THE LIVING BIBLE*)

ROAD MAP

Part 1 of this book repeatedly references the pivotal importance of practices or gestures. This chapter continues in that vein by way of an expansive description and theology of Christian practices. By "expansive" we mean to include practices self-evidently spiritual or religious—prayer, Scripture study, worship, and the like. In addition, Christian practices may also include eating together, shaping the life of a community, caring for our own and others' bodies, living simply, and more. We also hope to show how Christian practices are crucial to forming persons into virtues of Christian character, including desires of the heart. Ultimately, these descriptions invite further investigation into Jesus's revelation of God's reign. As a dimension of his incarnational ministry, Christ sanctified certain human undertakings as embodying God's way. He commended worship, healing, reconciling, and sharing God's abundance to his disciples and among others. Hence, we think the kingdom of God resembles communities practicing together along this joyful way. In addition, Christian life is fueled by Spirit empowerment. Therefore, we also attend to the work of the Holy Spirit in the task of nurturing faith.

Introduction

Nothing has energized the field of Christian education more over the past generation than the (re)discovery of the significance of Christian practices for nurturing faith. Focusing upon what Christians *do* in addition to what they profess reestablishes faith as a life lived in abundance for and with God instead of merely a set of propositions to believe before breakfast. Sustained Christian practices offer the possibility of linking otherwise fragmented beliefs together in lives that make sense. Practices also properly reclaim the entire body as the locus of faith. This includes the passionate desires of the human heart. As we shall see, practices are activities human beings do for and with one another, so they also reveal and help shape the relational and communal dimensions of faith. In sum, imagining faith as practice invites educational leaders to imagine forming persons into *living* faith where daily life and trust in God are woven into common cloth.

We also link practices to the joy of Christ's realm and to the Spirit's sanctifying work. These moves tie Christian practices to God's continuing mission on earth. We profess that God, who is the creator of history, entered history in the person of Jesus Christ, whose passion and resurrection restored that history to its proper course, one that will find consummation in due time. Christian practices remind persons of Jesus's kingdom-building work and the Spirit who sustains it. In a small way, they invite us to join it as well. In turn, faithful imagination—meaning here, the human capacity to experience and participate in God's saving work in the world—deepens. The result can only be described as joy!

Encroaching Challenges to Nurturing Faith	Engaging Resources for Nurturing Faith	Exclusive Uniquenesses of Nurturing Faith	Extraordinary Gifts for Nurturing Faith
Disorienting amnesia	Meaningful commemorations	Penetrating Scripture	Transformative hope
Autonomous determinism	Mutual disclosure	Interdependent kinship	Inspired trust
Interpretive pluriformity	Generous humility	Resurrected image	Restorative grace
Cultural constructionism	Intentional citizenship	Supernatural guidance	Countercultural faith
› Fragmented faith	Faithful gestures	Focused proclamation	Fortifying love
Conceptual bricolage	Probing reflection	Discerning community	Principled freedom

Theories of Practice from Aristotle through Aquinas to MacIntyre

Theories on Christian practice began to appear in the late twentieth century in a number of fields. In this chapter, we follow in particular virtue ethicist Alasdair MacIntyre, who is himself a student of Aristotle and Thomas Aquinas.[1] According to MacIntyre, Aristotle's primary concern was to live a "good life," one oriented to its proper end. In Aristotle's case, the good life consisted of responsible citizenship in the Athenian democracy, and in order to be responsible, the citizen had to cultivate the virtues of character toward that end. A virtue is a bodily disposition, a habit, cultivated to assist persons in pursuing this good life. The key to attaining virtue (and therefore the means to the good life) wasn't sitting in a classroom learning what virtue consisted of, but following a virtuous person and doing what that person does. Practice was therefore key to virtue. One became good by imitating exemplars. Consider how artists learn to paint or paint better by copying the work of, say, Van Gogh, or how golfers improve their swings by imitating Tiger Woods. Likewise, Aristotle counseled that doing good actions repeatedly disposed one to do the good habitually. Persons who recurrently behaved courageously, patiently, or justly came to be described as courageous, patient, or just—as bearers of virtuous character in other words, capable of doing the good reflexively.

Of course, there was more to attaining virtue than imitation. Aristotle also described "practical wisdom" as a primary virtue. It promoted the exercise of the right combination of virtues in the right proportion to one another to make appropriate responses to particular situations. Hence the life of virtue for Aristotle also required a dimension of artistry. Even this master virtue could become habituated over time. Though Jesus was not a student of Aristotle, he was a master of practical wisdom. He *bravely* skewered powerful religious "experts" over their presumptions of God's favor, while *humbly* enduring threats of violence against himself. In each case, he employed practical wisdom in concert with other virtues (here, both bravery and humility) toward the good end he was bringing about.

Aristotle's thought found its way into the Christian tradition through Thomas Aquinas (c. 1225–1274). Aquinas made creative use of Aristotle's program of training in virtue but offered important theological insights with respect to *Christian* virtues. First, he clarified the list of Christian virtues and distinguished them from Aristotle's. This was so because of their differing accounts of the good life. Where Aristotle envisioned the flourishing of the democratic polis (state), Thomas sought participation in the fullness of God's reign. Whereas an Athenian citizen may cultivate the virtue of persuasion in order to advance democratic interests, a Christian may require the virtue of patience amidst present suffering in order to hold on for the reign to be fully realized.

In addition, whereas Aristotle believed effort was the key to virtue, Aquinas realized that the most important Christian virtues were gifts of the Spirit. Effort alone could not engineer faith, hope, or love; those depend upon the gracious dispensations of the Spirit. Aquinas rightly asserted that those virtues originate in God and are given as gifts to Christians. Even so, Aquinas also believed it possible to unwrap these Spirit gifts, to put them to work, and thereby to grow in grace. As Paul exhorted the Philippians, "work out your salvation with fear and trembling" (Phil. 2:12–13). Like an orthopedist who repairs a skier's injured knee joint and then prescribes months of physical therapy to complete the healing, the Great Physician effects the repair by way of Christ through gifts of the Spirit but also prescribes therapeutic practices in order to harness the potential of these gifts. First the Spirit gives, and then the exercise of faith, hope, and love repeated thousands of times completes the healing. For Aquinas, as for Paul, faith is a gift given and then a work worked.

Another of MacIntyre's contributions is to lift up not only the relationship between virtues and practices but also their shared interdependence with stories. As noted previously, stories in this context are those grounding narratives that human communities employ to explain their origins and their destinies and, more basically, to illuminate their actions. According to MacIntyre, a practice becomes intelligible through a story. Suppose a neighbor spies MacIntyre in his yard with a rake. She may wonder whether the great philosopher is gardening, taking some exercise, or pleasing his spouse. The practice becomes intelligible only when the rake wielder shares his story. Further, MacIntyre contends that his character emerges out of the combination of the story and the practice. Together they identify him as gardener, fitness addict, dutiful spouse, or some combination of all three.[2]

Christian Practices

Christian educators and practical theologians Craig Dykstra and Dorothy Bass took these insights and built them into a way of nurturing faith around practices. They define Christian practices as "things Christian people do together over time in response to and in the light of God's active presence for the life of the world in Christ Jesus."[3] Each practice

- involves persons with what God is doing in the world and reflects God's grace and love;
- is learned with and from other people;

- possesses standards of excellence;
- comes to us from the past but will be shaped by us in the future;
- addresses fundamental human needs;
- is "thought-full," relies on beliefs, and develops in us wisdom;
- is public, not private;
- shapes the people who participate in it;
- comes to focus in worship;
- is a strand in a whole way of life.[4]

The connections to MacIntyre are clear: First, practices are learned from others in community, ideally under the guidance of exemplars. Second, practices are "thought-full," meaning in part that they are story-bound. For example, Christian practices related to sharing food with hungry people find their precedent in relation to biblical stories of famine, feasting, and God's provision, and especially to stories of Jesus satisfying persons' deepest hungers. Third, Christian practices may shape or "form" Christians in virtue, including wisdom. The practice of sharing food with hungry persons can make one generous, hospitable, compassionate, and grateful.

As with the examples immediately above, Bass and Dykstra make explicit the theological connections between practices and Christian life that MacIntyre does not. They assert that Christian practices offer the means to get involved with what God is doing in the world. Satiating hunger, reconciling wounded relationships, restoring persons to health and wholeness, and stewarding the nonhuman creation are all dimensions of God's mission to which practices can link us. In effect, through practices, we become participants in and agents of God's grace.

Some may suggest that practices amount to works righteousness. Not so, say Bass and Dykstra. Christian practices are responses to God's action in Christ by the power of the Spirit. Remember, God gives the gifts; we respond by unpacking and learning to use them. That said, practices may then become further means of grace. Our personal transformation continues as we participate in practices of God's transformation of the world. Grace abounds!

Bass and Dykstra's definition and related criteria for Christian practices are broad and inclusive. Religious and spiritual practices of the sort that Christian educational leaders have employed to nurture faith ever since New Testament times easily qualify. Prayer, study of Scriptures, and worship all get two thumbs up. The authors also stretch our imaginations, however, by expanding their accounts of practices to include hospitality, honoring the body, and household economics—undertakings that are not automatically or exclusively "Christian."[5] This is an important piece of their agenda for at least two reasons. First, it illustrates the close ties between Christian practices and Christian stories. While everyone eats to live, Christians transform eating into their own practice when, in light of the Scriptures, they welcome strangers to their tables, when meals become occasions for shared gratitude in response to God's provision, when they eat in a way mindful of their dependence upon the nonhuman creation, and when their meal sharing invites remembrance of the Food of Eternal Life.

SPIRITUAL LEARNING

Spiritual learning is often regarded as the heart of religion. It may be defined very broadly to cover those attitudes, beliefs, and practices that animate people's lives and help them to reach out toward supersensible realities. This suggests two functions or dimensions of spirituality: the horizontal and the vertical.

On the *human-horizontal level*, spirituality is a set of attitudes and values, with the beliefs and practices they undergird, that gives rise to and partly constitutes human psychological well-being. This aspect in part maps onto James Fowler's concept of a universal human faith, as a disposition for and activity of creating or finding meaning, and knowing, valuing, and committing oneself to what one takes to be ultimately meaningful. (For Fowler, religious faith differs from other forms of faith only in having specifically religious objects: centers of value and power in which people believe, and religious master stories by which they live.) Donald Evans's "attitude-virtues" may be seen as the ideal affective components of this essentially human yet salvific spirituality. For Evans, basic trust, humility, self-acceptance, responsibility, self-commitment, friendliness, concern, and contemplation are intrinsically valuable states that are also the main constituents of human fulfillment. As pervasive stances for living, or "modes of being in the world," they are expressed in—and give rise to—both beliefs and worship in religion, and beliefs and conduct in ethics.

Evans also recognizes the *vertical dimension* of spirituality, particularly in his claim that the attitude-virtues are necessary conditions for authentic religious experience, as our trust in God enables us to discern God. John Hick acknowledges this dimension in his reference to a "fifth dimension of our nature which enables us to respond to a fifth dimension of the universe": "the transcendent within us" that answers to "the transcendent without."

It is not unusual for something broadly comparable to the horizontal dimension of spirituality to be explicitly required as an aim of public education. As one might expect, this sometimes leads to controversy: for there is no neutral account of the learning outcomes that are of spiritual value. Christian education focuses on characteristically, if not always uniquely, *Christian* spiritual attitudes, values, beliefs, and practices, so as to assist children (and the adults they will become) both to flourish as human beings as they cope with their life experiences and to relate to the Christlike God in religious experience, prayer, meditation, and worship. Inevitably, it is difficult to assess how effective such teaching and learning is in leading to human flourishing, and especially in realizing spirituality's vertical function.

JEFF ASTLEY

Second, Dykstra and Bass highlight practices not automatically deemed "Christian" in order to ground faith in the realm of everyday, ordinary, material reality.

For example, "household economics" does not immediately evoke sweet spiritual songs, yet it remains crucial to living faith. Here we focus on one facet of that practice: living simply. Once again, plenty of non-Christians seek to live their lives in ways not driven by consumption. There's even a magazine sold in North America titled *Simple Living*. (Ironically, its editorial/marketing strategy promotes selling more stuff to make life simpler. Only in the US!) Many Christians also seek to live simply in imitation of Christ. They avoid "cumber" (a term that derives from Anabaptist tradition) in hopes that their loves may be fastened upon God rather than things. Living simply may even become a practice of prophetic resistance for Christians abiding in consumerist societies. Unchecked consumerism is idolatry, the altars of which constantly tempt citizens of the Global North to worship. Living simply witnesses to the interconnectedness of Christian households with global economic systems. It further begets practices of stewardship for God's creation and solidarity with workers the world over. Like all Christian practices, this one confronts the temptation to lock faith in a vault labeled "spiritual stuff." The practice of living simply manifests faith as a way of life.

Now is a splendid time to pick up a thread from a prior chapter. Recall our discussion of emotion and desire as critical dimensions of faith. Part of what it means to claim that practices shape character is linked to their effect upon human desire. Struggling out from under mountains of stuff (aka simplifying our lives) can free us to attend to other loves, maybe even for God! By tuning the heart, practices lead us on God's way.

Theologizing Practice: Practicing the Kingdom

God's "kingdom" or "realm" is the name Christians give to the culminating end of God's mission. Even though it marks the primary theme of Jesus's teaching ministry, many Christians pay it little attention. We tend to be much more interested in the culmination of our individual lives—what happens to *me* when *I* come to an end. This explains the greater fascination with the eternal life of the soul or the resurrection of the body. The phrase "kingdom (reign, realm) of God" stands, however, for the end with a capital *E*, the end of everything God's mission seeks. This includes the end to human history and the full establishment of Christ's eternal realm.

This is what we know about the kingdom of God. On the one hand, Jesus speaks of it in the present tense, and the church professes that Jesus established it through his ministry, passion, and resurrection. On the other hand, suffering and sin continue to haunt our existence. The realm will be fulfilled only when Christ returns. It thus bears a tensive "here now but not yet" quality. Theologians speak of "realized eschatology" as the beginning of the end set in motion by Jesus. It is the presence of God's realm *now* in human history. "Future eschatology" points to the future culmination of God's saving work, the end of the end, brought about through the work of the Spirit of Christ.

What is the relationship between Christian practices and the reign of God? Jesus himself connects the two while preaching his first sermon at Nazareth. Reading from the book of Isaiah, he declares: "The Spirit of the Lord is upon me, because he has anointed me to bring good news to the poor. He has sent me to proclaim release to the captives and recovery of sight to the blind, to let the oppressed go free, to proclaim the year of the Lord's favor" (Luke 4:18–19). He then adds, "today this scripture has been fulfilled in your hearing" (4:21). In other words, the reign consists of what Jesus sets about *doing* in his ministry. Jesus *practices* the kingdom and invites his followers to do the same. Hence it is present for disciples to live into now. Whatever else this reign may be, it consists of a loving community, one where unjust hierarchies are being leveled, God's justice made manifest, and people flourish. At present, the church, when it is at its best, prefigures it.

The kingdom is also a space for practicing peace. Again, we look to Jesus's ministry. By Jesus's power, forgiveness is offered, broken relationships are reconciled, violence is overcome, and persons are freed from the anxiety that accompanies the search for daily bread. Peace may be a state of mind, but for Jesus at least, it is inextricably tied to just social practices.

Jesus's vision of peace was also informed by the Jewish concept of shalom. *Shalom* means "peace," of course, but is also a term used to describe the original state of creation. Eden was a place of shalom before the humans' sin sent them to another zip code. In addition to peaceable community, shalom implies sustainable relations between human beings and the rest of the created order and between members of the nonhuman creation too. ("The wolf shall live with the lamb and the leopard shall lie down with the kid" [Isa. 11:6].) In other words, shalom as peace means the restoration of God's creative intent. Christians may live into God's realm by practicing careful stewardship over what is entrusted to them.

The Gospel writers imply, and Paul makes explicit, a connection between the reign of God and Jesus as architect of the "new creation" (see Rev. 22:1–5). John depicts Jesus as the creative "Word" who spoke creation into being. Appropriately, according to theologian Murray Rae, the redemption Jesus accomplishes causes the "consummation" of creation.[6] Christ's realm as new creation is implied in John's story of the healing of the blind man. According to Rae, "Light and life are brought forth from darkness; blindness is replaced by sight."[7]

To summarize, we are offering an account of Jesus as a practicing Messiah for whom the kingdom of God is the consummation of his creative and redemptive work. This kingdom is constituted by a web of relations (foreshadowed by the inclusive church) knitted together through social/communal practices that enable its own flourishing and that of the entire creation. Some may object to our account on the grounds that it is too earthy and not sufficiently spiritual. After all, Luke's Jesus also says "the kingdom is not coming with things that can be observed" (Luke 17:20). The enigmatic nature of Jesus's teachings on the realm of God notwithstanding, we offer two responses. First, we readily concede that our biblical and theological portrait of God's kingdom as a community consisting of practices of flourishing is insufficient. It is a symbol, one that connotes a divine reality whose wonder outruns human estimations. With Paul we profess that Christ is "able to accomplish abundantly more than all we can ask or imagine" (Eph. 3:20). Yet we are confident of this much: *at the very least*, the reign of God looks like a community practicing hospitality, inclusion, reconciling relations, healing, and peace. Where those practices are underway, Jesus's realm is not far behind.

In the era after Jesus's resurrection, the Holy Spirit leads (or prods) us to the fulfillment of God's reign. Understandings of the work of the Spirit or her relation to Christian education have often been vague at best. Christian educators face temptations to conjure and create educational plans like so many sous chefs whipping up decorous dishes, but invoking the Spirit to bless their efforts only after the meal is prepared (if at all). Lest this claim seem overblown, one may simply browse the online catalogues of religious publishers. Therein one readily discovers the genre "curricu-tainment," emphasizing fun or fashion seasoned with a dash of comfortable religiosity. Even Christian practices are "sold" as the means guaranteed to usher in the kingdom. Carol Lakey Hess rightly stands this recipe on its head.[8] She suggests that educators first seek to discern what the Spirit is up to in their communities before conjuring their casseroles. She notes how the Scriptures testify to the Spirit, prompting communities to worship God, to offer compassion for neighbors, hospitality to strangers, agitation for justice. More pointedly, she suggests the work of the Spirit is twofold. First, the Spirit embraces persons in love in order to anchor them ontologically. It holds on to persons as God's beloved creatures. Christian practices of hospitable community and worship offer the graced potential for this Spirit embrace.

Second, the Holy Spirit propels persons beyond themselves toward encounters with others who may offer gifts of transformation in return. A number of students at Duke Divinity School teach courses in the women's prison nearby. Somewhat to their surprise, communal solidarity emerges in these classes across what had seemed uncrossable divides, a reality that would not have unfolded had the students or the incarcerated women resisted the Holy Spirit's loving promptings to step out toward others.

As with other faith-forming strategies, practices are no panacea. Wrongly deployed to improper ends, they can deform and damage persons. (See Elizabeth DeGaynor's response to this chapter in part 5.) We allow that this is the fate of all faith-forming efforts in an era still clouded by sin. Our educational labors will always be imperfect and always require amendment; Christian practices are no exception. Fortunately, we have inherited Jesus's preaching and practice of God's kingdom, as well as receiving the Spirit's guidance toward it. Faith-forming leaders will call upon these gifts repeatedly as means to set their paths straight.

Practicing God's Realm, Receiving Divine Joy

Jesus's parables of the kingdom in Luke 15 repeatedly emphasize its joyous character. Angels sing, and fathers hold feasts, when sinners enter it. Theologian Miroslav Volf describes joy as the affective "crown" of the Christian life. Joy is "a form of attunement between the self and world perceived as blessing, joy is, ultimately, the emotional dimension of the good life, of a life that is both going well and is being lived [practiced] well; complete and lasting joy is the emotional side of the ultimate good."[9] The psalmists attest to joy as a fundamental disposition of all creation (see, for example, Ps. 96:11–13). They link it to praise and thanksgiving to God for God's good gifts. Paul persists in joy amidst great suffering. Even while shackled in prison, Paul rejoices; he knows who's in charge, and it's not Caesar! Then there's the mom we know who takes her school-age kids on a picnic Easter Mondays, "because there's just too much joy to contain in a single day!"

However wondrous joy is to receive, joy is not a goal Christians ought strive to attain. Pursuing joy gets the cart before the horse. Seek first my kingdom, Jesus reminds his friends, and the rest will follow. As we see it, however, especially from our perch in the heart of the world's most consumerist society, joy (or at least happiness) is, in fact, a primary pursuit. We've lived long enough for the bumper sticker "The One Who Dies with the Most Toys Wins!" to come and go. We've observed Black Friday (the traditional kickoff to Christmas gift shopping in North America) morph into a week's "celebration" and now a month: "Shop on Your Time. Black Friday Deals Available throughout November!" Meanwhile the superrich snatch up customized floatplane adventures into the Chilean Patagonia—when they're not buying their own islands. Nor are the authors immune. The informal motto of a certain academic institution one of us knows well is: "Work Hard, Play Hard." In this scenario, fun and happiness become the rewards of work. One doesn't receive them as gifts; one *earns* them. Hard work therefore *entitles* persons to happiness.[10] Ironically, this sense of entitlement is a joy killer. Who's got time to receive joy, to be surprised at its coming, to be lifted into communion with its Giver, when we imagine we can buy it online with money we've earned for ourselves?

Living for God's realm leads to joy by focusing attention away from the self and upon God and neighbor. It results in practices that mix people together to promote the reception of each other as gift. Echoing Volf, it promotes a sense of life going well because life is being lived well. It invites practitioners to participate in the joy of their Master.

How Do Practices Work?

John Wesley, the eighteenth-century Church of England priest and founder of Methodism, spoke of "means of grace" capable of forming persons toward sanctification. Wesley did not possess the contemporary language of practice, yet he would have agreed that practice makes perfect. He thought it possible, if not likely, that persons could reach full sanctification (perfection in love) during their lifetimes. He instructed members of his "bands" (small groups devoted to mutual accountability for Christian discipleship) to use all the means God provides for receiving grace and growing in faith. These means included, among many, prayer, Scripture study, and eucharistic worship, as well as works of charity and mercy, especially alongside of the poor. Like Aquinas before him, and Bass and Dykstra after him, Wesley believed that the cultivation of good habits by living out Christian practices was key to nurturing faith.

Wesley scholar Henry Knight suggests that for Wesley, these means "worked" (offered the grace of God's relational love) by revealing God's "presence" and God's "identity."[11] By "presence," Knight means that grace may be experienced. The Spirit is present in worship, for example, offering her love, assuring its constancy, and prompting worshippers to be or do something for God's sake. The Spirit's presence is "lively"; it registers in the human heart. For the third and final time, we call attention to the sense that practices offer power to evoke and form human desire. Practices can teach the heart to love rightly. By "identity," Knight conveys that, for Wesley, practicing the means of grace revealed the nature of the triune God. Scripture study, for example, discloses God's story. It points to Christ as the revelation of God—a revelation key to identifying God's creative and redemptive mission. Practicing the means of grace promoted growth in grace through deepened awareness of God's graced actions from creation, to the present, and to the promised realm.

With allowances for differing contexts, Wesley's plan for "practical religion" resembles the practices of Christians in the book of Acts (chapter 2), the cate-chumenate of antiquity, the spirituality of the desert mothers and fathers, and Saint Benedict's monastic "rule of life." Like his predecessors, Wesley recognizes that what a body (personal and social) does is key to what a body loves. In response, he shapes a community whose practices offer persons every opportunity to simultaneously receive and pursue their properly loving ends. Of course, he was widely lampooned as too "methodical" by his contemporaries. They found the way of life he commended prosaic, repetitive, and uninspiring. They dismissed the joyful outpourings in song from Methodist Christians as so much pietistic excess. What if their joy was instead the result of knowing God, sensing God's presence, and living as God desires? What, in other words, if this joy was a gift of living an abundant life, an ecstatic outburst of God's realm?

Practices in Practice

During World War II, French Huguenot Christians living in and around the tiny village of Le Chambon sheltered thousands of Jews, mostly children, from Nazi death camps. Documentarian Pierre Savauge, himself protected by villagers during his infancy, sought to explore and represent their actions in the film *Weapons of the Spirit*.[12] He discovered a robust ecology of practices. The hamlet's residents sung and testified to their own history of persecution by French Catholics. Many had worshiped in the Protestant church, whose pastor, Andre Trocme, was an avowed Christian pacifist preaching christological themes of peace. Instead of guns, he urged congregants to take up "weapons of the Spirit." Other Christian readers of Scripture simply pointed to the Bible's identification of Jews as "God's chosen people" who therefore required protection. As the word spread, thousands more children found sanctuary in Le Chambon, while local families, who were already poor, welcomed them into their homes at great risk to their own safety, a practice that also entailed making room and stretching their meager budgets. Photographs reveal children everywhere in the village delighting in snowball fights, picnicking in orchards, and singing together. Recall what we observed about joy as a sign of God's realm!

Remarkably, Savauge's interviews twenty-five years later with those who participated in this "conspiracy of goodness" reveal no latent sense of heroism or even any acknowledgment that their actions were out of the ordinary. "It was just what you did," said more than one. How do we explain the compassion, bravery, and humility? We suspect that saving thousands of Jews from Nazi death camps was at least in part the result of a web of interdependent practices. Citizens' sung memories of religious persecution caused them to empathize with the Jews. In addition to those memories, their enforced simple living inspired a social economic climate rooted in long-established habits of sharing and caring. Weekly worship and regular group Bible study further strengthened this web of practices by linking communal life to biblical stories. Exemplary leaders practiced what they preached. One Christian school teacher identified so closely with his Jewish students that, to the day of his death in a concentration camp, his captors refused to believe he was not Jewish.

We wonder which or how many of the practices at Le Chambon could have been neglected before the web finally broke? Could the community have sustained its exemplary faithfulness without equally faithful worship? Without long-standing habits of hospitality? In the absence of biblical literacy or the imagination to link Scripture with life? It's impossible to know. It does offer, however, the invitation to ponder the faithfulness of present-day congregations and the web of practices required to sustain them.

Implications for Faith Formation: Practicing God's Realm Today

Readers need not look far to discover exemplary communities of Christian practice at present. A few may be fortunate enough to find them in their own congregations. In addition, many traditional monastic communities are recovering vigor, and we are now witnessing the emergence of "new monastic" communities at the margins of urban centers and in rural outposts around the world.[13] All of these are seeking to practice Christian life communally and with deliberate intention.

Communities of Celebration, Mutuality, and Inclusion

For example, we can see in L'Arche communities compelling witness to practices of God's realm. Founded by the Roman Catholic theologian Jean Vanier, L'Arche offers a permanent home to persons with intellectual and developmental disabilities, who share in community with other "abled" residents—some of whom are permanent, and some, mostly young adults, who stay for a season.[14] On the face of it, L'Arche's mission would appear to be the provision of care and dignity by "abled" persons for the "disabled": "normally developing" residents live together in cottages with "core" members, assisting them with everyday tasks, like bathing, dressing, and eating. Yet those who arrive imagining themselves as care*givers* regularly testify to *receiving* profound gifts of love, friendship, and simplicity from their friends with disabilities.

L'Arche communities seek to be spaces for celebration. Eucharistic worship is the primary festival, but birthdays, holidays, and frequent outings also fill the calendar. Unconcerned with appearances, persons with disabilities delight in worship and other festivities. Their joy is infectious. Regardless of whether they can articulate the four spiritual laws, core members of L'Arche are among Jesus's most compelling witnesses. They practice God's realm; indeed, they may be sacraments of it.

Considering how persons with disabilities were literally closeted or otherwise institutionalized until very recently (and still are in some parts of the world), readers can understand why we describe L'Arche and communities like it as practicing God's reign. At L'Arche, deathly isolation is exchanged for Christian community, physical abuse for therapeutic touch, friendship overcomes alienation, and everywhere folks are surprised by joy.

Teaching Practices and Practice-Linking

Faith-forming leaders will need to strategize how best to teach persons to practice their faith. Obviously, this teaching involves *practicing*. Practices are best learned in community by way of imitation, especially of expert or exemplary practitioners. Exemplars are persons whose lives testify to the efficacy of their faith practices.

But persons also become more accomplished in their practice when provided opportunities to reflect critically on them (a subject taken up more fully in the next chapter). A pastor friend of Fred's led a weekly Lenten study on simplicity in which the prescribed practice was to refrain from purchasing nonessentials for forty days and invite persons to donate a share of the money they saved to a mission effort of the congregation. The pastor quickly discovered that participants had a great deal to say about their experiences. They described how disruptive practicing simplicity was to their routines, how it redirected their attention, created space in their schedules, and how they struggled even with defining "necessities." For example, what about new Easter outfits? They also devoted time to learning about and praying for the people their money was assisting. Undeniably, the chance to reflect upon their practice deepened the group's learning far more than the practice alone could have.[15]

To take this reflection component another step, Christian practices invite a form of "practice-linking" not unlike the "story-linking" described in chapter 5. Practice-linking invites reflection upon the impact of different practices on one another. It considers how, for example, additional practices like worship, Scripture study, or even a Lenten communal pilgrimage behind a cross assist in contextualizing and interpreting the practice of simplicity. Among other benefits, practice-linking situates simplicity within stories of God's simple abundance. Worship redirects simplicity from self-denial to gift of praise. Deepened simplicity creates potential for offering more generous hospitality to others. In sum, practice-linking draws attention to the cumulative formative impact of the entire ecology of Christian practices. Inviting persons to reflect on the interrelationships between and among practices assists in developing expertise upon a specific practice while cultivating imaginative connections to the whole.

Conclusion

Thoughts come and go in an instant, but practices occupy time and space. They hold the potential, therefore, to lend stability and coherence to Christian life by virtue of their consistency and repetition. They offer resistance to powers that fragment human experience into unrelated bits. They instantiate deep personal and social memories in human bodies. Practices are often public too. For better or worse, they disproportionately influence personal and corporate Christian witness. From the perspective of faith formation, Christian practices simultaneously nurture faith and constitute it. They provide embodied connections to Jesus's way. They teach our hearts to love what God loves. Best of all, participation in an ecology of practices may incorporate practitioners proleptically into the joy of Christ's reign.

Even so, practices are not adequate to faith formation isolated from other strategies. They, too, may distort faith, including in ways that resist conscious attention. It is important to learn to *think about* practices as a means to ward off mindless activism or unconscious deformation. We turn to that task next.

Interactive Dialogue

1. Where have you witnessed or been part of Christian communities actively practicing hospitality, simplicity, peace, or inclusion? What were your impressions?

2. The chapter argues for establishing "ecologies" of practices over a singular emphasis upon one or another practice. Why? How, for example,

may the practice of hospitality be made more faithful by practicing it in tandem with corporate worship and Scripture study?

3. When have you sensed that your practice was a participation in God's reign? Was joy in the mix? How does Christian joy overlap with happiness and distinguish itself from happiness?

4. According to the authors, what is the relationship between practice and grace? How does their assessment compare to what you understand of your own faith community or tradition?

For Further Reading

Bass, Dorothy C., ed. *Practicing Our Faith: A Way of Life for a Searching People.* 2nd ed. San Francisco: Jossey-Bass, 2010.

Bass, Dorothy C., and Susan R. Briehl, eds. *On Our Way: Christian Practices for Living a Whole Life.* Nashville: Upper Room, 2010.

Bass, Dorothy C., and Don C. Richter, eds. *Way to Live: Christian Practices for Teens.* Nashville: Upper Room, 2002.

MacIntyre, Alasdair. *After Virtue.* South Bend, IN: University of Notre Dame Press, 1981.

Sauvage, Pierre. *Weapons of the Spirit.* Los Angeles: Pierre Sauvage Productions/ Friends of Le Chambon Foundation, 1987.

Winner, Lauren F. *The Dangers of Christian Practice: On Wayward Gifts, Characteristic Damage, and Sin.* New Haven: Yale University Press, 2018.

CHAPTER TEN

Prophecy, Reflection, and the Freedom of Discerning Community

We do not learn from experience . . . we learn from reflecting on experience.

—JOHN DEWEY

Teaching is a catalyst that calls everyone to become more and more engaged.

—BELL HOOKS

ROAD MAP

After multiple cautions about the too narrow focus upon cognitive competence as the principal means to nurturing faith, this chapter returns to a consideration of the need for *thinking* in faith formation, especially in the form of critical reflection. Readers may justifiably inquire: Why, after so many chapters decrying the limits of thought and extolling instead the epistemic virtues of intuition, affect, aesthetic attunement, wondering imagination, and embodied habit, would we return to mentation, cognitive processes, and the exercise of reason? The truth is we have never opposed exercising the mind in relation to nurturing faith. What we oppose is the Western legacy of epistemological distortions—mind over body, thinking over feeling, theory over practice—as applied to faithfulness. Critical reflection, when allied with other ways of knowing, can help persons to see themselves and their world in new ways. For Christians, critical reflection can even disclose their sinful inclinations to distort the gospel for self-serving ends. Reflection, therefore, can lead to prophecy, wisdom, and the hope of transformation.

Introduction

Fred recently finished reading his first Agatha Christie novel, *Murder on the Orient Express*. As the title implies, a man is killed (stabbed twelve times; spoiler alert—it's a clue!) while a small group of train travelers rolls through eastern Europe toward Paris. Famed detective Hercule Poirot happens to be aboard and agrees to investigate. He sets about interviewing the other passengers. His process is methodical. He takes notes at each interview. He creates lists and grids describing such details as physical evidence, chronology of events, suspects, alibis, possible relationships between the travelers, and motives. Periodically, he reviews the gathered information with two friends. He also retires to his own compartment to reflect further. At the conclusion of the book, with all the suspects gathered in the dining car, readers marvel at Poirot's eye for detail and his genius for deduction as he explains what exactly transpired the night before. Clearly Poirot is one smart man; his intellectual capacities (actually Ms. Christie's) are highly developed.

This chapter explores the role of thinking not as an aid to crime solving but in relation to faith. Acting without thinking or thinking without acting may be equally detrimental to faith; one tends toward activism (all walk and no talk), the other toward verbalism (all talk and no walk). Neither is ideal. Hence our focus is upon self-aware, critically reflective thinking that contributes to following Jesus's way. The chapter also depicts the role of critical reflective thinking in personal and social transformation. On the personal level, transformation can be manifested as Christian practical wisdom, a way of perceiving divine guidance and living into it. On the societal level, transformation can entail communal discernment of injustice (sometimes described as a "prophetic task") and the efforts to overcome it. Christian educators properly seek to elicit both kinds. The chapter concludes, therefore, by describing an exemplary Christian educational method that proceeds by way of shared reflection in pursuit of Christian transformation.

Encroaching Challenges to Nurturing Faith	Engaging Resources for Nurturing Faith	Exclusive Uniquenesses of Nurturing Faith	Extraordinary Gifts for Nurturing Faith
Disorienting amnesia	Meaningful commemorations	Penetrating Scripture	Transformative hope
Autonomous determinism	Mutual disclosure	Interdependent kinship	Inspired trust

Encroaching Challenges to Nurturing Faith	Engaging Resources for Nurturing Faith	Exclusive Uniquenesses of Nurturing Faith	Extraordinary Gifts for Nurturing Faith
Interpretive pluriformity	Generous humility	Resurrected image	Restorative grace
Cultural constructionism	Intentional citizenship	Supernatural guidance	Countercultural faith
Fragmented faith	Faithful gestures	Focused proclamation	Fortifying love
▸ Conceptual bricolage	Probing reflection	Discerning community	Principled freedom

Coming to Terms with Critical Reflection in Education

We could define critical reflection, the kind of thinking we advocate here, as *"faith seeking understanding."*[1] Many Christians are wary of critical thinking, because they find it irreverent or even idolatrous, or because critical thought can threaten established authority. Admittedly, thinking past the limits of their finitude got Eve and Adam kicked out of the garden. But thinking can also unmask and overturn injustice. Strong thinking on the part of Moses's mother outwitted Pharaoh, saved her son, and helped secure Israel's eventual liberation from slavery.

One proper end for Christian critical reflection is *practical wisdom*. Wisdom, at least in part, is born out of reflection upon lived experience. Typically developing human beings do this natively. Seldom will a child touch a red-hot stove burner twice. Christian practical wisdom, however, is the result of focusing deliberate conscious attention upon previously unexamined dimensions of our lives in Christ. A lifetime of reflection upon Christian Source and sources in relation to Christian living can form persons and communities who exemplify or even embody the abundant life.

Another proper end for Christian critical reflection is *transformation*. Transformation overlaps with practical wisdom, but we offer two additional characterizations of it here. First, as was the case for Job, transformation can be prompted by reflection upon experiences of unjust suffering. Transformation in this instance involves acquisition of a "critical eye" for discerning circumstances from God's perspective. As the chapter will show, critical reflection is often employed to unmask distorted social structures in order to free persons from them. It also does so for the sake of transforming persons and communities into more faithful approximations of Christ's kingdom. Second, transformation can also occur when critical reflection recognizes its own limits. As Job ultimately confesses, God's ways sometimes remain unknown even to those who passionately seek communion with divine mystery. This form of transformation frees human beings from falling in love with their cleverness, from imagining, for example, that there will always be cutting edge technological solutions to complex planet-wide problems instead of depending upon the wisdom God has already offered. This second form of transformation requires Christians to remain humble in the mystery even as they pursue abundant life over lesser forms of life, for they recognize that short of the eschaton, their efforts toward transformation will require repeated transforming.

To reiterate, *thinking* is not a pox on Christians. Flawed as it may be, this book is a product of conscious, deliberate thinking. It reflectively deploys evidence and reason to criticize certain perspectives in the effort to highlight better ones. And, hopefully, readers make sense of these pages, utilizing their own tools for reasoned reflection. Thinking, especially thinking critically about our thinking, can lead to better and more truthful ways of knowing. That kind of deliberate, careful, critical reflection as an aid to faith is what we hope to elucidate here. We do so while remaining acutely aware of the full complement of human ways of knowing, so often neglected and whose influence upon thinking often goes unnoticed.

Thinking can thus lead to certain kinds of *learning*. Both are prompted by experience. Educator Jack Mezirow, whose insights we will follow here and in the next part, defines learning as a "process of using a new or revised interpretation of experience as a guide to future action."[2] For Mezirow, human beings are "propelled by the need to understand and order the meaning of our experience." We cannot *not* interpret experience (whether consciously or outside of awareness). Humans are always in the process of making meaning. Indeed, "the human condition may best be understood as a continuous effort to negotiate contested meanings."[3] While Mezirow acknowledges and appreciates that learning may be acquired tacitly as through enculturation, he focuses upon deliberate, systematic teaching to induce deepened and more truthful understandings of self and world.

Critical Reflection for Personal Transformation

Consistent with our own objectives, Mezirow's educational goal is for learners not only to acquire more information or practical tools toward mastery of a skill, but also for teaching and learning to lead to learners' transformation: "Transformative learning refers to the process by which we transform our taken for granted frames of reference (meaning perspectives, habits of mind,

mind sets) to make them more inclusive, discriminating, open, emotionally capable of change, and reflective so that they may generate beliefs and opinions that will prove more true or justified to guide action."[4]

Being transformed requires learners to make better sense of the subjects they consider; they gain better *perspective*. Their "sense making" becomes more sophisticated and subtle, often resulting in a completely different vision of the subject matter and, indeed, of themselves. According to Mezirow, their *agency* is transformed as well. Greater understanding offers reasons for better and more intentional action.

A simple illustration can explain what Mezirow envisions. A group of privileged college students travel to an impoverished city in Central America for an immersion experience in its language and culture. Prompted by a wise teacher-facilitator, the students also conduct ad hoc sociological and economic analysis. Touring a garment factory inspires the instructor to invite the students to draw connections between people's poorly compensated labor and the students' own wardrobes. The students return home not only with new and more accurate awareness of the sources of the clothing they purchase so inexpensively (it was no longer possible to imagine those J. Crew shorts as originating on a rack in a shop) but also equally determined to make more responsible and just choices when buying their clothes. This is transformative learning.

Mezirow contends that transformational learning requires *critical reflective discourse*. "Discourse" is a form of "dialogue devoted to searching for a common understanding and assessment of the justification of an interpretation or belief." It involves a "critical assessment of assumptions," and it leads toward "clearer understanding."[5] However, certain *pedagogical preconditions* are needed in order to make critical reflective discourse possible. It should occur in a community of learners. There should be frank acknowledgment of the power dynamics within the learning group, along with efforts to level asymmetries of power. Passive assimilation by students of the teacher's knowledge risks reinforcement of oppressive power dynamics through subtle or explicit coercion and does not permit the freedom of communal inquiry. Every voice must be welcome at the learning table. For learning communities to offer transformation, they must assist students in finding and then owning their voices, and this requires a commitment from all members of the community to listen to one another, sometimes listening each other into speech, as with assisting a student in conjuring the right language to express what they are seeking to articulate. Critical reflective discourse transcends argumentation for the creation of shared insight.

Transformations are often prompted by *disorienting dilemmas* (described in chapter 1) that shake up learners' prior *frames of reference*—mostly tacit sets of assumptions about how the world works, what counts for good or bad, what knowledge consists of, and visions of the purposes of life.[6] The students whose cultural immersion in Central America disrupted their frames of reference were fortunate to have a wise teacher to guide them; they were encouraged to name their experiences of cognitive and emotional disorientation. The results—at least for some—were steps toward a better frame of reference. Imagination is also key here as the means for students to link their own economic choices to other people's livelihoods.

For Mezirow, transformation not only means a shift in the frame of reference (seeing things from a different perspective), but also transformed learners grow to see themselves as new persons. Developmental psychologist Robert Kegan sheds light on the psychological nature of this transformation. According to Kegan, transformation involves not merely *what* persons know but also *how* they know it. We return one last time to the college students. Not only could the students begin to stand apart from and recognize social and economic forces that previously had operated upon them outside their awareness, but they also re-*cognized* themselves. They made steps toward new *self*-constructions as "citizens of the world" rather than just clueless consumers.

According to Kegan, the curriculum of life continually throws us "in over our heads," always challenging us to learn to swim anew (to make what we are subject to an object of reflection).[7] Newborns, previously fused with their environment (the warm, dark, wonderful womb), suddenly transition into a new space. By grasping, tasting, and touching objects in that space, they learn not only to name their environment but also to experience themselves as separate from it—a first awareness of "self." Eleven-year-olds who have finally mastered childhood suddenly find themselves run over by the race car that is adolescence. A more adequate self-construct will be required. Newlyweds who have only recently learned to be an intimate couple together find that hard-earned intimacy challenged by the birth of a child. A more adequate self, please!

Facing transformation can feel liberating or terrifying or both at once. Recently one of us welcomed an auditor into an introductory Christian education course at a theological school. Mother to two small children, she is the volunteer education coordinator in her parish. Not having attended college, she found the class intimidating at first but proved herself a capable reader and interpreter of texts and ideas. At the end, she reported with confidence, "I can do this, and I want to do more of it." Serendipitously, after the end of the semester, her parish called a new pastor with an expressed commitment to ministries of nurturing faith. Prompted by the pastor's vision, the congregation consulted with this woman, discovered her love for learning the practices of educational leadership, and offered to pay her tuition toward requisite degrees *and* to compensate her for her work in the parish! She was elated but also anxious—feeling in over her head. Her former frame of reference (her mostly tacit construction of self and world) was being pulled out from under her like a cloth on a perfectly set table. Who would care for her children? What about her relationship with her husband? How would she manage these new roles—student and minister—in addition to those she already carried? She mused that she would need to become "two people." We suspect that what will be required instead is one person transformed by a new frame of reference. If she is fortunate enough to receive loving support from family, church, and school, a transformed self may be birthed in this journey.

Transformation is analogous to a snake periodically shedding its skin. Old skins wear out; plus, their bearers outgrow them, hence the need to shrug off the old one in order to grow into the new. Put differently, the old must be deconstructed before the new can be created. But that time in between shedding the old and growing the new makes skin shedders incredibly vulnerable. And that is another reason why human beings find transformation so threatening. Transformation requires entering a liminal time and space where nothing makes sense anymore. The old frame is inadequate, but the new is yet to be constructed. Resistance is completely understandable and even to be expected.

A college student hears for the first time in a Bible class that Genesis 1 is more theology than science or history. Sensing an existential slippery slope, the student says: "Wait a minute! What does that say about the rest of the Bible? What does that mean for all that I believe? What does it do to my deepest commitments? Where then is 'truth'? Is this teacher a tool of Satan?"

Threatened here by critical theological reflection are not only the student's assumptions about the meanings of biblical authority and Truth with a capital "T" but also the student's very self-identity built upon those foundations.

So far, we have not investigated the Christian use of transformational learning. We promise that will follow. For now, it is enough to suggest that, however risky, God is in the transformation business too.

Critical Reflection for Social Transformation

A key inspiration for Mezirow's theorizing of thinking, learning, and transformation is the work of Paulo Freire—a twentieth-century Brazilian educational scholar who was called upon by his government to teach his country's peasantry how to read and write. Freire was also a Christian influenced by the liberation theologians of Central and South America. He ached over the suffering of the poor in his country and attributed the vast gulf between them and the country's elite to unjust economic and political systems. Not surprisingly, then, Freire discerned that traditional ways of teaching literacy—"See Jane run. Run, Jane, run!"—taught nothing about social reality and therefore only served preexisting dynamics of social power. He criticized this "banking concept" of education where the elite "deposit" only what they want others to know—effectively preserving their dominance over them.[8]

By contrast, Freire's strategy, more than teaching persons how to read, was to teach them *critical cultural* and *social* literacy. He sought consciousness raising, an awakening of the people to the oppressive sociocultural dynamics of power that gripped them. He and his team of educators visited villages where they proposed to establish "culture circles," searching first for "generative themes," points of energy, and tension in the community (the lack of basic health care, for example) that could catalyze critical awareness.[9] Once the researchers recognized a number of these generative themes, they commissioned artists to create simple but evocative drawings of village life in which the themes were embedded. Imagine, for example, a sketch of a man fallen in the street next to a cantina. Participants in the literacy circle immediately recognize "Juan," whose wife is sick but cannot afford to travel to the doctor, much less pay the medical bill. They report that Juan drinks out of despair.[10]

At this point, the facilitators in the culture circles introduce a "problem posing" educational method.[11] They ask probing reflective questions of participants: Why is Juan's wife sick? Why can't they afford health care? Why is there no clinic or medicine in this village even as there is an abundance of beer? Freire reports that participants in settings like these quickly begin to formulate insights into their situation. In effect, they learn to step outside of the sociocultural forces in which they were formerly immersed and to name them for what they are. Before coming to consciousness, they were mute. Now they find a common voice. They recognize that their fate is not foreordained from the creation of the world. In fact, their present state is the result of historical, social, economic, and cultural forces, a web of power relations embedded in and seemingly determining "normal" life. In response, they learn to see how human beings created these conditions; therefore, human beings can change them. For Freire, by awakening to the nature of reality, the oppressed could then take action to overturn it, to transform it, and to take up agency for their own liberation.

Mezirow and Freire share much in common. They both employ critical reflection aimed toward consciousness-raising, which they believe catalyzes transformation. (Each can also point to evidence of transformation by way of their methods.) Mezirow, especially when in dialogue with developmental psychology, emphasizes the epistemic transformation of individuals from a limited frame of reference to a larger, more accurate one. He also notes how the effect is to provide persons with a new sense of self-identity. Freire, on the other hand, envisions transformation as a communal project enabling oppressed people groups to struggle against forces of domination toward freedom. He worked to help poor communities claim their rightful share of social power. These distinctions reflect the differing contexts and agendas of the theorists, one working for "nontraditional" adult college students and the other on behalf of poor South American villagers. Their models have been adapted and adopted not only by educators who want to foster in students critical thinking about their own thinking but also scholars of all stripes who see their own teaching as a means to advocate for and foster justice.

FREEDOM

Christian freedom is understood as a present possession that anticipates a future, fuller realization. Like all freedoms, it is both freedom *from* (the law; sin and other species of spiritual bondage; evil and death; and the fear of God's condemnation) and freedom *for* (a life of obedient following of Christ, bound to righteousness in response to the gift of God's grace). This freedom is not to be understood as untrammeled license to behave in any way we wish, but specifically as the freedom to "choose life" (Deut. 30:19) and the "glorious liberty of the children of God" (Rom. 8:21).

More generally and publicly, a strong case is made for the right of all human beings to the liberty to pursue their own self-realization through social and political freedoms, including freedom from discrimination, freedom of speech and worship, and freedom to receive an education. Realistically, however, these are not unlimited freedoms.

Human and Christian freedom are brought together in many accounts of Christian education. Thomas Groome writes that we need to adopt these twin immediate purposes within the ultimate purpose of the kingdom of God and maintains that his description of freedom is sufficiently comprehensive to include all the values of the kingdom (justice, peace, reconciliation, joy, hope, and so on). Groome insists that we must concern ourselves with all three dimensions of freedom in Jesus Christ, not only the ("first" and "ultimate") spiritual and ("interior" and "psychological") personal aspects but also "freedom within our social and political contexts."

Freedom in Education. Both liberal and liberation education (and theology) utilize the language of freedom (from Latin *liber*). *Liberal education* reflects the classical understanding of the proper content and method for the education of the learner as a "free man," and it particularly seeks the education of the learner's mind for its own sake. This type of education increasingly came to involve learning the skills of autonomous, cognitive evaluation (criticism) of received views. *Liberation education* is founded more on moral criticism. It focuses on the other in the person of the poor and whoever suffers sociopolitical subjection, and seeks to educate their consciousness of their condition, as well as providing the skills and knowledge to escape it. Both approaches tend to oppose more traditional, transmissive, and authoritarian understandings of education.

Many types of Protestantism have historically embraced some sort of religious liberty. The Second Vatican Council also celebrated the gospel's "sacred reverence for the dignity of conscience and its freedom of choice" and required that Catholics engaged in spreading religious faith should refrain from actions that carry even "a hint of coercion" or dishonorable forms of persuasion.

However, the educational rhetoric about freedom of choice within religion, and more widely, is often overblown. Human freedom is never unlimited. Elmer Thiessen has argued for a properly qualified notion of *autonomy*, dismissing the idea of an absolute independence of mind and unrestricted critical competence within the learner as romanticized and unrealistic. An outward freedom *to express* religious belief is one thing; an inner freedom *of* belief is something very different. The latter is more limited than many assume, because our beliefs are not our direct creations. In the end, our beliefs are forced on us by our perception of the strength of the evidence and arguments we uncover. "The freedom that the learner can exercise is not a freedom to adopt one belief and reject another, but a freedom to engage in actions that have much more indirect, and sometimes unpredictable, consequences on her beliefs."

JEFF ASTLEY

Feminist scholarship is one case in point. Consistent with the practices of critical reflection toward transformative learning, feminists have dug under the surface of things to expose the web of patriarchy that so long prevented women from recognizing or living out their full humanity. Feminist scholar Mary Belenky, for example, shows how the polarities we have long taken for granted—male/female, mind/body, thinking/feeling, separate/connected, creative/re-creative—are wrapped in implicit bias. In each case, the first term is associated with masculinity and, in the West, is valued more highly. That pole, according to Belenky, "sets the standard" and "stands in opposition to its negative."[12] Belenky's work, along with that of her feminist and womanist sisters, is helping to nurture new generations of young women (and men) to critical awareness and more just self-understandings. In this effort, many have learned to resist patriarchal powers that do them violence. This struggle toward liberation is ongoing for women and for all kinds of people groups presently dominated by oppressive powers. The need for transformational learning continues.

Theological Themes in Critical Reflection

Undoubtedly, readers will have already sensed that the themes of this chapter—reflection, transformation, prophecy, justice, and wisdom—are theologically flavored. We make plain their theological resonances below in order to offer a clearer account of the ministry of Christian education as a theological enterprise. We also hope readers will gain new insight into the ways their ministries are tangled up with the identity and mission of God.

Paul the apostle is very clear about the transformational nature of the gospel. As Christ died for sin, he insists, so the baptized die to sin. Joined with Christ, they become new creations, no longer subject to its power. Paul, therefore, repeatedly presses the churches in his circle of influence to become who they are. He exhorts the Christians at Rome not to be "conformed to this world, but be transformed by the renewing of your minds so that you may discern what is the will of God—what is good and acceptable and perfect" (Rom. 12:2). He urges the same upon the Ephesians: "Clothe yourselves with the new self, created according to the likeness of God in true righteousness and holiness" (Eph. 4:23b). The baptismal undertones of these texts make plain Paul's conviction that, like baptism itself, transformation is a gift from Christ for participation "in Christ" both personally and corporately. Transformation in Christ enables the baptized to interpret the world from God's point of view and to live into that vision. On the other hand, that Paul repeatedly feels compelled to teach on the nature of transformation suggests how difficult the transformed life can be to "learn," let alone live (Eph. 4:20). It requires a community committed to continuous discernment, as well as to "speaking the truth in love" (Rom. 12:2; Eph. 4:14–15).

While Paul's language obviously differs from the language employed by Mezirow and Freire, he nevertheless describes a process very similar to critical reflection. He challenges Christians in the New Testament communities to think in depth about the gospel he has taught them in order to discern whether their lives truly reflect it. It is a process that requires comparison and contrast, deductive and inductive reasoning, communal assessment, plus critical and creative imagining. It invites an honest accounting. It asks participants to consider how things are and how they might become otherwise in light of their participation in Christ's body.

These are dimensions of self-conscious deliberation. It is a process of critical reflection because it demands not only assimilation of knowledge or accommodation to it but also judgment about how the knowledge pertains and what to do about it. Equally important, for Paul, the truth of the gospel must be shared in love. No one may be coerced into thinking the party line. Discernment proceeds by way of patience and humility in shared conversation.

Paul also seems to recognize how receiving Christ's gift of transformation was equally fearsome for Jew and gentile alike.

On a somewhat different plane, it can be helpful to compare transformation with "formation." Educational ministers sometimes describe formation as the ecology of teachings and practices utilized to "mold" or "form" persons into Christian faith and life. As we have noted in descriptions of the ancient catechumenate, formation is often described in the metaphorical terms of God the potter and humans the clay. Though the list varies, formational ministry generally seeks to teach biblical and doctrinal literacy, practices of Christian living, and Christian virtue. Critics complain that this formational process can be implicitly domesticating, meaning it can pass along untested assumptions about the church's cozy relation to state power, for example, along with its uniquely Christian content. Historically, these different knowledge domains were sometimes simply "handed over" for the sake of assimilation into the church, while the critical edge of the gospel was silenced. The church said, in effect, "Want to be a Christian? Memorize what we tell you, do what we say, and we will let you in."

Following Walter Brueggemann, we envision a connection between transformation and the prophetic task.[13] Brueggemann suggests that torah proclaims Israel's foundational story: We were slaves in Egypt, we cried out, God delivered us from slavery and into the promised land. This story frames Israel's existence by establishing its identity and destiny. Prophecy, on the other hand, speaks out against Israel's continuing temptation to forget its own story or to domesticate it. ("The story means only that the poor should be given a fair chance at success.") Prophets rage against Israel's accommodation to the Canaanites' religion, its geopolitical aspirations to empire, and its neglect of the poor. Yet prophets deliver their new word by invoking (the old) torah: "Do not forget that you were once slaves in Egypt."

For Christians, transformational learning will also always partake of the prophets' critical imagination. Prophets speak disruption on God's behalf. In a society where comfortable, if unfaithful, spiritual decay can set in like so much pleasant rigor mortis, prophets speak words of disequilibrium. They upset the apple cart. They decry the festering sores just beneath otherwise supple skin. Powers mobilize against prophets to shut them up, but prophets won't allow Israel to forget where it has come from.

Nurturing faith today continues to require teaching skills for critical reflection in order to maintain constant vigilance against domesticating the gospel—that is, making it endorse our present, often unfaithful, ways of life. Contemporary prophets point to the uncomfortable fact that North American churches remain largely racially divided. They insist that schooling for poor children match the quality of schooling for children of the elite. They tend to persist in their efforts to the annoyance of many.

How do prophets undertake their prophetic task? Brueggemann notes that prophets' primary weapons are poetry and ritual symbol. They utilize playful tools to speak truth to power. They march wearing funny hats, they employ satire, they offer roses to bayonet-wielding troops; armed with shopping bags, they face down tanks. Thus, critical reflection partners with creative aesthetic imagination to illuminate the emperor's nakedness. Effective prophecy catalyzes social transformation.

In addition to prophecy, a second transformative result of critical reflection can be Christian practical wisdom. In the Scriptures, wisdom attempts to make sense of experience to serve virtuous ends. It points out, for example, how "a soft word turns away wrath," or how farmers who till their land instead of sowing wild oats will have food enough to eat (Prov. 15:1; 12:11). Like other results of critical reflection, this form of wisdom arises out of "discernment," reflecting upon present experience or a tradition of experience to promote flourishing. Less than revelatory, it derives from the school of life. It operates in the realm of cause and effect. It teaches that responsibility goes hand in hand with awareness. This form of wisdom offers the stuff for building a life that prophecy imagines.

Alternately, Brueggemann also notes how biblical wisdom consists of insight into the *limits* of human knowledge. Job expertly deconstructs his friends' arguments for Job's own suffering. He believes he has an open and shut case before God. In the end, however, he acknowledges that God alone is the source of wisdom and that much of God's purpose remains hidden.

Implications for Nurturing Faith

The "Shared Praxis" Approach to Christian Education of Thomas Groome

Christian educators have appropriated critically reflective discourse toward specifically Christian ends. Thomas Groome's "shared praxis" approach sets the gold standard for this process. "Shared" in this case means that this approach to education is undertaken in community and is essentially relational. "Praxis" means "reflective action" or "active reflection."

THOMAS H. GROOME

Thomas H. Groome was born in Ireland into a Roman Catholic home and spent much of his early teaching career working in Catholic high schools. He later taught theology and religious education at Catholic University of America (1975) before joining the faculty of Boston College as an assistant professor of theology (1976). He serves as chairman of the Religious Education and Pastoral Ministry Department and professor of theology and religious education at Boston College.

Groome's important contribution to Christian education—making him arguably one of the most influential theorists in the late twentieth century—came with the publication of his book, *Christian Religious Education: Sharing Our Story and Vision*, in 1980 (subsequently revised and still in print). In it he explains the tension between the resources of the Christian community (Scripture, history, tradition) and learners' present experience. "Shared Christian praxis" consists of five pedagogical movements: (1) naming present action; (2) hearing the participants' stories and visions; (3) telling the Christian community's story and vision; (4) seeing the dialectical hermeneutic between the story and participants' stories; (5) and negotiating the dialectic hermeneutic between the vision and participants' vision.

JAMES P. BOWERS

Hearkening back to educator John Dewey (and Aristotle for that matter) and similar to others mentioned in this chapter, Groome presumes that human beings are constantly making meaning out of their lived experience. A farmer experimenting with a new crop informally theorizes what conditions might best promote its growth. The farmer reflects upon similar crops, upon which of his fields seems to be most hospitable to the widest variety of plantings, and which season is likely the most conducive to this new one's growth. This reflection is further informed by consulting books and talking with neighboring farmers. He plants the crop and stewards it to harvest. Along the way, he discovers which of his hunches were correct and which require modifying. He is engaged in *praxis*, a dialectical partnership between action and reflection. The actual practices of planting and stewardship enable him to construct a better theory of farming, but that theory is always in service of a more fruitful future harvest. Nor should we imagine a stark separation between reflection and action. Instead, in life, as in farming, there is continuing reciprocity between the two. We act and we reflect, we reflect and then we act, and on the cycle goes.

Like Freire before him, and Mezirow his contemporary, Groome makes this natural process of meaning-making the explicit focus of his educational approach. Unlike these others, however, Groome's particular genius is to fashion shared praxis as an expressly Christian undertaking, interposing the "Christian Story or Vision" into the reflective process. Learners are not left to reflection on their own experience alone to discern their way forward; they are actively supported by the resources of Christian faith, including Scripture and the theological tradition.

What does shared praxis look like on the ground? Below we present a stripped-down shared praxis session in order to provide readers a concrete example of Groome's approach.[14] The session outlined below, shaped by five "movements," considers Christian stewardship of the created world.

Movement One: Naming Present Praxis of Creation Care

- How are you and your faith community involved in stewarding God's creation?

Like most of the movements in shared praxis, this one proceeds by way of thoughtful/evocative questioning. In this case, participants are simply invited to describe their own praxis in relation to the stated theme. Responses to this particular question can be as varied as the participants—adopting pets, planting gardens, preserving farmland, limiting resource consumption, walking instead of driving, taking children outside, recycling, and so on. Participants may also wish to describe what they see going on locally and globally. Beginning with participants' own experiences invites them into shared conversation. There is no presumed prior knowledge about the subject or expected correct answer in order to join in. Participants simply are welcomed to share their lives in relation to the theme. Implicit here is the assumption that participants' lived experiences may *already* reflect God's gracious activity in this domain. They are not empty vaults awaiting a knowledge dump.

Movement Two: Critical Reflection on Present Action

- In what ways does your present praxis of stewardship seem adequate? Inadequate?
- What factors beyond yourself influence your own stewardship of creation or that of communities you inhabit?
- Is creation care a primary or secondary Christian practice?

In this movement, Groome invites participants to go beyond description in order to reflect critically upon their practices. Similar to Freire and Mezirow, this movement seeks to awaken consciousness, to bring to awareness the meanings of participants' practices of creation care along with their previously unreflective assumptions about it. Together, for example, they may discover how different communities enact different kinds of recycling policies, which, in turn, impact their personal efforts.

Movement Three: Making Accessible Christian Story/Vision

The session proceeds with public reading of Genesis 1:26–2:3, 15, followed by reflection on the following questions:

- How is this story suggestive of humanity's relationship to and with creation?
- What does "dominion" mean? "Subdue"? What have these terms meant historically to Christians of the Global North?

Next a different translation is presented. Old Testament scholar Ellen Davis suggests that these terms are ambiguous in Hebrew and could be translated differently. In place of "have dominion over" and "subdue" (Gen. 1:28), she proposes "exercise skilled mastery among" the creatures. Instead of "till [the garden] and keep it" (2:15), she offers "work [the garden] and serve it, to preserve and observe it." Students are then invited to reflect upon how the nuanced translations of the Scripture impact their consideration of stewardship and creation care.

This movement distinguishes Groome from conventional educational advocates for critical reflection. Insertion of the normative vision/story makes clear that there is an authority at work beyond our own experiences or capacities for self-scrutiny. The story reveals the Christian God as loving creator, one who makes promises to humanity—flourishing life in creative abundance—but also demands stewarding God's good gifts. Hence Christian care of creation involves more than "living simply so others may simply live." It is also a practice of gratitude and praise for who God is and what God does. To care for creation is to participate in God's creative/redemptive mission.

Movement Four: Dialectical Hermeneutic to Appropriate Christian Story/ Vision to Participants' Stories and Visions

- How do these renderings of the creation story affirm, question, or call us beyond our present practices of creation care?

In movement one, participants were invited to describe their present practice, to tell stories of themselves as stewards. We allowed that they could already be "good and faithful stewards." Movement four invites participants to deeper reflection upon their own stories in light of their encounter with the biblical story. This involves imagination because, as we have insisted, the Christian story is infinitely fathomable. Perhaps the opportunity to imagine stewardship as benevolent participation with creation instead of "resource management" will enliven new dimensions of the practice for participants. Perhaps participants unmoved by the shrill apocalyptic of the environmental movement will respond better to the grace, abundance, and vulnerability of God's good gift. Either way, there is transformation in the air!

Movement Five: Decision/Response for Lived Christian Faith

- How might you most faithfully respond to what you have discovered today?

Though Groome's approach is a critically reflective one, it is crucial to note that it begins with life (present praxis) and returns to life (renewed praxis). Groome echoes what we have urged throughout—Christian faith is more a life to be lived than a subject taught. That said, he does not dictate a "correct" response. Participants in this sample session may find themselves feeling more deeply in love with creation and Creator. They may take up what they judge to be a more effective personal practice of stewardship. They may opt to work together to influence congregational or community practice. Indeed, the "shared" in shared praxis illustrates how faithful judgment, discernment, and action are relationally bound—just like human beings themselves!

As elegant as it is, Groome's approach is just one in a rich trove of Christian pedagogies utilizing critical reflection upon life in learning groups based upon mutual loving support. Especially in communities where oppression and suffering are daily realities, critical pedagogies are employed all over the world to aid Christians in unearthing the causes of their suffering (making what they are subject to an object of reflection) and in discovering God's mission for their liberation. In other words, critically reflective pedagogies possess a prophetic edge.

Critical Reflection for Fighting Oppression

In her book *The Spiritual Lives of Young African Americans*, Almeda Wright suggests that the faith of Black young people is "fragmented," meaning there is little connection between their experiences of God, the problems they face, and potential action to overcome them. In response, she commends an "integrating spirituality" that invites living abundantly in the face of everyday oppression (which for some youth of color includes daily threats of physical violence).[15] Fostering integrative faith includes formation through practices historically important to the Black church—telling the stories of exemplary forebears, testifying, praying, and singing. Like all Christian practices, these doings form a deeply embodied communal identity. In the case of young African Americans' formation, these practices also serve to affirm their full humanity and to shape their imaginations for abundant life as hope-filled joyous resistance to oppression.

Wright also advocates utilizing critically reflective pedagogies for effecting transformation in Black youth. In this she allies herself with educational ministry's prophetic task. Her vision includes personal transformation, the coming to consciousness espoused by both Mezirow and Freire, which she characterizes as "somebodiness."[16] Second, she contends that individual transformation vests young people with agency, the capacity to join with others to name oppression and effect social and structural change toward liberation. Finally, Wright envisions young people's transformation of their own religious institutions, norms, and structures. Wright, too, invokes Brueggemann, encouraging youth toward a prophetic "disruption for justice" in the church itself in order for it to become the proper countercommunity the current generation of African American young people requires. She allows this will be a difficult and continuing task for young Black Christians, since keepers of torah seldom concede the possibility of new revelation. Yet listening for a prophetic word and speaking it publicly will be essential in the African American (and entire) church, not least because racism continues to mutate and evolve like a virus.

Conclusion

Critical reflection when practiced communally and bent to Christ's realm is an essential ingredient in nurturing the faith of the church. It can serve Christians well by assisting them in scrutinizing personal and communal infidelity. In addition, by bringing unreflective assumptions to consciousness, it can open the way to more faithful vision and practice. We caution once more, however, that critical reflection must find its place in the ecology of human and divine knowing, including imagination, desire, and the virtuous gestures of the body, personal and corporate. Bringing our thinking alongside our wondering, our God-given love for justice, and our practicing faithful life will help ensure that the objectifying work of critique may lead toward loving engagement with God and neighbor.

Interactive Dialogue

1. When have you been invited to reflect critically on matters or practices of faith? Were your responses to the process appreciative or defensive? Why? In light of your own experience and the accounts of the chapter, what are the potential risks or benefits of critical reflection?

2. According to the chapter, why is critical reflection often associated with the task of prophecy? How are true prophets distinguished from false ones?

3. Discuss how Thomas Groome's "shared Christian praxis" method blends practice with reflection. What is required from educational leaders to lead this process well?
4. Compare and contrast wisdom and prophecy.

For Further Reading

Brueggemann, Walter. *The Creative Word: Canon as a Model for Biblical Education.* Philadelphia: Fortress, 1982.

———. *The Prophetic Imagination.* 40th anniversary ed. Minneapolis: Fortress, 2018.

Freire, Paulo. *Pedagogy of the Oppressed.* New York: Continuum, 1994.

Groome, Thomas H. *Sharing Faith: A Comprehensive Approach to Religious Education and Pastoral Ministry: The Way of Shared Praxis.* San Francisco: HarperSanFrancisco, 1991.

Mezirow, Jack, and associates. *Fostering Critical Reflection in Adulthood: A Guide to Transformative and Emancipatory Learning.* San Francisco: Jossey-Bass, 1990.

———. *Learning as Transformation: Critical Perspectives on a Theory in Progress.* San Francisco: Jossey-Bass, 2000.

Wright, Almeda M. *The Spiritual Lives of Young African Americans.* New York: Oxford University Press, 2017.

Part Three

Colleagues in Nurturing Faith

Sociologists commonly refer to three questions related to the way we engage religion: What do I believe? (religious ideas); How should I act? (religious commitment); and Who am I? (religious affiliation).[1] Belief, behavior, and belonging. These are the themes around which our educational mission for the global church revolves, especially here in part 3: to help children, adolescents, and adults articulate their understanding of Christian belief; to achieve increasing correlation of belief and behavior; and to live out these concepts in a community of belief where belonging is a sacred gift, a birthright, and a safe place to fall. To accomplish these things, we turn (and constantly return) to our sacred documents.

What is the ultimate end for Christians in their study of the Bible? Study these words from Colossians 1:9–12:

> And so, from the day we heard, we have not ceased to pray for you, asking that you may be filled with the knowledge of his will in all spiritual wisdom and understanding, so as to walk in a manner worthy of the Lord, fully pleasing to him: bearing fruit in every good work and increasing in the knowledge of God; being strengthened with all power, according to his glorious might, for all endurance and patience with joy; giving thanks to the Father, who has qualified you to share in the inheritance of the saints in light.

Observe the purposes of reading Scripture. The apostles Paul and John talk of renewal and formation: "My dear children, for whom I am again in the pains of childbirth until Christ is formed in you . . . Behold! I am making all things new!" (Gal. 4:19; Rev. 21:5). In Colossians, Paul is more descriptive of the process for achieving this "newness," the "re-formation," no, "*transformation*." (See figure 2.)

The starting point is to be filled with the *knowledge of God's wisdom* (Col. 1:9). The purpose of this is not merely to gain knowledge in a passive, fact-accumulating way but also to absorb these biblical truths into one's *life*. The point is that Christians would live rightly—that is, walk worthy of the Lord (1:10). As the truth confronts Christians, this requires a *response* to the challenges from Scripture (1:10), an obedient action to conform. The result of this obedience is then to produce *fruit* (1:11), which enables the Christian to reduce nonconformity to the nature of God within and to *know God better*. Not know more *about* God, but to know God and be changed or educated into God's intentions and story (1:12). And, having gained greater knowledge of God, to return to his revelation for further study—and to repeat the cycle again and again in community.

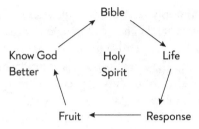

Figure 2. *The Flow of the Teaching Experience—Colossians 1:9–12*

This schema revolves around the person and work of the Holy Spirit, who is active in each part of this five-part process. God the Holy Spirit is the source of *inspiration* for the Scriptures. The Holy Spirit brings *illumination* to life. The Holy Spirit *motivates* response for living. The Holy Spirit brings about *fruit* as a result of right living. And the Holy Spirit *enables* Christians to know God better. David Hunter well summarizes this point: "Engagement is the experience we are having or ought to be having as Christians, namely, our encounters with God, our responses to this action, God's confrontations with us. The opposite word is *detachment*—connoting separation from any conscious sense of confronting the living God and dealing with his action in the world."[2]

To be clear, the purpose of studying the Bible is *not* to know the Bible better but to *know God better*.[3] Bernard of Clairvaux (1090-1153) brings perspective: "There are those who seek knowledge for the sake of knowledge; that is *curiosity*. There are those who seek knowledge to be known by others; that is *vanity*. There are those who seek knowledge in order to serve; that is *love*." To know God is to gain deeper love for his creation and his mission in the world. One's study of the history, archaeology, theology, and the genres of the Bible does not have a proper end in mere accumulation of interesting, even spiritual, information. The result is always knowing, loving, and serving God in a more insightful way. And learning God is the primary means of nurturing faith, the continuing drumbeat of this book.

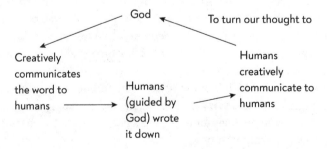

Figure 3. *The Divine-Human Communication Process*

And an important consideration of faith communities is how to best assist children, adolescents, adults, and persons with disabilities in learning the truths of the Bible. (See figure 3.) God has revealed to humans, and humans are instrumental in the discovery of strategies to guide others in knowing God.

When we teach the Bible to students, we must observe a purposeful approach that elicits learning. The Bible has an historical, contemporary, and future-oriented context. Learners are seekers of relevance, practicality, and applicability—attributes that are of foremost importance. (See figure 4.) Thus, the teaching efforts of a faith community must account for the concept of time and its connection to the experience of students. *First,* teachers should creatively "hook" students: to capture personal interest and motivate continued participation in what is intended. The teacher knows the importance of what is to be taught, but the students may need motivation to persist in the learning process. The hook gets their attention, sets goals, and is a natural link to Bible study. *Second,* teachers should introduce the "book"—that is, the biblical perspective on the topic at hand. This clarifies the meaning of biblical passages and helps students acquire information and understand meaning. *Third,* teachers can provide a "look" at how the relevant life situation of the student can be integrated with what is being learned and embodied. The "look" explores what the book implies for living today, guiding individuals to think through questions and issues that inevitably arise. *Fourth,* teachers anticipate a "took"—that is, what is taken from the study for our lives.[4] This personal application helps students pinpoint how they could and would respond to the call to faith. The challenges of Christian education are many. As teachers pray for the guidance of the Holy Spirit, engage proven educational teaching and learning practices, and know the needs of their students, effective Christian learning is more likely to occur.

Our task, then, in part 3 is to apply our propositions from parts 1 and 2 for nurturing faith in God's people of all ages. Too many books are heavy on theory and light on practice, or—as is the case with too many practical theology books—light on theory and heavy on practice. We contend there is no good theory without practice and no good practice without theory. We wish to treat this important educational mission of the church with integrity: to have an appropriate use of various academic domains—sociology, education, and theology—and weave them together in faithfully executed strategies for nurturing faith with children, adolescents, and adults.

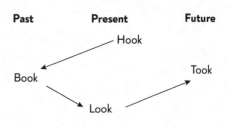

Figure 4. Learning as Past-Present-Future

God's people . . .	Nurturing through . . .
Children	Atmosphere
Adolescents	Passion
Adults	Vocation

As an operational plan for part 3 (see the chart above), we argue that the church's ministry with children must provide an overarching *atmosphere* for learning faith (chapter 11); that adolescents are most likely to engender faith when coupled with *passion* for faith formation (chapter 12); and that adults respond most favorably to learning the Christian way when *vocation* is at the forefront and emphasizes help in wrangling biblical perspective for the myriad of dilemmas of postmodern living (chapter 13).

Part	Theme
1	Cultural Dynamics for Nurturing Faith
2	Criteria for Nurturing Faith
3	**Colleagues in Nurturing Faith**
	➤ **Children (chapter 11)**
	➤ **Adolescents (chapter 12)**
	➤ **Adults (chapter 13)**
4	Contexts for Nurturing Faith
5	Conversations in Nurturing Faith

CHAPTER ELEVEN

Nurturing Atmospheric Faith in Children

No child under the age of fifteen should receive instruction in subjects which may possibly be the vehicle of serious error, such as philosophy or religion, because wrong notions imbibed early can seldom be rooted out.

—ARTHUR SCHOPENHAUER

Dear God, how did you know you were God? (Charlie) / Dear God, Are you invisible or is that just a trick? (Lucy) / Dear God, my grandpa says you were around when he was kid. How far back do you go? Love, Dennis / Dear God, I think about you sometimes even when I'm not praying. (Elliot) / Dear God, if you watch in church on Sunday, I'll show you my new shoes. (Mickey D.) / Dear God, I don't ever feel alone since I found out about you. (Nora)

—CHILDREN'S LETTERS TO GOD, COMPILED BY
STUART HAMPLE AND ERIC MARSHALL

ROAD MAP

What would you say is the goal of a faith community's ministry with children? No, really. We would be hard-pressed to find many in the church who voice negativity as we consider the Christian education of children, but the variety of responses and the trajectory of them would surprise and confound in their lack of cohesiveness or comprehensiveness. While we wish to be charitable and ascribe what happens for children as well intended, many simply have less of an intentional plan and more of a desire to serve or provide activities or to replicate an exciting program other churches are known for.

Good intentions are not enough; keeping children busy and distributing healthy snacks do not begin to set about a coherent plan for nurturing faith in children. Yes, one can see the logical flaws in those skimpy ideas, but to conceive of the prime objectives for ministry to and with children presumes clarity, perspective, and tangible means.

This chapter takes on obstacles to nurturing faith in children and tackles misguided stereotypes that too typically drive less-than-effective ministry. To be faithful to our task, we must address the influential weight of cultural effect upon children, the ill-fitting ideas of schooling, along with the parental priority of nurturing faith and the supplementary role of the faith community. We think the socializing atmosphere intentionally created by caring church leaders makes the biggest splash in nurturing faith in children.

Introduction

Education of any sort is inextricably and profoundly about the future; it exists to perpetuate shared beliefs and values, as a transmission device to bind generations, and to extend a way of living and thinking across time. Education has as its implicit goal to enrich the present and push to the future. We have a different take on this notion and will return to this later in the chapter. Educational endeavors may be grateful for how knowledge and practices have come to us from the past, and they anticipate a renewal, or ratification, of these ideas for new landscapes and a new time. While some of our learning from the past may be sentimental or a celebration of things experienced firsthand by others, one of the continual challenges of education is to make it relevant for contemporary life—the cohesive welding of knowledge to practice. The same task is to be achieved in one's reading and practice of biblical truth. Walter Brueggemann claims that biblical knowledge has a social dimension and it incorporates intangible dimensions such as memory, but always in the context of obedience to Yahweh.

Age	Nurturing through . . .
› Children	Atmospheric Faith
Adolescents	Passionate Faith
Adults	Vocational Faith

Of course, for purposes of this book, we consider theories and strategies for parents (and grandparents) and faith communities—all rooted in historical contexts—to assist their offspring in navigating a meaningful, personal, sustaining relationship with God. We discuss several challenges, which have the potential to diminish accomplishing this task, as paramount for consideration. Finally, we present the strategic goal of nurturing children through atmospheric faith (see the chart above).

The Mandate for Nurturing Faith with Children

Several theses guide our thinking about helping faith communities and parents consider the relationship of Christianity with children: we strenuously disagree with Schopenhauer's epigraph above, *first* because the Old Testament commands parents to teach their children in the ways of God, and the New Testament clearly teaches that Jesus calls children to himself, and *second*, the most favorable soil for sowing seeds of faith is in the soft hearts of children, and *third*, children possess capacities for faith, trust, and dependency that must be cultivated.

And since about half of the seven billion inhabitants of this planet are under twenty-four years old, this is an incredible opportunity for the church to inculcate the transcendent truth of the Christian faith that it claims in its youngest members.[1] We believe there is a substantial burden on churches to do this well—with sustaining effect and with a sound understanding of perpetuating the mission of God in the world.

While admittedly fewer international research projects detail the effective rate of faith transference between the generations, there are a number of quality investigations piloted in the United States. Happily, a substantial percentage of Americans share the same religious identity as their parents. Three recent and substantial studies bear that out—*General Social Survey, Pew Religion and Public Life surveys*, and *Faith Matters Survey*.[2] More specifically, while more than half of evangelical Protestants remain observant members of their parents' faith, the same is true for fewer than half of "Anglo" Catholics and mainline Protestants.[3] Research demonstrates that not only is there a higher birth rate among evangelical parents, but they are also more apt to keep their offspring within the family's religious tradition.[4]

Another important determinant of numerical growth is the current age distribution of each religious group—whether its adherents are predominantly young, with their prime childbearing years still ahead, or older and largely past their childbearing years. (See figure 8.)

In 2010, more than a quarter of the world's total population (27 percent) was under the age of fifteen. But an even higher percentage of Muslims (34 percent) and Hindus (30 percent) were younger than fifteen, while the share of Christians under fifteen matched the global average (27 percent). These bulging youth populations are among the reasons that Islam is projected to grow faster than the world's overall population and that of Hindus and Christians are projected to roughly keep pace with worldwide population growth.

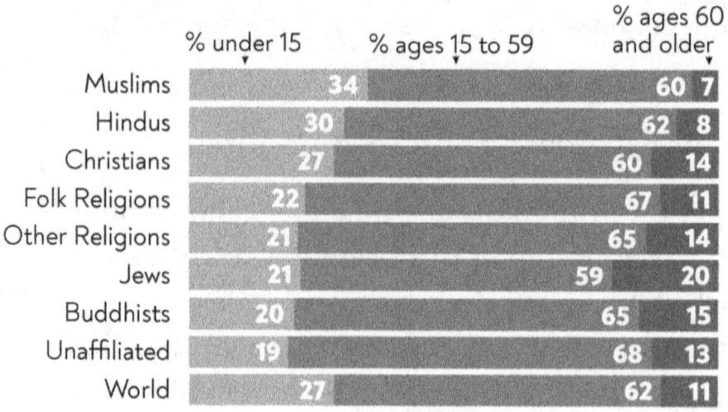

	% under 15	% ages 15 to 59	% ages 60 and older
Muslims	34	60	7
Hindus	30	62	8
Christians	27	60	14
Folk Religions	22	67	11
Other Religions	21	65	14
Jews	21	59	20
Buddhists	20	65	15
Unaffiliated	19	68	13
World	27	62	11

Source: The Future of World Religions: Population Growth Projections, 2010–2050 PEW Research Center

Figure 5. *Age Distribution of Religious Groups, 2010*

All the remaining groups in figure 5 have smaller-than-average youth populations, and many of them have disproportionately large numbers of adherents over the age of fifty-nine. For example, 11 percent of the world's population was at least sixty years old in 2010. But fully 20 percent of Jews around the world are sixty or older, as are 15 percent of Buddhists, 14 percent of Christians, 14 percent of adherents of other religions (taken as a whole), 13 percent of the unaffiliated, and 11 percent of adherents of folk religions. By contrast, just 7 percent of Muslims and 8 percent of Hindus are in this oldest age category.

Foundational Insights on Educating Children in Faith

In a broader sense, "education," in addition to being future-oriented, as discussed above, composes the sum total of those processes whereby society transmits from one generation to the next its accumulated social, intellectual, and religious experience and heritage. In part, these processes are *informal and incidental*, arising from participation in certain forms of social life and activity.[5] In another sense, more *formal educative processes* are designed to provide the immature members of society a mastery over the symbols and technique of civilization, including language (reading, writing, and speaking), the arts, the sciences, and religion, and to enlarge the fund of individual and community knowledge beyond the measure furnished by the direct activities of the immediate environment.

This understanding considers, then, melding a less structured *socialization* approach (a powerful communicator of values and social norms) with the more structured *schooling* model (which may be significant if the interests of the learner can be anticipated). The most judicious means of successfully accomplishing this mixture of strategies has long been the source of many instructive Christian-education debates.[6]

Christian education among ancient and modern peoples alike reveals these two aspects and their relevance for a balanced and meaningful growth in faith with children. On its informal side, it consists in the transmission of Christian ideas and experience by means of the reciprocal processes of *imitation and example*. Children, by participating in the religious activities and ceremonies of the social group, imbibe the spirit and ideals of the preceding generations, and in turn, these are modified by the particular economic and industrial conditions under which the entire process takes place.

A Christian education of children (and adolescents, as we will highlight in the next chapter) begins with the conscious and systematic effort on the part of more spiritually mature members of a social group to initiate the less mature members by means of solemn *rites and ceremonies* into the mysteries and obligations of their own faith community. In a study of Islamic, Jewish, and Christian schools, philosopher Walter Feinberg deduced that identity formation is crucial in helping children know to whom they belong. Through faith communities, "boundaries are constructed, roles marked off, relational possibilities circumscribed, and a collective identity stamped."[7]

And by this process, children learn their true *identity*—in Christ, in the local church, and in the global community of faith. McAdams describes that it is these stories we live by, explaining also how our childhood memories and experiences guide our story and offer meaning and identity.[8]

How, then, shall we define the church's attempts to infuse faith within its children? Simply stated, the education of children in Christian faith is the purposive, determined, and persistent quest by both natural and supernatural means to expose, transmit, or otherwise share with children God's message of good news, which is central to the Christian faith. Its ultimate end is to cultivate a life transformation of children by the power of the Holy Spirit so that they might be conformed to the revealed will of God as expressed in Scripture, and chiefly in the person of our Lord and Savior, Jesus Christ.[9]

While Jesus commanded the apostles to teach, no concrete directives were offered on how this would be accomplished. The church is left to discern the specifics. With cultural cues, educational wherewithal, childhood developmental research, and biblical and theological instincts, a strategy for communicating and living faith with children can be engaged.

Perhaps the most formative Christian education of children is that which is the most subtle. This could be said for the typical customs through which humans become members of any community, including the faith community. This, of course, aptly describes the incremental, almost subliminal, process of socialization.

An enlightening study by Princeton University sociologist Robert Wuthnow claims that adults interviewed did not remember the doctrinal instruction they received as youth. He quickly adds, however, this does not mean that they learned nothing about religion from their parents. What they recalled fondly about religion—and what often drew them as adults back to the church—were the rituals and sacred objects that were at the center of their religious upbringings.[10] The truly memorable and lasting aspects of a religious upbringing are imprinted in the home with one's family. Christian educators, whether parents or church teachers, older siblings or mentors, coaches or extended family members, should strive for religious infusion as much as for religious instruction. Training children in the right way may involve creating an environment in which spirituality is fully and deeply embedded, rather than merely drilling down on Bible verses, creeds, and catechisms. This seems to echo Horace Bushnell's working hypothesis: "Home is the church of childhood." (See the sidebar "Prayer and Children," pp. 257–58 below.)

Two primary agencies then are most determinative in the faith formation of children—the question is, How do we prioritize and distinguish between the *parental* role and *the church's* role in this process? This can be a ticklish discussion but a necessary one.

Some Christian parents delegate the task of nurturing faith to churches or parachurch organizations, perhaps due to a convincing cultural message that views specialized experts as best suited to the task.[11] To be sure, faith communities have a vital and supportive role in the spiritual growth of children (as well as adolescents and adults). Indeed, this is a major thesis of our book. Yet the primary responsibility is given by God to parents.

Clues to how faith is nurtured are found, among other places, in Deuteronomy 6:1–9. Succinctly summarized, the most favorable conditions conducive for life-changing impact are experienced best within a family context where loving, consistent, and committed relationships with God and family members are exhibited. Three circumstances seem to effectually foster the absorption of faith from one generation to the next.

First, a parent-teacher must be absorbed in the reality they are teaching to their children. "These are the commands, decrees and laws the LORD your God directed me to teach you to observe in the land that you are crossing the Jordan to possess, so that you, your children and their children after them may fear the LORD your God as long as you live by keeping all his decrees and commands that I give you, and so that you may enjoy long life. . . . These commandments that I give you today are to be on your hearts" (Deut. 6:1–2, 6). The most noted obstacle to gaining the Christian faith from parents, as reported in numerous research studies and anecdotal stories, is the dissonance between what a Christian parent claims as being so and how one actually lives at home, in the community, and in the workplace.

Second, a parent-teacher must have intimate relationships with those being taught. "Hear, O Israel: The LORD our God, the LORD is one. Love the LORD your God with all your heart and with all your soul and with all your strength. . . . Impress [these commandments] on your children" (Deut. 6:4–5, 7a). Social science expounds those factors that enhance teaching/learning as follows: frequent, long-term contact; warm, loving relationship; exposure to the inner states; observed in a variety of life settings; consistency in behavior; correspondence between one's behavior and beliefs of community; and explanation of lifestyle.[12] Naturally, as applied to Christian-education settings, these factors have rich value for introducing the faith in a meaningful, mentoring way.

Third, the parent-teacher's instruction must spring from real-life issues and natural situations. "Talk about [these commandments] when you sit at home and when you walk along the road, when you lie down and when you get up. Tie them as symbols on your hands and bind them on your foreheads. Write them on the doorframes of your houses and on your gates" (Deut. 6:7b–9). Humans are most ready to learn when the subject matter arises out of personal interest and in response to in-the-moment life circumstances, crises, and development tasks. The "curriculum" of Jesus's teaching, for example, most often arose from spontaneous questions or events; it rarely was preplanned, structured, or occurred in a formal "classroom." We turn now to an examination of how churches have traditionally educated children, which seems more often than not to lack the criteria expressed above.

A Traditional Strategy for Nurturing Faith with Children: Schooling as Miscalculated Model of Learning

One of Mark's favorite groups to engage are volunteer teachers and leaders in local churches. These kindhearted folks are generous with their time by giving of themselves to ministry with and to children. They are insurance agents, cashiers, social workers, coaches, and physicians, and they use their talents with little regard for what they will receive in return. At the same time, some are not as familiar as they might wish they could be with educational theory and practice, or with theological or biblical education. To be clear, neither formal education nor an academic degree is a prerequisite to have tangible benefit in children's ministry. Conversely, some volunteers do have academic credentials and educational experience yet lack effectiveness. Nevertheless, as professors in formal academic theological education positions, we believe even a rudimentary understanding of educational theory, human development through childhood, sociocultural dynamics of faith communities, and theological acumen are invaluable in conceiving of and practicing leadership in nurturing faith.

The reality that exists in many local churches is that too few have thoughtfully, strategically considered how children might best be inculcated in the beliefs and practices of a dynamic Christian faith. And because of a dim notion of what should be done, the Christian education of children has defaulted to the familiar practices of public education. It is fair to say that in many ways, the history of American education parallels, and even engulfs, the story of Christian education in churches and parachurch organizations, including mission agencies. Here's why.

It is difficult for Christian educational philosophy to separate itself from surrounding influences in public education. There are inherent similarities due to the nature of the educational task. Both Christian and secular education address all the same philosophical categories—epistemology, ethics, anthropology. Both employ pragmatic methodologies of teaching and learning.

In fact, the church seems most often to utilize the resources and insights of modern education in the following four models. First, the *assimilation model* unquestioningly accepts secular education theory, and the distinctives of Christian education are blurred as a result. Second, the *Bible-only way* of instruction rejects identification with secular education. Third, the *socialization model* maintains that education is better caught than taught. And fourth, the *amalgamation model* desires to combine the best elements of each.

Christian education has utilized all these models at various times and in various geographies. Our contention is that the evolution of modern American education has had a profound effect on the development of Christian education. In fact, Christian education would not be the same today without the influence of public education—for good and ill. Furthermore, a significant influence on public education was the business/factory principles of Frederick Taylor and his *scientific management*. He designed techniques for maximizing productivity from human labor. As a result, rules were instituted for the workers that replaced individual judgment, and management was based on measurement and standardization. This idea spread to the government—to eliminate waste, to be efficient. Almost immediately, educational administrators attempted to bring this system into the schools. The school became a factory where *efficiency*, at the expense of meaningful learning, replaced experience with productivity.

Several plausible reasons explain the swift and powerful leap of business-management practices to the school arena: *first*, the rise of the business person as a figure of leadership and herald of the American dream became a valued symbol of social progress; *second*, educational administrators sometimes made efficiency a high priority as a tangible way to preserve their jobs and to quiet the critics, who were often business leaders on school boards; and *third*, due to increasing immigration and overcrowded schools, new schools were constructed, which meant increased taxes from a population who wanted to see both *measurable* improvements in test scores and thrifty spending.

The science of efficiency not only impacted public education but also found its way into Christian education. Noted developmentalist Robert J. Havighurst reported in *The Educational Mission of the Church* (1965) that by the 1920s, the "scientific-pedagogy" approach in Christian education was "well established" and was growing in parallel with the developing pedagogy of secular education. In fact, Shailer Mathews, a clergyman at the University of Chicago, praised Taylor's scientific management work as a "practical philosophy destined to replace haphazard, traditional methods. The church should be a *business establishment*."[13] Oh my!

Unfortunately, both Havighurst's and Mathews's projections have rung true, to some extent, in the educational practices within Christian communities. For example, some curricula envision the concepts and information a four-year-old (or twelve-year-old or forty-year-old) should know, then teach the bits and pieces of information to produce the desired end result. The "end," however, should not be the focus of Christian education; the "process" of spiritual maturity and faith nurturance should be. Christian development is not routinely quantified or empirically measured; more often, progress can be seen, heard, and sensed in one's development. The tenets of business and scientific management seem inappropriate for nurturing faith.

So, let's wall off some distinct notions of Christian and public education and their relationship to nurturing faith. The oversimplified thesis argued here is that the education of the secular school should be more *intellective* than children's Christian education, which should also emphasize *affective* education. That is not to say that public education should not teach to the affective mode or that Christian education should not teach to the cognitive mode. Yet each has its own *predominate* emphasis due to its unique objectives.

Christian education with children needs to more clearly understand that its primary educational usefulness can be accomplished in the teaching and learning of attitudes, values, and beliefs. Certainly, a part of the curriculum will necessitate didactic teaching. Yet Christian education should reexamine the role and function of knowledge in the task of faith development.

So, to recap, a reexamination of the philosophy churches employ with the faith formation of children can frustrate even the best intentions by confusing a wrongheaded notion of knowledge or information with a knowledge of God. And there is another huge elephant in the room, which seeps from our cultural landscape, that affects children and the concept of children immensely. We examine this next.

Cultural Incursion: Protection, Innocence, and Premature Exposure

Western culture, while trumpeting love for children, more often complicates, even contaminates, the experience of childhood by its competitive, overexposed posture.[14] This chapter was written just as the movie *A Beautiful Day in the Neighborhood* was released, starring Tom Hanks as the beloved Mr. Rogers. He is held with loving regard by millions of children for helping them think about issues of image, esteem, and culture.

In addition, Mr. Rogers's decades on PBS's *Mister Rogers' Neighborhood* (1968–2001) have been memorialized in the 2018 feature-length documentary *Won't You Be My Neighbor?*[15] *Time* magazine called it one of the top ten films of the year. Besides the show encouraging children to feel and share when difficult and confusing issues present themselves, and besides assuring children they are "special," Rogers is concerned that children live in physically and emotionally safe, stable, and sheltered environments. These themes are echoed in the investigative work of Tufts professor David Elkind.

The thesis of Elkind's classic works *The Hurried Child* and *All Grown Up and No Place to Go* is that fast-paced, techno-savvy Western culture has prematurely exposed children to adult experiences and information, which results in an unnatural stress. As these children are rushed too quickly toward adulthood, it reduces their ability to form coherent self-images and promotes instead a scattered sense of values and place, *a patchwork self*, blurring the boundaries of what is age appropriate, by expecting—or imposing—too much too soon, and forcing kids to grow up far too fast.

Now, of course, this is not universally the case even in Western culture. Many children exist and thrive in protective, loving home environments. Our point is to call out conditions in any culture that intentionally or unintentionally place children at risk and compromise the nature of childhood through premature exposure to adult concerns. Elkind speaks of *adultified children*, a condition whereby childhood—as a safe, stable, protected time to experience and process new information and experiences—is compromised. Do these conditions ring true with your childhood experiences, or were you pressured to grow up too fast?

For some, boundaries are compromised; fences safeguarding life stages are torn down due to accelerated exposure for immature children who are not prepared to deal with the emotional, social, and physical effects it brings. And, some would observe, that not only is the line blurred between childhood and adolescence; the same condition exists between a heretofore preexisting safety wall between adolescence and adulthood. This state invents (even celebrates) a sort of *childified adulthood*, a condition whereby adults remain in a seemingly permanent state of immaturity.

Even as Christians assemble in community, they bring with them the cultural forces they encounter in schools, neighborhood, workplaces, and the media. Noted theologian Dietrich Bonhoeffer soberly says, "The ultimate test of morality of a society is what it does for its children." Our society claims to be rock-hard fiduciaries of children under their care, but in fact some recklessly mistreat them, while inadequate policies prevent flourishing.[16]

Children are at risk, sadly, even in faith community settings, and need protection. The clergy abuse scandal is a horrible tragedy that has existed not only within the Roman Catholic Church but also in Protestant settings. Environments that represent Jesus must be above reproach, especially with respect to their weakest, most vulnerable members.[17] Screening volunteers for ministry to children, including FBI background checks and developing explicit policies governing appropriate adult/child ministry interactions, can offer some assurance to parents and children at least as a start. In addition to physical protection, children must be safeguarded in emotional ways—by demonstrating respect and loving-kindness in their formal and informal interactions. Likewise, children must be shielded from dogmatic ways of interpreting faith that stifle curiosity and exploration of emerging understandings of a loving and tender God. Typical means of "managing" children—marked often by control and induced passivity through authoritative means (including intimidation and even fear)—must be replaced with a welcoming posture that views children as contributing, significant members of faith communities together with adolescents and adults. A grace-filled, inclusive atmosphere should permeate, saturate, and be appreciably observable in the care offered by churches and parachurch organizations in the nurturance of children.

What is your perspective? Does contemporary culture foster emotionally and physically safe conditions? Do its educational contexts instill character to cope with the complexities of life? Does contemporary culture provide grounded, stable role models through popular music, television, and other media to promote sound environments for social engagement with the issues and people encountered? Does culture's love-affair with sensate thrill, often associated with risky behaviors, make for a realistic practice of life serving others?

What is gained and lost when the innocence of childhood is forfeited due to cultural drift? What is the effect upon negotiating adolescence and adulthood without the necessary time of personal and socioemotional development intended by a safe, stable, loving childhood? To be sure, the ramifications of adultified childhood claim casualties among the young in our faith communities, making our best efforts at nurturing faith perilous.

Faith formation, Westerhoff proposes, is participation in and the practice of a particular way of life. Strictly speaking, we learn then from the academic field of cultural anthropology and its forming influences referred to as "enculturation," a way of forming people by infusing culture within. The question for the church is, Who is forming children with the greatest influence—home, school, media? And can the church stake out a more intentional and influential stance? Children are a heritage from God (Ps. 127:3) and have been gifted a communal status among God's people—a place to belong. And the role of this faith community is to serve as a "parallel society," acting to resist the often hostile, hurried, antifaith culture in which children exist.[18]

Given these sociocultural realities, what makes the most sense for conveying faith in a season of extremes, where religion is increasingly marginalized?

A Proposed Strategy for Nurturing Faith with Children: Atmospheric Faith

Mark has a front-row seat of children's ministry in his large nondenominational church. His daughter-in-law is "pastor to children" and superintends hundreds of children and adult volunteers. Through years of volunteering in this important ministry, in addition to parenting four of his own children, who are now married adults practicing faith with their own combined eight children, he has observed several tentpole practices that make the spiritual formation of children more likely.

1. Education in faith with children should evoke wonderment, interest, and curiosity.

Attempts that manifest boredom and passivity are the antithesis of what we seek.[19] We will know our approach has gone off the rails when the imaginations of children have become arrested or numbed to the grandeur of the presence and workings and majesty of God. The education of children should convey openness and exploration and not oppression or authoritarianism. This is not meant to imply that the stories or adults lack authority, but that our approach is to be bathed in graciousness and love.

These stories are entrusted by the older members of the community and extolled with faithful duty to the younger in-process novitiates. The stories of the faith are shared with delight by adults who are convinced of the truthfulness and authoritative reality of these narratives. These stories are nothing less than "articulations of a specific worldview, the shaping of a reliable order, and serve as a barrier against cultural chaos."[20] The majestic nature of these stories initiates children into the "secrets," as Brueggemann labels them, of the community and offers them rituals with which they find safety within these protective walls. These secrets *bind* children to the community and to God.[21]

This type of education is explicit and unapologetic in conveying the Christian faith's construction of reality, its power sources and most prized values, and its ways of living and standards of conduct within a normative socializing community. The stories, the rituals, the assurances, and the congruence of words and actions, communicated in welcoming ways, are altogether a powerful teacher.

To lean into this style of nurturing faith with children, teachers should do the following:

- *Incite wonder*: Trust Jesus in a way that transforms how I love God, myself, and the world, to know God and meet God's family. Remember that every phase is a time frame in a child's life to leverage distinctive opportunities to influence his or her future.[22]
- *Encourage exploration*: Do not make children feel inferior for mixing up factually incorrect information. Foster opportunities for children to ask all sorts of questions, even uncomfortable ones. Create a supportive environment for the ways and words children express themselves in prayer. Do not overexplain details or theological issues.

PRAYER AND CHILDREN

Generally, two broad categories are considered when Christian educators and Christian parents study the subject of children and prayer. The first category is teaching children *to* pray—that is, to instill in children the value and purpose of prayer. The second category is teaching children *how to* pray—that is, to teach children the scriptural and traditional forms of prayer that become the foundation for a lifetime of conversations with God. Both of these categories can be addressed by the instructor concurrently and by example at the earliest moment of a child's life and faith development.

Teaching children the lessons of prayer begins with appropriate modeling both within and without the home. In Hebrew, the word *horim*, referring to parents, and the word *morim*, referring to teachers, have the same meaning: to teach or to instruct. This instruction is necessary to instill both the habit and the ritual of prayer. This process is one that acknowledges the omnipresence of God and that encourages children to engage in dialogue with God as they do close friends.

Practicing God's presence by talking to God teaches children that living the Christian life is about communicating with God and fostering a constant attitude of prayer. The importance of this fact is not lost on children whose instructors show through example that God both desires and requires the attention of his people. Acknowledging God at meals by beginning with a prayer of blessing and concluding with a prayer of thanksgiving is one way that this is achieved practically in the Christian home.

Christian parents learn from Jewish tradition to be an example for prayer by saying a blessing over their children every Sabbath, following God's command to Moses: "Speak to Aaron and his sons, saying, Thus you shall bless the Israelites: You shall say to them, The LORD bless you and keep you; the LORD make his face to shine upon you, and be gracious to you; the LORD lift up his countenance upon you, and give you peace. So they shall put my name on the Israelites, and I will bless them" (Num. 6:23–27). Christian parents can begin praying with and praying over their children early in their lives, that they will grow by God's grace into mature followers of Christ and that they might live blessed lives and witness before others.

Through example, children learn the appropriate approach for prayer. Prayer should not be looked upon as an encumbrance upon the activity of life. Instead, prayer should be regarded as a natural accompaniment to daily living. Prayer is the opportunity to communicate directly with God, following great people of God in the Scriptures, including Jesus, who approached God to unleash burdens, to give thanks, to bless God with praise, to intercede for others, to ask God's forgiveness for confessed sins, to ask God to provide for a specific need, to complain about their circumstances, and to lament their losses.

R. KEVIN JOHNSON

---

2. Education in faith with children should consciously practice a two-pronged holistic strategy.

In John Westerhoff's *Will Our Children Have Faith?* (2000), he reminds that two modes of spiritual consciousness are possible—intellectual and experiential. The latter is characterized as predominately nonverbal, creative, nonlinear, and relational activities, whereas the former takes up theological truths contained in the stories of God's people. Both are essential for a fuller, holistic view. We have earlier objected to a classic schooling type of education in faith that camps in a cognitive approach. Yet we intend not to exclude facts, dates, and places that are indeed part of understanding the mission of God and the church's historic heritage. To balance the teachings and learning methods, we urge left- and right-brain expressions.

Some offer rewards to children for memorizing Bible verses or sections of catechisms as a way of learning. However, without a proper understanding of the words or concepts conveyed, little meaningful learning occurs. Mark enthusiastically enjoys watching children's programs in which his grandchildren can recite Scripture or theologically informed songs. He wonders, though he keeps this to himself, what they are able to explain from those verses or songs in their own words and how their lives are now changed to exhibit greater faith. While these church programs are cute, the degree to which spiritual formation occurs may be suspect.[23] Neuroscientists report that memorized data have little lasting effect on people's identity or values over time. Nevertheless, there may be a case to be made for some memorized core prayers, formulas of faith, and moral codes.[24]

For example, when children are taught to ask questions from the Old Testament—such as "What do these stones mean?" (Josh. 4:12) and "And when your children say to you, 'What do you mean by this service?' You shall say . . ." and other similar opportunities for educational questioning (Exod. 12:26; 13:8; 13:14; Deut. 6:20–21; Josh. 4:6)—the purpose is to gain answers of instruction. In other words, what Israel knows and how Israel knows it are linked.

To lean into this style of conceiving nurturing faith with children, teachers should do the following:

- *Pay attention* to doctrines and creeds, as well as awe and wonder; faith stories of instruction, as well as mystery and senses; rituals and practices, as well as values and relationships. In other words, the blending of knowing about God and experiencing God.
- *Practice rituals.* Rituals are repetitive, symbolic actions, in both words and deeds, that manifest and express a faith community's sacred story. These actions, rituals, are the basis for a spiritual life and growth in faith. Our symbols of worship are the most powerful of all.[25]

3. Education in faith with children should recognize them as active, participating members of the community of faith now.

Many religions have practices for passing religious identities on to children deeply embedded within them. Evangelicalism, by contrast, has long embraced the notion that everyone must choose their own religion. The nineteenth-century expansion of evangelicalism into the Protestant mainstream intensified conversion as a live option, as evangelists preached revivals and traveling pitchmen brought tracts and Bibles to people's doors. Irreligion, whether in the occasional growth of real atheists or agnostics or in the constant fears of imagined "infidels," also played an important role. American Christians came to define themselves in contrast to irreligion and thought of their children as having to exercise a deliberate choice to become Christian, rather than simply being Christian by baptism or upbringing.[26]

It was to this view that Connecticut pastor-theologian Horace Bushnell famously penned, "A child should grow up as a Christian and never know himself as otherwise." He believed in the child's development of an awareness of the relationship that has been initiated by God in and through baptism, the role of *the child's community* in fostering that relationship, and the child's understanding of, and response to, that relationship.[27]

How do you and your faith tradition reconcile these two very different approaches to being part of the faith community? This is a crucial issue for children in the faith community. Is a conversion experience expected (normally accompanied by a salvation story complete with a date)? Or should a child be considered part of the community of faith by virtue of the trust placed by God in that community? Or is another blend of these preferable? How one answers this question has direct and significant implications for how ministry with children is designed and practiced.

HORACE BUSHNELL

Horace Bushnell (1802–1876) was born in Bantam, Connecticut, and was the oldest of six children to a Methodist father and Episcopalian mother, who both were of Huguenot descent and rejected Calvinistic predestination and total depravity. Bushnell grew up on the family farm and was greatly influenced by the piety of his mother. Despite his youthful religious doubts, at age nineteen, Bushnell joined the New Preston, Connecticut Congregational Church, which his parents attended, and entered Yale College three years later. When a revival swept Yale, Bushnell experienced conversion and turned from law to enter Yale Divinity School.

When Bushnell assumed the pastorate of North Church in Hartford in 1833—where he would serve until his retirement—the last major influence that would shape his theology and understanding of Christian formation was in place. Within the context of pastoral responsibility for an urban, middle-class congregation and the challenges of responding to revivalism's exaggerated emphasis on crisis individual conversion experience and Princeton theologian Charles Hodge's charges of heresy, Bushnell would articulate a theological perspective mediating between New England Calvinism and American romanticism and craft an organic understanding of the Christian education of children. His approach would represent an attempt to blend differing emphases into a larger vision of Christian faith—a theology of comprehension. Bushnell argued for the centrality of human experience in knowing God, an integrated view of God's ordinary and extraordinary presence and work, and an understanding of biblical and theological language as poetic, aesthetic, evocative, organic, and lacking scientific or logical precision. He believed the appeal of Christianity was primarily to the heart and spirit.

Horace Bushnell has the dual distinction of being considered the "father of the Christian education movement" and the "father of American religious liberalism." Bushnell's pioneering efforts to move beyond the impasse between rigid Calvinistic theological rationalism and naturalistic theological liberalism eventually earned him the disapproval of both camps—resulting in charges of heresy, from the former, and in opposition for the Hollis Professorship in Divinity at Harvard, from the latter. Bushnell's contribution to Christian education found expression in his most famous work, *Christian Nurture*. Easily misunderstood if not read within the context of nineteenth-century American revivalism, Bushnell famously declared, "*The child is to grow up a Christian, and never know himself as being otherwise.*"

Bushnell never intended his words to deny the human inclination for sin, undermine belief in the need for Spirit-initiated transformation, or even represent a rejection of the need for revival. Bushnell had actually led revival services for his North Church congregation and affirmed the reality of miracles and spiritual gifts in the New Testament and in his time. What Bushnell argued against was "an extreme individualism" that sees children as sinners needing dramatic conversions regardless of godly parental influence.

Bushnell's contribution to Christian education was his broader theology, represented by efforts at integrating how God works supernaturally and naturally. He clearly believed the work of the Spirit and the grace of God was central to Christian nurture. He helped to draw attention to the educational needs of children as children and anticipated the twentieth-century emphasis on socialization as a primary means of formation. While he emphasized the role of the family in Christian nurture, his categorization as a theological liberal caused much of his work to be ignored by evangelicals.

JAMES P. BOWERS

---

4. Education in faith with children involves a generational mix.

Lawrence Cremin in his classic *American Education* proposes that education is fundamentally about passing on a heritage, a way of being, to another.[28] Mark's parents and grandparents told stories and practiced rituals that communicated to him what it meant to be a Lamport and a Christian (including being a Chicago Cubs fan! He is still not sure whether being a Cubs fan is part Lamport or Christian or both!). The apostle Paul reflected back to Timothy, "You have been taught the holy Scriptures from childhood, and they have given you the wisdom to receive the salvation that comes by trusting in Christ Jesus. All Scripture is inspired by God and is useful to teach us what is true and to make us realize what is wrong in our lives. It straightens us out and teaches us to do what is right. It is God's way of preparing us in every way, fully equipped for every good thing God wants us to do" (2 Tim. 3:15–17 NLT). Timothy learned wisdom from adults about the mission of God and nurturing faith.

To lean into this style of conceiving nurturing faith with children, teachers should do the following:

- *Embrace generational contributions.* Education has to do with the maintenance of a community through the generations. Its constructs most often are resilient and contain proportional doses of stability and flexibility, continuity and discontinuity.
- *Welcome tradition and transformation.* Intergenerational input can safeguard against rigid fossilizing and transient relativizing. The kind of education in faith we envision with children is radically subversive, which elicits cultural resistance due to its countercultural vision of the world. This is not a surprising outcome for Christians but is instead to be expected, embraced.

5. Education in faith with children presents an authoritative, unflinching devotion to the God of the universe.

Some parents are fond of the idea of taking their children to church (or dropping them off) and perhaps are drawn to the comfort of accommodating middle-class values they may assume to be affirmed by hospitable churches—values that serve as a means of fitting in and not standing out. Unfortunately, pleasant cultural domestication could be an expectation for churches' ministry to children—to keep them within the bounds of the faith in a fun, entertaining environment. However, there is no hint of anything such as educational acclimatization to social mores in the scriptural record.

Children need to be exposed to the holiness and unequalled greatness of God in our educational pursuits. As the Bible insists, there will be no other gods but the God of creation. This is the God who loves children and calls them to participate in devotion and service. For this God has defeated the other gods, and we affirm the divine reckoning of life with alternative stories and alternatives hopes. The ritual of the "stones" roots children in history, in truth, in confidence, and in a true-north community of faith. The stories properly ground us in faith.

This is contrasted with a most sobering observation provided by Amy Erickson, in the foreword to Brueggemann's *The Creative Word*: "Especially in more liberal churches, which are the churches I know best, educators tend to have a vague sense that it's important for children to know the Bible. However, my impression is many people in progressive churches harbor suspicions that the Hebrew Bible is at best irrelevant and at worst violent and oppressive. So they struggle with not only how to teach the Bible to children but why to teach it."[29] One may wonder whether this is a contributing factor of the decimation of mainline Christianity over the last several decades.

To lean into this style of conceiving nurturing faith with children, teachers should do the following.

- *Inculcate confidence in the truth of God.* The stories of God and God's interactions with people as recorded in Scripture resist the wrongheaded notions in culture of privatized faith or relativized faith. These encounters with truth through story ground timeless faith in children.
- *Prepare children to encounter cultural pushback.* Every time we hear a story from God, Brueggemann argues, "it means an assault on and refutation of another" version of truth or a cultural story; it is a subversive alternative to an imperial consensus.[30] And a certain hostility comes when a religion is presented that flies in the face of the accepted epistemology of the dominant cultural regime. Childhood is when these dueling contentions can be learned.
- *Offer the fortifying love of the faith community.* The reality is that education for faith with children is not to be viewed as a safety net but as fraught with risk, a countercultural risk; it is a subversive activity that, if properly taught and embraced, will have consequences. But then that is why God offers the gift of the faith community—to comfort the disenfranchised, to affirm the disbelieved, to celebrate the commonalities of the Christian destiny, and to provide hope in these darkened, antitheistic days.

Propositions for Nurturing Faith with Children

As a result of our pushback against the adultification of children, the church must be a place of protection and preservation. As a result of our displeasure with a misplacement of a formalized "schooling" model as it pertains to spiritual matters, the church must engage children with experiences, lovingkindness, and a place to explore. As a result of a reexamination of the appropriate God-appointed roles, we affirm the primacy of parents in nurturing faith, supplemented by the welcoming, loving community of faith. We also recognize that some children do not have access to two biological parents and that sometimes grandparents and other relatives, as well as baptismal parents, are ideally situated for nurturing faith in children.

As a result of these concerns, we have proposed age-appropriate and theologically informed principles for a faith-nurturing ministry with, to, and for children. The overriding concept that should wash over us is the *atmosphere* in which adults encounter children in the faith community. This atmosphere is best described as a welcoming hospitality (not production warehouses or impersonal programs). It is at once a loving, gracious presence of adults and adolescents (not age segregated); an experiential, festive backdrop (not overly structured, rules-dominated time); a place of interpretation for our faithful encounters with God (not whitewashed, moralistic stories); and a holistic, experiential knowledge of God.

These propositions may be tested in full as millennials (born after 1980) seem to display less religious belief than those of previous generations. If their parenting priorities reflect their beliefs, fewer children may encounter God and communities of faith.[31]

Conclusion

Mark and his wife lived in London recently and attended a wonderful Church of England parish. Several times, they were privileged to participate in a "welcome service" for children within its parishes. One of the prayers of that service expresses so beautifully the intentions of our educational efforts with children in faith: "*May he/she learn to learn to love all that is true, grow in wisdom and strength and, we pray, come to faith and to know the joy of your presence in his/her life with the fullness of your grace; through Jesus Christ, our Lord. Amen.*"[32] What a succinct and wonderful sentiment of experiencing both children and one's interactions with knowing, loving, and following God in the context of the church and in culture. Our intention in this chapter is to practically consider exactly how the intentions in this prayer might be accomplished.

The key influences of faith formation of children are parents and family, the community of faith, and culture.[33] Therefore, parents and churches should consider intentional strategies for welcoming children into faith communities. Obviously, public commitments for supporting families in raising children, such as baptisms and dedication ceremonies, are significant teaching events. Also critical to the faith formation of children is their intentional inclusion in corporate worship and children's church as a meaningful place to express their emerging realizations about God and the spiritual life. In addition, events that regularly engage intergenerational experiences nurture trust and provide a forum for developing adult, mentoring relationships.[34]

In sum, spiritual formation for children largely comes through relation-ships, symbols, rituals, and senses. The processes that influence growth of children's faith are communicated by belonging and participating within a vital faith community. This faith is modeled by the members of the faith community through interpreting and living biblical instruction with the members of the community, and encouraging growth experiences in the context of faith.

Interactive Dialogue

1. What do you make of Schopenhauer's quote in the epigraph at the start of the chapter? Does teaching children the Christian way, as opposed to a variety of religions, unfairly brainwash them?
2. Why do you suppose churches have adopted so many of the public school's methods for educating children in faith? What are the conse-quences of doing that?
3. If the spiritual nurture of children is the primary responsibility of par-ents (see Deut. 6:1–9), what role then should churches and/or para-church organizations have in this process?
4. The authors suggest five proposals for nurturing faith in children. If you were to add a sixth one, what would it be? How have you seen this to be effective in the spiritual formation of children?

For Further Reading

Beckwith, Ivy. *Formational Children's Ministry: Shaping Children Using Story, Rit-ual, and Relationship*. Grand Rapids: Baker, 2010.

Csinos, David M. *Children's Ministry That Fits: Beyond One-Size-Fits-All Approaches to Nurturing Children's Spirituality*. Eugene, OR: Wipf & Stock, 2011.

Fischer, Becky. *Redefining Children's Ministry in the 21st Century*. Mandan, ND: Kids in Ministry International, 2005.

Mercer, Joyce. *Welcoming Children: A Practical Theology of Childhood*. St. Louis: Chalice, 2005.

Stonehouse, Catherine, and Scottie May. *Listening to Children on the Spiritual Jour-ney: Guidance for Those Who Teach and Nurture*. Grand Rapids: Baker, 2010.

Wuthnow, Robert. *Growing Up Religious: Christians and Jews and Their Journeys of Faith*. Boston: Beacon, 1999.

Yust, Karen Marie. *Real Kids, Real Faith: Practices for Nurturing Children's Spiritual Lives*. San Francisco: Jossey-Bass, 2004.

CHAPTER TWELVE

Nurturing Passionate Faith in Adolescents

Adolescence is a "vernal season of the heart" when "life glistens and crepitates."

—G. STANLEY HALL

Youth look for the church to show them something, someone, capable of turning their lives inside out and the world upside down. Most of the time we have offered them pizza. We are painfully aware that we have sold them short.

—KENDA DEAN AND RON FOSTER

ROAD MAP

In his early youth worker days, Fred was vexed by fourteen-year-old "Anna" (not her real name). She was reserved and not inclined to the gregarious youth ministry broomball games Fred championed. In spite of broomball, Anna somehow agreed to participate in a mission trip to Mexico. While in mission, Anna led Bible school arts and crafts activities for younger elementary children over five days. In addition to displaying artistic gifts plus skills to teach art, Anna demonstrated relational skills with the children despite the language barrier. In class, she would sit next to them and point to features of their artistic creations. The children often responded with commentary in their own language. Anna listened and nodded, her body language demonstrating the loving attention her speech could not. These children were very sad to see Anna go. Having long since lost touch with Anna, Fred cannot say how this time in mission impacted her. He can report Anna's impact on him, however. It marked the beginning of a transition from imagining youth ministry as giving Christ *to* youth to inviting youth to participate *in Christ*. This chapter unpacks the theology and practices of this reimagining.

Introduction

The conventional wisdom on adolescents suggests they are a boiling cauldron of hormones, a storm surge of desire induced to act without thinking, a big bundle of impulsiveness that drives them to all sorts of risky behaviors. Young people "lead with their hearts."[1] They give themselves over completely to something or someone without regard to consequences. They dive in headfirst before first checking the depth of the water. Studies seem to confirm this account: drug and alcohol abuse, criminal endeavors, mental illness, and sexual activity (to name a few) all escalate dramatically during adolescence.[2] The conventional solution, therefore, has sought to protect youth from the danger they pose to themselves and others through the creation of "safe" communities (schools, teams, clubs, youth groups) where their passion and its negative behavioral consequences can be mitigated.

Age	Nurturing through . . .
Children	Atmosphere
▸ Adolescents	Passion
Adults	Vocation

But what if the passion of young people is not the root of their problem? Youths' passion can just as readily land them in the arms of God after all. We think passion itself is not the culprit. By contrast, we assert that the passion of the heart so evident in adolescence is not merely a phase to be survived until reason and relative sanity can be restored in adulthood but also a spiritual gift to young people, intended for sharing with God, church, and world. In light of our portrayal of human beings as "lovers" more than "thinkers," in chapter 6, we likewise contend that youth actually exemplify for the rest of us a crucial dimension of what it means to be human. We would do well to pour out our hearts in love as completely as they do. Consequently, the task of nurturing faith, rather than squelching young people's desire, will seek to connect it to God's unfailing pursuit of them in Jesus Christ. Christ is a worthy recipient of young love, because Christ, uniquely, can return and fulfill it. He alone is "big enough to take it," to meet fire with Fire. Phrased differently, we think that youth are *compelled* by Christ (2 Cor. 5:14–15) toward graced relational participation *in Christ*. They are moved ("im-*passioned*") toward him because he is first moved by them to draw them into himself. Along the way, Jesus transforms youthful passions, fashioning them as new expressions of praise in worship and "all in" participation in missional community.

Unfortunately, just as youth have become primed for Christly action (relational participation in Christ), they often are prevented from full participation in congregations. They are marginalized because they are kids. The authors judge it better that youth shake up the worshiping community with praise, try ministry for themselves, agitate for justice like so many Old Testament prophets, and willingly bear Christ's cross than be confined to the balcony to text each other. Instead of "protecting" youth from themselves and a dangerous world (and ourselves from them!), we propose commissioning and empowering them as the most passionate members of Christ's body to bear Christ into the world.

What Is Adolescence?

Just as childhood and adulthood are taken-for-granted categories of human existence, so is adolescence. However, the term was not even coined until the late nineteenth century.[3] Since then, it has been bolstered by an amalgam of biological, psychological, sociological, economic, and cultural claims that have only strengthened its pretension to ontological status. We grant that adolescents are biologically different from children and adults, and we judge it important for faith formational leaders to understand these differences. Finally, however, we characterize adolescence as a social construction. It is principally the creation of historic sociocultural forces whose impact on young people more often than not has prevented their flourishing. We unpack this claim below.

The beginning of adolescence is associated with the onset of puberty. Puberty includes the maturing of secondary sex characteristics, rapid bodily growth, and, as we have learned more recently, explosive neurological development.[4] Obviously, one outcome of puberty is the capacity to practice procreation. Yet that is just the tip of the iceberg. Neurological development can also lead to increasing self-awareness—catching one's self in the act of being, for example. It can foster empathic interpersonal perspective-taking (walking in another's shoes). It may prompt construction of a "self-identity."[5]

We find the deepening passion of youth to be the driver of this new way of being. Surging affective energy, including sexual energy, propels adolescents toward ends they desire. Moreover, young people become capable of feeling (reflecting upon) the powerful emotions that move them. Developmentally speaking, where children are mostly subject to their emotions, adolescents may to a certain extent make emotions the object of scrutiny. For example, youth may ask, "Is this what love feels like?"—a question that would never occur to a child.

On the other hand, adolescents may become so deeply impassioned that any effort toward reflection is overwhelmed. Neuroscience observes an asymmetry in brain development at this stage of life. Where emotion systems sprint off the start line like the proverbial hare, other cognitive systems, constituting what is called the "executive function," crawl tortoise-like into action. Only after a period of a decade or more does the brain's executive function begin to apply the brakes to the impulsive desires of the heart.[6] Hence adolescents' greater propensity for risk-taking behaviors. Passion can move young hearts to acts of great bravery or inexplicable violence.

Passion also propels young people into relationship with someone or something. Relationships certainly include involvement with persons (first true love, devotion to a mentor) or communities (live and die for TEAM) but may also catalyze other kinds of commitments—to causes, creativity, excellence, or some other perceived good. As Christian educator and youth worker David White points out, the American Revolution was mostly waged by a bunch of college-age kids.[7] Passion may also go unrequited, however. A youth who can give herself completely to another in love becomes vulnerable to unprecedented despair when love is not reciprocated. Adults who care for youth dare not underestimate the depths of interrelational suffering they undergo when propelled by the vulnerability of love.

The passion of youth is also subject to formation. Passion's ends are neither given nor automatic. This can appear counterintuitive, especially in a place like the United States, where passion is reduced by popular culture to one end—SEX. Youth are conditioned by American culture to believe that the totality of their desire should be fulfilled through sexual encounter. They watch as their bodies are sexualized through the media. They learn from the market to use their sexuality to harness power or status. This tacit construal of desire is so pervasive that an adolescent who dreams out loud an alternative vision of life is likely to be mocked for not "getting any" lately.

When passion is reduced to sex by principalities and powers, adolescents are left without a vocabulary to describe the other consuming loves of their lives. What to make of this delight I experience when exercising my mind? How to explain this determination to change the world? What is it when my band or team or project group is totally gelling? What or who is drawing me beyond myself toward the infinite? If sex is all there is to passion, then these wonderings can be explained away as repressed sexual desire, or, worse, they never come to consciousness in the first place.

The period of adolescence has lengthened in the developed parts of the world. In 1960, Americans married at about age twenty-one, marking the end of their adolescence. In 2013, the age of marriage was on average twenty-eight.[8] Without marriage and other markers of adulthood, like jobs or parenthood, so-called emerging adults continue their liminal season of betwixt and between, no longer child but not yet adult.[9] Fred's twenty-something daughter, speaking the vernacular of her generation, describes herself as "adulting."

Adolescent Oppression

Young people find themselves swimming against multiple social cultural currents they do not often recognize, let alone learn to resist. These are endemic of systemic sin and constitute barriers to their flourishing. A partial list includes the following:

- the aforementioned objectification of youthful bodies and consequent exploitation by the marketing/consumerist complex;
- immersion in a virtual world covertly distorting their passions;
- vulnerability to what once were considered adult problems—violence, abuse, crushing economic burdens, incarceration, and mental illness;
- lack of agency for contributing to their own flourishing;
- isolation in demographic ghettos away from children or adults.

In addition to being subject to the barriers with which all youth must contend, youth of color, youth with nonheteronormative sexual identities, and young people with developmental or physical disabilities also face racialized or gender oppression, plus social isolation or bullying.

Selling Bodies

At present, the bodies of youth are glorified. They have become icons of human potential. Their strength and virility offer stark contrast to the aged or infirm. Pulsing with the energy of life, they distract the rest of us from our mortality. Moreover, young women in particular are made over by media and patriarchy to simultaneously symbolize innocence and sexual provocation.

This iconic power of youth is in large measure the creation of marketing forces. Ultimately, these forces objectify what they celebrate. Young people's bodies, their creativity, and their passion are packaged to appeal to the market, including young people themselves. This process turns them into commodities. Instead of human beings with unique gifts and burdens passionately participating in the journey toward deepened flourishing, youth are cast as body parts, sex appeal, or attractive risk for the purpose of stimulating further consumption.[10]

That consumer capitalism is heretical religion and unsustainable on a finite planet goes without saying. Our concern here is its impact upon young people themselves. Consumerism not only commodifies adolescents but also seeks to convert them into the "faith." Gorgeous Olympic athletes market credit cards not only because the world is gaga for their beauty and vigor but also because economic forces are out to evangelize the next generation of consumers. In reality, few young people can live up to the image of themselves as portrayed by the media/marketing complex. Nor do they yet possess the experience or wisdom to imagine differently or to free themselves from its tentacles. Whatever agency they may wish to acquire is repeatedly sidetracked toward buying this product or that experience.

The Medium Is the Message Is the Smartphone

Risking anachronism, we suggest that the smartphone is the single most important formational instrument in the lives of youth at present. This generation of young people, described as "digital natives," is the first to be immersed from birth in this technology and the cultural transformations it is driving. Language is changing (LOL). Images overshadow words (smiley face). Memes are the new form of satire. Social media promises exposure and intimacy without bodily presence or risk. According to a poll directed by the nonprofit Common Sense Media, teens consume approximately nine hours a day of media, while so far there exists little understanding of its long-term impacts. "We're conducting the biggest experiment on our kids," according to director Jim Steyer. It is a "digital transition—without research."[11]

The authors are not Luddites, at least not on purpose. Yet we feel enough ambivalence about technology to offer this caution. It seems to us that the internet, as it has been constructed, seeks (literally) to capture the desires of young people. The infinite clickability of the web promises fulfillment around every turn. But at least three concerns arise. First, young people's attention is made fragmented and fleeting, instead of sustained and focused. Nicholas Carr, author of *The Shallows: What the Internet Is Doing to Our Brains*, worries that young people will find it more difficult to develop or sustain complex critical thinking skills as a result. He suggests empathy is equally at risk for lack of deep attending. Imagining life in another's shoes and then caring about it takes time.[12] Second, over the long term, there is realistic concern for the formation of young people's passions. It is a truism that most of the traffic on the web is pornographic; its ubiquity sends strong messages to youth on the meaning and proper ends for their desire. In other words, the web is not a neutral medium for free expression. It not only trades on the passions of youth but also disposes their loves to what the web itself wants them to love. In Augustinian terms, the love intended for God becomes distorted by the web, causing it to miss its mark. Third, youth face relational fragmentation and the loss of communal participation. Today young people hang out together while absorbed in their phones. They are together . . . alone. In contrast, for Fred, growing up in the era prior to personal devices attached to headphones, lengthy bus rides on school and church adventures featured raucous dance-offs in the aisle, cheerleading contests, belting out TV show theme songs, total bus neck rubs, spontaneous worship, and endless conversation. We were together . . . together.

ADOLESCENT RELIGIOUS IDENTITY

Identity research was first popularized by the developmental psychologist Erik Erikson (1902–1994). He defined eight psychosocial stages, in which the fifth stage, *identity* vs. *role confusion*, is located in adolescence. During this time, adolescents are faced with the difficult tasks of negotiating their rapidly changing bodies and a felt need to separate from parental attachments. Erikson theorized that the primary goal in adolescence is to develop *ego identity* (*ego* comes from the Latin nominative pronoun "I"), in which simple identifications made during childhood are integrated into a coherent sense of self in adolescence.

Erikson described each psychosocial stage as a favorable balance of the positive element (i.e., identity) over the negative element (i.e., role confusion). If a young person has more role confusion than identity, that person faces an *identity crisis*, which may encumber each of the consecutive aspects of human development. The term *identity crisis* became Erikson's most popular concept and gave many teenagers and young adults a structure through which to understand their own experiences. Erikson also described virtues that are achieved at each stage. For *identity* vs. *role confusion*, the individual achieves the virtue of *fidelity*, in which young adults begin to display a consistent level of commitment and faithfulness (fidelity) to how they know and understand their own selves.

James Marcia (1966) used Erikson's work in identity to formulate an overall measure of identity, separating identity into statuses of *identity diffusion*, *moratorium*, *commitment*, and *achievement*. Simply stated, a teenager may have a strong sense of an achieved gender identity but may have a crisis in religious identity.

These identity domains may move higher and lower in salience on a daily basis for adolescents. Thus, cognitively, a teenager is commonly processing multiple areas of identity and is likely to be unaware of how the domains implicitly move from the foreground of consciousness into the background. Religious identity, in particular, is one of the most important forms of identity attachments for young adults. Teenagers with religious experiences from childhood often seek to construct maximal religious experiences in their affiliations as a form of identity play. But this is often conventional (Marcia's *identity foreclosure*) in that adolescents are displaying attachments and not identity integration.

Christian Education and Adolescent Religious Identity. Helping develop educational programs that facilitate religious identity in adolescence may be one of the most important aspects of Christian education. It has been shown that identity attachments (more simple forms of nonreflective acceptance), even when formed/experienced with strong emotions, do not have the staying power of identity integration. A typical pattern of Christian education in America is one in which a vibrant program in adolescence is unmatched during early adult years—the precise time that real identity crises arise (differing from Erikson's original location of the crisis in adolescence).

Those who are seeking to assist individuals in religious identity formation are ultimately trying to help adolescents and young adults to move from identity attachments into a deeper (explicit and implicit) form of religious identity integration. Many theorists argue that this requires a reflective time in an individual's life in which the person breaks loyalties and allegiances of childhood and adolescent peer groups in an effort to integrate narrative and meaning into one's identity without the force of outside groups. For the most part, there has not been much practical research specific to religion in studying how to help adolescents and young adults during any identity crisis oriented around faith. Work in the related area of narrative theory suggests that prompted activities for spiritual autobiography, intergenerational experiences, and group-identity reflections might be promising areas to study. Practical theologians also need to speak to whether the role of Christian educators is to simply keep religious individuals in the church after an identity crisis, or whether the church itself should be impacted and open to change by individuals who have formed, after some reflection and growth, an integrated sense of religious identity.

DAVID M. BELL

Not convinced? Follow the money. Apple alone is so profitable, it hoards nearly $300 billion (a third of a *trillion*) in cash.[13] Much of this cash comes from sales of iPhones, the choice of nearly 80 percent of teens. Clearly, Apple and other media/technology giants have considerable motivation to continue to harness the desires of the young.

Growing Up Too Fast

Adolescents are forward looking. They are more inclined to anticipate high school and beyond than to pine away nostalgically for the good old days of second grade. Once, adolescence was imagined as a relatively safe space and a time to come to terms with changing bodies and to try on different possible roles on the journey toward adulthood. Admittedly, this vision of adolescence as a protected space was from the start constructed out of middle-class assumptions about wealth and the illusion of security it provides. It also privileges the emerging "individual" over the relational group.

Beginning with David Elkind's *The Hurried Child*, advocates for children and young people have painted a more ominous picture of premature pressures toward adulthood.[14] This pressure is refracted differently according to class. In wealthy families, it looks like harried, overscheduled kids sprinting from ballet to soccer to string lessons to SAT prep classes between Ritalin snack breaks—all of this calibrated to shape a winning portfolio for attaining admission into the good life. It has turned into elitist social Darwinism where only the fittest (of the socially fittest) survive. In one compelling example of the effects of this pursuit, practical theologian Brian Mahan offers a poignant description and theological analysis of young people mourning their disappointing AP scores.[15] Unfortunately, the "failures" of elite youth are manifested in increasing rates and severity of mental illness, drug addiction, and suicide.[16]

Poor youth also suffer with mental disorders, substance abuse, educational failures, and risk for suicide—but for different reasons. Instead of pressure to succeed, they feel pressure just to survive. They are much more likely than their elite peers to work to support the household or to provide childcare for younger siblings. They are more likely to be victimized by physical and sexual abuse. Often their parents cannot afford to pay for opportunities to acquire cultural capital through music lessons or family vacations.

Sexism and racism compound all these obstacles for young women and young people of color. They somehow must learn to navigate in a society dominated by patriarchy, White privilege, and implicit bias. As testimony to the reality of racism, the Children's Defense Fund documents what it calls the "Cradle to Prison Pipeline." The statistics are chilling. For example, a Black boy born in 2001 has a one in three chance of going to prison. A White boy has a one in seventeen chance.[17]

Going It Alone Together

Despite the pressure to become adults and their exposure to adult responsibilities and problems, young people are prevented from attaining the agency (the capacity to act to improve their own lives) that accompanies adulthood.

It cannot help that teens have become an increasingly isolated demographic. Two journalists working independently in the 1990s chronicled two very different groups of young people; one followed teens in suburbia, and the other described teens marginalized by poverty.[18] Remarkably, each writer independently depicted teens as inhabiting a world of their own, a space seldom trespassed by parents or other caring adults. They experimented with drugs, had sex, and engaged in criminal behavior without their parents' knowledge. That young people break adult rules is not exactly a revelation. What was new according to the authors was the extent of their abandonment by the adult world. The task of reaching adulthood fell to youth themselves without much help getting there. In other words, adolescence functions as a kind of socially enforced internment.

Nurturing Passionate Faith in Young People

What will faith formation for youth consist of in the twenty-first century? We have tipped our hand by way of the previous critical descriptions. It will seek to draw out, not squelch or flee from, the passions of youth while forming their all-consuming loves to God. It will strive to empower them as passionate participants in God's mission, capable of addressing and overcoming sociocultural forces that oppress them and haunt all of creation. Finally, it will teach for critical reflection, especially seeking to cultivate and act in response to theological imagining to articulate God's vision for new creation.

MENTORING ADOLESCENT BOYS

In 1904, G. Stanley Hall published his groundbreaking psychological work, *Adolescence: Its Psychology and Its Relation to Physiology, Anthropology, Sociology, Sex, Crime, Religion, and Education*, in which he noted adolescence to be "*the period during which boyhood spirituality was either developed or buried forever.*" The naturalness of Hall's vision meant not only that boys needed proper guidance attuned to their savage, rugged nature but also that only masculine men who understood a boy's disposition could provide him with this particular instruction.

Deemed "character building," adolescent male mentorship defined the work of newly founded, church-supported organizations, including the Boy Scouts of America, the YMCA, and the Boys' Brigade. Masculine mentors acted as the lynchpin of their efforts, building relationships and making disciples through the shared experiences of summer camp and athletics.

Echoing the rhetoric of the early twentieth century, the most vocal Christian responses to these boy troubles were twofold: reasserting the virtue of masculinity and reclaiming a dominant, masculine place for men from the perceived encroachment of ecclesial feminization. A tool for both the evangelization of apathetic young men and the cultivation of masculine disciples, mentorship was crucial to this "rescue" effort. Reiterating psychologists like Michael Gurian, Christian author John Eldredge railed against the pathologization of "masculine" behaviors by an overly feminized culture. Eldredge's book *Wild at Heart* presses Christian men to reclaim their God-given masculinity, characterized by an aggressive, boyish wildness bound by the heroic Christianity of the chivalric knight. Furthermore, fathers and mentors must guard the natural wildness of adolescent boys from the cultural pressures of feminization, helping them harness their masculinity as they transition into manly, godly men.

As heirs to the concept of adolescence, the church must interrogate the ideological foundation of adolescent male mentorship at work today. In particular, Christians should begin to examine the misogyny often present as a silent corollary to masculine bravado. Motivated by perceived boy troubles, masculine movements and their proponents continually cast women in opposition to men. Whether it is asserted that women are unable to understand boys or that imposing "feminine" qualities subverts male development, the underlying logic remains the same: only men can really train boys into men. This rationale marginalizes women's critical role in mentoring boys while simultaneously construing women as inferior to men. Such notions of masculinity, then, shackle women *and* men to an image that defines identity and molds character.

Mentorship can also replicate hierarchies along socioeconomic and racial lines. The psychological literature on adolescent boys and the character-building efforts of the twentieth century were largely aimed at White, middle-class populations. The issues of minority, foreign, homosexual, and working-class boys were typically ignored.

The masculine ideal occupying the center of male mentorship efforts risks becoming a false idol in whose image all must be cast. If Christ is the image in whom we are created, should not Christ be at the center of our mentorship aims? If Christians are to take Jesus's call to discipleship seriously, mentors and adolescent mentees alike must follow Christ into the baptismal waters. In baptism, the entire person enters into the death and resurrection of Jesus Christ. Masculinity, enmeshed as it is in our subjectivity, must also enter into this liminal space to face death and be reborn. Displacing any other systems of formation that claim supremacy, Christ now comes to define a person's being more than "manliness." Masculinity is not jettisoned altogether but must become subservient to Christ so that it might be regenerated by our true Image.

DEREK JONES

Forming and Transforming Passion through Participation

Having previously documented the passions of youth, we return to Kenda Dean to make the crucial theological connection. Dean suggests that the endless desires of youth to give themselves completely to something or someone may be matched only by God's desire for them: "The Christian story both authenticates adolescent passion and turns it inside out, redeeming, redirecting, and redefining it with a more profound Passion still: the suffering love of Jesus Christ. As a result, youthful passion serves the church both as a sign of the *imago Dei*, and as an energy source of enormous potential. By acknowledging the Passion of Christ, adolescent passions give way to faith; and, fueled by the energy of fierce love, this faith inevitably leads to ministry."[19]

Elsewhere, Dean sums it up this way: "Christ's passion transforms adolescent desire into sacrificial love."[20] Yet, we wonder, What does this look like walking around in shorts and T-shirts? Worship, fully inclusive Christian community, and mission are each practices where young people may encounter the passion of God and, by grace, find their own passions formed and transformed.

Worship

Passion compels relational beings to reach out beyond themselves in love, for, paradoxically, it is loving relationships that make us whole. Young people and all human beings are drawn to love God. In addition, as C. S. Lewis says, "we delight to praise that which we enjoy. . . . The praise not merely expresses but completes the enjoyment."[21] In other words, youth who are primed for passion (in this case joy) are also wired for worship. Worship provides the thin space where the tinder of young love may be ignited by the flames of the Spirit.

Like King David, youth can flat out break it down before the Lord. When invited, they readily dance, sing, step, sway, play, testify, and shout praises to God. This too is a result of their proclivity to passion. It is crucial for their faith formation that young people be granted time and space to exercise this desire to worship. They are compelled to meet and enjoy the living God. It is equally crucial for congregations to learn how to receive passionate youth worship as a *gift*. No, it may not yet be modulated according to the tastes of adult worshippers; guitar-hero ambitions or the "wrong" kind of gestures can seem excessive and embarrassing, like David's naked gyrations before God in front of the Jerusalem social circle. But since when does God become human, live a radically singular life, die a catastrophic yet purposeful death, and rise again in the flesh only to shy away from excess? God leads with the (Sacred) Heart too. God is all in! An extravagant God welcomes youthful extravagance. So what if the kids make a spectacle of themselves. God is spectacular![22] Faith communities hoping to survive past 2050 simply must find ways to invite the young to contribute their passion to the primary worship assembly. If worship is dead, youth will seek out the living somewhere else. Inviting the passionate participation of youth will require leaders of congregational worship to incorporate some of youths' cultural vernacular. It will invite (and risk) creativity—including appropriation of new media and forms of expression, of biblical preaching that addresses the fears and hopes of young people, their suffering as well as their successes—and offer embodied wholehearted responses of communal lament and celebration.

On the other hand, liturgical innovation toward passion does not mean everything old must go. "Contemporary worship" is not automatically the answer to "staid traditionalism."[23] In its nearly two decades of existence, Duke's Youth Academy (DYA) for Christian Formation has demonstrated that ancient liturgical rites—including, for example, communal confession of sin, sharing Christ's peace with one another, joyously sung prayers of Great Thanksgiving, and daily reception of Holy Communion—can become (again) for youth powerful means of participation in the joy of the triune God. That these practices may at first seem anachronistic to some youth likely testifies to church forgetfulness about where to go to receive grace. DYA's pedagogical strategy for liturgical formation includes explicit teaching on the history and theology of Christian worship, intentional inclusion of youth in worship as participants/leaders/planners, and opportunities to reflect on worship and its organic ties to all of Christian life. When youth are considered partners in the creation and performance of worship, at least two things happen. First, they begin to take seriously their role as bearers of word and sacrament for the assembly. Second, their youthful passion and experience inevitably infuse new life into old bones. Ultimately, through worship rich in word and sacrament, youth find ample opportunities to pour out their hearts to the Christ who is pouring his own into them.[24]

Mission

Recently, youth ministry has claimed a missional focus. Admittedly, its early efforts were tainted by colonialist motivations—privileged youth from the Global North encouraged to imagine themselves delivering Jesus to the "less fortunate" in the Global South. Thoughtful youth and youth workers quickly realized, however, that Jesus was way out in front of them. Instead of delivering Christ, missions became pilgrimages to encounter Christ in situations far more freighted with suffering and joy than was afforded by padded life back home. Said one youth worker devoted to outwardly focused missional youth ministry, "Mission is how Jesus breaks open my kids' hearts." In another case, an alumna of DYA sought to replace "helping" or even "saving" with "pilgrimage" and "friendship." She took initiative to cultivate friendships with youth in a congregation in Central America. She next recruited young people from her own church to go and visit these new friends. Her motivation, instead of flying south to "help out," was to deepen Christian friendships, to learn about life in another context through the eyes of her peers, and to share burdens and hopes with them.[25]

Like worship, mission is a ministry practice that invites young people to lead with their hearts. Not yet steeled by adult defenses, they willingly give their love to others, and they risk vulnerability with little regard for its consequences. Correspondingly, the Scriptures testify to Christ's presence through encounters with strangers, especially poor ones (Matt. 25:31–46). Mission, therefore, is another vital space where young love can meet Christ's love. Christian friendship reaching across social and cultural boundaries transforms hearts, establishing a new benchmark for faithfulness going forward. The passion of youth can testify to a church whose members are "known by their love."

Fred's experience with youth in mission suggests that it summons youth's "best" selves. He has watched them toil sacrificially at difficult tasks—painting, cleaning, building, cooking, teaching, caring for children, leading worship, serving, witnessing—much of which prompts head scratching from skeptical parents back home. Youth in mission often fall in love with the people they meet. They witness boldly through word and deed. They believe without ambiguity that God is with them as they do God's will.

Of course, as with worship, no missional effort is perfect. As noted, mission can devolve into top-down charity from rich to poor, and it can be twisted to testify to the "blessedness" of North American Christians in contrast to less cumbered brothers and sisters elsewhere. Nevertheless, faith formational leaders will continue to risk calling young people into mission. They will bear in mind that mission belongs first and last to God (*missio Dei*), not to the church or its youth.[26] They will teach youth to read the Scriptures missionally in order to see God's intent in the world and then to "read" the world, seeking to join God's saving work where they find it. They will imitate Christ's ministry and model humility, seeking as much to receive Christ through new friendships as to share Christ.

MENTORING ADOLESCENT GIRLS

Mentoring adolescent girls is an especially important practice of Christian education because girls face sexism within and outside the church and often struggle with loving themselves and finding their bodies acceptable.

The first task of mentors of adolescent girls is to participate in the church and discover their own passionate faith. When adolescent girls are connected in relationship with adults who are passionate about their faith, these girls are more likely to be passionate about their own faith and be formed into disciples of Christ throughout their lives.

The mentoring relationship must be based on participating in the living, active presence of Christ. The relationship is about loving the adolescent girl and being present with her as a member of the body of Christ. Ministry with girls is part of Christ's own ministry. Helping a girl discover her giftedness from God, discern her call from God, and respond to the world around her as a Christian can all be part of what comes out of a mentoring relationship. However, the goal of the mentoring relationship must be the relationship itself; the relationship must not be a means to an end, like becoming a member of the church or making some doctrinal affirmation.

Practical theologian Joyce Mercer discovered that Christian adolescent girls are very open to being "spiritual apprentices" but that they often have difficulty finding adults to apprentice them. Girls are looking for genuine relationships with adults who can guide them. Serving as adult mentors of adolescent girls is an opportunity for the hope to be realized.

Adolescent girls face particular challenges to their Christian formation from within their churches and society at large. Mentoring adolescent girls means forming an alliance with girls against the pressures and forces that threaten their humanity and therefore their spirituality. Depending on the context of the adolescent girls, there are a number of forces with which a mentor must engage. There may be pressures of sexual activity, promiscuous dress, gang involvement, consumerism, and the pressure of "success." Forming an alliance with girls against systemic oppression and damaging familial and social structures in the very personal way they show up in girls' lives is a central task of the mentor. In this way, mentoring is a practice of liberation and a way to embody the freedom of Christ in relationship.

Although males can be mentors of adolescent girls, it is also important for girls to have adult women in leadership positions in the church acting as models and mentors for them. It is particularly helpful when leadership roles in the church are open for girls' participation. Girls need to see female bodies affirmed in this way in the life of the church. Mentoring adolescent girls often requires the mentor to advocate for the girl to the leadership of the church. Mentoring adolescent girls is a practice of helping them to see, believe, and ultimately act in a way that affirms that their bodies are the "site and mediation of divine revelation." In order for them to come to this realization, adolescent girls need mentors who listen to them, love them, act on their behalf, and model this kind of faith.

EMILY A. PECK-MCCLAIN

Nor does mission necessarily look like leaving home for an exotic destination. Practical theologian and youth worker Benjamin Connor describes mission by way of his ministry with young persons with disabilities. His account examines faith communities and depicts the reality of blooming friendships between normally developing young people and their friends with disabilities. Connor notes that the body of Christ, too, is a disabled body; therefore, full inclusion of persons with disabilities "amplifies [the church's] witness" and is a central manifestation of God's mission. For our part, we are moved by the willingness of all kinds of young persons to join God's mission in this way. Fred lives just a block from an urban neighborhood where theology students live together with young adult friends with varying disabilities. It is a community marked by laughter and joy; it provides a glimpse of God's realm.

Participation through Passion

Passion and participative action are inextricably linked. As noted, to be in passion is *to be moved* by some other—including, potentially, God. Passion, therefore, is already incipient action. Christ himself is moved by young people to draw them close to himself. In turn, they are moved bodily to participate in Christ's body through worship and mission. Passion, therefore, is reciprocal and relational. We may imitate Christ because God in Christ lovingly imitates us through the incarnate Son's own passionate life, death, and resurrection.

If passion is incipient action, then the ministry of faith formation vigorously will seek to build upon youths' passions toward youths' agency, their capacity to act upon their worlds in redemptive ways, including for worship, missional outreach to the world, and missional inclusion of all kinds of persons in Christian community. In theological terms, this means faith-forming leaders will seek to equip youth to take up their baptismal ministries. Just as Jesus was Spirit-empowered and called to ministry through his baptism, so are persons baptized in his name. Again, this is not the same as keeping kids safe. Jesus's ministry was not safe. Nor does it mean allowing the young to grow to adulthood before we ask anything of them. They are primed for action *now*.

At the same time, we don't envision throwing youth to the wolves. Wise youth workers will scaffold youth's growing agency by surrounding them with many healthy adults who live and breathe Christ's baptismal call in their own lives. With the support of mentors, youth will be vested with real responsibilities. This includes energizing their capacity to dream God's dreams, followed by acting upon them while at the same time recognizing that their efforts are likely to be partial and imperfect. (So it is for all of us.)

Conclusion

A bullet point description of adolescent characteristics typically describes and extols their transition from concrete to abstract thinking. Cognitive abstraction makes possible capacities as varied as doing algebra and appreciating metaphor. It is also the raw material for critical consciousness, thinking beneath surface appearances of things to their root causes. Youth are emergently capable of thinking critically about the social conditions that impact their lives.

David White describes a group of young people under his care who became impassioned over shared experiences of racial profiling in their Los Angeles neighborhood. Their passion led to an exploration of the juvenile justice system. Supported by Christian youth workers, teachers, and allied judges and attorneys, these young people next established teen courts in their schools, where the rates of recidivism were approximately halved compared to those cases handled through the justice system.[27] Simply put, Christian young people became agents of justice for their peers. Evelyn Parker, another youth worker and practical theologian, describes this scenario as "emancipatory hope."[28] More than wishing, it empowers youth to *act* toward the hope they envision.

White's guidance included the essential step of consciousness-raising. He helped these young people to ask together, What kinds of young people did they witness being detained by police? Why? What assumptions guided the officers in their practices of detainment? What happened to Black boys who came into contact with the juvenile justice system? Did they receive the same protections as other detainees? Fact-finding by the group uncovered systemic bias against African American male youth. America's treasured equality of opportunity and its assumptions of innocence before guilt seemed not to apply to them. In the vernacular of the day, these youth and their adult mentors "got woke." Coming to consciousness was, in turn, key to their emancipatory hope leading toward action.

Recently in the United States, many high school students have awakened to the reality of gun violence being perpetrated upon them and their younger peers. Some have become convinced that if adults will not or cannot act to protect them, then they must act on their own behalf. In response, many are speaking out, demanding their constitutional rights for life and liberty. Political activism by young people against mass shootings of young people is met with everything from skepticism ("they're too young to understand the complexity of the issues") to indifference ("they don't vote"). Nevertheless, this is a case where the passion of youth to flourish has ignited their desire to learn why it is that society is not protecting them (the work of consciousness-raising to acquire perspective) and then to *do* something about it. Adult power is vaguely threatened; political interests wish the kids would go back to video games and cheerleading.

Congregations, at least that those who do not believe in divine sanction for the possession of weapons of mass death, dare not twiddle their thumbs in response. The kids are aroused! Like prophets, they are speaking truth to power. Will we point them to an equally aroused Jesus—he who lived and died for nothing less than their abundant life of peaceful flourishing—or will we just wait it out and hope they become distracted again? If we in the church wait too long, if we do not invite their passionate action consistent with God's peaceable mission, we risk losing our youth for good.

Passion means suffering another or suffering for and with another. This suffering springs from love. God's incarnation in Christ's life, death, and resurrection is the hallmark of God's loving passion for youth and for all of us. Nurturing faith in youth will unfold at the intersection of their passion and God's.

Interactive Dialogue

1. Draw a diagram (mental or actual) that locates you in relation to other constituencies in the faith community of your adolescence. For example, were you close to the center or more at the edges? Where would you locate other persons or groups? How did this location impact your faith and the faith of your adolescent peers?
2. In light of youth ministry's long history of focusing upon community and fellowship, why do the authors concentrate on worship and mission?
3. Compare and contrast the evangelical appeal for teens to accept Jesus into their hearts with this chapter's emphasis upon the passion of Christ and the passion of youth.
4. Defend, modify, or reject the assertion that adolescents as a group are oppressed.

For Further Reading

Connor, Benjamin T. *Amplifying Our Witness: Giving Voice to Adolescents with Developmental Disabilities.* Grand Rapids: Eerdmans, 2012.

Dean, Kenda Creasy. *Almost Christian: What the Faith of Our Teenagers Is Telling the American Church*. New York: Oxford University Press, 2010.

Edie, Fred P. *Book, Bath, Table, and Time: Worship as Source and Resource for Youth Ministry*. Cleveland: Pilgrim, 2007.

Parker, Evelyn L. *Trouble Don't Last Always: Emancipatory Hope among African American Adolescents*. Cleveland: Pilgrim, 2003.

White, David F. *Practicing Discernment with Youth: A Transformative Youth Ministry Approach*. Cleveland: Pilgrim, 2005.

Wright, Almeda M. *The Spiritual Lives of Young African Americans*. New York: Oxford University Press, 2017.

CHAPTER THIRTEEN

Nurturing Vocational Faith in Adults

I am made and remade continually. Different people draw different words from me.

—VIRGINIA WOOLF

Beyond the desert of criticism, we wish to be called again.

—PAUL RICOEUR

ROAD MAP

Poised to enter his seventh decade of life, Fred senses the question of Christian vocation in fresh ways. Whom might he become, and what might he do for God when he is no longer chained to a laptop? Where and how is he being called? For help in discerning, he has looked to the witness of others as they navigate similar transitions. One admired pastor reported that she paid attention with new eyes to the hopes and burdens of her community, then asked herself repeatedly what God was seeking to do with her in that setting once she was no longer leading a congregation. In a personal manner, she was employing the same methodology of this book. She sought to interpret her context in light of her biblical and theological understanding of God and God's mission, then to serve that mission through her own gifts, passions, and considerable wisdom.

This retiring pastor's path resonates with Buechner's famous definition of vocation: *"The kind of work God usually calls you to is the kind of work (a) that you need most to do and (b) that the world most needs to have done. . . . The place God calls you to is the place where your deep gladness and the world's deep hunger meet."*

This chapter explores adult faith formation, a process we deem essential to equipping Christian adults for discerning and living out their callings, first and foremost their calling to discipleship. In addition, we hope this chapter will help educational leaders invite adults to consider and reconsider their own vocations in light of their changing circumstances, the unfolding of new gifts and deepening insights into God's redeeming mission.

Introduction

For the first four centuries of its existence, adult faith formation was a priority for the church. We have frequently alluded to the catechumenate practiced in this era, a years-long church-based ecology of practices, teachings, moral testing, and rites culminating with dramatic baptismal initiation. Such intensive adult formation was presumed necessary in a mostly non-Christian world where other gods held court in the temples down the street and even the Roman emperor fancied himself divine. Given the fact that most adults of that era were not cradle Christians, the church understood itself as called to mission for Christ—sharing the good news of the triune God's saving intent for the whole world. In addition, the public persecution of Christians in that era required deep and intentional practices for shaping disciples capable of withstanding it—including even the possibility of martyrdom.

Age	Nurturing through . . .
Children	Atmosphere
Adolescents	Passion
⟩ Adults	Vocation

Things began to change with the conversion of Roman emperor Constantine to Christianity early in the fourth century, however. Once Christianity became the established religion of the empire, persecution of Christians diminished. In addition, Christianity quickly spread throughout the known world to the point where there appeared to be few adults left to convert. Though this is an oversimplification of history, it became possible for the church to imagine it had fulfilled its missional call to carry the gospel to the ends of the earth. The church's resources for faith formation were channeled to the children of believers.

In this chapter, we argue that it is once again time to reclaim and prioritize *adult* faith formation. As we have suggested, the culture of the Global North no longer consists of a comfortable Christendom. Drifting along with the cultural current is more likely to land one in a coffee shop on Sunday morning than in church. New and cradle Christians alike will need explicit and intentional training on how to be disciples of Jesus who live in settings that do not presume faith or are actively hostile to it. In addition, contemporary Christian adults journey through exceedingly complex sociocultural realities, where once-presumed certainties are regularly swept away like sand dunes in a storm surge. For much of human history, for example, persons were born and died in the same place. Their work, their families, their living spaces, and their communal relations were inherited or assigned. For better or worse, life was characterized by stability. Identities were mostly fixed. By contrast, today's adulthood presents many adults with a bewildering array of options. One may identify as one sort of person in one setting and another sort of person in other settings. Indeed, the concept of identity has become so fluid as to be dismissed as a fiction. Even adults who seek to form their identities in and through participation in Christ will be confronted with complex (and changing) possibilities and challenges throughout their lives. This dynamism makes the discernment of Christian vocation, a calling to be God's person and join God's mission, an urgent and continuing task for adulthood. The chapter will consider dimensions of vocation that adult faith formation rightly seeks.

Dynamic Adulthood

In the past, adulthood was conceived as a period of welcome stability following upon the ceaseless changes of childhood and adolescence. We now recognize that adulthood is just as dynamic as any other season of human life. Young adults continue to develop physiologically, while older adults must regularly come to terms with the biological changes that accompany aging. In addition, adulthood may prompt social and psychological adjustment when, for example, persons enter the workforce, marry, face questions about the process of gendering, become parents, or retire. Different generations of adults are also formed into differing (and sometimes competing) worldviews. Seventy-somethings do not see the world in the same way as thirty-somethings! Finally, and in relation to all the above, the faith of adults may wax and wane. It is possible that the passionate faith of younger years may transform into something like wisdom for maturing Christians. A brief glance around the planet suggests that wisdom is in short supply these days, so the authors welcome the possibility that Christian faith formation may nurture it in adults.

Young Adulthood

Young adults range in age from their twenties into their early thirties. Fred, who is parent to twenty-something-age children and regularly teaches students in this age range, can testify to their continuing physical development. He is often amazed by the bodily transformations his students undergo between the end of a spring semester and their reappearance at school in the fall. They are still growing!

Neuroscience, too, finds evidence of continuing brain maturation through at least the midtwenties.[1] This brain development may assist with complex cognitive tasks, including the so-called executive function, which enables problem-solving and impulse control, which in turn contributes to more effective regulation of the passions of adolescence. Psychosocially, young adults may begin to consolidate a sense of personal identity after trying on multiple roles during their teens, though they may continue to inhabit a plurality of identities. Young adults enter more purposefully into relationships—they *have* relationships rather than being *had by* the relationships of their youthful years. In the Global North at least, they often live increasingly independent from families of origin. This may catalyze the process of identity consolidation. Young adults begin to choose which dimensions of their familial identities to retain and which to jettison. Some young adults are entering the adult world in earnest, taking up careers, marrying, and having children, all of which tends to further consolidate identity. Others continue to experience identity as a fluid and transient dimension of their lives.

It is important to acknowledge widespread perceptions of a delayed entry into adulthood for this cohort. Jeffrey Arnett even posits a new life stage between adolescence and adulthood, which he calls "emerging adulthood."[2] For a host of reasons—including the need for ever more years of educational training in order to enter the workforce, growing student debt, and recent difficult economic conditions—persons within this demographic are postponing careers, marriage, and parenthood until their late twenties or thirties. If Arnett is right, faith communities that once banked on attracting young adults by offering wedding services and support for parenting will need to rethink how to minister to what today's young adults often experience as a more liminal season.

The defining experiences of this generation as a demographic cohort are also key to understanding them. Millennials, persons born between the early 1980s and the mid-1990s are formed by certain global events—the destruction of the World Trade Center towers in 2001 and the subsequent "War on Terrorism," plus the economic collapse of the late 2000s. Unsurprisingly, they tend to be distrustful of traditional institutions, including economic capitalism, government, and congregations.

According to the faith-development theory of James Fowler, young adults may feel the need for critical reappraisal and explicit articulation of a faith that, until this time, was tacitly embodied. This process—including deconstruction and demythologizing of previously reliable sources of authority, as well as their reconstruction—can be personally painful but may also yield an owned faith that proves more responsive to adult circumstances.[3] Churches are not unaccustomed to the disappearance of young adults from their attendance rolls during this season but have always counted on marriage and parenthood to bring them back—roles that young adults are deferring. What we don't entirely understand yet is whether this historically temporary generational diaspora is becoming permanent for millennials.

JAMES W. FOWLER III

James W. Fowler III is an American sociologist of religion and ethicist born into a Methodist pastor's home in Reidsville, North Carolina, in 1940. Fowler completed degrees at Duke (1962), Drew (1965), and Harvard (1971). Following a stint as associate director of Interpreter's House (1968–1969), he taught at Boston College and Harvard University Divinity School, where he was introduced to Lawrence Kohlberg's research on moral development. He pursued postdoctoral studies at the Center for Moral Development at the Harvard Graduate School of Education (1971–1972) and taught applied theology and directed a research project on faith and moral development at Harvard Divinity School (1969–1975). He moved on to Boston College (1975–1976) before beginning his long teaching career at Emory University's Candler School of Theology (1977). Fowler was named the Charles Howard Candler Professor of Theology and Human Development in 1987 and was for many years director of the Center for Research in Faith and Moral Development at Emory University. He served as the founding director of the Center for Ethics from 1994 until his retirement in 2005.

A minister in the United Methodist Church, Fowler describes himself as a "classical liberal Protestant." Fowler—influenced by the theology of Paul Tillich and Richard Niebuhr and the developmental psychology of Jean Piaget, Erik Erikson, and Lawrence Kohlberg—has a keen ability to integrate insights from various disciplinary perspectives in his theorizing and can converse easily across various fields of academic study.

Over the last thirty years, few people have had a greater impact on Christian education, ministry studies, and pastoral care since the publication of his groundbreaking *Stages of Faith: The Psychology of Human Development and the Quest for Meaning* (1981). Fowler's theory of "faith development" has reshaped the manner in which Christian educators, pastors, and pastoral counselors, as well as many outside the church, think about religious development and how to practice one's vocation. While Fowler is widely credited with bringing a helpful perspective on faith as universal, more than belief, experiential, and varying in conceptions of its maturity, there is critical dialogue about his theories. No fewer than four volumes addressing criticisms and implications of his work have been published. Some critique the Kohlberg-like reliance on abstract reasoning for achieving the highest stages of faith in Fowler's scheme as overly rationalistic, if not elitist. Even Fowler has raised questions about the cultural transportability of his theory. Overall, however, his creative and integrative work on how faith functions and develops has been generative of much consideration of the process and goal of Christian formation.

JAMES P. BOWERS

Midlife Adults

Adults in this phase, spanning approximately their mid-thirties to early fifties, are often at or near the peak of their intellectual and physical capabilities. Many require every bit of this fitness-for-life to meet the growing demands of leadership responsibilities at work and home. Some may be awakening to hints of finitude as well, either personally or through the experience of caring for their aging parents.

Middle adults continue to consolidate a sense of identity though wide relational networks at work, in social and civic gatherings, including via social media, and through shared experiences of childrearing with other midlife adults in the community and in congregations. This cohort has also moved beyond the apprentice phase. They have accumulated sufficient lived experience not only to perform more proficiently in the workforce and at home but also to take on mentoring roles for younger generations.

Some middle adults undergo a "midlife crisis." The recognition of having lived out half of one's days on earth can prompt deep reflection upon the shape and value of that life, which in turn may stimulate reprioritizing and recalibration. Responses range from pitiful efforts to retrieve one's youth (as in the caricature of the slightly paunchy man buying a sports car), to seeking out employment more consistent with one's values, to prioritizing relationships over strivings for "success." The social psychology of adult development helpfully observes that however painful undergoing these life crises may be, with the right kind of relational support, persons may be assisted toward the construction of more fitting self-identities and richer appraisals of life. As we mentioned in part 1, in every season, life is constantly throwing us in over our heads, forcing us to learn to swim all over again in shifting environments. Obviously, the church could play an important role here by buoying up middle adults in God's relational love, while providing resources to support their risky transformations.

Fowler suggests that faith at midlife may again change epistemological frames just as in earlier stages.[4] Where young adults often seek to articulate an owned faith, one that is explicit and rationally defensible, middle adults, because of the growing complexity of their lives, may become open to faith that makes room for mystery and even ambiguity. They may become more comfortable with paradox, with the possibility that two competing claims may be true at the same time. They may perceive more deeply the mysterious death-in-life and life-in-death that mark salvation in Jesus. Once absolutizing views of right and wrong may be required to come to terms with a child's profession of a nontraditional sexual orientation or gender preference. They may experience life in Christ as a "bright sorrow" where joy and pathos comingle. Middle adults may also freshly awaken to the power of ritual and symbol to communicate this presence-in-absence they experience as God.

Maturing Adults

This season (from the fifties into the early seventies) often prompts still another round of life transitions. Persons within this demographic may reshape their working lives. Even as consumer culture depicts their retirement to a life of leisure, adults are increasingly working with vigor well into their seventies (by choice or necessity) or adjusting their work/life balance to include volunteering and supporting extended family. Maturing adults also are experiencing and coming to terms with symptoms of physical decline. Like middle adults, many in this group continue to grapple with the dual demands of caring for aging parents and the slow transition of their young-adult children into full adulthood.

Social psychologists suggest that maturing adults may turn in earnest toward contributing to the future. They may, for example, work to create a legacy. To this end, some write memoirs, or, in one case we know, dream and then create a primary-care health clinic as an arm of a community's ministries with homeless persons—an enormous undertaking! They may also devote themselves to the future through the nurture of grandchildren. Grandparents often play an active role in day-to-day childrearing and may provide critical sources of cultural capital for the young. Grandparents, for example, in addition to sheltering children after school while parents work, may cart them to the special storytelling event at the local library. By investing themselves in younger generations, maturing adults contribute to the flourishing of children *and* themselves.

By contrast, maturing adults, dogged by disease, isolation, or poverty, may despair of any legacy. The authors have noted elsewhere how loneliness has become a public health crisis for senior adults in England. Faith-forming leaders will, therefore, actively seek to tap the generative potential in this generation, while acknowledging frankly the challenges maturing adults face.

At present, this demographic is increasingly composed of the influential baby boomers. Because this generation is enormously large, its experience has exercised outsized influence over the rest of the population. Boomers were famously idealistic in their youth. Living through, first, the Vietnam War and, second, Watergate, they became notably distrustful of older generations and their machinations of power. Determined to fashion a more equitable and peaceable society, they also experienced and engaged in movements undertaken by people of color for civil rights and women for liberation from patriarchy. As maturing adults, they are sometimes accused of retreating to the comforts of a status quo they fought so hard to overcome. Always self-interested, present-day boomers are determined not to grow old. This determination has led to near manic practices of personal fitness, nutrition, and self-affirming spirituality.

GENERATIONAL ISSUES

Social scientists have studied the characteristics of various generations. These generalizations may be predictive when a generation is in its infancy or descriptive as a generation matures and reaches for adulthood. The "greatest generation" (born before 1946) is known for their propensity for self-sacrifice. Generational studies really seemed to make their mark on popular culture and local church ministry with the advent and maturation of the baby boom generation. Born from 1946 through 1964, this generation made up the post–World War II baby boom. Due to their sheer size, the baby boomers left their mark on everything, with significant cultural changes. As midgeneration baby boomers moved into adulthood in the 1970s and 1980s, visionary churches began to take note of them and create ministries to attract them to their churches. It is no coincidence that the rise of the role of the children's pastor in church educational ministry coincides with the era when baby boomers were beginning to have children of their own. As adults, baby boomers became known for outsourcing many things in their lives and the lives of their children. Their children's spiritual education was something else they were willing to outsource, and the local church was more than willing to accommodate them.

Baby boomers in the church were also at the forefront of the contemporary worship movement, bringing their own musical preferences into the church.

After the baby boomers came the baby busters, so named because their numbers were not as large as the baby boom generation. Gen Xers, as they are also known, were born between 1965 and 1984. They have been called slackers, because they often seemed not to have the competitive drive of the baby boomers, and they were the first generation of the twentieth century to deal disproportionately with divorcing parents and blended families. The rise in the emphasis on youth ministry in churches is largely due to this generation. It was largely members of Generation X who populated the emerging church movement in the United States in the late twentieth century and who were the first to incorporate technology as a daily part of their personal and professional lives.

The millennials or Generation Y were born between 1985 and 2002. Millennials in the United States number around seventy million. They are the first generation to be defined by their technology use as being wedded to their cellphones and tablets while creating relationships through texting and social media. They have endured helicopter parenting, and as they age into young adulthood, many of them who grew up in churches are leaving these churches disillusioned by what they see as the church's intolerance and inauthenticity.

Children and youth need to be exposed to adults other than their parents as an important part of their spiritual formation and development; so those charged with the educational ministry of the church need to think seriously about ways to bring the generations together in the community of faith rather than develop more ways to pull them apart. It is important for children and youth to hear the personal stories of faith from those older than them. Intergenerational relationships are important for everyone in the church. And it is this kind of faith community that is most conducive to the spiritual formation of its members and is best at modeling to the world what Jesus meant when he told his disciples that the world would know his love when they saw the disciples love for each other.

IVY BECKWITH

Older Adults

The media frequently observes that "seventy is the new sixty" or "eighty is the new seventy." Improvements in health care, diet, and fitness in older generations often contribute to extended life spans and greater enjoyment of later years. Still, it becomes less possible to deny finitude when bodies begin to wear out and peers decline and die. The threat of isolation, poor health, or dementia grows. In addition, current older adults in the United States worry about insufficient retirement savings and inadequate health care coverage. Yet many older adults retain family and social networks, they remain intellectually curious, and continue to live relatively vigorous lives. Their basic stance toward life continues to be trusting, hopeful, and loving.

Unlike in much of the rest of the world, older adults in the Global North typically become marginalized socially and culturally. Once, they exerted authority over families and junior workers, and now they are the recipients of impatient eye rolls and groans when counting out actual dollars and cents in the grocery store checkout line. Again, however, the experience of decentering can also become life-giving. Their perceived lack of power makes possible new avenues of expression. Who knew, for example, that a former American president could become such an accomplished painter? Their wisdom, too, is an asset. Older adults, freed from the expectations and demands of leadership, may exercise a prophetic voice against the hubris of younger generations. In a frenzied world, we know countless older adults who patiently weave and reweave the social fabric through their support of farmers markets, handcrafting guilds, Habitat projects, communal flood and fire recovery, the stewarding of church grounds, providing meals for shut-ins, and the restoration of ecosystems. Because of their marginalization, this embodied wisdom often flies beneath the radar. We members of younger generations owe an enormous debt of gratitude to older adults.

A Brief Excursus on the Limitations of a Developmental Framework

This is as good a place as any to acknowledge that life does not always follow the script that developmental psychology prescribes. Many persons who lack economic or social capital simply cannot *afford* a midlife crisis, for example. Others, forced to live amidst social inequities, including racism, classism, patriarchy, and homophobia, spend their entire lives in crisis, a situation that can wear down capacities for resilience and adaptive change. What Richard Bondi calls "accidents of history" (see chapter 9), those dimensions of personhood that impact human identity but that we do not choose, are sometimes actively imposed upon persons against their will.

African theological ethicist and priest Emmanuel Katongole describes how an early career transition to Europe and later to the United States prompted the discovery that he was "black" (a racialized condition he had never experienced in Africa).[5] For the first time in his life, he faced limits on where he could live and what he could say. As W. E. B. DuBois brilliantly observed more than a century earlier, Katongole suddenly discovered what it meant for him (and all people of color) to be a "problem" to White dominant societies.[6] Though it is not impossible, as Katongole powerfully testifies, many persons of color find it difficult to flourish under conditions of racial injustice. Life does not unfold "happily ever after" for oppressed people in the ways developmentalism would prefer. If not active oppression, still other adults face life-threatening disease, violence, disability, job loss, death of spouses and friends, and divorce. Unlike the too easy predictions and prescriptions of the developmental model, human beings are as likely to *regress* as *progress*. While there is potential for growing practical wisdom and flourishing in midlife and beyond, the accidents of history may instead sweep persons toward cynicism and despair. With these limitations in mind, our own view is that a developmental framework for adulthood does at least provide a sense of the potential for navigating expanded complexity and living joyfully as persons of faith. In addition, it makes clear how adulthood is a widely variable season. Leaders concerned with nurturing adult faith will also need to be alert to both personal and structural threats to growth in faith, as well as the need to create opportunities to consider and practice deepened faith in response. Faith leaders may equip adults to "live free in Christ" despite oppression or to work peacefully to overcome oppressive forces.

It is also important to acknowledge that a developmental view of adulthood largely excludes adults with mild to severe developmental disabilities. These persons may never exhibit the cognitive competence or agency displayed by their more typically developing adult peers. Yet persons with disabilities have gifts to share with Christ's body and the world. Their simplicity, dependence, and vulnerability testify to the rest of us our own vulnerability before and dependence upon God. They are called to a vocation of witness!

Faith-Forming Implications of Dynamic Adulthood

Addressing Diverse Needs and Motivations for Adult Faith Formation

These brief descriptions of the seasons of adulthood suggest important implications for nurturing faith in adults. First, there is no single approach to faith formation that will adequately cover the entire adult life span. Educational leaders will need to take into account the sometimes dramatically different generational perspectives, psychosocial environments, prospective life transitions, and epistemological frames for faith that adults experience, and then address them accordingly. Put differently, and with the help of Roman Catholic Christian educator John Roberto, faith-forming ministry with adults will address "the unique life tasks, needs, interests, and spiritual journeys of people at each stage of adulthood."[7]

Roberto offers a number of down-to-earth suggestions toward these ends. First, he describes how adult learning is driven by adults' "intrinsic motivations" and self-perceived need for mastery of some task or role.[8] Newlyweds enroll in a couples class, divorcees connect in small groups to heal and discover how to be single (and whole) again, a first child prompts urgent inquiry into the mysteries of parenting, or retirement may quicken renewed vocational discernment. Roberto urges churches to carry out faith formation responsive to these motivating transitions. Second, and following from the first, adult faith-formation ministries will presume that not only the motivation but also the *agency* for faith formation resides more with adults themselves than with any agenda of educational leaders. No longer passive recipients of learning (if they ever were), adults learn best by building upon their previous learnings in light of lived experience. Finally, and in response to his previous claims, Roberto advances the intriguing image of the adult faith-forming leader as "curator."[9] Since there can be no one-size-fits-all model for adult faith formation and because adults are participative agents in their own faith formation, Roberto encourages faith communities to best serve adults by responsibly networking them to a broad ecology of faith-forming resources and offering these through a variety of platforms. These platforms will range from carefully chosen web materials, to online classes, to mentoring relationships, to educational gatherings at the church or in the community. Roberto believes that adults will gravitate toward the offerings that best match their own situations.

LIFE SPAN DEVELOPMENT

Defined stages of childhood development have been proposed by scholars such as Piaget, Erikson, and Freud. These have been appropriated not only in a descriptive but also prescriptive way, allowing diagnoses of early and late development, along with, in some cases, exceptional ability, disability, and medical or psychological issues. The focus of these theories has primarily been on the cognitive domain. Stages of physical maturing accompany the cognitive, and Tennant adds studies into self-development and identity as a third category; together the three are understood to provide a picture of growth and progress across the full range of human dimensions. Within a religious context, Fowler's *Stages of Faith* introduced a faith dimension to human development, extending this beyond childhood into a lifelong activity. However, Fowler's understanding of faith as a human universal is controversial, and many dispute that his schema accurately represents the faith journey of adherents to specific religions such as Christianity.

Spirituality, spiritual intelligence, and spiritual development are now increasingly recognized as significant throughout the life span, although these areas are not necessarily explored and promoted from within a religious context. As is the case with much Christian education, ongoing dialogue must take place between the Christian and the secular, allowing each to contribute to the other. Many attributes—especially wisdom—that are valued by Christianity are gained throughout the life span through experience. There is some evidence to suggest that a distinctively Christian wisdom can be developed through the capacity for theological reflection, and also that reflection itself has an embedded developmental progression that can be deliberately fostered. Lifelong learning, therefore, becomes a key dimension to life span development however it is conceived, challenging the idea that all aspects of human being remain stable or that there is necessarily a gradual deterioration of cognitive abilities after maturity, and affirming the notion that although there might be biological deterioration, ongoing learning and personal experience compensate for this. In addition, Christian theology offers profound insights into the nature of human being that should guide and inform understandings of both the ageing and maturation processes.

ALISON LE CORNU

Faith Formation for Adult Vocation

While the responsibility and agency for faith formation is properly entrusted to adults themselves, Roberto does not counsel an "anything goes" approach to nurturing adult faith. He presumes that the end goals of adult faith formation will promote "ongoing conversion to Jesus in holiness of life," "active membership in the Christian Community," and preparation to "act as disciples in mission to the world."[10] In our view, Roberto is pointing to shaping adult Christians toward vocations—knowing, being, or doing something for God's sake.

Christian baptism is the entree to vocation. Through baptism, persons die to the power of sin (if not its influence) and are born anew through the power of the Spirit (John 3; 2 Cor. 5). Passage through the baptismal waters also invites participation in the life, death, and resurrection of Jesus (Rom. 6). Put differently, baptism re-creates human beings for participation *in* Christ. Baptism makes us members of Christ's body for the sake of joining Jesus's mission to reweave the loving relationship between Creator and creatures. Baptism is at once gift and lifelong calling to discipleship; it empowers followers of Jesus to take up his reconciling ministry.

Practical theologian Kathleen Cahalan also links adult faith formation to vocation. For her, as for the authors, vocation first presumes the universal baptismal calling to discipleship—all Christians are to become Jesus's people in the world—but personalizes discipleship based upon unique Spirit gifts bestowed upon individuals who inhabit specific contexts. Consistent with the apostle Paul, Cahalan suggests that the Spirit gives different gifts to different persons, while insisting that these gifts are to be offered for the upbuilding of the body and for the wider common good.

Cahalan further specifies the need for adults to discern vocation around three evolving aspects of the self: (1) how to live out one's permanent baptismal *covenantal* commitments through faithful relations with God, neighbors, friends, parents, siblings, spouses, children, and nonhuman creatures; (2) what *service* one is to offer God in concert with a community devoted to Christ's mission; and (3) who one *is to be* in Christ in relation to one's gifts and accidents of history.[11]

1. Covenanting

The baptismal waters sustain us throughout our lives. Our permanent baptismal incorporation into the triune God also sustains us in other lifelong covenants—lasting relationships between persons, communities, and the whole of creation. Joining in faith communities, friendships, marriage, or parenting, as well as life shared with siblings and one's own parents, are all baptismally "wet." Faith is nurtured and tested as adults learn to practice charity, patience, and mutuality with one another, not to mention forgiveness and reconciliation. As we have said, faith is a relational gift of a relational God for the sake of flourishing relationships. The baptismal web of relationships that adults weave and are woven into provides the arena for living faith.

Parenting, for example, turns out to be vitally important for nurturing faith in children and adults alike.[12] As noted, the modern language of faith *nurture* (along with this book's title) is attributed to New England pastor Horace Bushnell in the nineteenth century. Bushnell proposed that the home become "the church of childhood" where "the child is to grow up Christian, never knowing himself to be otherwise."[13] This proposal came as a constructive response to what Bushnell believed had become a too formulaic and reductive revivalism, one where it was presumed necessary for faith communities first to break children's rebellious wills by convicting them of their sin, and only then to explain their need of Christ's saving grace. For Bushnell, this method was cruel and manipulative on at least two counts. First, it required a vision of a child's sinful depravity from birth, whereas Bushnell's own experience with children told him they enter the world a blend of good and evil and learn to become sinners only over time. Second, he resented the required individualism presuming children to be radically free decision-makers, depraved by sin yet somehow masters of their fate, capable of freely choosing to follow Christ. Instead, he pointed to children's pliability to the good and ultimately to life in Christ when nurtured by loving Christian parents.

Bushnell was a man of his time; he was a bit too enamored with the nuclear family as a dimension of the emerging middle class, and he could not yet recognize his patriarchy. He presumed, for example, that moms would be the primary "pastors" of the church of the home. Nevertheless, his insights into faith nurture as a relational phenomenon, and to the covenantal responsibilities of parents for lovingly nurturing faith in children, remain with us today.

2. Serving the Common Good

The call to discipleship is a call to communal life. Disciples are bound to one another in Christ as witnesses to God's coming realm. They must also learn to look beyond themselves and toward a bruised world. Hence, a second dimension of vocation is serving (ministering to) not only our own children or others within Christ's body but also a world hungering and thirsting for righteousness. This service is not optional. Adult Christians will necessarily discern ways to practice servant ministry in concert with God's mission.

A pastor in Baltimore responded to racial tension in that city by involving his congregation in growing and distributing food. His community networked with African American farmers outside the city to help to establish farmers markets on church properties. Folks living in "food deserts" (urban areas without access to healthy fresh food) came out in droves to purchase fresh fruits and vegetables at fair prices. Farmers found a stable market for their produce with no distribution fees gouging their profits. The weekly gatherings provided the church with the opportunity to better know and care for its neighbors—all this because a pastor understood that vocation called him and his people to participate in God's mission by stepping out to serve the common good.[14]

Once, the church assumed that the only persons who received this sort of vocation were the professionally religious. Priests got called; everyone else got a job. In the present day, the relationship between work and Christian vocation for service is more nuanced if also more complex. We owe a debt to Martin Luther for recognizing that vocation can belong to lay Christians just as readily as to people wearing collars. Luther saw that it was possible to be God's farmer, God's baker, and, perhaps Luther's favorite, God's brewer. Though Luther did not coin the phrase "the dignity of labor," he did level the hierarchical distance between clergy and laypersons by elevating ordinary work as a means to give glory to God. Barbara Brown Taylor speaks of the need to reemphasize Luther's "priesthood of believers" at present. She observes that when bringing up the topic of vocation with parishioners, they assume she intends for them to "do more" or "be more." Like Luther, she recommends instead becoming "God's person" in one's work as teacher, banker, truck driver, and so on.[15]

Yet this view also requires interrogation. Is it vocationally acceptable to be God's hedge-fund manager or God's nuclear-weapons contractor? Is this what it means to serve the common good? But then, what about laborers who have no choice for feeding their families other than to work long hours at industrial meat-processing plants where there is little dignity to go around either for the workers or the animals they slaughter? Is one's job always one's vocation?

Fortunately, Jesus's disciples and Paul demonstrate an alternative. Many of the disciples were fishermen, a craft they relied upon to support themselves before and after their years with Jesus. Paul was a tentmaker whose job funded his vocation for ministry. In these cases, vocation is distinguished from employment. At present, those who seek vocations of service and whose jobs do not afford them this opportunity often do so through volunteering. For example, adults with vocations for baptismal (or biological) parenting often volunteer in classrooms or with parent-teacher associations. In this way, they expand their familial callings to nurture their own children to caring for *other people's children*, which, of course, contributes to the common good. In a slightly different example, Fred knows a lay Christian, a marketing executive by trade, who has led a Young Life club, a Christian outreach ministry to high school students, for more than forty years! In his case, the job brings bread to the table and provides a roof over his head, but his vocation is youth ministry. He is a modern Paul.

To reiterate, discerning and then taking up baptismal ministry for the sake of others is an integral (not optional) component of adult faith. Fortunately, as we have seen, many of the transitions that Christian adults must navigate present opportunities for renewed attention to issues of vocation. Becoming a spouse, a parent, a job seeker, or a retiree all invite persons to ask (again), "What would God have me know, do, or be in this season of my life?" Effective faith-forming ministry with adults will accompany them on this journey by ensuring that question (and visibly the font) is ever before them, along with the resources—curricular and relational—to search for answers. In addition, a missionally minded faith community like this one in Baltimore, one that is itself outward-facing and compelled by Christ and the Spirit to serve the world, demonstrates tangible support for adult vocations through the practices of its own communal life. In this case, vocation belongs to the entire faith community and is not left to the mysteries of personal discernment.

3. Being in Christ

Cahalan's threefold treatment of discipleship and vocation concludes with identity. Baptismal covenanting *with* Christ and working *for* Christ are related to being (and ever becoming) *in* Christ. Catholics describe this destination as "divinization," while Protestants typically call it "holiness."

For Fred, this growth in the character of Christ seems halting at best. Writing in first person for a moment about one area of my own *being*, it has taken me much of a lifetime to challenge some of the un-Christian cultural expectations of my own gendering as a man. For example, in the effort to help my son emulate Christ's peace, I never taught him how to fight (though I'm aware now of ways I tried to form him to be "strong" so he wouldn't be picked on in the first place). In addition, I no longer reserve displays of vulnerability exclusively for my spouse (though I am still wary around folks I don't know well). I now also reject claims from college football coaches that losing is worse than death (though I've noticed myself becoming risk averse over time to minimize the possibilities of failure). My halting "growth" (if that is what it amounts to), therefore, is as much about learning to confess sin and receive the grace of Christ's forgiveness as it is any spiritual "progress" I make. Perhaps spiritual progress is synonymous with growing humility.

Yet this stance seems inadequate. I've seen faculty colleagues who are parents to young children struggle against forces in our institution that tell them in effect, "you don't have time to be a parent if you expect to earn tenure." I've heard colleagues of color testify with righteous anger to the persistence of racism even within a school committed to the training of Christian leaders. Being conflict averse, until recently I mostly practiced "duck and cover" when these issues boiled over into public disputes. I see now, however, that staying out of the fight was a privilege afforded to a southern White man in an historically southern White male institution. Female colleagues and colleagues of color could never purchase the pass I received for free. In addition to confessing and becoming humble about my privilege, I needed to *do* something. Though far from adequate, in recent years I have sought to better *listen* to hard and painful stories from colleagues and students who do not share my accidents of history, to amplify attention to writings and research from persons living out their faith in differing contexts from mine, and (again haltingly) to speak out about injustices instead of hiding. I'm not seeking either forgiveness or accolades here, only trying to describe how God continues to call even maturing adults to deepened vocations of baptismal being—to transformed character, in other words, which also deepens what it means to retain covenantal relationships and to serve the common good. This isn't a "happily ever after" story; it is the emergence of a different sense of calling upon my life, one I'm trying to take seriously.

Conclusion

Adult Faith formation, though often neglected, may be a rich and multifaceted ministry. Sensitivity to the various "stages" of adulthood will aid faith-forming leaders in creating nuanced adult formational settings and offerings. Keeping eyes on the prize of discipleship as the primary adult vocation will properly orient it. As we have seen in other chapters, nurturing adult faith is not only a good in and of itself; it raises the bar for effective faith nurture in the young and young in Christ. Mature Christian laypersons also serve to hold pastors accountable for their temptations to clericalism.

Interactive Dialogue

1. Why do the authors counsel attending to multiple stages of adulthood when seeking to lead adult educational ministry for faith formation? Do you agree? What are the practical implications for practicing this ministry?

2. How is the language of baptismal vocation used in the faith communities you know? Why do the authors assert its importance for adult Christians?

3. What is required for Christians to become wise? What lets you know when you are in the company of a wise Christian?

For Further Reading

Cahalan, Kathleen A. *Introducing the Practice of Ministry*. Collegeville, MN: Liturgical, 2010.

Fowler, James W. *The Stages of Faith: The Psychology of Human Development and the Quest for Meaning*. San Francisco: HarperSanFrancisco, 1981.

Roberto, John, ed. *The Seasons of Adult Faith Formation*. Naugatuck, CT: Lifelong Faith, 2015.

Part Four

Contexts for Nurturing Faith

ontexts matter for faith formation. Where and when persons find themselves in time and place, their social locations, and what dimensions of character have accrued to them through lived experience all impact how they conceive of and respond with faith to God's good news. And because contexts matter, there can be no single approach to faith-forming ministry—no generic one-size-fits-all model suitable to every context. Nor, because of differing contexts, will various formational approaches envision identical formational ends. Particularities of context will influence both educational means and the various objectives faith-forming ministries seek to realize.

While the claim that context matters may seem to some readers to be self-evident, it is a relatively recent discovery. To be more precise, contexts have *always* impacted formational ministries even as *awareness* of this truth did not really bubble up before the twentieth century. For example, the catechumenate, the process of formation into belief and practice in anticipation of baptismal initiation into the church of antiquity, unfolded very differently in differing regions surrounding the Mediterranean Sea. In Rome it emphasized an orderly progression of belief and practice toward the font, marked by undergoing scrutiny by church elders at important thresholds along the way. Though in its early versions the intent was to form Christians who could *resist* the power of empire, it used means (progression through stages, submission to hierarchical authority) very familiar to Roman citizens. Alexandria, on the other hand, was home to several philosophical schools prior to and alongside the rise of Christianity. There, too, catechumens journeyed toward baptismal waters, but unsurprisingly, considering its familiarity with the culture of schooling, Alexandria's version of the catechumenate cultivated intellectual rigor oriented toward faith "enlightenment"—faith as a way of knowing commensurate with schooling. In the Christian East, home to expressions of religious mysticism, the catechumenate sought primarily to cultivate participation in the mysteries of the Holy Spirit. Indeed, in the initiating rites, anointings with the oil of the Spirit sometimes eclipsed the significance of baptismal washing in water. From the beginning, contexts mattered![1]

It is likely, however, that these communities were less aware of their own or others' distinctives. They operated intuitively, doing what made sense for faith formation. Interestingly, when scholars in the twentieth century began to unearth ancient catechetical practices, they at first perceived a unified system, a singular catechumenate albeit with slight variations from place to place.[2] From a postmodern perspective, we recognize this as a peculiarly modern imposition. Captive to a modern social imaginary that imposed uniformity at the expense of noticing difference, early modern liturgical scholars could not see how contexts were shaping faith-forming practices. Not seeing contexts also turns out to be a function of power. Being "in charge" tends to make dominant social groups oblivious to difference or to perceive it as deviating from what is "normal." In a postmodern imaginary, however, belated recognition of contextual differences between different catechetical patterns and emphases has caused scholars to debate whether it even makes sense to group these diverse formational processes as species of the same *genus catechumenus*. In short, they (and through them *we*) may now recognize the significance of context for faith-forming approaches and outcomes.

From a strictly educational perspective, twentieth-century scholars, including John Dewey, Maria Montessori, and others, set the stage for the educational appreciation of context. Dewey called attention to the significance of learners' lived experience for shaping their education. Indeed, Dewey felt that learning proceeded by way of experience for the purpose of reflecting upon it toward deepened experience. Different experiences led to different outcomes. Montessori, whose training included biology and medicine, conceived of children and young people as developing organisms. Her educational method, therefore, came to be described as "learner centered" in contrast to traditional "content centered" approaches. In addition, Montessori required teachers to possess intimate understanding of each pupil in order to match educational ends to student gifts or needs. These insights from Dewey and Montessori opened the door for the fuller appreciation of the significance of context to follow.

Educational concern for context became a primary consideration in the work of Brazilian educator Paul Freire (see again, chapter 10).[3] Influenced by Hegel, Marx, and also by the then emerging field of liberation theology, Freire readily perceived how situations of oppression impact educational agendas. He describes how education may be utilized by elite "oppressors" to preserve their power over the "oppressed" of that society by reproducing (and thereby justifying) relations of domination. Poor people learned, for example, that it was proper for them to remain poor. By contrast, Freire's own educational approach begins by inviting learners to name their very *contexts* of oppression. For Freire to name or to "see" was to bring to consciousness and therefore to objectify social conditions of oppression with the hope that this critical consciousness would then mobilize oppressed peoples to act toward their own liberation. Freire's genius was not only to establish the significance of contexts for education but also to bring context to the center of his liberative educational agenda.

Beyond this agenda for liberation, Freire's work calls educators to the critical awareness that there is no "neutral" education; every educational approach enacts power for good or for ill in the lives of students. Freire also liberated educators from their captivity to the schooling paradigm by demonstrating how liberative education may be deployed broadly and beyond the walls of schools toward institutional and societal transformation.

Many of these same critical educational insights also animated the then new Black theologies and feminist and womanist theologies, and they continue to inform theologies of sex and gender, disability, and ecology, plus varieties of indigenous theologizing in the present day. These theologies proceed by way of making contexts explicit, especially contexts of suffering, oppression, or marginalization, because these are regarded as foundational for describing where God's liberating mission is ongoing.

In light of this hard-won contextual awareness, present-day faith-forming leaders will consistently reflect on their contexts for ministry as integral to shaping formational goals in that setting. They will get to know their people, cultivating an informed perspective on their gifts and wounds, their deepest hopes and the social or personal barriers standing in the way of God's trans-forming work. Even as they continue to operate in traditional contexts, like the parish or in church-related schools, they will remain critically aware about how those contexts may, without proper attention, lead to outcomes antithet-ical to the gospel—parish insularity or school competitiveness, to name but two. Not only will leaders undertake contextual analysis on behalf of those they serve; they will also teach learners to consider the importance of contexts for themselves and for learning to love neighbors as God loves them.

This part explores three traditional contexts for undertaking faith-forming ministries—the church, the Christian school, and the seminary. L. Gregory Jones describes how these contexts were likened by previous generations to partners in a "relay race."[4] Churches were to be the leadoff runners in the race; their aim was to instill in Christians basic beliefs and practices. Christian schools and colleges took the baton next; building upon foundational beliefs and practices, they linked these to the wider world of human knowledge and endeavor, including language, literature, social studies, mathematics, and sci-ence. Their mission was to form in students a Christian "worldview" (seeing the world as God sees it) in order to take up faithful life as Christian adults in a worldly society. The final leg of the race (for those still running the course) was theological education in seminaries and divinity schools. This was to be a context for deep and sometimes critical reflection upon beliefs, practices, and worldview and for training in the pastoral arts.

While allowing that some are still formed by running this "race" in consec-utive legs, Jones acknowledges a number of flawed assumptions in play. With Jones we find the metaphor quite linear and artificially compartmentalized. Neither education nor life itself unfolds with such assembly-line efficiency or predictability, and nor is "progress" inevitable. A twenty-one-year-old college senior may meet Christ for the first time at a campus ministry and then enroll in seminary the very next fall, never having been exposed to the "first leg" of formation into Christian beliefs and practices that the model presumes. Or, a high school junior, in agony over his parents' divorce, asks and demands from his youth director answers to profoundly theological questions, unwilling to stay the course until college or seminary to receive the answers.

Limitations notwithstanding, the relay race does at least call attention to contexts that remain important for faith formation at present. Parish, Christian school and college, plus seminary continue to perform important roles in nurturing faith even as each is becoming aware that each one of them is called to form persons' whole way of being—that, in other words, there is as much overlap between them as specialization. For example, at Duke Divinity School where Fred teaches, faculty and staff recognize how community worship and ministry field-education placements are just as vital as classroom teaching to nurturing students' faith.

It seems fitting that Christian educators continue their work in traditional settings like the ones we describe in this part. The goal of nurturing faith, however, will also cause educational leaders to imagine new possibilities in these traditional contexts. For example, church educators, instead of listening to their own voices echoing in their own silos, may offer themselves to the parish choir retreat where, in addition to practicing music, musicians will be assisted by these educators to explore theologies present in the lyrics of choral works and in the music itself. Or they may journey with the hurricane response team to the coast where, in addition to working alongside team members, they will help them to reflect on their baptismal vocations for serving those in distress and to reflect critically upon long-term strategies for minimizing the impact of "natural" disasters. Elsewhere, school-based Christian educators may need to break out of their captivity to the schooling paradigm, the assumption that learning begins and ends at the door of the classroom. At the Methodist Theological School in Ohio, Christian education faculty and students have worked to establish a working farm on campus where growing and harvesting crops, eating the fruits of their labor together, and ongoing reflection upon these practices have become a significant piece of the school's curriculum.

Contexts matter in myriad ways! Ultimately, however, they invite faith-forming leaders to innovate toward effective and faithful ways of ministry. May we all attend to the Spirit's work of new creation as we labor in our own contexts to do the good work of God.

Part	Theme
1	Cultural Dynamics for Nurturing Faith
2	Criteria for Nurturing Faith
3	Colleagues in Nurturing Faith
4	**Contexts for Nurturing Faith**
	➤ **Congregations (chapter 14)**
	➤ **Christian Schools (chapter 15)**
	➤ **Theological Education (chapter 16)**
5	Conversations in Nurturing Faith

CHAPTER FOURTEEN

Nurturing Intergenerational Faith through Congregations

One generation shall laud your works to another,
and shall declare your mighty acts.

—PSALM 145:4

When your children ask you in time to come, "What is the meaning of
the decrees and the statutes and the ordinances that the Lord our God has
commanded you?" then you shall say to your children, "We were Pharaoh's
slaves in Egypt, but the Lord brought us out of Egypt with a mighty hand."

—DEUTERONOMY 6:20-21

ROAD MAP

Once during his lean years as a cash-starved graduate student, Fred served
as a summer youth worker to a small congregation. Their stated goal for
his ministry was to increase the level of youth activities in order to attract
a half dozen more families with youth to the church, thus establishing the
critical mass to justify hiring a permanent youth minister. Their vision for
youth ministry consisted of twenty kids, a bus, and a (young) adult paid
to drive them around in it. Yet as soon as he set foot in the congregation
and for the rest of the summer, Fred noticed young people attending worship with adults, plus singing in the adult choir and accompanying it with
musical instruments. He enjoyed the intergenerational drama troupe that
frequently supported the pastor's preaching. He marveled at how youth
were vitally important to the success of the annual chicken barbecue
fundraiser, standing side by side with adults grilling chicken and ringing
up sales. He led a Vacation Bible School class that had for years featured
youth and adults participating together. The "youth" mountain camping

trip included as many folks over thirty-five and younger siblings of youth as youth themselves. When asked to give an account of himself at the end of the summer, he confessed failure to attract the requisite new families. He nevertheless described to the congregation how they were already practicing a vital, communally based, intergenerational ministry fully inclusive of youth. Was this assessment correct?

Introduction

Faith is the gift of Spirit birth. Yet faith doesn't drop straight out of heaven and hit folks over the head. Faith is normally cultivated in and through communal relationships—mediated by and through the faithful. This chapter seeks, therefore, to reappraise and reaffirm faith *communities* as essential to faith's nurture. This claim ought not surprise readers in light of prior theological accounts in part 2 describing divine interrelationship in and through the Trinity, divine-human relationship manifested in the incarnation of Christ, and the constitutive interrelation and mutual dependence of all creation—creatures created for comm-*unity* with God and one another—and of the theological necessity for (if flawed existence of) the church. The relational nature of God, creatures, and faith itself mandates relational approaches to its formation.

Faith Context	Nurturing Faith through . . .
› Congregations	Intergenerational Nurture
Christian Schools	Integrative Nurture
Theological Education	Intentional Nurture

But more than merely insisting that faith is born out of relationships and rightly housed in congregations, however, this chapter seeks to show *how and why* faith communities are or may better become essential greenhouses for nurturing faith. As we have emphasized, faith is as much a life stance and disposition as it is sure knowledge. Receiving its love-directing, imagination-shaping, identity-forming, and life-orienting power requires immersion in communities living out faith's values, visions, and practices. In addition to the witness of Scripture and the theological tradition, this chapter also explores educational and social science literature to help explain how congregations play a vital role in nurturing faith. In particular, we focus on the uniquely *intergenerational* nature of faith communities and their resulting complex cultures capable of catalyzing faith formation in young and old alike.

Challenges to Faith Communities

Ultimately, the church exists as a witness to God's saving work through worship and mission (Ps. 68:3). As is so often the case in faith formational ministries, means and ends overlap. Christians worship God and strive to join God in mission because they are called to these ministries, because they offer the means to deepen faith, and because they are expressions of faith itself. Let's take a closer look at the challenges congregations must overcome when it comes to fully claiming the communal nature of faith formation.

These are not the good old days for congregations, at least in North America and Europe. Whereas the Western church once rested comfortably in the bosom of nominally Christian culture and "Christian-ish" social institutions (imagine singing Christmas carols at the public school holiday concert or reciting the Lord's Prayer each morning before class as was the case in many cities across the United States not so long ago), the present finds faith communities ever more isolated at the margins of society. Some churches are graying, shrinking, and even closing, and the number of persons professing Christian faith is shrinking. In the United Kingdom, for example, great cathedrals often house cafés and libraries to pay the rent. Sunday attendance has dropped precipitously.

In addition, as sociologists of religion Smith and Denton show, even for Christians actively participating in faith communities, faith knowledge and practice often are profoundly lacking. These researchers demonstrate that even some of the most devoted Christians often possess only a limited vocabulary for faith, meaning they cannot fully articulate the nature of God and the mission of redemptive purpose. The study also reports that Christians lack steady practices of faith. Few pray consistently and even fewer pour out their lives in loving service to others. In sum, according to Smith and Denton, most professed Christians live as "Moralistic Therapeutic Deists" (MTDs) thoroughly confused about the nature of God and what the gift of baptismal incorporation into God calls them to.[1]

On the one hand, it is easy to blame the shifting cultural tide for congregational decline. There is no denying the negative impact of metatrends addressed in part 1 of this book; secularism, individualism, nominalism, and certain dimensions of postmodernism undeniably contributed to the eclipse of Christendom in the Global North. On the other hand, denominations and individual congregations comfortably ensconced in the privilege Western culture afforded them for generations effectively took their eyes off the prize of faith formation. Unlike Joseph in Egypt, these communities neither foresaw nor prepared for the years of famine presently starving the faithful.

Fifty years later, those of us who can recall these "good old days" are experiencing whiplash. How quickly things changed! When the tide of Christendom suddenly ebbed, congregations were not prepared to become countercultural communities.[2] Either through forgetfulness or colonization by the wider culture, they had lost the distinctive language, gestures, practices, dispositions of the heart, and vision—that is, the ingredients of *faith*—to bear Christ for one another, much less the world. They had also lost the means to form faith in members and new converts, and, more problematic still, the imagination to see the wealth of faith-forming resources already residing within their distinctive practices of worship and mission.

Congregations as Communities That Nurture Faith

C. Ellis Nelson was the first Christian educator of the modern era to recognize how congregations play an instrumental role in forming faith in their members. Working in the midtwentieth century and influenced by the insights of the then relatively new field of cultural anthropology, Nelson perceived that faith is communicated through "a community of believers" as they seek to discern and live out faith's implications together.[3] To grasp the significance of this insight, it helps to recall this period as the era when the self-chosen personal relationship with Jesus Christ predominated. As noted in parts 1 and 2, it was possible then to imagine faith as an exclusively individualistic pursuit. Nelson further noticed how faith communities educate their members not only through their explicit teachings of biblical and theological content but also, for example, through their budget-shaping processes and attention to or neglect of current social issues.

One of Nelson's students, Roman Catholic educator Maria Harris, crystalizes her professor's important insight by defining Christian educational curriculum as "the entire course of the church's life."[4] In short, she suggests that a congregation manifests a holistic ecology of faith meanings and practices, which proves to be the critical environment for nurturing it. John Westerhoff, another student of Nelson's, similarly describes the church's catechetical efforts consisting partly in a process of "enculturation." According to Westerhoff, "enculturation" includes settings where faith is nurtured formally, as when persons attend Sunday school or Bible studies or prepare for baptism and other rites of passage, but it also occurs through informal processes of socialization.[5] Repeated participation in communal gestures, ritual symbolic practices, shared stories, informal mentoring, practices of compassion and mercy, and patterns of loving relationships are all contributors to religious socialization. Nurturing faith, therefore, seems to require formation in explicit beliefs, practices, and worldviews (products of formal catechesis) and also in tacit imaginings or dispositions. French anthropologist Pierre Bourdieu describes this dispositional housing as a *habitus*, an intuitive "feel for the game," of participation in a particular culture.[6] In the case of the game of faithful Christian life, a Christian *habitus* consists of more than words can explain. Obviously, too, acquiring a feel for the Christian game requires *playing* it with others in the faith community.

JOHN H. WESTERHOFF III

John H. Westerhoff III was born in Paterson, New Jersey, in 1933. His mother took him to Sunday school "out of duty," but it was a powerful visionary and mystical experience in a revival service of a small church that greatly impacted him. Westerhoff became a student at Ursinus, at Harvard, and at Columbia, where he completed a doctor of education degree before being ordained in the United Church of Christ.

Westerhoff became convinced of the singularly important formation of liturgy and of the larger community of faith, and determined to focus on adult education as a most essential aspect of parish work. He would take these convictions into his work as professor of religion and education at Duke Divinity School and as editor of *Religious Education*. Westerhoff's greatest contribution has been to present socialization as a model for the work of Christian formation. Through various publications, but especially in *Will Our Children Have Faith?* (1976, then revised and still in print), he has argued for a catechetical—faith initiating and forming experience—process of participation in the life of the faith community, its liturgy, and the influence of its adult members as a central means of Christian formation.

Westerhoff's understanding of the nature of Christian education as the pastoral activity of catechesis taking place in the dialogue, activities, and liturgical practices of the faith community stands over against "schooling" models and instructional approaches. While not rejecting the role of instruction, he considers it primarily helpful for facilitating the mastery of propositional truth.

JAMES P. BOWERS

Nelson and his disciples also revealed the limitations of the "schooling paradigm" for nurturing faith. In the US at least, congregations, influenced by the common school movement of the late nineteenth and early twentieth centuries, came to consider the form of education practiced in the Sunday school to be the adequate and exclusive means for forming Christians in faith. Yet schooling tends toward "learning about" rather than "living out." In addition, schooling in the church often was considered a separate undertaking from, say, worship or mission, as if the latter have nothing to teach Christians on how to be faithful.

As perhaps the most important, if unintended, consequence, church schooling often reinforced generational separation, which contributed to the communal fragmentation of the church today (more about this below). At present, a common Sunday morning pattern in the United States features children attending Sunday school while their parents gather in the sanctuary for worship. Perhaps this was a workable solution when the wider culture supported Christian teachings, values, and practices. (We have our doubts.) In a post-Christian culture, however, schooling may remain an essential ingredient for faith formation, but it is not sufficient by itself. The insights of Nelson, Harris, Westerhoff, and others reveal the equally significant role played by communal enculturation and socialization—dynamics we don't ordinarily perceive because they do their formational work tacitly and implicitly. Armed with these insights, however, faith formational leaders can readily detect how children absented from worship and other domains of congregational living are being deprived of immersion in crucial dimensions of the faith-forming cultural ecology. They need to play the church's game in order to gain a feel for it.

Congregations as *Intergenerational* Communities That Nurture Faith

The conversation around forming faith in communities has focused more recently on their distinctive and nowadays nearly unique multigenerational character. It is worth pausing for a moment to acknowledge just how unusual the church is in this respect. Any given Sunday may find three or four generations of a single family in church praising God together! This, while the generations are ever more segregated in the broader society.

As readers know, young people spend most of their time in school with their peers. Similarly, parents go off to work, an adults-only space about which their children know little. Retired persons are expected to opt for their own separate living communities often equipped with gates—apparently to prevent infiltration by the younger generations. Generational segregation is itself partly a fictional construct designed to sell more products targeted to the specific "needs" of children, tweens, teens, emerging adults, young adults, and so on. It is also partly the result of growing affluence. Beginning in the late nineteenth century, nuclear families began to accumulate sufficient resources to live independent from their elders. On the other hand, poorer families and families composed of recent immigrants not yet converted to consumer capitalism are more likely to include two or more generations under a single roof.[7] Unlike a previous era where, for example, multiple generations lived and worked the family farm together, age-level ghettos have assumed normalcy in the Global North.

The church is not immune to this separation disease. As noted previously, members of different generations are as likely to be shunted in different directions on Sunday morning as they are to be found harmonizing "Amazing Grace" together in the sanctuary. Shamelessly, not too long ago, church growth "experts" actually advocated creating purposefully homogenous congregations populated by people of the same age, race, ethnicity, education, and social status—on the principle that like attracts like. Were Jesus still in the grave, he would be turning in it.

In light of this mixed record, advocates now distinguish between, on the one hand, "multigenerational" congregations that just so happen to register members from age nine days to ninety-nine years on their rolls and, on the other, "intergenerational" congregations who view their demographic breadth as a gift from God to be stewarded as a ministry resource for the flourishing of all. In their remarkable and lively book, Holly Catterton Allen and Christine Lawton Ross describe this intergenerational ministry as "creating frequent opportunities for various generations to communicate in meaningful ways, to interact on a regular basis, and to minister, worship and serve together regularly."[8]

Allen and Ross advocate intergenerationality for all the reasons described above (namely that faith is formed in and through communities and relationships) *and* because they believe faith formation in community happens best when it becomes a purposefully intergenerational communal endeavor. Their theological rationale largely overlaps with our own, but they also cite a number of supportive learning theories and social scientific studies, a few of which we summarize here.

They note how Albert Bandura, in his social learning theory, proposes that learning does not always proceed by way of direct transmission of knowledge or personal experimentation. Much learning also comes through "observation and modeling."[9] (Think of children watching and imitating their parents in worship.)

Further, framed in developmental terms, the authors contend that intergenerational communities offer more complex webs of relation than age-segregated groupings. Encounters with persons different from ourselves are more likely to confound and call into question personal attitudes and life practices previously taken for granted. Children learn to think and act in new ways through close relational ties with different kinds of persons more experienced than they. Similarly, adults are invited to reconsider the nature of faithful life when stimulated by the faithfulness and passionate questioning of children who do not yet take for granted the "normal" expectations of their faith tradition. Intergenerational faith formation is reciprocal, not just top down.

Even so, mature Christians are more likely to possess greater Christian practical wisdom than novices. Citing psychologist Lev Vygotsky, Allen and Ross note how the character of an intergenerational social setting can promote learning. Instead of conceiving learning as an individual undertaking, Vygotsky describes a "zone of proximal development" where persons are helped to perform higher level tasks by sharing in them together with more experienced members of a community. The authors, therefore, contend that the best way to learn something new is to be connected to "those who are just ahead on the learning journey."[10]

Finally, Allen and Ross cite the work of Lave and Wenger, on "situated learning" within "communities of practice." Studying midwife apprentices, among others, the investigators describe how persons are formed through "genuine participation" in the activities and roles they aspire to. This participation enables acquisition of "knowledge" and "skills" for midwifery but also absorbing "the ethos" and ultimately identifying with "the community" of midwives—that is, they *become* midwives.[11]

For Allen and Ross, the implications of these studies for faith formation are straightforward. Not only does nurturing faith require knitting persons together in a web of communal relations, but also less mature Christians depend upon opportunities for shared discovery and practice with more mature ones in order to grow in their faith. At the same time, mature Christians may find themselves awakened to new dimensions of faithfulness through these encounters with novices. In addition to deepening faith knowledge and practice, this kind of intergenerational learning also leads to deepened claims on persons' identities and vocations. In theological terms, not only do I know and do Christian things, I become incorporated into Christ (a matter of identity) and live my life toward Christ's realm (a matter of vocation) through participation in Christ's body incarnated in the local faith community.

Emeritus Christian educator Charles Foster, still another of C. Ellis Nelson's students, focused his entire career on the faith community as the crucible for faith formation. In Foster's most recent book, he describes the need to recover what he calls a "catechetical culture," an intergenerational community where the grammar of faith formation (faith's language and practices) is sustained and reinforced both formally and informally throughout the congregational ecology.[12] A catechetical culture works by way of fostering opportunities for young or new Christians to reaffirm and reflect upon their faith learning and practice with sufficient frequency to internalize it. Repetition is key. One expression of a catechetical culture finds parents quizzing their children about Sunday school learnings on the way home from church. Foster proposes intentional cultivation of this process of intergenerational reverberation across all levels of the congregation. He envisions children or new Christians included fully in congregational practices of hospitality and celebration, for example, so that they not only are immersed in the game of Christian life but also are naturally included in the conversations and mutual storytelling that accompany it. To *repeat,* faith is reinforced in its recurring performances *and* through both the spontaneous and intentional conversations springing up in the midst of the ordinary (and extraordinary) events of community life where the meanings and stories of these performances are told and retold for the benefit of all. *Repetition is key.* Purposeful creation and practice of catechetical culture provides the means to ensure such repetition.

We have heard of the Christian automobile mechanic who took on the ministry of caring for his congregation's aging bus and van during his off-time. Not only did he maintain these vehicles, however, he invited three teenagers from the church to help him out. After spending sufficient time wrenching auto parts, a sense of shared purpose and fun (along with greasy hands) began to grow between them. Almost naturally, the mechanic shared stories of his life and faith and invited his young friends to do the same. The language and practices of faith and even faith itself were shared and reinforced through this intergenerational web of relationships. While obviously the young people were dependent upon the adult's greater experience as a mechanic and a Christian, he quickly recognized how these friendships were deepening his own sense of purpose and vocation. He was growing in faith too! This was a site for reverberation and repetition of faith insights, an important expression of the catechetical culture Foster advocates.

Like Allen and Ross, Foster recognizes that intergenerational catechetical cultures will need to be reengineered and promoted in faith communities where generational segregation has become the norm. In the final part, we offer examples of what this refashioning of congregational life may require and look like.

Intergenerational Community Faith Formation in Action

Leadership for Congregational Change

Intergenerational renewal will require intentionality of purpose, imagination, and strategic planning from faith-forming ministry leaders, along with steadiness, patience, and hope. Leaders convicted by the need to cultivate intergenerational faith-forming communities will have studied and internalized the compelling theological and educational rationale for such a venture. They should be able to articulate a vision clearly and convincingly to key allies and stakeholders in the congregation, perhaps by leading them in exploring these themes together and then, with the help of stakeholders, gradually expanding the supportive network for this sort of renewal. Further, leaders will remain eyes-wide-open about resistance to reshaping their communities along intergenerational lines. Remember, different generations have come to assume that segregation by age is *normal* and even *good*. Adolescents, for example, are currently conditioned to regard children as annoying and adults as clueless, *at best*! Parents prefer to worship without interference from their children because they assume worship is *properly* an adult thing. In the rare cases where parents imagine it important for their children to be present in congregational worship, children are often bored by the adults-only nature of the practice. Nor can these heroic (or is it crazy?) parents expect relief or even a break from anyone else in the congregation, because *everyone* is operating out of the tacit assumption that they are bounded individuals whose responsibilities do not extend down the pew or across the aisle to a five-year-old. Children may be perceived as violating adults' "right" to worship in peace. Hence the need for clarity of vision and purpose, passion, patience, and persistence in recruiting allies. A congregational leader seeking to create an environment of intergenerational faith formation is not only undertaking a wholesale revision of ministry practice; she is also attempting to fashion an entirely new culture where assumptions about what is normal and good (children actively participating in communal worship?!) are also being transformed.

Access for All

In addition to the vision and determination to make intergenerationality less strange, *accessibility* for all kinds of participants will be a key consideration. Worship, mission, and faith formation will somehow need to "speak" to a broad range of experience and development. Since adults possess the most power in a faith community, congregational life is typically built around their experiences and expectations. In addition, adult modes of communicating and what passes for adult learning styles tend to predominate in faith formation, worship, and missional undertakings. Finally, many adults flinch at the prospect of intergenerational efforts because they presume things will require "dumbing down" to accommodate less mature participants.

At this point, we briefly recall the discussion in part 2 of humans as lovers more than thinkers, beings moved by their hearts to seek ends they desire. We also recall the educational inference that follows upon this anthropology. Forming hearts to love what God loves is far less a matter of speculative reasoning than practicing to instill good affective habits. The human heart is stirred toward the good by what it perceives to be beautiful—a gripping story, a powerful symbol, a moving song, an exemplar of lived compassion. This is equally true for all age levels.

Taking this anthropology seriously suggests that those educational practices we presume to be more basic (and seemingly childish) remain essential (and retain priority) for all Christians. If one hopes to love as God loves, there is no substitute for a lifetime of practice. Similarly, seeing the world through God's eyes is less a matter of rational explanation than it is joining a good story.

Fred began to sense the importance of story for adults by way of an unlikely teaching scenario. Each fall semester in an introductory Christian education course at Duke Divinity School, he includes a session on "Godly Play," a storied approach to the Christian education of children. In the early years, he only described this method and its rationale to his students. They learned *about* it, in other words. Serendipitously, however, a former student named Phyllis became a Godly Play instructor and later a Godly Play certified trainer. Together Phyllis and Fred decided that it might prove more effective not just to talk about Godly Play (a typical adult learning ploy) but also to *participate* in it. Phyllis wisely chose to share with the class the Godly Play story of Israel's exile to Babylon followed by the eventual return (of some) to rebuild the temple at Jerusalem. Seated on the floor with students gathered around her, Phyllis's mesmerizing storytelling was punctuated by the crunch, crunch, crunch sound caused by her marching small wooden figures (symbolizing the exiles) in a serpentine pattern across a box of sand (symbolizing the desert) from Jerusalem to Babylon and back.

GODLY PLAY

Godly Play invites children into a spirit of playful orthodoxy that combines a deep rooting in classical Christian language with creative openness. This is accomplished by associating the Christian language system with the creative process to make existential meaning, which has implications for learning, which is good pedagogy, but also has implications for knowing God personally, which is good theology.

Godly Play also involves children and adults in mutual blessing. This follows Jesus's saying that to become spiritually mature, one needs to become like a child. Adults cannot make the spiritual journey for children, so they need to equip them to make the journey for themselves. At the same time, by profoundly being who they are, children teach adults to wonder again and renew the graceful unity they had as children.

Godly Play does not attempt to force, manipulate, convince, or bribe children to think and feel in a certain way about God. Instead the art of how to make meaning with Christian language (sacred stories, parables, liturgical action, and contemplative silence) is taught so children can better cope with their existential limits—death, aloneness, the threat of freedom, and the need for meaning. The short-term goal is for children to enter adolescence with an inner working knowledge of the Christian language system. The long-term goal is for them to become a graceful people as adults.

Godly Play assumes that young children already have experienced the presence of the mystery of God in an undifferentiated way. This is a reasonable assumption, because evidence has also been accumulating in the physical and social sciences that the evolution of our species has been ongoing, because we are fundamentally creative spiritual beings. Jerome W. Berryman's *Godly Play: A Way of Religious Education* (1991) describes how Godly Play combines developmental psychology and Montessori education with God's lively presence, theology, play, and the creative process to articulate an approach for mentoring children's moral and spiritual development. It discusses the ultimate game, the importance of laughter, and the structure of a Godly Play experience. Six aspects of the spoken and unspoken process of Godly Play are discussed: wonder, community/ethics, the participants' existential limits, the nature of religious language, the importance of associating religious language with the creative process to make existential meaning, and how to use the deep structure of the holy Eucharist to guide the process's flow.

The Godly Play curriculum spirals upward and out from the core lessons, to extensions, enrichment lessons, afterward lessons, and synthesis lessons. The eight volumes of *The Complete Guide to Godly Play* describe this pattern. Volume 8 contains an overview of the foundational literature for Godly Play and the most complete summary of the spiral curriculum to date. In general, the core presentations are for children from three to twelve years of age. The extension, enrichment, and afterward lessons are for children from six to twelve years. The synthesis lessons are for older children from nine to twelve years.

JEROME BERRYMAN

With story complete but eyes still focused on its setting, Phyllis began to "wonder" about the story as the Godly Play method prescribes: What must it have been like to leave home? How did the people of Israel learn to "sing a new song" in a foreign land? What about that desert?

An extremely nervous participant observer in the first iteration of this process, Fred worried that his adult students would feel condescended to by being forced to submit to an approach designed for children. He'd noticed a few eye rolls at the outset of the storytelling and expected a massive snark attack when students were invited to wonder out loud in response. Instead, he marveled at how completely most students gave themselves over to it. More than a few of them named their own acute sense of exile, having left home for divinity school. Others confessed struggling mightily to sing their faith songs in this strange new academic key. Still others wondered whether what they were learning here in "Babylon" would translate back home in actual ministry settings.

Fred and Phyllis also provided opportunities for student reflection on the Godly Play approach after the conclusion of the session. It is no exaggeration to state that students regularly describe these sessions as offering a vital zone for faithful imagining and reflection upon their callings in response to participation in the biblical story. They also acknowledge that ways of learning many deemed childish (Godly Play also includes a period of time for participants to quietly "work" in response to the story through artistic means, either by "playing" with the story's figures and props, journaling, painting, drawing, and so on) opened their hearts to deep faith imagining and wonder.

Obviously, these are not truly intergenerational learning sessions. Yet they do indicate how approaches to faith formation enabling "participative relationship with" the subject of one's learning as opposed to the more typically analytical adult pattern of "distanced abstraction from" the subject matter remain important to persons at all developmental levels. We "grown-ups" would do well to recover these capacities for deep playfulness that children embrace with gusto.

Forms of Intergenerational Learning

Allen and Ross explicitly counsel intergenerational story-linking. As part of an actual intergenerational learning session and as a means of response to a study of the life of young David as described in 1 Samuel, they offer the following prompt: "God who delivered David from the bear, and the lion, and from Goliath has delivered me from . . ."[13] The authors provide samples of actual responses. Each one is a powerful testimony of living faith. In addition, no matter how young or old, all participants learned from hearing *others'* links with the story. How better, for example, for less mature Christians to learn how more experienced brothers and sisters come to terms with fear? What more effective means for more mature Christians to be reminded of the struggles of their younger peers and to engage them with empathy and compassion?

The authors recommend other highly participatory learning styles too. Better to act out Scripture or at least read it dramatically than to read it silently. Similarly, they contend that issues at the intersection of faith and life ought to be engaged through vivid case studies or artistic encounter. That many (though not all) adults *can* learn through analysis or verbalizing or internalized processes of rational abstraction from principles does not necessarily mean that they *ought* to. And that adult learning tends to utilize pedagogies to match does not mean that it *ought* to, at least primarily. Like children, adults continue to learn through experience or through active participation in faith practices. Put differently, ways of knowing and learning deemed primary for children remain critical for adults even as they go mostly unacknowledged.

Charles Foster, the advocate for catechetical cultures, offers another vehicle for intergenerational faith formation. He proposes that congregational "events" become the focus of faith formation in churches.[14] Examples of events can include a church's annual homecoming Sunday, worship during Advent/Christmas, the fish-fry fundraiser, building a new sanctuary, instituting a health mission for the surrounding community, or offering hospitality to neighbors. Citing the "eventful" character of Jesus's ministry, Foster suggests congregational events can incarnate and recapitulate Christ's saving purposes.

In order to harness the full formational power of these events, Foster recommends adopting a threefold pedagogical pattern: preparation *for* the event, participation *in* the event, and reflection *upon* the event. If we take building a new sanctuary as an example, presumably faith-formational leaders will plan to include everyone in the community in the entire process from start to finish. Full inclusion of all will allow for frequent catechetical reverberation of the community's old (and new) stories, meanings, and hopes.

The *preparation* phase could include pilgrimages to and through the old sanctuary (if one exists)—noting its sacred spaces and the dimensions of its design promoting a sense of transcendence and intimacy, and listening to stories of older members about their experiences in the sanctuary. Lifelong members may well recall their baptisms, weddings, weddings of their children, funerals of beloved brothers and sisters, and other rites of passage all in that space. Preparation might also include considering new or different features incorporated to reflect evolving worship patterns. What might be required to increase access and inclusion for children, elderly persons, or persons with disabilities? Perhaps they could be asked! We know of a church that built a very large baptismal pool at the entrance to its new sanctuary. Baptism had become a primary symbol in the congregation, one that animated its sense of living as a covenant family before God as well as its ministries and missions in the community. The congregation desired more visible and vigorous baptismal ritual/symbolic practices to reflect the vision and efficacy that a baptismal ethos already provided for the community. Finally, preparation might also include fundraising for the building, a task that could easily be shared across the congregation.

Participation in this case might look like regular updates on construction progress, special gatherings to celebrate punctuating moments (as when a crane lifts the steeple to its perch), tours of the construction site, actual shared work on the new building—from raising rafters to installing pew Bibles (everyone can participate somehow), culminating with a glorious communal worship celebration and dedication when the sanctuary is complete.

Postevent *reflection* is equally important. Faith-forming leaders will carve out multiple opportunities to invite persons to tell stories of their experiences of raising the new sanctuary, to describe where and how they saw God at work in the midst of it, how they relied upon God to do what they couldn't, where there may have been a need for forgiveness and reconciliation, and what they dream God will do in that new space for generations to come.

Readers may sense here how much more richly immersive is this eventful approach to nurturing faith than an hour of school on Sunday mornings. It illustrates how faith is fruit of faithful participation in communal life. Faith formation is made more intentional, however, through the practices of preparation and reflection. In those explicitly catechetical settings, stories, meanings, imaginings, biblical and theological links, prayers, critiques, and wonderings are shared in relation to the event. These settings provide the crucial opportunities for recollection, rehearsal, and repetition with enough frequency for faith to become embedded in persons' hearts, minds, bodies, and souls.

Forming Faith through Worship and Mission

Worship and mission constitute two primary formational events in the church. These eventful practices are contexts where the crucified and risen Christ has promised to be present, where two or more gather in his name, or where the poor, incarcerated, hungry, or naked are cared for—Jesus is there! Worship and mission are spaces of revelatory encounter with the living God, therefore, and are ripe with potential for faith formation and transformation.

As with explicit educational undertakings in the church, the *intergenerational* efficacy of these primary congregational practices requires highlighting. We confess to bemusement at the need to remind congregations to worship and serve *together* as one body, yet that is where we find ourselves. There's no denying the segregation of worship according to style preferences or generational taste. Similarly, mission, to the extent congregations understand it, often is confined to a "trip" that youth "take." Space does not allow for rehearsing once more the theological argument for why congregations should worship and serve as one body. Instead we focus upon the *how* questions, specifically, how to create the conditions for intergenerational participation in these events.

In *The Church of All Ages: Generations Worshiping Together*, Howard Vanderwell and others offer insight into how the church became generationally fragmented, what prospects the biblical and theological tradition offer for reform and renewal, plus down-to-earth strategies for reclaiming intergenerational worship.[15] In the spirit of Foster's eventful education, Vanderwell recommends that everything related to worship, from planning to worshiping to reflecting upon it, becomes purposefully generationally inclusive. Pastors and other worship leaders will create settings where they regularly listen to members' (from children to senior adults) thoughts and imaginings on biblical texts linked to their preaching, on issues that are central to persons' lives and that require prayerful intercession or homiletical attention, on musical participation, and so on. In addition to vital feedback, these worship-planning processes offer opportunities for worship leaders to teach the meanings of worship, including the rites that compose it.

Worshiping together also requires accessibility and equipping persons with the agency to offer their gifts. Unsurprisingly for Vanderwell and his contributors, accessible worship means getting out of our heads and making room for bodies, hearts, and spirits. His context as a pastor in the Reformed tradition shows a bit at this point; a great many Pentecostal and free-church traditions are way out in front of him here. Even so, we readily affirm that children and persons with developmental disabilities (and normally developing adults too) gain greater access to worship (and to the living God) through bodily gestures and heartfelt participation. Worship should be *moving* (double entendre intended)! Yet this does not require forfeiting a community's historic worshiping tradition. Scripture remains at the center of worship for Vanderwell and his denomination, except he now proposes it be read antiphonally by a child and her grandfather, for example, or interpreted dramatically by members of the congregation, or illustrated in the church bulletin or by projection on a screen. Sermon outlines should be made available, differently composed for different developmental levels. Sermons ought also to become more conversational and storied.

Our own sense is that faith communities may also reawaken to the power of sacramental performance and practice. Even communities that do not officially regard sacraments as means of grace can recognize their eventful character, how they offer the opportunity to participate in God's unfolding story of salvation. When practiced robustly, receiving bread and cup alongside one's brothers and sisters in Christ provides a "feel for the [Christian] game." It offers immersive participation in brokenness, in sharing that heals, in abundance and gratitude. Ritual practices speak more than words can say, evoking doxological wonder and avoiding abstraction in the process. They help shape the Christian habitus across the span of age and ability.

As with worship, we welcome the growing attention to mission in the church. The church exists to serve a missionary God who is working to restore all creation to God's realm. In addition to witnessing to God's mission through worship, congregations may also participate (in a small way) in God's missional purposes. Mission can mean "trips." Much biblical precedent exists for this frame. Mission can also mean deepened efforts toward hospitality locally in order to welcome strangers into the community.

As described in a previous chapter, Fred is a veteran of multiple mission trips. Through trial and error (mostly error), he learned many lessons along the way. Pertaining to this discussion, he noticed how for youth and adults, the practice of "leaving home" and seeking common purpose together broke down generational separation and lubricated intergenerational friendships. He once witnessed a retired painter patiently explaining safety procedures to a high school student who was about to ascend a very tall ladder to get at hard-to-reach trim on a church sanctuary. Later that day, the painter confessed to everyone how grateful he was not to go up the ladder himself and how appreciative he was of the student. The two of them were inseparable for the rest of the trip and remained friends back home.

Fred also realized how these journeys offered the possibility of linking all the practices of Christian life together in mutually interpretive and reinforcing proximity—what another youth worker calls "the dance."[16] These settings readily lend themselves to connecting Scripture to serving neighbors, to worship, and to living simply in Christian community together. This ecology of practices strengthens their graced formational impact.

In addition, Fred eventually stumbled upon a rough form of eventful education (before he'd read the book!) by beginning to include daily intentionally intergenerational reflection on the presence and work of Christ with and in this mission, God's concern for the poor, and the invitation to young and old Christians alike to sense and name God's pleasure in their efforts. Young people were frequently moved by the vulnerability adult participants confessed in these settings about their fears of overcoming language and culture barriers, plus their complex responses to the enormous poverty that sometimes left them despairing. Adults rejoiced at the willingness of young people to cross these same boundaries and to take them along for the journey. Mutual reflection also helped prevent drawing the wrong conclusions about mission: "I'm delivering Jesus to these people." Nope, he's already there. "I'm helping these people." Perhaps, but they are offering gifts to you too. Intergenerational mission created the conditions for everyone to express his or her "best self." Its purposeful social dislocation fostered the complex conditions required to transform old assumptions into more faithful ways of knowing, doing, and being. Its sustained dialectic of experiential action and careful reflection fostered the kind of catechetical culture where faith meanings and practices could grow and become more permanent.

Conclusion

As webs of communal relationship, and through their unique callings to worship and serve the triune God, congregations are uniquely suited to the task of nurturing faith. In the days ahead, leaders in faith formation will need not only to recognize but also intentionally foster and harvest these relational dynamics in their ministries. In addition to occasions for explicit teaching and learning about faith, they will fashion catechetical cultures where faith by the power of the Spirit is "caught" by engaging together with others in the life that constitutes it. Faith formation will require all hands on deck; nobody gets a pass. Members of generations formed to prefer their own company will need to be re-formed to include all. Fortunately, as we've noted, Jesus is present to and actively abetting *every* effort to break down boundaries and create communities of inclusion and intimacy. Reclaiming faith communities as intergenerational spaces of formation is therefore consistent with God's mission. Communities investing in this way of life are moving with the grain of the universe.

Interactive Dialogue

1. Reflect upon the congregation you know best. How well and in what settings do members of different generations interact? What might be improved?
2. Do you agree with the authors' contentions for the necessity of intergenerational communal processes of faith formation? Why or why not?
3. The chapter contains a number of broad strategies for communal faith formation. How might you imagine employing one or more of them? How would you go about it?

For Further Reading

Allen, Holly Catterton, and Christine Lawton Ross. *Intergenerational Faith Formation: Bringing the Whole Church Together in Ministry, Community and Worship.* Downers Grove, IL: InterVarsity, 2012.

Foster, Charles R. *Educating Congregations: The Future of Christian Education.* Nashville: Abingdon, 2006.

———. *From Generation to Generation: The Adaptive Challenge of Mainline Protestant Education in Forming Faith.* Eugene, OR: Cascade, 2012.

Vanderwell, Howard, ed. *The Church of All Ages: Generations Worshiping Together.* Herndon, VA: Alban Institute, 2008.

Wright, Wendy M. *Seasons in a Family's Life: Cultivating a Contemplative Spirit at Home.* San Francisco: John Wiley & Sons, 2003.

CHAPTER FIFTEEN

Nurturing Integrative Faith through Christian Schools

Many have taken the Christian faith to be a simple and easy matter and have even numbered it among the virtues. This is because they have not really experienced it, nor have they tested the great strength of faith.

—MARTIN LUTHER

Verbal language, both spoken and written, has dominated Christian education for too long. Perhaps as far as Christian faith is concerned, we have attached too literal an interpretation to the primacy of the word. By sanctifying the oral and verbal traditions, we have lost something of the richness of the early church where the great truths of the community were enshrined in shared experience.

—JOHN WESTERHOFF

ROAD MAP

A former ministerial student of Fred's once designed a final project for a Christian education course around land stewardship. As it happened, a congregation he served for a unit of summer field education had received the considerable gift of a farm! They were contemplating how best to utilize this gift. For the assignment, "Dan" (not his real name) imagined inviting the senior-high youth with whom he'd worked closely over the summer to fully engage in this discernment process. In light of his Christian education course work and his upbringing as a "nature boy," Dan envisioned a participative, problem-posing curriculum that would unfold over weeks and months. It included repeatedly walking the farmland in order to come to know it intimately. It invited participants to trace the stories of the land as told by recent and historic inhabitants and to listen to the stories the land itself was telling by attending to its geologic, geographic, and ecological dimensions. Equally important to these sorts of considerations were theological ones. Dan proposed to involve participants in close theological studies of divine and human relations to creation, and to "land" in particular. He knew that the Scriptures, the Old Testament especially, thematized land as a dimension of Israel's covenantal gift and obligation to God. He imaginatively characterized Jesus as "chief steward" of creation. Dan believed that his integrative educational approach would prompt further reflection on how best to steward this gift.

All good, yes?! Brilliantly conceived project, beautifully undertaken. Yet Dan confessed that he struggled to find a proper context to locate it. In his imagination, it was way too demanding of time and energy for a church fellowship group or a Sunday school class. When I asked him about setting it up as a formal course project in a school, he immediately allowed that it involved traditional subject matter taught in schools—science, cultural history, biblical and theological studies, and more. But he almost as quickly rejected that setting too. His intellectually integrative and practically oriented project, he said, "was too school-ish for church" but totally unlike the classes devoted to specific subject matter he took as a kid educated in Christian schools.

Introduction

Dan's dilemma and subsequent reflections capture something of the problems and possibilities for Christian schooling. On the one hand, unlike their secular counterparts, Christian schools are free to invoke God's presence and redeeming intent in their educational efforts. They may experiment and innovate with curriculum and pedagogical methods that integrate academic and practical, faithful ends. On the other hand, Christian schools have often uncritically appropriated the dominant paradigms for schooling—rigid curriculum parsed into discrete knowledge domains contained in fifty-minute chunks, top-down models of transmitting educational content (teacher talks, students listen), standardized testing as primary means to assess learning, and valuing efficiency above exploration, imagination, and problem solving.

Faith Context	Nurturing Faith through . . .
Congregations	Intergenerational Nurture
➤ Christian Schools	Integrative Nurture
Theological Education	Intentional Nurture

With its focus upon schooling Christians, the bulk of this chapter centers upon educational and theological considerations required to engage and promote effective school-based Christian education of primary and secondary students. This task is doubly complex. Not only must Christian school leaders negotiate the complex web of educational variables (curriculum, pedagogy, teaching, and so on) necessarily addressed by every school; they also must shape their educational considerations in light of particular theological convictions. After describing these considerations, the chapter examines one particular tradition of Reformed Christian schooling in the US as a study in what this process might look like when carefully unfolded and properly integrative of faith and educational practice. The chapter also briefly samples the broad and diverse range of possible Christian educational pathways beyond church-related schools, including public schooling and home schooling.

Theological, Social, and Cultural Impacts upon Christian Schooling

To speak of "Christian schooling" as if referring to a singular entity is already to oversimplify a complex, multifaceted reality. Not only does the schooling of Christians witness to widely diverse sets of practices and institutional settings throughout its history, present theological, social, and cultural forces only intensify this pluralism. This part names three factors that variously condition the educational efforts of Christian schooling.

1. Past and Present Associations of Schooling with the State

Presently, church (school) and state relations range from mutual support between state and largely Christian schools, careful separation between the entities (as in the US), to varying degrees of indifference or hostility between the two.

In some parts of Europe, including Great Britain and certain Scandinavian countries, for example, teaching about Christianity in government-funded public schools has long been the norm. Early on in the history of these countries, the church came to be understood as the religious wing of the crown and later the state. Where nation-states perceived themselves to be Christian, state-supported Christian schooling followed suit. The persistence of this pattern is surprising, considering that many of these same countries are nominally Christian at present. Perhaps as a concession to this reality and to growing non-Christian immigrant populations, teaching religion focuses more upon teaching about Christian doctrine and history and less upon spiritual discernment or active discipleship. In addition, where state-mandated religious education was once exclusively Christian, present curricula often feature studies of other great religious traditions in addition to Christianity.

The story in the US unfolded somewhat differently. Some groups of early European colonists (the Puritans, for example) brought with them to Massachusetts their esteem for Christian schooling as key to the life of faith.[1] This commitment spread westward with their descendants to places like Ohio, where Protestant Christian schooling was almost immediately incorporated into the new state's constitution.[2] Puritans and their descendants clearly believed that Christian religion was properly constitutive of public life; its purpose was to shape the polis Christianly. Elsewhere in the colonies and in the new republic, different flavors of Christianity shaped their respective publics differently. Quaker schools in Pennsylvania taught tolerance and resisted violence.[3] In Anglican-leaning South Carolina and Georgia, there was less fervor for schooling in general. Altogether, this original church/state pluralism prevented the founders not only from establishing one branch of Christianity as a national church but also from constructing a consensus theological expression of what would become common (public) schooling in the nineteenth century.[4]

2. Degrees of "in the World but Not of the World"

Christian schools also fall across a range of possible locations with respect to their relations with wider society. Christian fundamentalist schools often expressly commit themselves to inoculating students against worldly secular humanism and scientific overreach, forming them instead into biblical principles of holiness by way of obedience to biblical authority. Nineteenth-century members of the Roman Catholic Church (RCC), upon immigrating to the US, discovered their own "in but not of" flashpoint in the form of a predominantly Protestant culture, one that extended to the then emerging public schools. These schools proved to be Christian (not a problem for the RCC) but also heavily flavored by *Protestantism* (therein lay the rub). Ultimately, Catholicism founded its own parish church schools, a form of partial withdrawal from this too Protestant world, as a means to educate its young people into the distinct religious knowledge, practice, and ethos of the RCC.[5] Catholicism wasn't alone in the effort to preserve and transmit a distinctive religious identity. Some Protestant traditions also resisted the common schooling movement. For example, the Christian Reformed Church (CRC) founded parish schools in order to educate their young into the distinctives of their own faith. (More about the CRC below.)

3. Secularism and Postsecularism

As discussed in parts 1 and 2 of this book, secular epistemologies (ways of knowing), including empiricism and technical rationalism employed by schools, have come to dominate and even exclude other ways attuned to affective, imaginative, or bodily experiential knowledge. In addition, secularism by definition excludes the possibility of revelatory encounters with transcendence as a reliable way of knowing. As a result, what was initially Protestant Christian public schooling in the US became thoroughly secularized by the late twentieth century. Growing religious diversity within schools also contributed to the consignment not only of specific Christian convictions but also of considerations of transcendent mystery more generally to the null curriculum (what is not taught) in public schools. This curricular caveat rightly concerns Christian parents across the theological spectrum.

INFLUENCE OF PUBLIC EDUCATION

The influence of public education has affected education within Christian settings in a myriad of ways. Horace Mann (1796–1859) is considered the "Father of the public Common School era," which began in the mid-1830s and ended around 1900. As the first leader of the Board of Education in the state of Massachusetts, he argued for its establishment in order to discipline the unruly children of the nation into responsible, educated citizens. With regard to Christian education, Mann called for schools to be nonsectarian in nature; however, he clearly stated in his *Journal of the Common School* that Christian morals grounded the schools, that these morals were found in the Christian faith, and the Bible was welcome within the schools.

For the Christian educator, a pursuit of academic knowledge is born from a commitment to a Christian worldview, seeing all of creation through the lens of an accepted creator, who is sovereign and involved in the working out of the created order. There is a clear, linear purpose to knowledge, and it finds its roots in the Christian tradition. Humankind is part of a larger cosmic order, and there is a plan and a purpose in mind (Col. 1:12–23; Jer. 29:11). In contrast to this, the philosophical basis for public education does not necessarily hold this worldview, although Christian educators teaching within the public schools may. Other philosophies that undergird a public education rationale include an essential, or utilitarian, philosophy that states that education is for the purpose of creating citizens who can contribute to the working of society; a reconstructionist philosophy, which states that the purpose of education is to prepare individuals to critique and reconstruct society; or a perennialist philosophy, which is designed to promote the furtherance of a common core of academic knowledge that is passed down from generation to generation. These other philosophies can be incorporated into a Christian world-view, but the Christian perspective is not a part of the overarching philosophy.

A second issue where there is tension is the role of teaching Scripture. Early in its history, America had been a nation where the Bible and Christian theology and practices were commonly taught. In fact, many of the early reading texts were taken from Scripture passages, with the design that teaching a child to read and teaching scriptural, moral principles were done at the same time. Regardless of whether it was intentionally practiced or not, the Christian faith was accepted by most Americans as true. However, in recent decades, a commitment to Christian principles has been eschewed by the public school system, with the rationale that adherence to them would discriminate against children and families who hold to different religious traditions and faiths, or to none at all. In an effort to be as democratic as possible, public schools have sought to not teach about religion at all, resulting in most of the people of this nation not realizing the important and central role that faith has played in many of the academic subjects studied, such as history, English/language arts, biology and science, government, social sciences, mathematics, and philosophy.

A third issue is that of funding. Many Christian educators believe that if all citizens pay taxes, then they should also have the freedom to decide which schools their children will attend, thereby having the freedom to apply the funding to the schools of their choice. Others, however, believe that a democratic government should not fund faith-based schools, regardless of the faith being practiced, in order to adhere to the constitutional amendment calling for a separation of church and state.

LAURA BARWEGEN

At present, proponents of postsecularism argue, contrary to the claims of secularists, that religion and religiosity are not going away even in the Global North. In addition, in some cases, these accounts once again promote considerations for how and why education—even public education—ought to be religious if it is to be a complete education.[6] To be clear, this isn't a return to the mythological good old days that never were when schools in the US were "properly Christian." We've already noted how the vaguely Protestant "common schools" failed to earn the trust of many actual Christian constituencies. Postsecular educators do, however, claim that theological ideas ought to be invited to make their case alongside of scientific and philosophical ones even in nonreligious educational communities. This turn is already evident in "secular" universities, including some members of the prestigious Ivy League, where courses with titles like "Life Worth Living" are widely subscribed by students.[7] Typically a member of the theological faculty joins other nontheologians in teaching courses designed to invite students to imagine lives of flourishing for themselves and their communities. Christianity is not afforded pride of place in these curricular offerings, but its extraordinary reservoirs of wisdom for responding to questions of vocation and meaning are put on display in a positive light for all to consider.

Theological and Educational Considerations for Christian Schooling

Apart from the shared descriptor of "Christian," faith-based schools can be as different as individual congregations.[8] They are animated by a range of theological and educational commitments and practices. Insight into a school's history of beliefs and practices can assist its leaders in deepening and reforming its mission. To that end, tables 15 and 16 below depict differing theological and educational emphases.

Table 15. Differing Theological Orientations

	Juridical	Therapeutic
God	Judge/sovereign/ transcendent	Physician/relational/ immanent
Pre-fall humanity	Perfect/self-determined	Innocent/incomplete/ vulnerable to sin's power
Sin	Guilt/powerlessness/ inherited bondage/depravity	Infirmity/incomplete/ vulnerable to sin's power
Soteriology	Pardon for guilt	Healing/restoration/pro- gression towards *theōsis*
Grace	Imputed/imparted	Participatory/ response-able
Pneumatology	Impersonal power	Personal relational presence
Mission	Worship, witness	Eradication of sinful disease

The juridical orientation is so named because of its predominant metaphors for God (judge, sovereign ruler) and for its correlative vision of redemption as the just outcome of divine jurisprudence. In a judicial system, the judge must maintain impartiality, which requires separation from the accused. Justice must be rendered, and, if necessary, guilt punished. As readers readily detect, the logic of this paradigm requires that Jesus pay the just (if enormous) penalty for human sin through his death on the cross. Jesus's passion combined with his resurrection also restore human standing before and right relation with God. Human beings in this scenario are "at the mercy of the court." The condition of sin utterly destroys the divine image within. Humans cannot envision the good, much less do it. Only the Son can assuage their guilt, and only the Spirit proceeding from the Son can restore their lost image of God. Consequently, human beings redeemed by the divine judge take up the Christian life by displaying gratitude for divine mercy through worship and witness.

The therapeutic orientation aligns with its own primary metaphor for God (physician) and its related emphasis upon redemption as a process of divine healing. Like the juridical, this scenario depends upon divine initiative. Only God can heal the sin-sick soul or society. Unlike the juridical, however, the divine healer invites persons to participate in a small way in their restoration to wellness. They may take up therapeutic personal spiritual disciplines or work to eradicate the disease of sin in the world as avenues for the Spirit to perform its transforming work. This paradigm differs from the juridical in that it envisions the image of God in human beings as defaced or distorted but not totally lost. Humans may still, indeed must, take some response-ability in God's graced, saving mission. Humanity's fall from grace caused by sin, therefore, was less an inexplicably tragic reversal of original perfection than a happy fault that permits subsequent growth in grace. It further envisions this growth as a dimension of intimate relational partnership between humans, human communities, and the immanent Holy Spirit.

Each of these paradigms illuminates different dimensions of God's redemption in response to differing accounts of sin. While it may be the case that Protestants better recognize themselves in the juridical account while Catholic and Orthodox Christians lean toward the therapeutic, most Christian communities embrace a blend of these accounts along with others.

Table 16. *Differing Educational Orientations*

Educational Paradigm	Content-Centered	Learner-Centered
Educational goal	Mastery of transmitted knowledge	Construction of new knowledge
Learners	Passive recipients	Active participants
Curriculum	Subject matter as verified through revelation, reason, science, or historical investigation	Life as experienced
Pedagogy	Transmission	Discovery
Authority/truth	Resides in subject or teacher	Resides in learner

As is true for theology, education wrestles with its own tensions. These, too, play out across differing orientations, as noted in the chart above. They force educators, first, to reckon with the meaning of "knowledge" and its intent. Questions about knowledge that educational leaders should be asking themselves include the following: Is knowledge to be conceived as a giant server farm, full of data to be downloaded to the brain, or is it the capacity to manipulate information in order to solve problems or create something new? Ought knowing be confined to so-called intellectual capacities, or could we call purposeful bodily movement, as in dance and sports, or musicality, as with singing or playing an instrument, expressions of knowledge?[9] Does knowledge reside beyond persons, or is it to be drawn out from within them? Ought knowledge lead to deeper contemplation or prompt persons to action?

Second, and related to knowing, educators consider the nature of learners and learning. Are learners "sponges," passively absorbing any and all input, or agents of their own learning who choose to construct knowledge in light of their own experiences and in order to seek self-chosen ends? Are the content of and means to promote learning appropriate to all students, or ought they be tailored to suit individual gifts and needs?

Third, theories of knowing and learning drive considerations of curriculum and pedagogy. Should curriculum simply present predetermined subject matter, or should it invite wonder about possibilities? Are the best pedagogies ones that proceed by way of relation to learners' experiences, or does personal experience get in the way of learning important lessons?

In light of the considerations above, readers will concede that the educational tasks of formalized schooling are exceedingly complex. Perhaps this explains why schooling (in the US at least) perpetually frustrates school administrators, teachers, parents, and students themselves. It also suggests why schooling is repeatedly subjected to calls for reform. There's no single answer to any one of these questions and no end to the different possible configurations of answers to all the questions. Positively, the chart and the questions it raises help explain the emergence and continuing influence of varying configurations of schooling.

Below we describe examples of schooling illustrative of different possible positions across this educational spectrum. The specific focus is upon pedagogical strategies (how schools teach their curricular content), but, in the process, it demonstrates implications for the other educational dynamics, including the nature of knowledge, how learners learn, and what curriculum should be taught.

1. Direct Transmission

In her ethnography of fundamentalist Christian schooling, Susan Rose describes one high school strongly committed to transmitting its version of Christian educational content. The school purchases its curricular resources (and even its furniture!) from a for-profit educational corporation in Texas. Each student is expected to independently complete prepackaged assignments and pass proficiency tests before moving on to the next assignment. Tests assess student mastery of subject matter, not their ability to critically assess it or their capacity to use it toward constructing new knowledge.[10] The fundamentalist curriculum explains, for example, that energy and environmental crises are "myths . . . perpetuated by secular humanists"; it doesn't offer competing accounts of these issues, and nor does it invite students to offer critical responses out of their lived experience.[11] Overall, the school's educational intent is direct transmission of unambiguous educational content, which students are expected to master and then internalize uncritically. The school's educational authority and its construal of knowledge are not open to questioning. Doubtless, school leaders would declare that God as known through a particular reading of Scripture is the school's ultimate authority.

2. Indirect Transmission

This approach to education derives from the humanist tradition. Its proponents include Mortimer Adler, E. D. Hirsch, and others.[12] They seek to reclaim educational content for establishing a basis of shared cultural literacy in the US in order to sustain social cohesion. One educational method toward cultural literacy is the so-called Great Books curriculum. This curriculum has been adopted by a number of high schools and liberal arts undergraduate institutions, including Christian ones. The premise here is that students become educated to the extent that they are introduced to and learn to channel the best and brightest minds of human history. The curriculum emphasizes reading primary sources—what Augustine has to say for himself, for example—instead of what others have to say about his work. This approach is sometimes criticized as overly conservative because it seems to reassert the privilege of elite European male scholars who lived in the past. There's no compelling reason, however, that the canon of Great Books must be limited exclusively to dead White men. Only persons who have not yet read Simone de Beauvoir or Zora Neale Hurston could deny their place among history's most creative thinkers. A canon of great books may be amended or expanded to include a diversity of voices. A second criticism is the seeming overemphasis on content itself without due attention to student considerations of it. According to Yale educator Elliot Eisner, however, these critics misread this curriculum's intent. Instead of simply imbibing great thinking, this approach emphasizes constructing reasoned arguments about it. Eisner points out that student debate is crucial to developing a "critical understanding of the values and premises that underlie important works."[13] Students are to develop their own viewpoints by learning to garner and then deploy reasoned evidence in support of them.

Overall, this approach could be described as "indirect transmission." In contrast to the previous example, students are not expected to receive ideas passively and submit to them without question; they are encouraged to make sense of authors' claims and to argue over their merits. Students play an active interpretive role in their learning. They do not choose what to learn, however; that content is provided to them. Nor is the lived experience of students at the forefront.

3. Guided Discovery

A variety of educational examples that are best described as "guided discovery" may be found in the book *Ecoliterate: How Educators are Cultivating Emotional, Social, and Ecological Intelligence*.[14] In one case, faculty and students at a private day school in a small southern city became concerned about electric power generation as a contributor to climate change. After learning that the electricity for their community was produced at a coal-fired power plant, they decided to travel to the source of the plant's coal, which turned out to be a mine in southern Appalachia. Students and teachers toured coal-processing facilities and interviewed plant officials, local politicians, plus a variety of citizens, including both miners and persons actively opposed to mining. From all reports, students and faculty alike were deeply moved by what they experienced. Teachers then offered a series of problem-posing questions to assist students in reflecting upon what they encountered. Their questions included the following: What are the visible and less visible costs of this form of power generation? Who is responsible for it? How have your views on the matter become more complex as a result of our investigation? Without saying as much, they also mixed together questions from specific curricular domains, including math, history, science, and social studies: What economic policies continue to support and sustain coal-sourced power generation? What choices do residents of the places we visited have in this matter? How does the history of Appalachia influence present energy policy in our part of the country? What else do we need to learn in order to make sense of the problem? Finally, as is often the case with discovery-oriented curricula, students and teacher worked together toward solutions. The point, after all, is not merely to acquire information but also to solve problems. Students decided that it made the most sense in their context to implement low-tech energy conservation measures at their school.

We describe this curricular approach as "guided discovery" because while teachers play an important role in shaping the educational setting plus the goals and objectives for it (hence the *guided*), their learning goals for the students are more open-ended, less predetermined. They seek to empower students for their own learning and to cultivate their agency for active responses (hence the *discovery*). In addition to the students' experiences within the learning situation, their accumulating lived experience in the world plays a strong role in determining what exactly they will learn. This approach is also, therefore, more student centered. Curricular content is actively present and utilized, but it is deployed in the service of learners instead of learners being subject to it.

4. Free Discovery

Montessori education is a step closer to pure or free discovery. Named for its founder Maria Montessori, this way of education presumes that students, like all biological organisms, are driven toward development. Montessori's response was to shape the school as a rich learning environment designed to stimulate children's passionate pursuit of lived experience, including especially the development of their own gifts and interests.[15] Practically, that means less emphasis on abstract content and more occasions for touching, seeing, singing, painting, pretending, running, dancing, coloring, tasting, listening, and, yes, napping. Montessori schools are equipped with an abundance of balls, blocks, and modeling clay plus child-sized kitchens, garden tools, and musical instruments. (Books too!) There are fewer ordered rows of desks and more pillows spread out across the floor. Though we exaggerate a bit for effect, students are "turned loose" to explore their educational environment and therefore to experience and therefore to learn. In this case, the student is the primary subject matter. Teachers, instead of operating as drill masters, serve as encouragers, interpreters, and guides for students.

Notice, at this point, what a great distance we have traveled from (near) direct transmission to (almost) free discovery in these four models of formal education. At the extremes, the pedagogical approaches and also their convictions about educational goals, as well as their understandings of knowledge, learning, learners, and authority, could not be more different. Aspiring leaders of schools require critical insight into a school's educational philosophy and practice, because every approach, by emphasizing one or another educational value, deemphasizes or leaves out entirely some others. An exclusive emphasis upon transmission of content risks neglecting learners' lived experiences, their passions and interests, and their unique gifts. An exclusive focus upon learners can yield self-interested students who know little about the world and care less for anything beyond their own agendas. Obviously, this is why most (but not all) schools feature a blend of educational commitments and practices.

A Case Study in Deliberative Vision and Practice in Christian Schooling

By now readers may anticipate the double complexity of Christian schooling. In addition to the challenges of framing educational theory and practice, schools must also consider how differing theological orientations will impact their educational mission. Put positively, Christian schools ought to integrate educational orientations consistent with their theologies and vice versa.

The Christian Reformed Church in North America, a small denomination with Dutch European roots, has consistently demonstrated thoughtful vision and practice for Christian schooling.[16] From its inception, the CRC insisted upon the chartering of schools for educating the children of its congregations Christianly. Down to the present, a large percentage of CRC parents send their children to church-affiliated primary and secondary schools. In addition, Calvin University in Grand Rapids, Michigan, has become a hub for training teachers in CRC schools and for sustaining the important work of theological/ educational reflection that informs its approach to schooling.

In the book *A Vision with a Task: Christian Schooling for Responsive Discipleship*, the contributors powerfully display a CRC perspective that integrates theological vision and educational goals, means, and ends. The authors contend that vision is crucial for a school since, ideally, all of its educational undertakings will become forms of response to it. The authors propose their own vision for formal Christian education as "responsive discipleship."[17] It includes four dimensions. First, according to the authors, a Christian school should "educate for a life of worshipful kingdom service, for a life of God-imaging love, truth, and justice."[18] Second, cultivating student giftedness presumes that students are beloved creatures endowed by the Spirit with graced capacities to serve God and kingdom. Education, therefore, will both draw out student giftedness and pour in biblical and theological inheritance in order to properly orient those gifts. In addition, this blend of drawing out and pouring in requires clear and strong expectations from the teacher for student growth, while encouraging student agency for their own learning.[19] Third, "sharing joys and burdens" follows from Reformed theological convictions for covenantal regard and obligation. Christian schooling will prioritize community out of its convictions for human interdependence as God's means to promote human flourishing.[20] Fourth, with respect to shalom, the authors urge that the school itself seek to manifest kingdom justice, peace, joy and flourishing within its walls *and* that students be educated to work toward shalom throughout the created order.

These dimensions of discipleship are characterized as "responsive" in light of the Reformed conviction that Jesus Christ, the Word who graciously spoke creation into being, has also redeemed this creation through his passion and resurrection. Response in the form of living the kingdom way is possible because God in Christ has made it possible. In addition, redeemed creation is charged with God's grace. Educationally speaking, students may participate in this world as a means of response to God. Though sin remains a continuing distortive threat, in Christ creation may nonetheless be engaged as a reliable (even revelatory) source of truth, goodness, and beauty. Further, convinced of God's sovereignty over everything on heaven and earth, CRC educators subscribe to the idea that truth itself is capacious; it may include human scientific, philosophical, and artistic expressions in addition to specifically religious ones. Put more strongly, the CRC presumes that knowledge *begins* with God; therefore, *all* knowledge—even science—is fundamentally religious. In practical terms, to learn about and participate in traditional educational subject matter (language, math, science, etc.) may reliably contribute to deepened faith in God. Trust in God's sovereignty also means students may be educated to engage the world respectfully and lovingly without fear or apology. This Christological-creational theology of the CRC teaches students to be outward-facing.

This account has already begun to demonstrate in general terms what one intentional blending of theological and educational theory and practice may look like. In CRC schooling, Reformed theological emphasis—divine sovereignty, covenant community, redeemed creation—promotes "worldly" education, trusting that the world is an arena where God is working out divine purposes. Even so, CRC education maintains distinct reasons for participation in the world—ultimately to witness to and work for God's glory.

What about matters of curriculum and pedagogy? The CRC's middle-way theology yields similar patterns of concrete educational practices. To be sure, there is *content* to be *transmitted*—God's sovereign power and benevolent rule, the divine economy of salvation, the promise of covenant community, and the fulfillment of God's realm on earth in Christ by the power of the Spirit. To this end, courses in biblical and theological studies stand on their own, explicitly incorporated into school curricula as freestanding courses, but also included as important contributors in courses devoted to language, math, science, history, and so on. CRC educators recognize the limits of a content-only curriculum, however. Reliance upon a logical structure of knowledge and focus upon cognitive mastery of it must be balanced with aesthetic/religious invitations to "experience Christ" or experience creation "in its rich many-sidedness" in order to "evoke a response of praise, wonder, and worship."[21]

Therefore, the group of educators associated with *A Vision and a Task* also recommends that students not only learn about God's creation but also *experience* and *participate* in it (understanding and relating to other creatures, being immersed in the complexities of social orders, discovering how to shape just ones, exploring the vast diversity of cultural histories and products, etc.) as appropriate educational means. Specifically, the authors advocate integrative curricular units that draw students into active participation in their own learning. They encourage creative undertakings toward lived outcomes—assessing the viability of a frisbee golf course on school grounds and then constructing it, building a house in partnership with Habitat for Humanity, or producing a school musical. (We suspect they would be very open to Dan's proposed project described at the outset of this chapter.) While these projects draw upon discrete subject matter, their emphasis is on nurturing student creativity, problem solving, and agency—their "responsive discipleship," that is. This integral curriculum draws upon nearly all the ways of knowing as well—intellective, aesthetic, embodied, affective, rational, critical, and imaginative.

Traditionally, CRC education has sought to cultivate in its students a Christian worldview. They aim to instill awareness of God and God's redemptive purposes so that students' lives may be patterned in response to it. Again, to possess such a stance is to presume, first, that the world is worthy of Christian *viewing*. Contrary to some sectarian theologies born out of fear of the world (where, for example, the world is likened to a den of tree-hugging secular humanists), CRC theologizing encourages students to embrace the world but always with an eye to God's purpose and glory. Recently, some scholars studying CRC schooling have questioned the effectiveness of educating for a Christian worldview. James Smith observes that graduates of CRC institutions, while knowing Christian content, nevertheless pursue economic self-advantage, materialistic lifestyles, and high social status similar to their non-Christian peers. In the language of this book, in spite of Christian schooling, they tend toward Christian nominalism. This situation causes Smith to call for education attending to the formation of student *desires* rightly oriented to God and neighbor.[22] Others have taken note of the struggle of the CRC to racially integrate its schools and to make schooling affordable for low-income families.[23] These criticisms imply that CRC schooling has sometimes reproduced systemic sin instead of glorifying God. In short, CRC schools are both in and of the world in ways they intend and do not intend.

We chose to highlight schooling in the CRC because of its historic commitment to Christian education and the thoughtfulness with which it brings its own theological tradition to bear upon competent and faithful educational vision and practice. We regard these tasks of visioning and planning as essential and continuous for those who aspire to leadership roles in Christian schools. We also admire the CRC's willingness to sustain this difficult process over generations and even to air out failures publicly. Given the rapidity of cultural change and the persistence of sin, only sustained educational reform and renewal will be adequate to the task of schooling for faith's nurture.

Church in the Education of the Public

There are other proposals in addition to that of the CRC. Progressive Christian educators Seymour, Foster, and O'Gorman argued as early as the 1980s for the church to reassert itself in the education of the public. According to the authors, original efforts in Christian education in the US were catalyzed by missional service among the poor *and* by the assumption that education was to be undertaken so that Christianity could influence public life. At the turn of the twentieth century, the progressive religious-education movement seemed poised to deepen this public mission toward just social structures. Unfortunately, according to the authors, progressive Christian educators sometimes became enamored with "scientific" and "professional" educational innovations (specified learning objectives, graded curricula, teacher training, etc.) and focused their efforts upon educating persons already within the church while forfeiting the broader progressive vision for social reform. In short, progressive Christian education became, in their words, "domesticated."[24]

Although Seymour, Foster, and O'Gorman do not propose an institutional frame for housing their proposed Christian educational mission to the public, they do reclaim insights from early progressive religious educational leaders to fund their vision. With George Albert Coe, they maintain that "religious education is not a part of general education. It is the whole of which our so-called secular education is only a part or phase."[25] They also urge renewed attention to transcendence and to the "discernment and mediation of the sacred dimensions of reality," the absence of which has created a "void" in the public imagination.[26]

By the end of the twentieth century, the dreams of Seymour, Foster, and O'Gorman for the church to engage the public must have seemed quixotic at best. Religion seemingly eclipsed, secularism reigned in most forms of public schooling and had come to dominate mass culture. Efforts toward church co-operation in the religious education of the public failed or were discontinued due to lack of interest. Yet forty years later, religion, or at least awareness of transcendence, refuses to die. As postsecular educational philosopher David Lewin observes, educators have begun to acknowledge that "conviction and critique are not irreconcilable."[27] Lewin creatively proposes the biblical term *behold* as suggestive for an approach to nonsectarian public-engaging religious education. For Lewin, *behold* serves to gather students' attention and bears witness to something new, perhaps even revelatory. As a theological term, it connotes both "being held" (in love) and the students' need to see for themselves.[28] It suggests the importance of creating nonsectarian educational spaces for encounter with the primary or luminous experience from which persons' deepest convictions emerge. To be sure, proposals like this one for restoring religion and religious experience to public schooling aren't seeking the retrieval of Christendom, but they do rebuke the flat "no" with which secularism once denounced religion, and especially Christianity.

Whither Christians? Private, Public, or Home Schooling?

Parents, at least those with income to spare, face complex choices for the formal education of their children. While the chapter has considered most closely the theological convictions and educational dynamics that factor into Christian, and often church-related schooling, the majority of Christians in the US send their children to public schools, while a minority opt for home schooling.

Public schooling is the only option for some families. Private schools often charge steep tuition rates, thereby shrinking their applicant pools. Nor should readers assume that public schools represent education of the last resort for Christian families. Christian commitments to social justice and diversely inclusive communities may prompt parents to send their children to public schools as a first choice. This book has repeatedly commended entering into community with persons who see and live in the world differently from ourselves as critical for nurturing faith at present.

At the same time, it is important to acknowledge that not every public school realizes these ideals of diverse inclusion. Poor students often are confined to underfunded, underachieving schools and school systems, while students in more prosperous communities realize the advantages of extra economic and human capital deployed to their educational benefit. More than one person of faith has prophetically called Christians to support public schooling no matter where their own children go to school. Says Nicole Baker Fulgham, director of The Expectations Project, "When you realize that half of the kids in low-income communities don't graduate from high school, . . . we have to ask ourselves as a nation, as people of faith, do we believe in a God that somehow just gave academic and intellectual potential to kids with more money or kids who are not black or brown?" She continues, "From a purely moral standpoint, that's an injustice that we as people of faith should be acting to eliminate."[29] Political scientist Ted Williams III agrees with Baker Fulgham and goes on to say, "the opportunity for Christians to serve their communities through its public schools could not be greater." He champions the adoption of nearby public schools by local congregations whose members can contribute skills for tutoring, mentoring, and fundraising. He believes these relationships will then move Christians to take on systemic issues like inequitable funding across school systems. Interestingly, Williams advocates for public schooling while acknowledging that his own children attended Christian schools. He is aware that parents choosing to send their children to Christian schools face a double economic burden—the cost of private tuition plus taxation to fund public schools—yet he does not shrink from either obligation.[30]

HOME SCHOOLING

Home schooling is an alternative to parochial, private, or public schooling. The home school movement is representative of an extensive social dynamic of families (primarily in Western contexts) who believe that education of children is the ultimate responsibility of parents. The movement became prevalent during the last quarter of the twentieth century (predominantly with younger children) and did so in a manner that was unexpected. Parents separated themselves from generations of customs and laws to provide education to their children in their own homes, which, of course, does have biblical foundation (Deut. 6:4–9; Prov. 1:8–9; Eph. 6:4); those traditions were primarily the result of child-labor laws and societal changes that placed more children in schools. When the home school movement began, many of those who chose this educational alternative were reacting against public school curricula and environments. Consequently, as students entered their high school years and academic demands became more costly and rigorous, parents would often transfer their children to formal schools. The classical education model greatly helped to resolve this initial deficiency. In the early 1980s, there were approximately twenty thousand home school students in the United States, and current estimates by the National Center for Education Statistics factor some 1.5 million. Home schooling has increased in other countries, such as Australia, India, and the United Kingdom.

One foundation for modern home schooling was Dr. Raymond Moore and his wife Dorothy, who are often regarded as the grandparents of the movement. The Moores published *Better Late Than Early: A New Approach to Your Child's Education* in 1972, in which they expressed the philosophy that children learned more effectively when they were developmentally prepared. They directly opposed the perspective of public schooling by contending how it is better for younger children to be educated at home in an environment of love and support. Another formative basis for home schooling was the work of British educator Charlotte Mason, which was revitalized by the publication of Susan Schaeffer Macaulay's book *For the Children's Sake: Foundations of Education for the Home and School* (1984). Moore and Mason understood home schooling as an opportunity for Christian expression. Others, such as agrarian theorist Ralph Borsodi in his *Flight from the City* (1933) and educator John Holt (who established the *Growing without Schooling* magazine in August 1977), argued secularly for home schooling. Holt published *Instead of Education* (1976) to encourage parents to abandon any efforts toward reforming the public education system and promoted the notion of "unschooling."

Home schooling represents a historic effort to maintain family intimacy and to recover the role of parents in the education of their children. Families have regained a common purpose and work through home schooling and have become healthier as a result (as evident in the fact that homeschooling families tend to have twice as many children as other families, and they are less likely to be affected by divorce). Home schooling has also resulted in reclaiming and updating classical education.

RON J. BIGALKE

Many other Christian parents decide to school their children at home.[31] As with other decisions about schooling, parents cite diverse reasons for this choice. Goaded by the religious right in the US, some homeschooling parents fear the prospect of secular education and refuse to risk the spiritual vitality of their children by exposing them to what they perceive to be a godless or even evil environment. Theological problematics aside (Is there any space that God does not inhabit?), these parents rightly intuit that spending six to ten hours a day for thirty-something weeks a year over twelve years *in school* will be a deeply formative process. Even so, this attitude seems not to acknowledge the many Christian teachers and administrators serving in public schools, not to mention the strong proportion of students of faith who attend them or the proliferation of biblical courses and Christian fellowship groups within public-school systems. Other homeschooling families are motivated less by fear and more out of the conviction that God has called them to this educational task and given them the gifts to do it well. Sometimes naming special educational challenges their children face, they say, first, "no one knows my child's needs better than I," and, second, "schools as bureaucratic institutions are not always well suited to meet those needs." In addition, some homeschooling parents report enjoying putting their own education to work as teachers; plus, they appreciate the freedom to inculcate God's stories of grace and love into their children's education and to explore the theological implications of their children's learning. Home schooling also typically consumes fewer hours in a day than traditional schooling, thereby freeing children to play, pursue special interests, or contribute to the good of the household. Even as parents frequently sacrifice earned income to homeschool their children, they may in the case of larger families offset the loss of earned income by saving tuition money otherwise owed to a private Christian school. Homeschooling parents also seek to attend to their children's social development. An array of sports and social clubs for homeschooled children has sprouted up to address those needs.

Here a cautionary note sounded throughout this book bears repeating once again. To the extent that home schooling or any form of schooling shields learners from repeated, constructive encounters with persons and cultures different from their own as represented by diverse students and teachers bearing diverse upbringings and attitudes, that condition will negatively impact faith formation in the twenty-first century. In addition, to the extent that home schooling in the US continues to be a White, middle-class phenomenon, this withdrawal from the world could diminish or derail the very Christian motivations for pursuing it in the first place. If not at home, every effort should be made through church or extracurriculars to cultivate in homeschooled children friendships across cultural and racial lines.

Conclusion

Effective formal schooling, while always an educational aspiration, often makes only fleeting appearances in real life. Effective *and* faithful education is perhaps even more difficult to realize. It requires vision, educational expertise, and practical theological wisdom for integrating faith and practice. These same attributes make it a rich endeavor, one that could easily constitute a life's vocation. We deeply admire those teachers and administrators who balance wise reflection upon educational vision and practice with creative artistry for shaping learning communities where learners are celebrated and encouraged. This same practical wisdom is requisite for theological education, the training and formation of pastors and church workers. This is the subject we turn to next.

Interactive Dialogue

1. Was your secondary schooling oriented more toward mastering content or solving problems? How did you regard it then? What are its lasting formative impacts upon you today?
2. Which theological motifs and blend of educational theory and practice would be most important in developing an approach to educating oppressed or marginalized students?[32]
3. Construct your own animating vision for formal Christian schooling.
4. Discuss what would be required of a Christian secondary school (administration, faculty, students) to implement Dan's proposal (see road map) as an educational undertaking.

For Further Reading

Dewey, John. *Experience and Education.* New York: Touchstone, 1938.

Eisner, Elliot W. *The Educational Imagination: On the Design and Evaluation of School Programs.* 3rd ed. Upper Saddle River, NJ: Pearson Education, 2002.

Hirsch, E. D. *The New Dictionary of Cultural Literacy: What Every American Needs to Know.* New York: Houghton Mifflin, 2002.

Montessori, Maria. *The Montessori Method.* Radford, VA: Wilder, 2008.

Stronks, Gloria Goris, and Doug Blomberg, eds. *A Vision with a Task: Christian Schooling for Responsive Discipleship.* Grand Rapids: Baker, 1993.

CHAPTER SIXTEEN

Nurturing Intentional Faith through Theological Education

Theology, to be Christian, is by definition practical. Either it serves the formation of the church or it is trivial and inconsequential.

—STANLEY HAUERWAS AND WILL WILLIMON

What other vocation is entrusted with the witness to God's self-disclosure and the task of awakening appropriate responses to it? Because of the momentousness of the task . . . we do ourselves injury by not having thought deeply about the nature of ministry.

—THOMAS C. ODEN

ROAD MAP

Nurturing faith occurs not only in congregations or faith-based day schools but also in the more formal arena of theological schools. While training for ministry is conveyed in an array of classroom courses, spiritual formation is also a critical element of this brand of learning. This chapter assists those involved in administering and teaching in theological schools in understanding the role of possessing a sound educational philosophy, educational principles, and educational practice. A robust literature exists to ground us, including H. Richard Niebuhr's *The Purpose of the Church and Its Ministry* (1956), H. Richard Niebuhr, Daniel Day Williams, and James Gustafson's *The Advancement of Theological Education* (1957), Edward Farley's *The Fragility of Knowledge* (1988), and Charles R. Foster, Lisa Dahill, Lawrence A. Goleman, and Barbara Wang Tolentino's *Educating Clergy* (2006).[1] In this literature, one would discover an expansive discussion of the relationship of belief and practice in a theological education that would generally have reinforced while expanding their own vision of nurturing the faith of future leaders in the churches.

Introduction

Mark had the pleasure of speaking to about a dozen academic deans and presidents of theological schools, who had come to study and decompress for a semester at the Centre for Theological Education. This creative opportunity for reinvigoration and new engagement was the brainchild of Dr. Graham Cheesman and held on the campus of Belfast Bible College (Dunmurry, Northern Ireland). One of the more fascinating discussions with this rather geographically, ethnically, and theologically diverse group of men and women revolved around the purpose of theological education and how it might best be conceived in formal and informal settings in the twenty-first-century postmodern world. We jointly concluded that too little time is spent thinking about the educational philosophy, psychology, and practices of theological education.[2] Let's start with the role of the professor and teaching.

Faith Context	Nurturing Faith through . . .
Congregations	Intergenerational Nurture
Christian Schools	Integrative Nurture
‣ Theological Education	Intentional Nurture

Conceiving the Craft of Professor in Theological Education

Any reflective professor wonders about his or her effectiveness as an educator: "Why do I do certain kinds of things and not others? What evidence about how people learn drives my teaching choices? How often do I do something because my professors did it?" I certainly ask such questions. I regularly remind myself that the teacher has not taught until the learner has learned. Teaching is a serious and important intellectual and creative work, an endeavor that benefits from careful observation and close analysis, from revision and refinement, as well as from dialogue with colleagues and the critique of peers.[3]

How is teaching excellence to be defined? Ken Bain, director of the Center for Teaching Excellence at New York University, asserts that outstanding teachers are those professors who achieve remarkable success in helping most of their students learn in ways that make a sustained, substantial, and positive influence on how those students think, act, and feel.[4]

In *What the Best College Teachers Do*,[5] Bain identifies six recurring features that mark the most effective higher education professors. The results emerge from a fifteen-year study of nearly one hundred college professors in a wide variety of fields and universities, and offers valuable answers for all tertiary educators, including theological educators.

The short synopsis is that it is not as much what professors *do* as what they *understand* specifically about learning. Lesson plans and lecture notes matter less than the special way professors comprehend the subject and value human learning. The bottom line is that instructors are successful only to the extent that they enable their students to learn.

The objective of this chapter is to describe the most effective practices for teaching and suggest correlations with the teaching task of the theological educator. The ultimate goal of this exercise is to coax professors in theological institutions to reconsider their innate and explicit conceptions of educational philosophy, psychology, and practice.

Best Practices for Teaching in Higher Education

Try this exercise over the next few courses: Ask students to name and describe the habits of the best teachers they have encountered in their higher education learning environments. As you listen to the students recall with fondness and appreciation, compare these observations with these best practices from Bain's important study.

Best Practice Number One

The best professors know their subject extremely well. They use their knowledge to develop techniques for grasping fundamental principles and organizing concepts that others can use to begin building their own understanding and abilities. The best teachers are active and accomplished scholars, artists, or scientists. They read, think, and write. They follow the important intellectual developments in their field. They sometimes explore related fields outside their own. They enable learners to construct not only understanding but also meaning and application. In other words, the most effective professors can do intellectually, physically, or emotionally what they expect from their students. They think metacognitively about their discipline—analyzing its nature and evaluating its quality.

Best Practice Number Two

The best professors create critical learning environments. These are learning cultures where people confront intriguing, beautiful, or important problems. The routine quest is exploring authentic tasks that challenge students to grapple with ideas, rethink their assumptions, and examine their mental models of reality. While teaching methods vary, these conditions are best fostered to the degree that learners feel a sense of control over their education; work collaboratively with others; believe that their work will be considered fairly and honestly; and try, fail, and receive feedback from expert learners in advance of and separate from any summative judgment of their effort.

Best Practice Number Three

The best professors prepare to teach as a serious intellectual endeavor. Lectures, discussion parts, problem-based sessions, and so forth are treated just as intellectually demanding and important as their research and scholarship. The best teachers begin with questions about student learning objectives rather than about what the teacher will do. In short, methods are used as a means to the end: student learning.[6]

Best Practice Number Four

The best professors have high expectations for their students. Simply put, the best teachers expect "more." And more often than not, high expectations yield high learning results. They favor learning objectives that embody the kind of thinking and acting expected for life. They expect but also stimulate high achievement.

Best Practice Number Five

The best professors value their students. With what can only be called simple decency, the best professors display openness, reflect a strong trust in students, believe that students want to learn, and they assume, until proven otherwise, that they can.[7]

Best Practice Number Six

The best professors evaluate their efforts. All the studied professors have some systematic program (some more elaborate than others) to assess their own professional growth and to make appropriate changes.[8] As with most involved in practice-oriented endeavors, those who are most effective for the long haul seem to be able to flex their approaches and orientations for maximum result.[9]

Theology and education need to go hand in hand; it is a necessity, not a luxury. But what can theological educators learn from these best practices?

Abraham Joshua Heschel puts the ultimate role of the professor in focus with this insight: "What we need more than anything else is not textbooks but text-people. It is the personality of the teacher which is the text that the students read; the text they will never forget."[10] Now let us move from the professor to consider what obstacles in theological education prevent professors from being as effective in teaching as they might be.

Prevailing Misperceptions of Educational Philosophy, Psychology, and Practice in Theological Education

Educational philosophy is the foundation from which our educational psychology springs. In other words, our most robustly held beliefs about the nature and purpose of education manifest themselves in how teaching and learning is fashioned. Furthermore, our most strongly held assertions about educational psychology invariably display themselves in educational practice. Educational practices are more observable, whereas educational psychology and educational philosophy must often be inferred. While practice is vital, it is determined by more fundamental suppositions, therefore making these even weightier. (See figure 6 below.) An imperative obligation is for theological educators to plumb the depths of our most vigorously held beliefs about our inimitable brand of education.

Three prevailing and fundamental misperceptions beleaguer the landscape of theological education, and theological educators may be conspicuously culpable. These obstacles, it is posited (perhaps controversially we admit), are a flawed grasp of *educational philosophy* that caters more to knowledge than thinking; a confused notion of *educational psychology* that promotes teaching over learning; and a rickety impulse of *educational practice* that promotes the nature of theology more as academic rather than ministerial.

Educational Philosophy: The Role of Knowledge and Thinking in Theological Education

Every educational process has explicit and implicit assumptions about its purposes, methods, and intended outcomes for teaching and learning. Given the content and ultimate concerns of the theological disciplines, what are the most appropriate assumptions for those who are professors in the realm of theological education? Obviously, how a particular theological school or any particular professor answers this question then reveals an inherent educational philosophy, which in turo drives methods and outcomes.

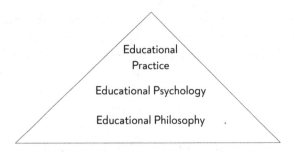

Figure 6. Foundational Elements of Developing Intentional Educational Design

Five "families" of educational philosophy inform educational practice. Whether formal or informal education, whether education with children, adolescents, or adults, whether public or private education, one of these five following families is at the heart of any educational mission:[11]

1. *Academic rationalism* has as its major goals acquiring knowledge and preserving heritage. The basic concept at the heart of this educational philosophy is *knowing*. Obtaining knowledge is the highest value.

2. The *development of cognitive processes* has as its major goals processing knowledge and applying information. The basic concept at the heart of this educational philosophy is *thinking*. Critique and analysis are the highest values.

3. *Curriculum as technology* has as its major goals mastering skills and training for tasks. The basic concept is *doing*. Proficiency at physical or social or moral or technical skills is the highest value.

4. *Personal relevance* has as its major goals seeking one's greatest interests and satisfying one's internal motivations. The basic concept is *being*. Realizing one's potential through the pursuit of self-selected learning is the highest value.

5. *Social reconstruction and social adaptation* has as its major goals addressing societal ills and meeting societal needs. The basic concept is *becoming*. Changing and adapting to society are the highest values.

The most pressing question is, of course, *Which one of these is the most appropriate educational philosophy for professors who teach theological education?* Should it primarily be knowing theological information, or knowing how to think theologically, or developing theological skills, or developing theological interests, or changing society based on theological principles?[12]

BEHAVIORISM

Secular behaviorism is a branch of psychology that states that behavior is influenced through systems of stimuli and responses. John B. Watson established behaviorism as a response to psychoanalytical theory, which explains behavior through an examination of thoughts, memories, and psychological crises. Instead, behaviorism is concerned with defining humans by their actions or responses. There are two subcategories of behaviorism:

- *Classical conditioning* occurs, according to Ivan Pavlov (1849–1936), when a formerly neutral stimulus is associated with an unconditioned stimulus to become a conditioned stimulus. A ringing bell is the identified neutral stimulus, which does not cause any response in the dog, until it is paired with the unconditioned stimulus of food, which causes the response of salivation. Now, instead of being neutral, the ringing bell has been conditioned to evoke the salivation response in the same manner as the food. Pavlov claimed that this conditions involuntary and emotional or physiological responses.
- *Operant Conditioning* is attributable to B. F. Skinner and is similar to classical conditioning, in that they both posit that human nature is conditioned by the environmental context and that there is a stimulus-response association that causes the conditioning. However, operant conditioning involves a choice, which is the response and which precedes the stimulus. According to Skinner, humans choose behaviors that are reinforced, or rewarded, and that move toward greater likelihood of survival or pleasure and avoid behaviors that are punished or harmful.

Early on, Christian response to behaviorism was strong and negative. The main concern was the apparent disregard that behaviorism had for the dignity of persons and claims that human nature is solely a result of the environmental contexts. A Christian perspective claimed identity was found in the very likeness of the Godhead (Gen. 1:27), as well as with a specific place in the created hierarchical order (Gen. 1:28–29). In addition, humankind has been redeemed by Jesus Christ with the promise of resurrection (1 Cor. 15) and reign with Christ (Rev. 20:6). Behaviorism, that humans are equal to the animals, negates the claim of Scripture. A second critique of behaviorism is its claim that humans develop in response to environmental stimuli, not, as Scripture states, in response to God's work within us. Throughout the New Testament, we are told that God himself offers the gift of the Spirit for those who will accept it and be filled (e.g., Luke 11:13; John 20:22; Acts 2:4). The Spirit itself provides the power for humans to grow into Christlikeness and have communion with the Father.

In the late 1970s and 1980s, however, behaviorism was reintroduced into the dialogue of Christian education and the Christian faith. Today, the conversation surrounding stimulus/response behavior and the existence and participation of the

Christian soul has been moved from the psychology field of behaviorism and into the developing psychological field of neuropsychology. Some of the questions that Christian educators must ask themselves are whether they see behavioral science applied throughout Scripture, such as in the rewards and punishments to the Israelites for following or not following the Lord, or the eternal reward of life everlasting for the acceptance of Jesus Christ as Lord and Savior, or the reward of the verbal praise "Well done, good and faithful servant" (Matt. 25:21).

LAURA BARWEGEN

Our view is that the development of cognitive processes is the most appropriate educational philosophy for theological education.[13] To be sure, there may be two or more other of these families that concurrently make a necessary contribution; no educational philosophy exists in isolation. And admittedly, all of these have some significance in theological education, but, in our view, our ability to think, to analyze, to critique, and then adapt to contextual practice is critical.[14]

Consider, for example, Jesus's educational intentions in the so-called Sermon on the Mount as a template for guiding how Christians should live as a faithful sojourner. So, yes, it is important that believers learn information about the kingdom of God; develop life skills for living in the kingdom; pursue motivating interests in the kingdom; and seek to alter society toward kingdom values. Nevertheless, it is perhaps more consequential to teach the faithful to learn principles that can be applied to changing societal conditions—that is, learning to think critically, to think theologically. The most desired educational result might be a changed society, but the most effective means to achieve that is fostered by an educational philosophy that nurtures theological thinking and application.[15]

As a theological education consultant, Mark is asked to evaluate courses, degree programs, and overall educational philosophy statements of theological schools in the United States and Europe. One of the most persistent imbalances he finds is the degree to which learning objectives, delivery systems, teaching methods, and learning assessments promote the knowledge-content without enough emphasis on critical thinking or cultural adaptation or ministry practice of that knowledge. Granted, the evaluation of cognitive knowledge is easiest to test through written examinations and essays, but the accumulation of knowledge is not the most desired product of theological education.

Professors who teach biblical studies know that such knowledge of academic vocabulary and textual languages is to be ultimately utilized in hermeneutical applications in preaching and teaching the principles of Scripture for Christian living. Professors who teach theological studies know that they lay a foundation of historical decisions and theoretical constructs that ultimately aims at informing the practical life of the church.[16] Neither of these pursuits—

biblical or theological study—is in and of itself the ultimate end but serves as a valuable but ultimately subservient means to another end, the faithful proclamation of the orthodox faith with contextual effectiveness in our modern circumstance. (See p. 370 below for a schema of the various subdisciplines contained in the "theological encyclopedia."[17] In the language of this graph, "ministry theology" contains the domain of "educational ministries" and our themes in this book regarding "nurturing faith.")

How do these sentiments align with the previously identified best practices of professors? (See table 17 on p. 361 below.) Our claim that the educational philosophy of development of cognitive processes (emphasizing thinking) is to be preferred over academic rationalism (emphasizing knowing) confirms Bain's best practice number two: the idea of creating critical learning environments. While it is vitally important that the best professors know their subject extremely well (best practice number one), they also understand this content-knowledge is best used as a means to an end, and not the end.

In sum, a flawed grasp of *educational philosophy* exists wherein professors of theological education cater more to the passive acquisition of content-knowledge over the more critical ability of teaching students to think theologically with an eye to applying the Christian faith and mission to the changing conditions of the world.[18]

CONE OF LEARNING

Edgar Dale (1900–1985) was born in rural North Dakota and later served as professor of education at Ohio State University (1929–1970). He made many contributions to the field of education and is sometimes referred to as the father of modern media in education. In 1946 he developed an icon that is still recognized among educators today. The premise of his theory represented in his Cone of Learning is that students tend to remember more by doing than by hearing. Actually, the original name for the cone developed by Dale was the Cone of Experience, focusing on the methodologies of teaching delivery and their effectiveness in retention. As seen in the figure that follows, Dale argues that the greatest retention (hence the large foundational base) is found in methodologies that include *saying* and *doing*.

The least retention (represented by the small peak of the pyramid) is found in simply hearing something read. His concluding assumption is that teachers who move from the passive to participative in their methodologies will experience a corresponding increase in retention among their students. Ironically, most traditional (and more frequently the default) teaching methods gravitate to the top of Dale's cone rather than the bottom where the retention is greater. Whereas expediency, budget, and context may limit the options in Dale's cone, the implication is that the lower levels of the cone are to be pursued by teachers who desire effective retention in teaching.

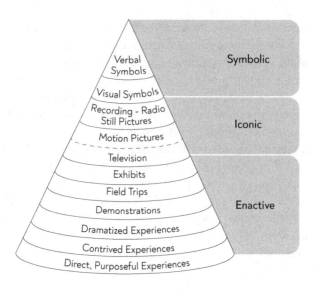

Figure 7. Cone of Learning

It is important to note what Dale's cone does not imply. First, it does not imply that teaching and learning *must* move from the bottom to the top of the cone. Second, there is no implied hierarchy of value in one level of the cone over the others. Third, there is no correlation between age and levels of the cone (i.e., older students do better with higher levels of the cone, and younger with lower levels of the cone). Fourth, simply using a video clip or field trip will not automatically cause the student to reach the goal of the lesson. Poorly done videos or ill-planned field trips may actually undermine the goals of the lesson.

A number of subsequent versions of Dale's cone have been created. Some of those have included percentages of retention listed with each level of the cone. Although these percentages would seem to empirically validate Dale's theory, those figures cannot be verified. Still, the theory seems to have pragmatic support.

Presuming the theory of Dale's cone, teachers would be wise to ask the following questions.

1. Where do most of my teaching methods lie on Dale's cone?
2. How can I begin to move my students' experience from symbolic to engaged?
3. What can I do to make learning more sensory (engage hearing, taste, touch, sight)?
4. When are students able to apply this lesson to real-life context?

LARRY H. LINDQUIST

Table 17. *Proposed Stance for Theological Education Correlated with Best Practices*

Educational Category	Proposed Theological Educational Stance	Best Practices for Teaching Theological Education
Educational philosophy	Critical thinking outlasts knowledge	Nurtures critical learning environment; knows subject well
Educational psychology	Learning trumps teaching	Values students; expects much from students
Educational practice	Theology must ultimately be practical	Prepares rigorously; conducts self-assessment

Educational Psychology: The Role of Teaching and Learning in Theological Education

What is the role of teaching and learning in theological education? How do professors best elicit learning? Barr and Tagg speak of the differing perspectives of an "instructional" model and a "learning" model.[19] The former is a fairly passive lecture-discussion format in which faculty talk and most students listen. This is a common scenario employed by many professors of theological education but is contrary to almost all research study on optimal settings and methods for student learning. The aim in the learning model is not so much to improve the quality of instruction—although that is not irrelevant—as it is to improve continuously the quality of learning for students. The learning model ends the lecture's privileged position, honoring in its place whatever approaches serve best to prompt learning of particular knowledge by particular students. We submit that the mission of neither theological schools nor their professors is merely instruction but rather that of producing learning with every student by whatever means work best.[20]

If professors of theological education acknowledge that learning must have preeminence in the educational arena, then specific knowledge of how students pursuing a theological education learn is an important endeavor.[21] In fact, we might argue that professors' awareness of adult learning theory ranks alongside knowledge of an academic discipline for maximal effect.[22] The case remains that whereas most professors of theological education are well qualified in their biblical or theological disciplines, many have not undertaken any formal study in adult learning theory. Unfortunately, some highly educated academics are at a loss to communicate that knowledge effectively to their clientele.

What principles can be gleaned from adult learning theory to engender greater learning in theological education? Most adult learning theory over the last quarter century quickly encounters the concept of *andragogy* (*andr-* meaning "man" and *agōgos* meaning "leading"), which is contrasted with pedagogy (*paid-* meaning "child"). In the minds of many within the adult education field, andragogy and Malcolm Knowles have become inextricably linked.[23]

For Knowles, andragogy is based on five crucial assumptions about the characteristics of adult learners that are different from the assumptions about child learners on which traditional pedagogy is premised:[24]

1. *Self-concept*: As we mature, our self-concept moves from one of being a dependent personality toward one of being a self-directed human being. (It should be noted, however, that this concept is culturally bound and arises out of a particular discourse about the self that is largely based on Western values for its expression.)

2. *Experience*: As we mature, we accumulate a growing reservoir of experience that becomes an increasing resource for learning. Thus follows the belief that adults learn more effectively through experiential techniques of education, such as discussion or problem solving.

3. *Readiness to learn*: As we mature, our readiness to learn becomes oriented increasingly to the developmental tasks of our social roles. The relevance of study becomes clearer as it is needed to carry out a particular task. Adults tend to learn things that are useful or interesting or because something fills us with awe, but educators should not underestimate just how much adults learn for the pleasure it brings.

4. *Orientation to learning*: As we mature, our time perspective changes from one of postponed application of knowledge to immediacy of application, and accordingly our orientation toward learning shifts from one of subject-centeredness to one of problem-centeredness. However, as Brookfield acknowledges, "Much of adults' most joyful and personally meaningful learning is undertaken with no specific goal in mind. It is unrelated to life tasks and instead represents a means by which adults can define themselves."[25]

5. *Motivation to learn*: As we mature, our motivation to learn is internal. This assumption, as Tennant purports, views adults' readiness to learn as "the result of the need to perform (externally imposed) social roles, and that adults have a problem-centered (utilitarian) approach to learning."[26]

Our contention is twofold: the most appropriate educational psychology tenets for theological education are (1) those that advocate learning and believe that theological institutions exist as places for ministerial learning and practice;[27] and (2) those that consider as vital the unique needs of adult learners, and elevate such needs over the top-down, passivity-inclined, learner-dependent models.[28]

How do these sentiments coalesce with the previously identified best practices of professors? Our notion that the educational-psychology stance based on learner outcomes is to be preferred over teaching outcomes confirms Bain's best practice number five, the emphasis on valuing students and their life circumstances. While it is vitally important that the best professors expect much from their students (best practice number four), they should also understand that theological learning is relevant for effective ministry preparation, experiential for enhancing ministry skills, and missional for creative participation in the ongoing restorative story of God.

Simply put, the most effective professors of theological education consider the motivations, life experiences, vocational urgency, and practical applications not only of the content taught but also the assignments given and the nature of the classroom environment.

CONSTRUCTIVISM

Constructivism is a learning theory rooted in the psychology of how humans learn, acquire knowledge, and make sense of the world. According to this theory, learners do not passively acquire knowledge or information; rather, the learner *constructs* knowledge. Given this perspective, teaching and learning methods that focus upon experiential learning, active learning, hands-on experiences, and learner-centered activities find support in constructivism. These methods are defended from the constructivist argument by noting that people learn most effectively when they do so by direct experience, engaging activities, reflection upon these experiences and activities, making sense of the experiences, and solving problems for themselves. Since constructivists perceive learning to be the process of an individual actively constructing knowledge, they tend to emphasize learning environments that require the learners to explore, experiment, and reflect.

While some refer to constructivism as a learning theory, scholars embrace it in on different levels. On the one side, radical constructivists assert that all truth is relative, and that it can be known only within an individual learner. As a result, this form of constructivism is sometimes rejected by Christian education scholars because of the implications for divine revelation and central truths of the Christian faith. At the same time, many embrace constructivism, acknowledging that truth exists outside the perception of the individual but that the individual still constructs a personal understanding of that truth, that people create new knowledge by building upon prior knowledge and experiences. This requires the learner be engaged, active, and reflective in the learning process. Because of these differences, some educators may refer to themselves as constructivist in pedagogy or methodology but not necessarily constructivist in philosophy.

BERNARD BULL

In sum, a confused notion of *educational psychology* exists to the degree that teaching takes precedence over learning for professors of theological education. Adult learners wish to take ownership of their theological education and learn in relevant, practice-oriented yet deeply grounded ways, ways that rhyme with the principles of adult learning theory. These forms of democratic and participatory experience are more likely to translate into both present and future meaning.[29]

It is, therefore, no wonder—in view of our conviction that some theological education professors and institutions execute ill-advised educational philosophies and educational psychologies—some educational practices are askew.

Educational Practice: The Nature of Theological Discourse in Theological Education

Many Christians today not only are uninformed about basic theology but even seem hostile to it. How has the notion of "theology" and "theologians" gotten a reputation of being boring, irrelevant, impractical, or ethereal? So, what is the purpose of theology in theological education and the mission of the church?

Christian theology is reflecting on and articulating the beliefs about God and the world that Christians share as followers of Jesus. By reflecting, Grenz and Olson claim,

> we use our minds to organize our thoughts and beliefs, bring them into coherence with one another by attempting to identify and expunge blatant contradictions, and make sure that there are good reasons for interpreting Christian faith in the way we do. Reflection, then, involves a certain amount of critical thinking—questioning the ways we think and why we believe and behave the way we do.[30]

So, theological reflection is an essential element of ministry and therefore extremely valued by laity and leaders in our church, right? Apparently not. Morgan reports a poll, funded by Murdock Charitable Trust, set out to discover US churchgoers' priorities when seeking a pastor. Both pastors and laypeople rated "theological knowledge" *last* out of five qualifications "most important for a good pastor," whereas seminary professors rank it first.[31]

The article further contends that theological education faces a crisis of confidence by churches.[32] It is a familiar tension between ivory-tower theory and leading-edge practicality not necessarily serving the church with the dexterity expected. While theological schools persist in graduating students conversant in Greek, Hebrew, and classical theology, they do not seem acculturated to ministry in a post-Christian world.[33]

Moreover, while churches may have lost a measure of confidence in theological schools, in recent years, these same schools have whispered concern over the higher percentage than expected of their alumni who seem not to be involved in ministerial roles within a very short time of launching into the profession, and they wonder why. Many reasons are possible, but what is the nature of discourse in theological education, and what should it be? And how do our educational practices affect theological learning for ministry preparation?

Grenz and Olson describe five types of theology (see figure 8):

1. *Folk theology* is unreflective believing based on blind faith. It rejects reflection because deep spiritual piety and intellectual reflection are considered antithetical to one another. Various Christian bumper stickers, choruses, clichés, and legends epitomize it. The chief characteristic of folk theology is its attachment of unquestioning belief to informal, unsubstantiated oral traditions and subjective feelings, and it refuses to measure them by any kind of grounds for believing. Folk theology is inadequate for most Christians; it encourages gullibility and simplistic answers to difficult dilemmas that arise from being followers in a secular world. This brand of thinking confuses "simple, childlike faith" with "simplistic and childish faith."[34]

2. *Lay theology* appears when ordinary Christians begin to question folk theology with its childish, simplistic clichés and legends. It arises when Christians dig into the resources of their faith, putting mind and heart together in a serious attempt to examine that faith. Lay theology may lack the sophisticated tools of logic, historical consciousness, and knowledge of biblical languages, but it seeks to bring Christian beliefs into a coherent whole by questioning unfounded traditions and expunging blatant contradictions.

Figure 8. *Grenz and Olson's Five Types of Theology*

3. *Ministerial theology* at its best uses tools ordinarily available only through some kind of formal course work—a working knowledge of biblical languages or at least an ability to use concordances, commentaries, and other printed helps; a historical perspective on the developments in theology through the ages; and keen systematic thinking that involves recognizing inconsistencies among beliefs and bringing beliefs into coherence with one another. But the ultimate purpose is to raise up those who are called to use their spiritual gifts to nurture congregations and parachurch organizations in order to continue the story and mission of God.

4. *Professional theology* attempts to raise students above folk and lay theology to ministerial theology by inculcating in them a critical consciousness that questions unfounded assumptions and beliefs. Professional theologians' main contribution lies in serving lay theologians and ministers, in teaching pastors in theological institutions, and writing books and articles to aid lay and ministerial theologians in their journeys of reflection.

5. *Academic theology* is a highly speculative, virtually philosophical theology aimed primarily at other theologians. It is often disconnected from the church and has little to do with concrete Christian living. While it is extremely reflective, it may cut off reflection from faith and merely seek understanding for its own sake.

What, then, should be the nature of discourse, given these categories of theology, for professors in theological education? We contend that folk and academic theology are of little consequence to the church. These brands of God-talk do nothing to advance faith but pervert the import of both faith and reason. Further, we vigorously protest that to the degree professors of theology intentionally or unintentionally promote shoddy or simplistic theological thinking, on the one hand, or purely philosophical speculation removed from the mission of God, on the other hand, it makes illegitimate the *raison d'être* for theological education.

Perhaps the real question to pursue as a guiding compass for theological education is, What is the deep need of the church? The answer is expertly informed leaders who know Scripture and can correctly interpret and adeptly apply it; culturally aware leaders who understand the mission of God and entreat the church to join in with the Spirit of God in the present world; and personally grounded leaders who handle troubled people and organizational difficulties that build communities of faith.

We, therefore, contend that the most important task of theological education is to single-mindedly advance ministerial theology.[35] What the church—and those who prepare for ministry in it—really needs is a grounded theological understanding of faith (the opposite of folk theology), while acknowledging that this is not its ultimate purpose (the goal of academic theology).[36] The ultimate purpose of grounded theology promotes maturity in faith, a kingdom perspective on life in the world, and motivation for continuing the mission of God to alienated people. These are the *real* needs of the church—to love, obey, and serve God faithfully with the mind as well as the heart.

The most appropriate educational practice for theological education should be to inculcate an inquisitive faith that is not afraid to explore the world of ideas (lay theology) in people in our churches; to develop the knowledge, perspectives, and competencies necessary to lead churches in faith and mission (ministerial theology); and to promote a vigorous and scholarly defense of the Christian faith to unbelievers and resources for reflection for nurturing faith of believers (professional theology).

How do these sentiments coalesce with the previously identified best practices of professors? Our position is that the most important educational practices of theological education must be focused on the intentional and rigorous preparation of ministry students as a serious and intellectually stimulating endeavor, which corresponds with Bain's best practice number three. Moreover, we submit that the most effective theological education professors will routinely and conscientiously conduct self-assessments of their roles as catalysts for student learning—that is to say, the preparation of ministry leaders, which attends to the proper purposes of their task.

In sum, a rickety impulse of *educational practice* exists to the degree it promotes the nature of theology more as folk or academic rather than ministerial. In cases where the former sort of theological education subsists, churches have every right to protest: "Forget formal theological education as it is practiced without regard to authentic service to the church; we will teach candidates for ministry what they need to know." This motivating concern then continually pushes theological education to be constantly reengineering its practices so that theological education and church practice are in sync.

Conclusion

The theological educators' three main tools are the biblical message, the theological heritage of the church, and contemporary culture. And within contemporary culture, we can make use of empirical research and the critical theory from various academic domains that inform professors of theological education in the most effective habits of their task. For the sake of excellence in theological education, an educational philosophy that promotes critical thinking over acquisition of knowledge is required. For the sake of quality in theological education, an educational psychology in which student learning and ministry competency trumps teaching is indispensable. For the sake of rightly prioritized theological education, educational practices that engage in ministerial theology are urgently needed for a church that will produce effective leaders for mission in the contemporary context.

Although its origins are dubious, the provocative aphorism "Christian education is neither" is one we appreciate.[37] We suppose a précis of the major argument of this essay could be similarly stated: "Theological education is neither"; it is not "theological" unless it considers the nature of its mission to be ultimately ministerial; and it is not "education" unless it takes seriously the learner as focal point of the process.

Interactive Dialogue

1. How have you experienced the six best practices of professors, as described in the opening part? How has classroom teaching/learning nurtured your faith?

2. The authors offered their choice among the five families of educational philosophy as a priority for theological education (namely, the development of cognitive processes). What do *you* think is the most appropriate educational philosophy for theological education? (If you are a seminary student, which does your school advocate, as implied by its culture, curriculum, and classrooms?)

3. How do you prioritize the relationship of *thinking* compared to *knowing*, *teaching* compared to *learning*, and *ministerial* theology compared to other types (in figure 8)?

4. What *is* and *ought to be* the relationship of theological education to the nature of the church, and nurturing faith?

For Further Reading

Banks, Robert J. *Reenvisioning Theological Education.* Grand Rapids: Eerdmans, 1999.

Brookfield, Stephen. *Developing Critical Thinkers: Challenging Adults to Explore Alternative Ways of Thinking and Acting.* San Francisco: Jossey-Bass, 1999.

Bruner, Jerome. *The Culture of Education*. Cambridge, MA: Harvard University Press, 1997.

Gonzalez, Justo L. *The History of Theological Education*. Nashville: Abingdon, 2015.

Grenz, Stanley J., and Roger E. Olson. *Who Needs Theology? An Invitation to the Study of God*. Downers Grove, IL: InterVarsity, 1994.

Hess, Mary E., and Stephen D. Brookfield. *Teaching Reflectively in Theological Contexts: Promises and Contradictions*. Malabar, FL: Krieger, 2008.

Jones, L. Gregory, and Stephanie Paulsell, eds. *The Scope of Our Art: The Vocation of the Theological Teacher*. Grand Rapids: Eerdmans, 2001.

Schuth, Katarina. *Seminaries, Theologates, and the Future of Church Ministry*. Collegeville, MN: Liturgical, 1999.

Shaw, Perry. *Transforming Theological Education*. Carlisle, UK: Langham Creative Projects, 2014.

Tennant, Mark. *Psychology and Adult Learning*. 2nd ed. London: Routledge, 2005.

Warford, Malcolm L., ed. *Practical Wisdom on Theological Teaching and Learning*. New York: Peter Lang, 2004.

Additional Resources

Theological Encyclopedia

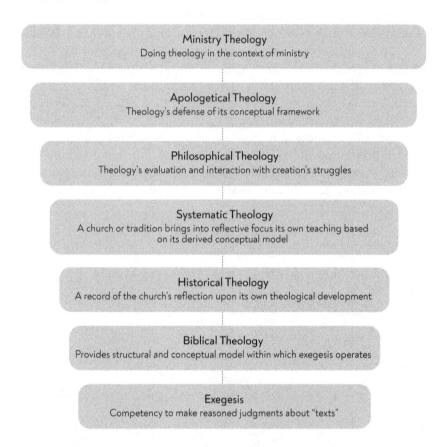

Ministry Theology
Doing theology in the context of ministry

Apologetical Theology
Theology's defense of its conceptual framework

Philosophical Theology
Theology's evaluation and interaction with creation's struggles

Systematic Theology
A church or tradition brings into reflective focus its own teaching based on its derived conceptual model

Historical Theology
A record of the church's reflection upon its own theological development

Biblical Theology
Provides structural and conceptual model within which exegesis operates

Exegesis
Competency to make reasoned judgments about "texts"

Self-Assessment Categories for Faculty Growth Plans

The following are categories from which faculty members should conduct a self-assessment as a starting place to develop a professional growth plan. These are categories that concern the work of a faculty member: (1) performance as a teacher, (2) scholarly and professional activity, and (3) institutional usefulness, with relevant subcategories of each major division.

    I.   Performance as a Teacher
        A.   Stimulates reflective thinking, an inquisitive attitude, and motivates learning through modeling.

    B.   Communicates an enthusiasm for the subject matter and teaching that encourages students.

    C.   Exhibits an unusual ability to relate the Christian faith to one's discipline and the learning process, providing institutional leadership in this regard.

    D.   Demonstrates unusual willingness to enhance the learning process beyond traditionally structured classes.

II.   Scholarly and Professional Activity and Attainment

    A.   Engages in extensive formal training in one's discipline.

    B.   Publishes scholarly works.

    C.   Presents papers at professional meetings.

    D.   Completes professional consultations and speaking assignments.

    E.   Fulfills leadership positions in professional organizations.

    F.   Receives special honors or recognition in one's disciplinary areas.

III.   Institutional Usefulness

    A.   Serves willingly as chair of committee, department, and division when called upon to do so by colleagues and the dean of faculty.

    B.   Shows unusual involvement with students outside the normal advising relationship.

    C.   Contributes to institutional development through the proposal of new programs and procedures.

    D.   Participates significantly in other institutional activities.

    E.   Sustains service in the larger community or church by completing special assignments.

Part Five

Conversations in Nurturing Faith

Marthe Cohn, as a young Jewish woman in the 1940s, risked her life as a member of the French Army's intelligence service to spy on Nazi troop movements during World War II. Later, when Cohn was in her nineties and living in the United States, she was asked by an interviewer whether she relied on her faith during her time as a spy. Her response? "When you live under such pressure you have no time to think about religion. You just do what you have to do to survive."[1]

Naturally, few of us have such harrowing experiences as Cohn's, yet her comment would appear to be the antithesis of what we might desire for readers of this book—namely, that difficult situations are not a time for thinking about one's faith. To have faith and to think about it and rely upon it would be *exactly* what we would wish.

In this final—and briefest—part of the book, we return once again (as we introduced in chapter 10) to *"thinking"* as an intentional strategy for nurturing faith. In this case, we are interested in critical and strategic thinking for shaping a process of faith formation. Thus, here we shall openly explore how leaders—clergy and laypersons—in churches and parachurch ministries around the globe should plan intelligently to nurture faith in adherents, at least as much as humanly possible, while still allowing, of course, for divine partnership.

To accomplish this exploration, part 5 is composed of just two chapters, followed by our rejoinder. In chapter 17 we lay our cards on the table and propose a teaching agenda for the global church in the twenty-first century. This is not merely to offer content but rather to unfold the means by which our teaching and learning are bound to have greatest impact for nurturing faith. Then, in chapter 18, we have asked six noted scholars to engage, test, and wrangle with our ideas for the sake of seasoned clarity in the sacred task of forming faith in and with children, youth, and adults. Indeed, all our previous chapters have led intentionally to culminate here in a purposeful plan to be adapted and contextualized for its faithful implementation in your faith community. This will require thinking, something that when done within the social dynamic of groups and committees can be challenging.

The renowned Irish playwright George Bernard Shaw (1856–1950) once quipped: "Two percent of the people think; three percent of the people think they think; and ninety-five percent of the people would rather die than think." Amusing, yes; true, debatable. In a similar vein, and likewise pulling no punches, noted Christian philosopher and spirituality author Dallas Willard (1935–2013) once surmised: "I know of no current denomination or local congregation that has a concrete plan and practice for teaching people to do 'all things whatsoever I have commanded you.' Very few even regard this as something we should actually try to do, and many think it to be simply impossible."[2]

Of course, Shaw's sentiment is satirical in its candid observation, but Willard's indictment is sobering. Both seem true, and both seem relevant for the state of the church's role in nurturing faith in much of the world. Lack of critical thought has long plagued local churches and parachurch organizations in their otherwise well-intended efforts to educate Christians.

Now we are quick to agree that "reason" is not the only way of knowing—certainly not. We freely declare an epistemological frame that values affect, aesthetics, the body, and habit as well. We agree with James Fowler, as an example, in his *Faith Development and Pastoral Care*, in which he argues that congregations usually display stage three faith (which does not make faith itself an object of reflection) and that this arrested development discourages those inclined to ask questions about it from doing so. We suppose we are reacting here to our displeasure with an incipient anti-intellectualist strain that persists in some quadrants of United States' Christianity. Perhaps this malady is learned from popular culture.

Consider the role of *thought* in contemporary culture. The myth of the advance of society due to undeterred technological and medical invention grows uncritically. Listen to political rhetoric, as an example. The *good-ness* of progress is not questioned. People assume those products and ideas that are outmoded are limiting and, conversely, that anything state-of-the-art is expedient and superior. The doctrine of *newness* promises a better experience, that life will be happier and easier. But the reality is that Westerners work *more* hours (not fewer) as each decade of "technological efficiency" passes; fewer contemporaries are happier, as evidenced by a multiplicity of measures—marriage/divorce statistics, job turnover ratios, financial indebtedness, mistrust of human institutions, and so forth.

Let's be honest, *thinking* about how best to nurture faith and make use of traditional practices has been a low priority. Reacting or replicating has been standard practice in many educational programs in the church, parachurch organizations, and mission agencies. Considering the effect of postmodernism on the Christian message, a number of strategies that nurture faith have emerged, but none has gained consensus—which is itself unsurprising given postmodernism's fear of totalizing discourse. The careful evaluation of how public education philosophy and practice influences Christian education has not been entertained evenly with intentionality, though we attempt to do it here. The enterprise of educating in faith should regularly consider what is taught and why, how, to whom, and under what conditions. Much of the reasoning and practice extant in our faith communities for educating in faith has long been forgotten. And so we do now what we have been doing because change is undesirable and thinking is difficult. Three sources would be well worth the reader pursuing in this vein: David White's chapter "Loving God with Your Mind" in *Practicing Discernment* and his chapter "Pedagogy for the Unimpressed" in *Awakening Youth Discipleship* are devoted to critical thinking as a faith-forming strategy for teens, and they offer strong insight on ways present culture distracts from thinking for that demographic.[3] For the rest of us, Nicholas Carr's *The Shallows* demonstrates how the internet is designed to fragment attention, thereby diminishing the capacity for sustained thought.[4]

Christians are *made*, not born. The "making" process of Christian initiation—or "christening," as some would say (notice the word "Christ" as the root)—is nothing less than the process of being (trans)formed into a new being. And it just does not happen without clear plotlines. Paul sketches the idea, urging us that we should be "admonishing and teaching everyone with all wisdom, so that we may present everyone fully mature in Christ" (Col. 1:28; see also Eph. 4:11–17; 1 Tim. 4:7; Heb. 5:14).

Festering cultural conditions—namely, the Babel-izing cry of postmodernism (a million voices unable to communicate with one another, where truth gets lost amid the chatter); the default mechanism of religious nominalism; the church's own tendency toward imperialism; and the wrong-headed notions of educationalism—must thus be considered in light of this all-important spiritual task. Can we think about the effect each of these has for nurturing faith in our own context? That much is owed, due to the importance of the end result—growth toward spiritual maturity or stalled in embryonic stages.

Uncritical engagement with societal conditions is responsible, at least in part, for the less than stellar reputation the church now has with popular culture and with its own members. This is one of the loudest themes in Diana Butler Bass's *Christianity after Religion: The End of Church and the Birth of a New Spiritual Awakening*. She wonders aloud whether the presence of discontent, doubt, disillusionment, and despair are indicators of the end of one phase of Christianity and the beginning of a transformation of faith. This untoward mood causes some to be bored and drop out because their (albeit misguided) understanding of the Christian way sees it as dull or perhaps simply just a rather lame "baptized version" of the same secular story, and others flee for their lives.[5]

Brown University professor William McLoughlin distinguishes between revivals and awakenings. And while revivals are typically individual religious renewals, awakening movements begin when old systems break down. Bass suggests that it is the latter that now may be at hand. This, of course, is the drumbeat of the so-called emerging church spokespeople, who offer a whole raft of literature to make this very case.

Perhaps something new is afoot. Some things need to change for the good. The reputation of the church in the postmodern world is more than tarnished—sometimes deservedly. For example, when Christians are in the news, it is usually because of something they have done wrong; they are planted on the wrong side of a cultural war or exposed for hypocrisy, or worse. What the world rarely gets to see is the grace that flows from the belief that we are all sinners in need of forgiveness.

Not long ago, readers may remember the tragic shooting of nine members of an African Methodist Episcopal Church in South Carolina by a White supremacist. The family members of those slain at the Charleston church bore witness to this central tenet of Christianity by saying to the killer: "We forgive you." This countercultural act of forgiveness did not go unnoticed. *National Review* writer Charles C. W. Cooke noted, "I am not a Christian, and I must say: This is a remarkable advertisement for Christianity."[6] Exactly! This is precisely the tack the church must take to gain a hearing in contemporary society. So, what must be our teaching agenda to nurture faith for the global church?

Part	Theme
1	Cultural Dynamics for Nurturing Faith
2	Criteria for Nurturing Faith
3	Colleagues in Nurturing Faith
4	Contexts for Nurturing Faith
5	**Conversations in Nurturing Faith**

    ➤ **A Teaching Agenda for Nurturing Faith for the Global Church (chapter 17)**
    ➤ **A Conversation among Practical Theologians (chapter 18)**
      1 Transformative Revelation (Percy)
      2 Interdependent Kinship (Wright)
      3 Resurrection Humility (Dykstra)
      4 Countercultural Faith (Oh)
      5 Kingdom Practices (DeGaynor)
      6 Probing Reflection (Groome)
Rejoinder and Epilogue (Edie and Lamport)

A Teaching Agenda for the Global Church
in a Postmodern World

The belief that all genuine education comes about through experience does not mean that all experiences are genuinely or equally educative.

—JOHN DEWEY

I know of no current denomination or local congregation that has a concrete plan and practice for teaching people to do "all things whatsoever I have commanded you." Very few even regard this as something we should actually try to do, and many think it to be simply impossible.

—DALLAS WILLARD

ROAD MAP

In part 1 we identified two major inhibitors of nurturing faith in the current cultural climate—the postmodern disavowal of absolute truth and a religious nominalism that normalizes belief without authentic commitment to the Christian faith. Here we develop further a theme introduced in part 1—*how concepts of schooling and education inhibit and inform the faith formation of Christians.* Descriptions of inconsequential noneducation, subversive miseducation, and transformational education will demonstrate how we stall or advance our efforts in churches and parachurch organizations to nurture faith. After all, the bottom line is that nurturing faith is an educative process that requires an intentional teaching agenda informed by sound theory and practice.

The Uniqueness of Christian Teaching and Faith

In the field of social psychology, the term *illusory superiority* is a cognitive bias whereby a person overestimates his or her own qualities and abilities in relation to the same qualities and abilities of other persons. As such, illusory superiority is one of many "positive illusions" relating to the self that are evident in the study of intelligence, the effective performance of tasks and tests, and the possession of desirable personal characteristics and personality traits. This undesirable condition seems to be a present reality across the educational spectrum.[1] Consider the following: Somewhat amusingly, research indicates that the percentage of teachers who rate themselves as "above average" to be a rather remarkable 94 percent! And the percentage of teachers who rate themselves in the "top quartile" is also an overconfident 68 percent.[2] Quite revealing indeed—a crystal-clear example of illusory superiority and a vivid indication that not all teachers know as much about their efforts and results as they think. Could a similar lack of insight be true of education in the faith?

While education and schooling in a general sense are related to the process of learning we discuss in this context of nurturing faith, these two types of education are dissimilar in critical ways. And our awareness of several distinguishing marks certainly differentiates Christian learning from other forms of learning. First, the *goal* is saving transformation, awareness of redemption as embodied in faithful personal and communal life before the triune God. Second, the *subject* matter is revelation as contained in or spoken through the divine Word who is Christ and who is known through Scripture and Christian tradition. This subject matter is always also a *matter of being*. For Christians, to know the content of God's revelation is important, but ultimately subservient to participating in (both receiving and sharing) divine love. Third, the *dynamics* of Christian education are guided by the Holy Spirit, who is called Teacher, and challenges, convicts, and empowers Christians to be transformed. These are not the hallmarks of classic or cultural education.

Nevertheless, a sound understanding of social science research and educational theory must guide our strategies for nurturing faith. Yes, a unity of theological content and contextual principles of educational theory and practice is a necessity for effective teaching, not an optional luxury. What obstacles may exist in Christian education that prevent teachers from being as effective as they might be?

To be effective also requires an understanding of what makes for *ineffective* Christian education. Specifically, it (1) misunderstands God and divine purposes; (2) misuses biblical content merely as historical data; (3) ignores a vital partnership with the home and family; (4) discounts the scope, sequence, and purpose of the curriculum materials; (5) maintains unbalanced interaction between biblical content, sharing interactions with the faith community, and meaningful engagement in service to the world; (6) fails to prepare students for life in the real world; (7) shields students from experiences in life involvement; and (8) miscalculates the dynamics of spiritual development. Much is at stake to avoid the ineffectiveness rampant in the other context of the educational enterprise, and great effort is incumbent upon those who will engage Christians in faith-shaping, reality-testing education.

Translating John Dewey into Our Faith-Nurturing Agenda

One non-Christian educator has been of immeasurable assistance in identifying educational ideas more in line with the very different agenda of nurturing (as opposed to mastering merely content about) faith. We speak of John Dewey (1859–1952), an American educational philosopher. Born in New England and raised in a theistic-believing home, he came to discount God.[3] Thomas Groome calls him one of the three most important educators of the twentieth century (along with Maria Montessori and Paulo Freire).

Dewey was critical of the standard way of educating, since schools were isolated from the struggle for a better life and dominated by medieval conceptions of learning. He argued that schools should be a genuine form of active community living, not a place set apart for the learning of lessons. He therefore devoted himself to fashioning an alternate form of schooling, one in which passivity, the mechanical massing of children, and uniformity of curriculum and method were replaced by activity, group participation, and adaptation to the needs of the student. He insisted on an interrelatedness of doing and knowing.

There are two ideas for the reader to hold in tension as we continue to pursue further consideration of Dewey's approach: first, it is the notion of the *interrelatedness of knowing and doing* that holds interest for us in nurturing faith; and second, *the goals of public education have unduly influenced the practice of education in the church.*

Central to applying what Dewey has to offer for those of us who wish to educate in faith is the relationship of knowledge, experience, relationships, and outcomes.

Education, says Dewey, must employ a progressive organization of subject matter in order that the understanding may illuminate the meaning and significance of contemporary life issues. Experience is educative only to the degree that it modifies the learner's outlook, attitude, and skill. Education, then, is historical and social, orderly and dynamic.

CURRICULUM

Curriculum has a Latin root that refers to "the course over which one runs" or journeys, which can include a planned route or a passage through life from birth to death to afterlife. For life's passage itself, God is the ultimate teacher, and all of creation is subject to revelation, formation, and learning across the life span and in community as disciples in lifelong learning.

For planned Christian education, curriculum can be defined more formally as the *content* made available to students and their actual learning experiences guided by a teacher. That *content* includes information, formation, and transformation for head, heart, and hand, impacting all of life. In other words, curriculum is the game plan for the practice of teaching. In exploring teaching and planning for it, the three phases of preparation, instruction, and evaluation need to factor into curricular thought and construction.

Preparation looms prominent in curricular planning and needs to be context-specific and addressed to particular persons involved in learning while teachers draw upon their Christian curricular and educational foundations. These foundations include Scripture, theology, philosophy, history, and the social sciences, along with a host of insights from diverse studies such as fine and applied arts, economics, political sciences, life sciences, physical sciences, systems theory, management theory, engineering, and even mathematics. From these wells, teachers creatively and critically draw key insights to organize their curricular plan honoring their particular perspective, voice, and gifts. Even with the use of a published or set curriculum, teachers need to adapt their plans to the persons and settings under their care. In preparation, teachers consider a wide range of methods, each of which has its strengths and weaknesses.

Instruction is suggestive of different plays or moves that teachers provide for order and ardor, for form and freedom in teaching relying upon the work of the Holy Spirit through prayer, attentive listening, and discernment in the process. In relation to teaching moves, the image or metaphor of dance emerges when teachers attempt to anticipate and respond to serendipitous elements not predicted in preparation.

Evaluation of curriculum and its actual implementation is highly emphasized in educational practice with a broad focus on assessment and outcomes. Such evaluation honors the need for accountability but may fail to honor those things not readily measurable in the actual use of a curriculum. The place of serendipity, surprise, and wonder is an essential part of an educational experience that allows room for the Holy Spirit in the practice of Christian education while teachers and learners sustain a teachable spirit honoring the place of continuity and change in the life of the Christian community and wider world.

ROBERT W. PAZMIÑO

Over the centuries, educational theorists continually debated whether motivation for learning was something engendered internally within a person or whether it was formed from the outside, shaped by external pressure. And Christian education has traditionally centered on the latter: teaching that explores bodies of knowledge, in a future-oriented framework, received by passive recipients, handed down from on high to others by teacher imposition.

One of the prevailing myths of Christian education is that it prepares the younger generations for the future. Unfortunately, this leads students—through the strategies employed in conveying this idea—to docility, passivity, and unconsidered obedience (or nominalism) rather than an active engagement that considers the relevance and importance of believing in *this place* and at *this time*.

We contend that this future emphasis is wrongheaded and lessens the urgency of the gospel. It also gives rise to these questions: How does teaching of any kind impose itself on the innate curiosity and freedom of the learner? What are the roles of the teacher and content and experience in Christian learning? How can the young (and old) become acquainted with the past—including the biblical record of God's self-revelation—in such a way that this acquaintance is a potent agent in appreciation of the living present?

Noneducation, Miseducation, and Education

Incentives for learning in the church are sometimes externally based or rewards oriented, which seem not to achieve the internal change sought in lasting faith formation. Since the mission of God is vibrant and dynamic and ultimately world shaking, one's truest thoughts about it should evoke thoughts of meaning and significance, not dread and dullness. So, what are educational factors that inform and inhibit faith? We shall discuss the latter first.

Three outcomes (the first two, unfavorable; the third, desirable) are normally the result of any educational attempt, whether it be formal or informal learning: *inconsequential noneducation, subversive miseducation, or transformational education*. These three conditions can be observed across the spectrum of church and parachurch attempts at Christian nurture. We cannot change what we do not acknowledge, so let's describe them.

Inconsequential Noneducation

The concept of schooling has been a part of the church's teaching because Jesus commanded to teach all the things he had taught to others. As a result, various approaches to this educative endeavor have emerged through the centuries.[4] Over the last two hundred years, many churches sponsored Sunday schools to partially achieve this mission, and—with varying results—some came to equate the mind-numbing tedium from their weekday school experiences with the corresponding schooling on Sundays. And it did not help that many of the same methods, including learning by rote, passivity, and discipline, mimicked public/secular schooling strategies.

Dewey is famous for his observation that all experiences are not necessarily educative. We argue, in fact, that many well-intended educational events are noneducative, accomplishing nothing of value toward the objective of nurturing faith. Any experience is noneducative when disconnected from one's previous experiences or from the life of the student, such that learning or growth is not realized. When Christian education results in nonexperiences, whether enjoyable or not, nothing takes hold, and the cause of fostering faith as a way of life goes nowhere.

Of course, the optimal condition for Christian education is to be educative, meaningful, engaging. Therefore, the task is to plan for and discriminate between experiences that are worthwhile and those that are not. Naturally we would prefer that all educational attempts result in valuable, appealing, and developmental learning, but some educators simply do not know what constitutes such learning—because of their own ineffective models of teaching and learning, the given environmental circumstances that limit effectiveness, or wrongly conceived notions about how faith is to be nurtured.

A palpable concern of the educator is with the situations in which learning may take place, which in turn depends on what is done by the educator and how (for example, significant are not only the words spoken but also the tone of voice used). In addition, educators must understand and appreciate the needs, life-development stages, and capacities of individual learners. Further, there is a need for education to see itself as an integral partner with other congregational ministries—worship, mission, and so forth.

The tenor of any educational atmosphere is reflected by how the necessary parties, namely, the teacher and student, are viewed in a given culture. Societies, as reflected in their governments and communities, may be more authoritarian or democratic. This is often correlated with the view of how the teacher and student is perceived—at a given point in a continuum between strict to egalitarian to permissive. Can anyone suitably dispute the belief that respectful, democratic social arrangements promote a better quality of human experience in learning the Christian faith? Are there any satisfactory or ethical arguments to be made whatever for coercion or manipulation in Christian education? Of course not.

Education is always navigating the time dimensions of relevance to past, present, and future. But the idea of using the present to prepare for the future contradicts itself. We always live at the time we live and not at some other time. The present affects the future. It is an unwise educational venture that sacrifices relevance in the present for a remote future. The educator has maximal responsibility for the quality of the present experiences of the learner. To reflect is to look back over what has been learned so as to extract meaning to present experiences. More to the point, nurturing faith means attention given to the *present* life and circumstances of the learner. When this element is overlooked, the irrelevance of Christian living can be wrongly mistaken for a faith that is either historic or future oriented. This is correlated with the issue of Christian vocational agency too. As noted in previous chapters, children and adolescents in our faith communities are more than merely Christians in training; the church requires their gifts for its present faithfulness.

Subversive Miseducation

Any experience is noneducative that has the effect of arresting or distorting growth in further experience. Experiences may be so disconnected from one another or from the life of the learner that learning (or growth) is not realized and may even stall completely. This is a problem, especially if we consider that faith is something that is never completely or perfectly obtained; it is something for which we must continually strive. Augustine says that God is love and that what we love when we love our God *is* God, and that when "nonbelievers" go off in search of other things, whether it be sublime things, like justice, or very low-down things, like satisfying lust and greed, they are really engaged in a more or less enlightened search for God, except they do not realize that it is God for whom they search.[5]

Miseducation (or even noneducative experiences) may even operate to leave a person arrested at a low level of development in a way that limits later capacity for growth. Experience simply does not just transpire inside a person; it has social and interactive dimensions. Consequently, every genuine experience must have an active side that works to change a person.

Of course, even unpleasant learning environments may produce experiences, but not good ones. Some educational attempts are of a wrong kind— rendering students callous to ideas and causing students to lose the impetus to learn. One consequence heard often of education experienced in the church is described by boredom, drudgery. So, we must be concerned with the *quality* of experiences.

Transformational Education

We return again to the Master Teacher and subject our grid of noneducation, miseducation, and education to Jesus's intentions and observed results. Jesus's teaching was largely incidental (albeit highly contextual)—coming in response to occurrences as he encountered them in his peripatetic life. Those men and women he encountered were often in crisis—physical or spiritual difficulty, or both—and as a result embraced new information toward resolving their predicaments. Jesus's teaching was enlightening because it intersected with people's lived experience and deepest hopes. Such a dynamic is the gateway to *transformational* education. Research related to transformative learning theory speaks of *disequilibrium* as a factor in change.[6] Cognitive dissonance or disequilibrium is caused when new information or experience cannot be easily integrated into one's current ways of knowing. It does not fit with what we have come to know. Cognitive stress with its information overloads or discourages learning and must be considered in the face of significant times of information intake. How is such disequilibrium encountered and resolved to evoke growth?

Brookfield describes the stages: *a trigger event* (which causes unease); *appraisal* (reflection on what is happening); *exploration* (for ways of coping or responding); *strategy testing* (to discover which new way works best); and *integration* (synthesis with other aspects of life).[7] This is the framework for transformational experiences—learning that ushers change, growth, and new experience.

What about a practical interactive exercise right here? Respond to this question: *Which of the following would best indicate to you that a student has learned the parable of the good Samaritan?* While you may be tempted to pick multiple responses, pick just one, and be ready to defend your response.

A.   The student memorizes and recites the entire parable word for word from your preferred translation.
B.   The student tells the parable in his or her own words.
C.   The student explains an example of someone being a "good Samaritan."
D.   The student decides to sit and have lunch with an outcast who is rumored to have AIDS.

So, what is your answer? One's response to this question is remarkably indicative of one's conscious or unconscious philosophy of education for Christian learning. The multiple-choice answers move from lower-order thinking and learning to higher-order thinking and learning. While there may be merit—to varying degrees of significance—to A, B, and C, ultimately, D, in our view, is preferred as the most effective means of nurturing faith. Yes, they may even build upon one another in the process of the student arriving at befriending an outcast, but ultimately Christian learning should promote action, change, and growth.

The fact is that transformational learning has checkpoints the student must encounter and progress through—normally in this sequenced order:

- Is the student paying *attention*?
- Can the student *comprehend* the teaching?[8]
- Does the student *believe* the teaching?
- Will the student *remember* the teaching?
- Will the student's *attitude* change to conform to the teaching?
- Will the student *act* differently?

The endgame of Christian teaching and learning is to evoke an action-oriented response.[9] It is easy to voice as a goal but much thornier to achieve it. Neuroscience explains that thinking is a process of activating synapses in the brain, while learning is a process of growing new neural networks between synapses.[10] Humans experience constant stimuli as we move through the day, and most information goes no further than sensory memory (within moments it is gone). To move to a sustainable level, information must first enter short-term or working memory, and it does this because of some reason that makes us pay attention.[11] But for information to transition from short-term to long-term memory, information must rise to the level of recollection based on need or relevance. Indeed, the entrance of information to one's long-term memory is often accompanied by actions, attitudes, and responses that are part of and also become a body of automatic, assimilated knowledge. This is the deep learning that alone nurtures faith in a meaningful way. Learning is a process of making new connections—both physical (between synapses) and metaphorical (between ideas or new information and existing knowledge). When a student encounters new information, he or she connects it with previous knowledge. Connecting new knowledge may invoke unlearning misinformation or misconception. Important then is the opportunity for testing this new information and, for Christians, living it in new practical ways.

JANE VELLA AND CURRICULUM PLANNING

Curriculum planning is a term that is used widely to refer to planning and implementing educational experiences for children and adults. Historically, there have been many models for curriculum planning, including Ralph Tyler's (1949) classic model that proposed a four-step planning process for any and all educational situations: determine the needs of the learners and the situation, design the learning event, organize and implement the plan, and evaluate the outcomes. Some, such as postmodernists and critical theorists, have challenged the notion of curriculum frameworks and indeed the purposes of education, noting that such frameworks and steps do not account for power imbalances in the learning situation or the context of the learning.

One of the more accessible frameworks for curriculum was proposed by Jane Vella (1994) in her book *Learning to Listen, Learning to Teach*. Building on her experience of education as a Maryknoll sister in international development contexts, and her immensely practical understanding of how to teach adults, she provided a set of twelve principles for learning. Though she prefers the word *planning* to *curriculum*, Vella's twelve principles are an amalgam of both the work of Tyler and of Malcolm Knowles.

Vella's first step in educational planning is to determine the needs of the learners through dialogue with them. The second (*creating safety* in the learning environment) and the third (*establishing sound relationships*) speak to the need to have respect between learners and teachers. The fourth principle, using *sequence and reinforcement*, is a reminder for educators to move from most simple to most complex ideas, and to constantly reinforce previous learning. The fifth principle, *praxis*, combines reflection with action and encourages learning by doing. Vella's sixth principle builds on earlier principles in stressing that learners need to play an integral role in *deciding* what happens in a learning event. The seventh principle, learning with *ideas, feelings, and actions*, suggests that educators take the whole person into account when teaching. The eighth principle stresses *immediacy* or teaching what people will find useful. The ninth highlights the importance of *dialogue* (not discussion) and mutual listening in a learning environment. The tenth principle (*teamwork*) and the eleventh (*active engagement* in learning) support working together with learners and helping them become fully engaged. The last principle, *accountability*, focuses on whether the learner has learned all he or she wanted or needed to know. The stress in each principle is on the learner and the learning environment and offers a practical and useful framework for Christian education. She reinforces the need to be learner-centered and to have an active, engaged learning environment. Her principles strengthen our insight into the need to work *with* learners when we plan and teach. Finally, she reminds us that with careful planning, Christian education can be a rewarding and engaging process.

LEONA M. ENGLISH

Learning, then, is more likely to occur if teachers pay more attention to how students *process* information. Consideration of how students learn will also be an informing factor in nurturing faith. For example, people have innate tendencies toward one of the following four preferred ways of learning: some are *visual* learners; others learn by *hearing*; some learn best by *reading*; still others by *doing*. These styles of learning enhance the quality and rapidity and depth of one's encounter with new knowledge and experiences. Similarly, teaching styles are ways that material is communicated by an individual or community.

These preferences—whether consciously displayed or not—should take into account students' tendencies for learning.

For some time, research on learning styles has emerged pertaining to several fronts, including that of cultural context.[12] Other factors also seem relevant for nurturing faith. For example, learning styles may also be influenced by gender.[13] The male brain tends to specificity in tasks and building systems around content; women tend to see multiple implications and the big picture. Men tend to go from theory to practice; women from practice to theory.[14]

Wisdom and Our Modest Proposal for a Teaching Agenda

Do you gauge the epigraph from Dallas Willard (at the top of the first page of this chapter) as haunting or fanciful or perhaps both of these? Even if more than a grain of truth resides in this statement, leaders and teachers in churches around the globe need discernment to know and enact the most effective strategies for nurturing faith. This, in a word, is *wisdom*. Wisdom is needed for leaders to know, will, and do what is right in creating Christian communities in which faith can be nurtured.

Walter Brueggemann, the eminent biblical scholar to whom we have earlier referred, proposes that *wisdom* comes to be the work of intelligently alert and restless people who will not settle for the easy, obvious, or conventional positions.[15] The teaching agenda of the global church in a postmodern world then prays for wisdom to set our agenda.

With that as our intended launching point, we propose several observations for leaders, teachers, missional strategists, and pastors attempting to nurture faith and the wisdom needed for theologically pragmatic decisions:

- While wisdom for nurturing faith is best derived in community, Berger and Luckmann nevertheless show that every community tends to make an easy move from *our way* to *the way*, thereby forming absolutes derived from experience.[16] But experiences, like programmatic fads, are intermittently reliable, and dogmatism should be avoided.
- As a result of persistent observation, one tends to generalize and concretize. Education in faith with children, adolescents, and adults is highly theological and does its best work when it coaxes discernment and patience and lives within contradictions and uncertainties and long-term hope (1 Cor. 13:12).
- Wisdom for nurturing faith may not be immediately apparent. Wisdom holds in tension a reasonable knowledge of the world and passionate trust in God: faith seeking understanding.[17]

- Wise decisions regarding nurturing faith normally have reflective, contemplative aspects that do not move quickly to clichés. Wisdom is mature and comes about through theologically informed reflection.
- There is a certain mystery about wisdom in nurturing faith, about moving from unknowing to knowing. And there is a patience involved as we wait for it and a respect for not knowing in the meantime. Therefore, wisdom concerns not speculation but obedience and ultimately ends in doxology (Prov. 3:5–8; 8:34–35).

Here, then, mustering the wisdom we have at this time, we offer these proposals for the global church.

Agenda Item #1: Nurturing Faith Prioritizes Formation over Education

The act of nurturing is messier and less easy to assess than the act of educating. The task of Christian educators is not merely to develop an individual's potential but rather to induct believers into the faith community. It is to give the skills, insights, words, stories, and rituals that pilgrims need to live this faith in a world that neither knows nor follows the one who is Truth. We are not content with life, with the limits that the present and the possible press upon us, but we strive and strain for something or other; we know not what.[18]

George Lindbeck compares emerging into the Christian way to learning a new language, a comprehensive way of living. We learn certain words, grammar, and syntax that enable us to say certain things and not to say others. The enculturation this language provides gives a new perspective on life and *forms* Christians into a particular person. The truth imbued in our personal stories, while imperfect and subjective, is powerful. Through socialization, people acquire a particular culture and are better able to sustain it within the wider society.[19]

Agenda Item #2: Nurturing Faith Stakes Its Concerted Effort on Identity Formation

In a pluralistic society, the predominant culture is more concerned with openness than identity; in fact, identity is sometimes forfeited for cultural compliance. Thus, one's family becomes extremely important, since the family is one of the few units left in our society that takes identity seriously. If the family fails—and sadly that is increasingly evident in Western culture—then the developing person is left at the mercy of other subcultures, who become familial surrogates. We are speaking of the nuclear family in this case. But while we agree that divorce or single-parenting are not ideal, ad hoc families—including, extended relations, fostering parenting, adoption, and baptismal families—can prove, in some cases, to be effective surrogates and as nurturing as biological parents.

Some Westerners exist in a society that is all about identity politics and, as a result, is fractured and bitterly divided.[20] We argue that one of the imperatives for Christians is not just to espouse a Christian identity over and against the world but also to be Christians *in* the world and *for* the world. Yet humans are historical beings who not only make history but are also made by history, products of the interactions of others—more than we like to admit. And so, what it means to be Christian is that we are a people who affirm that we have come to find our true destiny only by locating our lives within the story of God. This is the Christian's calling and *identity*.

Decisions not reinforced by the community tend to be short-lived, fads really. A Christianity without Christian formation is no match for the powerful social forces at work within our society. The Christian community makes it possible for a person to walk this path for the rest of life. Children and youth in our faith communities must be granted the gift to see themselves in a sort of apprentice-mentor relationship with older (or at least more mature) Christians, in which the young look over the shoulders of those who are attempting to be Christian in today's world. "The love of God is my north star, but it only provides me a starting point, not a finish, a first word, not a last. Everything depends on the follow-through, on facing up to this Augustinian question, '*What do I love when I love my God?*'"[21] We serve what we love.

Agenda Item #3: Nurturing Faith Rallies Its Forces toward Committed Discipleship

Being Christian is more like learning to paint or to dance than it is like having a personal experience or finding out something about oneself. It takes time, skill, and the wise guidance of a mentor. Discipleship implies discipline—forming one's life in congruence with the desires and directives of the Master. Formation implies the existence of an intentional, visible community made up of people who are willing to pay the price of community.

"Religious trust is a *deed*, something that demands our response, without pretense or dissemblance, that costs us our blood and our tears. . . . Otherwise it is a hollow bell, a tinkling cymbal, a lot of noise (1 Cor. 13:1)—or a list of propositions drawn up at a conference of well-fed theo-logicians."[22] Madeleine L'Engle claims that those who *believe* they believe in God but without passion in the heart and without anguish in the mind, without uncertainty, believe only in the *idea* of God and not in the being of God. Some less-than-reliable teachers or TV preachers, God bless them, tell us that faith must be "certain," otherwise it is waffling, and what good is that? By "certain" they do not mean transparent, for faith is through a glass darkly, not face to face (1 Cor. 13:12).

In a contested account, Austin Miles weaves a story of his troubled religious experience—moving from show business to ordination and traveling speaker in the Pentecostal tradition and Assembly of God denomination, with regular appearances and close friendships with Jim and Tammy Faye Bakker, to his loss of credentials, and then his faith.[23] He came from unbelief and was groomed, mentored, discipled, and educated to be a superstar in this wing of the Christian world. Observe in the following quotation the incommodious form his religious regimen took. (It is unsettling, to say the least.) As Miles began to be socialized into the Pentecostal tradition, he later reflects, laments, and accuses:

> Gradually, I stopped reasoning things out and stopped looking beneath the surface of events. Passively, I let my thoughts be programmed into that unquestioning, blind faith that the pastors carefully instill in the faithful as the only way to know God. That narrowing of my view, that closing of my mind, had become a vise that choked off free will and intelligent action. Instead, I let them fill my mind with stereotyped thoughts and falsified feelings. The displacement of my true thoughts and feelings produced a euphoric state and a sense of release from the evils, cares, and responsibilities of this world. It was like sweeping those things under the rug. There was no room to question or challenge: such thoughts were simply enemies of faith. The pastor to whom one would submit would always be there to assist, to guide, and to have the last word.[24]

These are tortured words. (Reread them.) Although they are melodramatic and make the point in fulsome exaggeration, clearly here our concern for nurturing faith in Christians is that a culture of learning must emerge in a way that emphasizes the very freedom that Miles gave up. Christians need freedom for active, engaging, critical thought rather than a passive acquiescence and mere acceptance.

The Latin poet Terence wrote that since what we wish for is impossible, we would have more peace if we sought only the possible.[25] Seems safe, but lacking mettle. To believe what seems highly credible, or even likely, requires a minimum of faith; whereas to believe what seems unbelievable, what seems impossible to believe, is really faith. (Pretend you are Mary hearing the angel's announcement [Luke 1:26–38]—unbelievable!) May our teaching agenda for the global church not settle for *only* the possible.

Interactive Dialogue

1. Describe a transformational-learning experience you have had that impacted your faith, and what transpired to foster this learning.
2. In light of the Dallas Willard quotation at the start of this chapter, if money were no object, what could your faith community do to incorporate the three agenda items (formation, identity, discipleship) into practice for nurturing faith in children, adolescents, and adults?
3. If you were to add a fourth agenda item for nurturing faith in the global church, what would it be? Why does it rise to the level of inclusion?

For Further Reading

Blair, Christine Eaton. *The Art of Teaching the Bible: A Practical Guide for Adults.* Louisville: Geneva, 2001.

Brookfield, Stephen D. *The Skillful Teacher: On Technique, Trust, and Responsiveness in the Classroom.* 2nd ed. San Francisco: Jossey-Bass, 2006.

Galindo, Israel. *The Craft of Christian Teaching: Essentials for Becoming a Very Good Teacher.* Elgin, IL: Judson, 1998.

Palmer, Parker J. *The Courage to Teach: Exploring the Inner Landscape of a Teacher's Life.* San Francisco: Jossey-Bass, 2007.

Smith, David I., and James K. A. Smith, eds. *Teaching and Christian Practices: Reshaping Faith and Learning.* Grand Rapids: Eerdmans, 2011.

CHAPTER EIGHTEEN

A Conversation among Practical Theologians

Do not try to make the Bible relevant. Its relevance is axiomatic. Do not defend God's word but testify to it. Trust the word. It is a ship loaded to the very limits of its capacity.

–DIETRICH BONHOEFFER

Faith is not safe. Faith is not faith all the way down, so that the gaps and crevices of faith are filled with more faith and it all makes for a perfect, continuous and well-rounded whole. Faith is always—and this is its condition—faith without faith, faith that needs to be sustained from moment to moment, from decision to decision, by the renewal, reinvention, and repetition of faith which is . . . continually exposed to discontinuity. Faith is always inhabited by unfaith, which is why the prayer in the New Testament makes such perfect sense, "Lord, I do believe, help me in my unbelief" (Mark 9:24). For my faith cannot be insulated from unbelief; it is co-constituted by unbelief, which is why faith is faith and not knowledge.

–JOHN D. CAPUTO

Let's remind ourselves of the roads we have traveled in this book. The concept of "faith" is of vital import for knowing God and cooperating with the global mission God intends. As a result, nurturing faith is the paramount educational mission of the global church. Yet several obstacles have served to lessen the effect of the church's efforts in this regard. We acknowledge the church's less than stellar record of preserving, defending, and championing human dignity evenly through the centuries; as a result, we concede that the church has been the cause, in some ways, of stunted faith. Impediments reside not only inside the church but also outside—such as the uncritical acceptance of modernity or postmodernity, and how it may seduce Christians to its version of truth. In addition, an odd brew of nominalism, nationalism, and traditionalism paint skewed images of authentic faith.

We have proposed a reasoned practical theology to inform theories and practices of nurturing faith in transcultural ways, which may be custom fitted to the global church. (See the chart below.) Our ways of thinking have been applied across the life span of children, adolescents, and adults, as well as preliminary endeavors in functional strategies for congregations, faith-based day schools, and theological education.

Here in this final part, we are attempting an experiment—to have six noted practical theologians reflect on, respond to, refine, and refute our ideas.[1] The perspectives of these scholars have no doubt been shaped to some degree by their own faith tradition: Elizabeth DeGaynor, Episcopal; Craig Dykstra, Presbyterian; Thomas Groome, originally from the Republic of Ireland, Roman Catholic; Kirsten Sonkyo Oh, United Methodist; Martyn Percy, Anglican from the United Kingdom; and Almeda Wright, American Baptist Church.

What follows, then, are six separate responses to our main theological propositions for nurturing faith (outlined in chapters 5–10). Each author has engaged with a specific chapter and presents here their own take on our ideas (see the chart below). Following these six pieces, we offer a rejoinder. Our hope is to further stir the pot and elicit new insight. Perhaps you will wish to interact as well with any of the concepts here, with a class or group.

Author	Related to Chapter ...	Encroaching Challenges to Nurturing Faith	Engaging Resources for Nurturing Faith	Exclusive Uniquenesses of Nurturing Faith	Extraordinary Gifts for Nurturing Faith
Martyn Percy	5	Disorienting amnesia	Meaningful commemorations	Penetrating scripture	Transformative hope
Almeda Wright	6	Autonomous determinism	Mutual disclosure	Interdependent kinship	Inspired trust
Craig Dykstra	7	Interpretive pluriformity	Generous humility	Resurrected image	Restorative grace
Kirsten Sonkyo Oh	8	Cultural constructionism	Intentional citizenship	Supernatural guidance	Countercultural faith
Elizabeth DeGaynor	9	Fragmented faith	Faithful gestures	Focused proclamation	Fortifying love
Thomas Groome	10	Conceptual bricolage	Probing reflection	Discerning community	Principled freedom

RESPONSE 1

Reflections on the Nature of Revelation and Religious Experience

Martyn Percy

I am grateful to Fred Edie and Mark Lamport for their measured and exquisite articulation of nurturing faith—and that it addresses the nature of revelation and religious experience. They are right to point out that Pentecostal influence, and the emphasis placed on religious experience by those in the charismatic movement, have done much to reshape our understanding of revelation during the twentieth and twenty-first centuries. They helpfully point out that although revelation has traditionally come through the normative fourfold mediation— of Scripture, tradition, reason, and experience—it is the last of these that has so significantly altered the landscape of Christian belief. So, in what follows, I want to push a little at the frontiers of their essay and expand a little on some of the issues that might flow from what they have both so ably articulated.

I recall hearing Bishop David Jenkins—an Oxford theologian who became a famously controversial Bishop of Durham (serving 1984–1994; he died in 2016)—preaching a sermon in which he said that God's revelation and our religious experience were *not* one hundred percent compelling. That is to say, God always left room for us to respond and wanted us to respond only in love, and not to be forced to do so. Consequently, God always left us space for alternative interpretations of divine action, which would include doubt—and even faithless rejection. God did not come to us in binding propositions, but in love. And because of that, education had to be rooted in love, and also left open for alternative horizons.

I have always warmed to this hesitant, nonhubristic Anglican vision for pedagogy, revelation, and religious experience, and I find it alive and well in these chapters from Lamport and Edie. It is implicit throughout their approach. Maurice Wiles's *God's Action in the World* also comes to mind.[1] Wiles's work is a kind classic Anglican apologia for the ways in which God works in the world. The approach taken by Edie and Lamport resonates richly with this tradition.

That said, we need to remember that all our religious experiences—a bit like those we have of love—are complex, nuanced, and balanced. They hover between conviction and circumspection, between belief and bafflement. We can handle them reductively if we wish. But humanity is always a sum greater than the parts. Poetry, mystery, and experience can ground us in conviction, but without giving us certainty. We cannot be sure, and yet we can somehow *know*. So nurturing faith, and theological education, becomes an important schooling in those spiritual senses that we may possess.

This is partly why I think that Edie and Lamport's insights are an invitation to develop an academic mind alongside some empathy for our spiritual sense. This form of practical theology—integral to any spiritual development—is, in other words, an invitation into risk-taking. One of those risks, clearly, is developing analysis that may cause us to doubt or reframe our original or foundational convictions and cherished spiritual experiences. But this is important work, for example, replacing hubris with humility, because it is too easy to deceive ourselves, spiritually. Revelations and religious experience do not leave us unchanged, unchallenged, or unjourneyed. So our minds will be expanded by the walk with God, and old ideas expended along the way. If we believe in revelation, then what we thought we understood yesterday might cause us to revisit our frameworks of knowledge in the future.

We also discover, in the process of entering into a dynamic relationship with revelation, that (to borrow a phrase from J. B. Phillips) our God is too small. Revelation and religious experiences enlarge our vision of God, and they can deepen our wisdom. So the imperative in faith is to cling on, but lightly, or to let go and trust. It is not to try and grasp, or so tightly clutch, that which was familiar and (hitherto) true, because God will always show us more. This is not to canvas an abandonment of orthodoxy for the uncharted waters of fathomless liberalism. Rather, it is to affirm and acknowledge that no Christian ever possesses all the truth or, indeed, very much of it. Rather, the truth possesses us.

Therefore, we are to walk humbly with God, knowing that the God who reveals himself in the things we find comforting and affirming also comes to us in the discomforting and disturbing—something the apostles Peter and Paul knew all about in their visions and revelations. God will not be bound by our constructions of orthodoxy. God will reveal himself both in and beyond our frames of reference. As Simone Weil famously remarked: "For it seemed to me certain, and I still think so . . . that one can never wrestle enough with God if one does so out of pure regard for the truth. Christ likes us to prefer truth to him because, before being Christ, he is truth. If one turns aside from him to go toward the truth, one will not go far before falling into his arms."[2]

All revelation and religious experience need to undergo an ongoing discernment though the development of our wisdom. And what better way to resource wisdom than through learning! The more we learn, the better we wrestle. And the better we wrestle, the more humble we become before the face of God, who alone is the source of true wisdom.

The story of revelation in the twentieth and twenty-first centuries is one of evolution. Just think about the weather, for a moment. God no longer sends the rain and sunshine. God does not make the weather, as the old Book of Common Prayer "Collect for Harvest" had it. But instead, we now pray for the wisdom and compassion to use this weather—and the harvest—well, and for good causes, and with gratitude. God no longer acts alone. Rather, God is at work through people, times, places—contexts and cultures—reconciling the world to himself through love and mercy. We are asked to join that work and foster it.

Moreover, our understanding of God, revelation, and religious experience over the last two centuries has been transformed by our collective experience of trauma, suffering, and evil. It was Bonhoeffer who said God loved us enough to see Christ pushed out of the world and onto the cross. In terms of the evil we experience, God usually meets us in weakness, compassion, and love—not in absolute power. Most people will know the so-called serenity prayer—or at least the first part of it. Very few, however, know that the original was written by Reinhold Niebuhr in the darkest days of the Second World War: "God, grant me grace to accept with serenity the things that cannot be changed; courage to change the things which should be changed; and the wisdom to know the difference. . . ." Rather fewer know the next part of the prayer, however. And this is a vital complement to the hope of transformation—in the wake of the revelation and experience of God that Edie and Lamport outline: "living one day at a time, enjoying one moment at a time, accepting hardship as a pathway to peace; and taking, as Jesus did, this sinful world as it is. Not as I would have it, but trusting that you will make all things right, if I but surrender to your will. So that I may be reasonably happy in this life; and supremely happy with you forever in the next."

Many soldiers were given this prayer as they left America for Europe, or indeed England for Normandy on D-Day. An Anglican understanding of revelation and religious experience is inherently humble and temperate. It can still say that God hears the prayer from the depths of the trenches, or the beaches of Normandy. Because God has become one of us—entered into our earth, our soil. Even to the extent that the Son of God lived in occupied, oppressed, and contested territory. He has loved us enough to live for us, as one of us, and among us. He is no stranger to our despair. He is *with us*; this is what Emmanuel means. He loves us where we are and walks with us in the valley of the shadow (Ps. 23); he is comfort in the dark and desolate places.

So, we are not spectators anymore, watching God in the distance. Or for that matter, subjects being watched by God from a distance, who makes occasional nonbinding interventions in human affairs and created order. Rather, in Christ, we are richly and inextricably bound up in God, who revealed himself in the form of a servant (Phil. 2). And the way forward to process God's revelation and our experience of that is to see this work as one of ongoing incarnation—the divine continuing to incorporate the human. God, in Christ, reconciling the world to himself.

God now works through you and me. This is how the hungry are to be fed; the naked to be clothed; the prisoner and the sick to be seen, heard, held, and healed. Just as Jesus is the body language of God in the Gospels, so are we, in this post-Acts phase of the church, to live. That makes me a confident Christian but also a cautious one. A rather ordinary one, actually. And it is a poem about an ordinary God that expresses the deep legacy that modern theology has placed upon us.

> "Do you believe in a God
> who can change the course of events
> on earth?"
> "No, just
> the ordinary one."
>
> A laugh,
> but not so stupid: events
> He does not, it seems, determine
> for the most part. Whether He could
> is not the point: it is not
> stupid to believe in
> a God who mostly abjures.
>
> The ordinary kind
> of God is what one believes in
> so implicitly that
> it is only with blushes or
> bravado one can declare,
> "I believe," caught as one is
> in the ambush of personal history, so
> harried, so distraught.

> The ordinary kind
> of undeceived believer
> expects no prompt reward
> from an ultimately faithful
> but meanwhile preoccupied landlord.[3]

Let me end on a scriptural note—an indecisive one drawn from the Gospels. Mark's Gospel begins very abruptly, and it ends in the same way. He concludes his narrative with these words: *ephobounto gar* in Greek, "for they were afraid" (16:8). What kind of conclusion is that to the greatest calling of all—to begin to preach and proclaim the resurrection of Jesus? The salvation of the world is now set in motion. But "they were afraid" hardly inspires confidence.

Yet as Eugene Peterson points out in his meditation on ministry, and through the lens of the book of Jonah in the Old Testament,[4] this word *gar* is transitional. No Greek writer would end a sentence with *gar*. It is a word that gets you ready for the next part of the sentence, except there isn't one. So Mark 16:8 is an end but not a very good one, which is why other later revisions of the text soon began to supply their own end, including the disciples running off, happily believing and rejoicing.

But I much prefer the original "cut." Mark finishes midsentence, I think, deliberately. *Gar* leaves us off balance, midstride. Where will the next step be? This is artful reticence; a conclusion is withheld from the disciples and the reader. It is up to us to say what happens next. In other words, the Christian faith cannot be wrapped up as a finished product. The frame is open, the picture not completed. As Peterson says, "write a resurrection conclusion with your own life." What will your next step be?

Ultimately, the assertions from Fred Edie and Mark Lamport leave us in a good place. It cannot be a place of certainty, for the very nature of religious experience, like that of love, is not a certainty.[5] However, love—rather like religious experience—is known through deep, blessed assurance. It is taken on trust and comes through faith. Such things are part of the mystery of humanity. But they are also, precisely, how God comes to us: love in, through, of, and for humanity. Such knowledge is wonderful. For any of this to be believed in, there will be some requirement for faith, facts, and feelings to be aligned. Such grounding is merely the basis for all deep, abiding human being, our relationality and communion with one another. It is also the grounding for our reception and perception of God—who dares to meet us in vulnerable love rather than binding power, and who, moreover, comes to us in the risk of our humanity, with all its frailty and suffering, so that we can come to know the presence and the love of such abiding divinity.

Kinship and Difference: Relationships Aren't Easy

Almeda M. Wright

Reflecting on theological anthropology, or what it means to be human considering the revelation of God, often pushes us toward discussions of our lowest common denominator. Often theological anthropology is only a discussion of the sinful and problematic nature of humanity. And while the authors include some of this in the chapter—from the opening vignette of the abusive father and husband, who also loved worship, to recounting many historical views of humanity, which reduce humans to one primary (and often negative) mode—they helpfully do not leave us there. They instead attempt to help readers articulate the ways that views of humankind as only rational or as "a bunch of animals" are too limited and should be supplemented (if not fully replaced) by exploring what humanity looks like when we focus on hearts, bodies, and minds.

Edie and Lamport open chapter 6, "Humanity, Embodiment and the Trust of Interdependent Kinship," with a quotation by Desmond Tutu: "My humanity is caught up, inextricably bound up, in yours. I am, because you are. To live this reality is to live the truth." This quotation points to a larger African philosophy of *ubuntu*, loosely translated as "the quality of being human" and expressed in the idea that "I am because you/we are." Reflecting on this quotation, the authors name relationality as a key element of humanity and one that is essential to our theological understandings. They force readers to wrestle with the significance of a focus on relationships for Christian formation, and to ask how does our theological anthropology, or even an understanding of *ubuntu*, and humans in relationship help us to imagine life together?

At its best, we hope that attention to relationships helps us respect our mutual interdependence and to become better friends, neighbors, and members of a shared earth. I say "at its best" because we cannot overlook the reality that our interconnectedness is a double-edged sword. Our mutuality reminds us that we can do immeasurable good when we work together. It also reminds us that careless and selfish acts can have lasting impacts on many beyond us, for generations. To be human in relationships does not mean that there is no sin/sinfulness or destruction. It simply means that we have a different entry point into the theological anthropology conversation and a different vision of what our lives together might be, in relationship with one another, with creation, and with God.

The authors lift our embodied and imaginative selves as correctives to views of humans as only or primarily rational. In support of this, toward the end of the chapter, they begin to outline how imagination is the vehicle of human relationality in Christian education. However, I was left to ponder several questions related to how we imagine life together. How does Christian education serve to push us toward better relationships with those like and unlike us? For example, no matter how much I want to move away from narratives of individual sinfulness or sin as fundamental to our human nature, even when I start from the place of humans as embodied, relational people, I find myself wrestling with the underside of relationships. I wrestle with scenarios of how things go horribly wrong because of the interconnectedness of humanity and society. Simply seeing our interconnectedness does not always remedy the impact or harm of centuries of exploitative relationships.

For example, my excitement about the turn to embodiment, relationships, and imagination in theological anthropology and faith development also comes with a caution to make sure that we continue to attend to the reality that these are not correctives that can be made without attention to histories of oppression and abuse. Take for instance some of the ways we engage categories of difference in what makes us human. The authors cite Richard Bondi's characteristics of humanity, in which the third element is "what [Bondi] calls the human 'subjection to the accidents of history.'" The authors go on to explain that these "accidents" can include gender, birth order, family, social location, race, and so on. If I am generous, I understand that Bondi is trying to convey that some things in our lives (that are essential and even controlling parts of our human nature and embodied selves) are beyond our control, but to call these "accidents of history" is offensive on one level (to be born female is not an accident or does not have the negative connotations that accident brings), and on another level, it removes responsibility for the creation of systems of oppression and participation in those systems. One's gender or race is not an accident, even if it is beyond one's control. Likewise, being oppressed or discriminated against because of one's gender or race is also not an accident; there are systems in place that sustain these. Furthermore, our work as religious educators must attend to these inherited (if not chosen) elements of humanity and our human relationships as well.

This chapter further pushed me to think through another dimension of religious education related to this caution to wrestle with the negative side of relationships (and to correct for the myriad injustices that have been wrought because we are interconnected). I was left wondering about how we nurture faith and relationships across lines of difference. The authors suggest story-linking as an example of imagining our lives together, considering God's revelation and history. As it is described by Wimberly and the authors, story-linking is an intragroup biblical reflection process where a group is asked to draw upon the resources of their shared faith and cultural community to begin to link their individual lives to the lives of their ancestors and faith exemplars to form creative responses to dilemmas or problems in their lives.[1] And while this can be expanded to larger contexts and possibilities, it does not explicitly help us to consider what happens when we think about how the Christian faith pushes us to connect across lines of differences.

In truth, most Christian education happens within culturally homogeneous contexts—even when we attempt to be intentionally inclusive or to utilize multicultural resources. However, until I read this chapter, I had not stopped to really wrestle with what happens when we must think about Christian education across lines of difference. I have always encouraged students to use story-linking in their own contexts (and have had to push some European American students to think more creatively when they attempted to say that they could not think of their own cultural story or when they simply wanted to draw upon the stories of others first and not necessarily on American histories or family histories), but I have not pushed them to apply it as an intergroup process (or to widen the realm of communal and cultural stories to include a much broader base of narratives).

However, my point here goes far beyond whether we can find common and shared stories to help us reflect on biblical and ethical truths. Instead, I am also pointing to the ways that we must constantly attend to moments when being in community may not be the easiest because the relationship is fraught with injustice, power imbalances, and distrust. The authors also employ Delores Williams's *Sisters in the Wilderness* as an example of the story-linking process. In this work, Williams connects the story of Hagar with the experiences of African American women who were enslaved, abused, and used as surrogates, but who also cultivated their own agency in relationship with God. But I had to also ask what happens if we continue to use the Hagar analogy, how does attention to relationality and even imagination help us in Christian formation contexts where some are more apt to see themselves in the actions of Sarah, and others more like Hagar? Does this type of Christian formation that emphasizes mutual interdependence and kinship also create space for addressing directly the fact that some in the Bible and even in our contemporary contexts tend toward mistrust? I argue that good theological anthropology helps us to see that there are no pure categories or that it is not helpful to have such rigid binaries, but we cannot gloss over the realities of different experiences of life, faith, and biblical texts. Thus, we must wrestle with how faith formation can help us in this way. The authors conclude this chapter by asking the readers to reflect on their claim: "cultivating Christian imagination requires sustained relationships with different kinds of Christians." I agree with Lamport and Edie, but I also wonder whether the authors have considered the cost or harm of some of these sustained relationships and whether we can also imagine what it might be like to be formed in faith that builds relationships based on mutual kinship—that has not glossed over the need to repent and to lament the pain of past and current relationships.

Participation in the Means of Grace

Craig Dykstra

In the first seminar I took as part of my PhD program, D. Campbell Wyck-off, professor of Christian education at Princeton Seminary, assigned Edward Farley's then new book, *Ecclesial Man: A Social Phenomenology of Faith and Reality*. That was more than forty years ago (as the title reflects), but the book posed a series of questions that has shaped the trajectory of my entire career as a Christian educator, parish pastor, theological educator, and foundation officer. Here are the questions Farley posed:

> In recent years the theological community has entertained what might be called a nasty suspicion about itself. The rumor did not arise within that community itself but, once implanted, it had a certain self-fulfilling effect. Could it be that there are no realities at all behind the language of this his-torical faith? Could it be that the testimony, the storytelling, the liturgical expressions of this faith refer to entities that have only phenomenal status? Could it be that the mode of existence which this historical religion calls faith involves no cognizing, no apprehendings, at all? Are Christian theo-logians like stockbrokers who distribute stock certificates on a nonexistent corporation? In this situation the "reality" of the corporation, its size, type, power, and promise, turns out to be simply the broker himself.[1]

Farley's answers to these questions are consistently "no." But he takes them seriously. And over the course of his book, he develops his response into an emphatic "yes" that testifies that there is, in fact, a way of living in a specific kind of community of faith that came into being in and through Jesus Christ. It bears within it "a life-world altering message, a distinctive imagery, and a novel sort of intersubjectivity" in and through which a powerful individually and commu-nally experienced "alteration of existence toward redemption" becomes possi-ble.[2] The word that names this fundamental reality, says Farley, is *ekklēsia*.

This book by Edie and Lamport, *Nurturing Faith*, it seems to me, takes on a task quite similar in character to Farley's and comes in the end to similar conclusions. The authors of this book describe profound and persistent challenges to nurturing faith that are consistent with the many "nasty suspicions" prevalent in our own contemporary culture and ethos. More importantly, however, the elements described in this book as "engaging resources, exclusive uniquenesses, and extraordinary gifts for nurturing faith" bear within them precisely the kinds of life-forming activities, distinctive linguistic patterns, powerful images, and fundamental ethos and intentionality in community that are constitutive of the Christian "faith world" in and through which new and true life is born, experienced, and lived. This is "good news" indeed!

Early in chapter 7, "Jesus, Sin, and the Grace of Cruciform Resurrection," Edie and Lamport make it clear that the "life-world" of *ekklēsia* into which we are called and enabled to live comes to us as a *gift*. Through his life, death, and resurrection, Jesus Christ "reveals God's identity and mission while drawing us into the joy of divine triune existence" and "invites faithful participation in himself, in his living body, as members of the new creation"—a new creation in and through which our constant struggles with sin and death are ultimately transformed and overcome (p. 169). The gift we are given not only comes *from* Christ. It comes in the form of *participation in* Christ. The new life is, in fact, life in God.

The task before us as Christian educators is to ask how it is that we can help fellow human beings (children, youth, and adults) to recognize and receive this gift of life. Lamport and Edie rightly highlight the power of story, metaphor, symbol, and ritual. In this regard, they follow in the tradition of Stephen Crites, who, in a brilliant essay entitled "The Narrative Quality of Experience," argues that narrative, symbol, and ritual are intrinsic to being human. They are a genre by means of which "the constitutive elements of human thought, feeling, and behavior are woven together into a particular self—a person who has his or her own character and way of being in the world."[3] At the same time, they are means by which God reveals God's self to us.

In his classic book, *The Meaning of Revelation*, theologian H. Richard Niebuhr said: "By revelation we mean that special occasion which provides us with an image by means of which all the occasions of personal and common life become intelligible. . . . Through it a pattern of dramatic unity becomes apparent with the aid of which the heart can understand what has happened, is happening and will happen to selves in their community and which the heart uses to understand life's meaning."[4]

For Lamport and Edie, as well as for Niebuhr, that "special occasion," that "image," is Jesus Christ: the *eikōn* of God—"the essential channel through which the revelation of God (and human redemption) is offered" (p. 173). In Christ, life becomes intelligible as we are enabled to draw upon means of grace that are both essential to living a specific mode of human existence and that are given to humanity as a gift of God's own saving generosity—even in the face of sin and death.

The gift and the call are to "participation in Christ," "participation in the means of grace," and "participation in his body, the church." More concretely, such participation is relational. We participate with others in certain "graced practices" that give shape to a shared, common life in and through which "Christ enables the 'flourishing of human actors' through relationships characterized by mutual encouragement and self-giving" (p. 183). In and through such participation, God's gift of "restorative grace" is both given and received.

This theological vision of Christian faith and life has significant implications for our understandings of the fundamental aims and dynamics of Christian education. Indeed, it calls for and requires much more powerful forms of Christian education and congregational life than currently seem prevalent in our society and culture. Fortunately, we have been blessed in recent years with the creation of a number of new, theologically rich, educationally powerful, and communally intensive forms of education and formation in Christian faith and life—particularly for adolescents and young adults. And Fred Edie is one of the earliest pioneers in this regard.

Edie's superb first book, *Book, Bath, Table, and Time: Christian Worship as Source and Resource for Youth Ministry*, provides both a compelling case for and a rich description of a full-bodied program of intensive theological education and Christian formation for high school–age youth. Both his theological vision and the formational practices around which he builds his educational program focus on the formative power of the *ordo*—the church's worshiping tradition that comes to us from ancient Christian liturgical practices and orders of worship. As Edie explains: "The *ordo* constitutes a living communal ecology: one that included initiating persons into Christian faith through baptism (bath), then continued to nurture them in faithfulness to their baptismal callings through sustained participation in the book (Bible), table (Eucharist), and Christian timekeeping. Thus, the *ordo* 'ordered' not only worship life on Sundays but the entirety of the church's life before God. Patterns for worshipping became patterns for communal living."[5]

This is a powerful claim in and of itself. But it becomes a good deal more powerful when we can see what happens when high school–age young people gather together to live the *ordo* in community for two full weeks at Duke Divinity School's Duke Youth Academy for Christian Formation. While they are there, the high school–age young people not only *learn about* Christian community. Much more significantly, they *experience and reflect upon* what for them is a new way of living.

Each day begins with morning prayer, in which the students and adult mentors share leadership responsibilities. In the course of the day, the community gathers for a two-hour plenary session during which a member of the Divinity School's faculty leads the community in studying themes ingredient to baptismal theology and then meet in covenant groups devoted to learning about, planning for, and reflecting on community worship. Throughout the two weeks, they visit a variety of kinds of churches located in diverse contexts; spend time in the academy's "Arts Village" cultivating their artistic imaginations and engaging with Christian artists of a wide variety of kinds; and go out into the larger community to serve in many diverse contexts "to hug, sweat, speak, and hammer in the name of Christ" and to "discover that Christ is already present in situations where some had imagined they were delivering him."[6] The evenings end as the day began—in worship of a kind that strives, as Edie puts it, "to 'play' heartily with book, bath, table, and time" and in covenant groups in which the members of the community "are invited to connect what they have learned about the significance of the *ordo* and their life in the *ordo* by way of the baptismal covenant with their practices of living together" as well as to "discern God's calling on their present lives and their unfolding futures."[7]

The theological vision that Lamport and Edie provide in this chapter is strong and compelling from beginning to end. The "Road Map" that summarizes this chapter sets the stage accurately, and the biblical and theological resources on which they draw throughout this chapter are rich. Their emphases on "relational participation in Christ's body" and on "graced practices" that both mark and shape the Christian life are fundamental to any true understanding of how God in Christ both saves and redeems us. As we work to create and sustain formational and educational contexts that have the power to enable people of all ages to experience and participate deeply and wisely in forms of worship that become patterns for communal life in Christ, we learn both to confess our sin more deeply and battle against powers of destruction more ardently, all the while praying for and living into transformed lives of mutual flourishing and joy.

Redeeming Hope: An Alternate Kingdom Informing Culture

Kirsten Sonkyo Oh

In light of the profound polarity defined somewhat by particularized social locations in our North American society, I am increasingly aware of the necessity of hope that can only be symbolized and ritualized in the Christian practice of baptism where the body is defined by rebirth and tied together in a fellowship of love: "Baptism signals our initiation into a *people*. Through baptism God constitutes a peculiar people who make us a new *polis*, a new religio-political reality ... that is marked by the obliteration of social class and aristocracies of blood."[1]

As such, in the baptismal covenant, the faith community is asked a binding question: "Will you nurture one another in the Christian faith and life and include these persons now before you in your care?" Subsequently, the congregation vows, "With God's help we will proclaim the good news and live according to the example of Christ. We will surround these persons with a community of love and forgiveness, that they may grow in their trust of God, and be found faithful in their service to others."[2] Insofar as the liturgy of baptism is put into practice, the church is a community of disciples who bear one another's burdens by nurturing each other in faith and life. Of such a faith community, John Wesley writes, "Sympathize with and assist each other in all your weaknesses, grievances, and trials. This our Lord peculiarly recommends; this he makes the distinguishing mark of his disciples."[3] The Christian faith community, then, is not simply countercultural. That is, this faith community does not only do the opposite of a particular societal culture. Rather, it is a result of the work of the Holy from another culture altogether, the Trinitarian community that is a nonhierarchical community of a divine dance (*perichōrēsis*).

Professors Edie and Lamport rightly provide a deep understanding of the church in biblical images and theological tradition of the church. The gift and uniqueness of the church as an agent of reconciliation and a countercommunity within our culture. As such, they assert the need for the church to be an inclusive communion—one that not only tolerates but also welcomes difference with humility and hope. Their indictment of a racialized church—still a problem today—is clear: "Instead, clouded by its own untested assumptions of superiority, [the pre-Reformation European church] justified enslavement, genocide, and conquest as God's providential intent" (p. 197). And as long as the hierarchy of color still lingers,[4] the church will remain divided along racial, political, socioeconomic lines. Further, such division runs deeper in the diverse terrain of theological differences within the church.

I unequivocally concur with Lamport and Edie that the quest for the unity of the church is biblical and a missional part of the church's DNA. Jesus prays for this unity in John 17 and the apostle Paul calls the church to be united with the physical metaphor of the body in Ephesians 4. It is also the picture of the eschaton in Revelation 5, 7 and 9. Their impressive inclusion of the two major failures of the church, in chapter 8, opens up the opportunity to extend those failures with a caution to steer clear of unholy unity, a unity that should *not* be preserved.

The story of Babel warns us about an unholy unity that was particularly destructive. Some have read in Genesis 11 the story of Babel that described an ideal unity: everyone in the whole earth spoke one language, they all migrated together, and they all shared the same goal of building a city and a tower to make a name for themselves in order to stay together. In the initial reading of the story, a jealous God comes down and creates linguistic confusion. However, employing a hermeneutic of suspicion, Ray Gaston lends insight into the fragile, detrimental unity of this speciously united group with these queries: "Just maybe, the universal language was imposed—one group imposing their language upon others. Just maybe the apparent order was maintained by an oppressive regime and the tower built by slaves. Just maybe, the fear of being scattered in the story is the fear of the oppressors that the oppressed will rise up against them and their own awareness of the tenuous hold they have upon power."[5]

Gaston's description of the unity we find in Babel comes at an enormous cost for those who are the oppressed: the ones who are actually building the cities and the towers, the ones who were coerced to assimilate to the dominant culture, the ones whose cultural artifacts were calamitously erased from the public sphere. Their forced marginality eschewed their cultural identities as something to be hidden or even jettisoned so that unity, questionable as it may be, could be preserved. Similarly, José Míguez Bonino evokes Genesis 11 as "the condemnation and defeat of the imperial arrogance and universal domination." Míguez Bonino notes that historical narratives repeatedly and "commonly imposed their language on the conquered as a way of unifying them all under the vision of a people destined for greatness by a self-made divine sanction."[6] Reading Babel through these lenses, God is the powerful liberator of the oppressed. God releases the captives to speak in their own languages, practice their ethnic cultural rhythms, and recalibrate their cultural identities. In essence, God is returning to the purpose of God's creation—to multiply, be fruitful, and subdue (dispersedly) the earth.[7]

The churches in the United States have had a historical past that also created structures of injustice with unequal distribution of power and domination. The church became embedded rather than prophetic in society, seeking to dominate in a turn toward a Babel-like existence. For example, speaking specifically of the Protestant church, African American theologian Stephen G. Ray points out, "Throughout the twentieth century, many theorists contended that the unique character of the Protestant movement predisposed it to an inordinate esteem of social, political, and economic structures of power."[8] Concomitantly, "African Americans in frustration left the white churches *en masse* to form their own churches. Denied equal participation in the existing churches, 'the move toward racially separate churches was not a matter of doctrinal disagreement, but a protest against unequal and restrictive treatment.'"[9] Michael Emerson and Christian Smith report that this mass exodus of African Americans from integrated churches occurred in the late nineteenth and early twentieth century as Jim Crow laws were being formed to separate and subjugate African Americans. This unfortunate yet necessary departure shows fracturing due to dominance and power. Could this historical dividing be God's intended idea of liberation like the story of Babel?

Nevertheless, critical race theory suggests that the socially constructed understanding of "race" stemmed from the sixteenth and seventeenth century to justify the subjugation of a group of people into the servant class. According to Fumitaka Matsuoka, this "race" construct seeped into Christianity with the dangerous ideology of "chosenness" that gave way to social hierarchy dependent on skin color to help propel the global expansion of the European West.[10] Hence, the plurality of voices sanctioned through postmodernity may be the church's opportunity to liberate herself from a modernist rationality of one "normative" concept of the "biblical truths." That is, these biblical truths are often the products of scriptural interpretations by the dominant voices of the White, Euro-American males whose interpretations were given the great privilege of being the normative and authoritative voices.

The admission that no biblical interpretation of Scripture is done in a vacuum, that all interpretations are colored by social locations and social construction, does not reduce "biblical truths." If social constructionism is understood as "the emphases on the interactional and communal context as the meaning maker,"[11] the authority of Scripture is strengthened in that recognition, which inadvertently encourages a global, contextual reading of the text that broadens and deepens the various scriptural commentaries and interpretations. In fact, Black, feminist, Latin American, Asian American, African, and postcolonial perspectives shed light on the more complex and robust readings of Scripture as already seen in the reading of Genesis 11. By incorporating cultural intelligence from various social locations, these nuances enrich the meaning of the biblical text.

Acts 2 establishes this contextual, global Christian communal nature of the church without dominance of one over against another: "All of them were filled with the Holy Spirit and began to speak in other languages, as the Spirit gave them ability. Now there were devout Jews from every nation under heaven living in Jerusalem. And at this sound the crowd gathered and was bewildered, because each one heard them speaking in the native language of each" (Acts 2:4–6 NRSV). Here, no language, culture, or journey of faith is neglected or devalued. This is a unity that respects and fulfills the scattering and diversification of peoples from Babel. Here, "Otherness is not denied but embraced in this differentiated and complex unity of Pentecost."[12] Indeed, "the faith we seek to nurture requires us to step with humility and hope into relations with others not like us" (p. 199) and to privilege those voices that have long been silenced by dominant scriptural interpretations and the theological tradition we often cite and teach.[13]

The gift of an irresistible citizenship is the offer of an alternative community. I envision with Edie and Lamport a church that is not simply countercultural but one that represents an alternate culture of the kin(g)dom of God: one that corresponds, interacts, informs, and even transforms our culture precisely because it exists outside of our culture altogether.[14] Its cultural system is not an entity that stands in conjunction with or oppositional to; rather, it is an entity that is made up of the "called out ones," as the Greek, *ekklēsia*, envisages. This alternative community proclaims her utter dependence on God's grace for salvation and confesses her faith in the finished work of Christ through the rebirth at baptism into Christ, at which point the divisions in the church are torn down. These disciples are knowers and followers of Jesus. The one who "dismantled the dominant culture and nullified its claims. The way of his ultimate criticism is his decisive solidarity with marginal people and the accompanying vulnerability required by that solidarity," according to Walter Brueggemann.[15]

As ones in Christ, we belong to an alternative community through our baptism, and in such belonging, our decision to trust God and follow Jesus shapes, orients, and constitutes our lives. As an alternative community who inhabit the irresistible citizenship of Trinitarian community, our distinctive theistic epistemology, values, and virtues lead us to the prophetic role of the church. Therefore, we face the reality of racial tensions, learn racial literacy, accept one another's human proclivities, and share the grace of God between one another as sisters and brothers in the new creation with our racial and cultural identities intact. This is the hope for a truly unified church that looks to mirror not our surrounding society but the eschatological preference found in Revelation 5, 7, and 9. This eschatological vision of the ultimate community of God constitutes all—disciples of Jesus from every race, class, nationality, and language—worshiping together in mutual fellowship of love.

Lived Faith in Communities of Charitable Critique

Elizabeth DeGaynor

Human beings are not brains on sticks; we are holistic entities of heart, body, mind, and soul. Yet some theologians have subscribed to a rationalistic dualism that valorizes mind over body, sometimes going so far as to see the body as the source of evil. Christian formation practitioners, especially those who focus on lived faith, acknowledge that our bodies contain wisdom, often before we can articulate it. James K. A. Smith asks us to consider what shapes us "to be a certain kind of people whose hearts and passions and desires are aimed at the kingdom of God." Answering this question considers our desires and the ways our identities are formed by sacred and secular liturgies that "train our hearts through our bodies."[1] Christian practices move us beyond stated beliefs and force us to live them. Jesus became incarnate and modeled ministry, and God continues to move through the world. We are invited to join in that work aimed toward shalom (peace, wholeness). *Phronēsis* (embodied wisdom) deepens our understanding of the contours of a faithful life, hopefully all the way into our bones.

Edie and Lamport's vision of formation is connected to virtue ethics and is focused on enlightening communities about the essential nature of practices for individual and social good.[2] Katherine Turpin problematizes the (sometimes oblivious) optimism of a virtue ethics approach to Christian practices, which often fails to account for ways that disciplined practice can transmit domination and oppression as easily as virtue and wisdom. Turpin uses Michel Foucault and Pierre Bourdieu to remind us that practices can be used as tools of violent but subtle discipline, aligning us to cultural values that do not lead to our flourishing, pitting us instead against our best interests, often without our awareness. We are formed into ways of being that favor those at the top of the social ladder. Christian practices may serve as an alternative counterformation that resists such hierarchy, but the two are not easily separable. While acknowledging the positive corrective that Christian practices offer to cognitive understandings of faith, Turpin worries about framing religious practice "as a source of virtue and connection with God that is backed up by the gracious intervention of God to ensure positive outcomes."[3] The corrosive influence of White supremacy could allow us to ignore negative outcomes or to excuse our sinful distortions if we position ourselves as those who know God better and do God's will best.

The roots of hierarchical power problems go all the way back to Aristotle, with whom virtue ethicists often begin. Although we may agree that being habituated into living a "good life" steeped in virtue is important, especially for the flourishing of the polis (state), the issue of who counts as a "citizen" in that state is left unexamined. What about women, slaves, or disabled persons? Thomas Aquinas clarifies the vision with his Christian lens on virtues, seeking to participate in the fullness of God's reign as the source of our flourishing, but there is an inclination toward universal rather than contextual being in the world. Edie and Lamport helpfully distinguish differences: "Whereas Aristotle believed effort was the key to virtue, Aquinas realized that the most important Christian virtues were gifts of the Spirit" (p. 206). Along with them, I'd like to suggest a both/and of divine grace and human action, rather than leaning exclusively on the holiness of the latter to avoid dealing with the brokenness of the former.

News of Jean Vanier's decades-long abuse of multiple people connected to L'Arche communities recently became public.[4] L'Arche's values were distorted by power dynamics and faulty theology: "Vulnerability and mutuality can eclipse individual dignity instead of nurturing it. Add the patriarchal theology of the priest Vanier saw as his 'spiritual father'—Thomas Philippe reportedly once silenced a victim's protests by calling himself an instrument of God—and the danger comes into focus."[5] The abuse of power in a community meant to protect and honor those with disabilities seems especially egregious in its hypocrisy. Shocking and yet not surprising. It is always fallen human beings who are trying to live out their faith, and we never do it perfectly. Some, however, do it predatorily. Vanier used the veil of his iconic power status to cover his acts of misconduct, and he—like John Howard Yoder—refused to admit wrongdoing, offering instead distorted theological justification for his behavior and the claim that such relationships were "reciprocal." Furthermore, members of communities are often disinclined to believe allegations.[6] The specter of sinful misconduct is not sufficient reason to abandon Christian practices, but it is sufficient cause to put safeguards of external oversight and times of critical reflection in place.

Lauren Winner offers an incisive critique of having too much unqualified hope in practices. She explains that "practices have been embraced as a way of fixing something in or for the church; practices have been embraced as a strategy of recuperation, repair, or reform," and they may well have the capacity for such, but "because nothing created is untouched by the Fall, Christians should not be surprised when lovely and good, potentially gracious Christian gestures are damaged, or when human beings deploy those Christian gestures in perpetuation of damage."[7] This reality means that our practices may well lead to layers of deformation, despite our hopeful aims. Or more insidiously, they might be aimed toward malformation from the outset. We must seek ongoing reflection in order to repent and repair the way we inhabit the world.

I write this during the coronavirus pandemic, and epidemiologists are demanding social distancing to the extreme of sheltering in place. Christians, especially congregational leaders, are trying to figure out what church looks like when members of the body of Christ are separated or what worship means when it is not communally embodied.[8] My denomination (Episcopal) is debating about the Eucharist as simultaneously sanctifying and a potential site of virus transmission. It is oddly striking to be living in a time when physical distance may be construed as the most faithful way to love our neighbors. Even this can be steeped in the privilege of those who have safe homes in which to be sequestered and access to resources that we can afford to hoard, even if it means others go without.[9] M. Shawn Copeland asks what becomes of theology when suffering bodies are placed at the center of our inquiry, asserting that doing so "uncovers the suffering body at the heart of Christian belief." She enjoins us to turn toward solidarity, a critique of self, society, and church, which begins with *anamnēsis*, the intentional remembering of the exploited victims of history, along with "acknowledgment and confession of sin, authentic repentance—change of heart, change of life, change of living."[10] All of these practices are further enriched through ongoing relationships and creative actions for social justice.

Edie and Lamport rightly acknowledge the interdependence of virtues and practices embedded in stories, including those found in Scripture. Narrative is how we make sense of ourselves.[11] But as someone who teaches theological reflection on literature, I have become increasingly aware that our popular stories are often slanted toward the powerful. Because I believe God can be found in all places, but perhaps especially on the margins (cf. Howard Thurman's *Jesus and the Disinherited* and Rowan Williams's *Being Human*), I have made it a priority to look for stories that center on characters who might otherwise be invisible (e.g., Pecola in *The Bluest Eye* by Toni Morrison). Close reading of such stories is a faithful Christian practice of listening to voices that have been silenced, and it attunes us to hear similar voices in our own communities.

I have been especially struck by what kingdom-shaping practices look like in the lives of young people. Since I first served as a mentor to high school students enrolled in Duke Youth Academy (DYA) in 2007, I have returned in varying roles, including my current one as academic ministry coordinator. The fruit of this work includes witnessing young people offer prophetic witness to adults about what is possible in intergenerational community, from expressions of joy and lament to acts of reconciliation. I have also been part of the faltering that inevitably occurs in groups of Christians, even when we are trying to be faithful, from irritability and insensitivity to racialized conflict. Much has been learned in our ongoing processes of recognition, reflection, and response.[12] Edie and Lamport are correct: At their best, Christian practices can and do "offer resistance to powers that fragment human experience into unrelated bits. . . . [They] simultaneously nurture faith and constitute it" (p. 217). But practices must be inhabited carefully to fortify their capacity to do so. This includes consideration of social location, deepening our understanding of what we are doing and why, and aiming for correlation of beliefs and actions. Insofar as we are willing to reflect critically on who we are, what we intend, what is happening, and how we might revision our actions, we can move toward more faithful practices.

Evelyn Parker has spent decades working with African American adolescents and the congregations in which they worship. She coined the term "emancipatory hope" to name an intricately woven life of both pious and political existence that focuses on critical consciousness and critical action so that racial, economic, social, and political domination is eradicated. Rather, "to possess emancipatory hope is to expect transformation of hegemonic relations of race, class, and gender and to act as God's agents ushering in God's vision of human equality."[13] Like the eschatological imagination offered by Edie and Lamport, emancipatory hope faces the present realities with the expectation of what can/will be. I join them in such hopeful work.

RESPONSE 6

Knowing for Living Faith

Thomas Groome

By way of epistemology, modernity championed an ahistorical and allegedly objective rationality focused on empirical data, excluding the emotive and experiential (and thus the mystical) from human knowing. As might be expected, such scientific rationality was inimical to Christian faith. Indeed, modernity expected its pretentious enlightenment to "abstract" faith from people's lives and from society (*à la* Charles Taylor), it being no more than irrational superstition. Such an epistemology could well sour Christian religious educators against critical reason in the affair of faith, seeing the former as only a threat to the latter.

Professors Lamport and Edie, however, take a wiser approach. Of course, they readily recognize the limitations of modernity's abstract reasoning. Yet they rightly insist that a certain mode of critical thinking is essential to informing, forming, and transforming people and communities toward *living* Christian faith. For faith's sake, such reflection should engage memory and imagination as well as reason—all three reflective faculties. Then, critical thinking that is located historically and culturally, that engages the rational and emotive, that transcends the dichotomy of theory and practice, can encourage in people a critically conscious and convicted faith that shapes their very being as Christian and advances the realization of God's reign in Jesus Christ.

To this end, Edie and Lamport draw upon and craft a compelling statement from many of the leading proponents of a consciousness raising and empowering mode of knowing/becoming for Christian religious education. This includes the prophetic voices of Paulo Freire, Jack Mezirow, Robert Kegan, Walter Brueggemann, and Almeda Wright. Having portrayed such a holistic epistemology as essential to truly knowing and knowing truly Christian faith, they propose an appropriate pedagogy to implement it. Flatteringly, they review my own proposal of a *shared Christian praxis approach* with appreciation.

This chapter 10 makes a very convincing argument for an empowering, emancipatory, and wise way of *knowing* Christian faith, one that invites believers far beyond "mere believing" (Metz), and religious educators far beyond "banking education" (Freire). In proposing such a holistic way of knowing, the authors are on good biblical grounds—as they note. It is surely significant that the biblical terms for "to know"—the Hebrew *yada* and the Greek *ginōskō*—also mean "to make love." This signals that the Bible encourages a way of knowing that engages both head and heart to shape the very being of people as people of God.

With appreciation for Mark and Fred's good work, I offer three following reflections.

As I read their review of my own work, I'm prompted to highlight again why I prefer to speak of a *praxis* way of knowing (Freire) over an *experiential* one (Dewey, Montessori)—though I admit that this distinction is subtle. *Praxis* is a reflective mode of knowing from one's life and actions in the world, whereas experience can at times be nonreflective and accepting—received more than initiated, passive more than agential. Then, precisely because a praxis way of knowing entails reflection upon one's own life and sociocultural context, it engages the emotions as well as the mind, the heart as well as the head. As people name and reflect critically upon their lives in the world, they are, metaphorically, sharing their own stories and visions—their very selves— and one cannot name and reflect upon oneself dispassionately.

Second, the authors quote approvingly Saint Anselm's definition of theology as "faith seeking understanding." I note, however, that Anselm and the theologians of his eleventh-century context and thereafter, imagined only *themselves* as doing the thinking involved in theologizing. They presumed that theology was for trained experts who would inform the faith of the common people—expected to passively accept and simply believe their teachings. By contrast, we live now in a postmodern era that requires every Christian to think critically about the challenges of living their faith in the midst of the world. They need to reach beyond reception and even beyond cognition to a personal conation of Christian faith, to a wisdom way of knowing that shapes their very being. In sum, all Christians now are called to be theologians and to "do" theology in order to nurture their lives of faith. This can be encouraged by the epistemology and pedagogy that Lamport and Edie propose.

Third, I want to expand beyond Anselm's notion of "understanding"—or at least as we would typically understand the term today; no pun intended. Here I draw upon the work of the great Catholic philosopher and theologian Bernard Lonergan. Among his many contributions to contemporary Christian thought, Lonergan did a service in outlining what he called the "dynamics of cognition"—the conscious activities we perform when we achieve what he referred to as authentic knowing. He named them as *attending, understanding, judging*, and *deciding*. He claimed further that we can readily recognize these cumulative activities in the operations of our own consciousness, performing them as we do a thousand times a day. And in portraying the complete cycle of cognition, Lonergan was attempting to reunite what Kant had separated— theoretical and practical reason.

So, the fourfold dynamic of cognition begins with *attending* to the data of whatever is to be known. It then reaches toward *understanding* the data, to comprehend its meaning. While understanding alone may be sufficient for theoretical knowing, authentic cognition entails two further activities. It needs to push onward to *judging* whether one's understanding is true or false, and what it might mean for one's life. And the dynamic is completed only by *deciding* what to do with or because of what one knows. This fourfold dynamic of attending, understanding, judging, and deciding is realized by what Lonergan calls the transcendental imperatives of *be attentive, be intelligent, be reasonable*, and *be responsible*. Note again that the fourfold dynamic clearly unites theoretical and practical reasoning—contra Kant's separation.

The four dynamics of cognition/conation are well reflected in the shared Christian praxis approach that Edie and Lamport outline. We can think of movements 1 and 2 as *attending* to the data and coming to critically *understand* one's own life in the world—present praxis. Movement 3 *attends* to and attempts to *understand* the data of Christian story and vision, the truths, values, and wisdom of our faith and the possibilities and responsibilities they mean for our lives. Then movement 4 reflects Lonergan's notion of *judgment*, even as it emphasizes (more than Lonergan does) coming to see for oneself and making the faith one's own. And movement 5 reflects the completing dynamic that Lonergan names as *deciding* what to do with one's knowing. In the shared Christian praxis approach, the decisions encouraged in the fifth movement can be cognitive, affective, or behavioral—depending on the theme, context, occasion, and so forth.

The dynamics of cognition reflected in the movements of a shared Christian praxis approach, then, encourage an integration of *life* (movements 1 and 2) and *faith* (movement 3) into *living* faith that is convicted and chosen (movements 4 and 5). This kind of pedagogy that brings *life to faith* and *faith to life* can encourage *living* Christian faith.

And by *living* faith (echoed well by Fred and Mark), I mean a faith that is *alive*—ever springing up and being refreshed with the kind of gospel/water that Jesus promised to the Samaritan woman and to Christians ever after (John 4:1–42). It is to be *lived*. As Jesus repeated so often, in one way or another, it is not enough to profess Christian faith; one must do the will of God in order to belong to God's reign (see Matt. 7:21–23). And *living* faith is ever *life-giving* for the person (John 10:10) and for the life of the world (John 6:51). Likewise, living faith engages all of our human capacities: our *heads* for personal conviction; our *hearts* for trusting and praying; our *hands* for doing God's will.

In sum, our Christian religious education requires a holistic epistemology and then a corresponding pedagogy in order to encourage, by God's grace, *knowing* for *living* Christian faith.

Take up the shield of faith, with which you can extinguish all the flaming arrows of the evil one.

—EPHESIANS 6:16

The Christian way is different: harder and easier. Christ says, "Give me all. I don't want so much your time, your money, your work: I want you! I have not come to torment your natural self, but to kill it. No half-measures are any good. I don't want to cut off a branch here and there, I want to cut the whole tree down. Hand over the natural self. I will give you a new self. I will give you myself; my own shall become yours."

—C. S. LEWIS

The Law of Unintended Consequences

In the wake of Facebook CEO Mark Zuckerberg's congressional grilling in April 2018 over the platform's role in disseminating political propaganda during the 2016 US presidential election, the spread of misinformation has proliferated with the rise of social media. Adam Fisher, author of *Valley of Genius: The Uncensored History of Silicon Valley (as told by the Hackers, Founders, and Freaks Who Made It Boom)*, talked to over two hundred people in the valley—including CEOs and billionaires—for the book. He perceived—almost to a person—a kind of disappointment or fear or trepidation about what it was that they had created and its *unintended consequences* in spite of best intentions.[1]

John Westerhoff's *Will Our Children Have Faith?* (1976) exposed the well-intentioned but counterproductive strategies of "schooling" Christians four decades ago.[2] He called for a radical reconfiguration of how Christians should be formed. The church acknowledged he was right but seemed not to be able to muster the enthusiasm to do much about it. We wonder what it will take for churches to jolt themselves into the profound realism that much is in need of reformation—and not with a feather duster but with a fire hose.

Until such reformation occurs, with respect to the results of Christian formation, people will continue to attempt the double-whammy of *catfishing* and *punking* God. A "catfish" is someone who pretends to be someone they are not and who creates false identities, particularly to pursue deceptive romances. To be "punked" is to have a joke played on someone, usually in public. Some people pretend to be in love with God and even create false religious identities all the while hiding behind a disingenuous image. The result is collateral damage: the voice and mission of God are at once *gelded* and *muted*. To be "gelded" means to deprive of virility or vitality, to weaken and emasculate. To be "muted" is an emotion or action that subdues or restrains.

In sum, we claim that the *law of unintended consequences* is at work—namely, some faith communities mislead by affirming less than faithful character, commitments, and behaviors. The consequence is a life of nondiscipleship. The mission of the church must lovingly nurture faith. A Christian is a disciple, and faith is the fuel.

Galvanizing Issues of Convergence

Our most dearly held convictions for nurturing faith in the global church, as affirmed and challenged by the response contributors, are the following.

Martyn Percy

How divine revelation is apprehended—whether through Scripture and tradition or faith experiences in Christian living, as Martyn Percy points out—needs to be governed by love. His hermeneutical advice is synonymous with our call for *generous humility*, as we have termed it. Being overly certain about the nature of God and what the divine intends is tantamount to "owning" God. With such certainty, fences are built to keep out contrary views and to protect the established orthodoxy. To be generous to those who experience God in alternative Christian ways, however, means accepting ambiguity and living by the faith we speak of in this book. It is also demonstrated by trust in the Holy Spirit to lead in truth. Some are simply not equipped or comfortable to operate this way. Percy appropriately reminds us of J. B. Phillips's challenge that our (version of) God may be "too small." For those who "own" God and have been encouraged to be confident in their hermeneutic conviction, this may be a most unwelcome apprehension. Our affinity for Martyn's incisive remarks gives us courage to embrace human frailty even as it bids for a faithful clasp to gain traction in the life of faithful living before God.

Almeda Wright

The sobering reality for Almeda Wright is not only the value of interdependent kinship but also the costs of sustaining it given the life circumstances and cultural realities that disciples carry with them. We agree. Relationships are not easy! While the *optimistic* side of us wishes to recall the (baptismal) theological reality that "In Christ, there is neither Jew nor Greek, there is neither slave nor free, there is no male or female" (Gal. 3:28), the *realistic* side acknowledges that sinful human dynamics (our susceptibility to the passion of hatred for others, for example, or our inclination to misuse the capacity for reason against truth and love) remain present and distort believers' relationships. Wright is correct, therefore, to call attention to the long history of relationality, where, again and again, powerful persons have abused relationships by exploiting vulnerable ones.

Wright's constructive criticisms call to mind the spirituality of the desert fathers and mothers of late antiquity. In these monastic communities, monks and nuns continually placed themselves and their relations to neighbors under the microscope of self-examination and mutual accountability. They understood relationships—marked by the turbulence of embodied passions, mystified motivations, and the give and take of vulnerability and dominance—to be the terrain upon which they worked out their salvation. Because of their commitments to unflinching self-appraisal and relational accountability governed by love, however, they regularly discovered occasions to confront their own sinful failure to love, to lament it, and to seek forgiveness from and reconciliation with harmed neighbors. Doing so requires Christian faith: faith that God does in fact redeem human beings from sin and restores them to new life; faith that the neighbor is a gift from God and that the neighbor and I will work out our salvation together (or we will fail separately); and faith that the truth will set us free. Desert monastics were convinced that confession led to freedom!

This vision of transformation through persistent self-scrutiny and interpersonal accountability is perhaps less than Wright is seeking. It does not fully account for historic patterns of oppression or asymmetries of power between persons or communities. These effectively prevent the forging of relationships before they may blossom. We elucidate a relational anthropology, however, because of its classical vision for human interdependence lately lost to individualism and because it takes into account many of the psychic, epistemic, and bodily complexities of embodied Christian existence in the world. Acknowledging these human predicaments is a necessary step on the journey to just societies.

Craig Dykstra

Consistent with our own stance, Craig Dykstra contends that the church is necessary for growing in faith. This "gift of participation" in the church, as he says, is analogous to receiving the "firstfruits" of a heavenly community, a glimpse of our place with God and the eternal community after earth. The Western propensity for staying apart—the resistance of being folded into a possibly freedom-limiting and independence-reducing situation (and therefore continuing to wallow in our own untethered beliefs and practices without insight into the misguided notions we hold absent communal accountability)—prevents and even robs persons of this gift. Of course, "gifts," such as the church, must be received.

To the extent that persons refuse participation with others, they deny themselves a primary means by which to enter into the shared presence of God. And this deeper meaning of participation, graced incorporation into the living Christ, the body of Christ, and God's mission for the world, is what Dykstra is after. We are grateful, therefore, that he names similar practices of formation to those we endorse. Distinctive Christian rituals, symbols, stories, and practices of living not only form persons into Christ; they also become graced means of participating in Christ. *We contend there is no more significant means of nurturing faith than through entering into the reality-reorienting presence of God through the faith community.*

Kirsten Sonkyo Oh

To follow the herd is instinctual. And Christian kingdom values are bound to get a resolute pushback from the popular culture that Kirsten Sonkyo Oh so aptly describes. For the church to display countercultural values and thinking takes courage in the face of criticism and hope in the God whom they serve. The conundrum that H. Richard Niebuhr foists into theological discussion regarding five typologies for how the church and culture might interact has been at the same time aggravating, provoking, and variating. While culture eschews prescribed morality and subservience to any higher authority, the church, which is to be nothing less than Jesus's ministry in the world, voluntarily acknowledges a source of truth that is beyond itself and willingly yields as servant to the authority of God. And furthermore, while culture rails in its self-referential pronouncements and bullying attempts to constrain people to toe the cultural line, followers of Jesus pull strength from the Christian community and resist what is opposed to the Christian ethic. These alternative voices each tell compelling stories. But obedience inevitably faces opposition. Faith is required to stand for God and resist popular stances on social, political, and ethical issues. Jesus forewarned believers that if the world hated him, it would certainly hate the church and the countercultural views embraced by its kingdom values. While cultural drift is awash in destructive values, a countercultural yet sensitive and loving church is the only hope the world has. What is the issue? If the church forfeits its voice and turns down the contrast between itself and the world, the message of God will be muted, perverted, or both. Yet, if the church unabashedly proclaims its powerful message but disregards the grace and gentleness of the gospel, the audience will be lost. Each generation and each culture faces the dance of how the church can best extol wisdom and the boundless love of God in fulfilling the brave Christian mission in the dark world.

Elizabeth DeGaynor

According to Elizabeth DeGaynor, our enthusiasm for *practices* as expressions of bodily, affective, communal, and aesthetic dimensions of faith *and* for their resistance to a construal of faith as nothing more than inward spirituality *and* for their accessibility to children and persons with developmental challenges come at the expense of acknowledging their subjection to sin. Supported by critical theorists, she adroitly describes the dangers of uncritical adoption of Christian practices as the sole strategy for faith formation. Practices are not automatically good. They can form persons into unjust patterns of imagining and acting, made even worse because they are embedded as personal habits and in social mores that resist critical scrutiny. Communal practices can perpetrate evil, including upholding hegemonies of power about which practitioners either are unaware or imagine to be good. One case in point from our chapter is the (de)formation of Christians as consumers. Consider cases of practices gone awry, as with the racial segregation of congregational worship in North America. Blacks and Whites worshiping separately, a practice that came to be viewed by many as normal and even good, in addition to inscribing theological error upon faith communities, functioned as one more means to enforce Jim Crow oppression upon African American Christians.

DeGaynor's points are well taken and undoubtedly correct. We should have been more circumspect in our appraisal. Yet if we are accurate in assertions for human knowing as thoroughly embodied and for God's reign as the embodiment of a vision for a polis ordered by Jesus's way (not incidentally one characterized by joy), then Christians will remain a people of practice. We will continue to gather (imperfectly) for worship filled with praise to God and to reach out (haltingly) to care for our neighbors (including partnering with them in pursuit of more just societies). In other words, we acknowledge that practicing faithfulness will require the *practice of vigilant scrutiny of our practices*, the courage to repent from or renew them when we see how they have begotten unintended consequences, and the grace to renew them.

DeGaynor encourages the necessity of pursuing faith formation across multiple fronts, in this case the requirement for critical reflection alongside of the practice of Christian life. Ultimately, her contribution to this work testifies to a theme carried throughout; faith-forming ministry leaders will bring multiple approaches and perspectives, an *ecology* of tools and strategies, to the task of making Christians.

Thomas Groome

There is perhaps no one who is more influential to our own collective thinking about the nature of *knowledge* in the Christian realm than Thomas Groome. His cogent approaches to "knowing God" in the spiritual dimension have resonated with us for decades, and we are indebted to his insightful, biblical applications and heuristic sensibilities for nurturing faith. What is most pressing in the here and now—that is, our postmodern backdrop—is the need more than ever for the acquired skill of critical thinking and an understanding of how this is sculptured within intentional Christian living. The temptation *not* to make knotty value judgments regarding faith and subsequent behavioral practice is alluring in the smorgasbord of cultural indulgence. But the exercise of character and discernment implored by Groome and Lonergan means our faith communities call us to *be attentive, be intelligent, be reasonable,* and *be responsible.* Growth in faith depends upon our willingness to make determined and sacrificial choices while moving in personal and spiritual maturity toward a clear vision of the kingdom of God.

Faith in, Obedience to, and Praise for God

The Christian faith is a way of life together, membership within a people. Acceptance or rejection of this faith is a "yes" or "no" to the enculturation of the church. Formation through socialization is not an optional matter for human beings; to be a person is to receive some version of culture. The question is not, Will some community shape us? It is inevitable. The question is, Will the community that forms us and identifies us be true or false?

The primary task of being educated in the Christian tradition is not the achievement of better understanding, but faithfulness. Indeed, we can come to understand only through faithfulness, as that story asks for nothing less than our lives.

Faith, inasmuch as it is a reorientation of our life away from the seductiveness of narcissism, is a deterrent from self-grounding and an invitation to self-transcendence. Karl Barth, perhaps the greatest theologian of the twentieth century, regarded endless fascination with ourselves as the ultimate reference, as the weightiest problem.[3] Walter Brueggemann likewise insists that the "thou" of the Psalms (i.e., God as the other) is counteraffirmation against self-referential location.[4]

Thus, faith enables obedience. And who knows where this obedience may end? Oswald Chambers reminds, "*We have no right to judge where we should be put, or to have preconceived notions as to what God is fitting us for. God engineers everything; wherever He puts us, our one great aim is to pour out a whole-hearted devotion to Him in that particular work.*"[5] The message of the gospel calls us to obedience in living out the mission of God. John Calvin, in his magnum opus *Institutes of the Christian Religion*, concludes: "But not only faith, perfect and in every way complete, but all right knowledge of God is born of obedience."[6] And one comes to know God and grow in faith by doing something—that is, obeying. Obedience is not a substitute for knowledge, but it is a way to knowledge of God, and faith. Truth be told, we would rather err on the side of obedience and then belief as a path to God. This book, we suppose, could have also been titled "nurturing obedience" or "nurturing praise," as these are the consequences of faith. As Ron Highfield proposes, "God's very being and action drive us to seek him, demand that we imitate him, and compel us to praise him. . . . We cannot know God without passion, longing, seeking, following, and praising. To know him is to praise him, for he is most worthy of praise."[7] So perhaps Thomas Groome's praxis is the clearest means for gaining faithful obedience.

Humans are created with remarkable potential because God has designed them in the image of the divine and bestowed many gifts upon them. He desires for them to love him, love their neighbors, and carry out redemptive mandates to all. However, because of the fall, humans are depraved in their thoughts, actions, and loves and are unable to love or live rightly. Even so, the means of restoration is found in the church's ministry of Christianly educating its members. Through transcendent worship, the faith community, thoughtful reflection upon God's revelation, and engagement with the world, believers can be transformed to think rightly, do rightly, and love rightly. The *nearness* of God lets us live not with knowing but rather with commending faith. As Psalm 119:151 counsels, "But you are near, O God; and all your commands are true."

Parting Plea—Compromise Elsewhere

Martin Scorsese's 2016 film *Silence*—the gut-wrenching true story of Christian martyrdom in seventeenth-century Japan—is likely to leave a thoughtful Christian with a sadness that may take some time from which to recover. After seeing the relentless, sacrificial, perservering faith of hidden Christians who refused to apostasize during the first two hours of the movie, two of the main characters, Portuguese Jesuit priests (played by Liam Neeson and Andrew Garfield), did apostasize in the end.[8] In spite of the knowledge of and experience with the community of faith, they abandoned their mission and relinquished the Christian faith because of doubt, expediency, and avoidance of suffering.

The same sadness experienced as a result of watching the movie (or reading Shusaku Endo's original novel) qualifies the concern and burden we have for some Christians who are at risk in throwing over their faith placed in the God of the universe. This grave circumstance and, correspondingly, this great opportunity have motivated us to write this book: Faith for all its delicate vulnerability remains the strong bridge to locating life's destiny in God. It is to be clutched, strengthened, protected, exercised, and nurtured with a relentless determination and bolstered by our communities of faith.

In the midst of a world culture where this calibre of faith is patently misunderstood, grossly misrepresented, and often artlessly rejected, promoting a fresh sense of authentic faith is an urgent task. Such reorienting is an act of imagination that is sculpted in response to yearnings that are all around us—yearnings for love, yearnings for community, yearnings for a future of flourishing. As C. S. Lewis chastized, "We are half-hearted creatures, fooling about with drink and sex and ambition when infinite joy is offered us, like an ignorant child who wants to go on making mud pies in a slum because he cannot imagine what is meant by the offer of a holiday at the sea."[9] Now is the time to embrace the life of faith and be nurtured in its fullness.

We leave readers with these words: When the Son of God returns, will he find *faith*? Without *faith*, it is impossible to please God. Increase our *faith* (Luke 18:8; Heb. 11:6; Luke 17:5).

Interactive Dialogue

1. If you were writing a response to any aspect of this book—the themes, the diagnoses of cultural issues, the proposals intended to nurture faith, and so forth—what would you say?

2. Pick the response that you resonated with most. What was it that drew you to agree? What would you say to the author?

3. Now that you have completed reading the book, what insights were most meaningful to you, and to what extent has your thinking changed from the time you began reading?

4. What will prevent churches and parachurch organizations and small groups and other faith communities from implementing the most salient aspects for nurturing faith in spite of the clear agenda for doing so? And what can leaders do to be change agents in this regard?

ACKNOWLEDGMENTS

We consulted a number of colleagues along the way—and with beneficial effect, we believe, in the ultimate writing results. So many of the themes Fred develops in his writing percolate across the entire faculty of Duke Divinity School. He is their most enthusiastic student. Strong commitments to justice on the part of colleagues in the Religious Education Association also influence his work. Fred is grateful for long-standing intellectual friendships with Chuck Foster, Jack Seymour, Anne Wimberly, Craig Dykstra, Susan Eastman, David White, and Joyce Mercer. Former graduate students Liz DeGaynor, Emily Peck-McClain, and Amanda Pittman (doctors now all!) helped shape his teaching and research too.

Mark is convinced that his thoughts are more cogent and sensible thanks to the advice of the following scholars, theologians, and practitioners: Jack Barentsen, Ivy Beckwith, Dean Blevins, Philip Bustrum, Graham Cheesman, Mara Crabtree, Finola Cunnane, Marian de Souza, Therese Lamport, Ron Michener, Peter Osborn, Larry Richards, and Charles Taliaferro. He also is indebted to Greg and Heidi Herbruck for a warm and welcoming environment to write in their Fort Myers, Florida, home during a frigid spell in Grand Rapids, Michigan. Bryan Froehle (St. Thomas University, Miami) and Byard Bennett (Grand Rapids Theological Seminary, Michigan) read multiple chapters and offered astute observations.

Very helpful critiques of our preliminary documents were provided via publisher's request from Kenda Dean (Princeton Theological Seminary); Chuck Foster (longtime professor at Candler School of Theology, Emory University); and an anonymous reviewer. Judith M. Heyhoe (editor to the faculty, Duke Divinity School) shined her eagle eye on our chapters to better blend our voices, wordsmith, and otherwise execute marvelous quality assurance.

Michael Thomson, then senior acquisitions editor at Eerdmans, who has since changed teams, and David Bratt, executive editor, extended sage advice and carefully shepherded the project through the six-year process. They were at once encouraging and optimistic, congenial and visionary. We are fans! We are also indebted to Amy Kent, Jenny Hoffman, and Lydia Hall, who handled the myriad of production details.

A huge debt of thanks to our fantastic team of indexers: Ronald J. Bigalke Jr., Mel Wilhoit, Mark Eckel, and Philip Bustrum.

We are honored by several luminaries—Chuck Foster, Tom Groome, Kirsten Sonkyo Oh, Elizabeth DeGaynor, Martyn Percy, Almeda Wright, and Craig Dykstra—who lent support by their insightful writing of the foreword and responses. (See their biographies on pp. 435–37.)

Last, but in no way least, we freely acknowledge that our thinking has been fine-tuned, our proposals tested, and we have even been "schooled" by our own engaging students at (for Fred) Duke Divinity School (Durham, North Carolina), (and for Mark) Evangelische Theologische Faculteit (Heverlee, Leuven, Belgium), Tyndale Theological Seminary (Badhoevedorp, Amsterdam, The Netherlands), Instituto Bíblico Português (St. Antão do Tojal, Lisbon, Portugal), and Seminario Teológico Centroamericano (Guatemala City, Guatemala).

Generous permission has been granted for adaptation of material in the following publications.

For sidebars:
George Thomas Kurian and Mark A. Lamport, eds., *Encyclopedia of Christian Education*, 3 vols. (Lanham, MD: Rowman & Littlefield, 2015).

For graphs in chapters 1 and 3:
"The Future of World Religions: Population Growth Projections, 2010–2015," Pew Research Study, http://www.pewforum.org/2015/04/02/religious-projec tions-2010-2050/.

For other material adapted herein:
Mark A. Lamport and Darrell Yoder, "Faithful Gestures: Rebooting the Educational Mission of the Church," *Christian Education Journal* 3 (Spring 2006): 58–78; *Christian Education Journal* 3 (Fall 2006): 362–64.

Mark A. Lamport, "The Most Indispensable Habits of Effective Theological Educators: Recalibrating Educational Philosophy, Psychology, and Practice," *Asbury Journal* 65 (2010): 36–54.

Mark A. Lamport, "Unintended Outcomes, Curious Inventions, and Misshapen Creatures: Juxtapositions of Religious Belief and Faith-Formed Practice and the Renewed Case of the Educational Mission of the Church," *Asbury Journal* 63 (2008): 95–113.

Mark A. Lamport, "Stealing Sacraments: What Protestant Educators Can Learn from Other Religious Traditions," *Christian Perspectives in Education* 2 (2008): 1–24.

Foreword Contributor

Charles R. Foster is professor emeritus of religion and education at Emory University's Candler School of Theology. Throughout his career, questions about the relationship of religion and education in the formative practices of Christian congregations and American culture have dominated the agenda of his teaching, research, and writing. He directed the Carnegie Foundation for the Advancement of Teaching and Learning study of clergy education 2001–2005. Foster is an ordained United Methodist minister. His publications include *Educating Congregations: The Future of Christian Education* (Abingdon, 1994/2006), *From Generation to Generation: The Adaptive Challenge of Mainline Protestant Education in Forming Faith* (Wipf & Stock, 2012), and with coauthors *We Are the Church Together: Cultural Diversity in Congregational Life* (Trinity Press International, 1996), and *Educating Clergy: Teaching Practices and Pastoral Imagination* (Jossey-Bass, 2006). He earned his MDiv from Union Theological Seminary in New York and EdD from Teachers College, Columbia University.

Response Contributors

Elizabeth DeGaynor (ThD/MTS, Duke Divinity School) is assistant professor of practical theology and Christian formation at Virginia Theological Seminary. She previously served as associate director of the Master of Arts in Christian Practice degree program at Duke Divinity School, along with teaching courses in Christian education and youth ministry. DeGaynor's current areas of research and writing include considering how theological reflection on fiction can shape community, and offering theological analysis of online pedagogies. She is coediting a revision of *Journey to Adulthood* (J2A), a youth ministry program of spiritual formation for sixth through twelfth grade (Church Publishing, 2020), and is a lay member of the Episcopal Church.

435

Craig Dykstra (PhD, Princeton Theological Seminary) is senior fellow in leadership education at Duke Divinity School and an ordained minister in the Presbyterian Church (USA). Before coming to Duke, he was senior vice president for religion at Lilly Endowment, where he had served since 1989. Dykstra's most recent scholarly work focused on pastoral and ecclesial imagination, as well as Christian practices, as key concepts for thinking about what it means to live the Christian life, to organize the discipline of practical theology, and to reenvision the work of pastoral ministry. He is coeditor with Dorothy Bass of *For Life Abundant: Practical Theology, Theological Education, and Christian Ministry* (Eerdmans, 2008). His books include, among others, *Growing in the Life of Faith: Education and Christian Practices* (Westminster John Knox, 2005) and *Practicing Our Faith: A Way of Life for a Searching People* (Jossey-Bass, 2010). At Duke, Dykstra conducts research, writes, teaches, and consults with Christian leaders about ways in which religious institutions can flourish in their missions and ministries in the context of our rapidly changing society and culture.

Thomas Groome was born in County Kildare, Republic of Ireland, and holds the equivalent of an MDiv from St. Patrick's Seminary in Carlow, Ireland, an MA from Fordham University, and a doctoral degree in religious education from Union Theological Seminary/Columbia University. A senior professor of theology and religious education at Boston College, Tom is also the director of the Church in the 21st Century Center at BC. His publications include his most recent book *Catholic Spiritual Practices: Treasures Old and New* (Paraclete, 2012); *Will There Be Faith? A New Vision for Educating and Growing Disciples* (HarperCollins, 2011); *Reclaiming Catholicism: Treasures Old and New* (Orbis, 2010); *Sharing Faith: A Comprehensive Approach to Religious Education and Pastoral Ministry* (Wipf & Stock, 1999); *What Makes Us Catholic: Eight Gifts for Life* (HarperCollins, 2003); *Educating for Life: A Spiritual Vision for Every Teacher and Parent* (Crossroad, 1998); *Faith for the Heart: A "Catholic" Spirituality* (Paulist, 2019); and his classic *Christian Religious Education: Sharing Our Story and Vision* (Jossey-Bass, 1980).

Kirsten Sonkyo Oh (PhD, Fuller Theological Seminary), an ordained elder in the United Methodist Church, is the ecclesiastical faculty member at Fuller Theological Seminary for United Methodist students, supporting their ordination process. She also serves as professor of practical theology at Azusa Pacific University, teaching undergraduates in the areas of Christian ministry and youth ministry. Oh has a dozen publications in various aspects of practical theology and focuses her research on intercultural narrative counseling, intersections of identity and pastoral theology, utilizing multidisciplinary approaches. She currently serves as a cochair of the Faith and Order Table of the National Council of Churches. In addition, she serves as a mentor to Women of Color Scholars through the General Board of Higher Education of the United Methodist Church.

The Very Reverend Professor **Martyn Percy** (PhD, King's College, University of London) is the forty-fifth dean of Christ Church, Oxford, England, and a member of the Faculty of Theology at the University of Oxford. He writes and teaches in two interrelated arenas: contemporary ecclesiology (specializing in Anglicanism, fundamentalism, and new Christian movements); complemented by practical, pastoral, and contextual theology, with significant work on Christianity and contemporary culture. His recent books include *Anglicanism: Confidence, Commitment, Communion* (Routledge, 2013), *Thirty-Nine New Articles: An Anglican Landscape of Faith* (Canterbury, 2013), and *The Futures of Anglicanism: Contours, Currents, Charts* (Routledge, 2017), and *The Oxford Handbook of Anglican Studies*, editor (Oxford University Press, 2015). His work is now the subject of a book, *Reasonable Radical? Engaging with the Writings of Martyn Percy*, edited by Ian Markham and Joshua Daniel (Pickwick, 2018). Percy has the distinction of being the only living theologian mentioned and quoted in Dan Brown's *Da Vinci Code* (chapter 55).

Almeda M. Wright (PhD, Emory University; MDiv, Harvard University; BS, Massachusetts Institute of Technology) is a professor of religious education at Yale Divinity School. Her research focuses on African American religion, adolescent spiritual development, and the intersections of religion and public life. Prior to Yale, she taught at Pfeiffer University and Candler School of Theology at Emory University. Professor Wright's publications include *The Spiritual Lives of Young African Americans* (Oxford University Press, 2017) and a book coedited with Mary Elizabeth Moore, *Children, Youth, and Spirituality in a Troubling World* (Chalice, 2008). Wright is an ordained minister of the American Baptist Churches and has been on the staff of Union Baptist Church in Cambridge, Massachusetts, and Victory for the World United Church of Christ in Stone Mountain, Georgia.

Foreword

1. Lewis Sherrill, *The Rise of Christian Education* (New York: Macmillan, 1950); Mary Boys, *Educating for Faith: Maps and Visions* (Cambridge: Academic Renewal, 1989); Karen Tye, *Basics of Christian Education* (St. Louis: Chalice, 2000); Robert Pazmiño, *Foundational Issues in Christian Education: An Introduction in Evangelical Perspective*, 3rd ed. (Grand Rapids: Baker Academic, 1988).

2. Frederick Packard, *Teacher Taught: An Humble Attempt to Make the Path of the Sunday School Teacher Straight and Plain* (Philadelphia: American Sunday School Union, 1839); Frederick Packard, *Teacher Teaching: A Practical View of the Relations and Duties of the Sunday-School* (Philadelphia: American Sunday School Union, 1861); Horace Bushnell, *Christian Nurture* (Eugene, OR: Wipf & Stock, 2000 [1861])); George Albert Coe, *A Social Theory of Religious Education* (New York: Charles Scribner's Sons, 1917); H. Shelton Smith, *Faith and Nurture* (New York: Charles Scribner's Sons, 1941).

3. Robert W. Lynn and Elliott Wright, *The Big Little School: 200 Years of the Sunday School* (Birmingham, AL: Religious Education, 1971).

4. Jack L. Seymour and Donald E. Miller, *Contemporary Approaches to Christian Education* (Nashville: Abingdon, 1982). Seymour continued to map developments in the field in *Mapping Christian Education: Approaches to Congregational Learning* (Nashville: Abingdon, 1997); and *Teaching the Way of Jesus: Educating for Faithful Living* (Nashville: Abingdon, 2014).

5. C. Ellis Nelson, *Where Faith Begins* (Richmond: John Knox, 1967); Lawrence O. Richards, *A Theology of Christian Education* (Grand Rapids: Zondervan, 1976); Thomas H. Groome, *Christian Religious Education: Sharing Our Story and Vision* (San Francisco: Harper & Row, 1980); Maria Harris, *Teaching and Religious Imagination* (San Francisco: Harper & Row, 1987); Anne Wimberly, *Soul Stories: African American Christian Education* (Nashville: Abingdon, 1994).

Introduction

1. Randy Maddox, *Responsible Grace: John Wesley's Practical Theology* (Nashville: Abingdon, 1994).

2. Stanley Hauerwas, "The Gesture of a Truthful Story," *Theology Today*, July 1, 1985, 181–89.

3. Perhaps Justo L. González expresses this thought more adeptly: "The notion that we read the New Testament exactly as the early Christians did, without any weight of tradition coloring our interpretation, is an illusion. It is also a dangerous illusion, for it tends to absolutize our interpretation, confusing it with the Word of God" (*The Story of Christianity*, vol. 1: *The Early Church to the Dawn of the Reformation* [San Francisco: HarperOne, 2010], 3).

4. N. T. Wright, *Simply Christian: Why Christianity Makes Sense* (New York: HarperOne, 2006), 209.

5. Jim Samra (PhD, University of Oxford) is senior pastor of Calvary Church (Grand Rapids, Michigan). This material is from his "2 Corinthians 3–5 and the Limitations of Behavioral Science," *Bulletin of Ecclesial Theology* 7 (2020): https://www.pastortheologians.com/bulletin. This theme also prominently emerges in Ryan Jackson, *New Creation in Paul's Letters* (Tübingen: Mohr Siebeck, 2010).

6. Diana Butler Bass, *Christianity after Religion: The End of Church and the Birth of a New Spiritual Awakening* (San Francisco: HarperOne, 2012), 56.

7. Find this three-part pattern in, among other places, Luke 12:13–21 (prelude, 13–15; orientation, 16–19; disorientation, 20; reorientation, 21); and Luke 14:15–24 (prelude, 15; orientation, 16–20; disorientation, 21–22; reorientation, 23–24).

8. Our thinking has been enhanced by the profound insights of Charles F. Melchert, *Wise Teaching: Biblical Wisdom and Educational Ministry* (Harrisburg, PA: Trinity Press International, 1988).

9. Charles R. Foster, *Educating Congregations: The Future of Christian Education* (Nashville: Abingdon, 1994).

10. This puts the teaching ministry of Jesus at the very center. Of course, this is unavoidable, since Christ is at the crux of *Christ*ianity. Admittedly, Christian education is not only all about Jesus's practice or principles. He wrote no letters (like Paul did), did not compile law (as in the Pentateuch), and did not compose any songs (as did David). While we are inclined to say that his person and work is central to all of Christianity, his teaching is contextualized to his time and his mission and does not necessarily demonstrate a comprehensive vision of what the church's educational mission might be. The entire Scripture is necessary for that, and even then, church tradition offers teaching examples that are good for contextualization but not necessarily found in this form in Scripture (e.g., Augustine's *Confessions*, the theological question-and-answer method of Aquinas, or of the catechisms, etc.).

11. D. Campbell Wyckoff, "Theology and Education in the Twentieth Century," *Christian Education Journal* 15 (1995): 12–26. Noted Christian educator Kendig Brubaker Cully calls D. Campbell Wyckoff the "architect of education."

12. D. Campbell Wyckoff, *The Gospel and Christian Education: A Theory of Christian Education for Our Times* (Philadelphia: Westminster, 1959), 98.

13. Wyckoff, *Gospel*, 23. The original "six questions" articulated underwent modification over the course of his career and morphed near the end of Wyckoff's writings into eight. Thomas H. Groome, who acknowledges a "resonance" between his own position and Wyckoff's, used Wyckoff's six foundational questions as an organizational framework for his own book; see Groome, *Christian Religious Education: Sharing Our Story and Vision* (San Francisco: Harper & Row, 1980), 151n36.

14. As we reflected upon our design, the flow and rationale of Thomas Groome's seminal works had almost unconsciously seeped into our thinking, most notably from *Christian Religious Education* but also from his more recent *Will There Be Faith? A New Vision for Educating and Growing Disciples* (San Francisco: Harper One, 2011).

15. We are helped in our thinking through the highly instructive and thought-provoking tome by Jack L. Seymour, *Teaching the Way of Jesus: Educating Christians for Faithful Living* (Nashville: Abingdon, 2014).

16. Richard Osmer's practical theological method informs our thinking as well as the organization of this book.

17. Rebecca Konyndyk DeYoung, *Glittering Vices: A New Look at the Seven Deadly Sins and Their Remedies* (Grand Rapids: Brazos, 2009), 183.

18. Arthur F. Holmes, *All Truth Is God's Truth* (Downers Grove, IL: InterVarsity, 1983).

19. In 1521 Melanchthon published "Loci Communes Theologici," the first systematic explanation of Protestant theology. Further explanations of these interrelated concepts may be found in J. P. Moreland and William Lane Craig, *Philosophical Foundations for a Christian Worldview* (Downers Grove, IL: IVP Academic, 2003), 18–20.

20. See his classic, *Christian Nurture* (Eugene, OR: Wipf & Stock, 2000 [1861]).

21. Marcus J. Borg and John Dominic Crossan, *The Last Week: What the Gospels Really Teach about Jesus's Final Days in Jerusalem* (San Francisco: HarperCollins, 2007), 209.

22. Mark is rooted by his sixteenth-century Swiss Brethren ancestors who were persecuted for their Anabaptist faith, which convicts him now in fighting off his looming baby boomer impulses. The perseverance and sacrifice of his forefathers act as an inhibitor to his temptation toward self-serving generational tendencies.

23. A further nurturance in faith for Mark has been parenting four children in the Christian way. The grace of God and the prayer of the faith community were forefront in the journey, which has included faithful grandparents and other family

members. It is possible they taught him more about faith than he taught them. That notwithstanding, and with much thanks and relief, as millennials, they are now all deeply involved in the life of their local churches, married to fantastic people of Christian faith, and are embarking upon the same generational task of educating their own children in faith. You are a great joy to me, Rachel, Aaron, Emily, and Amy; and so are you, Daniel, Michelle, Christopher, and Zachary! May the mission of passing on faith take deep root in their children (eight) and their progeny.

24. Truth be told, faith is not one of Mark's spiritual gifts; it is, however, his wife's most operative one. Unbeknownst to him, Mark's wife prayed for several years that he would write this book. It was not his idea. When he was (eventually) convicted to take on this writing challenge, he dragged Fred into the process. A most fabulous decision!

25. Fred has written chapters 5–10, 12–15; Mark has written the introduction, chapters 1–4, 11, 16–17, and the rejoinder/epilogue. We have each read and reread each other's chapters and alone are responsible for any errors of omission or commission that may be embedded.

26. Maddox, *Responsible Grace*.

27. George Thomas Kurian and Mark A. Lamport, eds., *Encyclopedia of Christian Education*, 3 vols. (Lanham, MD: Rowman & Littlefield, 2015).

Part One: Cultural Dynamics of Nurturing Faith

1. Here is the image. Look familiar? http://www.warnersallman.com/collection/images/christ-at-hearts-door.

2. Thomas H. Groome, one of the "response" authors, mirrors essentially the same "enchanted world" as Mark's, except his upbringing was in an Irish village (somewhat east of Illinois!), as found in *Will There Be Faith? A New Vision for Educating and Growing Disciples* (San Francisco: HarperOne, 2011), 435n7. And this "world" is likely gone forever, explains Yuval Levin in *The Fractured Republic Renewing America's Social Contract in an Age of Individualism* (Basic Book, 2016), due to a long process of unwinding and fragmenting after World War II.

3. David B. Barrett, Todd M. Johnson, and Peter F. Crossing, "Status of Global Mission, Presence, and Activities, AD 1800-2025," *International Bulletin of Missionary Research* 32 (January 2008): 30.

4. David Barrett, George T. Kurian, and Todd M. Johnson, *World Christian Encyclopedia: A Comparative Survey of Churches and Religions in the Modern World*, 2 vols. (Oxford: Oxford University Press, 2001).

5. The number of Christians in China is not known with any exactitude, but it is no doubt a spectacular number—although probably lower than the number for the United States.

6. Charles Taylor, *A Secular Age* (Cambridge, MA: Harvard University Press, 2007).

7. While this is a generalization, we understand some Latin American regimes have brutally repressed Roman Catholic Christians. Consider Oscar Romero.

Chapter One

1. Ruth Tucker, *Walking Away from Faith* (Downers Grove, IL: InterVarsity, 2002); David Kinnaman, *You Lost Me: Why Young Christians Are Leaving the Church . . . and Rethinking Faith* (Grand Rapids: Baker, 2011); David G. Bromley, *Falling from Faith: Causes and Consequences* (Newbury Park, CA: Sage, 1988); Ross Campbell, *Kids Who Follow, Kids Who Don't* (Wheaton, IL: Victor, 1987); Tom Bisset, *Why Christian Kids Leave the Faith* (Grand Rapids: Discover House/ RBC Ministries, 1992); William J. Byron and Charles Zech, "Why They Left," *America: The National Catholic Review*, April 30, 2012, http://americamagazine .org/node/150484; "Leaving Christianity" provides dozens of stories and weblinks devoted to those who have left Christianity, see https://sites.google.com/site/leav ingxtianity/home.

2. See http://www.pewresearch.org/daily-number/americas-former-catholics. See also Lincoln Mullen, "Catholics Who Aren't Catholic," *Atlantic*, September 8, 2015; and Archbishop Charles J. Chaput, *Strangers in a Strange Land: Living the Catholic Faith in a Post-Christian World* (New York: Henry Holt, 2017). Chaput deftly explores the challenge: How do we as Catholics navigate the secularization of America, and the moral crisis it has spurred?

3. Andrew M. Greely, *Religion in Europe at the End of the Second Millennium* (Herndon, VA: Transaction, 2004); Noelle Knox, "Religion Takes a Back Seat in Europe," *USA Today*, August 11, 2011. (A more detailed version of this article can be found at http://usatoday30.usatoday.com/news/world/2005-08-10-europe -religion-cover_x.htm.)

4. See Howard V. and Edna H. Hong, *The Essential Kierkegaard* (Princeton: Princeton University Press, 2000).

5. We derive no pleasure from observing that disenchantment, lethargy, and irrelevance are found in other educational enterprises in our world. Perhaps—no, it is very likely—even the practices and strategies inherent in general schooling unduly influence and contribute in a dilatory way to marginal results in Christian education.

6. Religious switching is not presumed to be the sole category for loss of faith. Disaffiliation from tradition and institution certainly comes into play as well. Here we wish to emphasize that formational processes internal to the Christian community are a primary cause of religious nonobservance, and that is undesirable. As professor Byard Bennett notes, social scientific literature often links the decline in

religious salience principally to changes in the broader society. It is often assumed, for example, that a choice of different economic models restructures social arrangements and creates a public sphere that is neutral with respect to transcendent (noneconomic) commitments, limiting the work that religion does within the scope of daily life. The primary figure in this discussion would be the Scottish sociologist Steve Bruce (especially his *God Is Dead: Secularization in the West* [Malden, MA: Blackwell, 2002]), but the existential security thesis of Pippa Norris and Ronald Inglehart (in *Sacred and Secular: Religion and Politics Worldwide*, 2nd ed. [Cambridge: Cambridge University Press, 2011]) has also been widely discussed.

7. John H. Westerhoff, *Will Our Children Have Faith?* (Harrisburg, PA: Morehouse, 2000), 18.

8. Catherine Evtuhov, *The Cross and the Sickle: Sergei Bulgakov and the Fate of Russian Religious Philosophy* (Ithaca, NY: Cornell University Press, 1997), 212.

9. This data comes from the Pew Research Center, "The Future of World Religions: Population Growth Projections, 2010–2050," April 2, 2015, http://www.pewforum.org/2015/04/02/religious-projections-2010-2050/#projected-growth-map.

10. Some believe the term *atheist* should not exist. No one ever needs to identify one's self as a "nonastrologer" or a "nonalchemist." As novelist Dan Brown asserts in his best-selling *Origin* (New York: Doubleday, 2017), 290, "atheism is nothing more than the noises reasonable people make in the presence of unjustified religious beliefs." This theme is more fully developed in noted skeptic Sam Harris's *Letter to a Christian Nation* (New York: Vintage, 2006).

11. Unaffiliated religions are expected to rise over that same time from 16 percent of the population to 26 percent. By 2050, the United States will have more Muslims (2.1 percent of the population) than Jews (1.4 percent). In South America and the Caribbean, Christianity will see a slight dip over the next four decades, from 90 percent in 2010 to 89 percent in 2050. Over that same time, the religiously unaffiliated population will add 45 million, increasing from 8 percent of the population in 2010 to 9 percent in 2050.

If the current trends continue beyond 2050—which is a big *if* considering unforeseen events that can happen over a forty-year span (war, famine, innovation, etc.)—then by the year 2070 the world's population of Muslims would roughly equal that of Christians.

Other chief findings from the report: Islam will grow faster than any other religion over the next forty years. Atheists, agnostics, and other people who do not affiliate with any religion, though increasing in countries such as the United States and France, will make up a declining share of the world's total population. In Europe, Muslims will make up 10 percent of the overall population. In the United States, Christians will decline from more than three-quarters of the population in 2010 to two-thirds in 2050, and Judaism will no longer be the largest non-Christian religion. Muslims will be more numerous in the US than people who identify as Jewish on the basis of religion. Four out of every ten Christians in the world will live in sub-Saharan Africa.

12. We acknowledge that some find the numbers from the Pew Research Center do not correspond to other studies on changes in religious identity, and there are questions about whether the data rest on a solid empirical foundation. For example, the projections for switching out of Islam are at best mere speculation, because there seems to be a dearth of reliable data on religious deconversion from Islam, and the number of converts to Christianity is too small to be a significant factor. Furthermore, folk religions tend to be retained when practitioners maintain multiple religious identities (i.e., in Hong Kong one might seek help from both Buddhist and Taoist religious professionals at different times in response to different needs). Other than that, there is a broad tendency of practitioners of folk religions to increasingly affiliate with transnational world religions. References to the growth in the Muslim population worldwide and in the US are often linked to higher birthrate rather than to religious switching.

13. Religious switching is likely to play a role in the growth of religious groups. But such patterns are complex and varied. In some countries, it is fairly common for adults to leave their childhood religion and switch to another faith. In others, changes in religious identity are rare, legally cumbersome, or even illegal. While it is true the religiously unaffiliated population is projected to shrink as a percentage of the global population (from 16 percent in 2010 to 13 percent by the middle of this century), it will nevertheless increase in absolute number. Recent censuses and surveys indicate there were about 1.1 billion atheists, agnostics, and people who do not identify with any particular religion. By 2050, the unaffiliated population is expected to exceed 1.2 billion. At the same time, however, the unaffiliated are expected to continue to increase as a share of the population in much of Europe and North America. In the United States, for example, the unaffiliated are projected to grow from an estimated 16 percent of the total population (including children) in 2010 to 26 percent in 2050.

14. In North America, Muslims and followers of "other religions" are the fastest-growing religious groups. In the United States, for example, the share of the population that belongs to other religions is projected to more than double—albeit from a very small base—rising from 0.6 percent to 1.5 percent. Christians are projected to decline from 78 percent of the US population in 2010 to 66 percent in 2050, while the unaffiliated are expected to rise from 16 percent to 26 percent. And by the middle of the twenty-first century, the United States is likely to have more Muslims (2.1 percent of the population) than people who identify with the Jewish faith (1.4 percent). In Latin America and the Caribbean, Christians will remain the largest religious group, making up 89 percent of the population in 2050, down

slightly from 90 percent in 2010. Latin America's religiously unaffiliated population is projected to grow both in absolute number and percentage terms, rising from about forty-five million people (8 percent) in 2010 to sixty-five million (9 percent) in 2050. For parallel information on the complex nuance of Europe's many and varied countries/cultures, see sources in footnote 3.

15. Philip Jenkins, *The Next Christendom: The Coming of Global Christianity* (Oxford: Oxford University Press, 2002).

16. All told, the unaffiliated are expected to add ninety-seven million people and lose thirty-six million via switching, for a net gain of sixty-one million by 2050. Modest net gains through switching also are expected for Muslims (three million), adherents of folk religions (three million), and members of other religions (two million). Jews are expected to experience a net loss of about three hundred thousand people due to switching, while Buddhists are expected to lose nearly three million.

17. Kinnaman, *You Lost Me.*

18. Gabriel Moran suggests that we move away from the terms *formal* and *informal* education because education always has form. His suggestion is to distinguish between "schooling," meaning school, and other forms of education—for example, family, work, leisure time. Thanks to Finola Cunnane for pointing this out.

19. Debra Dean Murphy, *Teaching That Transforms: Worship as the Heart of Christian Education* (Grand Rapids: Brazos, 2004), calls Christian education "a discipline struggling for legitimacy and respectability, a discipline whose intellectual complacency and lack of critical awareness have not only led to its marginalization in the academy but also left it bankrupt of the necessary resources to carry out the urgent task of forming and transforming the lives of Christians" (p. 22). Theologians accuse Christian educators of not being theologically informed; educators criticize theologians for neglecting the task of being educators. Theologians wrongly assume that because one may know theology one assuredly can teach it. Some churches are hindered by ministers who have little facility in or appreciation for the educational enterprise. Yet, theology is as useless without good education as Christian education is dangerous without informed theology (see Thomas H. Groome, *Christian Religious Education* [San Francisco: Jossey-Bass, 1999]).

20. Elias Aboujaoude, *Virtually You: The Dangerous Powers of the E-Personality* (New York: W. W. Norton, 2011).

21. Brian Mahan, Michael Warren, and David. F. White, *Awakening Youth Discipleship: Christian Resistance in a Consumer Culture* (Eugene, OR: Wipf & Stock, 2008); Charles R. Foster, *From Generation to Generation: The Adaptive Challenge of Mainline Protestant Education in Forming Faith* (Eugene, OR: Wipf & Stock, 2012).

22. Karen Mann, Tim Dornan, P. W. Teunissen, "Perspectives on Learning," in *Medical Education: Theory and Practice*, ed. Tim Dornan, Karen Mann, Albert Scherpbier, and John Spencer (London: Elsevier, 2011), 17–38.

23. James Smart, *The Teaching Ministry of the Church: An Examination of the Basic Principles of Christian Education* (Philadelphia: Westminster, 1954).

24. Charles Taylor, *A Secular Age* (Cambridge, MA: Belknap), 539–41.

25. Recent discussion of world religious traditions has centered almost exclusively on the question of salvation and reflected a three-prong typology of exclusivist, inclusivist, and pluralist. Perhaps some readers are suspicious, wary of any apparent accommodation to a mélange of world religions and their claims. This part is not a treatise on theological doctrine, but on how adherents of various religious traditions practice their beliefs in ways Christians could learn from in order to enhance their own faith and witness in the world.

26. Granted, the communities from which we are learning have suffered ongoing histories of minoritization, marginalization, and oppression. We are not intending to repeat past Christian privilege and a history of colonialism, where people with power feel free to simply take what they want/need in the name of faith without regard to marginalized communities from which they have taken. To refer to specific religious practices, as we have here, from the Mormon, Muslim, or Jewish tradition is undertaken with every intention of respect and gratitude.

27. Interreligious dialogue often turns on the question of mutually exclusive claims to salvation. The intent here, however, is to explore pedagogical processes of formation, a more modest undertaking. In other words, in this part, we make the effort to separate theology from education. Even this modest proposal is somewhat controversial. Gabriel Moran, cited above, contends that education is always nontheological, meaning that pedagogies may be exchanged across multiple contexts, including faith traditions. Debra Dean Murphy, also cited above, contends the opposite: pedagogies are always attached to particular theological claims, meaning that they are not automatically interchangeable.

28. Gerald R. McDermott, *Evangelicals Learn from World Religions? Jesus, Revelation and Religious Traditions* (Downers Grove, IL: InterVarsity, 2000), 10.

29. McDermott, *Evangelicals*, 14.

30. Mark must confess that the insights of the panelists and the response of the students to the ideas of alternate faith education philosophy and strategy make this learning exercise one of his favorites of the semester. Then, as the course evaluations are read, it appears to be one of their favorites too. Another comment may be noteworthy: the session is neither confrontational nor evangelistic but centers on gaining our guests' perspective on the issues. We find that the representatives seem to enjoy the dialogue, and they often gain a greater understanding of our Protestant educational enterprise as well.

31. For a penetrating analysis of the mercurial ascendancy of the Mormons by one of the finest sociologists in our day, see Rodney Stark, *The Rise of Mormonism* (New York: Columbia University Press, 2005). Stark claims that Mormonism has grown faster than any other new religion in American history. Between 1840 and

1980, it averaged a growth rate of 44 percent per decade; in the four decades from 1940 through 1980, growth zoomed to an astonishing 53 percent. If it maintains a 30 percent growth rate, Mormons would exceed sixty million by the year 2080; if 50 percent, then 265 million by 2080. See also a fine review of this book by Gerald R. McDermott, "Saints Rising: Is Mormonism the First New World Religion Since the Birth of Islam?," *Books & Culture* 12.1 (2006): 8–12. We acknowledge that various allegations are made against the Mormon Church and that bizarre sects exist within it; see, for example, best-selling author Jon Krakauer's riveting account, *Under the Banner of Heaven: A Story of Violent Faith* (Garden City, NY: Doubleday, 2003).

32. For a similarly appreciative Christian take on Mormon faith formation, see "Mormon Envy: Sociological Tools for Consequential Faith," in Kenda Dean, *Almost Christian: What the Faith of Our Teenagers Is Telling the American Church* (New York: Oxford University Press, 2010), 45–60.

33. *The Journal of John Wesley*, Christian Classics Ethereal Library, https://www.ccel.org/ccel/wesley/journal.vi.ii.xi.html.

34. For introductions to "cognitive disequilibrium" or "cognitive dissonance," see Bruce R. Joyce, "Dynamic Disequilibrium: The Intelligence of Growth," *Theory into Practice* 23 (1984): 26–34; "Cognitive Disequilibrium," in *Encyclopedia of Child Behavior and Development*, ed. Sam Goldstein and Jack A. Naglieri (Boston: Springer, 2011), 380; Leon Festinger, *A Theory of Cognitive Dissonance* (Evanston, IL: Row, Peterson, 1957).

35. It is brilliant, if somewhat fanciful, writing and reminds us of the Jewish roots of our Christian faith.

36. Paradoxically, in spite of Judaism's ancient traditions of passing on faith and religious instruction, cultural relevance and postmodern concerns have been raised recently. In 2006, Christians and Jews met at a two-day conference to discuss worship in America. Rabbi Dov Gartenberg of Congregation Beth Shalom, Simi Valley, California, and fifteen other Jewish leaders initiated the meeting with a desire to talk with evangelical Christians about new styles of worship and "emergent Judaism," as it has been labeled by some of its leaders. "We've got to learn from what our Christian colleagues are doing," said Shawn Landres, with Synagogue 3000, a progressive Jewish think-tank. Speakers at the conference said both faiths are struggling to stay relevant—particularly to young people—in a culture that is increasingly fast-paced and global (see Gillian Flaccus, "Dissatisfied Jews, Christians Share Ideas," *Grand Rapids Press*, January 21, 2006, p. C8).

37. Lauren Winner, *Mudhouse Sabbath* (Brewster, MA: Paraclete, 2004), ix.

38. Data compiled on North America (only) shows that a Christian's lifestyle is not discernibly different from that of non-Christians. For a well-researched and all-too-compelling case, see Ronald Sider, *The Scandal of the Evangelical Con-*

science: Why Are Christians Living Just Like the Rest of the World? (Grand Rapids: Baker, 2005). See also "Annual Barna Group Survey Describes Changes in America's Religious Beliefs and Practices," April 11, 2005, https://www.barna.com /research/annual-barna-group-survey-describes-changes-in-americas-religious -beliefs-and-practices, and "Barna's Annual Tracking Study Shows Americans Stay Spiritually Active, But Biblical Views Wane," May 21, 2007, https://www.barna .com/research/barnas-annual-tracking-study-shows-americans-stay-spiritually -active-but-biblical-views-wane.

39. William Hutchison, *Religious Pluralism in America: The Contentious History of a Founding Ideal* (New Haven: Yale University Press, 2003).

40. David Watson, *I Believe in Evangelism* (London: Hodder and Stoughton, 1976).

41. See Amy Plantinga Pauw's fascinating essay, "Attending to the Gaps between Beliefs and Practices," that applies this principle to the prophet Jonah and his misadventures, in *Practicing Theology: Beliefs and Practices in Christian Life*, ed. Miroslav Volf and Dorothy Bass (Grand Rapids: Eerdmans, 2002).

42. It seems the Christian practices that at least mainline Christians used to experience (reading Scripture after supper, bedtime or family prayers, the second Sunday service focused on the catechism and faith learning, etc.) have been abandoned or no longer accomplish their intended goals, appearing to have lost their relevance. Unfortunately, such practices have not been replaced with newer or more relevant ones. Would that be why so often only a nominal faith remains?

43. Michael Warren, *Youth and the Future of the Church: Ministry with Youth and Young Adults* (New York: Seabury, 1990), 20.

44. Cited in Marvin R. Wilson, *Our Father Abraham: Jewish Roots of the Christian Faith* (Grand Rapids: Eerdmans, 1989), 280.

45. Dorothy Bass, "Foreword," in *Educating People of Faith: Exploring the History of Jewish and Christian Communities*, ed. John Van Engen (Grand Rapids: Eerdmans, 2004).

46. For more on the social learning theories of Albert Bandura, see his *Social Learning Theory* (Englewood Cliffs, NJ: Prentice Hall, 1977) and *Social Foundations of Thought and Action: A Social Cognitive Theory* (Englewood Cliffs, NJ: Prentice Hall, 1986). Etienne Wenger's writings on communities of practice are very relevant here too, for example, *Communities of Practice: Learning, Meaning, and Identity* (Cambridge: Cambridge University Press, 1999).

47. Bandura's theory, with its emphasis upon observation and imitation as foundational for learning, along with this section's attentiveness to the formative efficacy of embodied practices (public ritual and personal prayer), can promote consideration of how persons with intellectual or developmental disabilities (IDD) may be included in a community's efforts toward faith formation. According to

Bandura, much learning begins not with thinking thoughts but with observing and doing actions. In addition, many persons with IDD readily respond to the affection of admired mentors. Faith formation ought therefore to include persons with IDD.

48. There is one more facet of Jewish religious education—that Jews pay for religious education in their synagogues—we are tempted to endorse for Protestants. Families are billed for tuition, a sizeable sum, and based on the tested theory that one values what one pays for, we surmise that with the financial investment comes a spiritual investment (at least, from parents footing the bill). But can you imagine the turmoil this radical notion would cause in a typical church? Mark was first introduced to this theory of the increased sense of quality education based on charging high tuition at a liberal arts college at which he taught—a college of highly valued academics. Perhaps if Christians paid for their Sunday school education, the quality of both what is taught (and how) and what is learned would improve.

49. See his *Translating the Message: The Missionary Impact on Culture* (Maryknoll, NY: Orbis, 1989); *Encountering the West: Christianity and the Global Cultural Process* (Maryknoll, NY: Orbis, 1993); *Whose Religion Is Christianity? The Gospel beyond the West* (Grand Rapids: Eerdmans, 2006). Of relevance for this nuanced subsection, see Sanneh's "Muhammad's Significance for Christians: Biography, History, and Faith," in *Piety and Power: Muslims and Christians in West Africa* (Maryknoll, NY: Orbis, 2003).

50. Bob McCahill, *Dialogue of Life: A Christian among Allah's Poor* (Maryknoll, NY: Orbis, 1996).

51. It is ironic that Muslims are often criticized for their radical faith commitment by Christians, who often exhibit a flaccid level of commitment—not too blatant, so as not to appear fanatical. Even more ironic, Christians in the United States sometimes accuse devoted Muslims of being "un-American," apparently presuming that Christian and US identities are identical.

52. Peter Berger, *The Sacred Canopy: Elements of a Sociological Theory of Religion* (Garden City, NY: Doubleday, 1969), 119. We are reminded by Finola Cunnane about Thomas Moore's book on *Care for the Soul*, in which he claims the great malady of our time is lack of soul, both individually and collectively. And when soul is neglected, he continues, symptoms such as obsessions, addictions, aggressions, violence, and loss of meaning abound.

53. Cited in L. Nathan Oaklander, *Existentialist Philosophy: An Introduction*, 2nd ed. (Upper Saddle River, NJ: Prentice Hall, 1996), 432.

54. Carl F. H. Henry, *Twilight of a Great Civilization: The Drift toward Neo-Paganism* (Westchester, NY: Crossway, 1988), 17.

55. For more on these, see the 9Marks website on building healthy churches, https://www.9marks.org/article/emerging-church-primer/ and http://freshexpressionsus.org/about.

56. Harold Bloom, *The American Religion: The Emergence of the Post-Christian Nation* (New York: Simon & Schuster, 1993), 196.

57. Murphy, *Teaching That Transforms*, 185.

58. For more on "kinesthetic learning," see Rita Dunn et al., "Impact of Learning-Style Instructional Strategies on Students' Achievement and Attitudes: Perceptions of Educators in Diverse Institutions," *The Clearing House: A Journal of Educational Strategies, Issues and Ideas* 82.3 (2009): 135–40; Harold Pashler, Mark McDaniel, Doug Rohrer, and Robert Bjork, "Learning Styles: Concepts and Evidence," *Psychological Science in the Public Interest* 9.3 (2008): 105–19; Frank Coffield, David Moseley, Elaine Hall, and Kathryn Ecclestone, *Learning Styles and Pedagogy in Post-16 Learning: A Systematic and Critical Review* (London: Learning and Skills Research Centre, 2004); Elizabeth Jane Simpson, *The Classification of Educational Objectives, Psychomotor Domain* (Washington, DC: Gryphon House, 1972); David Kolb, *Experiential Learning: Experience as the Source of Learning and Development* (Englewood Cliffs, NJ: Prentice Hall, 1984).

59. Bass, "Foreword," v, authors' emphasis.

60. This thesis is powerfully demonstrated in Alan Wolfe's profound writing in *The Transformation of American Religion: How We Actually Live Our Faith* (New York: Free Press, 2003). Lourens Geuze, one of Mark's students at Evangelische Theologische Faculteit (Heverlee, Leuven, Belgium), sees a correlation between vigorous insistence on personal individualism with an increasing tendency toward nondenominationalism of churches.

61. Andy Crouch, *Culture Making: Recovering Our Creative Calling* (Downers Grove, IL: InterVarsity, 2009).

62. From a sermon by A. W. Tozer, http://www.cmalliance.org/devotions/tozer ?id=23.

63. Students in Mark's course at Evangelische Theologische Faculteit (Heverlee, Leuven, Belgium) in May 2018 contend "lack of commitment to anything" is problematic for nurturing faith. This is manifested in an unwillingness to join, participate, and follow. Likewise, students in Mark's course at Tyndale Theological Seminary (Badhoevedorp, Amsterdam, The Netherlands) in June 2018 wondered whether "self-deception, biblical illiteracy, and time on task" might also be obstacles to faith development. Points taken in each account.

Chapter Two

1. Australian American actress Nicole Kidman recently returned to the foundations of her childhood faith because she was ultimately dissatisfied with the life she was attempting to live without God. She said she "longed for something all the fame and fortune could never fulfill." See https://www.foxnews.com/opinion /paul-batura-nicole-kidman-faith-catholic-vanity-fair.

2. See his *Explaining Postmodernism: Skepticism and Socialism from Rousseau to Foucault* (Tempe: Scholargy, 2004). One might find a suitable definition of postmodernism in Steven L. Bindeman, *The Antiphilosophers* (New York: Peter Lang, 2015), 1–2.

3. While most scholars eschew circumscribing postmodernism with precision, due to its indefinable qualities, nevertheless here is an attempt at least to paint its general facets. Reading through the list of binary attributes below will at least give the reader perhaps a clearer orientation to the nuances of this rather complex philosophical topic:

Descriptions of the postmodern spirit (the first characteristic in each phrase is preferred over the second): the individual to the universal; the psychological to the ideological; communication to communion; information to knowledge (truth); diversity to homogeneity; permissiveness to coercion; multicriteria to norms and dogma; an eclectic approach to a systematic one; what is vital and existential to what is logical and reasonable; opinion to ideas and thought; sentiments to reason; artisanship to art; aesthetics to ethics; syncretism to unity of belief; multiculturalism to culture; complete irrationalism to absolute rationalism; what is particular to what is universal or cosmopolitan; what is private and personal to what is public and social; egoism to solidarity; subjectivity to objectivity; personal impulses and instinctual feelings to objective norms and values; pleasure to asceticism and violence; options to obligations; frankness to secrecy; human needs to technological demands; multiplicity and difference to uniqueness and uniformity; micro to macro; minorities to majorities; local/concrete contexts to global contexts; marginal dissent to global consensus; microgroups to macrocommunities; emotional, sectarian communities to ecclesial communities; spontaneous leaders to legal or traditional leaders; personalism to authority; "deconstruction" of the inherited world to its affirmation; "decolonization" to colonization; the people, and ethnic groups, to the nation; adolescent immaturity to adult maturity; ambiguity to clarity and distinction; what is weak to what is strong; what is frivolous to what is serious; what is ephemeral, unstable, and transitory, to what is firm, stable, and lasting; leisure and partying to work; consumerism to production (Isaías Díez del Río, "Postmodernidad y Nueva Religiosidad," *Religion y Cultura* 39 [1993]: 55–91).

4. Nicholas Wolterstorff, *Lament for a Son* (Grand Rapids: Eerdmans, 1987), 76.

5. Professor Stephen Asma (Columbia College, Chicago) is irreligious but concedes societies need religion, and that its irrationality ("magical thinking," he stamps it) may even be the source of its power. He dismisses religion as a cultural analgesic and the function of a cultural response to life's problems. Religion can be energizing (also "anesthetizing," he surmises), but its rituals, says Asma, produce a therapeutic mechanism to assist people trying to navigate suffering. And emotion may offer quicker ways to solve problems than cognition, which for the unbeliev-

ing leaves the options for relieving life's painful experiences to aspirin, alcohol, hobbies, work, love, and friendship. See his "What Religion Gives Us over Science," *The New York Times International Edition*, June 5, 2018, 10–11. Possibly, but other empirical *emotional* attempts to mask life-pain are violence and terrorism, racism and marginalization, power and corruption. Some may assign these latter six evidences as a result of religion, but no true religion promotes these things; they result from human flaw, sinful choices, and lack of peace through Jesus.

6. Thomas Aquinas, *The Summa Theologica*, trans. The Fathers of the English Dominican Province (Benziger Bros. ed., 1947), https://www.newadvent.org/summa/3004.htm.

7. Adapted from August Comte, *The Positive Philosophy of August Comte*, trans. Harriet Martineau, vol. 3 (London: Bell, 1896), 305–8.

8. A fine telling of the "how we got this way" story can be found in Charles Taylor, *A Secular Age* (Cambridge, MA: Harvard University Press, 2007). He traces the roots of humanism through three streams of evolved awareness: that people (finally) became enlightened about the (previously mysterious) phenomenon of nature; that humans figured out that the foundation of societies is not the divine right of kings but the will of the people; and that we do not live in an "enchanted world" where we need God to sustain us.

9. Langdon Gilkey, *Naming the Whirlwind* (New York: Bobbs-Merrill, 1969), 39–71.

10. The quotation is from Fyodor Dostoyevski, *The Brothers Karamazov*, trans. Constance Garnett (New York: Modern Library, 1955), part 1, book 2, chapter 6. As a further word about the point of this subsection, James K. A. Smith's book *Who's Afraid of Relativism?* argues that relativism is more about our knowledge being contingent upon our "relative" embeddedness in life. In other words, we cannot discover truth from some point of outside neutrality and objectivity. This does not negate truth; it simply says that it is mediated to us contingently—which is part of being human.

11. Daniel Taylor, "Are You Tolerant? Should You Be?," *Christianity Today*, January 11, 1999, 43.

12. Stephanie Hanes, "Singles Nation: Why So Many Americans Are Unmarried," *Christian Science Monitor*, June 15, 2015, https://www.csmonitor.com/USA/Society/2015/0614/Singles-nation-Why-so-many-Americans-are-unmarried.

13. Randall Balmer, "The Generation of Faith," in *Growing Pains: Learning to Love My Father's Faith* (Grand Rapids: Brazos, 2000).

14. Free-thinkers among us may be intrigued by Dan Brown's fascinating and inventive perspectives in his novel *Origin* (New York: Doubleday, 2017) on how humankind morphs with technology into a new species, and the human forms we know now disappear! This is obviously a work of fiction, yet the twin themes of this best seller—where did we come from and where are we going—offer proposals

NOTES TO PAGES 62–66

very attractive to the postmodern mindset, that is, life exists without God, and the human destiny is intertwined with the inevitable captivity of artificial intelligence.

15. Richard N. Ostling, "Christianity Gets Credit for West's Freedom, Sociologist Claims," *Grand Rapids Press*, January 28, 2006, D7.

16. Allan Bloom, *The Closing of the American Mind* (New York: Simon & Schuster, 1987), 25–26.

17. This "logical conclusion" does not automatically have to go here, though it may. Postmodernism's response to modern certainty is skepticism. Skepticism can perform a prophetic iconoclasm under the right conditions.

18. Cited in Bruno Forte, "Parola e silenzio nella riflessione teológica," *Settimana di Camaldoli*, 2001, www.nostreradici.it/parola_silenzio.htm.

19. While Vattimo is decidedly pessimistic about the effects of postmodernism, others such as John D. Caputo and Richard Kearney portray postmodernism in a much more affirmative light.

20. We are inclined to agree with "complexifying" readings of the world, especially as modernity's chief failure has been its idolization of human pretenses to know with certainty. Thus, we might be accused of advocating tolerance based on the limits of our understanding. Yet as Christians, we believe we are called to love, compassion, and humility. These are not synonyms for tolerance, but like tolerance, they refuse the violence that so often accompanies monopolization of truth. We are reminded of the quotation from a few years back: "Christians have spent much of the twentieth century trying to be right, perhaps it is time for us to be good?" Perhaps that names the tension we continue to feel here. We would rather be accused of being "tolerant" based upon our love of others different from ourselves than beat the drum against the persecution of those accused of being "intolerant" in the name of Jesus. What do you say?

21. A. J. Conyers, "Can Postmodernism Be Used as a Template for Christian Theology?," *Christian Scholar's Review* (Spring 2004): 308–9.

22. Richard Bauckham, *The Bible in Mission: Christian Mission in the Postmodern World* (Grand Rapids: Baker Academic, 2004).

23. Conyers, "Can Postmodernism Be Used?," 308.

24. See Willie James Jennings, *The Christian Imagination: Theology and the Origins of Race* (New Haven: Yale University Press, 2011).

25. Jean-François Lyotard, *The Postmodern Condition: A Report on Knowledge*, trans. Geoff Bennington and Brian Massumi (Minneapolis: University of Minnesota Press, 1984), xxiv.

26. For example, see Sofia Lotto Persio, "Did Stephen Hawking Believe in God? What Physicist Said about the Creation of the Universe," *Newsweek*, March 14, 2018, https://www.yahoo.com/news/did-stephen-hawking-believe-god-093023745 .html. "In the past, before we understood science, it was logical to believe God created the Universe. Now, however, science offers a more convincing explanation.

What I meant when I said we would know God's mind was that we would know everything that God would understand if he existed. But there are no Gods."

27. To be fair, it is debated whether Lyotard would have Christianity in mind with respect to metanarratives. Perhaps the main thing about the metanarratives to which Lyotard refers is their oppressive "false legitimizing" power. He is addressing primarily overarching philosophical systems, science, or political frameworks (such as Marxism). These have been devalued because they could not fulfill their promises and their legitimizing (false) power has been revealed.

28. Radical postmodernism takes this further. Self-authority is more about modernism than it is about postmodernism. James K. A. Smith would argue this in *Who's Afraid of Postmodernism? Taking Derrida, Lyotard, and Foucault to the Church* (Grand Rapids: Baker Academic, 2008). The self as an isolated individual is gone. It does not exist because it has always been embedded so thickly in traditions, communities, and environments; thus the "self" can never emerge. This embeddedness and its inescapability are keys for postmodernism. This is where Heidegger's influence is central.

29. Ralph C. Wood, "Orthodoxy at a Hundred," *First Things*, November 2008, 42.

30. Ronald T. Michener reminds us that some postmoderns (Caputo, for example) are not arguing for getting rid of but integrating experience, feeling, and imagination into our discourse, since it has been so top-heavy with rationalism. In other words, some do not deny reason; they are simply saying that reason should not always be the "boss" that sets all the terms. This is where postmodernism shows much promise for Christian thinkers.

31. Harold M. Schulweis, *For Those Who Can't Believe: Overcoming the Obstacles to Faith* (New York: HarperCollins, 1994), 2.

32. Like Mark, Michener is a professor at Evangelische Theologische Faculteit (Leuven, Belgium).

33. See his astute entries "Christian Education, Postmodern" and "Postmodernism" in the *Encyclopedia of Christian Education*, ed. George Thomas Kurian and Mark A. Lamport, 2 vols. (Lanham, MD: Rowman & Littlefield, 2015), 1:255 and 2:971–72 respectively.

34. Harvey Cox, *The Future of Faith* (San Francisco: HarperOne, 2009).

35. J. Marion Snapper, "The Third Person in the Learning Process," in *Teach Me Thy Way* (Grand Rapids: The Christian Reformed Church, 1965), 126. See also Garrett Green, *Imagining God* (Grand Rapids: Eerdmans, 1989), and Eva Brann, *The World of Imagination* (Lanham, MD: Rowman & Littlefield, 1992).

36. See James K. A. Smith, *Desiring the Kingdom: Worship, Worldview, and Cultural Formation* (Grand Rapids: Baker Academic, 2009), 18–19, 32–34.

37. Does participation in faith practices in the context of community itself constitute faith? Or does the community performance exist to nurture faith in individuals? We say *both*. What do you say?

NOTES TO PAGES 72–76

38. The Christian flirtation with culture displays a profound overconfidence in the power to change culture. Andy Crouch reports in *Culture Making: Recovering Our Creative Calling* (Downers Grove, IL: InterVarsity, 2013) that of the 1.5 million titles in the Harvard University library collections published before 1900, *zero* included a reference to changing the world. In 2007, Google results for the same inquiry number 8.8 million. Crouch says: "We moderns certainly can't be accused of lacking self-confidence. The explosion of books about 'changing the world' fits our self-image—we are world changers. But the more carefully you listen to the people who study the mechanism of culture—sociologists and anthropologists and journalists—the more you begin to doubt that we can change the world at all. A major theme of contemporary sociology is not how we can change the world—it is how thoroughly the world changes and shapes us" (pp. 188–89).

39. Crouch, *Culture Making*, 176–77.

40. The persistence of stories, at least tacitly as social imaginaries, seems to rebut what Lyotard says. We will pick up and elaborate upon "story" as a means of nurturing faith in part 2.

41. Andy Crouch, "Rites of Passage," *Christianity Today*, June 1, 2003. Unintended consequences have arisen from the postmodern story with Christianity. Joseph R. Laracy considers further the ramifications of postmodernism on Christianity. He sees the rejection of grand narratives, fragmentation of knowledge, loss of the human subject, and the so-called "death of man" as having had particularly devastating consequences on both the academic study of theology and the practice of religion. Philosophers, theologians, and indeed entire ecclesial communities have seen historic Protestant communities, in an attempt to be "relevant" to postmodern humans, transform themselves in such a way that many Episcopal, Lutheran, Methodist, and Presbyterian families no longer feel the need to attend Sunday services. After all, options trump obligations. In the more extreme instantiations of the postmodern preferences, as have been expressed in the Unitarian Universalist Church and the post-church "Christianity" of Vattimo, one finds even less interest from *cercatori di Dio* (seekers of God). If there is no such thing as objective truth and God has not definitively revealed himself through his Son, why rouse yourself for morning "worship" at a Unitarian Universalist Church? All that remains is the man, alone on the sinking ship in the dark of night, clumsily trying to build a posthuman, post-Christian lifeboat ("A Postmodern Christianity?," *Homiletical and Pastoral Review*, September 7, 2013, http://www.hprweb.com/2013/09/a-postmodern-christianity).

Chapter Three

1. Particularly memorable was that two students were from Rwanda—one from the Hutu tribe and another from the Tutsi tribe. This bitter, deadly ethnic rivalry

is detailed with great insight in the movie *Rwanda* (2004). In our class, however, these men understood that their greater citizenship was not tribal but that of brothers in the peaceable kingdom.

2. We acknowledge that there may be various layers to this story, one intended to display how Christianity as a sectarian movement of the Spirit often seems to get flattened and domesticated by institutional concerns into nominalism. Critics of Christian colonialism, for example, may wonder why those views did not enter the conversation. They might also welcome the apparent lethargy in some branches of African Christianity as a signal not of the impotence of Christianity itself but the rotting of its oppressive European trappings (like equating Christian and national identities). We are no experts in African Christianity, but from the outside looking in, it seems to be exploding in more indigenized forms. It is possible that both realities may coexist, prompting African ministry students to profess frustration with Christianity expressed as a form of national or cultural identity, while elsewhere, celebrating vibrant African-ized Christianity catching fire. In sum, we wish to be sensitive to an alternate view, avoid the appearance of imperialism, and acknowledge the debate over the decidedly mixed legacy of European (and American) missionary efforts in those countries. Finally, to profess that whatever the church's mission has been in the past, the future of mission in Africa will be predominately African.

3. Gili S. Drori, John W. Meyer, and Hokyu Hwang, *Globalization and Organization: World Society and Organizational Change* (New York: Oxford University Press, 2006).

4. Vincent Donovan, a Roman Catholic missionary to the nomadic Masai tribe of Tanzania, wanted to counteract this trend as he presented the Christian message to them. His most interesting and missiologically profound observations and strategies are recorded in his classic, *Christianity Rediscovered*, published in 1978 by Orbis Press and still in print.

5. This remains, in Mark's view, a significant issue for the next generation as the projected growth of Christians would be driven largely by the continued expansion of Africa's population. Due to the heavy concentration of Christians in this region of high growth, Christians would increase as a percentage of the global population. Sub-Saharan Africa's Christian population is expected to double, from 517 million in 2010 to 1.1 billion in 2050. The share of the world's Christians living in sub-Saharan Africa will rise from 24 percent in 2010 to 38 percent in 2050. It bears consideration, however, that many factors could alter this trajectory. For example, if a large share of China's population were to switch to Christianity, that alone could bolster Christianity's current position as the world's most populous religion. At any rate, in countries with large Christian populations, trends could slow or reverse the increase in numbers as nominalism and nationalism take root.

6. Americans came to think of religion as a matter of choice because of a long

historical process. When religion was disestablished in the aftermath of the American Revolution, the removal of state encouragement for religion had the effect of encouraging people to decide matters of religion for themselves.

7. Nineteenth-century Roman Catholicism was often strongly marked as an ethnic faith by Protestant anti-Catholicism. There is a similar phenomenon among American Jews, some 22 percent of whom (32 percent among millennials) think of themselves as Jewish—but culturally, not religiously. It may be that, in time, religious communities that are relatively new in transient locations (e.g., Muslims and Hindus in Western cultures) will be subject to the same pressure and similarly come to think of their faiths more as a choice than as an inheritance. An interesting commentary on this can be found in Lincoln Mullen, "Catholics Who Aren't Catholic," *Atlantic*, September 8, 2015.

8. Nigeria also will continue to have a very large Christian population—projected to have the third-largest Christian population in the world by 2050, after the United States and Brazil. As of 2050, the largest religious group in France, New Zealand, and the Netherlands is expected to be the unaffiliated. Of course, these are projections. Generativity followed by decline may also be followed by renewal. This story is historically shortsighted and might best be measured against God's eschatological promises unfolding as we speak. Are we in decline or at Phyllis Tickle's "rummage sale" (see her *Embracing Emergence Christianity Participant's Workbook: Phyllis Tickle on the Church's Next Rummage Sale*)?

9. Andy Crouch, *Culture Making: Recovering Our Creative Calling* (Downers Grove, IL: InterVarsity, 2013). What seems true is that Christianity appears to become domesticated over time. There may be equivocation about to what extent the domestication comes through its encounters with culture, except that cultures are human creations and therefore enculturate sin. Imagining life as a journey toward some end, believing human beings are precious, these are culturally embedded convictions whose roots are Christian. Dean Blevins contends that consumerism/commodification is also a powerful influence (not only in the West but wherever notions of "the health and wealth gospel" abound), and that it probably has as much influence as nationalism and traditionalism. Vince Miller's *Consuming Religion: Christian Faith and Practice in a Consumer Culture* (New York: Continuum, 2004) has perhaps described this phenomenon best.

10. As found in Steven K. Green, *Inventing a Christian America: The Myth of the Religious Founding* (Oxford: Oxford University Press, 2015), http://www.salon.com/2015/06/28/god_is_not_on_our_side_the_religious_rights_big_lie_about_the_founding_of_america.

11. Robert P. Jones and Daniel Cox, "Most Believe in American Exceptionalism," PRRI, 2015, http://publicreligion.org/research/2015/06/survey-americans-believe-protests-make-country-better-support-decreases-dramatically-protesters

-identified-black. It is worth noting, and not surprising, since the question presupposes a God, that only 39 percent of people who don't identify with any particular religion (the so-called "nones") agree that America is a Christian nation.

12. Mark A. Noll, *The New Shape of World Christianity: How American Experience Reflects Global Faith* (Downers Grove, IL: IVP Academic, 2009), 59.

13. Noll, *New Shape*, 191.

14. See, for example, Stanley Hauerwas, *War and the American Difference: Theological Reflections on Violence and National Identity* (Grand Rapids: Baker, 2011).

15. Alan Wolfe, *The Transformation of American Religion: How We Actually Live Our Faith* (Chicago: University of Chicago Press, 2003), 254–55.

16. Jaroslav Pelikan, *The Vindication of Tradition* (New Haven: Yale University Press, 1984), 65.

17. Mary C. Boys, *Educating in Faith: Maps and Visions* (San Francisco: Harper & Row, 1989).

18. Charles Foster, *Educating Congregations: The Future of Christian Education* (Nashville: Abingdon, 1994).

19. N. T. Wright, *Simply Christian: Why Christianity Makes Sense* (New York: HarperOne, 2006), 207.

20. Ronald Sider, "The Scandal of the Evangelical Conscience," *Books & Culture*, January/February 2005, 8–9, 39–41.

21. Michael Horton, "Beyond Culture Wars," *Modern Reformation*, May–June 1993, 3.

22. Wolfe, *Transformation of American Religion*, 212.

23. Perhaps a disclaimer is wise here regarding such definitive descriptions and parsing in the boxes of the graph. We freely admit that while the descriptions can be heuristically helpful, they oversimplify. In this case, the culprit is the distinction of belief from practice. However, our main intent here is to examine the differences between what we say we believe and what we do, especially as a failure to act on what we believe is a form of hypocrisy.

24. Amy Plantinga Pauw, "Attending to the Gaps between Beliefs and Practices," in *Practicing Theology: Beliefs and Practices in Christian Life*, ed. Miroslav Volf and Dorothy C. Bass (Grand Rapids: Eerdmans, 2002), 33–48. I am relying on her observations here to make my point in these several paragraphs.

25. Pauw, "Attending to the Gaps," 35.

26. Pauw, "Attending to the Gaps," 37.

27. Pauw, "Attending to the Gaps," 48.

28. Until his death in the early twenty-first century, Christopher Hitchens was the most well-known foe of religion in general and Christianity in particular in the Western world. He famously described Christianity, Judaism, and Islam as "the axis of evil." One of his books, *God Is Not Great*, firmly established him as a leader

of the antireligion movement. He regularly debated any and all Christian takers on the question of whether Christianity was good for the world. Obviously, this work of Christian practical theology disagrees vehemently with Hitchens's claim that religion is the chief problem humanity faces. We think it is sin. Moreover, we contend that the effort to rid the world of religious faith, including Christianity, is quixotic. Antireligion is a glaring instance of wrong belief, wrong practice.

29. Rodney Stark and William Sims Bainbridge, *The Future of Religion: Secularization, Revival, and Cult Formation* (Berkeley: University of California Press, 1985), 1.

30. This camp took a major hit when renowned British atheist philosopher Anthony Flew, then 81 years of age, abandoned his former strongly held convictions to acknowledge that God does exist. The *scientific evidence* compelled him!

31. Max Weber, "Essays in Sociology," in *From Max Weber: Essays in Sociology*, ed. Hans Gerth and C. Wright Mills (New York: Oxford University Press, 1958 [1946]).

32. Philip Jenkins, *The Next Christendom: The Coming of Global Christianity* (Oxford: Oxford University Press, 2002).

33. David Barrett and George Kurian, *World Christian Encyclopedia*, 2nd ed. (Oxford: Oxford University Press, 2001).

34. David Lyon, *The Steeple's Shadow: On the Myths and Realities of Secularism* (Grand Rapids: Eerdmans, 1985), 1.

35. Martin E. Marty, *The Modern Schism: Three Paths to the Secular* (San Francisco: Harper & Row, 1969), 19.

36. Of a population of sixty million, the number adhering to non-Christian religions is still not large. Jews, Muslims, Sikhs, and Hindus combined represent no more than 5 percent of the British total, roughly the same non-Christian proportion as in the United States. But we cannot safely conclude that the remaining 95 percent of British people should be classified as Christian. According to a survey taken in 2000, 44 percent of the British claim no religious affiliation whatever, a number that has grown from 31 percent in 1983. More worrying still for the churches, two-thirds of those aged eighteen to twenty-four now describe themselves as nonreligious: almost half of young adults do not even believe that Jesus existed as a historical person. Only 40 percent of British identify themselves as Christians, and the degree of this identification is often slight. While twenty-five million are believed to be members of the Church of England, under a million of these supposed Anglicans can ever be found in church, even for Easter or Christmas. Between 1989 and 1998 alone, Sunday church attendance for all Christian denominations combined fell from 4.7 million to 3.7 million, a decline of 22 percent in just a decade. In a recent dispute over using faith-based charities to provide social welfare, prominent Labour Party politician Roy Hattersley protested, "This is an agnostic nation. People don't take [religion] seriously." It is difficult to

argue with his assessment—and the fact that he could offer it so uncontroversially amply illustrates the weakening of a Christian English conscience (Lyon, *Steeple's Shadow*, 94).

37. See Fred P. Edie, "Converging Streams: An Island Congregation's Practices of Pastoral Care," in *Greenhouses of Hope: Congregations Growing Young Leaders Who Will Change the World*, ed. Edie and Dorie Grenenko Baker (Lanham, MD: Rowman & Littlefield, 2010), chapter 5, 107–36.

38. Dallas Willard, *The Spirit of the Disciplines: Understanding How God Changes Lives* (San Francisco: Harper Collins, 1988), 258–59.

39. For more on this idea, see Mark A. Lamport, "Excellent Belief, Congruent Practice: Juxtapositions of Promise and Peril in the Educational Mission of the Church," in *Thy Brother's Keeper* (Eugene, OR: Wipf & Stock, 2010), 237–57.

40. Philip Jenkins, *The Lost History of Christianity: The Thousand-Year Golden Age of the Church in the Middle East, Africa, and Asia—And How It Died* (San Francisco: HarperOne, 2009), 275.

Chapter Four

1. Stephen Prothero, *Religious Literacy: What Every American Needs to Know—and Doesn't* (San Francisco: HarperSanFrancisco, 2007), 3.

2. Danièle Hervieu-Léger, *Religion as a Chain of Memory* (New Brunswick, NJ: Rutgers University Press, 2000 [1993]).

3. Carl E. Schorske, *Thinking with History: Explorations in the Passage to Modernism* (Princeton: Princeton University Press, 1998), a series of essays that reveal the changing place of history in nineteenth- and twentieth-century cultures. See more at http://www.macfound.org/fellows/89/#sthash.tZyYYi2q.dpuf.

4. Neil Postman, *Amusing Ourselves to Death: Public Discourse in an Age of Show Business* (New York: Penguin, 2005 [1985]), 136–37.

5. While the Pew Research Center published results of a Fall 2013 survey that finds Jews in the United States overwhelmingly proud to be Jewish, nearly one in five describe themselves as having "no religion." The gap is generational, with 32 percent of Jewish Millennials identifying as Jewish on the basis of ancestry, ethnicity, or culture, compared with 93 percent of Jews born in 1914–1927, who identified on the basis of their faith. "This shift in Jewish self-identification reflects broader changes in the US public," said Pew's Religion and Public Life Project. "Americans as a whole—not just Jews—increasingly eschew any religious affiliation," with 22 percent of all Americans identifying with no particular faith, it said. See https://www.pewforum.org/2013/10/01/jewish-american-beliefs-attitudes-culture-survey.

6. Although Mark went to midwestern elementary public schools in the 1960s, there was never homework assigned on Wednesdays—almost shocking to think of

now and recently confirmed by his parents to validate possibly faulty childhood reasoning—because that was the night for midweek church services!

7. See Craig Dykstra, *Growing in the Life of Faith: Education and Christian Practices* (Louisville: Geneva, 1999), xiii.

8. This is true enough for some, including adults with normally developing minds. The force of the anthropology chapter (6) and the congregation chapter (14) in this book demonstrate the tacit influence worship can exert upon heart and therefore habits of virtue. Jamie Smith would argue that this is less about what we choose and more about whom we love.

9. Don E. Saliers, "Liturgy and Ethics: Some New Beginnings," in *Liturgy and the Moral Self: Humanity at Full Stretch before God*, ed. E. Bryon Anderson and Bruce T. Morrill (Collegeville, MN: Liturgical, 1998), 17.

10. Debra Dean Murphy, *Teaching That Transforms: Worship as the Heart of Christian Education* (Grand Rapids: Brazos, 2004), 16.

11. Robert Putnam, *Bowling Alone: The Collapse and Revival of American Community* (New York: Simon and Schuster, 2000), and Jacqueline Olds and Richard S. Schwartz, *The Lonely American: Drifting Apart in the Twenty-First Century* (Boston: Beacon, 2010). Interestingly confounding, Apple CEO Tim Cook included in his June 2016 commencement address a caveat to MIT students: social media can turn us "antisocial" and "divide us" (https://www.usatoday.com /story/tech/news/2018/01/24/apples-tim-cook-dont-want-my-nephew-social -media/1061144001). The "connected world" of social media is another of the countless examples of American sociologist Robert Merton's "unanticipated consequences" of a given phenomenon, in this case, "disconnection" and "alienation." See his "The Unanticipated Consequences of Purposive Social Action," *American Sociological Review* 1 (1936): 895.

12. Despite news one may have heard about bombs and violence, Belfast is consistently named the safest capital of any European country.

13. This, we believe, is what Jesus intended by the metaphor of being *salt* and *light* to a given cultural context; the church extends a glimpse of what the kingdom is and buoys that culture, which, left to its own devices and impulses, would be markedly less civil. Mark's favorite commentator on this concept is John Stott, who has so lucidly exposed these ideas in *The Message of the Sermon on the Mount: Christian Counter-Culture* (Downers Grove, IL: InterVarsity, 1978).

14. Of course, the essential nature of community for faith formation must be worthy of a person's trust. We will take this up more fully in chapters 5 and 8.

15. Modern Greeks have an apropos phrase indicative of this concept, which translates literally "running without arriving."

16. Reported by Connie Cass, "In God we trust, maybe, but not each other," *Associated Press*, November 30, 2013. The full report may be found at https://ap news.com/article/77c9917145004f37b97ded87ffd31602.

17. Dietrich Bonhoeffer, *Life Together: The Classic Exploration of Faith in Community* (New York: HarperOne, 2009), 123. There is a tension between the authenticity of the individual and the tyranny of the community. Bonhoeffer seems to raise the nervousness. Issues of discipline and coercion are always to be considered in groups.

18. Thanks Dan and Jean, Bill and Yolande, Greg and Heidi, and Teresa!

19. C. Ellis Nelson, *Where Faith Begins* (Atlanta: John Knox, 1967), 10.

20. Regrettably, this is the theme of a whole genre of books.

21. Bonhoeffer, *Life Together*, 138–39. The question remains, how do those who have been failed by intimate faith communities allow themselves to trust again? Perhaps this is too tough to answer, yet we staunchly have confidence in the best intentions of the people of God.

22. Alister McGrath, *Christianity's Dangerous Idea: The Protestant Revolution—A History from the Sixteenth Century to the Twenty-First* (San Francisco: HarperOne, 2007), 93.

23. McGrath, *Christianity's Dangerous Idea*, 208–9.

24. Robert Plummer, ed., *Journeys of Faith: Evangelicalism, Eastern Orthodoxy, Catholicism, and Anglicanism* (Grand Rapids: Zondervan, 2012). To be sure, this is not a book on biblical interpretation but on how various traditions of Christianity interpret and practice Scripture in community, as exampled in representative journeys.

25. Stanley Hauerwas, *Unleashing the Scripture: Freeing the Bible from Captivity to America* (Nashville: Abingdon, 1993), 15.

26. N. T. Wright, *Simply Christian: Why Christianity Makes Sense* (New York: HarperOne, 2006), 191.

27. Harvey Cox, *How to Read the Bible* (New York: HarperOne, 2015), 207–9.

28. N. T. Wright, *Scripture and the Authority of God: How to Read the Bible Today* (San Francisco: HarperOne, 2013), 187.

29. A. J. Conyers, "Can Postmodernism Be Used as a Template for Christian Theology?," *Christian Scholar's Review* 33.3 (2004): 308–9.

30. From an interview in *Christian Century*, October 29, 1997, 972–78.

31. Reported in Rodney Stark, *The Triumph of Christianity: How the Jesus Movement Became the World's Largest Religion* (San Francisco: HarperOne, 2011).

32. Stark, *Triumph*, 410–12.

33. See Mark A. Lamport, "Unintended Outcomes, Curious Inventions, and Misshapen Creatures: Juxtapositions of Religious Belief and Faith-Formed Practice and the Renewed Case of the Educational Mission of the Church," *Asbury Journal* 63 (2008): 95–113; Mark A. Lamport, "Excellent Belief, Congruent Practice: Juxtapositions of Promise and Peril in the Educational Mission of the Church," in *Thy Brother's Keeper* (Eugene, OR: Wipf & Stock, 2010), 237–57.

34. Ernest Troelsch and C. Ellis Nelson point out that Christians are automatically encultured and embedded in multiple subcultures simultaneously.

35. Andy Crouch, *Culture Making: Recovering Our Creative Calling* (Downers Grove, IL: InterVarsity, 2008).

36. In October 2013, during a pilgrimage to Assisi, Pope Francis called for the Catholic Church and its faithful to rid themselves of earthly concerns, as Saint Francis did. Speaking in the hall where the medieval saint is said to have taken off his robes in a gesture of humility, Pope Francis said the Church should also "divest" itself and return to spiritual basics. "The Church, all of us should divest ourselves of worldliness," a visibly emotional pope said, adding, "Worldliness is a murderer because it kills souls, kills people, kills the Church." "Without divesting ourselves, we would become pastry-shop Christians, like beautiful cakes and sweet things but not real Christians." Pope Francis has called for a "poor Church for the poor" and has said he wants to overhaul the two-thousand-year-old institution, making it less "Vatican-centric" and closer to ordinary people. The Pope seeks to refresh Roman Catholic Christian education in an age of postmodernism and focus on the saint's message of poverty rather than that of interreligious peace. See https://www.bbc.com/news/world-europe-24391800.

37. McGrath, *Christianity's Dangerous Idea*, 463.

38. Dallas Willard, *The Great Omission* (New York: HarperCollins, 2006), 4.

39. Stanley Hauerwas, "The Gesture of a Truthful Story," *Theology Today*, July 1985, 186.

40. For more, see Mark A. Lamport and Darrell Yoder, "Faithful Gestures: Rebooting the Educational Mission of the Church," *Christian Education Journal* 3.1 (2006): 58–78.

41. We are enthusiastic about the synergetic relationship of John Wesley's so-called quadrilateral—Scripture, tradition, reason, and experience—for interpreting and living the Christian faith. While some might wish to acknowledge only "Scripture," God is operative, and faith is enhanced, by the dynamic interaction of all four.

42. Ruth Tucker, *Walking Away from Faith: Unraveling the Mystery of Belief and Unbelief* (Downers Grove, IL: InterVarsity, 2002). A third factor is deduced—difficult circumstances in life; and while significant, it is omitted here, as it does not coalesce with our main point. See also, Martin Marty's classic, *Varieties of Unbelief: From Nihilism to Atheism; From Agnosticism to Apathy: Explorations in American Religion* (New York: Holt, Rinehart and Winston, 1964), for a more theoretical model of this topic.

43. For more on this idea, see Mark A. Lamport, "The Most Indispensable Habits of Effective Theological Educators: Recalibrating Educational Philosophy, Psychology, and Practice," *Asbury Journal* 65.2 (2010): 36–54.

44. It is also interesting to note that Jesus asked over a hundred questions, as recorded in the gospels, and that this would appear to be an intentional and

significant teaching strategy. Since we can assume he knew the answers to these questions, his strategy was one of engaging learners in thinking, evaluating assumptions, and having meaningful dialogue.

45. It is a remarkable phenomenon to observe how prevailing societal customs and educational philosophies in a given region of the world mimic the same stances in Christian education practices in those same geographic regions. It is not surprising then—and Mark has observed it firsthand in Africa, Asia, and eastern Europe—that a teacher-dominated, content-centered, student-dependent, pedagogical model is more common in Christian education, much like the more rigid political environments in these regions. Conversely, in many cases, Christian education, at least in theory, in North American and western Europe more often leans toward a more egalitarian-based, learner-focused style—much like the democratic political arenas in these regions.

46. Stanley Grenz and Roger Olson, *Who Needs Theology? An Invitation to the Study of God* (Downers Grove, IL: InterVarsity, 1994), 25.

47. Amy Plantinga Pauw, "Attending to the Gaps between Beliefs and Practices," in *Practicing Theology: Beliefs and Practices in Christian Life*, ed. Miroslav Volf and Dorothy C. Bass (Grand Rapids: Eerdmans, 2002), 41.

48. Murphy, *Teaching That Transforms*, 131.

49. Mae Elise Cannon, *Just Spirituality: How Faith Practices Fuel Social Action* (Downers Grove, IL: IVP, 2013), 15.

50. J. I. Packer, *God Has Spoken* (London: Hodder & Stoughton, 2005), 43.

Part Two: Criteria for Nurturing Faith

1. Reported by Rob Waugh, "Atheists Are More Intelligent 'Because They Overcome the Instinct of Religion,'" Yahoo News UK, May 18, 2017, https://www.yahoo.com/news/atheists-intelligent-overcome-instinct-religion-111146334.html.

2. There are some interesting theories about the rise of "superhero" movies and its interface with religion during this first quarter of the twenty-first century. An internet search will reveal an array of comments.

3. Of course, knowledge is a spiritual gift (1 Cor. 12:8), but this is an ability to discern God, Scripture, and other conditions that, through the power of the Holy Spirit, guide individuals or faith communities in the mission of God. The warning against being "puffed up" (as Paul cautions us in 1 Corinthians 13) because of our knowledge is always to be heeded when we boast of special understanding or exceptional faith.

4. For more, see Joyce Ellen Salisbury, "Perpetua," *Encyclopaedia Britannica*, March 3, 2020, https://www.britannica.com/biography/Perpetua-Christian-martyr.

5. Readers may remember that the first usage of the label "Christians"—that

is, *Christianos* in Greek, "little Christs"—was by adversaries and mockers, who nonetheless recognized that Jesus's followers had become him—a spiritual manifestation of this point! See Acts 11:26.

6. Thomas H. Groome, *Christian Religious Education: Sharing Our Story and Vision* (San Francisco: Jossey-Bass, 1999), 91.

Chapter Five

1. Daniel S. Schipani, "Christian Religious Education in a Culture of Disbelief," *Religious Education* 92 (1997): 168.

2. Noel Leo Erskine, "How Do We Know What to Believe? Revelation and Authority," in *Essentials of Christian Theology*, ed. William C. Placher (Louisville: Westminster John Knox, 2003), 34.

3. Schipani, "Christian Religious Education," 168.

4. Donald Wood, *Barth's Theology of Interpretation* (Burlington, VT: Ashgate, 2007), 152.

5. See chapter 2 of Benjamin Connor, *Practicing Witness: A Missional Vision of Christian Practices* (Grand Rapids: Eerdmans, 2011).

6. The term recently was put to use by philosopher Charles Taylor but has also drawn attention from theologians. See Charles Taylor, *A Secular Age* (Cambridge, MA: Harvard University Press, 2007), 3–5. David Ford offered a response in his "God's Power and Human Flourishing: A Biblical Inquiry after Charles Taylor's *A Secular Age*," paper presented at the Yale Center for Faith and Culture, Yale Divinity School, March 23–24, 2008.

7. A theme taken up by Jürgen Moltmann, *The Trinity and the Kingdom: The Doctrine of God* (Minneapolis: Fortress, 1993), 150.

8. *Contact*, directed by Robert Zemeckis (Los Angeles: Warner Brothers, 1997), DVD, starring Jodi Foster and Matthew McConaughey.

9. Martin Buber, *I and Thou*, trans. Walter Kaufmann (New York: Charles Scribner's Sons, 1970).

10. See Parker Palmer, *To Know as We Are Known* (San Francisco: Harper, 1993), chapter 1.

11. Quoted in Schipani, "Christian Religious Education," 168.

12. Erskine, "How Do We Know What to Believe?," 35.

13. Hans Wiersma, "A Brief Introduction to *sola scriptura*," https://lutheranthe ology.wordpress.com/2011/01/18/a-brief-introduction-to-sola-scriptura/.

14. See Martin Luther, *Commentary on Romans*, trans. J. Theodore Mueller (Grand Rapids: Zondervan, 1954).

15. Alasdair MacIntyre, *Whose Justice? Which Rationality?* (Notre Dame, IN: University of Notre Dame Press, 1988), 12.

16. See, for example, Walter Brueggemann, *The Creative Word: Canon as a Model for Biblical Education* (Minneapolis: Fortress, 1982) or *The Prophetic Imagination* (Minneapolis: Fortress, 2001).

17. Wesley scholar Albert Outler named this fourfold basis for receiving revelation a "quadrilateral." See Albert C. Outler, ed., *John Wesley* (Oxford: Oxford University Press, 1964), iv.

18. Henry H. Knight III, *The Presence of God in the Christian Life: John Wesley and the Means of Grace* (Lanham, MD: Scarecrow, 1992).

19. Randy Maddox, *Responsible Grace: John Wesley's Practical Theology* (Nashville: Abingdon, 1994). "Without God," Wesley famously preached, "[we] cannot. Without [us], God will not." (Quotation is variously attributed to both Augustine and Wesley.)

20. See Richard Jenkins, "Disenchantment, Enchantment, and Re-Enchantment: Max Weber at the Millennium," *Max Weber Studies* 1 (2000): 11–32.

21. See Taylor, *Secular Age*.

22. George Albert Coe, *A Social Theory of Religious Education* (New York: Charles Scribner's Sons, 1929), 55.

23. Barth spells out his opposition to natural theology in *Church Dogmatics: The Doctrine of God*, vol. II/1 (London: T&T Clark, 2010).

24. Karl Barth, *The Word of God and the Word of Man*, trans. Douglas Horton (New York: Harper & Row, 1957), 14.

25. See James K. A. Smith, *Who's Afraid of Postmodernism: Taking Derrida, Lyotard, and Foucault to Church* (Grand Rapids: Baker Academic, 2006), 65.

26. William James, "The Will to Believe," in *The Will to Believe, Human Immortality and Other Essays in Popular Philosophy* (New York: Dover, 1960), section V.

27. Taylor, *Secular Age*, 12.

28. William H. Willimon, *Remember Who You Are: Baptism, A Model for Christian Life* (Nashville: Upper Room, 1980), 16.

29. The fourth-century early church father Chrysostom used the term *awesome*. See Edward Yarnold, *The Awe-Inspiring Rites of Initiation: The Origins of the RCIA* (Collegeville, MN: Liturgical, 1994), 57.

30. Thomas M. Finn, *Early Christian Baptism and the Catechumenate: West and East Syria* (Collegeville, MN: Liturgical, 1992), 5.

31. Stephen E. Fowl and L. Gregory Jones, *Reading in Communion: Scripture and Ethics in Common Life* (Eugene, OR: Wipf & Stock, 1998).

32. Fowl and Jones, *Reading in Communion*, chapter 5. *Stranger* and *outsider* are freighted terms in the present day. Often they are employed to maintain the boundaries and unequal power relations between privileged and marginalized communities. The Scriptures repeatedly witness, however, to God's primary concern for those perceived as outsiders, to welcome them into God's communion,

and to the ways these outsiders repeatedly confounded "insiders" who imagined they monopolized God's favor. Fowl and Jones therefore counsel the need for Christian readers to make the Scriptures strange to themselves again in order to resist this presumption of God's blessing and to listen instead for the truth.

33. Schipani, "Christian Religious Education," 165.

34. Brian Mahan, Michael Warren, and David White, *Awakening Youth Discipleship: Christian Resistance in a Consumer Culture* (Eugene, OR: Cascade, 2008), 53–54.

Chapter Six

1. Pat Conroy, *The Great Santini* (New York: Dial, 2002).

2. Some judge theological anthropology to begin and end with Jesus Christ, including especially his saving work on behalf of humankind. For organizational purposes only, we reserve comment on Jesus's redemption of creation from sin for the next chapter.

3. These musings on being are inspired by Thomas Groome, *Sharing Faith: A Comprehensive Approach to Religious Education and Pastoral Ministry* (San Francisco: HarperSanFrancisco, 1996).

4. René Descartes, "I Think, Therefore I Am," in *The Philosophical Works of Descartes*, vol. 1, trans. Elizabeth Haldane and G. R. T. Ross (New York: Cambridge University Press, 1970), 101.

5. Jean-Jacques Rousseau, *Emile*, trans. Barbara Foxley (New York: Dutton, 1969).

6. See Sigmund Freud, *The Ego and the Id* (New York: Norton, 1990).

7. See Sigmund Freud, *Civilization and Its Discontents* (New York: Norton, 2005).

8. See Robert Wright, *The Moral Animal: Why We Are the Way We Are* (New York: Vintage, 1994), or Richard Dawkins, *The Selfish Gene* (Oxford: Oxford University Press, 1989).

9. Oxford English Dictionary, "natural selection," https://en.oxforddictionaries.com/definition/natural_selection.

10. William James, *Principles of Psychology* (New York: Henry Holt, 1890), 449.

11. Gregory of Nyssa, *The Life of Moses* (New York: Paulist, 1978), 96.

12. Roberta Bondi, *To Love as God Loves: Conversations with the Early Church* (Philadelphia: Fortress, 1987), 59.

13. Bondi, *To Love as God Loves*, 60.

14. Augustine, *Confessions* 1.1.

15. This quotation commonly attributed to Pascal appears here considerably simpler and pithier than what he actually wrote. See *The Pensées* (New York: Penguin, 1966), 75.

16. James K. A. Smith, *Desiring the Kingdom* (Grand Rapids: Baker Academic, 2009), 50–51.

17. Smith, *Desiring*, see chapter 2.

18. Katherine Turpin, *Branded: Adolescents Converting from Consumer Faith* (Cleveland: Pilgrim, 2006).

19. Pascal, *Pensées*, 78.

20. Susan Eastman, "Imitating Christ, Imitating Us," in *The Word Leaps the Gap: Essays on Scripture and Theology in Honor of Richard B. Hays*, ed. J. Ross Wagner, C. Kavin Rowe, and A. Katherine Grieb (Grand Rapids: Eerdmans, 2008), and *Paul and the Person: Reframing Paul's Anthropology* (Grand Rapids: Eerdmans, 2017).

21. The jury is still out on the significance of mirror neuron networks. Neuroscientists remain skeptical that these alone can explain such complex behaviors as sociality or empathy. What remains undeniable, however, is the phenomenon of imitation persisting from infancy to adulthood. Persons not only imitate the body positions and gestures of others (yawning is a simple example); they also feel what they perceive others to be feeling.

22. Richard Bondi, "The Elements of Character," *Journal of Religious Ethics* 12 (1984): 205.

23. Bondi, "Elements of Character," 206.

24. Bondi, "Elements of Character," 207–9.

25. Bondi, "Elements of Character," 209–11.

26. Iain McGilchrist, *The Master and His Emissary: The Divided Brain and the Making of the Western World* (New Haven: Yale University Press, 2009).

27. Fred P. Edie, "Imagination," in *Encyclopedia of Christian Education*, ed. George Thomas Kurian and Mark A. Lamport (Lanham, MD: Rowman & Littlefield, 2015).

28. Anne E. Streaty Wimberly, *Soul Stories: African American Christian Education*, rev. ed. (Nashville: Abingdon, 2005).

29. Fred's own work attempts to link biblical stories of God's salvation to corporate worship as a space where those stories may be performed *and* to everyday practices of Christian life, like hospitality, eating together, and caring for creation. His hope is that aesthetic participation in bodily performance, in multivalent symbols, and in song and heightened poetic speech, Christians will not only acquire the means to imagine life with God but also find their hearts moved by the Spirit to embrace it. Fred P. Edie, *Book, Bath, Table, and Time: Christian Worship as Source and Resource for Youth Ministry* (Cleveland: Pilgrim, 2007).

30. Delores Williams, *Sister in the Wilderness: The Challenge of Womanist God-Talk* (Maryknoll, NY: Orbis, 2013).

31. Amanda Jo Pittman, "Knowing the Way: Scriptural Imagination and the Acts of the Apostles" (ThD diss., Duke Divinity School, 2016), 106–67.

32. Courtney T. Goto, *The Grace of Playing: Pedagogies for Leaning into God's New Creation* (Eugene, OR: Pickwick, 2016).

33. See, for example, Jerome T. Berryman, *Godly Play: An Imaginative Approach to Religious Education* (San Francisco: HarperSanFrancisco, 1991).

Chapter Seven

1. Catherine Mowry LaCugna, *God for Us: The Trinity in Christian Life* (New York: HarperCollins, 1991), 411.

2. Gregory of Nazianzus, *Nicene and Post-Nicene Fathers*, vol. 7 (Peabody, MA: Hendrickson, 1994), 440.

3. L. G. Whitlock Jr., "Cyril of Alexandria," in *Evangelical Dictionary of Theology* (Grand Rapids: Baker Academic, 2001), 314–15.

4. Alister E. McGrath, *Christian Theology: An Introduction*, 6th ed. (Hoboken, NJ: Wiley, 2016), 192.

5. Gregory of Nyssa, cited in Thomas M. Finn, *Early Christian Baptism and the Catechumenate: West and East Syria* (Collegeville, MN: Liturgical, 1992), 9.

6. Robert W. Jenson, "How Does Jesus Make a Difference?," in *Essentials of Christian Theology*, ed. William C. Placher (Louisville: Westminster John Knox, 2003), 202.

7. Those who like to propose Christianity as an escape from "empty" rituals will have to reckon with the ritualistic practices of its founder. Jesus was circumcised according to Jewish custom, made pilgrimage to the Jerusalem temple on holy days, worshiped at the synagogue on the Sabbath, received baptism from John the Baptist, and according to John's gospel baptized others (John 3:22). His transformation of the Passover celebration is also well documented. Jesus's interactions with foreigners and outsiders, his sense of what it meant to be a Jewish male, and even his eating customs were formed through his immersion in the culture of first-century Jewish Palestine. Jesus embraced but also reinterpreted these cultural "tools" and "products" to make his gospel known. That he (critically) embraced culture as a means to nurture faith assures Christian educators that they may do the same.

8. Friedrich Schleiermacher, *The Christian Faith*, ed. H. R. Mackintosh and J. S. Stewart (London: T&T Clark, 1999), 132.

9. See, for example, Stanley Hauerwas and L. Gregory Jones, *Why Narrative? Readings in Narrative Theology* (Eugene, OR: Wipf & Stock, 1997). See also Stanley Hauerwas, *The Peaceable Kingdom: A Primer in Christian Ethics* (Notre Dame: University of Notre Dame Press, 1986), 24–29.

10. C. S. Lewis, *The Chronicles of Narnia* (New York: HarperCollins, 1998); Isak Dinesen, *Babette's Feast* (New York: Penguin, 2011); Clyde Edgerton, *Walking across Egypt* (Chapel Hill, NC: Algonquin, 1987).

11. Robert Murray, *Symbols of Church and Kingdom: A Study in Early Syriac Tradition* (New York: T&T Clark, 2006), 31.

12. Sebastian Brock, *The Luminous Eye: The Spiritual World Vision of Saint Ephrem the Syrian* (Kalamazoo, MI: Cistercian, 1985), 42.

13. Sebastian Brock, *The Harp of the Spirit: Poems of Saint Ephrem the Syrian* (Cambridge: Aquila, 2013), 85.

14. Paul Boer, *Hymns and Homilies of St. Ephraim the Syrian* (Middletown, DE: Veritatis Splendor, 2012), 184.

15. Edward Yarnold, *The Awe-Inspiring Rites of Initiation* (Collegeville, MN: Liturgical, 2001), 100.

16. We borrow the language of *book*, *bath*, *table*, and *time* from Gordon Lathrop, *Holy Things: A Lturgical Theology* (Minneapolis: Augsburg Fortress, 1993). Lathrop employs this language to indicate that distinctly Christian worship practices are adapted from cultural practices. Kimberly H. Belcher, *Efficacious Engagement: Sacramental Participation in the Trinitarian Mystery* (Collegeville, MN: Liturgical, 2011), 44–47, builds upon this insight. She suggests sacramental participation is culturally and theologically efficacious when human beings recognize how these ordinary practices (take eating together, for example), besides accomplishing cultural goods (shared meals as building or renewing community), can also offer access to divine purpose and graced transformation (a shared meal as constituting the body of Christ).

17. Quoted in John Tinsley, "'Tell It Slant,'" in *Theological Perspectives on Christian Formation: A Reader on Theology and Christian Education*, ed. Jeff Astley, Leslie J. Francis, and Colin Crowder (Grand Rapids: Eerdmans, 1996), 89.

18. Susan G. Eastman, "The Shadow Side of Second Person Engagement: Sin in Paul's Letter to the Romans," *European Journal for the Philosophy of Religion* 5.4 (2013): 97.

19. Susan G. Eastman, "The Empire of Illusion," in *Comfortable Words: Essays in Honor of Paul F. M. Zahl*, ed. Todd Brewer and John D. Koch Jr. (Eugene, OR: Pickwick, 2013), 11.

20. Eastman, "Shadow Side," 99, 102.

21. Eastman, "Shadow Side," 102–3.

22. Eastman, "Empire of Illusion," 17.

23. Eastman, "Shadow Side," 107.

24. Susan G. Eastman, "Imitating Christ, Imitating Us: Paul's Educational Project in Philippians," in *The Word Leaps the Gap: Essays on Scripture and Theology in Honor of Richard B. Hays*, ed. J. Ross Wagner, C. Kavin Rowe, and A. Katherine Grieb (Grand Rapids: Eerdmans, 2008).

25. Emily Peck-McClain, *Arm in Arm with Adolescent Girls*, Horizons in Religious Education Book Series (Eugene, OR: Pickwick, 2018).

Chapter Eight

1. Ross Douthat, "Save the Mainline," *New York Times*, April 15, 2017, https://www.nytimes.com/2017/04/15/opinion/sunday/save-the-mainline.html?_r=0.

2. David Kinnaman, *You Lost Me: Why Young Christians Are Leaving the Church . . . and Rethinking Faith* (Grand Rapids: Baker, 2011), see especially part 2.

3. Joy K. Challenger, "Infused: Millennials and the Future of the Black Church" (DMin thesis, Duke Divinity School, 2016).

4. Cyprian, "On the Unity of the Church," *Christian History Institute*, https://www.christianhistoryinstitute.org/study/module/cyprian.

5. Peter Hodgson and Robert H. King, *Christian Theology: An Introduction to Its Traditions and Tasks* (Minneapolis: Fortress, 1994), 226–30.

6. Hodgson and King, *Christian Theology*, 225.

7. Hodgson and King, *Christian Theology*, 234.

8. William C. Placher, ed., *Essentials of Christian Theology* (Louisville: Westminster John Knox, 2008), 244.

9. Adolf von Harnack, *What Is Christianity?* (New York: Harper & Row, 1957), quoted in Gerhard Lohfink, *Jesus in Community* (Philadelphia: Fortress, 1984), 1.

10. Lohfink, *Jesus in Community*, 71.

11. Lohfink, *Jesus in Community*, 122–32.

12. Lohfink, *Jesus in Community*, 56–58.

13. Lohfink, *Jesus in Community*, 62.

14. "The Most Segregated Hour in America—Martin Luther King Jr.," YouTube, last modified April 29, 2014, https://www.youtube.com/watch?v=1q881g1L_d8.

15. According to the Pew Research Center, as of 2014 eight out of ten congregants attend services "where a single racial or ethnic group comprises at least 80% of the congregation." More hopeful, the remaining 20 percent attend worship where no single race or ethnic group predominates, up from 15 percent in 1998. Even so, individual congregations in the US remain far less racially and ethnically diverse than schools or other public-facing institutions. Michael Lipka, "Many U.S. Congregations Are Still Racially Segregated, but Things Are Changing," Fact-Tank: News in the Numbers, December 8, 2014, https://www.pewresearch.org/fact-tank/2014/12/08/many-u-s-congregations-are-still-racially-segregated-but-things-are-changing-2/+&cd=2&hl=en&ct=clnk&gl=us&client=safaried.

16. Willie James Jennings, *The Christian Imagination* (New Haven: Yale University Press, 2010), 18–19.

17. Jennings, *Christian Imagination*, 24.

18. Jennings, *Christian Imagination*, 31.

19. Jennings's primary focus is the church that accompanied European colonialist expansion. Originally, a pre-Reformation movement gravitating toward

Central and South America, it possessed Roman Catholic roots. As Protestantism emerged, that movement quickly became involved in colonialist Christianity in North America, West Africa, and South Africa, to name a few regions. Jennings's descriptions of colonialist Christianity also could apply widely to pre–Civil War churches in the American South, to the American Christian mission to its first peoples, or to the apartheid regimes of South Africa. Readers may believe the authors are painting the church with too broad a brush on this point. It cannot possibly be the case that the church was a uniformly racist institution. Admittedly, eighteenth-century British Christians were among the first to inveigh against slavery. Abolitionist churches in the northern US did not rest until slavery was abolished and were equally passionate about offering aid to freed slaves. Jennings might respond that opposing slavery and remediating the suffering it caused are not the same as coming to terms with racism and dismantling it along with White privilege.

20. Jennings, *Christian Imagination*, 182.

21. Jennings, *Christian Imagination*, 78.

22. Jennings, *Christian Imagination*, 93.

23. Jennings, *Christian Imagination*, 113 (our emphasis).

24. Dan Wilson, Emily Robison, Martha Maguire, and Natalie Maines, "Not Ready to Make Nice," Dixie Chicks, *Taking the Long Way*, Sony BMG Music Entertainment, 2006, CD.

25. Christena Cleveland, *Disunity in Christ* (Downers Grove, IL: IVP, 2013), 177–91.

26. Cleveland, *Disunity in Christ*, 81, 96.

27. Cleveland, *Disunity in Christ*, 26.

28. Cleveland, *Disunity in Christ*, 21.

29. Dorotheus, *Dorotheus of Gaza: Discourses and Sayings*, Cistercian Study Series 33 (Kalamazoo, MI: Cistercian, 1977), 138–39.

30. Sting, "Russians," *The Dream of Blue Turtles*, Sony/ATV Music Publishing, 1985, CD.

Chapter Nine

1. See Alasdair MacIntyre, *After Virtue* (South Bend, IN: University of Notre Dame Press, 1981).

2. MacIntyre, *After Virtue*, 206–8.

3. Dorothy C. Bass, ed., *Practicing Our Faith: A Way of Life for a Searching People*, 2nd ed. (San Francisco: Jossey-Bass, 2010), 5.

4. Bass, *Practicing Our Faith*, 6–11.

5. Bass, *Practicing Our Faith*, chapters 2, 3, and 4.

6. Murray Rae, "The Testimony of Works in the Christology of John's Gospel," in *The Gospel of John and Christian Theology*, ed. Richard Bauckham and Carl Mosser (Grand Rapids: Eerdmans, 2010), 295–96.

7. Rae, "Testimony of Works," 306.

8. Carol Lakey Hess, *Caretakers of Our Common House: Women's Development in Communities of Faith* (Nashville: Abingdon, 1997).

9. Miroslav Volf, "The Crown of the Good Life: Joy, Happiness and the Life Well Lived—A Hypothesis," August 20, 2015, https://www.abc.net.au/religion/the -crown-of-the-good-life-joy-happiness-and-the-life-well-lived/10097970.

10. "Hard work" here more likely means peering into a laptop than the physical labor of extracting precious metals from thousands of feet below the earth's surface.

11. Henry H. Knight III, *The Presence of God in the Christian Life: John Wesley and the Means of Grace* (Lanham, MD: Scarecrow, 1992), 8–15.

12. Pierre Sauvage, *Weapons of the Spirit* (Los Angeles: Pierre Sauvage Productions/Friends of Le Chambon Foundation, 1987), film.

13. See, for example, Jonathan Wilson-Hartgrove, *New Monasticism: What It Has to Say to Today's Church* (Grand Rapids: Brazos, 2008). See also Hartgrove's chapter "Living as Community," in *On Our Way: Christian Practices for Living a Whole Life*, ed. Dorothy C. Bass and Susan R. Briehl (Nashville: Upper Room, 2010), as well as the companion video to the chapter, on YouTube, https://www .youtube.com/watch?v=oqfDho7htlk.

14. Since writing this chapter, tragic news has emerged about Vanier. According to an internal report from L'Arche, their founder, now deceased, engaged in long-term patterns of sexual and emotional abuse of female associates. While the investigation found no evidence of this abuse extending to disabled members of L'Arche communities, the news is no less devastating to persons all over the world who believed in Vanier's vision and practice of inclusive Christian community. We believe that L'Arche communities continue to model Christ's joyous abundance for members, but we also see more clearly the dangers of romanticizing intentional Christian communities of practice.

15. The previously cited *Practicing Our Faith* and *On Our Way* readily lend themselves to teaching (and practicing) specific Christian practices with groups or classes. There is also a version for youth, titled *Way to Live: Christian Practices for Teens,* that is accompanied by downloadable curriculum designed to facilitate practices, along with reflection upon them.

Chapter Ten

1. "Saint Anselm," *Stanford Encyclopedia of Philosophy*, https://plato.stanford .edu/entries/anselm/#FaiSeeUndChaPurAnsThePro (accessed February 5, 2018).

2. Jack Mezirow and associates, *Learning as Transformation: Critical Perspectives on a Theory in Progress* (San Francisco: Jossey-Bass, 2000), 5

3. Mezirow, *Learning as Transformation*, 3.

4. Mezirow, *Learning as Transformation*, 7–8.

5. Mezirow, *Learning as Transformation*, 10–11.

6. Mezirow, *Learning as Transformation*, 16–17.

7. See Robert Kegan, *In Over Our Heads: The Mental Demands of Modern Life* (Cambridge, MA: Harvard University Press, 1998).

8. Paulo Freire, *Pedagogy of the Oppressed* (New York: Continuum, 1994), 53.

9. Paulo Freire, *Education for Critical Consciousness* (New York: Continuum, 2002), 41–84.

10. This is a stylized encounter, based in Freire's work, but largely of the authors' own creation. It is offered for illustrative purposes.

11. Freire, *Pedagogy*, chapter 2.

12. Mezirow, *Learning as Transformation*, 74–77.

13. Walter Brueggemann, *The Creative Word: Canon as a Model for Biblical Education* (Philadelphia: Fortress, 1982); see especially chapter 3.

14. Groome's own descriptions are more detailed and helpful than ours. See his *Sharing Faith: A Comprehensive Approach to Religious Education and Pastoral Ministry: The Way of Shared Praxis* (San Francisco: HarperSanFrancisco, 1991).

15. Almeda Wright, *The Spiritual Lives of Young African Americans* (New York: Oxford University Press, 2017), 235.

16. Wright, *Spiritual Lives*, 227. Wright borrows the term from womanist theologian Jacquelyn Grant.

Part Three: Colleagues in Nurturing Faith

1. Diana Butler Bass, *Christianity after Religion: The End of Church and the Birth of a New Spiritual Awakening* (San Francisco: HarperOne, 2012), 47–48.

2. David R. Hunter, *Christian Education as Engagement* (Charleston, SC: Nabus, 2013 [1963]), 38.

3. The former is bibliolatry, a misguided worship of the Bible, which, as odd as it may sound, is still as idolatrous as any other-than-God distractions.

4. This "hook-book-look-took" approach to encountering Scripture has long been associated with Lawrence O. Richards's *Creative Bible Teaching* (Chicago: Moody, 1998).

Chapter Eleven

1. Philip Jenkins, *The New Faces of Christianity: Believing the Bible in the Global South* (Oxford: Oxford University Press, 2006).

2. See General Social Survey, http://www3.norc.org/GSS+Website; Pew Research Center's Forum on Religion and Public Life, "Religious Landscape Study," http://religions.pewforum.org/reports; and Faith Matters Survey 2006 (computer file), Roper Center for Public Opinion Research Study USMISC2006-FAITH version 2, Saguaro Seminar (producer), 2006 (Storrs, CT: The Roper Center for Public Opinion Research, Cornell University [distributor], 2011), https://ropercenter .cornell.edu/featured-collections/faith-matters-survey-2006.

3. Robert D. Putnam and David E. Campbell, *American Grace: How Religion Divides Us and Unites Us* (New York: Simon & Schuster, 2010).

4. Michael Hout, Andrew Greeley, and Melissa Wilde, "The Demographic Imperative in Religious Change in the United States," *American Journal of Sociology* 107 (2001): 110.

5. See H. H. Meyer, "Education," *International Standard Bible Encyclopedia*, http://bibleencyclopedia.com.

6. One of the most cogent discussions is presented in John Westerhoff, *Will Our Children Have Faith?*, rev. ed. (Toronto: Morehouse, 2000).

7. Walter Feinberg, *For Goodness Sake: Religious Schools and Education for Democratic Citizenry* (New York: Routledge, 2006), 18.

8. See Dan McAdams, *The Stories We Live By: Personal Myths and the Making of Self* (New York: Guilford, 2005), and *The Redemptive Self: Stories Americans Live By* (New York: Oxford University Press, 2005).

9. Adapted from Mark A. Lamport, "Youth Ministry," *Encyclopedia of Christian Civilization*, vol. 4 (Oxford: Blackwell, 2011).

10. Robert Wuthnow, *Growing Up Religious: Christians and Jews and Their Journeys of Faith* (Boston: Beacon, 1999).

11. We certainly realize that some children in our local churches do not come from Christian homes, and in this case, the church by default becomes the necessary and primary educator in faith.

12. Lawrence Richards, *Christian Education: Seeking to Become Like Jesus* (Grand Rapids: Zondervan, 1988).

13. Shailer Mathews, *Scientific Management in the Churches* (Chicago: University of Chicago Press, 1912), 56, our emphasis.

14. Full disclosure—Mark started writing this chapter twice before this version. He was influenced by ire over how Western culture really treats children, as opposed to what they say about "our" children. He has tried to refocus on seeing the issue through God's perspective but will admit his righteous indignation may still show through.

15. http://focusfeatures.com/wont-you-be-my-neighbor.

16. To name just a few, the United States has among the skimpiest parental leave policies in the Global North, shields many poor children who lack access to pre-

school, encourages mass marketing to children, and watched significant increase in the rate of childhood poverty since the 1970s. As we write, federal, state, and local governments have rushed and continue to rush headlong to allow the younger among us maximum access to marijuana and vaping, and those governments are now being forced to backtrack after more suitable clinical research demonstrates public danger. Such haphazard behavior to expose the young to harm is reckless. To reiterate our point, some segments of culture claim to be an ally of the young by providing (and not limiting) them unseemly experiences and in the name of unrestricted personal freedoms.

17. We must confess there are few more egregious things we can think of—abuse of naive members of faith communities—that rankle us. In the name of righteous indignation, God will deal with such perpetrators. This negatively affects children's future regard for the Christian family, let alone presenting a false image of the church and the very nature of God!

18. See Marva Dawn, *Is It a Lost Cause? Having the Heart of God for the Church's Children* (Grand Rapids: Eerdmans, 1997).

19. Astonishment in God, his nature, his acts, and his love is not meant to cease during childhood; indeed, we are to find fresh insight and realization through life, that is, fresh every morning (Lam. 3:22–24).

20. Walter Brueggemann, *The Creative Word: Canon as a Model for Biblical Education*, rev. ed. (Minneapolis: Fortress, 2015), 27.

21. Cf. Brueggemann, *Creative Word*, chapter 1, especially pp. 22–23.

22. A helpful source in this regard is Parent Cue, http://theparentcue.org, and their ongoing research is compiled in The Phase Project.

23. So we are not accused of being blatant skeptics of such practices, we freely admit that participating with others in such exercises, while not fully graspable by the children at that present time, does not negate the aspect of faith community participation and the possibility that these words may be retained in their consciousness until such a time may come where greater abstract insight may occur. Two of Mark's grandchildren participated in a choir in which over the course of three years they memorized (and sang) the entire book of James. May God bless this to their minds.

24. See Thomas H. Groome, *Will There Be Faith? A New Vision for Educating and Growing Disciples* (San Francisco: HarperOne, 2011), 8–9.

25. See Clifford Geertz, "Religion as a Cultural System," in *Anthropological Approaches to the Study of Religion*, ed. Michael Banton (London: Tavistock, 1966).

26. See Elizabeth Caldwell, *God's Big Table: Nurturing Children in a Diverse World* (Cleveland: Pilgrim, 2011); and Elizabeth Caldwell, *Making a Home for Faith: Nurturing the Spiritual Life of Your Children* (Cleveland: Pilgrim, 2000).

27. See Shirley K. Morgenthaler, ed., *Exploring Children's Spiritual Formation*

(River Forest, IL: Pillars), 6. The author is Lutheran and understandably references "baptism" as opposed to "dedication," because of her theological orientation. We are satisfied with either notion in this definitional context.

28. Lawrence Cremin, *American Education* (New York: Harper & Row, 1970, 1982, 1990).

29. Brueggemann, *Creative Word*, x.

30. Brueggemann, *Creative Word*, 37–38.

31. See Emma Green, "Keeping the Faith," November 2014, http://www.the atlantic.com/magazine/archive/2014/11/keeping-the-faith/380799. Other research indicating correlations between religion and well-being may be found in the following: "Millennials in Adulthood," Pew Research Center, March 7, 2014, https://www.pewsocialtrends.org/2014/03/07/millennials-in-adulthood; John Wilson and Darren E. Sherkat, "Returning to the Fold," *Journal for the Scientific Study of Religion* 33 (1994): 148–61; Felix Neto and M. da Conceição Pinto, "Satisfaction with Love Life across the Adult Life Span," *Applied Research in Quality of Life* 10 (2014): 289–304; Felix Neto, "The Satisfaction with Sex Life Scale," *Measurement and Evaluation in Counseling and Development* 45 (2012): 18–31; W. J. Strawbridge et al., "Frequent Attendance at Religious Services and Mortality Over 28 Years," *American Journal of Public Health* 87 (1997): 957–61; A. Hoff et al., "Religion and Reduced Cancer Risk," *European Journal of Cancer* 44 (2008): 2573–79; and Lynda H. Powell, Leila Shahabi, and Carl E. Thoresen, "Religion and Spirituality: Linkages to Physical Health," *American Psychologist* (2003): 36–52.

32. "Welcome Service," *Book of Common Prayer* (The Archbishops' Council of the Church of England, 2000).

33. Sadly, we acknowledge that any of these three powerful socializing agents may foster, as well as deter, experiences of faith.

34. For sound research and practical ideas on this topic, see Jackson W. Carroll and Wade Clark Roof, *Bridging Divided Worlds: Generational Cultures in Congregations* (San Francisco: Jossey-Bass, 2002).

Chapter Twelve

1. Kenda Creasy Dean, *Practicing Passion: Youth and the Quest for a Passionate Church* (Grand Rapids: Eerdmans, 2004), 6.

2. Joe Magliano, "Why Are Teen Brains Designed for Risk-Taking?," *Psychology Today*, June 9, 2015, https://www.psychologytoday.com/us/blog/the-wide-wide -world-psychology/201506/why-are-teen-brains-designed-risk-taking. See also Arthur Allen, "Risky Behavior in Teens Can Be Explained in Part by How Their Brains Change," *Washington Post*, September 1, 2014, https://www.washingtonpost .com/national/health-science/risky-behavior-by-teens-can-be-explained-in-part

-by-how-their-brains-change/2014/08/29/28405df0-27d2-11e4-8593-da634b3343
90_story.html.

3. For an early treatment, see G. Stanley Hall, *Adolescence: Its Psychology and Its Relation to Physiology, Anthropology, Sociology, Sex, Crime, Religion and Education*, vol. 1 (New York: Appleton, 1922 [1904]). Of special interest to this chapter is Hall's description of adolescence, in the epigraph at the beginning of the chapter.

4. A nontechnical description may be found in Barbara Strauch, *The Primal Teen: What New Discoveries about the Teenage Brain Tell Us about Our Kids* (New York: Anchor, 2004).

5. Erik H. Erikson, *Identity: Youth and Crisis* (New York: Norton, 1968).

6. Magliano, "Why Are Teen Brains Designed for Risk-Taking?"

7. David White, *Practicing Discernment with Youth: A Transformative Youth Ministry Approach* (Cleveland: Pilgrim, 2005), 16.

8. Eleanor Barkhorn, "Getting Married Later Is Great for College-Educated Women," *Atlantic*, March 15, 2013, https://www.theatlantic.com/sexes/archive/2013 /03/getting-married-later-is-great-for-college-educated-women/274040/.

9. Jeffrey Arnett, *Emerging Adulthood: The Winding Road from the Late Teens through the Twenties* (New York: Oxford University Press, 2004).

10. See Chanon Ross, "Wicked Art: Marketing, Augustine, and the Demonic," *Liturgy* 29 (2014): 45-54.

11. Hayley Tsukayama, "Teens Spend Nearly Nine Hours Every Day Consuming Media," *Washington Post*, November 3, 2015, https://www.washingtonpost .com/news/the-switch/wp/2015/11/03/teens-spend-nearly-nine-hours-every-day -consuming-media/?utm_term=.adbad9b45ebd.

12. Nicholas Carr, *The Shallows: What the Internet Is Doing to Our Brains* (New York: Norton, 2011).

13. Anita Balakrishnan, "Apple Hits Record High, and Its Market Cap Nearly Reaches $900 Billion," CNBC, November 2, 2017, https://www.cnbc.com/2017/11 /02/how-much-cash-does-apple-have.html.

14. David Elkind, *The Hurried Child: Growing Up Too Fast Too Soon* (Cambridge, MA: Da Capo, 2007). See also Mary Pipher, *Reviving Ophelia: Saving the Selves of Adolescent Girls* (New York: Penguin, 1994).

15. Brian Mahan, Michael Warren, and David White, *Awakening Youth Discipleship: Christian Resistance in a Consumer Culture* (Eugene, OR: Cascade, 2008), chapter 5.

16. Elisha R. Galaif et al., "Suicidality, Depression, and Alcohol Use among Adolescents: A Review of Empirical Findings," *International Journal of Adolescent Medical Health* 19 (2007): 27–35. Available online at https://www.ncbi.nlm.nih.gov /pmc/articles/PMC3134404/.

17. Children's Defense Fund, "Cradle to Prison Pipeline® Fact Sheet," October

2009, http://www.childrensdefense.org/library/data/cradle-to-prison-pipeline -overview-fact-sheet-2009.pdf.

18. William Finnegan, *Cold New World: Growing Up in a Harder Country* (New York: Modern Library, 1999), and Patricia Hersch, *A Tribe Apart: A Journey into the Heart of American Adolescence* (New York: Ballantine, 1998).

19. Dean, *Practicing Passion*, 22.

20. Dean, *Practicing Passion*, 15.

21. C. S. Lewis, *Reflections on the Psalms* (New York: Harcourt, 2017), 111.

22. In all worship, it is the intercession of the Son by the power of the Spirit that transforms human worship into acceptable offerings before the Father.

23. "Contemporary worship" has been around long enough to gather a history. See Lester Ruth and Swee Hong Lim, *Lovin' On Jesus: A Concise History of Contemporary Worship* (Nashville: Abingdon, 2017).

24. We do not oppose youth's involvement in contemporary worship. We believe this movement has recovered a sense of majesty, grandeur, and even spiritual ecstasy appropriate to the worship of God. On the other hand, as with all worship, it too risks reducing young people's role in it to that of a passive consumer of a performance by worship "stars" instead of shared participation in the "people's work." In addition, the frequent absence of sacramentality offers youth fewer, not more, opportunities to connect with and rightly identify God as *triune* and, therefore, *missional*.

25. Gleaned from testimony at a DYA reunion, June 20, 2018, Duke Divinity School, Durham, NC.

26. Benjamin T. Connor, *Practicing Witness: A Missional View of Christian Practices* (Grand Rapids: Eerdmans, 2011), 33.

27. Mahan, Warren, and White, *Awakening Youth Discipleship*, 27-28.

28. Evelyn L. Parker, *Trouble Don't Last Always: Emancipatory Hope among African American Adolescents* (Cleveland: Pilgrim, 2003), 11.

Chapter Thirteen

1. Christian K. Tamnes, Ylva Østby, Anders M. Fjell, Lars T. Westlye, Paulina Due-Tønnessen, Kristine B. Walhovd, "Brain Maturation in Adolescence and Young Adulthood: Regional Age-Related Changes in Cortical Thickness and White Matter Volume and Microstructure," *Cerebral Cortex* 20 (2010): 534-48, https://doi.org/10.1093/cercor/bhp118.

2. Jeffrey J. Arnett, *Early Adulthood: The Winding Road from the Late Teens through the Twenties* (New York: Oxford University Press, 2004).

3. James W. Fowler, *The Stages of Faith: The Psychology of Human Development and the Quest for Meaning* (San Francisco: HarperSanFrancisco, 1981), 179-80.

4. See Fowler, *Stages*, chapter 5, "Conjunctive Faith," 184-98.

5. Emmanuel Katongole, "Greeting: Beyond Racial Reconciliation," in *The Blackwell Companion to Christian Ethics*, ed. Stanley Hauerwas and Sam Wells, 2nd ed. (Malden, MA: Blackwell, 2011), 72–74.

6. W. E. B. DuBois, *The Souls of Black Folk* (New York: Barnes and Noble Classics, 2003), 7.

7. John Roberto, "Faith Formation for All the Seasons of Adulthood," in *The Seasons of Adult Faith Formation*, ed. John Roberto (Naugatuck, CT: Lifelong Faith, 2015), 6.

8. Roberto, "Faith Formation," 17.

9. John Roberto, "Becoming a Faith Formation Curator," *Lifelong Faith* (Spring 2011): 20–25, https://meh.religioused.org/becoming_a_faith_formation_curator.pdf.

10. Roberto, "Faith Formation," 5.

11. Kathleen A. Cahalan, *Introducing the Practice of Ministry* (Collegeville, MN: Liturgical, 2010), 28. Cahalan's description of vocation is remarkably similar to Roberto's goals for adult faith formation. For perspective on the relationship of baptism to vocation, see Fred P. Edie, *Book, Bath, Table, and Time: Worship as Source and Resource for Youth Ministry* (Cleveland: Pilgrim, 2007).

12. To be clear, not all Christian adults are called to biological or adoptive parenthood. The nature of the baptismal covenant, however, does seem to call adult disciples to the love and nurture of other people's children.

13. Horace Bushnell, *Christian Nurture* (New York: Charles Scribner, 1861), 10, 20.

14. Edie Gross, "A Network of Black Farmers and Black Churches Delivers Fresh Food from Soil to Sanctuary," *Faith and Leadership*, https://www.faithandleadership.com/network-black-farmers-and-black-churches-delivers-fresh-food-soil-sanctuary?utm_source=FL_newsletter&utm_medium=content&utm_campaign=FL_topstory.

15. Barbara Brown Taylor, "Vocation," in *Pastor: A Reader for Ordained Ministry*, ed. William Willimon (Nashville: Abingdon, 2002), 24–25.

Part Four: Contexts for Nurturing Faith

1. See Maxwell E. Johnson, *The Rites of Christian Education: Their Evolution and Interpretation*, rev. and exp. ed. (Collegeville, MN: Liturgical, 2015), especially chapters 2–5.

2. Michael Dujarier, *A History of the Catechumenate: The First Six Centuries* (New York: William Sadler, 1979). To his great credit, Fr. Dujarier was among the first to recognize the historic significance of the catechumenate and its potential for faith formation in the late twentieth century.

3. Paulo Freire, *Pedagogy of the Oppressed* (New York: Continuum, 1970).

4. L. Gregory Jones, "Beliefs, Desires, Practices, and the Ends of Theological Education," in *Practicing Theology: Beliefs and Practices in Christian Life*, ed. Miroslav Volf and Dorothy Bass (Grand Rapids: Eerdmans, 2002), 185–205.

Chapter Fourteen

1. See Christian Smith and Melinda Denton, *Soul Searching: The Religious and Spiritual Lives of American Teenagers* (New York: Oxford University Press, 2005), 163–64. Through the authors' study teenagers, they suggest that teens learn this moralistic, therapeutic, and deistic "faith" through their families and churches. They warn that MTDs are colonizing and domesticating Christianity across North America. Unlike the God of the Old and New Testaments, the god of MTD is morphing into a feel-good god who validates our opinions of ourselves and otherwise comforts us but does not get involved with human history or call persons to cross-bearing for the sake of God's realm.

2. Post-Christendom has been especially hard on predominantly white middle class and affluent denominations and congregations in the Global North. Poor congregations and congregations composed of people of color never experienced the same measure of privilege and access to power Christendom afforded their wealthier and whiter neighbors. Their own countercultural stances, byproducts of the racism and classism they have endured, have provided them with resources to resist current antireligious cultural pressures.

3. C. Ellis Nelson, *Where Faith Begins* (Louisville: John Knox, 1984), 10.

4. Maria Harris, *Fashion Me a People: Curriculum in the Church* (Louisville: Westminster John Knox, 1989), 17.

5. John Westerhoff and O. C. Edwards, eds., *A Faithful Church: Issues on the History of Catechesis* (New York: Morehouse Barlow, 1981), 2–3.

6. Pierre Bourdieu, *The Logic of Practice* (Cambridge: Polity, 1990), 56.

7. Paula Span, "America at Home: Grandparents in the Attic, Children in the Basement," *New York Times*, February 17, 2018, https://www.nytimes.com/2018/02/17/health/multigenerational-shared-households.html?action=click&module=RelatedLinks&pgtype=Article.

8. Holly Catterton Allen and Christine Lawton Ross, *Intergenerational Christian Formation: Bringing the Whole Church Together in Ministry, Community, and Worship* (Downers Grove, IL: IVP Academic, 2012), 21.

9. Allen and Ross, *Intergenerational Christian Formation*, 92.

10. Allen and Ross, *Intergenerational Christian Formation*, 102

11. Allen and Ross, *Intergenerational Christian Formation*, 103.

12. Charles Foster, *From Generation to Generation: The Adaptive Challenge of Mainline Protestant Education in Forming Faith* (Eugene, OR: Cascade, 2012), 96.

13. Allen and Ross, *Intergenerational Christian Formation*, 224.

14. Charles Foster, *Educating Congregations: The Future of Christian Education* (Nashville: Abingdon, 2006), especially chapter 2.

15. Howard Vanderwell, ed., *The Church of All Ages: Generations Worshiping Together* (Herndon, VA: Alban Institute, 2008).

16. Dorothy Bass and Don Richter, eds., *Way to Live: Christian Practices for Teens* (Nashville: Upper Room, 2002), 2.

Chapter Fifteen

1. The Massachusetts Colony passed legislation in 1647 requiring schooling for children living in towns. For a full account of education in the American colonies, see Lawrence A. Cremin, *American Education: The Colonial Experience 1607–1783* (New York: HarperCollins, 1972).

2. David McCullough, *The Pioneers: The Heroic Story of the Settlers Who Brought the American Ideal West* (New York: Simon & Schuster, 2019).

3. Elizabeth A. O'Donnell, "Quakers and Education," in *The Oxford Handbook of Quaker Studies*, ed. Stephen Angell and Ben Dandelion (New York: Oxford University Press, 2015), 409.

4. Lawrence A. Cremin, *American Education: The National Experience 1783–1876* (New York: HarperCollins, 1980). Cremin traces the controversy over the proper religious orientation of America's new public schools.

5. Jack L. Seymour, Robert T. O'Gorman, and Charles R. Foster, *The Church in the Education of the Public: Refocusing the Task of Religious Education* (Nashville: Abingdon, 1984), 75–89.

6. David Lewin, *Educational Philosophy for a Post-Secular Age* (New York: Routledge, 2017), 1–7.

7. Yale theologian Miroslav Volf is one of the principal advocates for bringing Christian wisdom into academic conversations around the nature of human flourishing. See https://divinity.yale.edu/news/life-worth-living-goes-global.

8. Our description of theological positions is inspired by practical theologian Randy Maddox. See his book *Responsible Grace: John Wesley's Practical Theology* (Nashville: Abingdon, 1994). See especially chapter 2, "The God of Responsible Grace." We have simplified Maddox's nuanced account.

9. See Howard Gardner, *Frames of Mind: The Theory of Multiple Intelligences*, 3rd ed. (New York: Basic, 2011). Gardner was among the first to discount a centralized theory of cognition in the brain. Instead of conceiving intelligence as a singular capacity deployed across multiple tasks, Gardner proposed that discrete regions of the brain managed distinct tasks. Subsequent brain research offers qualified support for Gardner's theory. While not always tied to specific regions, different neural networks do seem to manage different intellectual tasks. The network involved in spoken language, for example, is distinct from the network that

supports musical expression. Gardner's work also expanded what counts for intelligence. Building upon Gardner, Daniel Goleman points to the significance of "emotional intelligence" for successfully navigating complex social settings. School leaders have become aware that students who can sense what they and classmates are feeling and can summon empathy for others tend to do better in school and, it turns out, in life. See his *Emotional Intelligence: Why It Matters More Than IQ* (New York: Bantam Books, 1995).

10. Susan Rose, *Keeping Them out of the Hands of Satan: Evangelical Schooling in America* (New York: Routledge, 1988), 113–22.

11. Rose, *Keeping Them*, 129.

12. Mortimer J. Adler, ed., *The Paideia Program: An Educational Syllabus* (Chicago: Institute for Philosophical Research, 1984); E. D. Hirsch, *The New Dictionary of Cultural Literacy: What Every American Needs to Know* (New York: Houghton Mifflin, 2002).

13. Elliot W. Eisner, *The Educational Imagination: On the Design and Evaluation of School Programs*, 3rd ed. (Upper Saddle River, NJ: Pearson Education, 2002).

14. Daniel Goleman, Lisa Bennett, and Zinobia Barlow, *Ecoliterate: How Educators Are Cultivating Emotional, Social, and Ecological Intelligence* (San Francisco: Jossey-Bass, 2012), 35–42.

15. Maria Montessori, "A Critical Consideration of the New Pedagogy in Its Relation to Modern Science," in *The Curriculum Studies Reader*, ed. David J. Flinders and Stephen J. Thornton, 5th ed. (New York: Routledge, 2017), 29.

16. The authors wish to thank Elizabeth A. DeGaynor, assistant professor of Christian education at Virginia Theological Seminary, for freely sharing her expertise in Christian schooling and especially her knowledge of schooling as practiced by the Christian Reformed Church. Her dissertation charts the history of schooling in the CRC along with its current efforts to take seriously its theological heritage, while navigating strong theological, educational, and cultural cross currents. See her "Learning (Re)formation: An Ethnographic Study of Theological Vision and Educational Praxis at Grand Rapids Christian Schools" (PhD diss., Duke University Divinity School, 2016).

17. Gloria Goris Stronks and Doug Blomberg, ed., *A Vision with a Task: Christian Schooling for Responsive Discipleship* (Grand Rapids: Baker, 1993), 16.

18. Stronks and Blomberg, *Vision with a Task*, 16–17.

19. Stronks and Blomberg, *Vision with a Task*, 23. Not incidentally, the presumption that students are diversely gifted will also raise critical questions about so-called ability grouping in classes. See pp. 24–25.

20. Stronks and Blomberg, *Vision with a Task*, 24.

21. Stronks and Blomberg, *Vision with a Task*, 202.

22. Smith, *Desiring the Kingdom*, 17–18.

23. See, for example, Christopher M. Meehan, *Growing Pains: How Racial Struggles Changed a Church and a School* (Grand Rapids: Eerdmans, 2017).

24. Seymour, O'Gorman, and Foster, *Church in the Education*, 108–9. In fact, they even take issue with the term *nurture*, suggesting that it signaled Christian education and should be focused on what goes on inside churches at the expense of its public mission.

25. Seymour, O'Gorman, and Foster, *Church in the Education*, 110–11.

26. Seymour, O'Gorman, and Foster, *Church in the Education*, 127–28.

27. Lewin, *Educational Philosophy*, 7.

28. Lewin, *Educational Philosophy*, 117.

29. "Nicole Baker Fulgham: Mobilizing People of Faith to Eliminate Inequity in Public Education," Faith & Leadership, July 14, 2014, http://www.faithandleader ship.com/qa/nicole-baker-fulgham-mobilizing-people-faith-eliminate-inequity -public-education.

30. Ted Williams III, "Why Should Christians Care about Public Education?," The Center for Public Justice, June 22, 2012, https://www.cpjustice.org/public /capital_commentary/article/546.

31. Our thanks to friends, neighbors, and colleagues for their willingness to share their motivations for and experiences with home schooling.

32. Learning groups desiring to complexify this question may wish to read "Skills and Other Dilemmas of a Progressive Black Educator," in Lisa Delpit's *Other People's Children: Cultural Conflict in the Classroom* (New York: Norton, 2006).

Chapter Sixteen

1. H. Richard Niebuhr, *The Purpose of the Church and Its Ministry: Reflections on the Aims of Theological Education* (New York: Harper & Row, 1956); H. Richard Niebuhr, Daniel Day Williams, and James Gustafson, *The Advancement of Theological Education* (New York: Harper, 1957); Edward Farley, *The Fragility of Knowledge: Theological Education in the Church and in the University* (Minneapolis: Augsburg, 1988); Charles R. Foster, Lisa Dahill, Lawrence A. Goleman, and Barbara Wang Tolentino, *Educating Clergy: Teaching Practices and Pastoral Imagination* (San Francisco: Jossey-Bass, 2006).

2. Mark's life has been inexorably entangled with and immensely enriched by formal education, uninterrupted for six decades, since he was four. Professors, books, and colleagues have pushed him in exploring the world of ideas. He owes much to them for causing him to think new thoughts, have vicarious experiences, and even feel great emotion. Thanks specifically to John Dewey, Peter Kreeft, Larry Richards, John Stott, and Ted Ward. These and others have shaped Mark's educational philosophy, educational psychology, and educational practice in his role as a

professor of theological education, for which he is extremely grateful. In addition, it has been a great pleasure for him to modestly assist in the mission of theological education in a recent European adventure: Belfast Bible College/Queens University (Northern Ireland), All Nations Christian College (England), Instituto Biblico Portuges (Portugal), Evangelische Theologische Faculteit (Belgium), and Tyndale Theological Seminary (The Netherlands). Finally, Mark is deeply appreciative to the wonderfully insightful, profoundly inquisitive, and multitalented students it has been his pleasure to encounter in and out of the classroom in the United States, Europe, Asia, and Australia. He is well aware they have taught him much more than he has taught them—a profound debt he owes.

3. Helpful books guiding professors in reflection on educational practice include Stephen Brookfield, *Becoming a Critically Reflective Teacher* (San Francisco: Jossey-Bass, 1995), and—more specific to the task of theological education—Mary Hess and Stephen Brookfield, *Teaching Reflectively in Theological Contexts: Promises and Contradictions* (Malabar, FL: Krieger, 2008).

4. The insightful and provocative writings of Neil Postman are relevant here, most notably in *Teaching as a Subversive Activity* (New York: Delta, 1971) and *The End of Education: Redefining the Value of School* (New York: Vintage, 1996).

5. Ken Bain, *What the Best College Teachers Do* (Cambridge, MA: Harvard University Press, 2004).

6. For more on developing educational methodology, see Stephen Brookfield, *The Skillful Teacher: On Technique, Trust, and Responsiveness in the Classroom* (San Francisco: Jossey-Bass, 2006); Barbara Gross Davis, *Tools for Teaching* (San Francisco: Jossey-Bass, 2009); Marilla Svinicki and William J. McKeachy, *McKeachy's Teaching Tips: Strategies, Research and Theory for College and University Teachers* (Belmont, CA: Wadsworth, 2010); Gary Morrison, Steven Ross, and Jerrold Kemp, *Designing Effective Instruction* (Hoboken, NJ: Wiley, 2006).

7. The results of Mark's doctoral dissertation research have served him well in and out of the classroom in this regard; see distilled versions in Mark A. Lamport, "Student-Faculty Informal Interaction and the Effect on College Student Outcomes: A Review of the Literature," *Adolescence* 28.112 (1993): 971-90, and Mark A. Lamport, "Student-Faculty Informal Interaction and Its Relation to Christian College Settings: Research and Implications," *Research on Christian Higher Education* (Fall 1994): 66-78.

8. See "Self-Assessment Categories for Faculty Growth Plans," pp. 370-71 above, a fine tool of self-assessment for professors, which assists in faculty growth plans. This was originally developed under the leadership of Richard F. Gross and R. Judson Carlberg, both academic deans and then presidents of Gordon College (Massachusetts), where Mark benefited from this tool for nine years of his career.

9. For very helpful resources, see Thomas Angelo and Patricia Cross, *Classroom*

Assessment Techniques: A Handbook for College Teachers (San Francisco: Jossey-Bass, 1993), and Dannelle Stevens and Antonia Levi, *Introduction to Rubrics: An Assessment Tool to Save Grading Time, Convey Effective Feedback and Promote Student Learning* (Sterling, VA: Stylus, 2004).

10. Abraham Joshua Heschel, "The Spirit of Jewish Education," *Jewish Education* 24.2 (1953): 15.

11. A very good overview on the most representative typologies in educational philosophy is Elliot Eisner, *The Educational Imagination*, 3rd ed. (Upper Saddle River, NJ: Prentice Hall, 2002).

12. Some will undoubtedly want to answer this five-pronged question in the affirmative, that all five educational philosophies are necessary for theological education. But that response avoids an intentionally focused educational philosophy that drives practice above all other choices.

13. Jesus asked over one hundred questions (as recorded in the Gospels)—and not because he did not know the answers!

14. For more on creating a classroom environment and teaching methods conducive to critical thinking, see Stephen Brookfield, *Developing Critical Thinkers: Challenging Adults to Explore Alternative Ways of Thinking and Acting* (San Francisco: Jossey-Bass, 1999).

15. We would argue more fully that the most effective educational philosophy for theological education, as stated above, is the Development of Cognitive Processes; and the most effective methods to implement this philosophy are Academic Rationalism and Curriculum as Technology; and the most effective motivation for these methods is Personal Relevance; and the most desirable educational outcome from this educational philosophy is Social Adaptation and Social Reconstruction.

16. Graham Cheesman, mentioned in the introductory paragraph, wonders whether the theological educator is doing his or her work "for the Church," or from within the church, or from outside the church. In other words, is theological education primarily an educational task that benefits ministry, or is it a ministry task itself that is done with good educational skills? He tends toward the second option with the proviso that the theological educator is not seeking to "do good" just to the church but also to society and the individual student, although this can be seen to be within the concept of "church ministry." We agree. For more on this line of thought, see L. Gregory Jones and Stephanie Paulsell, eds., *The Scope of Our Art: The Vocation of the Theological Teacher* (Grand Rapids: Eerdmans, 2001).

17. Edward Farley, in his *Theologia: The Fragmentation and Unity of Theological Education* (Eugene, OR: Wipf & Stock, 2001), strongly criticizes the theological encyclopedia because of its tendency to parse theology into separate domains: Bible, history, ethics, and so forth, which he further claims has distanced theology from the reflective habits of lay believers. Unlike Farley, Mark imagines "ministry

theology" as the crown of the various theological endeavors. For Farley, ministry theology was always merely applicative and not in and of itself a hermeneutical enterprise. In other words, unlike Farley, Mark reconstructs rather than rejects the theological encyclopedia and supports doing theology in the midst of the effort to live faithfully.

18. And because of the inevitability of the changing nature of culture(s), it is continually surprising to us how the curriculum of theological education is so loaded toward biblical and theological studies in contrast to minimal or nonexistent content in social and cultural analysis, especially of one's own culture. Why is cultural analysis necessary? In order to better speak, live, and conduct the mission of the gospel into the world. One (confidently) presumes that those who are members of a given culture will therefore certainly *know* their culture. However, it is largely true that those in a culture often do not objectively analyze or understand how we are influenced by our own culture. While Christians wish to be culture changers, sociologists uniformly report that cultures ultimately make us in their compelling image, including Christian institutions. For one of the freshest insights on this topic, see Andy Crouch, *Culture Making: Recovering Our Creative Calling* (Downers Grove, IL: InterVarsity, 2008).

19. Robert Barr and John Tagg, "From Teaching to Learning: A New Paradigm for Undergraduate Education," *Change* 27.6 (1995): 12-25.

20. See Robert Diamond, Judith Grunert O'Brien, Barbara Millis, and Margaret Cohen, *The Course Syllabus: A Learning-Centered Approach* (San Francisco: Jossey-Bass, 2008); Dee Fink, *Creating Significant Learning Experiences: An Integrated Approach to Designing College Courses* (San Francisco: Jossey-Bass, 2003); and Maryellen Weimer, *Learning-Centered Teaching: Five Key Changes to Practice* (San Francisco: Jossey-Bass, 2002).

21. It is supposed that many professors and institutions would agree with these propositions in theory, that learning is the goal. But the plain reality is that in theological education practice—as syllabi are designed, learning objectives are written, and learning activities are conceived—merely transmitting blocks of cognitive-based information composed of various theological subdisciplines is most conspicuous. There is a gap then between what we say we want in theological education and what its structures engender. Or, to use a distinction made by Chris Argyris and Donald Schön in *Theory in Practice: Increasing Professional Effectiveness* (San Francisco: Jossey-Bass, 1974), the difference between our espoused theory and our theory-in-use is distressingly noticeable. An "espoused theory" is the set of principles people offer to explain their desired behavior; whereas, the principles we can infer from how people or organizations actually behave is their "theory-in-use." At this moment, and perhaps contrary to many loud protestations, the Instruction

Paradigm is theological education's theory-in-use, while the espoused theories of many more closely resemble the Learning Paradigm.

22. See Mark A. Lamport and Mary Rynsburger, "All the Rage: How Small Groups Are Really Educating Christian Adults—Part 2: Augmenting Small Group Ministry Practice: Developing Small Group Leadership Skills Through Insights from Cognate Theoretical Disciplines," *Christian Education Journal* 5.1 (2008): 391-414.

23. The works that best distill Knowles's major principles are *The Modern Practice of Adult Education: From Pedagogy to Andragogy*, 2nd ed. (Englewood Cliffs, NJ: Prentice Hall, 1980); *Andragogy in Action: Applying Modern Principles of Adult Education* (San Francisco: Jossey-Bass, 1984); and *The Adult Learner: A Neglected Species*, 4th ed. (Houston: Gulf, 1990).

24. Knowles's ideas are not without controversy. Some critiques of andragogy, and in particular the work of Knowles, can be found in J. Davenport, "Is There Any Way out of the Andragogy Mess?," in *Culture and Processes of Adult Learning*, ed. Mary Thorpe, Richard Edwards, and Ann Hanson (London: Routledge, 1987), and Peter Jarvis, "Malcolm Knowles," in *Twentieth-Century Thinkers in Adult Education* (London: Croom Helm, 1987).

25. Stephen Brookfield, *Understanding and Facilitating Adult Learning* (Milton Keynes, UK: Open University, 1986), 99.

26. Mark Tennant, *Psychology and Adult Learning*, 2nd ed. (London: Routledge, 2005), 132.

27. Mark's designated title is "lecturer" at two of the theological schools he serves in Europe, a title he resists employing; sometimes, where appropriate, he clarifies this disinclination based on his views of teaching and learning.

28. It is a remarkable phenomenon to observe how prevailing societal customs and educational philosophies in a given region of the world mimic the same stances in theological schools in those same geographic regions. It is not surprising then, and Mark has observed it firsthand in Africa, Asia, and much of eastern Europe, that a teacher-dominated, content-centered, student-dependent, pedagogical model is more common than not in theological education—much like the more rigid political environments in these regions. Conversely, in many cases, theological education, at least in theory, in North America and western Europe more often leans toward a more egalitarian-based, learner-focused style—much like the democratic political arenas in these regions.

29. The writings of John Dewey, particularly in *Experience and Education* (New York: Free Press, 1997 [1938]); *Democracy and Education* (Teddington, UK: The Echo Library, 2007 [1916]); *How We Think* (Boston: Houghton Mifflin, 1998 [1933]); Jerome Bruner, *The Culture of Education* (Cambridge, MA: Harvard University

Press, 1997); *The Process of Education* (Cambridge, MA: Harvard University Press, 1977); Paulo Freire, *Pedagogy of the Oppressed*, 2nd ed. (New York: Penguin, 1996); and Ivan Illich, *Deschooling Society* (New York: Marion Boyars, 2000 [1970]), present compelling rationales for freedom and democracy in education.

30. Stanley Grenz and Roger Olson, *Who Needs Theology? An Invitation to the Study of God* (Downers Grove, IL: InterVarsity, 1994), 25.

31. Timothy Morgan, "Re-Engineering the Seminary: Crisis of Trust Forces Change," *Christianity Today*, October 24, 1994, 75.

32. It is a curious anomaly that there is a continual glut of those who desire careers as professors in theological education and simultaneously a continual dearth of those who desire careers in ministry leadership.

33. Somewhat surprising is the degree to which the curriculum for ministerial preparation has not appreciably changed over the course of the last half century, especially in comparison with other professions and realms of knowledge.

34. Yet this characterization is not intended to wantonly besmirch good-hearted but relatively uninformed people who have some degree of faith. On the other hand, this best seems to depict those who are more likely to be taken in by some theologically naive or unscrupulous television evangelists.

35. Lay theology is important but is most conveniently nurtured by ministry leaders through the life, nature, and mission of the church. While professional theologians rightly continue dialogue with their academically inclined peers, their first-order calling is to educate and train called and gifted men and women for ministry.

36. Some theological professors seem to harbor an academic recruiting agenda that seeks to convince ministry students that the more prestigious path to take is following their lead into the world of theological education. This may partially account for the "glut" and the "dearth" opined in note 32, above. On the other hand, Mark's much more common observation is the passion and heart that theological education professors have for those who are called to serve church-based and parachurch ministries. Indeed, some of the finest, most godly men and women he has ever had the privilege to know have been his colleagues (and role models and friends!) in theological education.

37. The aphorism is credited to Ted Ward, Mark's PhD advisor and mentor to a generation of theological educators, who unambiguously modeled the integration of education and theology, spending his career first in the School of Education at Michigan State University and then in the Department of Educational Ministries at Trinity Evangelical Divinity School (Illinois).

Part Five: Conversations in Nurturing Faith

1. Cohn detailed her story in *Behind Enemy Lines: The True Story of a French Jewish Spy in Nazi Germany* (New York: Three Rivers, 2002). See Holly Meyer, "Why This

Jewish Woman Risked Her Life to Spy on Nazi Troops during WWII," *Tennessean*, January 30, 2018, https://www.tennessean.com/story/news/religion/2018/01/30/why -jewish-woman-risked-her-life-spy-nazi-troops-during-wwii/1055173001/.

2. See Dallas Willard, "Spiritual Formation in Christ: A Perspective on What It Is and How It Might Be Done," in *The Great Omission* (San Francisco: Harper-Collins, 2006), 68–79.

3. David White, *Practicing Discernment with Youth: A Transformative Youth Ministry Approach* (Cleveland: Pilgrim, 2005) and *Awakening Youth Discipleship: Christian Resistance in a Consumer Culture* (Eugene, OR: Wipf & Stock, 2008).

4. Nicholas Carr, *The Shallows: What the Internet Is Doing to Our Brains* (New York: Norton, 2010).

5. Diana Butler Bass, *Christianity after Religion: The End of Church and the Birth of a New Spiritual Awakening* (San Francisco: HarperOne, 2012), 14–17, 38.

6. Reported by Kirsten Powers, "Christians Forgive Unspeakable Sins," *USA Today*, June 27, 2015, A8.

Chapter Seventeen

1. This same phenomenon is found on a macrolevel as well. Americans have extraordinary confidence in their place on the world stage. They are known for their assessment of the United States being "the best country in the world." This self-assigned ranking is not lost on those of other countries. Educationally, how-ever, a generation of testing places US students near the bottom when compared with developed nations in math and science. What Americans do have an extraor-dinarily high ranking in is self-confidence—a case study of "illusory superiority" that feeds such results as those provided about "teaching effectiveness."

2. Stanford C. Ericksen, *The Essence of Good Teaching: Helping Students Learn and Remember What They Learn* (San Francisco: Jossey-Bass, 1984).

3. "Dewey . . . does not readily yield to summary." Mary C. Boys, *Educating in Faith: Maps and Visions* (San Francisco: Harper & Row, 1989), 47.

4. Be reminded of the global variations that exist within cultures as prelimi-narily theorized in chapter 16, note 28.

5. John D. Caputo, *On Religion* (London: Routledge, 2016), 26.

6. See, for example, Stephen Brookfield, *Developing Critical Thinkers: Chal-lenging Adults to Explore Alternative Ways of Thinking and Acting* (San Francisco: Jossey-Bass, 1987); Patricia Cranton, *Understanding and Promoting Transforma-tive Learning: A Guide for Educators of Adults* (San Francisco: Jossey-Bass, 2006); L. Dee Fink, *Creating Significant Learning Experiences: An Integrated Approach to Designing College Courses* (San Francisco: Jossey-Bass, 2003); James E. Loder, *The Transforming Moment: Understanding Convictional Experiences* (San Francisco:

Harper & Row, 1982); and Jack Mezirow, *Learning as Transformation: Critical Perspectives on a Theory in Progress* (San Francisco: Jossey Bass, 2000).

7. Brookfield, *Developing Critical Thinkers.*

8. Children and persons with disabilities are likely to demonstrate varying levels of comprehension from this and other abstract concepts, such as the answer D, yet perhaps are likely to practice D. This makes the issue of comprehension admittedly complicated.

9. Brookfield, *Developing Critical Thinkers*; Cranton, *Understanding and Promoting Transformative Learning*; Loder, *Transforming Moment*; Mezirow, *Learning as Transformation.*

10. Mary-Ann Winkelmes, "Formative Learning in the Classroom," in *Practical Wisdom: On Theological Teaching and Learning*, ed. Malcolm L. Warford (New York: Peter Lang, 2004), 161–80.

11. Winkelmes, "Formative Learning," 130–36.

12. David Kolb, *Experiential Learning: Experience as the Source of Learning and Development* (Upper Saddle River, NJ: Prentice Hall, 1983).

13. Simon Baron-Cohen, *The Essential Difference: Men, Women and the Extreme Male Brain* (New York: Basic, 2004).

14. Perry Shaw, *Transforming Theological Education: A Practical Handbook for Integrative Learning* (Carlisle, UK: Langham, 2014), 238.

15. We freely acknowledge a debt to Walter Brueggemann (*The Creative Word: Canon as a Model for Biblical Education* [Minneapolis: Fortress, 1982], especially 28, 106, 154) for his original observations of this theme; we have adapted them to address the specific nature of this chapter.

16. Peter L. Berger and Thomas Luckmann, *The Social Construction of Reality* (Garden City, NY: Doubleday, 1966), 92–104.

17. Gerhard von Rad, *Wisdom in Israel* (New York: Abingdon, 1972), especially chapter 4.

18. Caputo, *On Religion*, 116.

19. Thanks to Will Willimon for his incisive, convicting wisdom expounded in "Making Christians in a Secular World," *Christian Century*, October 22, 1986, 914.

20. See, for example, Rebecca Traister, *Good and Mad: The Revolutionary Power of Women's Anger* (New York: Simon & Schuster, 2018).

21. Caputo, *On Religion*, 3.

22. Caputo, *On Religion*, 18.

23. This biographical (and all too graphic) account is from Austin Miles, *Don't Call Me Brother: A Ringmaster's Escape from the Pentecostal Church* (Amherst, NY: Prometheus, 1989) and has the *de rigueur* elements that make for a salacious soap opera, although sadly it is one of the creepiest accounts of religious manipulation and perverted control we have read in recent memory.

24. Miles, *Don't Call Me Brother*, 113.

25. Caputo, *On Religion*, 10.

Chapter Eighteen

1. Information about each of these scholars may be found in the list of contributors, beginning on p. 435.

Response 1

1. Maurice Wiles, *God's Action in the World* (London: SCM, 1986).

2. Simone Weil, *Waiting for God* (New York: Harper, 1973), 69.

3. Donald Davie, *To Scorch or Freeze: Poems about the Sacred* (Manchester: Carcanet Press, 1988), 49. Reprinted by kind permission of Carcanet Press, Manchester, UK.

4. Eugene Peterson, *Under the Unpredictable Plant* (Grand Rapids: Eerdmans, 1994), 195–96.

5. On this, see Robert Towler, *The Need for Certainty: A Sociological Study of Conventional Religion* (London: Routledge & Kegan Paul, 1984).

Response 2

1. This is not to imply that the story-linking process and pedagogy does not apply beyond African American Christianity. In fact, I appreciate Wimberly's work because of its ability to translate to other contexts. Anecdotally, I have found that students of all backgrounds gravitate toward this work every time I teach it. They connect with both the framework and the concrete steps she offers for helping people teach biblical texts in culturally and socially relevant ways.

Response 3

1. Edward Farley, *Ecclesial Man: A Social Phenomenology of Faith and Reality* (Philadelphia: Fortress, 1975), 6.

2. Farley, *Ecclesial Man*, 108–9.

3. See Stephen Crites, "The Narrative Quality of Experience," *Journal of the American Academy of Religion* 39 (1971): 291–311.

4. H. Richard Niebuhr, *The Meaning of Revelation* (New York: Macmillan, 1941), 80–81.

5. Fred P. Edie, *Book, Bath, Table, and Time: Christian Worship as Source and Resource for Youth Ministry* (Cleveland: Pilgrim, 2007), 7.

6. Edie, *Book, Bath, Table, and Time*, 29.

7. Edie, *Book, Bath, Table, and Time*, 31.

Response 4

1. James K. A. Smith, *You Are What You Love: The Spiritual Power of Habit* (Grand Rapids: Brazos, 2016), 115.

2. See https://www.umcdiscipleship.org/resources/the-baptismal-covenant-I.

3. John Wesley, *Wesley's Notes on the Bible* (Grand Rapids: Francis Asbury, 1987), 533. Here he writes on Galatians 6:2.

4. As Edie and Lamport remark, "It 'naturally' located white skin at the top of the hierarchy, shades of yellow, red, and brown in the middle, and very black ('burnt' or 'harmed') skin at the bottom" (p. 197).

5. Ray Gaston, "Re-Reading Babel and Pentecost: A Postmodern Polemic," *Modern Believing* 40 (1999): 37.

6. José Míguez Bonino, "Genesis 11:1–9: A Latin American Perspective," in *Return to Babel: Global Perspectives on the Bible*, ed. John R. Levison and Priscilla Pope-Levison (Louisville: Westminster John Knox, 1999), 13, quoted in Frank D. Macchia, "Babel and the Tongue of Pentecost: Reversal or Fulfillment? A Theological Perspective," in *Speaking in Tongues: Multi-Disciplinary Perspective*, ed. Mark J. Cartledge (Eugene, OH: Wipf & Stock, 2012), 41.

7. See Walter Brueggemann, *Genesis*, Interpretation: A Bible Commentary for Teaching and Preaching (Atlanta: John Knox Press, 1982), 99–100.

8. Stephen G. Ray, *Do No Harm: Social Sin and Christian Responsibility* (Minneapolis: Fortress, 2003), 98.

9. Michael O. Emerson and Christian Smith, *Divided by Faith: Evangelical Religion and the Problem of Race in America* (New York: Oxford University Press, 2000), 39.

10. Fumitaka Matsuoka, *The Color of Faith: Building Community in Multiracial Society* (Cleveland: United Church, 1998), 27–28.

11. Harlene Anderson, *Conversation, Language, and Possibilities* (New York: Basic, 1997).

12. Macchia, "Babel and the Tongue of Pentecost," 43.

13. Jung Young Lee suggests that as long as third-world theologians continue to validate their work by the criteria of Euro-American theology, which has long dominated racial and ethnic minorities, they will not be able to produce an authentic theology from their own perspective. In epistemological terms, marginal theology rejects the Western exclusivist either-or thinking and adopts the Eastern inclusivist epistemology of neither/nor and both/and. Neither/nor expresses the

in-between situation of marginality, whereas both/and its in-both. Jung Young Lee, *Marginality: The Key to Multicultural Theology* (Minneapolis: Fortress, 1995), 71.

14. See also the 1996 "Nairobi Statement on Worship and Culture," which proposes that Christian worship always has aspects that are transcultural (universal, transcending every culture); contextual (expressing particular cultures); counter-cultural (critiquing particular cultures); and cross-cultural (mixing and sharing different cultures). https://worship.calvin.edu/resources/resource-library/nairobi-statement-on-worship-and-culture-full-text.

15. Walter Brueggemann, *The Prophetic Imagination* (Minneapolis: Fortress, 2001), 82.

Response 5

1. James K. A. Smith, *Desiring the Kingdom: Worship, Worldview, and Cultural Formation* (Grand Rapids: Baker Academic, 2009), 18, 25.

2. Descriptions of ideologically varied ways of doing Christian formation can be found in Kathleen Cahalan, "Three Approaches to Practical Theology, Theological Education, and the Church's Ministry," *International Journal of Practical Theology* 9 (2005): 64–94.

3. Katherine Turpin, "The Ambivalent Legacy of Practice in Faith Formational Literature" (paper presented at Religious Educators Association 2018 Annual Meeting), https://religiouseducation.net/papers/proceedings-REA2018.pdf.

4. L'Arche International Summary Report, February 22, 2020, https://www.larche.org/documents/10181/2539004/Inquiry-Summary_Report-Final-2020_02_22-EN.pdf/6f25e92c-35fe-44e8-a80b-dd79ede4746b. In a letter written May 2015 regarding accusations made against Thomas Philippe, Jean Vanier wrote that he was "overwhelmed and shocked," but the recent report shows not only that he knew for decades but also that he enabled Philippe's misconduct and covered up multiple allegations.

5. "L'Arche's values of accompaniment, vulnerability, and mutuality are bigger than Jean Vanier," *Christian Century*, March 4, 2020, https://www.christiancentury.org/article/editors/l-arche-s-values-accompaniment-vulnerability-and-mutuality-are-bigger-jean-vanier.

6. For more on Yoder, see Soli Salgado, "Allegations of Sexual Harassment against John Howard Yoder Extend to Notre Dame," *National Catholic Reporter*, June 25, 2015, https://www.ncronline.org/news/accountability/allegations-sexual-harassment-against-john-howard-yoder-extend-to-notre-dame; Rachel Waltner Goossen, "'Defanging the Beast': Mennonite Responses to John Howard Yoder's Sexual Abuse," http://www.bishop-accountability.org/news5/2015_01_Goossen_Defanging_the_Beast.pdf.

7. Lauren Winner, *The Dangers of Christian Practice: On Wayward Gifts, Characteristic Damage, and Sin* (New Haven: Yale University), 3, 180. See also Amy Plantinga Pauw, "Attending to the Gaps between Beliefs and Practices," in *Practicing Theology: Beliefs and Practices in Christian Life*, ed. Miroslav Volf and Dorothy C. Bass (Grand Rapids: Eerdmans, 2002), 33–50. She offers insights about deformities of practice that often come from the outside, which requires us to open our conversational circle wider, to include nonmembers and secular resources found in feminisms and critical race theory.

8. Casey Cep, "The Gospel in a Time of Social Distancing," *New Yorker*, May 29, 2020, https://www.newyorker.com/news/on-religion/the-gospel-in-a-time-of-social-distancing; Melissa Florer-Bixler, "I Refuse to Participate in Worship That Leads to Devastation," *Sojourners*, March 25, 2020, https://sojo.net/articles/i-refuse-participate-worship-leads-devastation?fbclid=IwAR2qgmIzeiJnr4W-uposOf-n36XyvQB8ThpEtlxbM4DZSAZH1fd5PgmJ6iw.

9. Jason DeParle, "The Coronavirus Class Divide: Space and Privacy," *New York Times*, April 12, 2020, https://www.nytimes.com/2020/04/12/us/politics/coronavirus-poverty-privacy.html?smid=nytcore-ios-share; Charles M. Blow, "Social Distancing Is a Privilege," *New York Times*, April 5, 2020, https://www.nytimes.com/2020/04/05/opinion/coronavirus-social-distancing.html.

10. M. Shawn Copeland, *Enfleshing Freedom: Body, Race, and Being* (Minneapolis: Fortress, 2010), 1, 58, 126.

11. For a helpful description of narrative theology (also called postliberal theology), see Gary Dorrien, "A Third Way in Theology" and "Truth Claims: The Future of Postliberal Theology," *Christian Century*, July 4 and 18, 2001.

12. Charles Foster's model for eventful formation (prepare, participate, reflect) is helpful here. See *Educating Congregations: The Future of Christian Education* (Nashville: Abingdon, 1994), especially chapter 2.

13. Evelyn Parker, *Trouble Don't Last Always: Emancipatory Hope among African American Adolescents* (Cleveland: Pilgrim, 2003), 6–19. In the 2009 Religious Educators Association (REA) Proceedings, Parker adds the components of intersectionality and further awareness of internalized racism, along with focusing on one fruit of the Holy Spirit: courage to act for emancipatory hope. http://old.religiouseducation.net/proceedings/2009_papers.html.

Rejoinder and Epilogue

1. David Knowles, "Tech Leaders Lament the Mess They've Created," *Yahoo News*, July 25, 2018, https://www.yahoo.com/news/tech-leaders-lament-mess-theyve-created-090055838.html.

2. John Westerhoff, *Will Our Children Have Faith?* (East Malvern, Canada:

Dove, 1976). Subsequent editions and revisions were released in 1980 and 2000, which would seem to demonstrate they agreed with his assessment of ineffectiveness and kept it in press, but wholesale changes in how Christians are formed have been marginally reconceptualized.

3. Karl Barth, *Protestant Theology in the Nineteenth Century* (Valley Forge, PA: Judson, 1978), 33-178.

4. Walter Brueggemann, *The Creative Word*, rev. ed. (Minneapolis: Fortress, 1982), 139. See, among others, Psalms 22, 73, 77, 139.

5. Oswald Chambers, *My Utmost for His Highest*. https://jasontwombly.word press.com/category/oswald-chambers/.

6. John Calvin, *Institutes of the Christian Religion*, Library of Christian Classics 20 (Philadelphia: Westminster, 1960), 1:72.

7. Ron Highfield, *Great Is the Lord: Theology for the Praise of God* (Grand Rapids: Eerdmans, 2008), 401-2.

8. A more faithful example of courage in the face of the persecution of Roman emperor Marcus Aurelius is a Christian named Sanctus, who, when tortured, simply answered, "I am a Christian." The more he was tortured, the more he persisted in saying nothing but these words. Moved by this and many other signs of courage, some who had earlier denied their faith returned to confess it and die as martyrs.

9. C. S. Lewis, *The Weight of Glory* (New York: HarperCollins, 2001), 26.

Abington v. Schempp (1963), 99
Aboujaoude, Elias, 31
Abraham, 55, 61
adolescence, 266, 268–70, 272–74; oppression, 270; religious identity, 272
Adolescence: Its Psychology and Relation to Physiology, Anthropology, Sociology, Sex, Crime, Religion, and Education (Hall), 275
adolescent religious identity, 272; and Erik Erikson, 272; and James Marcia, 272
adolescents, passionate faith for, 275
adult faith formation, 287
adulthood, 284, 287; dynamic, 285; emerging, 288; faith-forming implications of dynamic, 295; learning theories of, 360, 361–68; mid-life, 290; older, 293; young, 287
adultified children, 254
adulting, 270
African American Christian education, 163, 165
age distribution of religious groups, 248
All Grown Up and No Place to Go (Elkind), 254
America as Christian nation, 80–81, 82–83
American Education (Cremin), 261

American Revolution, 269
amnesia, disorienting, 118, 149
andragogy, 362
Angelou, Maya, 135
Anselm, 97
anthropology, religious, 401; steps toward, 159
apartheid, 145
Apple (company), 273
Aquinas, Thomas, 54
Asma, Stephen, 452–53n5
Associated Press–GfK and General Social Study (1972), 103
Astley, Jeff, 228
Athens, 135
Augustine of Hippo, 32, 54, 61, 168; Augustinian, 272; *Confessions*, 158
autonomy, 228

Bainbridge, William Sims, 88
Ball, Peter, 89
Balmer, Randall, 60–61
Bandura, Albert, 42, 317, 449–50n47
"banking concept" of education, 226
baptism, as gift, 2
Barth, Karl, 129, 139
Bass, Dorothy, 45
Bauckham, Richard, 65
Beautiful Day in the Neighborhood, A (film), 254
behaviorism, 355; and classical condi-

tioning, 355; and operant condition-
ing, 355
Belenky, Mary, 228
Bell, David M., 273
Berger, Peter, 43, 88, 109
Bernard of Clairvaux, 242
Berryman, Jerome, 321
Blevins, Dean, 458n9
Blomberg, Doug, 161
Bloom, Allan, 62
Bloom, Harold, 44
Bohler, Peter, 37
Bondi, Richard, 159–62
Bondi, Roberta, 157, 158
Bonhoeffer, Dietrich, 33, 94, 255, 394;
   Life Together, 103, 105
Book of Common Prayer, 168
Bosch, David, 186
Bowers, James P., 104, 232, 261
Boys, Mary, 83
Boys' Brigade, 275
Boy Scouts of America, 275
bricolage, conceptual, 99, 101, 113, 118,
   125, 150
Brown, Dan, 453–54n14
Brown, Mick, 59
Brueggemann, Walter, 230–31, 236,
   246, 257
Buber, Martin, 132
Buddhism, 116
Bulgakov, Sergei, 28
Bushnell, Horace, 13–14, 250, 260, 298;
   contribution to Christian education,
   250, 259, 260–61; father of American
   religious liberalism, 261; father of the
   Christian education movement, 261;
   and Harvard Divinity School, Hollis
   Professorship at, 261

Calvin, John, 32
Calvinists, 138
Caputo, John D., 51, 394, 454n19
Carey, George, 89
Carr, Nicholas, 271
Catholics, 138, 144
character building, 275
Chesterton, G. K., 94
Chicago Cubs, 261
childified adults, 255
children, education in faith for, 248;
   proposed strategies for, 251, 263;
   schooling and miscalculated strategies of, 251; traditional strategies
   of, 251
Children's Defense Fund, 274
Children's Letters to God (Hample and
   Marshall), 245
chosenness, as dangerous activity, 413
Christian education, American
   Protestant: approaches to, ineffective, 378–79; distinguishing marks
   from other forms of education,
   378–79; myths, 383; "shared praxis"
   approach, 231; theory and questions
   of, 6. See also miscalculated models
   of learning
Christianity, major changes in European-Caucasian, 23
Christian Nurture (Bushnell), 261
Christian practical wisdom, 231
Christian schools, 331; a case study,
   342–45; differing educational orientations, 337; differing theological
   orientations for, 336; influence of
   public schools on, 334; Protestant
   and Catholic, 333; secularism and
   post-secularism and, 334; and the
   state, 332–33; theological and educa-

tional considerations for, 336; theological, social, and cultural impacts upon, 332–36

Christian stewardship, 232–35; critical reflection on present action, 233; decision/response, 235; dialectical hermeneutic, 234; making Christian story accessible, 233–34; naming present practice, 233

Christian story or vision, 232

Christian tradition, breadth of, 163

Christie, Agatha, 220

church, 188; as alternative community, 191, 194, 409; as business establishment, 253; and colonialism, 197; in the education of the public, 345–46; failures of, 3, 195–96; and its identity, 201; imagery of, 189–90; and implication for nurturing faith, 198–202; and inclusion, 196; and racism, 196

"citizens of the world," 224

Coe, George Albert, 139

cognitive abstraction, 282

communities, faith, 311; challenges of, 313; congregations as, 314; intergenerational, 314; kinship and, 401

Comte, August, 57, 58, 64

confrontation, 129

congregations that nurture faith, 314–15

Conner, Benjamin, 281

Conroy, Pat, *The Great Santini*, 149

constructionism, social, 99, 101, 118, 125, 150, 363

consumerism, 271

context in nurturing faith, 11, 99, 305–6

Conyers, A. J., 64, 65

Copernicus, 151

Coppola, Sophia, 52

Cornelius, 165

Cox, Daniel, 80

Cox, Harvey, 71, 108

"Cradle to Prison Pipeline" (Children's Defense Fund), 274

Creative World, The (Brueggemann), 263

Creel, Richard E., 33

Cremin, Lawrence, 261

critical eye, 221

critical reflection/thinking, 116, 117, 221; discourse, 223; fighting oppression, 235; personal transformation, 222–25; social transformation, 225–28; and Socratic method, 117; theological themes, 229

Crouch, Andy, 47–48, 72–73, 456n38

"cultural circles," 226; and generative themes, 226

cultural incursion, 254

cultural literacy, 226

culture, versions of, 428

curriculum, 384

Dante, *Inferno*, 151

Darwin, Charles, 154

David, King, 277

Davis, Ellen, 234

Dean, Kenda Creasy, 266, 277

DeGaynor, Elizabeth, response by, 414–17

Derrida, Jacques, 56

Descartes, René, 151–52, 156, 158, 159

detachment, 242

determinism, autonomous, 99, 101, 118, 125, 149

developmental framework, limitations of, 294

Dewey, John, 71, 93, 116–17, 159–60, 219, 232, 306, 379, 419, 485, 489, 491; translated for nurturing faith, 381–84

dilemmas, disorienting, 223

discipleship. *See* nurturing faith

discovery, guided, 340–41; free, 341–42

disequilibrium in education for change, 386

disorienting: amnesia, 118, 149; dilemmas, 223

"disruption for justice," 236

divine-human communication process, 242–43

Donovan, Vincent, 457n4

doubt, 32, 430; in Christian community, 33; as universal experience, 32

Duke's Youth Academy (DYA) for Christian Formation, 278

Dutch South African Church, 145

Dutton, Edward, 123

Dykstra, Craig, 75, 99, 173, 206–7, 209, 426; response by, 405–8

Eastman, Susan, 159

Edie, Fred, 164; education in faith, 262–63; inculcate confidence in truth of God, 263; offer love of faith community, 263; prepare children for cultural pushback, 263

education, 383–86; atmosphere in, 384; critical reflection in, 222; experiential, 93; and inconsequential noneducation, 383; and informal learning, 93; and subversive miseducation, 383; public education, influence of, 334. *See also* informal and incidental educative processes

educational design, foundational elements of, 356

educational mission of the church, 25

Educational Mission of the Church, The (Havighurst), 253

educational philosophy, 355–59; five families of, 356

educational practice, 361–67. *See also* higher education: best practices in

educational psychology, 359–61

Egypt, 163

Eldredge, John, 276

Elkind, David, 254, 274

emancipatory hope, 282

embodiment, 18, 148, 158, 163, 425–26

embracing generational contributions, 262

"enchanted world," Charles Taylor and, 23

encouraging exploration, 257

enculturation, 256

engaging religion, 241–42; modes of, 124

Engel v. Vitale (1962), 99

Enlightenment, 158, 166

epistemological distortion, 219

Erickson, Amy, 263

Erikson, Erik, 272–73

experience, 136–38; and John Dewey, 137; as educative, 379; religious, 397, 398

exploration, encouragement of, 257

faith, 53–55, 60–62; atmospheric, 256; challenges to communities of, 313; community, 409; fragmented, 99, 101, 118, 125, 149; living/lived, 11–12, 416, 418, 420–21; and the mission of God, 200–201; nature of, 1; and obedience, 429; and praise, 429; and relationship, 312; story of, 53–56. *See also* nurturing faith

faith development, and James Fowler, 374

faith formation, through worship and mission, 325

faithfulness, 429

Faith Matters Survey (Roper Center for Public Opinion Research), 247

"faith seeking understanding," 221

father of the Christian education movement. *See* Bushnell, Horace

Feinberg, Walter, 249

feminist scholarship, 228

Finn, Thomas, 142

Flew, Anthony, 460n30

flow of the teaching experience, 242

forgiveness, countercultural act of, 378

formal educative processes, 248

formation, 230; identity, 390; spiritual, 390

Foster, Charles R., 31, 83; foreword by, xvii–xxi

Foster, Jodi, 138, 140

Foster, Ron, 266

Foucault, Michel, 56

Fowl, Stephen, 145

Fowler, James W., and stages of faith, 289

frames of reference, 223

Francis, Saint, 135

freedom, 227; human and Christian, 227; religious liberty, 227

Freud, Sigmund, 153

Friere, Paulo, 225–27, 229, 232–33, 236, 306

Galileo, 151

Gartenberg, Dov, 448n36

General Social Survey (NORC [National Opinion Research Center] at the University of Chicago), 247

generations: baby boomers, 292; generational issues, 292; maintaining community between, 262; millennials, 291. *See also* intergenerational learning, forms of

Gilkey, Langdon, 58

Global North/South, 278

Gnosticism, 116

Godly play, 321–23; and Jerome Berryman, 321

Goto, Courtney, 165, 166

"got woke," 282

Grebel, Conrad, 203

Greco-Roman culture, 135

Green, Steven K., 80

Grenz, Stanley, 114

Groome, Thomas H., 124, 227, 231–32, 441n13; response by, 418–21; "shared praxis" approach to Christian education, 231

Guinness, Os, 32

Gurian, Michael, 276

Hagar, 164

Hall, G. Stanley, 266, 275

Hample, Stuart, 245

Hanks, Tom (as Mr. Rogers), 254

Hauerwas, Stanley, 107, 186, 351

Havighurst, Robert J., 253

Henry, Carl, 44

Hervieu-Léger, Danièle, 98

Heschel, Abraham Joshua, 41

Hicks, Stephen, 52

higher education, 350; best practices in, 353–54

Hirsch, E. D., *Cultural Literacy*, 98

Hitchens, Christopher, 459–60n28

Hitler, Adolf, 139

Hodge, Charles, 260

Holy Spirit, 242

home schooling, 346–48

hooks, bell, 219

horim (parents), 257

Horton, Michael, 84

human beings, 150; human nature, implications of for faith formation, 162; human portraiture, 150–59

human development over life span, 296–97

humility, generous, 424

Hunter, David, 242

Hurried Child, The (Elkind), 254, 274

Hutchison, William, 41

identity, 249, 272–73, 414; achievement, 272; commitment, 272; diffusion, 272; ego, 272; identity crisis, 272; identity vs. role confusion, 272; moratorium, 272; religious, 273

illusory superiority, 378

images of God, 192–93; grounded in theology, 192; images from created world, 192

imagination, 172; Christian, 404; and faithful imagining, 172; of God, 173; and mystery, 171

imago Dei (image of God), 277

imitation and example, 249

incarnation, the, 131–32, 170; and enfleshment in Christ, 174; theological musings on, 171–72

inciting wonder, 257

informal and incidental educative processes, 248

intergenerational learning, forms of, 323; leadership for congregational change in, 319–29; nature of faith communities, 312, 316–17

Irenaeus of Lyon, 51, 148

Ishmael, 164

Islam, 42–43

Israel, 163

James, William, 140, 155

Japanese American Christian spirituality, 166

Jenkins, Philip, 30, 62, 95

Jerusalem, 135

Jesus Christ, 43–44, 53, 55, 57, 65, 66, 69, 73, 77, 92; and analogical language, 1–2; orientation, disorientation, and reorientation, 5; teachings, content and method of, 5; transformative education and, 383–84. *See also* incarnation, the; participation in Christ

Jews, 165

John (apostle), 241

John of Damascus, 54

Johnson, R. Kevin, 257–58

Jonah, 85–87

Jones, Derek, 276

Jones, L. Gregory, 145

joy, 212–13

Judaism, 41–42

Justin Martyr, 117

Kant, Immanuel, 153

Kearney, Richard, 454n19

Kegan, Robert, 224

Kidman, Nicole, 451n1

Kierkegaard, Søren, 28, 58

kinesthetic symbolism, 44–45

kingdom of God. *See* practicing the kingdom

Klinenberg, Eric, 60

knowing and doing, interrelatedness of, 379

knowledge, 12; cloud of unknowing and, 13; of God's wisdom, 241; knowing and, 418; limits of human,

13; social and cultural construction of, 13; understanding and, 421–22; wisdom and, 12

Lamport, Mark, 256, 261
Laracy, Joseph R., 456n41
learning, 7; Christian, 383–86; cone of, 359–60; experiential, 7; from other faith traditions, 35–46; horizontal dimension of, 208; kinds of, 222; as past-present-future, 243; and processing information, 386; situated, 318; spiritual, 208; styles, 386; vertical dimension of, 208
Levinas, Emmanuel, 56
Lewis, C. S., 277, 423
liberal education, 227
liberation education, 228
love, 2–3; and knowledge, 400
Luddites, 271
Luther, Martin, 55, 134, 135, 330
Lyon, David, 89
Lyotard, Jean-François, 56, 65–66, 455n27, 456n40

Mahan, Brian, 274
Marcia, James, 272–73
Marshall, Eric, 245
Marty, Martin E., 89–90
masculinity, 275–76; ecclesial feminization, 276; manliness, 276
Mathews, Shailer, 253
McConaughey, Matthew, 140
McDermott, Gerald R., 35
McGilchrist, Iain, 162
McGrath, Alister, 106
Mendel, Menachem, 69
mentoring: adolescent boys, 275; adolescent girls, 280–81; and G. Stanley Hall, 275; and masculine ideals, 274
Mercer, Joyce, 280

metanoia (transformation), 116
metaphor and linguistic devices, 176–78
Methodism, 136
Mezirow, Jack, 222–26, 229, 232–33, 236
Michener, Ronald T., 70, 72, 455n30
Milton, John, 1
miscalculated models of learning, 251–53; amalgamation, 252; assimilation, 252; Bible-only, 252; socialization, 252
mission, 278–79, 281
Mister Rogers' Neighborhood (television series), 254
modernism, 61–63
modern thought, stages of, 57–60
Moore, Thomas, 450n52
Moralistic Therapeutic Deists (MTDs), 313
Moran, Gabriel, 447n27
morim (teachers), 258
Mormonism, 36–38
Moses, "new," 163
Murder on the Orient Express (Christie), 220
Murphy, Debra Dean, 44, 447n27
mystery, 142; necessity of, 143; paschal, 179

natural selection, 154
Nelson, C. Ellis, 105
Neoplatonism, 135, 157
Nietzsche, Friedrich, 43
Noll, Mark, 80–81
nominal Christian(ity), 76–85, 88–90; contributors to and manifestations of, 79–83
North America, 107
Northern Ireland, 102

nurturing faith, 3, 6, 13, 391; challenges to, 30, 98; with children, 245; distinctives of and gifts for, 115; implications of revelation and, 162; macrofactors of, 23–24; mission and, 11; thinking as a strategy for, 375–76; wisdom and, 389

Oden, Thomas C., 351
Oh, Kirsten Sonkyo, response by, 409–13
Olsen, Roger, 114
oppression, 402, 414, 423

Packer, J. I., 118
Palmer, Parker, 13
parallel society, faith society as, 256
Park, HiRho Y., 138, 156
Parker, Evelyn, 282
participation in Christ, 406–7, 426
Pascal, Blaise, 94, 158
paschal mystery, 171; theological musings on, 180–83
passion, 269–72, 277–79, 281–83
patchwork self, children and, 254
Paul (apostle), 54, 55, 229–30, 241, 261
Pauw, Amy Plantinga, 85
paying attention to doctrines and creeds, 259
Peck-McClain, Emily A., 281
pedagogical preconditions, 223
Pelikan, Jaroslav, 83
Percy, Martyn, response by, 396–400
Perpetua, Vibia, 123
perspective, gaining better through transformation, 223
Peter (apostle), 55, 165
Pew Religion and Public Life surveys, 247
Pittman, Amanda Jo, 165, 166

pluriformity, interpretive, 99, 101, 118, 125, 149
postmodernism, 56; as critique of empiricism and rationalism, 56; humanistic traits of, 66; results of, 70; story of, 62–73
Potok, Chaim, 39
power, 415; inequities of, 199–200
practical theology, and terms for nurturing faith, 9–10
practical wisdom, 221
practice, theologizing, 208; theories of, 205
practice-linking, 216–17
practices, 204, 206–9, 213–15; communal, 427; implications for faith formation, 215–17; kingdom-shaping, 417; and the reign of God, 210–11; theologizing, 209–12; and virtues, 206
practicing rituals, 259
practicing the kingdom, 209–10; and the reign of God, 212; and simplicity, 216
praxis, shared Christian, 421; movements of, 420
prayer, and children, 257
"problem posing," 226
professor, teaching craft of the, 350; best practices of, 352–53
prophetic task, 231
Protestantism, 111
Prothero, Stephen, 98
puberty, 268
Putnam, Robert, Bowling Alone, 102

realm, God's: and divine joy, 212; practicing, 215. See also practicing the kingdom
reason, 135–36, 155; interpreting God's

actions through, 156; relationship of faith and, 155

reflection, 114

reflective engagement, 159; implications for faith formation in, 231; and James Fowler, 160; and Paulo Freire, 160; and Donald Schon, 159; theological themes in, 229

Reformation, 135

relationships, negative side of, 403

religion, instinct of, 123; self-justifying stories of, 125

religious affiliation, 241; commitment, 241; ideas, 241

religious composition of the United States, 79; age distribution of religious groups, 248

religious education: of Jews, 40; of Mormons, 37; of Muslims, 43

Religious Education Association, 139

religious switching, 29–30, 46–48

resurrection, cruciform, grace of, 169, 183

revelation, 129–33; as knowing God, 396; mediating sources of, 133; in modern and postmodern world, 138–41; nature of, 396; and theology, 4

Reyes, Patrick Bruner, 117

Richards, Lawrence O., 15, 104, 485n5

Ricoeur, Paul, 285

rites and ceremonies, 249

ritual: as solemn ceremony, 39; ritual practice as formative, 40

Robinson, Robert, 27

Rodin, Auguste, *The Thinker*, 151

Rorty, Richard, 56

Rousseau, Jean-Jacques, *Emile*, 152

sacraments, 178–79; and participation, 177–78

Sanneh, Lamin, 42

Schipani, Daniel, 145

schooling and Christian education, 423; case study in, 342–45; home, 347–48; model, 248–49; one, 344–45; private, 346–47; public, 334–35, 346–48; theological and educational considerations for, 334; theological, social, and cultural impacts upon, 330

Schopenhauer, Arthur, 245, 247

Schorske, Carl, 98

Schwanda, Tom, 142

scientific management, 252; efficiency, 252–53

Second Vatican Council, 228

secularism, 88–90

self-identity, 268

selling bodies, 270–71

"sense making," 223

sexuality, 269–70

Shallows: What the Internet Is Doing to Our Brains, The (Carr), 271

shared praxis approach, 231

Sider, Ronald, 84

sin, 179–84; battling, 185

Smart, James, 33

smartphone, 271; digital transition, 271; young people as "digital natives," 271

Smith, James K. A., 71, 158, 159, 453n10, 455n28

Snapper, J. Marian, 71

social constructionism, 412

social Darwinism, 274

socialization, 103; approach, 248–50; intentional strategy of formation through, 104; theologies of Chris-

tian formation and, 104; and John Westerhoff, 104
social literacy, 226
societal conditions, critical engagement with, 375; and cultural influences, 63
Solomon, 69
spiritual consciousness, 258; experiential, 258; intellectual, 258
Spiritual Lives of Young African Americans, The (Wright), 235
Stark, Rodney, 62, 109, 460, 447–48n31
Steyer, Jim, 271
story, stories, 175; shared, 403, 416; story of God, 3, 4, 8
Streep, Meryl, 59
studying the Bible, and the Holy Spirit, 240; purposes of, 242; time orientation, 241, 386; ultimate end of, 242
superiority, illusion of, 378
symbol and ritual, 178
symbolism, kinesthetic, 44–45

Taylor, Charles, 23, 27, 34, 140, 453n8
Taylor, Daniel, 59
Taylor, Frederick, 252
teaching, growth plans for, 370–71; practices, 216; uniqueness of Christian, 378
teaching agenda for the global church, 379–93
teaching experience, flow of the, 242
theological education, prevailing misconceptions, 355
theological encyclopedia, 370
theology, types of, 363; for nurturing faith, 10
Thiessen, Elmer, 228

thinking in contemporary culture, 374
thinking in faith formation, 219
Thurman, Howard, 165
Tolstoy, Leo, 75
Tozer, A. W., 48
traditions, 134–35
transformation, 221; critical reflection for personal, 222; critical reflection for social, 225; radical, 8; vision of, 425
transformational experiences, 386; learning from, 391
transmission: direct, 339; indirect, 339
Trinity, 131–32
Tubman, Harriet, 165
Turpin, Katherine, *Branded*, 158
Tutu, Desmond, 148
Twain, Mark, 1

unintended consequences, law of, 423–24

Van der Linden, Dimitri, 123
Vattimo, Gianni, 63, 454n19
Vella, Jane, and curriculum planning, 387–88
Virgil, 53
virtue ethics, 414
vision, theological, 407
vocation, adult, 297–300

Warren, Michael, 41, 145
Weber, Max, 57, 88, 138
welcoming tradition and transformation, 262
Wesley, John, 34, 82–83, 136, 137, 141, 213–14
Westerhoff, John H., III, 28, 104, 256, 258, 315, 330; and socialization model of Christian formation, 315

White, David, 31, 269, 282
Wild at Heart (Eldredge), 276
Willard, Dallas 46–47, 94, 377; *The Great Omission*, 111
Williams, Delores, 164
Willimon, Will, 141, 351
Will Our Children Have Faith? (Westerhoff), 258
Wimberly, Anne, 163, 164, 165
Winner, Lauren, 39
wisdom and teaching, 391
Wolfe, Alan, 82, 84
Wolterstorff, Nicholas, 53
wonder, incitement of, 257

Won't You Be My Neighbor? (documentary), 254
Wood, Ralph, 67–68
Woolf, Virginia, 285
worship, 277–78
Wright, Almeda (response), 235–36; response by, 401–4
Wright, N. T., 83; *Scripture and the Authority of God*, 108
Wuthnow, Robert, 250
Wyckoff, D. Campbell, 6–7, 15, 405, 441n13

Yahweh, 246
YMCA, 275

INDEX OF SCRIPTURE REFERENCES

OLD TESTAMENT

Genesis
1:3	2
1:26–2:3	232, 233
1:27	357
1:28–29	357
2:15	233
2:18	162
11	410

Exodus
12:26	259
13:8	259
13:14	259

Numbers
6:23–27	258

Deuteronomy
6:1–26	249
6:4–5	249, 347
6:6	249
6:7	249, 347
6:7–9	249
6:20–21	259, 309

Joshua
1	69
4:6	259
4:12	259

1 Samuel
2:3	118
16:7	157

Psalms
23	400
68:3	313
78:4–7	97, 118
85:10–11	34
96:11–13	211
119:151	432
145:4	309

Proverbs
1:7	100
1:8–9	347
3:5–8	390
8:34–35	390
12:11	230
13:24	10
15:1	230

Ecclesiastes
1:14	69
2:11	69

Isaiah
11:6	209

Jeremiah
29:11	334

Jonah
1:9	86
2:9	86
4:2	86

NEW TESTAMENT

Matthew
6:7–8	83
7:3	198
7:21–23	423
10:39	3
11:5	146
13	143
16:15	143
16:18	25
21:23–27	143
25:21	356
25:31–46	279
27:12–14	143
28:19–20	3

Mark
1:22	169
4	143
4:38	143
8:35	3
10:25	3
10:51	143
15:39	130
19:16	143

Luke

1:26–38	393
4:18–19	209
4:21	209
6:32	191
6:46	143
7:22	146
9:25	143
10:25	143
11:13	357
14:11	3
15–16	143, 211
17:5	53, 432
18:8	53, 432

John

1:38	143
3:2	297
3:16	127
4:1–42	423
6:35	3
6:51	423
8:12	118
8:31–36	56
10:10	2, 423
16:25	2
16:29	1
17	410
20:22	357
20:29	2

Acts

1	213
2:4	357
2:4–6	412

Romans

1:20–22	58, 179
1:22–27	179
1:28	180
3:9	180

3:9–11	181
5:8	2
5:13	69
6	170, 182, 183, 297
6:20	180
7:15	181
7:17	181
7:21–23	2
12	188
12:2	228
15:13	69

1 Corinthians

2:1–5	142
4:1	142
5:7	170
8	136
11:1	159
12	188
13:1	389
13:2	390
13:12	110, 389
13:13	55, 111
15	357

2 Corinthians

4:6	2
5	297
5:14–15	268
5:17	2
5:21	182

Galatians

3:28–29	193
4:19	25, 55, 239
5:13–29	9
5:22–23	25

Ephesians

2	193
2:15–16	193

3:20	210
4	410
4:4	188
4:11–17	377
4:14–18	228
4:20	228
4:23b	228
5:32	142
6:4	347
6:10	184
6:10–18	30, 184
6:12	193
6:16	425

Philippians

2	399
2:12–13	205

Colossians

1:9–14	25, 239
1:12	332
1:15	171, 172
1:19	172
1:27	142
1:28	377
2:13–15	194

1 Thessalonians

2:13–14	12

1 Timothy

4:7	377

2 Timothy

3:15–17	262

Hebrews

4:14–16	131
5:14	377
11:1	124
11:6	55

11:8	55	1 Peter		7	410, 413
11:17–19	55	2:4	188	9	410, 413
12:1	54			20:6	357
		1 John		21:5	239
James		4:7	202	22:1–5	210
1:2–4	33				
2:14–26	11	Revelation			
2:19	11	5	410, 413